PRAISE FOR

MY WARS ARE LAID AWAY IN BOOKS

"A scholar of the old-fashioned, hard-boiled, heroic sort. Habegger leaves his reader with a feeling close to exaltation by his scrupulous, detailed, selective massing of the evidence of Dickinson's path to her work. . . . [He] has come closer than anyone else to getting past the closed door. . . ."

—Robert D. Richardson, *The Washington Post*

"This a a major achievement, and it is written in a language that makes it accessible to academics and general readers alike . . . this is now the definitive biography, and it will continue to illuminate the paths and roads of Dickinson travelers for decades to come. For which, thanks."

—Domhnall Mitchell, *Emily Dickinson International Society Bulletin*

"This sumptuously perceptive and scrupulously well-balanced biography of Emily Dickinson . . . conjures up a full-bodied, humanly realized person, not the ghosts or neurotic phantoms of spurious myths. . . ."

—Sam Coale, *The Providence Journal*

". . . a highly readable, unassuming work that overcomes many of the problems, editorial and biographical, that beset previous biographies and critics of Dickinson."

—Jay Parini, *The Philadelphia Inquirer*

"Refreshingly insightful and straightforward . . . [Habegger is] a good detective."

—Carmela Cuiraru, *The Wall Street Journal*

"Packed with fascinating information about and insight into Emily Dickinson, her family, and her friends, this superb biography . . . bring[s] us as close to this extraordinary poet and reclusive, self-dramatizing, and profoundly perplexing person as we are likely ever to get."

—William E. Cain, *The Boston Globe*

My Wars
Are Laid Away
in Books

ALSO BY ALFRED HABEGGER

Henry James and the "Woman Business"

Gender, Fantasy, and Realism in American Literature

The Father: A Life of Henry James, Sr.

My Wars Are Laid Away in Books

The Life of Emily Dickinson

Alfred Habegger

THE MODERN LIBRARY / NEW YORK

2002 Modern Library Paperback Edition

More permissions, as well as photo credits, can be found on pages 761–764.

Library of Congress Cataloging-in-Publication Data

Habegger, Alfred.
My wars are laid away in books: the life of Emily Dickinson / Alfred Habegger.
Includes bibliographical references and index.
ISBN 0-8129-6601-5 (pbk.)
   1. Dickinson, Emily, 1830–1886. 2. Poets, American—19th century—Biography. 3. Women and literature—United States—History—19th century.

PS1541.Z5 H32 2001   811'.4—dc21   [B]   2001019429

Printed in the United States of America
Modern Library website address: www.modernlibrary.com

2 4 6 8 9 7 5 3 1

For Nellie

Contents

Introduction

Any great writer who stands aloof from customs seen as fundamental is certain to be mythologized by posterity. For no one is this truer than Emily Dickinson, whose reclusiveness, originality of mind, and unwillingness to print her work left just the sort of informational gaps that legend thrives on. And yet there is no need to settle for the simplifying icons of her that pass for truth, including the icon of ineluctable mystery. In spite of the gaps, there are enough materials for a solidly documented narrative of her life covering the conditions that shaped her to the inner dynamics of her art and thought.

The present volume began with the feeling that it was time someone assess recent findings and claims relating to this poet, undertake a comprehensive review of the known sources on her, and conduct a determined search for new ones. Among the reflections that set me in motion (this was 1994) was the realization that it was two decades since the huge Dickinson midden had been sifted by Richard B. Sewall, still the best of the poet's surprisingly few biographers. Since then, the feminist revolution had brought a number of rich new insights, conjectures, and perspectives to bear on her, some wonderfully illuminating. R. W. Franklin was about to complete his new edition of her poems, and certain "theoretical" approaches and isolated finds had opened fresh avenues into her life and work. But the more I read and taught her and considered competing claims, the more I felt that the story of her struggle and her genius was not being told.

Among the many ways readers have made sense of Dickinson, two approaches stand out. The older of them regards her as a pioneer, working in isolation and developing fifty years ahead of time the fractured thought and language that were to be characteristic of high modernism. The modernist Dickinson was not someone who could be patronized as "eccentric," or explained as a product of New England Puritanism; it was her writing and not her person that merited attention. The other and more recent approach sees her as a woman of her time, an American Victorian intimately involved in female networks and responsive to female writers. This view builds on the groundbreaking 1975 article by Carroll Smith-Rosenberg, "The Female World of Love and Ritual," and a great deal of specialized historical excavation, and rightly emphasizes that Dickinson had friends to whom she regularly sent letters and poems.

Each of these two approaches gets a great many things right. But aside from the obvious fact that they are fundamentally opposed and irreconcilable, both distort her historical reality. Their inadequacies will appear as this book unfolds. What must be noted here is the dubiousness of construing this profoundly one-of-a-kind writer by first enrolling her in any group at all, no matter whether it is the contemporary group of close female friends or the future group of detached modernists.

It seems wiser to begin and perhaps end with a recognition of the things that make Dickinson stand out—her genius, her extremely tenacious affection, her avoidance of public life, her reluctance to publish. Whatever her final intentions for the nearly eighteen hundred poems she left behind, the fact that a great many were not communicated to friends warns us that we cannot assume, as we of course do with most writers, that she meant to be read and understood. What George Steiner has said of a poem by Paul Celan applies even more exactly to a large proportion of Dickinson's work: "At certain levels, we are not meant to understand *at all*, and our interpretation, indeed our reading itself, is an intrusion."

The tacit recognition that our reading of Dickinson *is* an intrusion has all along contributed to her appeal. One of the reasons readers at all levels respond to her with passionate enthusiasm is that, knowing something of her life and character, they approach her work with these in mind. Again and again, readers feel that, remote and difficult as she is, they are on the track of *knowing* her. They feel a heartbeat; they receive the words as primal and immediate, as coming straight from life. Sadly, this way of reading is generally a mistake, especially if we succumb to the illusion that we can zoom into her life and penetrate her secret being. One of Dickinson's paradoxes is that she both invites and deflects such intimacy. "Not telling" was one of the things she did to perfection. How that came to be is part of the story this book attempts to follow.

Coming to this project after having written about the James family, I was struck by an assumption pervading a great deal of the critical analysis of Emily Dickinson. With almost anyone else—Charles Dickens or George Eliot or Henry James or James Joyce or T. S. Eliot—it is taken for granted that the life has some sort of shape or curve, however complicated, and that if we know where on that curve a particular work is situated we will probably come to a better understanding of it. There is development over time, in other words, and this directional trend becomes a map by which readers steer. With Dickinson, however, it is often assumed there is no map, direction, or development—that her art was static or airless and that we don't need to know about her stages, sequences, contexts in order to catch on. Her critical expositors habitually move back and forth between her writings of the early 1860s and those of the 1870s and 1880s, as if to rule out in advance that a given work had much to do with the point she had reached when she wrote it, and that the points connected. It is as if this writer were freakishly unable to learn from experience, and wrote without traction all her life. This approach was made explicit some years ago by David Porter, an influential Dickinson critic, who based his analysis of her as modernist on such premises as these: that "a chronology of composition has so far been impossible to establish" and that "her art did not change over more than two decades of composition."

It is true and indeed notorious that Dickinson wrote in the same few verse forms all her life, and that she always sounds like Dickinson, and that readers are easily lulled. But her stitched manuscript books, loose copies and drafts, and poems sent to others *have* been dated with varying degrees of exactness, and thus we *can* follow her tracks in a very rough chronological sequence. The feeling that she somehow failed to grow arises less from the oeuvre as such than from the problems we encounter in trying to read it. Aside from the inherent obscurity of some of her work, we meet two sets of practical problems: editorial and biographical. Since she did not date her verse or write for the press, choosing instead to trust a fraction of her output to close friends while keeping most of it to herself, we don't know how to organize it, frame it, or even set it up in type. The biographical problems are equally daunting: many of her letters are not dated; those to key correspondents have been destroyed or tampered with; and those she received are almost entirely gone, making it next to impossible to understand some of her replies and assess some relationships. And then there is the dearth of recorded incident that resulted from her reclusiveness. Any honest attempt to narrate her life, especially certain phases, ought to begin by acknowledging such difficulties.

But that there *were* phases is certain. A premise of this biography is that chronology is vital to comprehending Emily Dickinson—that she not only developed over time but that her work often reflected the stages of her life. Her poetry shows a striking and dramatic evolution. The question of development is fundamental: again and again, in reading her, we need to think about her recent history and how it shaped her immediate future. While the poems are obviously not a diary, a great many bear the impress of current experience. Even when they stand at a certain remove from it, as almost all of them do, their meaning may elude us if we miss the connection.

To get a handle on Dickinson's relationships, especially with those to whom she sent her poems, biography has to carry out two different tasks. The first is to conduct a broad archival investigation in order to discern her friends' historical reality *apart from her*. The second (for which her girlhood letters offer an indispensable fund of suggestion) is to try to see what she apparently expected from friendship *as such*. Only by taking both steps is it possible to sense the distances between her and others, and how she tried to bridge them with her letters and poems, and thus how she came to craft that unique writing voice that speaks so directly and seductively to us. And only if we follow her step-by-step from the beginning, or rather from her parents' and *their* parents' beginnings, can we see the successive stages of her struggle and achievement.

By now, the tradition of parceling Dickinson out among her friends is well established. When Mabel Loomis Todd brought out her pioneering collection of the poet's letters in 1894, she organized it by recipient, devoting each chapter or segment of a chapter to a particular correspondence. Although Todd arranged matters so that the earlier correspondences preceded the later ones, her book did not finally present a coherent picture of the poet's life in letters. Eighty years later, when Sewall composed his two-volume life of Dickinson (for which he enjoyed access to restricted materials owned by Millicent Todd Bingham, Todd's daughter), he observed the same principle of organization, devoting each chapter to a particular family member or friend. One of the strengths of Sewall's two volumes, which for twenty-five years have set the standard, is the judiciousness with which they examine a number of legends and riddles. But because they present the poet's life as an amalgam of separate relationships and correspondences, the basic story of *her* life and work is not laid out. A recent and selective edition of her messages to Susan Gilbert Dickinson, her sister-in-law and close friend—*Open Me Carefully*, by Ellen Louise Hart and Martha Nell Smith—follows a similar procedure, trying to see Dickinson through a single lens. A great deal of other work in print and electronic media is organized in the same way.

If biography is a narrative that integrates everything, no matter how complex, into a single life's forward-moving braid, it would seem that the biography of Emily Dickinson has yet to be attempted. My purpose has been to tell the story that seems implicit in the documentary record that is available to us, and at the same time to let the reader behind the scenes by showing just where that record has been fractured. I have aimed at something serviceable for the general cultivated reader and the specialist alike—not an encyclopedic survey of every facet, acquaintance, and poem, but a comprehensive account of essential matters. Of course, I also pay attention to recent insights and contentions, and also to important unknown or untapped sources, such as the printer's copy for the 1894 edition of Dickinson's letters.[1] My chief regret is that constraints of

---

1. After the handwritten copy was prepared by Mabel Loomis Todd but before it was sent to the printer, a number of passages were blue-penciled, perhaps on the advice of Austin Dickinson, the poet's brother. Since many of these excisions came from letters whose manuscripts are lost, the smudged printer's copy, now at Yale's Manuscripts and Archives Library, is the only source for some of Dickinson's more personal epistolary remarks. Still unpublished, these have not been made use of by critics or biographers.

space have kept me from going into several poems about which I have much to say.

Four years after I began working full-time on this biography and just as my narrative had reached the year 1850, the date of Dickinson's earliest known poems, R. W. Franklin brought out his three-volume variorum edition of her poems. No book could have been more timely. Even though it fails to provide evidence or argument for most of its assigned dates (and, inevitably, makes mistakes), the edition is based on an exceptionally careful examination of original manuscripts and early transcriptions. Building on the editorial work of Thomas H. Johnson and others, Franklin goes well beyond it in establishing a plausible chronology and identifying the poems' recipients. The correction of certain key errors dramatically simplified my work, if for no other reason than that a good deal of distracting peripheral noise abruptly ceased.

But the person to whom I am chiefly in debt is my wife, Nellie Habegger, without whose eager, energetic, and shrewd assistance this biography could not have been completed. Helping me carry out the dusty research at library after library, where "the Habeggers" returned each spring or fall like Dickinson's birds or crickets, and then providing much-needed criticism, suggestion, and ridicule after reading at our kerosene-lit table my clumsy attempts to get it all down on paper, she is the silent but indispensable presence in this volume.

Textual Note

Although Dickinson's private copies of her poems sometimes list alternative words or phrases, as if she hadn't made up her mind, she always made a final choice when sending her poems to friends. I have generally done the same, assuming that that is how she wanted her verse presented to others. If she recorded a preference for a certain alternative (by underlining, say), that will be the one I select. In a few instances, the physical arrangement of alternative lines strongly suggests a preference. If there seems to be no authorial guidance whatever, I rely on my own taste and judgment. Following custom, I quote verbatim and retain idiosyncrasies of capitalization and punctuation. I have, however, silently dropped the apostrophes that Dickinson regularly inserted in possessive pronouns and occasionally in plural nouns, on the ground that such errors are as unrelated to her meaning as they are annoying. Like Franklin, I represent her "dashes," no matter how long, short, raised, lowered, or angled, with an en dash enclosed by spaces (–).

In referring to letters, I adopt Johnson's numbering, preceded by an "L," in *The Letters of Emily Dickinson* (abbreviated *Let* in the Notes section). For readers accustomed to Johnson's numbering of the poems, a first-line index to poems discussed provides his as well as Franklin's numbers. "Fr" stands for Franklin, whose classification system and sequence I follow.

A Note on the Paperback Edition

I have taken the opportunity of a new edition to amend factual errors or omissions and make a few alterations. An index on page 648 gives Johnson's numbers for those poems whose first lines are not given.

April 2002
AH

Part One

1636 – 1830

The arrangement of the stage as shown in the *Reunion of the Dickinson Family, at Amherst, Mass., August 8th and 9th, 1883.*

Chapter 1

*Amherst
and the Fathers*

Sometime between 1636 and 1638, Emily Dickinson's earliest American progenitors in the paternal line, Nathaniel and Ann Gull Dickinson, left the parish of Billingborough in Lincolnshire, England, for the raw British outpost of Wethersfield, Connecticut. One motive for their drastic move was a determination to practice without interference the militant late-Reformation faith known as Puritanism. The times were hot with rebellion against the Church of England.

In 1659 Nathaniel, Ann, and their children moved north into Massachusetts with a number of other families and established a town along the fertile Connecticut Valley deep in Norwottuck country. They called it Hadley, and Nathaniel played a leading role in organizing and regulating its municipal, educational, religious, and military affairs. When savage warfare broke out in 1675 between the indigenous peoples and the English, three of his nine sons were slain. When England's Puritan rule ended and those who had condemned Charles I to the headsman's block fled for their lives, they ended up in this frontier town, founded on righteousness and violence. And when a new town was carved out of Hadley's eastern parts a century later, in 1759, it was named for the man who would recommend using smallpox-infected blankets to "extirpate" the Indians: Lord Jeffrey Amherst.

By 1830, the year Emily Dickinson was born in Amherst, the area was thick with light-skinned farmers bearing her last name, and the ancestral zealotry had moderated into a quirky hardheaded stubbornness known locally as Dickinson grit. A Dickinson reunion held there in 1883 was attended by a huge number of Nathaniel's descendants, who listened to a minister declaim a versified panegyric composed by Elizabeth Dickinson Currier, one of Emily's aunts. The poem termed the clan's patriarchs "men of *muscle*, as of *mind*" and denounced any falling away from their evangelical zeal. What the ancestral legacy meant to the event's organizers is suggested by a photograph of the stage, which shows a slender gun standing on the floor next to portraits of Dickinson judges, generals, governors, and ministers. The weapon was said to have been "used in killing Indians and wolves."

Although Emily Dickinson would not have attended this pious family gathering, she was very much a member of the tribe—savvy, tough, resolute, heaven-obsessed, independent, unusual. In one of her most eye-catching poems, "My life had stood a loaded gun," she, or at least the speaker, almost seems to be the deadly Dickinson musket come to life:

> None stir the second time –
> On whom I lay a Yellow Eye –
> Or an emphatic Thumb –
>
> Fr764 (about 1863)

A later and less enigmatic poem concerns the unavoidability of "fighting" for one's life "In that Campaign inscrutable / Of the Interior" (Fr1230). Another, "My wars are laid away in books" (Fr1579), obviously retrospective, dates from about 1882, not long before the reunion. Hard battle resulting in victory or defeat was a central, lifelong metaphor for her. Far from being a wispy escapist, she was as martial a Dickinson as any of them. Yet she had no one's blood on her hands and paid little or no attention to family or local history, including her father's toast at Hadley's 1859 bicentennial invoking the by now moss-covered theme of New England's errand into the (so-called) wilderness.

What complicated this inheritance for the poet was that she was not only disqualified by her sex from entering public life but actively instructed *not* to define herself in terms of the collective struggles of her time. Unlike her father, Edward, a conservative bulwark of the public world as she knew it, she was relegated to the private sphere, and that at a time when specifically domestic and affectionate qualities were assigned to women and given an extreme emphasis and development. Also, sentimental writing by both sexes was in vogue. If Emily's letters and poems often express a kind of ultimate in exquisite tenderness, we should bear in mind that the energies that might have been expended otherwise in different conditions were, with her, compressed into writing that had to remain a part of private life, even when confided to close friends.

One of her poems from early in the Civil War sums up a woman's life and death by tracing her footprints into a deserted and unfamiliar place. Although the woman's path is untraveled by others, it is, paradoxically, already there, familiar, old:

> *'Twas the old – road – through pain –*
> *That unfrequented – One –*

These lines take us back to the old Puritan allegories of life's hard and lonely course, except that here the journey begins not in sin but in anguish. Observing the woman's tracks as if from just above, the speaker follows with breathless engagement:

> *This – was the Town – she passed –*
> *There – where she – rested – last –*
> *Then – stepped more fast –*
> *The little tracks – close prest –*

> *Then – not so swift –*
> *Slow – slow – as feet did weary – grow –*
> *Then – stopped – no other track!*

The footprints hint at an extreme and convulsive effort, which appears to have failed. But the story isn't over:

> *Wait! Look! Her little Book –*
> *The leaf – at love – turned back –*
> *Her very Hat –*
> *And this worn shoe just fits the track . . .*
>
> Fr376

In the end, we are assured the traveler has been translated to a bed in "Chambers bright." That her place of rest is made up by women, not angels, hints that her impassioned but unknown errand into the wilderness was in some way specific to her sex.

The only friends to whom Dickinson is known to have sent the poem were two first cousins on her mother's side, sisters, of whom she was especially fond. At the time she copied it in her secret manuscript books, about 1862, her own tracks were also extremely "close prest," resulting in 227 poems for that year alone, by R. W. Franklin's count. Her book, too, was dog-eared at love, and pain and solitude, and laughter and risk and freshness and power and so much more. Devious, disguised, and mostly obliterated, Dickinson's tracks are going to be harder to read than those of the risk-taking woman she wrote about. Is the poem about a single woman whose capacity for love drives her into panic, solitude, and death? At times it will look as if the poet was on that "unfrequented" road. But hers kept going where the other woman's stopped.

In 1850, writing the future president of Dartmouth College, Charles Hammond described Amherst, the town Dickinson passed, as "the land of the fathers," the place where "the ancient altars" were still honored and tended. To follow her road to greatness, we have to go back to her paternal grandfather, whose dedication to those altars helped set the terms within which she defined and dared to exercise her high calling—an artist's heroic errand into and out of a wilderness all her own.

All the Armor of Fortitude and Determination

Samuel Fowler Dickinson, the poet's grandfather, embodied much of her paternal heritage, being both a man of means and a man of thought—a promoter of education, a community leader, a defender of Calvinist orthodoxy. He rose to greatness as a cofounder of Amherst College, but he also proved an obsessive, unbalanced, and scattered man whose judgment went astray and whose life ended in a shambles.

After graduating from Dartmouth as Latin salutatorian in 1795, Samuel spent a year teaching school, an occupation he found too dependent on the "whims" of constituents. His lungs unwell, he underwent a conversion and began studying with the Reverend Nathanael Emmons, one of New England's most energetic and eminent Calvinists. Four months of Emmons convinced the young man he was not cut out for the ministry, but he continued to regard his instructor as a "great Divine." Indeed, judging from Samuel's intense lifelong drive, it looks as if he took to heart Emmons's curious "Exercise Scheme," a religious teaching that gave unusual emphasis to the power of the will and the obligation to use it.[1]

Returning to Amherst, Samuel put himself under the tutelage of Judge Simeon Strong, the town's leading lawyer and the owner of much valuable land in its center. In a letter to a college friend dating from this period, the young man wrote that "for entering the world we need all the armour of fortitude and determination." This statement, that of some-

---

1. A successor of Jonathan Edwards, Emmons taught the usual doctrines of God's Sovereignty and Human Depravity. However, for him depravity was not an inherited state (Original Sin) but a "voluntary opposition to God." Because his system made sinfulness a question not of what humans are but what they *choose* to be, it followed that they must exercise their wills in effecting their regeneration; hence "Exercise Scheme." The peculiarly American dynamism of this idea may have had a formative impact on Samuel.

to permit greatness to pass through

one putting the Exercise Scheme into motion, catches the embattled drive working within Samuel and some of his descendants: *all* the armor and determination was precisely what they required. His imagery gives us our first sight of the resolute will to be great that his granddaughter would quietly assert some sixty years later.

But Squire Dickinson, as he came to be known (the title being honorary only), was an overreacher, with little sense of his natural limits. Although he played a leading role in Amherst's affairs, he never acquired the calm and powerful reserve traditionally associated with a pillar of the community. Instead, as Elizabeth Currier recalled, he gave "himself but four hours of sleep, studying and reading till midnight, and rising at four o'clock he often walked to Pelham or some other town before breakfast. Going to court at Northampton, he would catch up his green bag and walk the whole seven miles. '*I cannot wait to ride.*'" Ambitious and public-spirited, he was also frenetic, the kind of man who undoes his own success. He acquired title to a great deal of land in and about Amherst, as had Judge Strong, but he couldn't carry the mortgages. In state elections, he was sent to the house ten times and once to the senate, but when he ran for a congressional seat in 1828 after opposing his district on the tariff issue, he was crushed 1,968 to 246, his hometown turning against him two to one. Three years later, addressing the regional Agricultural Society, he unloaded a vast collection of opinions on education, militia reform, Sabbath schools, ardent spirits, excessive government expenditures, and all aspects of farming. "He works very hard," a daughter reported in his old age; "he thinks he cannot get along without lending a helping hand to every man's plough."

The woman Samuel married on March 21, 1802, Lucretia Gunn of nearby Montague, was said by one of her daughters to be slow "to form acquaintances or attachments," which may mean either that she was withdrawn or that she was unfriendly. Her few extant letters, mainly to her son Edward (the poet's father), bespeak an ordinary and down-to-earth range of interests and a strikingly ungenteel directness: "We are engaged killing hogs to day of course must shorten my letter." "Do not recollect any remarkable occurrence except Mrs. Hicks who once attempted to cut her throat last week jumped into the well and put an end to her existence." In 1820 news of a revival inspired the hope her son would be converted "and not have to lament the 'Harvest is past the Summer is ended & you are not saved.' " Curiously, 1820 seems to have been the year she herself joined Amherst's First Congregational Church—twenty years after her husband. According to Martha Dickinson Bianchi, the poet's grandmother "was by tradition of somewhat tart disposition, and was often referred to in moments of bad temper as 'coming out' in her high-strung grandchildren. If a door was banged— 'It's not me—it's my Grandmother Gunn!' was an excuse glibly offered by the three small rascals."

Toward his children, Samuel was anything but a cold, uncaring patriarch. When a son became feverish, the Squire let everything go and "devoted my time, night & day, to him," writing this very letter "by his bedside." After another son contracted the same illness, the anxious father was "able to attend to little other business" despite his desperate need of money. Concerned about his daughters' education, he was so eager to have them attend a course of lectures by the botanist Amos Eaton that he urged Edward to come home at Yale's term break and escort his sisters. He added, uncoercively, "I do not mean to direct, but to express my desire, that you should do this."

By 1813 Samuel had fathered five of his nine children and it was time to enlarge his family's living space and mark his own civic prominence. Replacing the home previously standing on the site, he erected a spacious and imposing house that looked down on Main Street from a slight elevation. Amherst's first brick house, the Dickinson Homestead[2] was a symmetrical, hip-roofed structure in the Federal style, with four large rooms on each of its two stories. Although this was the building in which the poet was born and spent her first nine and last thirty years, it had yet to undergo the extensive additions and remodeling she would take for granted as an adult. The modifications seem to have begun quite early. A one-story wooden "office" (no longer standing) was attached to the west wall, and in 1821 a daughter noted that "Papa has had ten men

---

2. Originally the word designated a family's established dwelling place, including house, outbuildings, and land.

to work for him all the week they are to work upon his house." A year and a half later she triumphantly announced to brother Edward, "we have got some curtains to the west front-chamber, we expect to have our blinds up in two, or three, weeks, and when you come home you wont hardly know our house." The change from "his" to "our" speaks volumes. The Dickinsons' life at home was originally much more improvised than the stately mansion of the present suggests.

In 1817, well before the Squire's contributions to Amherst College began consuming his estate, he mortgaged this house for $2,500 (today roughly $75,000), an encumbrance he was never able to lift. The household that shaped the poet's father was marked by high dreams and ambitions, a generosity as reckless as it was shining, worsening indebtedness, and a series of desperate expedients concluding in disaster. Having known what it was like to live without the security and dignity that should have gone with his rank, Edward Dickinson would prove extremely protective of his own family, particularly his wife and older daughter.

Rolling Back a Flood of Error

One of the developments that dismayed Calvinists in Samuel's time was the growth of Unitarianism. Unlike the orthodox, who saw human depravity as so absolute that a divinely initiated regeneration was required, the Unitarians left a large space for human goodness. Where Calvinists saw true religion as necessarily containing elements of terror and psychic violence, Unitarians stood for serenity, a life of rational virtue, a view of Jesus as a model for imitation rather than a divine Savior. The war between these versions of Protestantism became extremely bitter in the century's second and third decades, giving rise to schisms between congregations and lawsuits over church property and a pervasive social division.

The orthodox saw Unitarianism as a betrayal of the founders, but that was not the only thing that roused a fighting spirit. The secularism that was stimulated by the war for independence, the erosion of the system in which a town was both a religious and a political corporation, the growth of an unchurched and ill-educated population in the West, and the Federalist Party's weakness in national politics: such developments helped fuel the broad conservative reaction that has been loosely termed the Second Great Awakening.

This movement had a vigorous life that extended into the poet's formative years, establishing revivals as a major aspect of congregational life and stimulating the development of new institutions—Sabbath Schools, societies for distributing Bibles and tracts and commissioning missionaries, and powerful advocacy campaigns for temperance, Sunday closing laws, and other reforms. Designed to keep certain social tendencies in check and reassert a version of the ancestral errand, these institutions served to foster the mysterious inner act based on surrender or submission and known as conversion. This was the system the poet was born into and grew up taking for granted.

One of the changes that most disturbed the orthodox occurred at Harvard's divinity school, which defected to Unitarianism early in the century. It was because conservatives saw Harvard as having dropped the torch that was its main reason for being—training a learned clergy faithful to the Reformation—that Amherst College was founded when and where it was, and with such fervor. "We have seen error attempting to roll its desolating flood through our churches," intoned Noah Webster at the laying of the cornerstone in 1820; "we have seen prostituted to the vile purpose of disseminating false doctrines, funds that were consecrated to the interests of truth." This angry sense of betrayal, widely shared, helps explain how a village that turned out many college graduates but commanded little real wealth was able to organize, endow, and set in motion a first-rate college.

Samuel Fowler Dickinson was one of the leading figures in the story, which began when he and Judge Strong's son Hezekiah and others organized Amherst Academy in 1812. When the three-story brick building opened its doors in 1814—to girls as well as boys—it was one of western Massachusetts's best private classical schools. Three years later the Squire was part of an ambitious fund-raising campaign to upgrade the Academy, the aim being to endow both a professorship of languages and a scholarship fund for indigent young men willing to become missionaries or ministers. After a mighty effort this campaign collapsed, only to be at once reborn when the poet's grandfather convinced a fellow enthusiast, Colonel Rufus Graves, that instead of scaling back their goals they should enlarge them. Realizing that a grandly imposing project might have more appeal than the improvement of an existing institution, these wild dreamers resolved to create an evangelical college rivaling Harvard and Williams, then the state's only colleges. Thus was set in motion a concerted effort to reverse what an early student called the "wide-spread defection from the faith of the fathers."

The first step was to raise $50,000, the minimum required by the charter (which had not even been approved as yet). And it was all or nothing: if the drive fell short, all subscriptions would be void and the project would collapse. To insure against this, Samuel and eight other supporters signed a "guaranty bond" in the summer of 1818, jointly committing them to a ceiling of $15,000. He also contributed the individual sum of $1,005. For a man already struggling with debt, such commitments were lavish to the point of recklessness. Fortunately for him, the pledge drive reached its goal in 1819.

When South College, the school's first edifice, went up in 1820–1821, Samuel was on the building committee and frequently intervened to rescue the shoestring undertaking. According to an early witness, the Squire

> would pledge his private property to the bank to obtain money that the work might go on. And when there was no money to pay for the teams to draw the brick or men to drive them, his own horses were sent for days and weeks till in one season two or three of them fell by the wayside. Sometimes his own laborers were sent to drive his horses, and in an emergency he went himself, rather than that the work should cease.

Sometimes he paid the workmen "out of his own pocket, while his wife and daughters toiled to board them." The intense domestic pressure can be seen in a distracted letter from wife Lucretia to son Edward: "They have compleated the College our affairs are still in a crazy situation." What "compleated" meant, as her oldest daughter explained, was that South College's roof was on and work had ceased for the winter. The craziness at home, whatever that was, reflected Samuel's obliteration of the line between the world at large and domestic life—a line his son would rigorously defend. Edward knew that zeal moves mountains, but he didn't want the zealot's family to foot the bill.

Zeal also tends to lose track of the proportion between means and ends.[3] Looking back, Edward Hitchcock, the college's third president and first historian, blamed the rapid early expansion of the physical plant for the load of debt that crippled the school in the 1830s, very nearly destroying it. If Hitchcock had wished to assign blame, he could have pointed at the Squire, who in 1821 undertook, as his daughter reported, "to build the [college] President's house." The next summer Samuel helped pay for the liquor—old rum and sling—at a function held in the president's yard.

The idea behind Amherst College was that a corps of pious and disciplined ministers and missionaries would roll back Unitarianism, counteract the disintegrative tendencies of American democracy, and carry an educated and resurgent evangelicalism from New England to the rest of the world. It was an idea with consequences: Robert College in Istanbul, American University of Beirut, and Doshisha University in Kyoto were all founded by the school's devout alumni (the last by Neesima Shimeta, class of 1870 and number one son of a samurai father serving a scholarly Tokyo prince). These institutions are among the results of the vision and energy of the poet's grandfather, on whose mind, as William S. Tyler noted, "the conversion of the world often pressed heavily."

The go-for-broke zealotry of Emily Dickinson's grandfather fed into her life in complex and intimate ways. She too, working under desperate conditions, became a creator ex nihilo, though only in the privacy and protection of her home—the same home he had built, wagered, and

---

3. In speaking of Samuel Fowler's zealotry and fanaticism, I am thinking of his extreme dedication, activism, and risk-taking. To judge by his dismissive 1831 remarks on "stern articles of faith," he was far from intolerant of others' beliefs.

lost. And she worked for different ends. So far from trying to save the world, one of the things Dickinson didn't do was *teach*, in this differing from almost all other nineteenth-century English and American writers of consequence.

Yale vs. Amherst Collegiate Charity Institution

To follow Edward Dickinson, the poet's father, through his college years and early professional training is to see how Samuel's fortitude and determination perpetuated themselves in a different form.

When Edward left for Yale in fall 1819, he found a larger and more stimulating world than anything his hometown had to offer. Defining the basic goals of education as "expanding [the mind's] powers, and storing it with knowledge," Yale's president clearly saw that the chief thing was to "throw the student upon the resources of his own mind." Essays and declamations were frequently assigned, and there were well-established student debating societies, which, in addition to sponsoring a good deal of speechifying, had well-stocked libraries. A more orthodox and socially conservative school than Harvard, Yale required every student from outside New Haven to be under the guardianship of a "patron." Any student who denied the divine authority of the Bible was threatened with expulsion. Anyone caught attending a "comedy or tragedy" was subject to a fine, and there were dozens of other proscriptions. Still, as far as Edward was concerned, all this implied surveillance was neither unfamiliar nor oppressive, and he soon informed his father he was "please[d]" by "the Government of College." What pleased him most, however, judging by the many letters he received from fellow students and never threw away (some addressed to "Friend Dick"), was the companionship of talented young men his age.

But Friend Dick had only a single term before the Squire required him to sell his furniture and return home. Since the new college was not yet in operation, that meant going back to Amherst Academy. At first Samuel tried to pretend the school offered as good an education as Yale and would be "equally beneficial," but before long the truth came out: he was swamped by "bills of this quarter." One of the ways the young man coped with this humiliating comedown was to try to keep up with the freshman class at Yale, or so one judges from a requested progress-report sent him by a former roommate.

Fortunately, Squire Dickinson's fortunes rebounded and Edward was able to return to Yale for the regular summer term. It was then that New Haven and its college were overwhelmed by an historic revival. The evangelist Asahel Nettleton arrived on August 5 and, staying till December, preached and prayed and otherwise assisted at private gatherings. The student body became quiet and serious and anxiously flocked to the meetings, which became so crowded, one participant noted, "that hundreds go away from the conference rooms, not being able to get in." Remarkably, as the long vacation came and went and Edward's sophomore year got under way, the religious feeling grew instead of being dispersed. There were more meetings, more conversions, more exhortations of the impenitent by their regenerated classmates. In Edward's first term, the entry to his room in Middle College had been in frequent uproar. Now "you could pass through no entry . . . without overhearing the low, earnest, supplicating voice of prayer." The popular senior-class "ringleader" experienced a dramatic conversion that became the subject of a tract, and the divinity school received its founding impetus. Some of Edward's acquaintances and classmates were changed for life, but his friends Osmyn Baker of Amherst and George Ashmun of Springfield held out, and so did he. His mother was not the only family member who pleaded with him. "If, Edward," his father wrote, "I could hear that you were among the number, who had embraced the Savior, how joyful the news! Pray for a new heart."[4]

As Edward's sophomore year ended, he received the dismaying news that he would have to drop out of Yale a second time and return to

---

4. One should note the gentleness of Samuel's religious suasion. In 1823 he wrote his son that "when a man is imbarrassed with disappointments—difficulties in business & the cares of a family—he seems to have no time to think of God & duty . . . I mention this as a serious fact for your reflection. My own experience shows the increasing difficulties in the way of being religious, as we advance in life." As a rule, Edward did not approach his own children in this confiding and equal spirit.

Amherst, whose tiny college was about to go into operation. The reason his father gave was the same as before: "*necessity*—inability to supply the money necessary at N. H." This time he softened the blow by allowing his son to "take a room in the College building, and have no connection with home except boarding." Although the boy didn't have to sell his furniture, the implied return to New Haven didn't materialize until he had spent his full junior year at Amherst Collegiate Charity Institution, as the new school was infelicitously known.

A year after Edward graduated, his debating society at Yale, Brothers in Unity, decided that Amherst's Charity Institution "would not be beneficial to the cause of science and literature." Judging from the letters Friend Dick received in fall 1821, he not only shared this disdain for the tiny, pinched school his father had helped invent, but regarded New Haven's larger, freer, and more arrogant college as his proper intellectual home. Osmyn Baker commiserated with him for having "to leave an institution where you may choose your associates and friends from 300, and enter one where that number is reduced to 50, and those chiefly of principles and habits of life very different from your own."

Edward's next-younger brother, William, a staunch ally and a shrewd, original, and bellicose character,[5] took an even dimmer view of the transfer from Yale. Afraid that Edward would be persuaded to finish his education at home, William urged him not to let "the trustees of the Institution triumph over your best judgement." The more he thought about it the angrier he grew:

I cannot leave this subject I know how it is *exactly*. . . . It is just like this. Im Mad to think of it. in the 1st Place Col Graves comes in good morning Mr ⓒ Dickinson. Very fine morning Sir . . . Well sir have you been to the institution this morning Sir I think you had better conclude to enter *here*. . . . *A* has given so much and B. [has

---

5. An obituary of William noted that "he had an incisive manner of speech and a dry humor" and "always clung to his point and not infrequently carried it." Thomas Wentworth Higginson's statement to Emily Dickinson that he could not imagine "two beings less alike than you & him" missed certain underlying similarities.

given] *ground* for the President House and C. *is going to SUB-SCRIBE.* . . . Mr D. you had better stop Here by the time you finish there will be a vacancy for you to set up *Law* Oh yes says Papa he may have my office as soon as he gets through. Well says Col Graves that is fine indeed you *cant* have *nothing* better than that. . . . I [Graves speaking] had better start for Indiana to day there's a man there that'll give $3.75

This fascinating passage dramatizes a basic issue the poet's father had to resolve in one way or another: what to do about the invasive zealotry that threatened to overwhelm him?

Although Edward was already well on the way toward becoming the stoically responsible man who did so much to shape the poet's life, his feelings sometimes broke out in odd performances. In early November, the discouraged collegian committed the one known public disgrace of his life. It began in the room of an academy student, where he and some other lads had a late oyster supper and a quantity of "cherry-rum and gin." At midnight they moved their party to the grounds of the Institution (still basically a construction site), where they "behaved in a very indecent and riotous manner, and made great disturbance . . . till one o'clock or later." Their mistake was to wake up a young professor of Greek and Latin, Joseph Estabrook, something of a dandy and not much liked. As a former Yale roommate pictured the scene, probably drawing on Edward's own account, Estabrook rushed outside and "expose[d] his *nakedness* to the rude night winds of winter, for the purpose of prowling among the devotees of . . . an innocent conviviality." Whatever the punishment was, one guesses from another friend's commiserating tone that Edward took it with scornful dignity: "I know not whether I ought to congratulate you or condole with you on the recent distinguished marks of attention which you have received from the faculty of *Amherst Collegiate Charity Institution.* Perhaps the greatest honour which that body can confer, is that of punishment." The episode brings out as nothing else the gap that had temporarily opened between the young man and his paternal legacy.

The final humiliation occurred when Edward returned to Yale for his senior year and, failing to secure a college room, took private lodgings with three freshmen for fall term. A warning he got from Baker hints at his grim response to this arrangement: "There is danger that your disposition will receive a tinge of sourness and discontent which will endure." But the indignity passed, and for his last two terms Edward shared a senior room with George Ashmun, the friend from Springfield who later became a prominent Whig and then Republican. Ashmun's letters suggest he must have been a profane and amusing companion.

Academically, Edward remained an average student, and even though he now matched his best previous grade, receiving a 2.4 in May 1823, was far from qualifying for top honors. Samuel, former Latin salutatorian, had communicated to his son the hope that he would earn "a respectable place among your classmates,"[6] but when the prize Commencement speeches were announced, Edward got the last one on the list, joining seven others in a "Dialogue." The many college essays he kept substantiate the impression he was not some sort of genius.

Surviving a Blackness of Darkness

In the three years between graduation and the beginning of his courtship, Edward prepared for his career by reading law with his father, assisting in his practice, and in 1825–1826 attending the nearby Northampton School of Law. This was a trying period for the young man, whose struggle to enter the world was jinxed by his father's growing troubles. What we see crystallizing is a certain kind of uncommunicative hardness, a principled severity based on determination and the shock of seeing what goes wrong when the man of the house proves an inadequate protector.

---

6. Cynthia Griffin Wolff's life of Dickinson offers a textbook example of how a weak factual base can turn a biography into unadmitted fiction. Claiming without evidence that Edward was a "superb student," Wolff wonders why his father didn't praise him for his "excellent work at Yale." The gratuitous problem then leads to a ringing psychological insight: "Samuel Dickinson did not much play the father's role with Edward. Instead, he treated the boy as someone to lean on and confide in. . . . Edward was left to 'father' himself."

Soon after Edward's final return from New Haven to Amherst, an ominous trend showed up in his father's recorded real estate transactions. In November of that year he mortgaged several properties to Oliver Smith of Hadley, a brother-in-law, for $2,000. Two months later he gave the Massachusetts Hospital Life Insurance Company additional mortgages worth $3,000. Four months after that, in exchange for $6,000, he gave Smith mortgages on a long list of properties including the Dickinson Homestead, now doubly encumbered. That was in May 1825. In August he sold his long-lived father's East Street farm fifteen days after his death, the money coming once again from his brother-in-law Smith, whose own foundations were now trembling. In January, acting together, the Squire and Smith made a questionable deal with their widowed sister-in-law, Lucinda Dickinson, and her underage children, assigning them several previously mortgaged properties in exchange for $5,000.

There is no doubt as to the basic meaning of these and other mortgages and sales: Samuel was trying to make interest payments and meet other debts by pledging and repledging all his capital. At the time Massachusetts (which still imprisoned for debt) did not have a modern insolvency or bankruptcy law establishing a procedure for giving fair and equal treatment to creditors, terminating hopeless debt, and starting over. Quite simply, there was no way out for Edward's father, who had to continue borrowing larger and larger amounts, in the process corroding the fortunes of his relatives Oliver Smith and Lucinda Dickinson.

The effect on Edward was to deepen the silent and stoical elements of his character. Again and again, as houses and commercial buildings and large acreages of farmland were exchanged for a few more months' breathing space, he was present at the transactional moment, affixing his name as legal witness. Although he left no direct record of his response to such events, his basic mood is easily surmised from a sympathetic letter sent to him by Baker: "I know well enough what a blackness of darkness that is which envelopes a young man in your situation."

A further complication was that the Squire not only expanded his public activities but forcefully enlisted his son's support, at times giving him an inside lesson on how things got done. Writing home from

Boston at the moment when Austin Dickinson, the college's lobbyist, was working to procure a charter from the legislature, Samuel commanded that "Master Dickinson's business *must* be done & I must know it, at least by thursday's mail—get security if possible—if not attach enough to secure it—the Auditors are very uneasy."

The effort succeeded, but on other occasions Edward risked being caught up in inflammatory and futile undertakings. The minister of Amherst's First Church, the Reverend Daniel A. Clark, was a learned but rough and forceful preacher who deeply offended the parish's wealthier members. (George Shepard, a professor at a seminary, recalled with admiration how certain passages in Clark's sermons "would come suddenly like a great rasp across the audience.") In an ill-considered attempt to preserve peace, Samuel pressed formal charges against him at a church meeting in December 1823 but then, leaving for Boston, failed to perform the impartial investigation that was required. When Edward was asked to do so in his place, taking depositions from Clark's former congregation in Connecticut, he declined, citing his "extreme youth and entire inexperience" and his fear of "receiving an injury to my reputation, at the very outset of my career." Prevailed on anyway, partly because "the charges were brought in my father's name," he never felt "more unpleasantly" than when entering the Connecticut stage on what would be his first big professional challenge. Edward didn't care for the minister, but as his account of his investigation shows, he did his best to remain impartial while collecting and sifting a sorry tangle of allegations (among other things, Clark was accused of having "pulled out the nails" from a house he occupied). In the end, when a council of ministers unanimously exonerated the man of Samuel's charges, Edward emerged unscathed, with a reputation for prudence and fair dealing.

Two months after Clark's acquittal and at the worst possible time for his own fortunes, Samuel cosigned a $3,600 guardianship bond for Hezekiah Wright Strong, his old ally in founding the academy and college. The result was that the Squire was apparently "obliged to furnish the money," sued Strong for restitution, and was awarded $3,800 in August 1824. Strong, however, not only avoided paying up but snagged the

Amherst postmastership that Samuel coveted for himself. Outraged at his debtor's coup, Samuel whipped off a letter of protest to the postmaster general that disclosed Strong's shaky finances and presented his own superior qualifications. Postmasterships paid well, and presently the Squire tried to get the job for Edward. Failing again, bitter and vindictive, he sued to have Strong removed from the guardianship of his own children, the grounds being that he was likely to appropriate for himself the funds reserved for their upbringing.

This was the other side of the principled tenacity the Squire had displayed in founding Amherst College. Some men might be chastened by financial distress, reducing their activities and acting with less precipitation, but he seems to have flung his nets wider and wider. In later years his descendants, his last daughter, Elizabeth, in particular, venerated him as one of the righteous in Israel, one who risked and lost everything for Amherst College—a family myth largely accepted by twentieth-century biographers. What was forgotten was that Samuel jeopardized his in-laws' wealth along with his own and recklessly intervened in others' affairs. Carried away by an exaggerated sense of his public mandate, he left a legacy of shame and hardship as well as pride.

Coping with this legacy in the years before his courtship and marriage helped make Edward Dickinson the husband and father he was. William and his other three brothers left Amherst to go into business elsewhere, but Edward came back, and although he looked for openings for an attorney in other towns, he took over from his unreliable father without leaving a single expression of exasperation. Unlike William, who was "Mad" to think of the pressures at home and turned them into an amusing drama, Edward learned the lessons of silence, honorable self-control, firm-jawed leadership, and the necessity of preserving family dignity. He had observed from close up a father's disaster, and after being repeatedly bruised by it, gained an unshakable belief in the priority of family security and the importance of buckling on *all* the armor of fortitude and determination. In this way, the poet's father came into possession of the loaded gun he would then pass down to his daughter.

There was a definite military quality in Edward—a sense of discipline, of readiness for combat, of standing at attention for life. In 1853, showing off the recently opened Amherst and Belchertown Railroad, he seemed to his daughter to be "marching around the town . . . like some old Roman General upon a Triumph Day." In his old age she reported that in going for kindling he "steps like Cromwell." It was in 1824 that Edward received his commission as ensign in his state's militia. Quickly promoted to major, he acquired the sword, sash, and plume that were part of the correct parade regalia and began writing "Maj. Dickinson" above the masthead of newspapers he considered worth saving. He was an earnest participant in musters and encampments, and was soon convinced by the slack discipline that militia officers should be "instructed by Graduates from West Point." That he backed such a reform (extreme for a believer in states' rights) shows how much he believed in order and general uprightness, and in the basic ideal of the citizen-soldier. As he said in a training-day speech, "It is a distinctive trait in the character of our Government, that the citizen & soldier are combined—that we have rights & possessions as citizens, which, as soldiers, we must defend." This fervently held view, nicely dovetailing with the young man's armored stoicism, had lasting consequences for his treatment of his wife and daughters, whose sex disqualified them from citizenship.

Early in 1826 Major Dickinson had "Camp duty" in the town of Monson, some twenty miles southeast of Amherst, in the course of which he sought a formal order to arrest a lieutenant colonel absent without leave and court-martial him under the articles of war. One evening, accompanied by a friend and fellow officer, he attended a chemical lecture given by the principal of Monson Academy. Chemistry was one of the sciences then in fashion, and it was both instructive and amusing to observe what happened when a fellow listener "took the Gas." But Major Dickinson was less interested in the demonstrations up front than in the young woman sitting next to him. Her name was Emily Norcross, she was attractive, pleasant, and not overly talkative, and she posed an emphatic challenge to the masculine authority he now possessed.

The Comparative Intellectual Powers of the Sexes

The opinions about women that Edward brought to his wooing of the poet's mother are made clear by his part in a memorized dialogue at the end of his junior year. The subject of the "colloquy" was a comparison of "the Intellectual Powers of the Sexes." It appears on the program of Amherst College's first commencement exercises, with the two participants identified as E. Dickinson and T. Packard. The script, in Edward's hand, has been preserved with his college papers.

The debate opens with speaker A ("unexpectedly detained by indisposition") asking speaker B how a question that recently "engrossed the attention of our fellow students" has been resolved. B replies that he will prove "the abilities of females" have been undervalued and that the two sexes have "equal" mental powers. A is surprised and asks how something so improbable can be demonstrated. The answer, B says, is that "the advantages which the sexes enjoy for improving their minds are very unequal." Before a young woman has a chance "to acquire a taste for the pursuits of literature and science," she finds herself "engaged in the affairs of domestic life." Would not a young man, no matter how enterprising, have *his* ambition "*damped* by the continued admonitions of his friends, that his abilities would not justify him in spending the time and money necessary?" Still, some females—Hannah More, Madame de Staël—*have* overcome such discouragements and "risen to distinction."

Speaker A answers that the Scriptures clearly make man "lord of the creation" and woman "subject to the man," and that everyone has always known that these are their relative positions. Since it is woman's nature "to depend on men for protection," "there is a dignity in the obedience of a female to her partner in life." Does it not follow that, just as women have less muscular strength than men, so "in literature and science, they are naturally inferior to us?" Why aren't women heads of state? Why don't they lead armies? Look what happens when they neglect their duties for their minds: they become "pedantic and masculine," as "intolerably loquacious and unyieldingly obstinate" as the Madame de Staël you claim to admire.

(pi-dan'tik)
pedantic = one who makes needless display of their learning

When B retorts that A has wandered from the subject and failed to show that women would not rival men if given a chance, A returns to the difference in the nature of the sexes: females may have "a more lively imagination . . . but in those branches of knowledge which require labour and perseverance and depth of thought . . . they have never yet shown themselves worthy of . . . equality with us." Seeing that no agreement is likely, B brings the debate to an end, but not before dedicating his life to correcting the low estimate of women's mental powers.

Although student presentations had to get higher approval, it was understood that they represented their authors' views. At the end of the manuscript, in Edward's hand, stand the participants' names, E. Dickinson and T. (for Theophilus) Packard, with an "A." under the former and a "B." under the latter. There is no doubt who speaker A was.

Edward's idea of women's subjection to men was standard in his time, but the stridency and fixity with which he defended it were his own. The young man's effort to cope with his father's failure left him holding the unyielding conviction that any females of *his* were going to get the most vigilant protection a man could offer. This was what he would bring to courtship, marriage, and paternity.

hegemony = domination in leadership
eg: The predominant influence of one state over others

Chapter 2

Emily Norcross of Monson

Voted That Brother Joel Be a Committee

By the time Edward Dickinson sat next to Emily Norcross at the chemical lectures, the town of Monson had become a classic hegemony, with a small, stable, closely related clique pretty much running its manufacturing, mercantile, educational, and religious institutions. The fastest way to identify the man who chiefly ran them is to study the local property tax list, which shows that in 1834, in the central district, the highest-taxed person, at $80, was Joel Norcross—Emily's father and Emily Dickinson's grandfather-to-be. The next biggest property owners were Joel's storekeeping brother-in-law Rufus Flynt, at $75; Joel's tavern-keeping brother, Amos Norcross, at $37; and another of Joel's brothers-in-law, Timothy Packard, at $36.

The figure for Joel only hints at the extent of his investments and activities. He was one of the major stockholders in the Hampden Cotton Manufacturing Company, whose factory and millpond were a short distance from the large family home. He had a large and prosperous home-farm and numerous additional fields, meadows, pastures, and woodlots. He was both a partner of his brother-in-law Flynt in the main general store and an active "County Trader," constantly buying, selling, and bartering large quantities of cordwood, lumber, beef, rye seed, barrels of cider, and so forth. The daybooks in which he recorded credits and debits have been deposited at the Monson Historical Society, and as one flips through them one gets an oppressive sense of the man's unflagging orderliness—the steady forward tread of a keen mercantile judgment. These documentary traces tell a very different story from what we read in Samuel Fowler Dickinson's desperate mortgages.

Joel was also a pillar of Monson's First Congregational Church, a more stable, active, and, as was said, "efficient" society than Amherst's feuding First Church. Working closely with the Reverend Alfred Ely, he helped organize and finance the Union Charitable Society, which supported missions and "feeble churches" and helped "poor and pious youth" prepare for the ministry. As the voluminous records show, he regularly served as vice president and on the onerous solicitation committee, though mostly leaving the mundane administration to others. His basic role is suggested by the minutes of an 1828 church meeting at which it was decided to build a chapel in Monson's satellite town in Maine. To get the job done, it was moved "that brother Joel Norcross be a committee to procure a plan," and also transmit the plan "together with the money"—as simple as that, and leaving it all up to him. The motion passed.

But Joel's most generous philanthropies were educational. Monson Academy, incorporated in 1804 and thus predating Amherst Academy, was one of western Massachusetts' outstanding academies prior to its decline in the 1830s. Although it got substantial state aid, the institution was kept afloat by local benefactors, chief among whom was Joel, his gifts amounting to $7,250. (The next biggest donor was Andrew Porter, owner of Monson's North Factory, at $3,200.) In today's money, Joel's

benefactions would come to roughly $200,000. One of the most impor-
tant things to keep in mind about Emily Dickinson is that *both* her
grandfathers dug deep in their pockets for education.

That Joel Norcross was basically in charge in Monson did not make
him some sort of New England Godfather. Regardless of the sources of
his public influence, it was articulated in public meetings, legitimized by
votes, and recorded in minutes, and thus a very different thing from the
secret power of nondemocratic village regimes. Still, we can take for
granted that this shrewd and public-spirited man frequently stepped on
others' toes. At his death at age sixty-nine, the principal of the academy
he helped create and sustain grudgingly observed that it was "pretty generally conceded that Monson has lost a benefactor in Mr Norcross
though many hated him heartily while he lived."

Sister Betsey and the First Female Praying Circle

Betsey Fay Norcross, Joel's wife and the poet's maternal grandmother,
was chiefly occupied with household affairs, as her daughter Emily, the
poet's mother, would be. When Betsey died in 1829, the dignified obituary written by her minister, Alfred Ely, emphasized her attachment to
home: "Humble and retiring in her disposition, it was in the bosom of
her family, and among those who observed her in domestic life, that her
prudence and affectionate regard to the happiness of all around her appeared most conspicuous." The passage could easily be applied to Dickinson's mother and, with qualifications, to Dickinson herself. Although
many have questioned the strength and value of the poet's maternal
legacy,[1] one writer going so far as to call Emily Norcross Dickinson a
mere "carrier of Dickinson traits," there were vital continuities between
Betsey, her daughter Emily, and her gifted granddaughter. Prominent

---

1. Until the late 1980s biographers tended to heap the Norcrosses with derogatory epithets.
Wolff dismissed Joel's letters as "awkward, uncultivated." Cody, the pioneering psychoanalytic
biographer, called the poet's mother "emotionally shallow, self-centered, ineffectual, conventional, timid, submissive, and not very bright." Such judgments no longer seem advisable following the research of Mary Elizabeth Kromer Bernhard and Martha Ackmann.

among them was a strong and exclusive adhesiveness to house and family. The poet's love of home derived in part from her mother's and grandmother's unusually "retiring" domesticity.

But Dickinson's maternal inheritance remains complicated, ambiguous, and hard to discern. There are hints of ambivalent feelings about her mother and a lack of solid information about the relationship. Happily, an unusual document dating from the last two years of Betsey's life, the sixty-page journal of the "First Female Praying Circle" in which she and other Norcrosses were active, opens up the tightly structured pieties of the mother's world. This journal helps us appreciate the pressures and expectations the poet had to deal with.

The Praying Circle was begun in 1827 by Hannah Porter, the dynamic wife of the man whose gifts to Monson Academy were second only to Joel's. A female version of the male organizations that ran the town, the Circle had a written constitution, a set procedure for each meeting, and a rotating secretary. It enjoyed the support of Reverend Ely and drew its members from the town's most influential families: its single largest contingent consisted of women belonging to the Norcross clan by birth or marriage. Its purpose was to promote the full evangelical agenda through prayer and devotion, discreetly administered pressure, and money-raising. What distinguished it from the town's other religious organizations was an explicit rule of secrecy, the constitution stipulating that "no member shall be at liberty to make any remarks respecting the meeting before others who are not members."

The journal shows how effective the Circle must have been in coordinating its members' hearts and minds. At each session they agreed on a shared "resolve" for the next two weeks—to pray for "our Literary Institutions," for example, or to raise $50 for a missionary society. Meeting in Betsey's home in April 1829, their second anniversary (she was hostess six times in all), they solemnly discussed their "union of sentiment & design" and how "greatly endeared" they had become to each other. Certain they had been gathered for great purposes, they decided to pray for a revival, and more, to adopt no other resolve until the revival came. It was their boldest move yet, a decision to take heaven by storm, as it were.

At the time Betsey had only several months to live and the First

Church was at a low point, having reaped only five new professions of faith in 1827 and not a single one in 1828. Like other orthodox churches, this one relied on intermittent revivals to bring in a harvest of new members from the younger generation. For six months Monson's women kept their resolve, praying and encouraging one another and working behind the scenes, and finally a revival began. As was mostly the case in New England, it lacked the ranting and emotional display seen in the West or among Methodists, but it still proved terribly solemn, intense, disturbing. The Reverend Asahel Nettleton (whose labors at Yale in 1820 had left Edward Dickinson unsaved) was called in to assist at the daily prayer meetings, and when the excitement ended there were about seventy new converts, including Betsey's younger daughter Lavinia. Revivals were often credited to the quiet efforts of devout women. The Praying Circle's journal for 1827–1829, a unique document of its kind, clarifies what that meant, and what the poet would be holding out against at key junctures.

One of the Circle's seven charter members was Phoebe H. Brown, the best-known woman hymnist in New England. Earlier in her life, before moving to Monson, Brown had experienced severe poverty. Once, taking an evening walk to a rich neighbor's estate—her one daily break from the care of her children—she was reproached for trespassing. In response she composed her most famous hymn:

> *I love to steal awhile away*
> *From little ones and care,*
> *And spend the hours of setting day,*
> *In humble, grateful prayer.*

In succeeding stanzas, the speaker tells how she loves to shed a "penitential tear," reflect on God's mercies, and picture the "brighter scenes in heav'n," and in all these ways renew her strength. The hymn concludes:

> *Thus, when life's toilsome day is o'er,*
> *May its departing ray*
> *Be calm as this impressive hour,*
> *And lead to endless day.*

Shifting the scene from earth to heaven in this way was a fairly standard program. In working it out, Mrs. Brown attained the bland, competent, and uplifting lyricism of her time, which, unlike ours, wanted poetry to serve public ends.

Her lyric was published in the mid-1820s in *Village Hymns for Social Worship*, a popular evangelical collection edited by (once again) Asahel Nettleton. According to a Connecticut Valley woman born the same year as Dickinson, this hymnal was one "we all carried." "I Love to Steal Awhile Away" appeared in many other hymnbooks and eventually became one of those songs everyone knew. The humble praying woman had achieved something (and this was not her only hymn) that would always elude the pious and popular Josiah Gilbert Holland, none of whose lyrics became hymns. Even Samuel Bowles, whose Sundays were about as pious as Mark Twain's, would find Brown's words on his tongue as he began a letter to Dickinson's brother: " 'I steal awhile away' from my Sunday devotions to pass to you and yours the compliments of the season." Bowles was *not* being reverent, and neither was Dickinson when she offered to send *Village Hymns* to her brother "by earliest opportunity." That was in 1853,[2] when she and Austin were the family's only unconverted members. Well aware that this now old-fashioned compilation was the last thing he wanted, she mockingly added, "I was just this moment thinking of a favorite stanza of yours, 'where congregations ne'er break up, and Sabbaths have no end.' " The hymn describing heaven in this ominous way was also in Nettleton's collection.

When Dickinson attended Mount Holyoke College in 1847–1848 and a revival swept the student body, Hannah Porter, the Praying Circle's founder, seems to have organized an informal circle of concern around the future poet. It is probable that the Circle, still very much alive, made the stubbornly unconverted young woman a focus of prayer and pressure.

If there was much that Dickinson took from the Norcross side, there

---

2. At the time Monson's poet was still visible. When Emily Norcross Dickinson attended Monson Academy's fifty-year jubilee in 1854, it was Brown who composed and delivered the official, preachy, and backward-looking poem (". . . For DUTY was the watchword then . . .").

was much she had to resist and reject, to define herself *against*. A part of this large maternal heritage was Phoebe H. Brown, public poet, the voice of congregations. To grow up with her as the accepted standard could spur a fresh mind into thinking about a more private form of authorship.

A Narrow Girlhood

Each of Dickinson's grandmothers gave birth to nine children and was kept busy by a vast array of pressing domestic labors. But "crazy" as Lucretia Dickinson's situation at home may have been, at least none of her children died before her. Betsey Norcross had to bury four of hers, including her two oldest, Hiram and Austin, who both died in their twenties. Hiram is thought to have been killed by the mysterious wasting disease known as consumption (tuberculosis). These tragic events had deep and long-lasting effects on the family. When Betsey died, attention was paid to the "severe afflictions, which she was called repeatedly to endure in the sickness and death of children." And when her oldest daughter, Emily, the poet's mother, gave birth to *her* first child, his middle name, the one he went by, was taken from the lamented Austin.

Another feature of the grandmothers' generation that had a discernible effect on the poet's life is that, where Lucretia had four healthy girls to help her, Betsey had only two who reached adulthood—Emily, born in 1804, and Lavinia, born in 1812. These hard facts suggest the poet's mother did not enjoy the easy girlhood her father Joel's wealth and standing might otherwise imply. Years later the younger sister recalled "how much care" the huge Norcross house (a converted tavern) entailed. Not only were there boarders to be looked after, but there was generally no more than one hired "girl." Much of the work had to be done by Emily, who served as Betsey's mainstay until Lavinia grew old enough to shoulder her part of the load. When Austin and five-year-old Nancy died in 1824, nineteen-year-old Emily must have joined in the hard bedside labor we can only imagine—"watching," wiping a sweaty forehead, holding a basin for spitting blood, helping an emaciated figure out of bed. The traces of this exceptionally responsible girlhood are to be read in Emily

Norcross Dickinson's mature character: a fanatical insistence on household order; a melancholy, inexpressive, relatively inelastic spirit.

The poet's mother went to Monson Academy, but for how long or how regularly we cannot say: the early catalogs are gone. In her time it was not assumed that students must be in continual attendance from one term to the next, keeping up with their age-mates. Because there were only two basic levels of instruction, junior and senior, with none of the rigid grade levels we take for granted, pupils often dropped out for one or more terms. Those whose help was required at home would simply interrupt their education.

The earliest trace of Emily Norcross's schooling dates from October 1819, when she was fifteen and participated in a Monson Academy "exhibition," a public display of students' achievements. A printed program, unearthed eighty years later and reproduced in a newspaper of 1902, shows "E. Norcross" taking the part of Rosamond opposite Queen Eleanor. The girl also played Susan, daughter of a missionary to the Cherokees, and Sylva, daughter of an "ancient Shepherdess" in a pastoral drama called "Search after Happiness." These performances were succeeded by a ball held in Uncle Amos's tavern, with Uncle Erasmus Norcross serving as one of four managers. An invitation signed by Erasmus was printed on the back of a playing card, as was customary. The evening seems to have had a surprisingly secular tone.

The next trace comes from 1821–1822, when a certain Caroline P. Dutch, then in her early twenties, served for one year as the academy's "preceptress." Her evaluation of Emily's performance, written on a neatly scissored slip of paper, was never discarded:

> Miss Emely Norcross, for punctual attendance, close application, good acquirements, and discreet behaviour, merits the approbation of her
>
> > Preceptress.
> > C. P. Dutch.

Miss Dutch also superintended the "Female Department" of the church's Sabbath School during her year in Monson. The daughter of a minister, she of course paid close attention to her pupils' religious and moral training. Her report on Emily Norcross puts the emphasis on effort and conduct.

But the teacher's painful formality did not preclude warm personal affection. On the notes Emily took of a sermon, written sideways below point number two ("How happy is the christian's lot"), we find this smuggled message:

> Oh! my dear Caroline
> > Remember me
> for
> > forever

If this was Caroline P. Dutch, she did remember. In 1823 she returned to Monson for a visit, and a few days later her punctual and discreet former pupil, then in New Haven, received the welcome message that her teacher "wanted to see you very much."

Remarkably, after marrying the Reverend William W. Hunt, this admired preceptress not only ended up in Amherst but became one of the poet's own early teachers at Amherst Academy. That this coincidence has escaped scholarly notice shows how badly the mother-daughter connection has been slighted. One wonders: Did the two Emily Dickinsons share notes on the instructor they had in common? Does the mother's attachment to Caroline help explain why the daughter was "always in love with my teachers," as she once said? Unfortunately, we have no record of the poet's feelings about this particular teacher.

Emily Norcross's one surviving schoolgirl composition is titled "On Amusements: A Dialogue between Mary & Julia." This may have been a collaborative effort designed for oral delivery at an exhibition: above Mary we find the name of Sarah; above Julia, Emily. Moralistic and uncombative, the dialogue begins with the other girl saying, "when we last met, we were conversing upon Amusements: you thought them criminal and injurious. I cannot think that your sentiments are correct for what can be more innocent than the Amusements of the Theatre, the Ball room, and the like." Remembering that the exhibition of 1819 had been followed by a ball, it is clear that this dialogue, stilted as it is, concerned the live local issues of the day. Speaking up for control and repression is Julia/Emily:

> O my dear Mary, what can be more pernicious to the youthful mind, than the Amusements which you are now pursuing: when you reflect upon the precious time which you have wasted in vain recreations, will it afford you any real satisfaction? O *No far* from that: be assured Mary that it will cause many a sigh and bitter remorse of conscience.

After a token defense of her position, the other girl is persuaded by Julia/Emily's "cheerful countenance" that "religion is not that melancholy gloomy thing which I have long imagined." Now quite reformed, she voices Julia/Emily's austere ideal of the pleasures and rewards of friendship: "Oh favour me with your society often for I think your conversation will ever be a sourse of instruction to me."

Compared to the pugnacious colloquy in which Edward and another young man fought it out on an issue of consequence, Emily's dialogue seems something of a charade, sadly controlled and unreal. If this contrast says something about the emphases in boys' and girls' education, it also exhibits one of the big differences between these two persons. Proper, formal, strained, Emily's part of the composition shows no pleasure in writing, no impetus to put herself onto the page. Instead, she persuades another girl to give up some amusing activities in favor of conversation seen as "a sourse of instruction."

All her life Emily Norcross seems to have regarded writing as a chore that bore no relation to the heart's needs; certainly, she proved an inexpressive and dilatory correspondent. In March 1824 her brother William, then at Yale, reproached her for a silence of six weeks. A few months later, trying another tack, he said he wouldn't "scold" her anymore for not writing. After she married and left home, her sister Lavinia was dismayed to find that "Emily does not *trouble* herself about answering my letters." Regarding Edward as more responsive, Lavinia confided that her sister's letters were "so short I must complain can she not fill a sheet." His own sister Lucretia was so put out by his wife's silence she sarcastically asked him to have her sign "her *name* in your next letter" lest she "forget how to write." The poet's mother's preferred methods for communicating with people at a distance were, one, not answering, and two, leaving the page mostly blank.

The most revealing pieces of writing from Emily Norcross's first two decades may be her sermon notes and outlines. Like other orthodox societies, Monson's First Church had two services each Sunday and thus two sermons to listen to. On June 3, 1821, when a visiting minister selected John 13:27 as his text ("That thou doest, do quickly"), she recorded his main points:

> 1st Life is short and uncertain
> 2nd The period for working out our own salvation will [be] short
> as short as our stay on earth

Another Sunday, as if preparing for parenthood, she dutifully noted all the things she would have to explain to her children. The fourth point was: "You must teach them . . . that the carnal mind is enmity against God and they possess the carnal mind." The sixth: "Further teach them the truths respecting death judgement and eternity." These outline-covered pages probably give an accurate picture of the laborious intellectual and spiritual labors the poet's mother grew up taking for granted. There was so much hard work, so much discipline, so much to take seriously. That her sermon outlines are mostly in ink tells us (given the awkwardness of using pen and ink in a meetinghouse pew) that she went to the trouble of recopying her original penciled notes. And all the while, technically unconverted, she could not regard *herself* as ready for eternity.

It is only because Emily retained a few penciled notes that we have that smuggled "Oh! my dear Caroline." This chance survival reassures us that after all there was life beneath the discipline. It also warns us how tricky it is to rely on written evidence (as we must) in order to make sense of someone who couldn't express herself in standard written formats. That, however, was just the kind of mother Emily Dickinson required.

In 1853, when Austin was away studying at Harvard's law school, Dickinson informed him that "Mother was much amused at the feebleness of your hopes of hearing from her." Mother's odd laugh—that abrupt unmuffling of a nonstandard mind—shows up at intervals in her letters. One January when her husband was away, she informed him, "The weather still continues mild not like winter at all. I think old zero has lost very much of his self respect." Several years later, writing in the same seasonal conditions, her fifteen-year-old daughter wondered if "Old Winter had forgotten himself." The huge bag of tricks accumulated by the poet got a start in her mother's small pocketful of wry.

Herrick's School

Emily Norcross's longest absence from Monson prior to her marriage took place in summer 1823, when the nineteen-year-old spent several months at a highly regarded girls' school in New Haven run by the Reverend Claudius Herrick. Previous alumnae included Maria Flynt, a first cousin living in Monson, and Harriet Webster, daughter of the lexicographer and later the wife of Professor William C. Fowler of Amherst College. Accompanied by a cousin, Olivia Flynt, Emily had her lessons in a large five-bay, two-story house on Elm Street, along with sixty-four other girls. (Three years later, when Olivia alone enrolled for a second term, enrollment was down to thirty-eight and the school seemed "much better.") The two Monson girls apparently lived with Elizabeth Whittlesey, the forty-nine-year-old daughter of a New Haven clergyman. On Olivia, at least, Miss Whittlesey's "rigid restraint" left a strong impression.

Although Emily made "but few" acquaintances, she clearly won over Reverend Herrick, who spoke of her three years later, according to Olivia, "with a great degree of interest—says he became very much attached to you." This report is another sign of the warm response the young woman inspired in teachers and age-mates alike. After she married, Miss Whittlesey trumpeted a message to Edward Dickinson announcing that she had "a pretty good opinion of you because you have so good an opinion of your wife." The passage suggests that those who liked Emily understood that her good qualities might not be universally appreciated.

Like many of Herrick's pupils, Emily Norcross enrolled for only one term, perhaps because of the press of work at home. The following year a younger brother took for granted she would be "attending to domestic affairs this summer," but still expressed the hope there would be leisure for "social intercourse or reading" and she would not be "continually pent up in the kitchen." His fears seem to have been on target: in his next letter, dated November 1 (the season when hordes of flies left barnyards for the warmth of houses), he could only trust that she was "victorious over your mortal enemies, the Flies." It may well be that a heavy workload kept the poet's mother from cultivating her mental powers and acquiring social ease.

Yet her own letters show how happy she was to leave New Haven for Monson, "my *dear dear* home," as she called it in a letter to her sister. A very local person, she was tightly bound to family and friends, familiar routines, a limited palette of country sights and sounds. When Olivia went back to Herrick's school in summer 1826, her letter to Emily developed the feelings she knew her cousin could enter into—how she yearned for "the retirement of our little village" and missed "that little circle of dear friends." She acknowledged a letter from Emily ("quite too short," to be sure) that "spoke of the dear little bird—the Whippoorwill—I have heard but one since I left home—I believe there are more of them in M[onson] than anywhere—The *Cat-edid* supplies its place here—presume you have not forgotten what fine music they used to make in Temple-street [Whittlesey's home]." "Fine music" is sarcastic, but the passage still strikes the right chords: Emily's strong local attachments, her love of rural tranquillity, and her alertness to sound—not just the dramatic whippoorwill but the background of locust- or cicada-song.

Forty years later, when Emily Dickinson had to go to Boston for medical treatment for her eyes, she asked her sister, "Do you remember the Whippowil that sang one night on the Orchard fence?" Both the poet and her brother Austin found a special meaning in the chirping of crickets in high summer. "Musicians wrestle everywhere" (Fr229) is how she began one of several poems that register the undertone of birdsong and insect calls. It was partly owing to her mother that the country's dispersed drone became one of the things she noticed and wrote about, while taking her own place in the chorus. She was her mother's daughter in ways not easily got at.

Chapter 3

1826–1828: Winning Emily Norcross

Nowhere do we get a more intimate picture of Emily Dickinson's domestic origins than in her parents' many courtship letters, all but one of which have been preserved. The only other extended exchange between the couple dates from the late 1830s, when their union had become close and stable and its tensions muffled. If we wish to parse the marriage that formed the poet, we must follow her parents' first negotiations.

On February 8, 1826, when the militia exercises and chemical lectures were over, Solomon Warriner, Jr., a friend of Edward, teased him about "the young Lady, who lived about a mile from our quarters, & near one of the Factories. It cannot be necessary for me to mention her name for I think the impression she made upon your heart, was too deep to be soon effaced." That same day Edward sent the young lady a resolute and dignified love letter. "From our short interviews," he wrote, "I imbibed an attachment for you, which I shall continue to cherish." Not mentioning his heart, he declared his "esteem" for one "in whom so many of the female virtues are conspicuous," and then he made a forthright declaration of his intentions: to "cherish a friendship, which . . . if reciprocated, might promote our mutual happiness." He was proposing, not marriage, but an exchange of letters that might lead to marriage.

It isn't known whether Emily Norcross was surprised by this unusually explicit and possibly premature declaration. Taking three weeks to reply, she evidently found it a tricky assignment to frame an encouraging yet suitably noncommittal response. She admitted his proposal gave "pleasure," feared "it would not be prudence in me to give you a definite answer at present," but then concluded with as definite a reply as Edward could have desired: "I shall hear from you with pleasure."

On each side, the correspondents had to contend with heavy constraints. As a student at Northampton Law School, Edward was weighed down with studies and with legal research carried out for his instructors. For her part, Emily not only had little free time but felt a paramount need to be circumspect. Fearing her privacy would be compromised by the postal system, she announced in her second communication that she "could not consistent with my present fealings send letters by mail"—meaning she would rely on trusted friends to carry them. She drafted this letter in her room "without any one persons knowing how I am occupied I fear I shall soon be enquired for."

Because Edward saw the exchange of letters as a formal precontractual process in which each party "would be perfectly plain & use the utmost freedom of remark," he made a strenuous effort to convey a lucid and emphatic idea of his opinions, ambitions, expectations. The opinion he voiced most often—that courage, resolution, and hard work can achieve great things—recalls his father's youthful credo that a man starting out in the world needs "all the armour of fortitude and determination." The last word was a favorite with Edward, who liked to underline it. "All that is wanting to make any man what he *would be,* is a *determination* to become such." "More depends on a *determination* to be contented . . . than we are apt to imagine." "A man can do almost any thing which he *determines to do*—the mind, says one, is omnipotent." In back of these steely affirmations stood two awkward facts: Emily already had a comfortable home, and all he had was a debt-burdened father and a future. "I know the risk is great, on your part," he candidly conceded.

Four months after Edward began the correspondence, having received two widely spaced letters and made two day-trips to Monson, he dispatched a sober proposal of marriage:

> Our last interview, which was much more free & unreserved than any former one, led me to a satisfactory conclusion respecting your qualifications, & convinced me that you possessed virtues calculated to render yourself & your friends happy.—And such reliance do I place on your candor, that I feel perfectly safe in making a most unreserved avowal of my esteem, & in declaring my wish to become a friend for life to you.

Following this came a long cautionary recommendation that Emily owed it to herself to investigate his character and history, to facilitate which he referred her to the men who ran the law school, to his fellow students, and to various clergymen, among them the Reverend Lyman Coleman, who was then courting her cousin Maria Flynt and who could speak for the petitioner's "character in College."[1] Adding a long account of his professional prospects, he urged her, first, to reach a decision at her convenience and, second, "to communicate it." That was the closest he came to an expression of passionate expectation.

In some respects this strangely eviscerated proposal was a product of its time. Although "friend for life" may look like a euphemism for wife, spouses and relatives *were* often referred to as friends—a usage the poet would retain long after others dropped it. Still, we cannot equate her young parents with the conventions and understandings of the period. Even for New Englanders, they had an insistent and unfashionable angularity, with obvious ceremony-cutting elements in their personalities.

---

1. For Emily, references had little value. On one of Edward's early visits, she told him we "ought to form our own opinions, or our own judgments" (his summary). Chances are, this struck him as naive—one more reason she needed his protection. Fifty years later, their daughter expressed the same idea to two friends whose faith differed from hers: "we cannot believe for each other."

There was a purposeful, starting-from-scratch highmindedness in Edward's proposal. Anyone can promise love and devotion in the usual phrases, but *he* was framing a marital constitution, trying to spell out exactly what Emily might be getting into.

During the couple's two-year courtship, Edward sent seventy letters and Emily twenty-four. If for him the correspondence promised a full and free exchange of views, for her it was a much neglected duty, a cause of discomfort, avoidance, shame. The more open and aboveboard he seemed, the more she was hamstrung by uncertainty and embarrassment: it was as if his aggressive candor worked against a matching response. Though she had promised only to "hear," not to speak, she would apologize at the start of her letters for not replying sooner, and in closing for not writing more. She announced she had something to say, or that "it would give me pleasure to answer all your enquiries," but that was it: nothing followed. On rare occasions she spelled out how her time was occupied—caring for sick family members, going to Hartford to lay in winter supplies, paying a round of visits when brother William's fiancée came from New York. Her usual rule, however, was to offer nothing but blanket excuses: "there are many things to prevent my writing of which you are not acquainted." Once the excuses became an obligatory feature, they began to generate their own rueful humor, as when, à propos of nothing, she added the postscript "I must leave the apologies"—the abruptness of which reminds us of the poet's sly trenchancy. But the general undertone was an uneasy feeling of not living up to her suitor's expectations: "I am sensible that I have never exercised that freedom [of expression] which I presume you have desired me to."

This uneasiness was caused in part by Emily's sense of inadequacy as a writer. Dutiful and laborious, she was still far from having mastered the rules of standard written English. Miss Dutch, the Reverend Herrick, and Edward's well-schooled sisters would have wondered at the misspellings, the opaque diction, the tangled syntax, and that unstable writing voice—its mix of vernacular elements and stilted propriety.

Still, not only was Emily capable of expressing herself with decision and vigor, but her odd sense of humor was always coming out. Edward's friend Solomon suddenly became "the wise man." A string of accidents led her to speak of Edward as enrolled in "the unfortunate society." Referring to the frequent trips from Belchertown of Maria Flynt's ministerial fiancé, Emily joked, "We consider Mr Coleman as almost a resident. I imagine he thinks cousin Maria would make but little progress in her favourite study, divinity, without frequent lectures." There is no prudery here, the language flows easily, and the speaker seems comfortably immersed in the local point of view ("we consider"). The passage shows how firmly the poet's mother was rooted in her family and native village before being transplanted to Amherst.

Edward's proposal of marriage went out in early June. Then came silence. He rode to Monson on July 5 but came home without an answer. Trusting that Emily's reasons for saying nothing were "good," he manfully kept up his end of the correspondence, using her first name now. He hoped her father would sanction the match, and offered to write him. Finally, on August 8, addressing Edward by his first name, Emily admitted his last letter had made her happy and hoped he had not inferred a lack of interest from her "poor returns." Her conflicted feelings are apparent in one of her hopelessly tongue-tied sentences: "Did I not rely with perfect confidence in what you have expressed to me I should not take the liberty to include your happiness with my own but at present I feal privileg to do it." Following this, she assured him she had read the "pamphlets" he lent her and explained why they were not yet returned. Having cleared *that* up, she returned to the business at hand, finally giving her answer:

> I think you must be convinced ere this that your intercourse with me
> is mutual although I have not explained to you my views as I have
> wished but I will improve this opportunity to acknowledge my warm
> and increasing attachment to you and that your proposals are what I
> would wish to comply with, but without the advise and consent of
> my father I cannot consistantly do it. As I regard his fealings very
> much should I meet his approbation I will then assure you of my
> confidence and affection.

Edward sent his formal request to Joel Norcross after he was out of law school and about to open an office in a new brick building in the center of Amherst (on the site of the present town hall). Deferential but emphatic, he covered all the main points: that Emily's "virtues" had inspired a "partiality for her," that his esteem was reciprocated "in a measure," that the two had "conversed freely & familiarly on the subject," and that he hoped to become "her legal guardian & protector." Again, references were sent along with a request to "communicate your opinion to Emily, or me, in any manner you may deem proper."

The result: not only did Joel fail to answer but Emily also fell silent. Was her father sending out inquiries? Were there reservations about Edward's uncertain prospects? The young man continued to send letter after letter, until, finally, taking silence for consent, he raised the delicate question "as to the time when it would be proper to consummate our union." But he didn't push, shrewdly allowing there was no hurry and that he must establish himself in his profession. "A few months! perhaps." This was the right approach, and a week later Emily signaled her agreement: "you may rightly conclude that my feelings are in unison with yours I am happy to learn that you are not disposed to be in haste the reasons you have advanced correspond perfectly with my fathers views."

Although the couple was now engaged, the negotiations leading to this result had been far less open than Edward had imagined. Many things conspired to muffle Emily: the dynamics of courtship, the requirements of modesty, her lack of skill in letter-writing, her close attachment to home. Indeed (and this may explain her father's silence as well as her own), she was so indispensable in the Norcross household that its members were probably unwilling to discuss her leaving. The following summer, when she spent a few weeks in New York City, her brother William noted that "her absence . . . produces quite a vacancy in our small family, and we look for her return with no small degree of pleasure." Ominously, Betsey Norcross was not only "indisposed" but "quite low," so that in February 1827 the best that could be said was that "we trust that she is gradually recovering." If Mother was dying, would she be able to spare Emily? If so, could the family make do? One effect of Edward's suit was to ask the Norcrosses to speak their own dreadful questions.

The opacities of the poet's mother's life cannot be blamed solely on her husband. The trick is to balance what she brought from Monson with the pressures attributable to him. Still, the daunting effects of his directness and determination should not be underestimated. Nor should something else the young attorney brought to the relationship: his vigorous understanding of the complementarity of his male authority and her "female virtues."

After receiving Emily's final consent, Edward published a forceful exposition of these sex-linked virtues. Even though this act took place three years before the poet's birth, it would seem to be one of her life's formative events—the framing of the constitution that would determine and govern her existence.

What Coelebs Required in a Wife

Edward had always been an affectionate older brother, with a strong sense of responsibility for his four sisters. Judging from early letters, such as the one in which Lucretia thanked him for his advice on education, it was assumed on both sides that it was his part to counsel and protect and theirs to listen and defer. Mary, his favorite, may have had reservations about his high-handed views on women, but she still complimented his "elegance of *style*" and deprecated her own "diffuseness." After Mary's death many years later, Edward was made guardian of her four girls, one of whom always treasured the memory of his loving support: "His bearing was almost stern in its dignity & nobility, but his nature was as beautiful, & sympathetic, & tender as a mother's. . . . As a child I feared him, until I found him out when trouble & difficulty came, & my Guardian became my strong, & tender, & lovingly-revered Friend." The tenderness was loyal and true—but it had to be understood who was boss. When sister Catharine failed to consult him before engaging herself to a man not yet established in business, her nervous anticipation of his response to the news—"You need not stare, or lift up your hands"—speaks volumes. When they next met, she found Edward silent, remote, and "very sober" and before long had to admit they didn't "seem to *make up* quite." He and most of the family didn't attend her wedding in Andover. Authority was taken seriously in the Dickinson family.

Edward's assumption that women were to be guarded by men was the conventional view in his time, but he was unusual in making a special study of female education. In the six years since his junior-year colloquy, the young man's interest in how to foster and protect the "female virtues" had grown intense and obsessive. Neither his fiancée nor his daughters would be able to ignore his fixed and vehement opinions on the subject, which go a long way toward explaining the poet's extreme sense of privacy and why publication was such an issue for her.

One of several ironies is that the person Edward was most indebted to for his formulations was a woman, the learned and prolific Hannah More.[2] A protégée of Samuel Johnson, More exemplified both the urbane culture of the eighteenth century and the evangelicalism of the early nineteenth. Her *Strictures on the Modern System of Female Education* assailed the emphasis on conventional accomplishments and the failure to prepare women of rank for the duties of marriage and motherhood. In America her most influential book was probably *Coelebs in Search of a Wife,* of which the Dickinsons owned an edition published in 1820. This plotless novel tells how Coelebs (Latin for "bachelor") sifts English society for the perfect spouse until his encounters with a series of foolish and vicious wives and daughters persuade him that "the women who bless, dignify, and truly adorn society" are in general "little known, because to be known is not their object. . . . If they occasion little sensation abroad, they produce much happiness at home." Not only did this become one of Edward's root ideas but he became determined to disseminate it.

---

2. Years later Edward presented Dickinson with an 1851 edition of an advice manual first published in 1821, *Letters on Practical Subjects, to a Daughter.* (His sloppy handwriting makes it hard to say whether the book was given in 1852 or 1862.) If she read it, she would have discovered that "the entire works of Mrs. More, the pride and glory of your sex, you cannot read too often or too attentively."

His forum was Amherst's first newspaper, *The New-England Inquirer*, a four-page weekly he helped found in late 1826 and whose initial editor was his friend Osmyn Baker. On December 22, not long after Emily Norcross agreed to marry him, Edward's five papers on "Female Education" began appearing. Signing himself "Coelebs," he set out his intentions for the series in a bland and urbane manner. With the second paper, however, things veered out of control with the declaration that he would say "just *what* I think, and just *as* I think," unmoved by either the smiles or frowns of "fair readers." As he developed the familiar view that the good of society requires women to be wives and mothers, a note of sarcastic defiance not present in More's equable novel began to be heard. How are we benefited, Coelebs asked, if women annoy men "with endless cant upon subjects of controversy"? Why should women attend college to prepare themselves for "a life of 'single blessedness' "? It would be preferable for young women to take the veil and spend their lives in nunneries than for men "to sit under the showers of wise reasonings, and learned arguments, which their consciousness of superiority would continually prompt them to pour out upon us." Summing matters up, Coelebs sketched a scene in which a pushy literary female takes the reins of polite conversation from her husband: "She will introduce your guests to the contents of the last 'Quarterly' . . . She will tell them of the beauty of one passage, or the defects of another . . . She knows the character of all our public men, and never hesitates to pronounce an opinion upon the policy of their measures." Such will be the baneful results of too much female education.

Even in 1827, these belligerent opinions struck many as extreme and ill-tempered, including the *Inquirer*'s editor, who called Coelebs "a little 'notional' " and printed the criticisms of two readers who signed themselves "A Lady" and "Tabitha." (A later editor would quote a minister who doubted that women were "constitutionally incapacitated for intellectual eminence" or that "there was a sex in the soul.") Stung, Edward dashed off an invective insinuating that "Tabitha" was not really a woman: "How long since she put off the garb of a man & appeared [in] female dress?" Rather than print this, Baker issued a stern public rebuke:

"Coelebs is utterly inadmissible. He will see at a glance the impolicy and injustice of publishing articles intended only to expose" other pseudonymous authors.

In his third paper, Edward conceded that works of literature might legitimately be read by women. All he wanted was "to guard them against that pedantic, positive, dogmatical & obstinate manner . . . which delights in argument." The charms of female character are modesty and forbearance, a "willingness to yield to the opinions of persons of superior wisdom."

The ferocity implicit in such views came out in full force in what was to have been the fourth paper. In this sarcastic tirade against fashion, Edward described a young woman who has been "ruffled & flounced & furbelowed" and then pictured the shocking consequence—her abandonment of home and duties for "parties of pleasure." Nothing was quite so sickening as to pass such a creature on the street and "see her turn around to *look at you.*" There was only one remedy: mothers must teach daughters that it is no hardship to "rise early, & attend to the duties of the house during the whole of the day," and that it is only by "constantly remaining *at home*" that they will find husbands.

Like the reply to "Tabitha," this essay also proved unpublishable. Returning to the subject of women's education, Edward used his fifth and final paper to list the intellectual pursuits proper for women. Departing from the strict orthodox view, he allowed that they could read the better kind of novels. Chemistry had a practical value in housekeeping. Botany, as his preliminary outline puts it, "refines & chastens" females. Painting and drawing serve "to make them *neat.*" To form their taste as letter-writers, they should study Addison and Steele's *Spectator* papers. The key point, emerging in Edward's concluding notation, was "Stay at home."

After the essay appeared, Edward reflected on his motives in a letter to his fiancée: "I know not why it is, but I have long . . . felt much interest in having [women] correctly instructed, & their tastes and judgments properly formed." Wishing "some disinterested person" would furnish a sensible account of women's duties and seeing no volunteers, he simply stepped forward. Judging from this statement, the young man had little understanding how snarled his feelings were regarding literary women. After meeting Catharine Sedgwick, New England's best-known woman novelist, he informed Emily she had "an interesting countenance—an appearance of much thought, & rather masculine features." To be sure, he would regret "to see another Madame de Stael—especially if any one wished to make a partner of her for life. Different qualities are more desirable in a female who enters into domestic relations—and you have already had my opinions on that Subject—More when we meet." No doubt there was more when they met.[3] Yet Edward had been glad to meet Sedgwick and felt "a conscious pride that women of our own country & our own State, too, are emulating not only the females, but the men of England & France & Germany & Italy in works of literature." When he read her latest historical novel, *Hope Leslie,* he admired the two heroines—one English, the other Pequod—and made a point of sending the book to Emily.

In fact, Edward repeatedly urged his fiancée to look at books by women. It is true he sent her the *Spectator* papers to refine her deplorable style and often quoted Edward Young's *Night Thoughts,* a great favorite, but the fiction he pressed on her consisted of dignified historical novels by women: Jane Porter's *Scottish Chiefs* and *Thaddeus of Warsaw* and Lydia Maria Child's *The Rebels, or Boston before the Revolution.* Edward's approval of this American novel by a woman who promoted numerous reforms reveals his early liberalism. But the liberalism seems to have wilted: years later his daughter gave a political activist the impression she had grown up without having "heard of Mrs. Child."

Unlike the original Coelebs, whose chosen bride is literate and cultivated as well as home-loving, Edward chose a signally unliterary woman. Indeed, one of his papers asks the question some might like to put to him: "How does it affect us . . . to receive an epistle from a valued friend, with half the words mis-spelled—in which capitals & small letters have changed positions—where a plural noun is followed by a sin-

---

3. There was also more in the fifth Coelebs paper, which praised "the productions of some of our Female Authors" but insisted their pursuit of fame ruled out "domestic happiness," thus mandating "their departure from Society."

gular verb?" To be sure, a similar question confronts admirers of the often ungrammatical poems written by the couple's daughter.

Far from abating, Edward's heated opinions about literary females and staying at home exerted an immensely complicating effect on his daughter's position as a writer of genius. To publish her poems or proclaim her ambition would have been extremely risky acts. Of the many things that conspired to both energize and silence Dickinson, her father's emphatic views were not the least salient.

The ironies could hardly be more extreme or punishing. Assuming a mask invented by a gifted woman, the poet's father set out to explain why women should not develop and deploy their minds. He chose to marry a (mostly) obedient and inexpressive woman who would not usurp his talking rights, and then he became a remote and often silent paterfamilias. He fathered one of the greatest of poets but probably never realized it.

It misses the point to think of Edward as a tyrant. Given his admiration of selected women writers, it would seem that in some tacit or subterranean way he *invited* his daughter to write. She herself drew attention to his conflicting messages when she told Higginson in 1862 that Father "buys me many Books—but begs me not to read them—because he fears they joggle the Mind." If by "the Mind" we understand "the female mind," this remark looks like a critical summation of Edward's Coelebs papers, which say, essentially, that, though women should be taught the alphabet, this is a risky operation that too often results in a crazy feminine rattle. If the paternal text was *You must not be a public author*, the subtext may have been *Write in private*.

Coelebs Gets His Wife

Just east of the building in which Edward had his office was the spacious home of Jemima Montague, an aging widow with family ties to both his parents. Although her husband's will gave her a secure lifetime tenancy, Samuel Fowler Dickinson had acquired the title to both the house and the seventeen acres that went with it. Not imagining any hitches, Edward informed his fiancée that he could have the place "any time I please, as my father has the control of it." He could either "*hire*, or *buy*, as shall be thought best."

A carpenter was found, and by early 1828 improvements were under way in the part of the house not occupied by the widow. It would soon be a fitting residence for an up-and-coming attorney and his respectable bride, and Edward pressed Emily Norcross to come and inspect the premises, so as to "have a voice in the style of making the repairs & improvements."

There was also the question of Emily's prenuptial visit to her future in-laws, about which one of Edward's sisters, Lucretia, was polite but pressing:

> We have Miss Norcross, been anticipating the pleasure of a visit from
> you this season, & much regret that it is inconvenient for you to
> come. I have only to add, that it would be very gratifying to all of us,
> & should you make it convenient at any time this winter, to spend a
> week or two with us; we should be happy to see you.

Was this easy propriety intimidating to a woman whose letters were generally awkward, incorrect, and late? The one and only time the bride-to-be appeared in Amherst was for Commencement on August 22, 1827—a public event that ruled out much close contact with Edward's family. She was accompanied by brother William and sister Lavinia and may not have stayed overnight. Edward invited, urged, begged, ordered, but she remained so unresponsive that he finally asked—a bleak and desperate joke—whether she intended "to remain at Monson after we are married?" It would be good to know how his sisters explained her peculiar standoffishness, but all we have is Mary's bland exculpatory statement of 1829: "I know Emily is not fond of travelling."

Finally, in January 1828, when the failure to visit had grown embarrassing, Emily sent her fifteen-year-old sister Lavinia to look at the remodeled house and be looked at by Edward's family. More open and expressive than Emily, Lavinia seems to have been an acceptable delegate. Mary Dickinson, teaching in South Hadley, was sorry she could not go home to meet her during her week in Amherst. But Emily missed her sister so much that (in an appealingly weird joke) she "was almost inclined to be homesick."

In the courtship's final months the couple became much more direct with each other, Edward in showing his annoyance and exerting his authority and Emily in speaking her mind and bridling at his control. Once, he scolded her for stepping out to so many evening meetings, which in his view served no purpose but to risk her health. When she advised him of a historical lecturer she planned to hear, he sent a long and earnest critique of the man. In reply, Emily issued a mild reproof and a plea for tolerance and freedom:

> Is it not singular that your feeling should have so commanding an influence over mine but it is to strong to overcome, but it is for us to be prudent and not to injure the reputation of others, but let their works prove them.

She was saying that Edward was too "commanding" and "strong to overcome" her opinions, and too prejudicial in judging the lecturer. Although her syntax may be an unpruned thicket, her series of "buts" eloquently conveys her anxious and inarticulate resistance. We are reminded of what she told Edward when he advised her to check with his references: people must make up their own minds. One of the things the poet's mother took to Amherst was a quietly persistent independence masked by outward obedience.

In answering this letter, Edward ironically professed his gratitude for his fiancée's advice and mocked her "decision of character"—the "air of *authority* & *independence* which you assumed." Using his favorite word, he was "determined to bring you out, a little—you have refused & excused yourself long enough." He, too, was becoming plainer and more sarcastic. "Don't you think it rather queer that I should '*find time*' to write to you, every day? and hear from you about once in a month?" begins his letter of January 31, 1828. Hers of February 9 opens with a short, flat (and exasperated?) sentence responding to his iterated requests to visit him: "One more invitation." "Your true sincerity I never would presume to dispute," she went on, "yet there are, and have been reason, to prevent me from acting in compliance with your wishes. Perhaps you will say they are all trifling, I am sensible that my feelings are unlike many others at least those within the bounds of my observation, but it is not necessary for me to explain to you why."

These exchanges bring out one of the besetting lifelong tensions within the Dickinson marriage. When Edward asserted his manly right of command, Emily did as she must without effectively explaining herself. Aware that her silent resistance undermined his authority, Edward could not help getting angry and then both accommodating himself and continuing to insist. He had wanted a quiet wife with all the domestic female virtues, and now, maddeningly, that was what he was getting. And the poet was getting a mother whose wayward obliqueness afforded a useful model for her own orientation to the world.

When Joel Norcross unexpectedly showed up in Amherst to inspect the Montague house, Edward was deeply gratified:

> Your father returns this morning, & while his horse is harnessing, I write a few words. We have been over all *our* house, and examined it, thoroughly—he has proposed some alterations, with which I am much pleased—he saw Wid. Montague, & will tell you all about her & the house, and what he thinks of our prospect of having a comfortable house.

Emily's father was a man of standing and judgment, and his presence, approval, and advice meant a great deal to Edward. The occasional progress reports he sent Joel still survive. One from early March announces "the family have left my house, & repairs are making as fast as possible."

Just as Lavinia was a kind of substitute for her older sister, so Joel stood in for Emily on questions of remodeling and furnishing. Among his valuable gifts to the young couple was a new cast-iron kitchen stove. When the four- or five-hundred-pound appliance was transported from Springfield and installed, Edward could not contain his delight: "It is not the rusty thing which your father, in his peculiar way of producing

an agreeable surprise in having things prove much better than he represents, would have us believe—but one of the neatest, & best looking
stoves that I ever saw." Smoothing the transition to married life, Joel had
already become a second father to Edward, a much more efficient and
reliable one than Samuel.

Last came the scrubbing. Well aware of Emily's insistence on order
and cleanliness, Edward assured her a week before the wedding that "the
house has been cleaned by a black woman, but I suppose it will have to
pass thro' other hands again, under your own inspection—I told her, that
if there was *one speck* left on the windows, they would be all taken out &
washed anew!—So you see, I have done my duty." The relaxed tone
shows that, among other things, the couple had achieved a degree of
companionable freedom.

Emily made it clear the ceremony was to be as simple as possible: no
groomsman, no bridesmaid. No longer straining for genteel effects, she
expressed herself with blunt decision in her last two letters.[4] On the
question of domestic help: "You speak of haveing a girl. I shall not consent to it at all." On her feelings at leaving Monson for Amherst: "I have
many friends call upon me as they say to make their farewell visit. How
do you suppose this sounds in my ear But my dear it is to go and live
with you." Her plainness, lack of inflation, and slight distance from conventional formulas ("as they say") reveal the difference between her and
her fiancé's well-educated sisters. They also remind us once again of her
unemphatic obliquity and insistence on the right of private judgment.
Such were the things that little bright eyes (and ears) would soon be
picking up, leaving Helen Hunt Jackson to wonder fifty years later at the
"curiously direct phrase" with which Emily Dickinson designated Mr.
Jackson—"the man you live with."

On May 6, 1828, the marriage was solemnized and the couple
moved into the rooms the groom had so anxiously and meticulously pre-

---

4. She had also become quite forthright in expressing affection. In summer 1827 she "could sit
by my window all the night but your society I would like to complete my happiness." Soon
after—she was the first to use the word—she wished she could give him "the parting kiss." Following her lead, Edward both adopted and censored the phrase, wishing "we could press the
parting hand, & give the parting ____s."

pared, on the assumption they were in his father's "control." A week later friend Solomon complimented him on his "thoroughly repaired" house. Coelebs was at home with his unliterary wife.

What She Didn't Mention

One of Dickinson's most haunting poems concerns the unreckoned costs of wifehood:

> She rose to His Requirement – dropt
> The Playthings of Her Life
> To take the honorable Work
> Of Woman, and of Wife –
>
> If ought She missed in Her new Day,
> Of Amplitude, or Awe –
> Or first Prospective – Or the Gold
> In using, wear away,
>
> It lay unmentioned – as the Sea
> Develope Pearl, and Weed,
> But only to Himself – be known
> The Fathoms they abide –

> Fr857

For the unnamed woman of this poem, marrying means dropping into a deep and masculine sea and drowning her individuality once and for all. Since the sea can "Develope" *both* "Pearl, and Weed," it is too soon to say whether her sacrifice was a mistake. Instead, what the poem dwells on is the transaction's silencing effect—the disturbing fact that the wife has nothing more to say about the promising things she has given up. Is she unwilling to voice the inner truth about her union, or is she unable? The poem's final claim is that only her husband can know the "Fathoms," depths, in which she now lives.

These lines, composed by early 1864, may be a response to the marriage of someone known to Dickinson, possibly her friend Eliza Coleman, who in 1861 married a dynamic and dominating minister during a heavy rainstorm. Does the poem also give Dickinson's sense of her parents' union? There is no doubt she saw her father as a figure of great power and her mother as small and pinched and overbusy, without that sense of questioning "Amplitude, or Awe" that she herself valued. Comparing her parents with the couple in the poem, we see in both an extreme asymmetry between the man's requirements and the woman's inarticulate compliance. Still, if the poem makes us think of Mrs. Dickinson, it is not quite her story: she probably did as much hard work before her wedding as after, there are few hints of amplitude or awe at any point in her life, and she was capable of ignoring her spouse's orders and obeying her own sweet will.

The poem says less about Emily and Edward Dickinson than about the way their daughter imagined the risks a woman takes in marrying. What the poem presents is the visionary insight the Norcross-Dickinson union stimulated in one of its products.

Woman's inarticulate Compliance

Chapter 4

1828–1830: Shifting Foundations

When Emily Dickinson was born, her parents were enjoying a calm interval between the insecurities of their first two years of marriage and the economic trials her father was to face in the 1830s. Edward would eventually prosper, yet his early financial stresses deposited a kind of Depression mentality in the poet—an uneasy sense of the fragility of foundations. As a teenager, she once dreamed that "Father had failed & mother said that 'our rye field which she & I planted, was mortgaged to Seth Nims.'" As reported, the dream gives the main speaking role to the hardworking mother, who announces that the crop she and her daughter have grown is in jeopardy thanks to Father. If the dream is to be trusted (always a question), it suggests the daughter picked up her parents' anxiety about financial insolvency. Curiously, the vision was real enough to the girl that she asked her brother to reassure her that Father hadn't failed.

Wiped Out

When Emily Norcross left her home in Monson on May 6, 1828, she moved into a house supposedly controlled by a powerful father-in-law. May 1 was the day property was officially valued by the town of Amherst. The assessment rolls for that date in 1828 show that Samuel Fowler Dickinson was held liable for the taxes on a number of pieces of real estate. Another indication of his public standing is his election that month by the Massachusetts legislature to fill a vacancy in the state Senate. May 30 was the day he swore his oath and took his seat.

Then, on June 11, one day before the Senate adjourned, Squire Dickinson "obtained leave of absence for the remainder of the session." A week later, having decided to open a new school "in the science and practice of The Law," he placed a tortured notice in the *New-England Inquirer*:

> This Prospectus is issued *with extreme diffidence;* in as much as it promises only the efforts of *an humble individual* . . . whose attention, for some time past, has been partially withdrawn from the Profession. Yet, believing that *perseverance,* united with *untiring application, and exclusive devotedness* to the object of pursuit, always possesses a redeeming spirit, as well as an overcoming power, the undersigned *is determined* to omit no exertion, and avoid no sacrifice, *to deserve,* what he humbly hopes *he may receive,* a portion of the public patronage.

Everything in this notice seems characteristic of the man: the bloodied tenacity, the prompt and public way in which he played his last desperate card, and the religious phrases derived from the Exercise Scheme the Reverend Nathanael Emmons had taught him long ago ("redeeming spirit," "overcoming power," "omit no exertion . . . *to deserve*"). All in all, the prospectus is so unrealistic and self-flagellating it seems fairly unhinged (and in fact, the school never got off the ground). But the most important implication here is not psychological but economic.

That the Squire was officially bankrupt is confirmed by the *Inquirer's* editorial endorsements of July 17 and August 28, which stated that the "pursuits and embarrassments" that had distracted him for several years "are so far disposed of and removed, that he is enabled to redeem the pledge already given, of devoting exclusive and persevering attention from this time, to the profession." In plain language, the hammer had fallen and Samuel was wiped out, with no more debts, projects, or properties and with only his knowledge of the law to sustain him. Edward was one of the paper's proprietors and apparently headed the prudential committee that managed its business side. There seems little doubt the editorial support of Samuel's unlikely new venture had inside authority and was meant to put the best possible face on his failure. That November the Squire was slaughtered in his run for the national House of Representatives, getting less than 10 percent of the vote.

What all this meant for the poet's parents is that in summer 1828, several weeks after marrying, they discovered they did not have secure possession of their half of Jemima Montague's house after all. Given the attention Edward had lavished on the place, and the high standards of domestic order Emily brought to it, the discovery must have been a shock. They were more alone in the world than they had realized.

The inexorable legal ramifications quickly worked themselves out. On October 29, Samuel's coadjutant, Oliver Smith, in deep trouble now, sold a long list of mortgaged properties, including the Jemima Montague place and the Dickinson Homestead. The purchasers were John Leland, the treasurer of Amherst College, and Nathan Dickinson, a goldsmith and a first cousin of Edward. Neither apparently wished to be harsh, but given the deal's huge face amount ($20,000), they had to turn the Montague place to the best possible account.

On December 8, with Emily about five months pregnant, Edward turned to her father for advice. Explaining that "the assignees" of Samuel's property were obliged to dispose of it, the young husband admitted his father's "misfortunes place me in rather a difficult situation respecting my house, [more so] than was anticipated when I made the repairs." He had to decide between two undesirable alternatives—renting what might at any time be sold from under him or buying what he could scarcely afford. The stoical young husband did not complain or accuse, but his dignified statement makes clear which of his two fathers he valued for judgment and counsel.

Edward's relations with his in-laws were to be unusually close and confidential. After hearing from Joel, he struck a new deal with Leland and cousin Nathan that gave him some sort of interest in his part of the house. Not only was the deal a "great bargain," but he believed he could sell out "for more than the amount of my purchase money." Eventually, this second agreement proved as fragile as the original one, but for now Edward was confident his tenancy had a solid footing.

The Work, You Know, Comes upon You

Among the congratulatory notes Emily Norcross Dickinson received after the wedding was one from Loring Norcross, her first cousin. Loring sent polite wishes for her and her spouse's "prosperity," then added a curious remark: "I think that the People in Monson rather Imagine that you both have ran a wild goose Chase, but time must determine."

Nothing reveals Emily's unfolding situation quite so vividly as the many letters she received from her younger sister. Breezy and indiscreet, Lavinia was both more sociable than the poet's mother and more inclined to express her opinions and her wide range of feelings. Judging from the First Church of Monson's Sabbath School records, she was also something of a whiz: at age thirteen she committed to memory no less than 1,343 Bible verses, 600 more than the top male memorizers. Lavinia took so much pleasure in communicating, that not only did she become the Norcrosses' delegated intermediary with Amherst but also the Dickinson children would feel closer to her than to their other older relatives. It is no accident that the poet's most relaxed and newsy letters went to the daughters of this lively, friendly, and expressive aunt.

The second of Lavinia's extant letters to her married sister went out over Joel's opinion that it is "foolish for me to write you so often." Dated two weeks after the wedding, it made clear how much Emily was missed in Monson and how "homesick" she was assumed to be. As time passed without a reply, however, Lavinia began to feel abandoned. Wishing to send "some intelligence from home," she couldn't help suspecting "it is of but little consequence to you tho 'there was once' no place like home." When a letter finally came, Lavinia "did not know as you would ever find time to write me but I am much encouraged." It was now her turn to perform the chore Edward had previously carried out—making the most of Emily's infrequent and meager replies.

What chiefly worried the Norcrosses was Emily's insistence on doing all the housework. She had been married three months when Lavinia transmitted some forceful advice from home:

> I hope you will give up your work in some measure for Mother worries a great deal about you if you do not favour your-self I think you will be very ungrateful to your husband and friends if you cannot do every thing you wish about your house you must consider you are out of health & let all the needless work go—your health depends on your own prudence remember.

Two months later Lavinia wrote, "I understand your health has not been as good I hope you will soon have some assistence in your domestic avocations."

After the laborious wife was finally coerced into hiring a servant, Lavinia found a woman willing to leave Monson for Amherst, then begged Emily to "favour yourself when she comes." But Emily found it as difficult to retain her help as others found it to keep her from working too hard, and within several weeks, judging from Lavinia's query— "has your girl returned?"—the servant was gone. When a new one was found, the Norcrosses breathed easier: "Now Miss Green is with you we feel that you will have good care—Mother sends love." But before long Miss Green was also out of the picture, prompting Lavinia to confide that "Mother has had much anxiety about your help which you will need before long." Finally, when Emily was seven months pregnant, her parents took matters into their hands by arranging to send their own girl, Mary. The next month Lavinia nervously summed matters up: "happy to hear you was in good health—hope you will be prudent—soon you will have Mary's assistence."

On Emily's side, we should note she had no female kin to help with housekeeping and child care, and that the cheap labor supply the huge Irish Catholic influx brought in was still in the future (apparently, New Englanders were not reliable domestic workers). In these circumstances, and given the Dickinsons' insecurities, the young wife presently made an ill-advised decision. In fall 1828 her husband had been approached by a leading Springfield attorney looking for a "regular family" to board his son and nephew, Richard Bliss and Henry Morris, then entering Amherst College. Since the school furnished no meals, students boarded with those who took an interest in the institution or wished to earn a modest income. In Edward's case, there was also a professional incentive to meet the request: Richard's father was a state representative and Henry's father was about to become a judge. Still, a letter Edward sent from Springfield left the decision "entirely with [Emily] to manage as you think best. The work, you know, comes upon you, and it is wholly immaterial with me, what you conclude." As usual, Lavinia had strong opinions, urging her sister not to "take boarders next term as it is so uncertain about help and Edward says you can do as you please." Spring term began in early February and ended in mid-May, and Emily was due in mid-April; the advice was sound. But it was ignored, as we learn from Lavinia's letter of March 17 asking to be remembered to the boys. Of course, the arrangement couldn't last, and when summer term opened, Edward explained to Richard "the reasons of our not taking boarders" anymore.

That Emily took on this extra work shortly before the birth of her first child reveals something about her as a housekeeper—her drivenness, her extreme thrift. It also shows how she adjusted to her and Edward's unsettled situation: putting her shoulder to the wheel, doing everything possible to promote their prosperity, doing it all perfectly and by herself and without adding to her husband's burdens or expenses. Even under the best of circumstances, a young married woman in charge of housekeeping had to see to a huge number of domestic operations, especially in storing and preparing food. In Emily's case, the unexpected financial troubles of her husband's family exacerbated her self-reliant and perfectionist tendencies.

The household manual Edward gave Emily about 1830 discloses

some of the attitudes and practices the poet grew up with. Written by Lydia Maria Child, *The Frugal Housewife* was aimed at families of "the middling class" who were struggling to get ahead. "Unlike all other domestic advice books of the period," writes Child's biographer, this one does not "take for granted that its readers rely on servants." One of its ruling maxims is that "patchwork is good economy." That is, "the true economy of housekeeping is simply the art of gathering up all the fragments, so that nothing be lost. I mean fragments of *time*, as well as *materials*." The book itself is a kind of patchwork quilt, consisting of hundreds of random rules, hints, tricks, recipes. "Never put out the sewing. If it be impossible to do it in your own family, hire some one into the house, and work with them." Child's directions on the right way to clean brass, leather, lamp wicks, freestone hearths, you name it, presuppose an endless supply of elbow grease as well as an exalted ideal of household cleanliness. The effect of such a book on a housewife already inclined to take the business too seriously is easily imagined. Emily's copy of the book, moderately worn, has what looks like a grease spot in the section on "common cakes." The one dog-eared page is in "How to Endure Poverty."

This frugality came to look quite primitive to the children. "Our amiable mother never taught us tayloring," the poet wrote years later, "and I am amused to remember those clothes, or rather those apologies made up from dry goods with which she covered us in nursery times." "Tayloring" meant employing a tailor or dressmaker instead of sewing it yourself; the word, identically spelled, shows up in an account of Joel Norcross. Edward's opinion was that his wife took domestic self-sufficiency too far: "You must not try to do things that expose you, for the sake of being too economical—& getting along, within yourselves."

Over time, Mother's devotion to thrift and order grew so extreme she became a kind of outsider in her own home, subtly detached from its pleasures and standards. In the early 1860s her daughter Emily concluded a letter written late at night by making a fantastic excuse for not transmitting Mrs. Dickinson's best wishes: "Mother would send her love – but she is in the 'Eave spout,' sweeping up a leaf, that blew in, last November." That the letter was probably written in August, long after the leaf got lodged in the roof gutter's spout, adds to the grotesqueness of the scene: the housewife out in the dark, tiny, singleminded, going into the spout for that last fallen leaf. Is this chore something the mad sweeper is only dreaming of, or is she imagined as actually in the pipe's flared opening with her miniature broom? Either way, it is an unforgettable picture of an obsessed New England housekeeper driven from the comforts of home and much too busy to send her love, let alone to write.

Sister! Why That Burning Tear?

On April 16, 1829, the Dickinsons' first child was born, a boy named William Austin. Everyone was inexpressibly relieved, and before long Edward was boasting about his "smart boy." Just as quickly, Lavinia twitted him on his fatherly pride, predicting the child "will go to College soon if he improves as fast as you mention he has." The advantages of being the firstborn son soon became evident to the keen eyes of his Aunt Lavinia, who wished that winter that she could see the baby "& govern him a little." To Edward she sent a warning, "You must not love him too well." It was a dangerous thing to become too attached to one's child.

The baby was coddled partly because he was the bright spot among shadows. That spring Edward felt "lifeless," full of "languor & weakness," a condition caused in part by an infected tooth he knew he should have removed. The previous year the pain had been so severe he felt an occasional "*jump,* which actually shakes my head." The use of ether for extractions being two decades in the future, the young father had not been able to make himself see a dentist. Lavinia's blunt opinion was that he had "not exercised much patience in his sufferings."

In Amherst's property valuations for May 1, 1829, Edward's once prominent father is shown for the first time as owning no real estate, and in Monson the Norcrosses were wrestling with the elemental challenges of sickness and death, sin, salvation, and immortality. After giving birth to her first child, Aunt Eliza Norcross (Erasmus's wife) remained "quite low" for a time (and never had another child), and in February Emily's brother Hiram died of consumption, leaving an infected widow and two young children. But nothing proved quite so agonizing as Mother's terminal decline.

By mid-July Betsey could no longer keep food down and was taking calomel, a mercury-based medicine. At month's end her poisoned mouth was raw, her vomiting was persistent, she had to be lifted when her bed was made, and Lavinia's bulletins were sounding desperate:

> You can have no idea how emaciated she is nothing but the skin covers her bones, she cannot yet take any thing to nourish her except a little water-gruel . . . she is very anxious to see you wishes after commencement is over to have your husband fetch you down you must not disappoint her.

Was it cancer? Feeling that she was in the "dark valley & shadow of death," Lavinia ended her letter with the plea "Emily do come & see us—I feel as tho' you must come & sympathise in our distress." That was on August 18. Commencement was not until the twenty-sixth.

Remarkably, it was that summer, while Betsey lay dying, that the great revival her Female Praying Circle had been working for the last two years finally got started. For herself, one guesses, the dying woman was not overly concerned; she would reportedly die in peace and with a "full assurance of a happy immortality." Still, *could* she die in peace with her daughters outside the ark of safety? That consideration undoubtedly lay behind the dying woman's insistence that Emily come home. If Emily was to be refreshed with the shower of blessings, she must come *now*.

But as of September 1, Edward had not yet driven his wife the twenty-two miles to Monson. On that day, writing at Mother's behest, William O. Norcross virtually required Emily to "come home & stay with her a few days." Joel had to be away, Mary (the "girl") was absent for her own health's sake, and it was obvious that Betsey could not "long remain with us." The revival was gaining power, and several members of the family including cousin Loring (but not Lavinia) had found the throne of grace. William would be in Amherst by ten A.M. on September 4, a Friday, driving Emily back to Monson that same day.

Taking her baby, Emily apparently reached home a matter of hours before her mother died early Saturday morning. Later that day William wrote to inform Edward of Betsey's death and relay instructions where to find his wife's black bonnet, veil, and collar, and the bandbox to carry them in; prepared ahead of time, perhaps, all were necessary now. And meanwhile the revival continued its crescendo under the direction of the Reverend Asahel Nettleton, who also came to Monson in early September. The following month William and Lavinia both found "relief"—in her words, "a peace of mind different from anything . . . ever before experienced." There can be no doubt that Betsey's protracted death and the coincidental revival marked a major and dramatic epoch in Norcross family annals.

For Lavinia, the drama had an almost suicidal intensity. In 1835, when she wished to transfer to the evangelical Bowdoin Street Church in Boston, the Reverend Alfred Ely drafted a brief account of her desperate 1829 conversion. Ely's letter, laid before the new church's Examining Committee and duly summarized in its minutes, stated among other things that Lavinia felt "she was a lost sinner without a hope in Jesus—After some time she shut her self up in her room and was determined to submit before she came out." This ultimate and solitary struggle, one of the great crises in the life of Emily Dickinson's closest aunt, took place a month or so after Betsey's death and funeral. One of the things we would like to know about the poet, given her own habits of seclusion, is what she knew about her aunt's ordeal.

Hoping to communicate her new sense of happiness, Lavinia wrote Amherst, "Yes the convert has enjoyment the world knows not of. I enjoy my mind very much." Sister Emily, on the other hand, dressed in mourning and still unconverted, found no such relief. So far from enjoying *her* mind, she seems to have been overwhelmed with grief and guilt. By marrying, she had abandoned the home that needed her. She had let Mother die without the comfort of knowing they would meet in heaven. And she had had her sister's constant reminders that Mother's anxiety about Emily's exposure to hard labor was "a great hinderence to the restoration of her health." The dutiful young wife and mother carried a very heavy load on her conscience.

These were the circumstances under which Lavinia composed a

poem designed to ease her sister's anguish. She may have written others as well, but this is the only one we have from her hand:

> *Sister! why that burning tear*
> *Stealing slowly down thy cheek*
> *To my friendly listening ear*
> *All thy little sorrows speak*

These lines from just before Emily Dickinson's birth could not be mistaken for hers, yet they exhibit something repeatedly seen in her writing—a consolatory purpose and an animating bond between an articulate sister full of insight and eager sympathy and a silent sister unable to express her choked sorrow. Reading the silent sister's thoughts, the writing sister tries to divert her imagination from the grave:

> *What if that heart once beating warm*
> *Lies low among the silent dead*
>
> *O look not there! but raise thine eye*
> *To higher climes where angels are*
> *Where pleasures never bloom to die*
> *Sister—our mother's happy there.*

The poem was neatly copied on an elegant and expensive sheet of boardlike paper with an embossed lacy border and scallops pressed in the corners.

We don't know for sure that Dickinson saw it, but it seems obvious that it was from such love-drenched sheets that her own profound explorations of desire and grief began.

Fresh Beginnings

Unlike Edward's father, cousin Nathan Dickinson, the new co-owner of the Montague place and the Dickinson Homestead, was on the rising half of the seesaw: in 1827 his taxable money at interest was put at $400; one year later, at $2,600. Emily happened to be in Monson when Nathan got married in June 1829, leaving Edward to put on record his contemptuous view of Nathan's method of bringing home his bride— "in an *old shackling waggon, without cushion* or *Buffalo-skin*—so much saved—'*out of their hydes*' which is all 'clear gain.' " "How would you like that way?" Edward asked his wife, clearly implying that Nathan's way of getting ahead was not going to be their way.

Nathan did extremely well in Michigan land and timber in the coming years, but for now it was necessary to economize what he could out of his and others' "hydes." Early in 1830 he let it be known he could not fulfill his part of the revised agreement concerning the Jemima Montague place. For the second time, in other words, Edward and Emily were threatened with the loss of their home and the money that had gone into refurbishing it.

As before, Edward turned to his father-in-law for advice, presenting a straightforward account of his situation and the various options. He was satisfied where he was, the old Montague house being pleasant and comfortable and "convenient, at all times, to my business." But he was reluctant to meet Leland's demand for "several hundred dollars more than I agreed to pay." The alternative was to buy from Leland a certain lot west of the Dickinson Homestead—"the best building lot for sale in our neighborhood"—and build a small house. Edward emphasized that he wanted advice only, not money, and also that he was acting in accord with his wife's wishes. He said nothing about having discussed the matter with his father.

Answering at once, Emily's father pointed out the drawbacks of Edward's two main options: the Montague place was exposed to fire, and building a house would probably be more expensive than anticipated (not to mention "loss of time and anxiety of mind"—two of Squire Dickinson's plagues). Joel's suggestion was that Edward rent for a couple of years rather than rush into a deal. But he pointedly left the question to his son-in-law: "After all I think you better able to judge what would be best for you and your little Family." A young provider could have wished for nothing better than this mix of sound Yankee advice and kindly diplomacy.

In the end Edward made a choice that had not been on the table when he wrote Joel. Probably acting in concert with his father, he bought the west half of the Dickinson Homestead from Leland and cousin Nathan for $1,500, a deal he was able to swing by signing a mortgage for $1,100. For a young attorney who still had his way to make, this was a heavy commitment. But there were strong favoring considerations: the property was Edward's boyhood home, the house was the grandest one in town, and it was not much of a walk to his office on the Common's northeast corner. Nathan and Leland retained possession of the east half of the house, but the west half was Edward's (with occupancy to begin in six months). Now, surely, his "little Family" would be safe from the threat of a sudden eviction.

Joel's letter of advice is postmarked March 9. The deed was signed March 30. At some point in the intervening three weeks, Edward reached an understanding with the Homestead's owners. Nine months later, on December 10, Emily Dickinson was born. Assuming she was conceived in March—the "Month of Expectation" one of her poems calls it (Fr1422)—a cheeky question arises here. Was she conceived by a couple celebrating the purchase and acquisition of their first home? Could she have been joined to the brick house that came to be her world even more closely than has been thought?

In May Edward took his first business trip to New York City. Three years earlier, when his fiancée went there, he had indulged some dire fantasies of urban filth and decay—the bad habits of "the lower classes," "the seducing arts of base men," the hordes of ruined women. Now, delighted with everything he saw, he walked so much he rubbed his heels raw and had to exchange his boots for shoes, "one of them slipshod . . . but never mind—they are not so particular here as they are in little villages." In the evening he went to the Park Theatre and saw what was billed as a "new opera," *Rokeby*. Writing home late that night, he pronounced everything in the city "grand & magnificent.—and just what I like." Then, his protective anxieties coming to the fore, he warned his wife against the risks of infection: "I trust you will be prudent, and not expose yourself to cold, or the *evening air*—take the medicine which I prescribed. . . ."

That summer, when Emily was four or five months pregnant, her sister hoped that she would "not be so much troubled with your help as you have been." Not only was that old problem still there, but once again she decided to take boarders, to Lavinia's surprise. As for Edward, he was "so much engaged in business this summer" that a letter carrier was advised not to "call on him at present as he was in a confusion state." It must have been an extremely busy time for a couple anticipating a change of residence. If Mary Dickinson Newman's experience when moving into a house is any guide, there would have been a great deal of "painting, papering, scouring" to be got through. There was also the bustle of Commencement in late August, with a house full of guests for Emily to look after.

Following the move on September 1, Emily found herself in her second shared living arrangement, separated by hallways and staircases from Edward's parents and younger siblings. Lavinia had no doubt her sister and brother-in-law would be happy in their new home. The only disadvantage she saw was in living "so far *from the city*." She may have been referring to the village business center a quarter mile distant.

That fall it was learned that Joel planned to remarry—a necessary step now that Emily and Betsey were gone and a firm hand was needed for the children still at home, Lavinia, Alfred, and Joel Warren. The new wife and mother, previously unmarried and in her forties, was startlingly unlike "retiring" Betsey Fay. Coming from an eminent clerical family, Sarah Vaill had been a teacher and was thought to be "quite a superior woman"; as Emily guardedly put it, she was "very well spoken of." Her shrewd and humorous father, the Reverend Joseph Vaill, pastor for fifty years of a Connecticut church, was to be the subject of a book-length biography in 1839. Sarah's extant letters, pleasant but a little starchy, are those of someone who made a constant point of being temperate, refined, helpful, good-humored.

To receive such a bride, the immense Norcross house had to be cleaned as never before. On November 11 the man who painted Monson's wagons and fences billed Joel for "painting floors at your House." A week later Lavinia informed her sister that "we are all full of business." The wedding was set for early January, and as the day approached Lavinia gave voice to a thought others might not have uttered: "what shall I call her? Can I say Mother. O that I could be far away from here—Emily you may depend I want to be with you." That was on December 6.

Notwithstanding such anxieties, it was a time of high hopes and fresh starts. The bankruptcy in Amherst had been weathered, and the deaths and other upheavals in Monson were receding into the past. The Dickinsons and the Norcrosses had both succeeded in reconfiguring and restabilizing themselves. A few days after Lavinia doubted she could say "Mother," Dr. Isaac G. Cutler was summoned to the west side of the Dickinson Homestead. The town's senior physician, he knew the building well, having gone there to deliver Lucretia's last babies. Afterward he added a line to his long record of deliveries:

Edward Dickinson Esqr   December 10   G [for Girl]

Opening his wife's Bible, Edward made a more detailed entry in the family record:

Emily Elisabeth, their second child
was born Decr 10. 1830. at 5. o'clock A.M.[1]

From all the signs, the baby was an easy one to care for. Six months after her birth, as the mother wrote a letter to her temporarily absent

---

1. The time of birth makes even less likely the old story that the birthchamber was being simultaneously repapered by Lafayette Stebbins, on the wife's insistence and against the husband's orders. This story, based on a 1944 letter by Mary Adèle Allen, first appeared in Jay Leyda's *Years and Hours of Emily Dickinson*. As Leyda's notes show, Allen got the story from a Mrs. Foote of Marblehead, who had been told it by an old man who advised her on gardening, Edgar Gregory, of Gregory Seeds. Gregory must have got it from his wife, born Flora Dell Stebbins in Amherst in 1871; her father was Lafayette C. Stebbins, variously a painter and farmer. But Lafayette was born about 1845, fifteen years *after* the poet, and *his* father, William, also a painter, lived in Wendell. Like most stories told about the famous, this one is obviously too garbled to be taken seriously.

husband (*he* had written every day), she conveyed an air of tranquil contentment: "I have retired to my chamber for a little space to converse with you—with my little companion on the bed asleep. . . . I am now counting the days when I hope that you will return into the bosom of your family. . . . I attended the tract society yesterday had quite an interesting meeting. I must leave you my dear to resume my usual employment which you may well suppose."

There is a one-word postscript following the signature:

Excuse

Was it because she hadn't written? Was it because she risked the "*evening air*" in order to attend one of the meetings her husband deprecated as unnecessary for women?

This was the home that awaited the sleeping baby.

Part Two

1830-1840

After the fire of 1838, David Mack, Jr., built a straw-goods factory in the center of Amherst, the appearance of which has been preserved on company letterhead. In the right foreground stands the commercial building erected by Samuel Fowler Dickinson in the 1820s. Looking east on Main Street, we see in the middle distance, on the left side of the street, the gabled Dickinson Homestead, purchased in 1833 by Mack.

Chapter 5

1830–1835: A Warm and Anxious Nest

In 1866, reporting an encounter in which Mrs. Dickinson hoped her grandson "would be a very good Boy," her daughter took immense pleasure in the five-year-old's answer: " 'Not very dood' he said, sweet defiant child!"

The pleasure grew with age. At fifty the poet sent this subversive encouragement to a group of neighborhood children: "Please never grow up, which is 'far better' – Please never 'improve' – you are perfect now." Among other things, she was making an irreverent allusion to St. Paul's yearning for heaven in Philippians 1:23 ("For I am in a strait betwixt two, having a desire to depart, and to be with Christ; which is far better"). Another letter toying with Holy Writ, in this case Jesus' saying "Except ye . . . become as little children, ye shall not enter into the kingdom of heaven" (Matthew 18:3), advised a devout friend: "Unless we become as Rogues, we cannot enter the Kingdom of Heaven." For the poet, our inborn disobedience had become wholly benign. It *qualified* us for paradise rather than causing our expulsion from it.

These charming provocations remind us that Dickinson was a nine-teenth-century Romantic who found some of her best material in the idea of childhood purity. They exhibit her insouciant defiance of a huge range of conventions and disciplines. They warn us not to see her as the product of a "blighted childhood" (Sewall's good phrase for the legend he effectively opposed) or to forget how she was always harking back to her beginnings and finding a perennial richness there. And they hint that as she looked back at her early years from the vantage of middle age, what she saw was someone who had probably been too good.

In narrating a subject's early years, a biographer tries to assemble the scattered and fragmentary evidence into a truthful portrait of a mind in process of formation. Among other things, that means not letting the occasional drama or sensation obscure the mundanity of life. With Dickinson, whose later retrospects were apt to be pungent, extreme, and free of context, not so much reporting as transforming the original facts, the work becomes doubly treacherous. We must not ignore the docu-mented grimnesses and certain shocking claims ("I never had a mother"), yet we have to keep the fundamentals steadily in view: the parents' devotion to their firstborn daughter and that daughter's attach-ment, adhesion, to them. When she was fourteen and a friend was left motherless, her response was to "pity her very much she must be so lonely without her mother." Young Emily was an affectionate and spir-ited child, and the home she grew up in had a close, regular, anxious feel. Her parents believed in simplicity, systematic planning, steady disci-pline, and hard work, but the work fell on their own shoulders rather than the children's and the punishments were less frequent than the re-wards. It is clear that Emily experienced major trauma as a girl, but probably not before 1844.

Which is not to say there were no shadows from the outset: tight liv-ing quarters, financial insecurity, insistent parental anxieties, threats of sickness, fears of death and the afterlife, and an extreme imbalance of power between father and mother.

The occasionally sinister conditions and the basically unblightable vitality: the challenge before us is not only to keep both of these in sight but to trace the explosive generative force of their union.

The Dangerous Evening Air

Edward and Emily Norcross Dickinson were surrounded by parents bereft of their children. Up the street lived Irene Dickinson Montague, Edward's aunt, who had lost three of her first four. In Monson there was Hannah Porter of the Female Praying Circle who had to bury all four of hers, the last one surviving to age thirteen, and in Easthampton there was Samuel Williston, the rich button manufacturer whose four children, girls, all died by the age of six, the first two in 1831 from "inflammation upon the lungs" and "Canker Rash." The latter disease was scarlet fever. Once, after young Emily woke up with a rash, her father vigorously conjured her mother not to let it develop[1] into "the Canker-rash." Among her aunts, Lucretia Dickinson Bullard lost her first child and Mary Newman her first three. Edward was in the vicinity of Andover, the Newmans' home, when the third one "*died* at 1. o'clock this morning!" as he informed his wife. He was glad to be able to show his sympathy for the desolated parents by attending the funeral. "I really feel for them much," he wrote.

Little Emily was two years old when Aunt Lavinia advised the Dickinsons that a two-year-old in Monson had been scalded to death "in a pail of hot water." "I mention this," she added, "that you may be careful about your children." The warning was superfluous: Edward was already in a constant state of alertness for illness, accidents, and criminal assault. This vigilance stemmed both from his sense of female vulnerability and from his own medical history, including what a sister once referred to as "your old complaint, the palpitation in the heart." In 1823, taking the stage to New Haven for his commencement, he had been in an accident that left his roommate George Ashmun with a broken leg.

---

1. As John Harley Warner points out, medical knowledge was less inclined to recognize "specific diseases" than to assume that attendant conditions "could nudge one disease into another."

In 1826 he had been greatly impressed when an Amherst sophomore caught cold, "neglected to apply for medical advice," and died. As a bachelor law student, he assembled a file of emergency remedies: for dysentery, take blackberry root; if you swallow prussic acid, take ammonia; if you're struck unconscious by lightning, let's hope someone douses you with cold water. By his mid-thirties he had known "the distress of rheumatism in my hyp & back." All his life Edward prescribed, doctored, ordered to bed, and warned against drafts, so that his home remedies became both an accepted ordeal and a standing family joke. Twelve years after he died, the poet heard of a case in which someone was thought to have been poisoned in her home, and the old joke instantly revived: "Dont you think Fumigation ceased when Father died?" She wrote that a month before her death.

Father's basic remedy was to require anyone with symptoms, including himself, to stay or return home and take to bed. In 1842, looking forward to visiting Austin in nearby Easthampton, he "was taken suddenly ill—& consequently has been an invalid to-day." Between him and his sister-in-law Lavinia there was a vigorous contest of wills over proper treatment: he would prescribe certain remedies and she would insist "he need not pride himself that he has cured me—for it is not so." Once, when she came to Amherst in the dead of winter, troubled and depressed, Edward gave advice that she refused, their standoff growing so bitter it was still unsettled by the time she left for home. She was "grieved to the heart" by the quarrel, and when her travel escort stopped for an hour's rest in Belchertown, she got off a hasty note to her brother-in-law hoping he would "have me in affectionate remembrance" after all. She reminded him he did not understand "all the bad feelings I have."

Like his father before him, Edward "watched" with the sick, sitting up all night at their bedside. Certain duties belonged to women, of course, but it was incumbent on the man of the house to be the vigilant protector. If there was serious illness in his absence, he must abandon all engagements and return home. If prevented from doing so, he must keep strict surveillance from a distance. Edward's early letters home always contained a regulation dose of health-related advice. When he left for

Boston in 1837 to lobby for troubled Amherst College, he was prepared to leave his post "if any of you are sick. . . . I must see to my family, before any & all other business." In 1874, when his son was absorbed in consulting with Frederick Law Olmsted about the landscaping of Amherst's common, Edward was so anxious about his grandson's "Rheumatism" he instructed the forty-five-year-old Austin on his primary duty in the case: "I would not neglect Ned for Mr Olmsted, even."

One reason Edward wanted his wife to stay at home was to avoid accidents, exposure to illness, damp drafts, the dew—the "*evening air*" he mentioned in his 1830 letter from New York. But in 1835, when she made an extended visit to Lavinia in Boston and he remained at home, he sent a very different prescription. Assuring her the children were happy with their temporary caretaker (his cousin Thankful Smith), he urged Emily to have "no anxiety about home, but try to enjoy yourself." She was to see as many of the "public institutions" as she could, including Bunker Hill, the hospital for the insane, even the Tremont Theatre, and wherever she went she should take a carriage regardless of expense: "forget all your cares." A few days later someone in Boston informed a correspondent that "Mrs. E Dickinson called in the Evening." The letter-writer was glad to have the visit but noted it *was* made rather late, after "Mother & Ann had retired." Mrs. E. Dickinson was making full use of that hard-to-get license to enjoy the evening air.

In Amherst, having received an upbeat bulletin, Edward was delighted "to hear that you was enjoying yourself so well." During his wife's absence, he attended court in Greenfield, the Franklin County seat, returning home late at night and leaving at five the next morning, but in spite of this grueling schedule he wanted her to "spend as much time & go as far as you desire to, now you have got started." The next year, when she made some sort of family visit to Springfield, he again pressed her to be carefree and self-indulgent and enjoy the urban spectacle.

How to explain the difference between these letters of 1835–1836 and that of June 1829, when Edward grudged Emily's time with her dying mother in Monson ("but *this* visit is to *last* till *sleighing*")? Though he still regarded himself as his wife's health monitor, he had gained a better understanding of her "nervous" qualities and requirements. He now knew that she suffered from what was not yet termed premenstrual syndrome, a topic the couple discussed with gingerly euphemism.[2] She had also undergone some poorly documented but threatening bouts of illness, one of them consequent on her third pregnancy, and of course she continued to drive herself to exhaustion. What Edward had figured out was that his wife's well-being mandated a periodic vacation from home.

One of the fundamental things young Emily grew up taking for granted was that Mother had a great deal of work, was often worn out, and must be spared as much trouble as possible. "Be kind to your good mother," Edward frequently reminded his children; "she has to work very hard to take care of you." That they must "not disturb Mother" or "make her any trouble" or always be running to her for help became a kind of refrain, a basic duty shaping both the mother-daughter relationship and the future poet's sense of the relative powers of men and women. Again and again the keen-eyed girl (regarded as frail herself) was asked to leave her dear mother alone—and thus to reflect on the disadvantages of growing up to be a woman and a wife.

Upheavals

On July 3, 1831, when little Emily was half a year old, her mother became a member of Amherst's First Church by profession of faith. What that means is that Emily Norcross Dickinson had experienced a satisfactory conversion and could now expect to be reunited with Betsey Fay

---

2. The rapid back-and-forth correspondence of 1838 makes matters clear. Edward left home for his first legislative term on January 1, apparently just before Emily's period. Two days later he was informed her "head-ache was very severe, . . . which I expected . . . I hope before you receive this letter, you will be relieved." On the fifth she assured him that "as regards my own health it is much improved since you left. The reasons need not be explained." On February 25, not quite two months later, Edward was "afraid your periodical head-ache will trouble you, this week—I hope you will not go out much . . . try to make your labors & cares as little as you can." The next time, having shown less understanding, he received this mild reproach: "My dear I do endeavor to be calm & I do wish to do evry thing in my power to comply with your requests. You know very well the state of my health was peculiar when you were at home which occasioned me to feel somewhat depressed, you must therefor excuse all that has passed."

Norcross in heaven. It appears the poet's first year was a time of peace and fulfillment for her mother.

Mrs. Dickinson entered the church as part of a wave of fresh converts. On the hill that year a total of twenty-six young men joined the Amherst College church, and elsewhere in New England and New York hundreds of communities were shaken by one of the most intense and widespread revivals on record. There is a fitting symbolism in the fact that, as the older Emily was caught up by the tides of the time, the one thing we know about the younger one is that at eleven months "little E. is as well as ever, and stands alone, a great deal."

As for Edward, although he had long since accepted the truth of the orthodox system, he had not yet tasted the inner surrender that would mark him as "saved." During courtship, his solemn admission that he was "not a christian" had prompted some gloomy reflections on death and eternity, and a hope that he and Emily could together undergo a change of heart, but now that she was safe and he wasn't, a new fear entered his letters: separation for eternity. Would *he* be the one left behind? One by one his siblings were being gathered in: Lucretia had proclaimed her faith at twelve, Mary joined Andover's South Church in 1831, Catharine entered Amherst's First Church soon after Emily, Frederick became a member of the college church, and Samuel Junior was redeemed in Georgia. When Edward was sent the news about brother Samuel, he couldn't help making a discouraged remark about "that happy future state of existence, for which we all ought to be ever in readiness, but which I am sensible I have always neglected—and fear I always shall."

Meanwhile, Edward became more active than ever in the First Parish. Congregational societies consisted of two overlapping entities, church and parish. Professed members constituted the church, the inner group, but the less selective parish was in charge of finances. Not infrequently, the influential men were unsure of their salvation and thus outside the church proper. After Emily's conversion, the structure of authority in the Dickinson family mirrored what was often seen in Congregational societies: the husband had the secular power but no religious voice; the wife, vice versa. For the next nineteen years Emily Norcross Dickinson had the unenviable position of being both the subordinate wife and the solitary Christian in the family. Here, *she* was alone, it being her task to carry husband and children to the throne of grace without having been granted abundant means.

One ironic result of the 1831 revival and the spread of benevolence—the "general moral reformation," Edward termed it—was a drastic reduction in his volume of business. In February 1832, going to Joel Norcross once again for advice, he confessed that lawyering had become so unprofitable it did "not at present afford me a support." He wasn't "pressed or embarrassed," but if he could raise $500 by April 1 he would feel much less anxious. Worried about the mortgage he had signed on March 30 two years earlier, he recalled in his next sentence that at the time he took this plunge his "prospects were very fair, and soon after . . . the change of times took place." Now there was so little work he was thinking of abandoning Amherst and the profession and looking for a responsible position in a bank or factory.

When Emily got pregnant at the beginning of summer, the pressure on the Dickinsons became just so much greater. Two months before she was due, sister Lavinia tried to anticipate the coming emergencies and declared her own availability: "Now if you cant get any [help] & you are unwell dont fail to let me know—dont suffer—for if it is necessary I can come & assist you." At the last minute, on top of everything else, came the old familiar domiciliary threat: on February 27 the *Hampshire Gazette* ran a notice by John Leland and Nathan Dickinson that the east half of the Dickinson Homestead—the part occupied by Squire Dickinson and his family—was to be sold at auction. It was a repetition of what had occurred twice before, the variation being that now there was to be an unpredictable public sale. There seemed no end to the aftershocks of the Squire's insolvency.

The day after this announcement, Dr. Isaac G. Cutler added a line to his record of births:

Edward Dickinson Esq.   February 28   G

Opening his wife's Bible between the Old and New Testaments, the father inked in the vital facts:

Lavinia Norcross, their third
child, was born Feb.ʸ 28.ᵗʰ 1833.
at 9. o'clock A.M.—

For reasons the record does not explain, Mrs. Dickinson took an unusually long time to recover. On May 29, three months after the delivery (her last), she was so unwell her sister tried to console her with someone else's hard luck: "There is a woman in [Monson] that has a child nearly 6 months old & now she cant walk a step without a crutch—so take courage some are worse than you & some better." Making matters worse, the infant proved much more troublesome than little Emily had been. Everyone hoped the baby would grow "more quiet," but at three months she was said to be "no better."

Once again, the growing family was going down the rapids with everything at risk. Caught between his reduced income and a large mortgage, Edward sold his half of the house back to Leland and Nathan on May 13. Nine days later the partners made the entire place over to General David Mack, Jr., the two deals no doubt being coordinated. Mack came from a rich and benevolent family in the western part of the county: his father contributed lavishly to educational and evangelical causes and became the subject of a pious tract, and he himself donated his $2,500 house in Middlefield to the local church. Chances are, the buyer regarded the Dickinsons as a fine family ruined in a good cause. The reverse of harsh, he allowed a year's grace before assuming possession; perhaps this was part of the deal. Still, Edward could hardly have been satisfied, occupying his own home at another man's pleasure.

Under these trying circumstances, with the mother sick and the baby crying and the big deal pending, it was decided to ease the situation by sending little Emily away.[3] A few days before Edward disposed of the Homestead's west half, Lavinia Norcross drove to Amherst to pick up

---

3. That the two older children did not sleep with their parents is implied by Lavinia Norcross's statement to her sister that brother William's family "sleep four in the bed yet but that is their business."

her two-and-a-half-year-old niece and then took her back to Monson in a spring thunderstorm.

Thanks to all these contributing causes and the timely and alert presence of Aunt Lavinia, we now get our first detailed report of Emily's early speech, temperament, behavior.

Passionate Aunt, Contented Child

From the beginning, Lavinia had been tremendously interested in her sister's children. "I want to see little Elizabeth very much, Austin likewise," she wrote in 1831 (using Emily's middle name to differentiate her from her mother). She worked on a blue bonnet for the child and eagerly anticipated seeing her or Austin in Monson in spring 1833—"if I am spared."

Lavinia added this proviso because of her tormented love of Loring Norcross. This young man was not only a first cousin but a quasi-brother, having been her father's ward from age five and living in the Norcross home for extended periods. A headstrong and rebellious teenager, in 1828 Loring admitted that since he had been "under the immediate Controll" of Joel Norcross, he had not acted "so as to merit & gain his respect." Now he was just beginning his long and unsuccessful effort to establish himself in business in Boston.

Uncertain it was "right for cousins to marry," Lavinia had spent "many sorrowful hours" worrying about the fact that she and Loring were "connected & . . . have been brought up together." She finally resolved to override these misgivings—just before picking up her niece in Amherst, where she revealed her intentions to her astonished sister. It isn't known what Emily thought of the match, but others took for granted the Norcrosses disliked "seeing *so near* a brother and sister made nearer." For some reason, this marriage made more talk than the truly incestuous 1838 union between Edward's younger brother Timothy and a *double* first cousin.

Lavinia took another chance halfway to Monson when she chose to outrun an approaching storm rather than sit it out in a tavern. The light-

ning approached more rapidly than she had anticipated, and as the travelers passed through the pine woods southeast of Belchertown, "the rain
wind and darkness came . . . the thunder echoed." Fortunately, the horse
merely "shook his head & galloped on." The intrepid aunt felt "wonderfully supported." Emily called the lightning *the fire*—the fire-stealer's
first recorded words. At first the child "felt inclined to be frightened
some—she said 'Do take me to my mother'[4] But I covered her face all
under my cloack to protect her & took care that she sh[oul]d not get wet
much." What chiefly worried Lavinia, as she later admitted to her sister,
was knowing "you would feel so anxious about us."

Emily quickly learned to play the Norcrosses' piano, probably the
first she had seen; she called it "the *moosic*." Grandfather Joel was "much
amused by her sports," and when she was taken to Betsey Fay's ancient
mother, still living, it was decided the little girl resembled her dead uncle
Austin. At church she behaved well for a two-year-old; the few times
she happened to "speak loud," Joel would "pat" her—though not, Lavinia
specified, "to hurt her or make her cry." ("Pat" has entered the record
badly misread as "slap.") The fond aunt sewed a tiny gingham apron for
her niece and in other ways lavished time and attention on her, remarking again and again in letters how happy and good she was and how
much pleasure she gave her caretakers and how well she ate and slept.
Twice the parents were assured the child was "perfectly contented."[5]
"She speaks of her father & mother occasionly & <u>little Austin</u> but does

---

4. The formality of speech was still in evidence three years later when Sarah Vaill Norcross, Joel's
wife, wrote that "Mr. Norcross, (as your little Emily would say,) started this morning for
Boston." Sarah's usual word for Joel in family letters was "papa." The child's preference for the
more formal term—adopted from her father?—clearly caught the family's attention. (That
Leyda erred in reading *Mr* as *Wm*, thus obscuring the point, becomes obvious if one compares
Sarah's way of forming both abbreviations in her letter to Mrs. Dickinson of May 1, 1835.)

5. Wolff claims the girl's "docile demeanor" (a loaded phrase) was "a response to horror, for her
aunt was engaged in nursing the mortally ill" Amanda, a consumptive sister-in-law thought to
be dying. It is true that the letters that report Emily's contentment also describe Amanda's decline, yet Wolff's overwrought interpretation has little to say for it. At the beginning of the visit,
Amanda joined the family at mealtimes, speaking "but little" and appearing "cheerful." After she
became bedridden, two women were hired as nurses, thus further segregating her from the ongoing life of the very large house. To claim that the invalid's condition left lasting scars on the
visiting two-year-old is to insist quite unreasonably on the legendary "blighted childhood."

not express a wish to see you—Hope this wont make you feel bad." The underlined phrase again shows Emily picking up the grown-ups' designation for her older and larger brother.

Some years later, after the birth of Lavinia's first girl, Edward reported that she was "fond of her child, & appears quite motherly." In her daguerreotype she is holding a later daughter and looking like an icon of fulfilled (but inwardly grieving) Victorian motherhood. "There never was a better child," Lavinia wrote the Dickinsons at the end of May, clearly hoping to keep little Emily as long as possible. "She is very affectionate & we all love her very much—She dont appear at all as she did at home—& she does not make but very little trouble." This is the one and only hint in Lavinia's letters that her niece had been unhappy or troublesome in Amherst—as well she might, given the difficult new baby, the mother's illness, and other problems.

Emily stayed with Lavinia about a month before her father took her back to Amherst. It was early June. The next morning the aunt came upon the little apron, left behind. "You cant think how I felt," she wrote her sister. "I cant tell you how lowly I was . . . I wanted to weep all the time."

In fall Lavinia wished "very much to see the children particularly Emily." The next year she peremptorily advised Edward, "You may expect to lose Emily Elizabeth some part of the summer if all things go right." The child was very attaching.

Half a House Won't Answer My Turn

On August 4, when baby Lavinia was five months old, she was well enough to be taken to her parents' church and baptized. Although Congregationalists did not consider baptism necessary for salvation and sometimes ignored it, the rite still counted for something in Amherst, where it was reserved for the offspring of parents "in full Church fellowship." This provision explains why Austin and Emily were not subjected to the rite, neither being eligible prior to Mrs. Dickinson's profession of faith in July 1831. But why not afterward? Though the picture is murky, the poet does seem to have remained unbaptized. The reason for being clear about this is to discern the freedom she took with the facts in her great poem, "I'm ceded – I've stopped being theirs," where the speaker abandons "The name They dropped opon my face / With water, in the country church" (Fr353). (For most of her life Dickinson spelled "upon" with two "o" 's.)

Meanwhile, Samuel Fowler Dickinson had not recovered from his financial collapse. When his daughter Lucretia married Asa Bullard, the old man's blessing to his son-in-law began with a statement of regret: "I wish I was able to give a fortune with my daughter." Although he headed the committee that enlarged the burial ground in 1832, the Squire could not regain his position in Amherst, and the next year he did what his son Edward merely contemplated: found a place elsewhere. Lane Seminary, a manual-labor school in the hills above Cincinnati, had recently been established by a group of militant evangelicals. Its mission, similar to that of Amherst College, was to train an orthodox clergy for the western states and territories. Appointed as steward, Samuel was to superintend the farming, printing, and mechanical enterprises by which students earned their keep. What he didn't know was that a charismatic young abolitionist named Theodore Weld was about to touch off one of the most remarkable student revolts in American reform history. On December 16, 1833, traveling by himself (his wife and younger children staying behind for the time being) the Squire left New England. Little Emily, three years old, never saw him again.

Soon, it was time for the Homestead's new owner to move in and for the Dickinsons to reshuffle themselves yet again. Having got wind of the coming changes, Lavinia wanted to know what the "arrangements [were] for the spring—What part of the house you occupy." About May first, Grandmother Lucretia and her daughters Catharine and Elizabeth vacated the east side and set off for Ohio. Edward and Emily and their three children moved across the hallways into the east half, and General Mack and his family took possession of the west half; in the process, the General indelibly impressed little Austin as "a man to command attention anywhere, tall, erect, of powerful build, with a head finely set, clear, exact, just, a believer in law and penalty for its breach. . . . I remember

my first sight of him—I was four years old—I thought I had seen God."
For the next six years the future poet and this Jehovah-like landlord
shared the same roof.

As a structural investigation has shown, Mack enlarged the attic
space by replacing the hip roof with gables, raised the roof line on the
north and south sides, and added a second story to the wooden "office"
on the west. The latter structure, long gone, can just be discerned on a
letterhead lithograph of Mack's downtown straw hat factory and distant
home. But as the new owners expanded their living space, the old ones,
losing the office, became more cramped. Since the household well apparently went with the Macks' part of the house, the Dickinsons' domestic routines became more exacting. Now, when the family ran out of
soft water from the roof-fed barrels, they had to resort to the less convenient barnyard well. Judging from Edward's urgent orders from
Boston in winter 1838, carrying water in from the barn must have been
one of the more demanding chores:

> When [Catharine, the hired girl] & Austin go after water, at the
> barn—tell them to be careful about the cattle hooking or hurting
> them. *You must not go into the yard, yourself,* on any account—there is
> no necessity for it, and you *must not do it.*

Primitive and unhealthy as it sounds, the arrangement was not out of
line with contemporary standards.

Judging from a startlingly frank assessment Edward sent his father-
in-law soon after Samuel left for Ohio—"I have always thought that
such a change in relation to my father would prove for my advantage
here, and be an additional reason for my remaining"—the son regarded
the old Squire as something of an incubus. And in fact, with one less
lawyer in town, Edward's business picked up. This proved to be the turning point in his fortunes; at last he was on the path to prosperity. Appointed to the town's school committee in 1832, he became a trustee of
Amherst Academy in 1835 and in August of that year succeeded John
Leland as treasurer of Amherst College. This position brought a salary
of $300 and, more important, recognition as a trusted fiduciary officer—

a major achievement for an attorney recently under the pall of his fa-ther's bankruptcy.

One month after this appointment, Edward complained to his wife, visiting in Boston, about their cramped living quarters: "I must spread myself over more ground—half a house, & a rod square for a garden, won't answer my turn." There is no doubt the young lawyer was in a phase of rising expectation, driven partly by success and partly by the dramatic economic boom of the mid-1830s. Land speculation was tak-ing real estate values to unheard-of levels, and Edward, a renter with lit-tle capital, could not help fearing that he was missing out. As before, he turned for advice to his canny father-in-law, who chose this time to sell some valuable factory shares, dispose of his needlessly large dwelling place, start building a Greek Revival house, and do some speculative buying. As Joel set off on an investment trip to Maine, Edward wanted Emily to get him to "speculate a little for me in '*Maine land.*'" It was time to make some real money: "if I don't speculate in the lands, at the 'East,' I must at the 'West.' . . . To be shut up forever 'under a bushel' while hundreds of mere Jacanapes, are getting their tens of thousands & hundreds of thousands, is rather too much for my spirit." "Don't think me deranged," he added, knowing his wife would wonder.

In Amherst, the mania focused on Michigan, and before long a number of prominent citizens were heavily invested there, among them cousin Nathan, who eventually moved to the territory and gained a rep-utation as "a good judge of Land." Instead of going West for himself, Edward relied on advice from Nathan and various investment partners in Massachusetts. He took the plunge in 1836 and within a few years owned land in Lapeer and St. Clair Counties on the Lake Huron side, and Ottawa and Kent Counties on the Lake Michigan side. None of it seems to have made much money for him.

"So your Western speculators have started," wrote brother-in-law Joseph A. Sweetser (Catharine Dickinson's husband) early in 1836, not committing himself as to their wisdom. When some of the Macks went out to look things over, they discovered as much fraud as good land. "*Many* will be disappointed," they cautioned Edward; "we cannot expect to be made rich by the speculation immediately." In Boston, Lavinia

Norcross's pastor preached against the "*haste to be rich*" and recommended steady labor as the one true way to wealth. After the Dickinsons ascended nearby Mount Holyoke, Lavinia teased Edward for trying to "look to the 'far west' & . . . get a glance of the silver & gold that grows in that luxuriant soil." From the sound of this, she, too, doubted the wisdom of buying raw land at a distance during a speculative boom.

In Amherst, Edward's land purchases were more prudent. In 1834 he bought three-eighths of an acre carved from the west end of Mack's Homestead lot. Two years later, in partnership with Mack, Luke Sweetser, and another, he locked up the adjoining "Triangle lot" to the west, the deed stipulating that the premises be "kept as an open park" for the purchasers' benefit. The first of these acquisitions coincided with what he had once called "the best building lot for sale in our neighborhood." Edward had plans, and the plans would one day mature. Globally, the rising young attorney couldn't resist the wild moneymaking schemes of his time. Locally, he had a cool head after all.

Did She Say Anything About Losing Her Luggage?

Unlike Edward, whose professional success brought a growing sense of freedom and aspiration, Emily seems to have been racing in place on the domestic treadmill. Except when she enjoyed an occasional respite in Boston or Monson, the advice she got from her sister and husband never varied. Lavinia in 1833: "You must not worry yourself more than you can help—for there is nothing so wearing as anxiety." Edward in 1838, sounding annoyed: "Why won't you try to avoid getting overdone—Leave undone some little matters which it is not important should be done."

In spite of the Dickinsons' fading economic worries, the problem of finding reliable domestic help was as far from resolution as ever. In January 1836, Edward's sister Lucretia was afraid that Emily would be "without help . . . [and] alone all this cold weather." In February, Joel Norcross wanted to know whether a newly hired woman had "arrived at the time—& . . . answers your expectations." The extremity of the Dickinsons' need is apparent from a staggering question Lavinia asked that same month: "Is the girl you used to have in prison yet?" Nothing is known about this person except that Lavinia regarded her as "deranged" and "a subject for the Hospital—she looked like a maniac when I saw her."

As for the impact of all this on the Dickinson children, it looks as if they were much better shielded from illness, cold weather, and physical labor than from their parents' protective anxieties. The one marked passage in the Dickinsons' copy of *The Frugal Housewife* concerns the amount of work children should be assigned:

> I would not that servile and laborious employment should be forced
> upon the young. I would merely have each one educated according to
> his probable situation in life; and be taught that whatever is his duty
> is honorable; and that no merely external circumstance can in reality
> injure true dignity of character. I would not cramp a boy's energies by
> compelling him always to cut wood, or draw water; but I would teach
> him not to be ashamed, should his companions happen to find him
> doing either one or the other.

This passage hints at the general assumptions about work in the Dickinson household: Austin and Emily were not to be brought up as menials, the work they performed was defined by gender, they were given simple household chores, and they were not given too many of them. In their early years, the children undoubtedly did less hard work and had fewer responsibilities than their mother had taken on. In a way, she was the family menial—which seems to be what she wanted.

As Edward's letters home indicate, he was always looking out for "the best methods of instruction & government" of his children. The family's child-raising manual, *The Mother at Home; or the Principles of Maternal Duty*, by the Reverend John S. C. Abbott, was full of sensible advice, which the Dickinson parents seem to have taken: "Guard against too much severity." "Do not be continually finding fault." "Do not deceive children." "Never punish by exciting imaginary fears." And yet there was so much guarding, so many precautions, that even as the parents tried to create the perfect shelter they instilled a great anxiety in its very heart. For the Dickinson children, it was both official truth and heartfelt conviction that home was paradise. Yet home also oppressed; and as time passed, the children, Emily most of all, perfected the art of living separately in close proximity.

What happened was that, beginning with the close attachment to her mother that expressed itself during the thunderstorm, the child absorbed much of her language, and a certain humor and toughness and sense of privacy, and many other things. But before long, because of Mother's illnesses and narrow ways and self-exhausting tendencies, and partly because of the family enterprise of sparing her, the older daughter had to develop a precocious independence.

This two-phase sequence helps us construe a statement that has given rise to some grim readings of the poet's life: "I never had a mother." In August 1870 she apparently spoke these words to Thomas Wentworth Higginson, who soon after jotted them down along with some of her other statements; he may have got them right. The inevitable inference is that she was never much attached to her mother, that the mother failed her emotionally, and that the result was a profound deformation.

In fact, the forty-year-old poet was undoubtedly referring, not to her early attachment to her mother, but to the second and more easily remembered phase. She was also probably reacting to Higginson's reverential article on mother love in the previous month's *Atlantic Monthly* and demonstrating her ability to think about this loaded topic more candidly than he. Having declared she never had a mother, she at once added, "I suppose a mother is one to whom you hurry when you are troubled." As the clarification suggests, what she was talking about was not so much her filial bond as her independence of mind, which had struck Higginson as one of her most remarkable qualities. Where had that come from? The poet's answer: from *not* running to Mother with her troubles, from learning how to deal in private with doubt, dread, awe. "There are depths in every Consciousness," she wrote in the 1870s, "to which none can go with us." When oppressed with fears and worries, the girl had done as Father ordered ("not disturb mother") and kept them to herself. One of the ways Emily Dickinson became herself was by not making a confidante of her burdened mother.

We have a very revealing report from the mid-1830s of the Dickinson children's sensitivity to their mother's anxious states. One of the things that worried her when traveling alone was that her luggage would be lost en route. This fear, possibly exaggerated, was by no means unfounded: others shared it, public conveyances were rough and primitive, and it was widely assumed that women had better be escorted. Women of Emily's class put a great deal of time and effort into their public outfits, the loss of which condemned them to not stepping out—enjoying the evening air. After Mother left for Boston in 1835, Austin woke up in the night and was told a letter had just come from her. The first thing the six-year-old boy did was to ask "very anxiously . . . whether she said anything about losing her luggage." We could not ask for better anecdotal evidence of the children's early love and concern for their mother.

Although most of Dickinson's recorded memories of girlhood probably date from after the 1830s, there is one that should be mentioned here because of what it says about her early feelings for and perceptions of her mother. "Two things I have lost with Childhood," the poet jotted down some time after Mrs. Dickinson's death in 1882: "the rapture of losing my shoe in the mud and going Home barefoot, ~~grasp~~ wading for Cardinal flowers and the mothers reproof which was ~~for~~ more for my sake than her weary own for she frowned with a smile." The passage captures many aspects of the writer's girlhood: the interest in flowers (learned in part from Mother); the questing, pleasure-seeking spirit; the accidental nature of her transgression; her sense that her mother was always weary; and her perception that the reproof did not come from the heart. There is both an implicit filial sympathy here and an unbridgeable chasm. We see how the daughter who later said she "was always attached to Mud" had begun to define herself against her housekeeping mother.

But underneath everything were Edward's protective anxieties, far more forceful than his wife's and always projected outward. "When I was a baby," the poet wrote in her fifties, "father used to take me to mill for my health. I was then in consumption! While he obtained the 'grist,' the horse looked round at me, as if to say ' "eye hath not seen or ear heard the things that"[6] I would do to you if I weren't tied!' " Like most early memories, this one stands in inexplicable isolation. The family record mentions no trips to the flour mill and has no overt references to the daughter's being "in consumption." It seems out of character that Edward of all people would expose a child with bad lungs to a mill's fine floating dust. Indeed, the writer seems struck with amazement that *Father* could have done that. Still, the sense of not being well and of being at risk from the horse's large, placid, backward-staring eye gives us the exact stamp of Edward's dire admonitions. "Do not get out and go near the horse, or you will be trampled," one almost hears him saying. Then, going about his business, he leaves the child sitting there and looking at that eye, her mind taking shape under the pressure of fears real and imaginary.

---

6. Dickinson liked to play with this familiar passage from Isaiah 64:4, already famously adapted by Paul in I Corinthians 2:9 and Bottom in *Midsummer Night's Dream:* see Fr132, Fr1261, and L92 and L1035.

Chapter 6

1836–1840: The Fire-Stealer's Girlhood

In a poem dating from the early 1860s, one of Dickinson's first-person speakers begins with a complaint about being shut up in a prosaic or literal reality, then turns her attention to a scene from childhood. Remembering how she was put in a closet as punishment for her loudness or volubility, she revels in her triumphant escape:

> They shut me up in Prose –
> As when a little Girl
> They put me in the Closet –
> Because they liked me "still" –
>
> Still! Could themself have peeped –
> And seen my Brain – go round –
> They might as wise have lodged a Bird
> For Treason – in the Pound –

Himself has but to will
And easy as a Star
Look down opon Captivity –
And laugh – No more have I –

Fr445

The last four words mark a return to the present. What they apparently say is that now, as in the past, she has "but to will"—has to do no more than *that*—in order to escape prison and achieve flight or song.

Dickinson's poems often lay claim to a kind of sovereignty traditionally identified with deity itself. What is striking about this one is that the consciousness of power seems to originate in childhood within a cage.

Early Schooling

One Sunday in 1839, during Edward Dickinson's second term in the state legislature, he visited the state prison near Boston in order to observe brother-in-law Loring teach a Sabbath School lesson. Afterward, he sent his children a report of an inmate's pitiable illiteracy: "The poor ignorant fellow took a [pin?] & pointed to each letter, & called it by name, but could not pronounce words. I instructed him how to pronounce several little words, such as 'and, in, to, the, of &c'—& he seemed much interested—said he wished he could have me teach him, every Sabbath." The father wanted to make sure his children understood the inestimable value of literacy.

Before Emily Dickinson went to Amherst Academy in the 1840s, she learned to read, write, spell, and do simple arithmetic in a common school, which she began attending by age five. Although the surviving family record doesn't identify the particular institution, it was probably the West Center District School, located at what is now 220 North Pleasant Street, a half-mile or so from the Dickinson Homestead. One of eight district schools, the two-story edifice was built of brick and dated from the late 1820s. Outside were a woodshed, a so-called necessary, and a stink rising from Colonel Horace Smith's adjacent sewer. The scholars were divided into two groups, age seven being the dividing line. Instruction would have been based on chants, drills, a standard speller, and so forth. *The New England Primer* and Westminster Catechism may have been reserved for home.

The reason for thinking Emily went to the West Center District School instead of a private one is that her father's election to the town's General School Committee in 1832 implies a commitment to public education. In 1841 he presided at a county school convention featuring Horace Mann, secretary of the state board of education, whose long address developed the proposition that our innate passions must be corrected and supplemented by learned knowledge. One of Mann's negative examples was the loving "but ignorant mother" who unknowingly exposes her darlings to the risk of consumption by tucking them into a tightly closed bedchamber in winter.

Curiously, the one point in Emily's early schooling on which we are well informed is that she was rigorously kept at home during spells of sloppy weather and sickness. Her father's first mention of her and her siblings' attendance makes it sound like an adventure well over: "the children went to school to-day—and are now all snug in bed." Health and safety were the overriding concerns, and not just for Edward: when Aunt Lavinia inquired whether Emily and Austin had started school, she at once added, "it is too bad to send them in the cold weather." Of course, the weather did not threaten the children equally: the same letter in which Edward instructed Austin to "be a nice boy—go to school—mind your mother" had these orders for Emily: "You must not go to school, when it is cold, or bad going—You must be very careful, & not get sick." When Lavinia was nearly five and probably a scholar, Edward identified the older sister as the one who needed protection. "Take good care of Emily, when you go to school," he commanded Austin, "& not let her get hurt."

Because of the sickness and "bad going" ("I never knew the mud so deep," wrote Mrs. Dickinson), Emily spent no more than two or three days at school during the first three weeks of January 1838. In February, writing home from Boston during a violent snowstorm, her father sent the following orders: "Don't let Austin be out too much in cold, stormy weather. Emily must not go to school, *at all*. Keep Lavinia from croup & fits." Even in mid-March, judging from one of Edward's letters—"I suppose Austin goes to school—let him be careful about getting cold"— Emily was not being let out.

Other parents seem to have been less fixated on their girls' liability to sickness. Among the children of Amherst professors, Helen Fiske was a rough-and-tumble tomboy and Rebecca Snell is known to have enjoyed "a good sledding day." For Emily more than for most girls, winter meant confinement. It isn't clear she ever played in the snow.

Some of the general assumptions behind Emily's schooling can be seen in Edward's advice to his girls (not his boy) during mild winter weather and "bad going." They were to "keep school, & not disturb Mother," or, again, to "keep school and learn, so as to tell me, when I come home, how many new things you have learned." To "learn" was to memorize discrete bits that could be exhibited orally, in a mimicry of classroom recitations or end-of-term examinations. To "keep school" was to do the lessons at home. Massachusetts led the nation in public education, yet the only mention of attendance in the Revised Statutes of 1835 asks ministers, selectmen, and school committees to use "their best endeavors" to encourage it. This was not laxity but a function of the times: as long as schooling was defined as memorization and recitation, the ritualized objectivity had the surprising effect of *preserving* children from subtler and more invasive classroom tyrannies. Later, as grade levels and lesson plans were invented and the teaching corps was professionalized, schools became a place where children were subjected to a process of elaborately stepped socialization. Because these graduated rigors came after Emily's time, she was free to set her own pace in ways we find hard to imagine.

Although it is impossible to quantify her school attendance, it appears she acquired much of her early learning at home, in the presence of a mother who spelled "feeling" with an "a." Does that help explain why Dickinson began "upon" with an "o" for most of her life, or why she and her sister and brother never learned, or bothered with, standard punctuation? In Emily's first letter, from age eleven, there are no periods or paragraphs and the "ou" combination in "would" and "you" looks like an "a." Yet the script is tiny, neat, and perfectly even, and, as we shall see in the next chapter, the composition is so fresh and fluent it is obvious the writer felt wholly at ease with a pen in her hand.

So it looks as if one result of the poet's early schooling was that she took to the air before quite mastering the ground. It is what we have just seen in "They shut me up in prose": the escape from ordinariness into freedom and fantasy.

Literature for Children

During courtship, Edward saw that his fiancée had access to a current magazine of light and decorous literature. Now he arranged for his off-spring to get a leading New England monthly for genteel juveniles: "My Dear little Children—I send you some of Parley's Magazine—They have some interesting stories for you to read. I want to have you remember some of them to tell me when I get home." *Parley's* contents are summed up in the six departments named on its cover: travel, biography, history, poetry, moral tales, and puzzles. Every issue had rhymed conundrums at the foot of the page and a sprinkling of curious reports from around the world. One of the issues Edward probably sent had an article on the Roman carnival that described the cross-dressing carmen "fanning themselves with a pretended delicacy" and their mistresses "strutting in breeches," but only to caution all good little readers that this sort of thing was "not to be tolerated in regular society."

Edward's purpose in bringing *Parley's Magazine* into his home was obviously to provide his offspring with an approved source of entertainment and stimulation. A tract the Dickinsons seem to have owned, *Mistakes of Parents*, warned that "sufficient pains are not generally taken to make home interesting and pleasant." "A happy home, is a heaven on earth" was part of Father's creed, and he was always taking "pains" to make his own a center of relaxed (not too relaxed) social pleasure. "All be pleasant to each other & try to make it pleasant & happy at home": this

odd imperative shows up in his letters at least as often as the more standard commands such as "don't deceive" and "obey your mother."

There was not a great deal of pleasant juvenile literature in the
1830s. Inevitably, one of the works that figured in Emily's experience
was Isaac Watts's eighteenth-century *Divine and Moral Songs for Children*. Song number 18, "Against Scoffing and Calling Names," was a versification of II Kings 2:23–24, where forty-two bad children mock the
prophet Elisha and receive their just recompense from two she-bears:

> *When children, in their wanton play,*
>   *Serv'd old Elisha so;*
> *And bid the prophet go his way,*
>   *"Go up, thou bald-head, go:"*
>
> *God quickly stopp'd their wicked breath,*
>   *And sent two raging bears,*
> *That tore them limb from limb to death,*
>   *With blood, and groans, and tears.*

The girl may have learned the song at her church's Sabbath School, which
met between morning and afternoon services and was in a flourishing
condition in the early 1830s. Decades later, when cousins Louisa and
Frances Norcross joined a rather more liberal religious study group, Dickinson recalled the ursine mayhem as epitomizing her childhood's harsh
faith: "I believe the love of God may be taught not to seem like bears."

Another of Watts's moral songs that Dickinson may have learned
was number 15, "Against Lying," of which one stanza goes:

> *The Lord delights in them that speak*
> *The words of truth; but every liar*
> *Must have his portion in the lake*
> *That burns with brimstone and with fire.*

In the 1880s a note Dickinson sent her nephew's teacher drew this contrast between the terrors of the moral law and Jesus' message:

"All Liars shall have their part" – Jonathan Edwards –
"And let him that is athirst come" – Jesus –

Like others, Dickinson came to see Edwards as the ultimate pur-
veyor of Calvinist terror. But it was Asa Bullard, her uncle by marriage,
who was the key agent in spreading the fear of death and damnation
among children of her generation.[1] Smooth and narrow, Bullard was a
different kind of believer from the Dickinsons. In the early thirties he
became editor of the *Sabbath School Visiter*, a leading children's evangelical monthly. This magazine offered a variety of brief homilies,
moral tales, reports from the mission field, exhortations aimed at parents and Sunday School teachers, and conversion statistics. Two features stand out for the modern reader: the drive to convert young
children and the emphasis on illness, physical dismemberment, and
early death. In Bullard's magazine, there was an insidious link between
God and bears.

Edward maintained amicable relations with Asa and Lucretia
Bullard and visited them on his trips to Boston (always seeing much
more of Loring and Lavinia, however). In February 1837, writing from
this city, he announced he was sending "the Sabbath School Visiter to
Austin & Emily—I tho't it would please them so I subscribed for it." By
this time, Emily, six, must have been literate.

The January issue featured the true story of "Charles's Last Sickness," in which, though little Charles died a painful death, he did not
complain and was not afraid. "So *you* would feel, if you loved Christ as
you ought," the story concluded; "but remember, you *must* die, whether
you love him or not."

---

1. Bullard remembered being ridiculed by other children after his conversion at sixteen. In his
four years at Amherst College, "the laws and rules . . . never came in conflict with my wishes."
As a student, he started a Bible class for the town's African-Americans, once getting up early
Monday morning to "have a good religious talk" with "Mother Phillis" (Phillis Finnemore,
judging from James Avery Smith's *History of the Black Population of Amherst*). In his senior year
he roomed with the Dickinsons, later marrying the Squire's daughter Lucretia. Defining himself by his service to the young and the disenfranchised, Bullard was a good organizer and sto-
ryteller, had a blinkered mind that moved easily in beaten paths, and often gave signs of various
unadmitted resentments. His sister was the wife Henry Ward Beecher wasn't faithful to.

The next story, "The Stolen Nails; or Little Sins," told of a "youth, who, when he stood on the gallows with a rope around his neck, wished to speak once more to his mother. She went up to his side before a great multitude of people, and put her face close to his mouth, and he bit off a piece of her ear." The condemned wretch is then allowed to sum up the moral of the piece: "Mother, if you had reproved me when I at first stole little things, I should not have come to this untimely end."

In the February issue the Dickinson children discovered that there was more to "Charles's Last Sickness." After "his sight failed," the four-year-old boy asked his mother where she was "with anxious and imploring tone of voice. . . . 'Here I am, my child, holding you.' 'Why, I can't *see* you, mother.' "

March brought "An Infant Missionary's Dying Gift," which told of Frederick Dewey and how he fell into a barrel of boiling water at the age of three and then gave the missionaries all he had, sixty cents, before expiring.

In April and May there was another two-part story, "The New Year's Present," about a pious dying boy who "marked a great many verses" in his Bible for his unconverted brother.

June and July had the moving tale of Abigail E. Dwight, who loved her Sabbath School lesson but suffered from an enlargement of the heart and when her father came it was too late: she "was a corpse and dressed for the grave."

July also told of "An Infant Christian," Martha Ann Graves, who was a month younger than Emily Dickinson and had serious religious interests from age two. She died, and now "the cheerful bird flits across her narrow house, where her dust sleeps waiting the resurrection morn." The contributor came from Amherst College.

In August the future poet probably read an excruciating true-life narrative, "The Lost Finger," in which twelve-year-old Elizabeth sticks an index finger into a hole in a "revolving card" at a factory and has the flesh torn away up to the first joint, leaving "about an inch of the clean, white, naked bone." "O!" adds the narrator, "the nerves of that very finger of my own, twitch and tremble as I write it." One of Dickinson's poems describes a woman speaker as sadistic as this story's writer: "She dealt her pretty words like Blades – / How glittering they shone – / And every One unbared a Nerve / Or wantoned with a Bone – " (Fr458).

"The Little Girl Who Loved Prayer" was the offering for September ("fell into a full cistern of water and was immediately *drowned*"), and so on through the last three months of 1837.

Did Edward realize how graphic and harrowing the reading material was that he had provided his children, and was the subscription renewed? The magazine continued to dwell on the deaths of young children[2] and "the *separations* death occasions," and also to vent a resentful illiberality, as when the nation's youth were assured that at the end of time the writings of Shakespeare, Scott, and Byron would be revealed as "utterly worthless" next to those of John Bunyan and Richard Baxter.

In the Dickinsons' commerce with the Bullards, one feels a colorless or perfunctory quality, as if the connection was kept up chiefly for family reasons. An 1839 letter by Edward undergoes a noticeable change in tone in turning from one brother-in-law to another: "Mr. J[oseph]. A. Sweetser came in from N. York today. . . . I was very glad, indeed, to see him, and he seemed as much so, to see me. . . . Mr. Bullard called to see me on Monday, & staid sometime—his family are now well. . . ."

Tellingly, Emily was not only very young when she joined the exchanges between her parents and the Bullards but was seemingly unaware of their routine or indoctrinational character. In February 1838, after she and Austin had received the *Visiter* for a year, her father wanted her mother to "tell Emily that I gave Uncle Bullard her bundle for his little children." Apparently, the thoughtfulness was Emily's alone; nothing was said of any gifts from Austin or Lavinia. It wasn't long before a reciprocal bundle arrived for the Dickinson children, prompting the acknowledgment that they were "much gratified with their little Books which uncle B. sent them."

---

2. Bullard's publication probably had an impact on a young reader in faraway Missouri. In 1841 it was announced that "between *fifty* and *sixty* new schools" had been established in that state, and the publications of the Massachusetts Sabbath School Society had been sent "into hundreds of schools and families. . . . The influence of these books . . . will be felt on thousands of the rising generation there in the far West." Exactly, and *Tom Sawyer* and "The Story of the Good Little Boy" (he dies) were among the results.

A certain picture, provisional and fragmentary, is coming into focus. It features a young girl, affectionate, generous, responsive, aware of adult concerns and precocious in language, who, once a month, owing in part to her father's best intentions, gets exposed to an insidiously sadistic version of official and approved reality. She is disturbed, but because she has learned not to run to her mother with her troubles, the matter escapes her parents' anxious but imperceptive oversight. It may not be major trouble, but it is something.

✦ The picture shows a seven-year-old compelled to develop a kind of self-reliance, to cultivate her vast powers of creative resistance, to sing her way out of the closet of death.

Letting Go of Aged Parents

In the mid-1830s the older Emily seems to have undergone a serious illness. Writing to Edward in May 1835, Loring Norcross was "very sorry indeed to hear that you have had so much affliction in your family." The next month, when Edward's sister Catharine arrived in Amherst after a year in Cincinnati, she assured her parents she found mother and children "quite well," repeating and underlining at letter's end that Mrs. Dickinson was *perfectly well.*" The insinuating emphasis points to something the record fails to clarify.[3] It was that fall she went to Boston for rest and recuperation. When she chose not to sail to Maine with her father and stepmother, the latter was relieved: the rough ocean passage "would have nearly *done her up.*" By November she was "much afflicted with the rheumatism," and Edward himself was so unwell a sister urged him to "go South before another winter comes—if you would preserve your health." No one outside the family knew more about their daily tri-

---

3. Mrs. Dickinson's uncertain health and the cramped living quarters may explain why she and her husband had no more children after Lavinia. Statistics for the time and place suggest that birth control was becoming the norm. According to Christopher Clark's economic study of Amherst and five other towns in Franklin and Hampshire Counties, the mean number of children born to women who married in the second, third, and fourth decades of the nineteenth century was 7.03, 6.22, and 4.47 respectively. The Dickinsons were part of this declining trend.

als than the Macks, one of whom hoped in June 1836 (writing from Michigan) "that health is restored to your family."

In the winter of 1837–1838 a catastrophic fire destroyed the heart of Amherst's business district.[4] As a sign of Edward's psychic investment in the village, on the night of the disaster, before learning the bad news, he woke up in Boston "from a distressing dream, in which I thought there was a great fire devouring my friends in Amherst." Having had the same nightmare the previous morning, he naturally wondered "what connection there was between the fire & my mind." He found he couldn't stop dwelling on the "awful & sublime" scene: "it haunts me by day & by night." Clearly, the man was much more than the dry rationalist he liked to impersonate.

The news from Ohio was no better. Samuel Fowler Dickinson was unhappy at Lane Seminary, feeling his hands were "tied too much." Following the famous Lane debates of 1834, the fervently abolitionist student body rose up against the faculty and trustees and decamped "almost in a body." The next year Samuel's daughter described him as "really sick or *unwell* a great deal." Mother Lucretia missed the folks back home and seemed to make no friends in the West, and sister Elizabeth, deprived of the right social training, was becoming "a wild, uneducated, boisterous girl." It was "*wrong* for people so old, to go from their first home & find another," Catharine felt. But Samuel had "determined never to return to the east." As was said to Edward about brother Timothy, "he is determined and you know enough of your own family to know what that word means with them."

In 1836 the former Squire took a job at another fledgling school, this one near Cleveland in northeastern Ohio—Western Reserve College. His announcement of the move was so incoherent his son in Georgia could not "make it out in his writing." The old man was more distracted and unmanageable than ever. And then came the news of his death on April 22, 1838, from "lung fever."

---

4. Two months later David Mack, Jr., bought the prime commercial lot north of the Common on which he erected Phoenix Row, seen in the foreground of the lithograph reproduced on page 73.

The shocked responses of Edward's three married sisters have survived. Lucretia Bullard unctuously reminded Edward, still unsaved, of the eventual family reunion in heaven: "Let us all follow his *last*, his *dying* message to us, & then *we* too shall go where he is." Catharine, less inclined to smooth matters over (she was the one paternal aunt the poet made friends with), wished Father "had expressed his feelings, as he drew near his end. . . . It would be a great comfort if he had said but [a] few words." Whereas Lucretia took a rosy view of his "almost uniform good health," Catharine shrewdly guessed that "his depression of spirits" had brought on his death. Stricken with guilt, she accused herself of having "poorly repaid" his paternal kindness and regretted that the children had not provided a secure home for their aged parents. The third sister, Mary, expressed a mixture of self-satisfaction and reproach: "I have ever been ready to do my full share . . . if some others would do the [same]." Chances are, she was not thinking of Edward so much as of William, the prospering family rebel, who years later erected a large memorial gravestone in Amherst's West Cemetery, as if to make up for old arrears.

Samuel's college accounts were in such a mess he hadn't been paid his salary. Catharine and Mary urged the widow to stay in Ohio until "you get *your dues* in the settlement of your affairs," but this was an evasion of the hard question facing the children: who takes Mother? Not only had Lucretia Gunn Dickinson become more demanding with age, like her husband, but in Catharine's view she wasn't capable of being "happy with any child." And in fact, she couldn't find a permanent berth after returning to the East. There were brief stays with two children, William and Lucretia, but her main support came from her sisters Hannah Whitmore of Sunderland and Clarissa Underwood of Enfield. Lucretia's letters from this period complain about boils, dizziness, the ingratitude of children. "Catharine wrote me not long since the reason why she does not make me a Home," she sourly informed Edward; "it is because her Husband does not like *Old Folks* it is likely the same reason operates throughout the family." She added a dire prediction of the neglect awaiting her children in their old age, then capped this with an apology as headlong and intemperate as her accusations: "I did not think of even entering upon this subject when I commenced pardon every thing improper I know I am made up of imperfections."[5]

"It would be best I do not ask to go to your house," she wrote Edward in one of her calmer moments, "for I know it is not convenient." Although he and Emily had taken boarders in recent years—Frederick Dickinson in 1835 and Joel Warren Norcross in spring 1836—these were healthy and adaptable boys who could sleep with the children. A difficult old woman would have been a heavy burden for a daughter-in-law frequently ill and always oppressed by household cares. There simply wasn't room in the Dickinsons' half-house for Lucretia. And so it had to be Elizabeth, the youngest and only unmarried daughter, who helped see her mother through her last months of life, and who was not quite seventeen when the old woman died of consumption on May 11, 1840, in the Underwood home in Enfield. The memory of this dismal period may have energized Elizabeth years later when she helped organize Worcester's innovative Home for Aged Females.

The Dickinson girls visited their grandmother at least once before her death: in September 1838, when Emily was seven, and she and Lavinia were dropped off at Enfield for a few days while their parents went on to Boston. From this or a later visit, the girl carried away a lasting memory of Lucretia's outspoken brother-in-law, Kingsley Underwood, a blacksmith incapacitated for work and devoted to reading, writing for the press, and composing satirical verse. Locally, Underwood had quite a name as a homespun wit, "the best read man of his town." Decades later, in a warm letter to Catharine Dickinson Sweetser, Emily recalled how this aunt had "listened with me to the great wheel, from Uncle Underwood's 'study,' and won me in 'divers other ways' too lovely to mention." "Divers other ways," a typically sly theft of Scripture, comes from Paul's Letter to the Hebrews,

---

5. If Lucretia Gunn Dickinson indulged in such tirades in her earlier years, as one of her 1821 letters suggests, this might help explain why Edward's 1822 colloquy and 1827 Coelebs papers showed a pronounced aversion to women who lectured men.

which begins, "God, who at sundry times and in divers manners spake in time past unto the fathers . . ." Did Uncle Underwood's study impress the poet-to-be as a special place for thinking and writing? Were she and Catharine listening to a nearby millwheel as it turned and creaked? Was Catharine on the scene because it was May 1840 and the Dickinson clan had gathered for Grandmother's funeral?

Hard Times

The boom years ended in 1837, making clear to Edward that his Michigan speculations were not going to pay off anytime soon. Spring brought a classic business panic, with banks suspending payment in gold, land plummeting in value, credit vanishing. Surveying the year's events in a Thanksgiving sermon resolutely titled "Rejoice with Trembling," Loring and Lavinia's minister recollected the panic's effect on commercial and financial circles—"the leaden hearts, the sleepless nights, the dismay of countenance, the fearfulness and trembling."

The resulting depression, persisting into the early 1840s, did serious damage to the fortunes of Emily Dickinson's closest relatives. In Boston, where Loring formed a partnership with his brother-in-law Matthew F. Wood (the families sharing houses on Bulfinch, Pinckney, and McLean Streets), the two commission agents had been handling large volumes of raw fiber and textiles, on credit, naturally. In 1838, indiscreet as ever, Lavinia let sister Emily know that "our husbands have felt the pressure of the times very much & have had an extension. . . . [S]till they are not discouraged at all." Under her signature, her spouse, probably annoyed at her blabbing about his business troubles, penned a short and sardonic postscript: "This letter was written by Mrs Loring Norcross." But Loring needed his clever wife's advice. A year later he claimed he and Wood had "paid all our notes" but then admitted that "what we may do hereafter is out of our power to say." When old Joel Norcross drew up his will in 1842, he left Emily's share directly to her but placed Lavinia's in a trust, an arrangement almost certainly intended to shield her large inheritance from her husband's creditors. That the document is in Ed-ward's hand suggests the trust was his idea.

In Brooklyn and New York, Joseph A. Sweetser was also struggling to stay afloat and slowly losing heart. After a succession of partnerships, he fell ill, lost weight, and by November 1839 was sounding quite somber: "My business has been small this year—The times bear hardly upon me and that with family afflictions sometimes give me a heavy heart." Mary Dickinson's husband, Mark Haskell Newman, urged the discouraged man to cut his losses and "not be *forever* sinking . . . Let yr pride and present business go, together—& rubbing all out begin anew." The advice was taken: Sweetser, Wheelwright, & Lathrop was allowed to die, and Joseph brought his family back to Amherst and took a job as cashier of the Amherst Bank. After a year or two in the village, where the Sweetsers joined the First Church, they returned to Brooklyn. Back on his feet now, on November 4, 1842, Joseph presented Catharine with one of his many anniversary poems celebrating their marriage. The poem was smooth enough, but the man's real talent was in the dry-goods trade.

No doubt Emily became better acquainted with the Sweetsers dur-ing their 1840–1842 interlude in Amherst. Her uncles included an edi-tor (Bullard), a publisher (Newman), and now a poet who wrote for private consumption. In 1858, when she herself began producing poems in earnest and in volume, she would send Uncle Sweetser one of her more mysterious and important letters.

Letters from a Legislator

Another way the hard times had an impact on the girl was through her father's ties to Amherst College.

Facing serious shortfalls, the school had been drawing down its sacred Charity Fund to meet annual expenses. Now, with money drying up all over, it was decided to apply for a grant from the same source that had re-freshed Williams and Harvard with large infusions—the General Court.

Accordingly, in fall 1837 Edward Dickinson was asked to run for a seat in Massachusetts' lower house and do what he could to secure an appropriation. Since he had no political ambitions as yet and hated to leave his home and office, he accepted with the idea he would be a one-issue representative, free to return to Amherst after the question was settled. The term of office was one year. He served in 1838, and after failing to win passage for the appropriation tried again in 1839.

At this period the Massachusetts House was hardly a place of luxury or comfort. There were over five hundred members, and they sat on un-cushioned benches in a large hall heated by wood stoves in the corners—sat mainly "in their overcoats and hats," as one of them recalled. Edward's letters home show that he was focused and diligent, made friends and allies, and slowly began to enjoy himself. Once, the speaker of the House invited him to a casual meal at home, no one else being asked. The representative from Amherst was a skillful political worker, but the times were unpropitious and there was a lingering feeling that the college was too sectarian. In the end, though the school's petition got good committee support, it was voted down by the House. The following year, sentiment was more favorable, but now there was no money and the petition could only be "referred" to the next legislature. The official record shows Edward making a last-ditch effort on the floor, trying to get the bill sent back to committee "with instructions to report a resolve thereon." His motion was defeated.

But if Edward's time in Boston proved a wash, the correspondence it stimulated constitutes an invaluable record of family relationships and the poet's early development. Every few days he penned a long message home, generally filling the sheet. His wife, Emily, wrote once or twice a week, leaving less blank space than formerly. The letters they produced in the first four months of 1838, more abundant and detailed than for any other period in their lives, permit some assured conclusions about the young poet's domestic situation and early formation.

For all its problems, the marriage seems to have become a happy and successful one. There are no more lofty disquisitions from Edward or opaque, tangled excuses from Emily. The two speak the same language now, answering one another frankly and promptly and with an evident feeling of comfort and security. In every letter they say how much they hate to be apart. They offer fond but dignified expressions of attachment. They are quick to show sympathy for one another's troubles. They often "reperuse" the other's letters. In a word, they work hard at the business of mutual accommodation, hold similar views of a husband's and wife's very different "duties," and take pleasure in performing them to each other's satisfaction. When someone showed signs of thinking their love had cooled now that they had been married so long, Emily "imagine[d] I could tell him a different story."

Quite telling is the way the Dickinsons handled the awkward fact that she was "saved" and he wasn't. To keep this difference from becoming a hidden sore point, or, worse, a constant source of edged allusion, the couple followed a certain daily ritual that indirectly reaffirmed their desire to be as one.

Several months before Edward's election, the Reverend Josiah Bent had been installed as the First Church's pastor, thus ending a troubled four-year period without an acceptable minister. A new fervency had become felt, rising to a climax on January 1, the day Edward left for Boston. It was a day of "Fasting & prayer," as Reverend Bent noted in the church record book, "a precious season, and promising to the cause of religion"; in the margin he drew a pointing hand. One result of this fresh spirit was that the Dickinson couple agreed to pray twice daily for Edward's conversion. "My Dear," he reminded her, "we will remember each other, morning & evening—tho' I am not what I should be—& what I hope your good example & influence will enable me to become." These reminders of his spouse's "promise" gave her a deep gratification in seeing him "thus disposed." "My promise is not forgotten to my dear husband," Emily would reply, with typically formal affection; "may you be what you so much desire to be is my earnest prayer." In this way, even though Edward was doubly apart—unsaved as well as in a distant city— the pair daily reenacted their eagerness to be united.

What particularly weighed on him was the knowledge that he wasn't ready for heaven:

If, as you believe, and I can't doubt, this life is a mere preparatory state for another period of existence, how important to act with reference to such a state—& yet how little we really do seem to consider it. I need not tell you that no day passes without my having some reflections on this subject, in connection with you, & our dear little children. The idea that we must be, at some time, separated, is too much for me to harbor—and the reflection that we might not meet again in a future state, is too much.

Years later his daughter expressed a similar idea with greater compression and generality: "Were Departure Separation, there would be neither Nature nor Art, for there would be no World."

That Edward was agonized by the prospect of separation and not the threat of hell says something about his personal investment in his family. It also prompts some questions about the nature of his anxious fear, which he may not have fully understood. Was he feeling the wage earner's regret at having to be away from his family each day and slowly losing touch? Was he intuiting the terminal remoteness he eventually fell into? Years later, as his daughter noted, he spoke of his life as having been "passed in a wilderness or on an island. . . . And so it is, for in the morning I hear his voice and methinks it . . . has a sea tone . . . a suggestion of remoteness as far [as] the isle of Juan Fernandez."

Given the good working relations the couple established in the 1830s, their union's permanent tensions stand out all the more clearly. The most salient of these concerned Emily Norcross Dickinson's health, "nervous" as well as physical. Putting the conflict at its simplest, Edward believed she exposed herself to needless risk, while she believed he worried about her too much. Over and over, with varying tones, they restated these basic positions. A snowstorm drew this from Edward:

Do not overdo—nor exert yourself too much—don't go out evenings, on any account—nor too much, in the afternoon. It is better for you, in cold weather to stay at home, pretty much. If you will ride to meeting [i.e., church], send Austin to ask Mr. Frink . . . to carry you.

Emily's reply that others were looking after her carried the muffled implication that her husband needn't worry about her so much or issue so many orders:

> My dear you are very kind to say to me to call upon Mr Frink when
> I wish, but when I tell you, that he has offered to do it, without my
> presenting my requests . . . we may well suppose that we have some
> friends.

Sometimes, however, she stated her position with simple dignity, and a steady recognition of *his* nervous states:

> You must not be to anxious for us You must try to sleep quietly nights
> as you say to me Last night I rested finely and I have enjoyed the
> comfortable affects during the day. which I presume you will be glad
> to learn.

But Mrs. Dickinson's times of calm well-being were few and short-lived. Once, when the man Edward hired to dispatch his routine business called on her, he found her "*looking very well,* but complaining of being very nervous." Her fears about the many things that might go wrong in her husband's absence were not unfounded. Robberies and assaults were always being reported, and one night, when Lavinia was attacked with the croup, her mother had to get up, "obtain" a light, and give the child "wine drops" to make her vomit (it worked). When Emily was "covered with the rash" and "complained of being tired," a doctor was called in, "a little course of medicine" was administered, and the girl was soon on her feet. If the wind rose in Boston, Edward feared it was driving against his wife's "chamber window" in Amherst and disturbing her rest. Often two-edged, his messages surely stressed her as much as they soothed. "Keep your doors all safely locked, nights," he ordered, adding hollowly, "tho' nothing is going to hurt you."

Since the First Church did not yet have a vestry, weekday events were held in the meetinghouse basement, later recalled as "a most uninviting room, low-ceiled and dark and half-subterranean." That was where the prayer meetings took place during the Reverend Bent's revival. On April 1, Edward laid down the law:

> One thing I forgot to charge you about [before returning to Boston]—that is going out, evenings, to attend meetings—as much as you may be *inclined* to go, my *positive injunction* is that *you do not* go into the *vestry*, on *any occasion*, for *any purpose*, in my absence. Now don't disregard this. I shall find it out, if you do. It is a most dangerous place—& I wonder that any body will venture into it.

There is no doubt Edward himself was part bear. Once, he sent the threat that if any of the children should die, "& you did not let me know that it was sick, before hand, I should never forget it." One would like to know whether his wife retained the memory of this terrible anticipatory vindictiveness.

What *we* should not forget is that the protective rage was in proportion to the anxious and tender love. Father's affection and ferocity, twisted to form an unbreakable strand, stretched around his children, his daughters especially, the older one most of all, forming her high-tension electrified perimeter.

The Best Little Girl in Amherst

Being the oldest child and a male and thus presumed to be hardier than his sisters, Austin was singled out again and again for special duties and privileges. As a designated water-carrier and general-purpose errand runner, he was entitled to brave the elements when females were compelled to stay indoors. Once, when Mother was at a wedding, she waited till it was nearly over and then sent Austin racing to the post office to see if she had a letter from Edward. Over time, the distinction grew more invidious, especially after Austin entered Edward's profession. From then on, Father would write to him about politics and business, and to his daughters about . . . little of importance. Judging from the record (incomplete, we remind ourselves), his relations with them steadily contracted.

But in 1838 it looks as if his connection with Emily was warm and rich, and well integrated into her growing sense of herself and the world. Indeed, the voluminous correspondence of that year suggests that Father distinguished his older daughter in subtle but immensely significant ways. On January 5 he sent brief messages to each of his children. That to Austin seems the most generic: "You must be a nice boy—go to school. . . . Get in your wood . . . be good, at the table, & help Mother all you can. I shall want to hear all about it." That to Lavinia shows she was seen as needing correction: "You must not deceive Mother—if you do, I shall know all about it." But that to Emily takes for granted an advanced moral and emotional development and has no threat of surveillance: "Be pleasant to your *little* [italics added] brother & sister, & help all get along as pleasantly as you can. I want to have you one of the best little girls in town." What one senses between the lines here—that Emily was the most responsive of the three, in rapport and eager to please—finds confirmation elsewhere, as when Edward warns Austin and Lavinia but not Emily against playing outside in the wind. The impatient and inconsiderate juvenile egotism that Aunt Elizabeth noted in Lavinia ("stands at my elbow, tearing me to stop") was nowhere recorded for the older sister.

The same picture emerges from the letters of Mrs. Dickinson, who also distinguished Emily as the advanced and thoughtful child, moving faster than her siblings toward responsible participation in the world of adult concerns. It is she who sent the bundle to the Bullard cousins and asked for "a little Emery" to scour her needles with—a request that tells us she was not only assembling her domestic toolbox but acquiring the ethic of frugality and self-help. (What Austin wanted was a penknife.) Though Mother often said the children missed their father, she transmitted no individualized messages to that effect from Austin or Lavinia. From Emily, however, we have two, each suggesting how competently the girl assimilated her parents' tone and at the same time how skillfully she worked out what *she* wanted to say:

[The children] are very desirous I should say to their Father they have been good children. Emily says she wishes I would write to you

that she should be glad to see you but she hope[6] it is all for the best
that you are away.

> [Emily] speaks of her Father with much affection. She says she
> is tired of living without a Father.

These statements show how conscious the girl was of her family's entire
dependence on Edward, powerful and all-sustaining and much-loved
and frequently, necessarily, absent.

In her maturity, Dickinson often intimated she had been anything
but a model child. As we have seen, she had a vivid memory of being reproved by Mother after wading in the mud. Although we must be on
guard against literal readings of her first-person poems, the importance
of being "still" in "They shut me up in prose" does evoke the Dickinsons'
tight half-house, with the Macks beyond the partition walls from 1834
to 1840. "We're nettles, some of us," says Marian Erle in Elizabeth Barrett Browning's *Aurora Leigh*, "And give offence by the act of springing
up." The passage is marked in Dickinson's copy.

What to do with this contradiction between the parents' picture of
the best little girl in Amherst and her mature sense of having been a
mud-loving nettle? It is obvious the spirited child must have broken
many rules, and also that her frequently absent father didn't have to contend with her or wasn't always apprised of her misdemeanors. But there
is a deeper answer, one that has to do with the girl's contrasting relations
with her father and mother.

---

6. Note should be taken of the mother's usage here, with its groping pidgin effect. Should we
label "hope" an overscrupulous or archaic subjunctive, or do we call it uninflected? Could the
passage have been dictated by her daughter, making "hope" *her* word? Whatever the answers,
Dickinson's poetry would make flagrant use of this unusual verb-form:

> *The General Rose – decay –*
> *But this – in Lady's Drawer*
> *Make Summer – When the Lady lie*
> *In Ceaseless Rosemary –*
>   Fr772B (J675)

For two illuminating discussions of the practice, see Lindberg-Seyersted, pp. 243–52, and
Miller, pp. 2–5, 63–69.

Before Emily's adolescence, we do not have one report or memory of Edward's having reproved or punished her. Instead, whenever the source of early parental chastising is specified, it proves to be Mrs. Dickinson. "Mother told me when I was a Boy," she told a nephew in the 1870s, "that I must 'turn over a new Leaf' – I call that the Foliage Admonition." The passage not only tells us the girl impressed her mother as often misbehaving, but that the daughter's disdain for maternal platitudes became a point of tension. Another memory, recorded on two scraps of paper pinned together, seems to rebel against Mother's pinched outlook, and also the doctrine of Original Sin: "We said she said [the?] Lord Jesus – receive my Spirit – We were put in separate rooms to expiate our temerity and thought how hateful Jesus must be to get us into trouble when we had done nothing but crucify him and that before we were born." It isn't known who the other child was or what this was all about, but it looks as if an innocent game was misread as blasphemy.

The point is not that Mother liked to punish (she didn't), but that there was real tension between her narrow mind-set and the daughter's wilder, exploratory impulses. "I always ran Home to Awe when a child, if anything befell me," the poet wrote Thomas Wentworth Higginson in the 1870s; "He was an awful Mother, but I liked him better than none." For the mature Dickinson, "awe" meant something like sublime terror. The girl realized she could not carry this burden to Mother, so she kept it to herself, pondering it, letting it become a kind of second home.

Simultaneously, the girl was giving some concentrated thought to certain patriarchal figures in the Bible—their power, love of dependents, private anguish. The story of the tragic conflict beween David and his loved son Absalom "haunted me when a little girl." She was especially troubled by the punishment meted out to Moses, who was not permitted to enter the Promised Land after leading the Children of Israel to its borders:

> It always felt to me – a wrong
> To that Old Moses – done –
> To let him see – the Canaan –
> Without the entering –

The poem ends with Moses gazing at the distant, forbidden place:

> *Old Man on Nebo! Late as this –*
> *My justice bleeds – for Thee!*
>
> Fr521

The same scene appears in two other poems, Fr179 and Fr1271. The girl was lastingly impressed by it.

Emily's rapt pity hints at the vigor and complexity of her juvenile feelings about the paternal order that mandated her own disabling exclusion as a female. On the one hand, her sympathetic interest in patriarchal leaders suggests how much she identified with Father in thought and fantasy. We may take this interest as a sign she was incorporating into her own psychic horizons his powerful determination, self-reliance, aloofness.

Yet, along with the sympathy for suffering patriarchs, went more than a touch of suspicion and defiance: to pity Moses, after all, was to question sovereign justice. According to the First Church's Articles of Faith, the Scriptures had been written by "Holy Men . . . moved by the Holy Ghost." On this point the girl had her secret reserves, or so she declared in the 1880s: "The Fiction of 'Santa Claus' always reminds me of the reply to my early question of 'Who made the Bible' – 'Holy Men moved by the Holy Ghost,' and though I have now ceased my investigations, the Solution is insufficient."

Above everything was the central mystery of "the Father," whom everyone was always addressing in public prayer. One of the hymns in *Watts and Select*, her church's hymnal in the 1830s, had a riddling and disturbingly exclusive quatrain:

> *"There's none can know the Father right,*
> *But those who learn it from the Son;*
> *Nor can the Son be well received,*
> *But where the Father makes him known."*

What made these words, spoken by Jesus, even more impressive was that they were sung to the tune of "Old Hundred" (composed by John

Dowland, incidentally). A gifted and alert girl might easily wonder what this hieratic male wisdom was all about, and why there was no provision for the Mother and the Daughter in the divine circuit of knowledge. Dickinson's possible response, composed in the 1870s, begins:

> Who were "the Father and the Son"
> I pondered when a child –
> And what had they to do with me . . .
>
> Fr1280A

There is one early memory that can be precisely dated: the poet's first Lord's Supper. This rite was celebrated every two or three months, following the regular Sunday morning meeting. Edward and his children and other nonmembers would stand up and leave and the pastor would then invite professed Christians to partake, so that Mrs. Dickinson would be the only one in the family pew who drank the wine and ate the bread. Young Emily may well have been curious about the unseen rite and her powerful father's mysterious exclusion (like Moses'?).

On January 7, 1838, when Edward was in Boston as Amherst's newly elected representative, his wife wrote him that at church that morning "Austin and Emily . . . staid with me during the communion season." The event hardly seems noteworthy, yet it made a lasting impression on the precocious seven-year-old, who felt she had been offered a rare invitation. Four decades later she recalled the occasion in a letter to Maria Whitney:

> Detained once at a sacrament, because too small to retire [by herself, that is], the Clergyman asked all to remain "who loved the Lord Jesus Christ" –
>
> Though the Lord Jesus Christ was a stranger to me, the invitation was noble.

In another letter recalling the same event, "rising" persists as an odd aspect of the moment:

The cordiality of the Sacrament extremely interested me when a Child, and when the Clergyman invited "all who loved the Lord Jesus Christ, to remain," I could scarcely refrain from rising and thanking him for the to me unexpected courtesy, though I now think had it been to all who loved Santa Claus, my transports would have been even more untimely.

In these two retrospective passages, the original experience seems to have been heavily overlaid with later materials, so that it is now seen through various intervening screens. But judging by common elements, the girl's initial reaction was a pleased surprise. There was an unexpected cordiality in Reverend Bent's invitation, and she took it seriously enough to want to respond, feeling she was being offered something rare and precious.

This response is what we might expect from a child with unusual linguistic and intellectual gifts, and who is eager to master the adult religious mysteries. Admitted for the first time into the presence of ultimate power, she gets a glimpse of the rare privilege awaiting her.

Part Three

1840-1847

The house on Amherst's West Street (today North Pleasant Street) that was
Emily Dickinson's home from 1840 to 1855. The porch in the photograph is
of a later date.

Chapter 7

First Years on West Street

The national economy was still depressed but 1840 was a banner year for Emily and her family. In spring they left the Homestead's east half and moved into a spacious house on what was then called West Street and later became North Pleasant. At the same time, the First Church secured its most effective pastor of the century, the Reverend Aaron Merrick Colton, a major influence on the poet's formative years. In November, the Democrats took the blame for hard times and the Whigs hoisted old William Henry Harrison into the White House, to the loud cheers of all Dickinsons, Norcrosses, and Sweetsers. And either that fall or the next spring, Emily began attending Amherst Academy.

It was in January 1840 that an itinerant portrait painter named Otis A. Bullard rented studio space above Pitkin and Kellogg's store and advertised his services in the *Amherst Gazette:* he would stay "a few weeks" and be available afternoons "from 1 to 4." Unlike the old Squire, who died without leaving an image of himself, Edward wanted permanent visual records of the family—"Mold[s]," his uncooperative daughter later called them. Sittings were arranged, and if the resulting portraits seem frustratingly generic as compared to the daguerreotypes about to take

America by storm, they do convey a few personal qualities. Looking at Edward, one is struck by the red hair, the tightly set mouth, the direct gaze and premature furrow—the whole impression of taut severity. His wife, Emily, whose eyes do not quite meet our own, presents (in Theodora Ward's apt description) "a face of gentle propriety with a deprecatory smile." The children's faces, much harder to delineate than those of adults, seem stamped by the same template. To individualize them, Bullard resorted to props, showing Lavinia, for instance, with a picture of her favored pet, a cat.

Of the three, Emily is the most fully characterized, holding a flower above a book opened to a drawing of a flower. Clearly, the nine-year-old is not only interested in plants but wants us to observe a connection she has spotted between the two worlds of print and nature. Her hair, like her father's and brother's, is emphatically red.

A Bold New England Voice

There was no one outside the family whose voice, language, and opinions were drummed into Emily more regularly than were those of the Reverend Aaron Merrick Colton.

Orthodox in doctrine, Colton was remembered as a gentle, peaceable, unostentatious man, fond of joking, a hater of slavery. One gets an idea of his character from the good habits enumerated in one of his sermons—

> habits of candor, and charity, in judging; habits of self-control, and the soft answer which turneth away wrath; . . . habits of friendliness, courtesy, gentleness toward all men; habit of a pleasant look and word to children, wherever you meet them—a whole mission in itself, and of the best; habits of keeping at home, and improvement of time; habits of observation, of study and reflection . . .

As a public speaker, Colton didn't aspire to the sedate polish of the more dignified school of ministers or the emotional heat of the type that "fire[s] up." Instead, he devised a laconic, not always correct, yet vividly expressive style that seems to have had a major influence on the future poet.

In early 1840, Colton was in his second year of graduate study at Andover Theological Seminary. What must have been a student essay, "Boldness in the Preacher," had already seen print. "There is *power* in boldness," it declared; "we bow to a decisive spirit. We do it instinctive homage." The ministerial student was not quite ready, however, to seek the homage of a large and prominent congregation.

Then, the Reverend Josiah Bent having died, the young man got an invitation from Amherst's First Church to "supply" the first two Sundays of March 1840. "Supplying" meant preaching for a stated fee without assuming other pastoral duties. Fifty years later, speaking at the church's anniversary celebration, Colton gave a sharply etched account of what happened next: how he arrived by coach on muddy roads, called as directed "on Edward Dickinson, Esq., then occupying the east part of Gen. Mack's house," and had tea there. On Sunday morning, contrary to agreement, the theological student found he was on the footing of an applicant for the empty pastorate. The next day, in Edward's law office, there was a two-hour confrontation with the church and parish committees, during which the young man was prevailed on to declare himself a candidate and be introduced to all the parish households by committee members. After the high-pressure recruiting operation ended, the poet's father offered a strategic and well-turned commendation of the victim: "That Colton is a marvel of a man—to visit two hundred families in one week, and tire out seven committee-men, and pat every woman's baby."

Edward probably made this statement at the April 1 parish meeting, which voted to "unite with the Church" in extending a call to young Colton. The vote was unanimous—a signal achievement given the bitter conflicts that had riven the society in the years since Samuel Fowler Dickinson pressed formal charges against the Reverend Daniel A. Clark. In the parish minutes Edward's name heads the three-man committee appointed to enact the resolution. There can be no doubt he was a key player in the devious campaign to restore congregational unity and snag a bold, first-rate preacher.

Before a candidate could be ordained, he had to prove his orthodoxy in a public grilling by a council of ministers. Colton's account of this ordeal nicely illustrates his elliptical manner. Here, in sentences that mostly do without subject or predicate, he produces the effect of rough private notes:

> Tuesday, June 9th [1840] . . . Documents presented and approved. Then the march to the church—moderator and candidate arm in arm, and followed by a large company, representatives of the churches. Something of *form* if not of comeliness in the times of old. Large gathering in the church. Stood nearly two hours for examination. . . . Coming out of the church after that ordeal, I was met at the door by a Mr. Clark Green, asking me to come to his house on the evening of the next day (Ordination day), and marry his daughter. Well, well; didn't this mean business and binding?

Colton may have wanted his hearers to have the same initial misunderstanding of "marry his daughter" that we do. A practiced writer and speaker, he knew how an ambiguity hanging in the air can operate on listeners, keeping them alert and thinking. There was *attitude* in his packed sentences, a running implication of trenchant opinions not spelled out. For a poet who was to ignore many rules and carry the art of economy to unprecedented lengths, listening to this voice was excellent training.

As impressive as Colton's spare humor was his emotional candor. After his ordination and his officiation at the wedding, he returned to his room in the Amherst House, on the corner of West and Amity Streets. Too tense to sleep, he pushed the curtains open in the middle of the night and looked down at the dark crossroads. Was he up to this work he had been inveigled into accepting? Suddenly, he felt a mad impulse, "a more than half purpose," to escape while he could. At the same time, the humorist inside voiced the town's response: " 'Strange freak; man called and settled, and ran away the first night.' "

This was the man whose preaching Emily Dickinson heard from childhood to early adulthood. At age sixteen, she thought his Thanksgiving sermon "excellent." But then came the momentous 1850 revival, following which her letters show signs of irritation at "his earnest look and gesture, his calls of *now today.*" In August 1852, seriously ill, he announced his resignation. The young woman was probably willing for him to go. But by then the gift he had brought was part of her—not the gospel as delivered to the saints, preached week after week for thirteen years, but the sustained exhibition of a man expressing himself in the kind of plain, honest, uncalloused English that grazed your funny bone. Colton's abrupt and pithy understatement exemplified the New England tone at its best—sly, pungent, comfortable with the vernacular, intelligent without ceremony, anything but bland.

The short quotations Dickinson was always introducing into her letters show how alert she was to the striking sentence or phrase, memorized on the instant (but often modified later). Judging from the many Bible verses she remembered hearing at church, the habit must have developed in childhood. Once, she evidently caught a minister intoning, " 'Oh thou who sittest upon the Apex of the Cherubim, look down upon this, thine unworthy Terrapin.' " Whoever "fired up" with that pious nonsense, producing a spasm of hilarity in at least one listener, it can't have been Colton.

Along with style, the young poet derived something else of incalculable value from her minister: a sense of the power of language. The leading idea in Colton's essay on boldness is that, however mild the preacher may be in private life, as vicar of Christ he speaks with sovereign authority and stands with founders and conquerors. Convinced that ministerial power must be articulated by the voice in well-thought-out "modulations and cadences," Colton took to heart his father's "criticisms, on one occasion, upon my own manner of closing the Lord's Prayer." In Matthew 6:13, this prayer concludes, "For thine is the kingdom, and the power, and the glory, for ever. Amen." These words, uttered again and again with attention to shades of meaning, took on a profound private significance for the poet-in-the-making. "When a little Girl," she wrote in her thirties, "I remember hearing that remarkable passage and preferring the 'Power,' not knowing at the time that 'Kingdom' and 'Glory' were included." Although we don't know exactly how Colton's musical delivery gave rise to this striking act of appropriation (*mine* is the power), the idea never left her. In her forties she urged her sister-in-law to "Cherish Power," which "stands in the Bible between the Kingdom and the Glory, because it is wilder than either of them." Here, too, supreme power is snatchable by mortals, though now its lawless energy is such that it must be hedged between—indeed, syntactically enclosed by—the two other entities.

Such were the lessons the quiet, red-haired girl sitting in the Dickinson pew was learning from bold (though not *that* bold) Reverend Colton.

A Grand Old House All Their Own

In spring 1839, as the depression persisted and the General Court declined to make an appropriation for Amherst College, Edward made his first substantial investment in local real estate since 1830. For $3,000, he bought a large frame dwelling place on West Street with over two acres of grounds. It was "a grand old house," as a later occupant recalled, with a traditional central chimney, wide plank floors, and "beams . . . of such hard wood the carpenters dreaded cutting into them." The long irregular yard made a dogleg south and east, running along the southern boundary of Amherst's burial ground. In the 1920s the house was razed to make way for a Socony Mobilgas filling station. At present, another station occupies the site.

In making this purchase, Edward gave the seller a $1,500 mortgage. He must not have felt stretched, however, for in March 1840, after Colton's first visit, he invested $3,000 in a second house—cousin Nathan Dickinson's former dwelling. The reason Edward could swing these deals in hard times was that he had his father-in-law's backing: Joel not only cosigned on a loan but made a $2,000 "advancement" on his daughter's future inheritance. Paying half this amount to his cousin, Edward covered the rest with a $2,000 mortgage. The risk was minimal: Nathan's three-acre place had a good location on the Common's east side, and it brought a steady income until 1856, when Edward sold it to the Newman estate for $6,000, to be a home for his orphaned nieces.

Judging from a remark of Loring Norcross to Edward—"we hope you will be pleased with your new residence when you get into it"—the Dickinsons moved from Main to West Street about April 1, 1840. Although the new home was less imposing than the former one, it was their own, it didn't have to be shared, and there was plenty of room for garden, orchard, and grapevines, and even for a small grove of pine trees planted by Austin. For the first time, the family knew what it was to have abundant space to themselves. However, the second-floor rear windows looked down on Amherst's burial ground, described by a local minister as treeless, "forbidding," and "repulsive." The place entered Emily's imaginative life in many ways, some playful, as when she found a buried homophone and "called the Ceme*tery Tarry*town" [italics added].

As befitted a rising county attorney with many public responsibilities, there was a continual flow of visitors for the women of the household to feed and clean up after. There were also occasional long-term guests, mainly relatives or student boarders. Ann Elizabeth Vaill Selby, a niece of Stepgrandmother Norcross, spent the summer of 1845. Edward's youngest sister, Elizabeth, lived there in April and May of 1842, and in 1844 was invited to return for "a 6 months visit." Jane Humphrey, one of five well-educated daughters of a doctor in Southwick, moved in while attending the academy. All of these seem to have been on an easy footing in the household. Mrs. Selby became an honorary "Aunt" and gave Emily piano lessons, and one morning Elizabeth rose at 5:30 "and got breakfast *before any of the rest were up.*" Since the eighteen-year-old was "afraid to sleep alone," or so Emily claimed, Vinnie—Lavinia—had to share her bed.[1] That left Emily with the slightly older Humphrey girl

---

1. This may be the place to note that the doctor's record of Elizabeth's birth on May 29, 1823, identifies her as male, and also that she married at age forty-three, had no children, and is referred to in a letter by the poet as " 'the only male Dickinson on the female side.' " The explanation that irresistibly comes to mind is: born genitally ambiguous. Another explanation is that the busy doctor made a mistake. As Dickinson's quotation marks hint, Elizabeth was the original speaker of the mot. Indeed, an early letter by the poet's niece reports a visit to "the Aunts yesterday" during which "Aunt Emily [said] she is always reminded by a Aunt Elizabeth of the ancient drama, which I will narrate. 'Little boy, I am your *Aunt Eliza,* the only surviving *male* relative on the female side!!' " Elizabeth could have been referring to the doctor's classification, or her own unusually brisk and managerial ways, or both.

as a sleeping companion, an arrangement she may have preferred, judging from the affectionate reminder she sent Jane afterward: "what good times we used to have jumping into bed when you slept with me. I do wish you would come to Amherst and make me a great long visit."

"Jumping" was how a lively pair of girls went to bed in an unheated room in winter, followed perhaps by a bit of snuggling. Lucy Fowler, who grew up in Westfield and shared Emily's social, economic, and religious coordinates, recorded years later that "our house was always full and no one ever aspired to a room or even a bed alone," and also that "the sleeping rooms were cold." Recalling early bedmates, this memoirist noted that she and a girl cousin "often slept together and a more sweet and capable and loving friend never lived." Once, on the spur of the moment, Lucy spent a night in nearby Feeding Hills with Abiah Root, one of Emily's special friends. "How grand I felt to be robed in one of Abiah's nightgowns and how we chattered after we were in bed."

Emily Dickinson also remembered such moments—remembered as she alone remembered. Writing her last known letter to Jane in the mid-1850s, she yearned for the domestic closeness they had known in 1841–1842: "How I wish you were mine, as you once were, when I had you in the morning, and when the sun went down, and was sure I should never go to sleep without a moment from you." This statement, quite intense even for the time, suggests one of the reasons why friends sometimes drew back from her.

Living on West Street for fifteen years, Emily completed her schooling, had a series of intense friendships, wrote a great many letters and a few poems, and reached her mid-twenties. The place became filled with vital memories, good and bad, so that when the day finally arrived when she and the rest of the family moved back to the Dickinson Homestead, newly remodeled and grander than ever, neither she nor her mother appears to have welcomed the change. West Street was home.

But it never quite became home for Father, whose eye remained cocked on the Homestead and the small property he had bought just west of it. In 1843 he enlarged this toehold by purchasing two adjoining tracts from Luke Sweetser. Edward had long-range plans for the neighborhood he had left. Slowly, piece upon piece, he was putting something together.

I Sent You There to Improve

Emily's first extant letters, spurred by her brother's and a girlfriend's unwelcome absence, were written when she was eleven. The basic pattern was already present: as she took up her pen she was flooded by memories of severed intimacy.

In fall 1841, with Amherst College continuing to decline, it was decided that Edward would have to return to the State House and try yet again to secure legislative support. Running for the Senate this time, he won by an impressive margin, 3,175 votes out of 5,184, showing how respected he was in Hampshire County and how well the Whigs were doing. He took his seat on January 5, 1842.

The other senator from Hampshire County, Samuel Williston of Easthampton, was the wealthy founder of the first endowed academy in western Massachusetts, Williston Seminary, which had opened its doors the previous month and was known to be aiming at a very high standard. The two senatorial colleagues undoubtedly talked about the school, particularly since Edward was dissatisfied with his son's performance in Amherst. On March 3 the legislature adjourned for six months and Father came home, freeing Austin from male guard duty. Amherst Academy's sixteen-week winter term ended March 22, after which (and a couple of weeks' freedom), the boy left for the last month or so of Williston's spring session. The paternal message that followed him—"I sent you there to improve"—suggests that a comprehensive shaping-up was expected.

Unlike Amherst Academy, with its constant turnover in staff, Williston Seminary had the resources to recruit and retain the best teachers and sustain a solid program from year to year. In other respects also, as Williston made clear in his unusual first-person "Constitution," his school maintained a high degree of control. He gave large sums for laboratory equipment but demanded that the sciences be "taught in their proper relation to *natural and Revealed Religion*" and that all permanent teachers believe in the depravity of man, the need for an atonement, "everlasting punishment of the finally impenitent," and so forth. There was also plenty of punishment here below: one boy "had 5 or 6 birch rods used up on his back" for "playing at meetings," and another received "a smart ferruling" for using profane language. Not only were pupils "*faithfully disciplined*" and "*thoroughly drilled*," but "bad orthography, bad penmanship or bad grammar" would not be endured. All in all, the institution posed an unbeatable challenge to Amherst Academy's regional dominance. Austin's friend Ned Hitchcock, son of Professor Edward Hitchcock, pronounced the new school "the best of any about here, for both boys and girls." When another boy transferred from Amherst to Easthampton and dreamed he was back at his old academy, he "did not like [it] much but soon awoke."

Austin roomed in the three-story Hampshire House, run by Luther Clapp and located across Easthampton Common from the seminary. After moving in, the boy got a paternal letter full of commands and permissions:

> Obey all the laws of the school—be kind and pleasant to all the scholars . . . if you have the head-ache, as you do sometimes, you must ask Mr. Wright [the principal] to excuse you from study. Be careful of your eyes—if they are weak, you must not use them.
>
> I think you had not better study more than one hour, in the evening, unless you wish to.

Austin was to concentrate on Caesar, improve his "writing" in some unspecified way, and be more distinct in his enunciation, giving "every little word its full sound."

The letter concluded with "love" not only from the family but from Sabra Howe, the innkeeper's twelve-year-old daughter. The touch was typical of the warm but laconic interest Edward expressed in his young children's concerns. Two years later, when Emily was away, he let her know Lavinia and some friends had spent the day playing with their dolls at Mrs. Caroline D. Hunt's (one of their recent teachers).

All of the other letters from home during Austin's month-long absence seem utterly characteristic of their authors. Aunt Elizabeth the drillmaster, much given to needling her nephew, asked him to bring his diploma home—"diploma for correct behaviour if nothing more."[2] Mother's abbreviated note was full of regulation phrases ("only a moment," "say a few words," "in haste") but still conveyed her fondness for her son and her eagerness to see him again and observe his performance in the public examination. "I anticipate much pleasure in visiting you," she wrote.[3]

Making a Hurrah with Pen and Ink

We read these letters, and then we turn to the two from Emily, and also the one she sent Jane Humphrey in the same four-week period. That we have nothing of hers from the next two and a half years shows how much has escaped us.

We hear her echoing her mother's pet phrases and anxious humor when she tells her brother, "I have the privilege of looking under the bed every night which I improve as you may suppose." We detect a lively interest in local gossip—the recent and well-publicized temperance dinner, the more "genteel" supper the college students are planning, and

2. An extant report, possibly from Austin's fall 1844 term at Williston, shows higher marks for academic work than for conduct. In recitation he was "perfect" on 152 occasions, "imperfect" on 60, "bad" on 5. His deportment was judged "unexceptionable" 34 times and "exceptionable" 20 times.

3. Since it is sometimes claimed that Emily Norcross Dickinson didn't love her children and never opposed her husband's will, a couple of commonplace details in Elizabeth's letters should be noted. That for April 21 ends, "Mother especially sends much love." That for May 10, read in conjunction with Emily's letter to Jane, shows that Mother went to Easthampton against Father's wishes after his sudden illness caused a change in arrangements.

In September 1841 and 1842 Mrs. Dickinson made visits to Boston, no doubt to her sister's family. A Fiske family letter of 1842 drops the fact that Lavinia was boarding out in her mother's absence but says nothing about Emily, who may have been in Boston at the time.

someone's insurance policy for "8 thousand dollars instead of 6 which makes him feel a great deal better." Her voice sounds an acerbic vernacular note as she tells how the Wilsons moved a house—"made out to get one of the Mt Pleasant Buildings to its place of distination which is a matter of great rejoicing to the public."

Punctuation is minimal, there are no paragraphs, and the transitions are abrupt and breathtaking: "My Plants grow beautifully – you know that elegant old Rooster that Austin thought so much of – the others fight him and killed him – answer this letter as soon as you can." Here and elsewhere, we hear the lively tones of an eleven-year-old immersed in childish things, or rather, immersed in the world in a childish way. We get a strong impression of an affectionate nature that does not feel the usual inhibitions. To Austin: "We miss you very much indeed you cannot think how odd it seems without you there was always such a Hurrah[4] wherever you was I miss My bedfellow very much." To Jane, the absent bedfellow: "I miss you more and more every day, in my study in play at home indeed every where I miss my beloved Jane – I wish you would write to me – I should think more of it than of a mine of gold." If one may judge by the writer's attentiveness to her recipients' concerns, the professed love was genuine: Jane was given news of an older sister teaching in Amherst; Austin was assured that Sabra had spurned another boy.

The report the girl sent her brother on his rooster's troubles is a striking piece of storytelling, far more detailed and vivid than anything in her parents' many surviving letters:

> . . . brought your Rooster home and the other 2 went to fighting him while I was gone to School – mother happened to look out of the window and she saw him laying on the ground – he was most dead – but she and Aunt Elisabeth went right out and took him up and put him in a Coop and he is nearly well now – while he is shut up the other Roosters – will come around and insult him in Every possible

---

4. Exemplifying the family's delight in quoting Emily, Elizabeth wrote Austin, "we are very lonesome without you—one reason as Emily says, is 'because you always make such a hurra.'"

way by Crowing right in his Ears – and then they will jump up on the
Coop and Crow there as if they – wanted to show that he was Completely in their power and they could treat him as they chose . . .

Coming from a child only eleven years old, the letters are altogether
extraordinary. The headlong energy of her self-expression; the directness
with which she says what is on her mind; the lavishness with which she
bestows her attention on the world around her; the innocence of that
gaze; the warmth; the constant flicker of humor, of irony; the already
well-stocked mind; the colloquialisms and odd mistakes: these varied elements show that the young writer already commands a very great
range.

Significantly, this amplitude is accompanied by an alert interest in
compositional effect. "This Afternoon is Wednesday," Emily informs
Jane,

and so of course there was Speaking and Composition – there was
one young man who read a Composition the Subject was think twice
before you speak – he was describing the reasons why any one should
do so – one was – if a young gentleman – offered a young lady his
arm and he had a dog who had no tail and he boarded at the tavern
think twice before you speak. Another is if a young gentleman knows
a young lady who he thinks nature has formed to perfection let him
remember that roses conceal thorns he is the sillyest creature that
ever lived I think. I told him that I thought he had better think twice
before he spoke – what good times we used to have . . .

This exuberant riff is the earliest surviving example of a kind of writing
at which the girl would excel in her teens and early twenties and for
which she attracted much local admiration and envy: the extravagant
spoof. It is a gifted performance, worked out in her head in response to
the young man's probably inept composition and his insulting remark on
young ladies, and offered now for her girlfriend's pleasure. Then, informing Jane how she paid him back, Emily reminds her with no transition of the fun they used to have jumping into bed . . .

While she wrote, Father was elsewhere in the West Street house nursing his "Rheumatism" and Mother was away in Easthampton watching Austin perform at the school examination. The fun of solitary mental play and the fun of human intimacy: for Emily Dickinson, the fun of writing was the thing that seemed to bring these two together, and that brought out the best in her. Was she imagining and inventing as much as she was remembering, busily devising an intimacy that didn't quite exist? Was it all mostly unreciprocated, leaving her out there pretty much by herself? Possibly. All we know is that by age eleven she was fully engaged in composing her transparent seductions.

Simultaneously, she was taking her first steps toward a new kind of freehand action poetry, playing with life as she knew it without tinkering for a final frozen printed result.

Legal Witness

About this time, the girl began leaving another kind of written trace. On September 1, 1843, her father sold eighty acres of Michigan farmland to Levi D. Cowls of Amherst. After the deed was signed, it was carried out west and an official copy made by the register of deeds in Lapeer County, Michigan. This copy attests to the surprising fact that twelve-year-old "Emily E. Dickinson" had signed as a legal witness.

This is the earliest of nineteen legal signatures Emily is known to have left on documents prepared by her father (listed in an appendix). One guesses that most of them were signed at home, not in his downtown office. Austin and Lavinia also acted as witnesses, but neither did so at so young an age as she: her brother's earliest known legal signature dates from May 12, 1843, when he was fourteen; her sister's, from December 8, 1851, age eighteen. She witnessed much less often than Emily, whose many signatures suggest she was more dependably available than Lavinia—more often at home. Still, that Emily began performing this occasional service at an early age is further evidence her father regarded her as signally responsible and grown-up.

Although it is unlikely that Emily paid close attention to the documents she signed, her signatures do show how much she lived on the periphery of her father's legal business and real estate investments. Again and again she was asked to take notice of transactions in which commitments were made *at that moment*. Such events helped constitute the world as she knew it.

If we take that fact seriously, and also remind ourselves that Loring Norcross and Joseph A. Sweetser, the uncles she was closest to, were high-volume dry-goods jobbers with strong Whig views on politics and the economy, we won't be surprised that this reclusive writer used the technical vocabulary of law and business far more extensively than other English or American poets of her time. Only a writer who was keenly aware of the legally binding and the commercially risky—of bonds, lawsuits, judgments, insolvencies, failures—could have written about love in the ways she did:

> *I gave Myself to Him –*
> *And took Himself, for Pay –*
> *The solemn contract of a Life*
> *Was ratified, this way –*
>
> *The Wealth might disappoint –*
> *Myself a poorer prove*
> *Than this great Purchaser suspect,*
> *The Daily Own – of Love*
>
> *Depreciate the Vision –*
> *But till the Merchant buy –*
> *Still Fable – in the Isles of spice –*
> *The subtle Cargoes – lie –*
>
> *At least – 'tis Mutual – Risk –*
> *Some – found it – Mutual Gain –*
> *Sweet Debt of Life – Each Night to owe –*
> *Insolvent – every Noon –*

Fr426

Imagining the exchange of mutual love as a legally irreversible transaction, the speaker anticipates the two possible and opposite results. In the
first, mundane love turns out to be more disappointing than had been
envisioned. In the second, there is the rapture of fulfillment, in which
one expends one's whole estate in repeated nights of love (with a man
rather than a woman, incidentally).

Few poets have been so caught up in high-risk plunges and binding
exchanges. A poem of 1859, "I had some things that I called mine"
(Fr101), plays with the idea of suing God for frost-killing her garden an-
nuals. In "What would I give to see his face?" (Fr266), from 1861, she
offers to sign a bond with Shylock pledging everything she values in nature for "*One hour* – of her Sovreign's face."

What would Edward have thought of these poems involving such
extravagant hypothetical exchanges? To ask the question is to see, instantly, how remote his daughter was from the staid Whig mentality she
loved impersonating and exploding.

Chapter 8

Amherst Academy

Afterward You May Rejoice

By today's standards, the school Emily attended off and on for seven years looks austere and forbidding. Prayer began and ended the day; teachers were authorized to administer "private or public admonition or degradation"; students were given long poems in blank verse that met the test of orthodoxy—Milton's *Paradise Lost,* Edward Young's *Night Thoughts,* William Cowper's *The Task.* Yet Amherst Academy was a more loosely run affair than tightly buttoned Williston Seminary. Since there was no endowment (all the fund-raising having gone into the college), the academy had to rely on tuition payments to meet expenses, and the teaching staff had every incentive to be indulgent—and seek a career elsewhere. Three of Emily's instructors were classroom veterans, but most of them (among the men) were fresh college graduates giving a year to education before continuing their professional study. One thinks of such teachers, the rising scholars and ministers of their time, as more apt to encourage talent than resentfully strangle it. On balance, the academy seems to have been a good place for a prodigiously gifted girl who needed the freedom to be herself as well as competent instruction.

Emily was fortunate in another way as well. Until shortly before she enrolled, Amherst Academy had been closed to girls, who were thus compelled to choose between traveling elsewhere for their education or attending Hannah White's Amherst Female Seminary. Students at this institution were allowed to sit on either side of a lecture hall at Amherst College and listen to Professor Edward Hitchcock lecture on geology, but it seems unlikely that Mrs. White offered Latin instruction comparable to what academy boys were given. Then came the disastrous 1838 fire, resulting in the closing of the Female Seminary and the admission of girls to Amherst Academy, including its prestigious "Classical Course."

Latin was taught by the principal, whose first-floor station between a large study hall and a small recitation room facilitated maximum surveillance. Girls were instructed in other subjects by a preceptress in a second-floor room, often in company with smaller boys. For Wednesday afternoon "Speaking and Composition" (Emily's phrase), everyone tramped up to the third floor, where, as Ned Hitchcock recalled, a "real nice hall" filled the entire space, with arched roof and abundant windows.

The catalog for 1840–1841 has the Dickinson sisters enrolled in the English Course, as was customary for entering students.[1] Emily was still in English in fall 1841, as a $4 tuition receipt attests, but by the following spring she was able to tell Jane Humphrey she had entered "the class that you used to be in in Latin." The catalog for her third year, 1842–1843, shows her continuing in Classical, with Lavinia, never much of a student, dropping back to English for the time being. The poet kept on with Latin until at least May 1845, according to a letter of that month, suggesting that in all (ignoring the terms spent at home) she had three and possibly four years of the language. In her last year at the academy, 1846–1847, she returned to English.

---

1. The annual catalogs published at the end of the school year listed all students enrolled without specifying which terms or how many they had attended.

A surviving school edition of Virgil bearing the written names of "Miss Emily E. Dickinson" and Abby Maria Wood shows just how substantial a foothold the poet acquired in the Aeneid. Abby had lost her father at an early age and from about 1838 resided in the household of Luke Sweetser, an uncle residing on the hill just north of the Dickinsons. By the time the young poet moved to West Street in 1840, she and Abby were in all likelihood "particular" friends, as Emily phrased the relationship in 1845. That year they spent their free time with each other during a term both passed at home; at school they shared the same table. Although they may not have translated the Aeneid side by side, Emily's comment that the two were "plodding over our books pretty much as ever" suggests they did work together. The edition of Virgil, recently acquired by Amherst College from Abby's descendants, is of interest for its penciled marginalia. Among these is a line from *The Task* that evokes the schoolgirls' occasional ennui: "Oh for a lodge in some vast wilderness." On the flyleaf, in Emily's hand, we read this penciled inscription:

> Forsan et haec olim meminisse juvabit   Aeneid 1 – 203.
> *Afterwards you may rejoice at the remembrance of these (our school days)*
> When I am far away then think of me – E. Dickinson.

The textbook seems to have been presented to Abby in 1855, when she married the Reverend Daniel Bliss and sailed for Beirut as a missionary wife. Such a gift would have been in character for Dickinson, always exceptionally generous in bestowing valued books.

For boys, Latin was a prerequisite for college and entry into the professions. A girl had no such incentive, nor did Emily share the taste for the witty application of Latin tags. But she would have been a very different poet if she hadn't studied the language, which, as Lois A. Cuddy has argued, helps explain her extreme dislocations of standard English word order and her use of such grammatical terms as "ablative." When she pictured *Epigaea repens,* trailing arbutus or mayflower, drowsing through the winter along with other plants that bloom in early spring, she used the scientific name with no sense of strain:

> *Hush! Epigea wakens!*
> *The Crocus stirs her lids –*
> *Rhodora's cheek is crimson –*
> *She's dreaming of the woods!*
>
> Fr85 (J142)

Few English-language poets have been equally comfortable with our abstract Latin-rooted vocabulary, or as skillful in combining it with vigorous Anglo-Saxon. One of Dickinson's poems exalting anticipatory over possessive pleasure ends in this way:

> *Inquire of the closing Rose*
> *Which rapture – she preferred*
> *And she will point you sighing –*
> *To her rescinded Bud.*
>
> Fr1365 (J1416)

The last line achieves a signature effect by attaching a Latin-based legalism to the simple "Bud."

No Dancing Lessons

Emily probably studied more subjects than those her surviving letters happen to mention: Latin, botany, geology, history, ecclesiastical history, "mental philosophy," arithmetic, algebra, and geometry. Every other week she and others were required to write a composition and read it to the assembled student body on Wednesday afternoon. On the off week, as an exercise in oral delivery, they were to read aloud "from some interesting book." Her recollection several years later of "the rhetoric of the gentlemen and the milder form of the girls" shows that the oratorical flourishes boys were expected to master were deprecated for her sex. Yet in spite of cultural prohibitions on women's public speaking, academy girls were encouraged to express themselves.

One of the school's selling points was that students could attend gratis certain scientific lectures at the college. When Emily studied geology in spring 1845, she seems to have followed the lectures of Professor Edward Hitchcock, Amherst's eminent scientist. Hitchcock was to conduct the state's first geological survey after making a special study of the fossil dinosaur footprints so abundant in Connecticut Valley shales. Brilliant, homely, dour, he was remembered for the way he handled a doubting voice on a legislative committee: "Reaching his hand down into the pocket of his old fur-collared camlet overcoat, he brought up from its depths two or three small fragments of rock. . . . 'Why, here they are; see for yourself.' " As Hiroko Uno has shown, the treatment of fossils and volcanoes in Hitchcock's *Elementary Geology* left a deep impression on Dickinson's imaginative life. The unexplained pushing-up of mountains became a powerful symbol in her poetry, as in "The mountains grow unnoticed" (Fr768).

Hitchcock's great point was that, so far from conflicting with religion, science actually proves it. Sewall believed his *Religious Lectures on Peculiar Phenomena in the Four Seasons* had a major influence on Dickinson's often symbolic treatment of the seasons, always a leading topic for her, and on her basic orientation to nature and immortality. In these lectures, seasonal phenomena richly prefigure life after death.

Virtually all academy textbooks incorporated the evangelical perspective. *The Improvement of the Mind* by Isaac Watts instructed young people how to use their mind so as "to subordinate all to the service of God." Thomas Cogswell Upham's *Elements of Mental Philosophy,* which Emily studied at age fourteen, set forth the traditional "faculties" of the mind at a time when psychology was not yet a science, linking such topics as perception, reason, memory, desire, and the imagination to the orthodox scheme of things. For Mary H. Jones, a cultivated Episcopalian who wanted her daughter to acquire "polish of manner" through French and dancing lessons, *Mental Philosophy* was a flagrant symptom of "the peculiar tendency of our society at Amherst." As far as this woman was concerned, the town was a tasteless "land of *factories equality* and *independence.*"

Although Mrs. Jones may have exaggerated the community's egalitarianism, she was not far off in her assessment of Amherst Academy.

The opposite of a genteel finishing school, it was the latest embodiment of New England's strenuous Puritan culture.

Disorganization

Although there is more to be said about what Dickinson got from her textbooks, the fundamental problem, given her startling self-emancipation from contemporary literary taste, seems to be what she carried away from school *as such*. How could someone who all but worshipped her teachers at Amherst Academy prove so independent of prescriptive authority?

Part of the answer lies in the school's troubled condition during Emily's period of attendance: the teaching staff was in constant flux, the program underwent frequent and sometimes drastic changes, and improvisation and personalized instruction became the norm. For a strong student, institutional drift can bring freedom and promote self-sufficiency—two things Emily would miss at strict Mount Holyoke. In addition, Edward's presence on the board of trustees and the prudential committee (the executive committee responsible for appointments) helped give his daughter an inside view of institutional difficulties.

During Emily's first three years of intermittent attendance—1840–1841, 1841–1842, and 1842–1843—a new principal and head teacher had to learn the ropes each fall from the man previously in charge. All of the young men who thus took charge of the school and its Latin classes—Joel Sumner Everett, William W. Whipple, and Daniel T. Fiske—had just graduated from Amherst College and evidently brought a certain energy and idealism to the work. Whipple, the girl's first Latin instructor, was so kindly and encouraging that a student later described him as "lovable." A local mother thought he was "excellent" but feared he "presses his scholars quite enough." As for Fiske, he seems to have been an exceptionally perceptive guide, as we shall see. Charles Temple was the girl's French instructor in 1842–1843, and probably in other years also, judging from the French words sprinkling her letters; it was Temple who cast her silhouette in 1845.

The "Female Department" saw even more turmoil. For the first two terms of 1840–1841 the person in charge was Miss Mary Maynard. In spring she was replaced by Mrs. Caroline D. Hunt, whose "distinguished reputation and long experience in teaching" were made much of in an advertisement; she was preceptress in fall 1841, when Emily is known to have attended. Hunt was advertised as staying on for the sixteen-week winter session, but when the following term began she had already yielded to Helen Humphrey, Jane's sister. That fall, the experienced Hunt returned for three terms, to be replaced by twenty-nine-year-old Jennette P. Dickinson in summer 1843.

Clearly, the dominant woman instructor in 1840–1843 was Mrs. Hunt, present for six or seven sessions of varying length. Since Emily's three known letters from this period were written when Helen Humphrey was in charge, we don't know what impression the longer-lasting teacher made on the girl. This blank in the record is doubly regrettable in that Hunt had been her mother's preceptress in Monson, under the name Caroline P. Dutch. One reason she returned to the classroom after marrying, unlike most women teachers, was that she had no choice: early widowed, she found herself impoverished with five young children to raise.

Hunt's career during Emily's time had some dramatic ups and downs. Following a school examination in July 1841, she was commended for improving "the *manners* of her pupils" and credited for their "excellent compositions" and "recitations in Botany . . . and intellectual philosophy." Ned Hitchcock remembered her as "a *smart* old woman," and versatile as well, teaching "drawing & penmanship & some other things." Her North Amherst pastor summed her up as a "lady of considerable culture" whose life was made wretched by poverty, inadequate housing, "delicate health," and a constitutional nervousness. His remark that "people became rather weary of her moods" could be an allusion to her troubles in the 1842–1843 academic year, which saw a dramatic attrition in the number of girls in the classical course, from twenty-five to ten. That October Hunt complained in private about her difficulties with the "daughters of her best friends." The following May, in "miserable" health, she was so discouraged about "the girls . . . talking against her," that she resigned as preceptress. Was Emily one of the talkers? Perhaps not, given her gentle comment to a friend two years later: "I have some patience with these – School Marms. They have so many trials."

With Hunt's departure, the trustees went on record in favor of a "permanent" teaching staff. Sensible as it was, the new policy seems to have led to greater instability than ever. Not only did turnover increase but supervision was so weak there were no annual catalogs for three years, beginning with 1843–1844. The institution's prestige declined, students left for rival schools, and there were abrupt curricular changes. German was introduced in winter 1846, only to be canceled when the teacher resigned in mid-term.

Ironically, Emily's relations with some of her instructors during this period of instability became all the more congenial and rewarding. In December 1843, the academy hired what was to be her favorite preceptress, Miss Elizabeth C. Adams, a thirty-three-year-old native of Conway. A practiced teacher and administrator, Adams had been principal of the female department of an academy in Syracuse, New York, from 1840 to 1842 before moving back to Massachusetts. Unfortunately, though she remained at Amherst Academy for four consecutive terms, Emily had to miss a good deal of school, this being the period of a major girlhood trauma (discussed in the next chapter). The principal for 1843–1844 was Jeremiah Taylor, fresh out of Amherst College and, according to one witness, a very "pleasant" teacher. Like his predecessors, he seems to have taken for granted that his temporary job did not require any large institutional vision. In spring 1844 he offered a bland assessment, "Amherst Academy 'holds on its way,' " and made plans to leave.

His successor, the Reverend Lyman Coleman, tall, handsome, ruddy, married to Maria Flynt of Monson and thus almost family (she was Mrs. Dickinson's cousin), was of a different stripe. His résumé was already long and mixed: tutor at Yale when Edward was a student; minister at Belchertown (resigning under fire); instructor in boys' schools. He had pursued advanced study in Germany, but his scholarship was not of the first rank and he would be an old man before finding a niche at Lafayette College, as professor of ancient languages. Bent on making big changes but out of touch with student needs, the fifty-year-old Coleman sought and received authorization "to dispense with a female teacher." This proving impractical, his advertisement the following term stated that he would be "assisted by a young Lady from Troy, of superior qualifications and success as a Teacher." The language suggests the new woman was not hired at the rank of preceptress. Since Coleman never named female staff in his public notices, her identity isn't known.

Still, Emily was not inclined to find fault. On May 7, 1845, two weeks into the term, she happily announced "we have a very fine school." Three months later, with the term about to end, she declared she had never enjoyed herself "more than I have this summer. For we have had such a delightful school and such pleasant tea[c]hers." There can be no doubt of her glowing response, yet, as her plural "we" tells us, she was also speaking for the community her father identified with and sought to direct. Precocious, "responsible," sharing the town's anxiety for its exposed academy, she was not yet ready to draw the sharp line between the collective mind and her own that would help define her as an adult.

But Coleman was too distracted to maintain control. In addition to teaching Greek and German at the college, he was worried about his consumptive daughter, the beautiful and accomplished Olivia, Emily's second cousin. In March 1846, the anxious father abandoned Amherst for a position in milder Princeton, leaving the school "quite broken up for this term," as young Joseph Lyman lamented. This boy had been studying German—with Emily—and now wished he was back in Williston Seminary for its "superior instructions."

Amherst's academy had never been weaker. The new acting principal, Jesse Andrews, was a senior at Union College in Schenectady. Student bills there convey a rough idea of how the young man juggled his commitments.[2] From January to April he sustained no charges, apparently because he was in Amherst keeping its school alive, but during Union's summer term he paid tuition and room rent—clear evidence he had turned the academy over to someone else. The advertisement he ran

---

2. Andrews seems to have become a sort of last-ditch hope for foundering schools. Turning up in north Mississippi in 1871, he undertook a rescue operation at Jefferson College, where, for $100 a month, he contracted to teach Latin and Greek and "all English branches usually taught in a preparatory School."

before heading back to Schenectady—"Particular attention will be paid to young men fitting for college. Competent instruction will be provided in the Female Department"—shows a continuing disregard for the girls' side. Yet once again it all fell out perfectly as far as Emily was concerned, the competent female proving none other than "dear Miss Adams," who now returned for a second stint.

Three striking facts about Emily's schooling in this difficult time are that the Prudential Committee was able to hire talented and congenial instructors, the girl is not known to have left a single complaint, and she was probably the only one in her circle who did not transfer elsewhere. When the Pittsfield Young Ladies' Institute opened in 1841, it was recognized as the best female academy in western Massachusetts and quickly attracted Amherst's brightest girls—Olivia and Eliza Coleman, Sarah Porter Ferry, Helen Fiske, Mary E. Humphrey, Martha Gilbert. With the possible exception of Abby Wood, *every one* of Emily's best friends of 1844 left Amherst Academy, Abiah Root switching to Mary B. Campbell's school in Springfield and Sarah Tracy and Harriet Merrill entering institutions as yet unknown. Even Emily's brother and sister attended school elsewhere, Austin returning to Williston Seminary in fall 1844 and Lavinia spending a year at Ipswich Female Seminary in 1849–1850.

The Dickinsons' real and imaginary fears for Emily's health probably explain why she alone never went to another academy. She evidently accepted the situation, determined to make the best of school and teachers, yet if the choice had been hers, she would have preferred a change. In fall 1845, assuming her friend Abiah was about to return to school in Springfield, Emily wrote, "I really wish I was going too." Four months later the wish had grown in intensity: "I suppose . . . you are enjoying yourself finely this winter at Miss C[ampbell]s school. I would give a great deal if I was there with you."

In early 1838, mid-1844, and spring 1848, Emily had to miss a great deal of school for reasons of health, but her longest forced absence was in 1845–1846, when, during a fifteen-month period starting in September, she was fully enrolled for only eleven weeks. "Mother thinks me not able to confine myself," she wrote that fall; "she had rather I would exercise." In winter there was a partial reprieve when she was allowed to attend Coleman's class in German: "father thought I might never have another opportunity to study it," she explained—several weeks before the teacher quit. In April, when Adams was rehired, Emily was determined to resume her schooling in spite of a "severe cough . . . attended with a difficulty in my throat & general debility" not to mention "bad feelings" (being "quite down spirited," as she later confessed). But four weeks before term's end and after "many a severe struggle," she had to withdraw, spending the rest of summer "in the fields" and making an extended autumn trip to Boston. Fall term had begun by the time she came home, so she sat that one out too, it being her decision this time. She finally resumed recitations in early December.

Adams was still preceptress, but at term's end she resigned to get married. Her successor, Rebecca M. Woodbridge, the twenty-year-old daughter of the minister in nearby Hadley, was a little more than half her age and possibly Emily's youngest woman teacher yet. Some ten days after the spring session began, the sixteen-year-old girl sent a friend an admiring description of the new preceptress. The sketch evokes both the collective buzz the attractive young woman set off among the schoolgirls and the writer's own responsiveness to the charms of face and figure:

> We all love her very much. Perhaps a slight description of her might be interesting to my dear A[biah]. – She is tall & rather slender, but finely proportioned, has a most witching pair of blue eyes – rich brown hair – delicate complexion – cheeks which vie with the opening rose bud – teeth like pearls – dimples which come & go like the ripples in yonder little merry brook – & then she is so affectionate & lovely. Forgive my glowing description, for you know I am always in love with my teachers. Yet, much as we love her, it seems lonely & strange without "Our dear Miss Adams."

One is struck by the way the writer fuses her strong personal reaction to Woodbridge with the group's collective feelings. Which conjugation is the real one here, "we love" or "I love"? Did the other girls also feel "lonely & strange" without Adams?

When Jesse Andrews left for Union College in 1846, another young man, Leonard Humphrey, stepped in as principal. Even though he, too, was in his last year of college (at Amherst), he was somehow able to take charge that summer. Humphrey brought in preceptresses instead of female assistants and proved unusually effective at restoring confidence. That fall, boasting that he had been chosen valedictorian of his class, Emily proudly declared, "we now have a fine school."

Although she had said this before, this time the academy's fortunes were on the rebound—as were her own. She had not only recovered from her most threatening illness to date but had also secured her parents' permission to leave home for a better school. Since the new plan was to enter Mount Holyoke Seminary in fall 1847, all her energies were now devoted to preparing for entrance examinations. Except when a severe cold kept her home in early 1847, she worked closely with her teachers from December 1846 through the following summer, becoming good enough friends with Humphrey that he later visited her at Mount Holyoke.

Dickinson and Humphrey shared a history of withdrawals from school owing to illness, but when the young man died in 1850 she felt she had lost a preceptor rather than a friend or equal:

> . . . the hour of evening is sad – it was once my study hour – my Master has gone to rest, and the open leaf of the book, and the scholar at school *alone,* make the tears come, and I cannot brush them away; I would not if I could, for they are the only tribute I can pay the departed Humphrey.

That Dickinson could picture herself as his abandoned student two years after her schooling ceased says something about the subtle pleasure of exaggerating her reliance on this, her first, "Master" (she had recently devoured *Jane Eyre* and was reading a lot of sentimental literature). Certainly, Humphrey could be seen as having saved the academy in its—and her—dark hour. But the chief thing to be noticed is the sense of close, personal dependency on teachers as such.

"Oh! I do love Mr. Taylor," she burst out when the former principal visited Amherst following a two-year absence. The responsive warmth, a product of both her ardent temperament and her teachers' attractive qualities, got an immense boost from the precarious institutional situation: the academy's fluctuating fortunes, the teachers' unpredictable comings and goings, the dramatic instructional zigzags. It was because Emily did not experience a program so much as a series of improvised student-teacher relationships that she later told Thomas Wentworth Higginson she "went to school – but in your manner of the phrase – had no education." Another consequence was that her dependency on preceptors became a model for what she expected from adult friendship, such as that with Higginson.

The girl was still in her mid-teens when she realized, with fine insight, that "it is my nature always to anticipate more than I realize." One of the things she would anticipate—or invent in retrospect—was the truly masterful authority. A poem from her early thirties on the loss of innocence says that in time one

> . . . gains the skill
> Sorrowful – as certain –
> Men – to anticipate
> Instead of Kings –

Fr701 (J637)

What seems to have happened was that this waiting for kings helped shape her own strong drive for sovereign power.

Although we will always wonder how one-sided Dickinson's friendships were, her attachment to teachers does not seem to have been unreciprocated. Teachers are on the lookout for the rare, responsive, generously endowed student, and Emily was noticed by at least two of hers. Elizabeth C. Adams once sent her "a newspaper as large as life" and "a beautiful little bunch of pressed flowers." But when Emily reciprocated with "a paper" (a composition?), no reply was received. "How much I would give to see her once more," the girl confided. When Adams did finally return to "wield the sceptre, & sit upon the throne," Emily was jubilant: "Oh! you cannot imagine how natural it seems to see her happy face in school once more." Of course, the two were not equals: the pupil never first-named the sceptered Adams and was not given private notice of her resignation and engagement.

The other teacher who recognized Emily was Daniel T. Fiske. Fifty years later, when Mabel Loomis Todd conducted a vigorous search for the poet's letters, Fiske recalled his twelve-year-old scholar with impressive clarity:

> I have very distinct and pleasant impressions of Emily Dickinson, who was a pupil of mine in Amherst Academy in 1842–43. I remember her as a very bright, but rather delicate and frail looking girl: an excellent scholar: of exemplary deportment, faithful in all school duties: but somewhat shy and nervous. Her compositions were strikingly original: and in both thought and style seemed beyond her years, and always attracted much attention in the school and, I am afraid, excited not a little envy.

This is the most rounded and dependable portrait on record of Emily as schoolgirl. Fiske must have been a keen observer,[3] as the impression he gathered and then retained for half a century accords in every particular with contemporary evidence, down to the implicit tension between the girl's exemplary performance in all school duties and her striking originality. Looking back from her early twenties, Dickinson caught that tension in noting how "*I* used, now and then, to cut a timid caper." In middle age she liked to pretend she had been a vagrant boy, and one of her late scraps says, "train up a Heart in the way it should go and as quick as it can 'twill depart from it." But it hadn't been that way for her as a shockingly grown-up yet precarious girl.

One reason her frailty registered with Fiske was that he was a pioneering advocate of physical education. An early manuscript lecture of

---

3. Like Jeremiah Taylor, Fiske went on to Andover Theological Seminary, became an ordained minister, and was awarded an honorary doctorate of divinity by Amherst College. Serving a Newburyport church for forty years, he wrote a number of scholarly reviews and articles. He lived to be eighty-three.

his assails "the imperfect ventilation of school rooms & churches" and says a good word for "the sports & shouts of children—their delight in mere noise without any special object—their fondness for running & jumping & other varieties of motion—their eagerness to be in the open air and sunlight." The young man who wrote that must have been an unusually benign schoolmaster. He would have enjoyed Dickinson's freedom-loving poem describing the letting-out of school at noon on Saturday:

> From all the Jails the Boys and Girls
> Ecstatically leap –
> Beloved only Afternoon
> That Prison does'nt keep –
>
> They storm the Earth And stun the Air,
> A Mob of solid Bliss –
> Alas – that Frowns should lie in wait
> For such a Foe as this –
>
> Fr1553

The poem gains force if we remember that its author had been far from robust in girlhood, and by her early fifties, when she wrote it, was a kind of prisoner.

Emily's early handwriting, tiny and neat and utterly unlike her sister Lavinia's careless scrawl, makes visible her tense girlish dutifulness. Once, as the end of a term approached, she confided to a friend that she was

already gasping in view of our examination, and although I am determined not to dread it I know it is so foolish. Yet in spite of my heroic resolutions, I cannot avoid a few misgivings when I think of those tall, stern, trustees, and when I know that I shall lose my character if I dont recite as precise as the laws of the Medes and Persians.

What loomed over her was not the teachers, always on her side (until she went to Mount Holyoke), but the patriarchal trustees. It was *the law* the young perfectionist was anxious about as she prepared for the academic contest in a community that put mind first and body second. That, and knowing she would be measured against her own sterling past performances.

Herbarium

Dickinson assembled two collections in her lifetime. The second, her bundles of poems found after her death, has become deservedly famous. The first, her sixty-six-page book of pressed flowers, has been all but ignored by her biographers.

The herbarium is a collection of dried plants kept in a large leather volume manufactured for the purpose. Eleven by thirteen inches, it has a dark green spine and an embossed floral cover and still carries the bookseller's sticker (G. & C. Merriam, Springfield). Inside are four or five hundred specimens of flowers, wild and cultivated. Once picked, they were neatly laid out, pressed, dried, and, with the help of a botanical manual, identified. The current scientific name, followed by two numbers, was written in ink on a narrow strip of paper placed over the stem and pasted to the page. Sometimes the upper parts were held in place by narrower strips. Roots are not shown, only the flowers and upper stem and one or more leaves. Each page contains several specimens in a neat and artistic arrangement.

Although it isn't known whether Emily's mother kept an herbarium, she was so fond of her cultivated plants that Edward sometimes reassured her when she left home that her plants were "safe & flourishing." As the Bullard portrait of the Dickinson children shows, Emily had acquired a similar interest by 1840. Two letters from 1842 and 1845, both written in May, name botany as a school subject. Possibly, it was in the latter year, when she was fourteen, that she began assembling her collection. "I have been to walk tonight," she informed a friend on May 7, "and got some very choice wild flowers." Have you made "an Herbarium yet," she went on to ask. "I hope you will if you have not, it would be such a treasure to you, most all the girls are making one. If you do perhaps I can make some additions to it from flowers growing around here." The pressed flowers sent by Elizabeth C. Adams may be in Emily's herbarium.

The textbook in use at Amherst Academy was Almira Hart Lincoln's *Familiar Lectures on Botany*. Formerly a teacher and acting principal at Troy Female Seminary, Lincoln (later Phelps) wrote this textbook under the guidance of Amos Eaton, a lecturer at the Rensselaer School and a botanical authority. Thanks in part to Eaton's encouragement of women scientists (his sister-in-law, Laura Johnson, was the author of *Botanical Teacher for North America*), Troy became a center for the propagation of botanical studies. It is surely no mere coincidence that Emily showed so much excitement about herbariums during the term the "young Lady from Troy" was employed by the academy.

The author of several other scientific textbooks, Lincoln Phelps was eventually elected to the American Association for the Advancement of Science—the third woman so honored. She shared the widespread view that botany was "peculiarly adapted to females; the objects of its investigation are beautiful and delicate; its pursuits, leading to exercise in the open air, are conducive to health and cheerfulness." But she also stressed the intellectual value of this science—its stimulus of the mind's capacity to group objects into "beautiful and regular systems." The mysterious numbers that Emily added to her identifying labels show how much her teacher emphasized this aspect of systematics. According to the Linnaean or "artificial" system, the number of stamens in a flower determined its "class," and the number of pistils its "order." Since, for example, the cardinal flower, *Lobelia cardinalis,* has five stamens and one pistil, it would belong in the fifth class, first order. Eaton's *Manual of Botany, for North America,* the book Emily may have consulted in order to identify her specimens, recommended that the label include these numbers to "facilitate the process of arranging specimens in the herbarium."

Emily followed Eaton's advice, up to a point. After writing *Lobelia cardinalis* and *Lobelia inflata* on her specimen labels, she added the numbers 5.1. to each. But then she placed these congeneric plants on different pages. One finds a few related species grouped together—buttercups, geraniums, anemones, violets, pipsissewa, and spotted wintergreen—but by and large her order of arrangement had nothing to do with the Linnaean system. She also included duplicates and became increasingly lax in her identifications. The effort to discern exact principles of order in the poet's later manuscript books seems undercut by the herbarium, which shows a declining interest in nomenclature, systematics, organization. Chances are, she did what most people would do: added specimens as they were collected and became ready. That may be how her poems were assembled, for the most part.

An early poem makes fun of the exact classificatory system she inked onto so many schoolgirl labels:

> *I pull a flower from the woods –*
> *A monster with a glass*
> *Computes the stamens in a breath –*
> *And has her in a "class"!*
>
> Fr117A

The stanza accurately describes the "artificial" system's stamen-counting procedure. By the late 1850s, when Dickinson copied the poem into her packets, this system had been pretty well discarded by botanists. One wonders whether she knew that.

The stamens and pistils that most flowers possess are the male and female sexual organs. That the poet thought of flowers as female suggests her love of plants owed more to culture than science. Although she always made use of scientific names and the technical terms of plant anatomy, the rich human meanings that flowers accrued for her had little to do with botany as such. Closely associated with particular seasons, flowers helped articulate the seasons of the spirit. Pressed between the pages of a letter, they became a medium of exchange between her and her friends, those of her own sex especially. Cultivated indoors, especially after a conservatory was added to the Dickinson Homestead, they became a consuming avocation.

One aspect of herbarium-making that left an indelible mark on the poet-in-the-making was her experience in the field. Nothing was quite so thrilling as the discovery or acquisition of a new kind, as when she was shown her first mignonette by Aunt Catharine or lost a shoe wading for cardinal flowers. The memory of that experience, not "5.1.," determined what *Lobelia cardinalis* came to mean for her. "I had long heard of an Orchis before I found one, when a child," she wrote at age forty-five, "but the first clutch of the stem is as vivid now, as the Bog that bore it." Her herbarium has the yellow fringed orchis (*Habenaria ciliaris*) and the larger purple fringed orchis (*H. fimbriata*). One of these may be the trophy of that avid clutch.

In later years fragrant daphne became the "dearest" of flowers for her, but always with this qualification: "except Wild flowers – those are dearer." With many of these, such as the brilliant and fugitive cardinal flower,[4] a late-summer bloom that prefers the shade "of some black and winding brook" (Higginson's words), there were strong personal associations. "One of the sweetest Messages I ever received," the poet wrote in her fifties, "was, 'Mrs [Susan] Dickinson sent you this Cardinal Flower, and told me to tell you she thought of you.' " But young Emily was also "haunted" by the white saprophytic Indian pipe and "ecstatic puff-ball," which get nutrition from decaying plant matter instead of chlorophyll and sunlight. When Mabel Loomis Todd sent her a painted panel of Indian pipes in 1882, the poet generously replied: "That without suspecting it you should send me the preferred flower of life, seems almost supernatural. . . . I still cherish the clutch with which I bore it from the ground when a wondering Child, an unearthly booty." One Amherst woman remembered a spot called Rattlesnake Gutter as "the only place to my knowledge where we could find the spectral Indian pipe." Todd's depiction of these flowers was reproduced on the title page of the first edition of Dickinson's poems.

This consuming interest in finding and collecting is best appreciated by those who, like Colette or Vladimir Nabokov or E. O. Wilson, become absorbed as children in a sector of the natural order. Persisting for

---

4. As Robert L. Gonsor has pointed out, Dickinson described this flower's spectacular action in her lines "Bright Flowers slit a Calyx / And soared upon a stem" (Fr523). This dramatic efflo-ration served as an image of a painful female splitting for the sake of a higher-order existence. The image may inform her mysterious breakout poem, "I saw no way – The heavens were stitched" (Fr633).

a time from one growing season to the next, Emily's passion was regularly frustrated by winter. "When Flowers annually died and I was a child," she recalled, "I used to read Dr Hitchcock's Book on the Flowers of North America.[5] This comforted their Absence – assuring me they lived."

Chances are that Emily's parents saw her quest for specimens as a salutary outdoor activity, and that she expanded her herbarium in summer 1846, when a persistent cough and depressed spirits required her to drop out of school and (as she put it) "ride & roam in the fields." After her death, Lavinia told an inquirer that "when we were little children we used to spend entire days in the woods hunting for treasures." A girlhood friend, Emily Fowler, recalled "two excursions to Mount Norwottock, five miles away, where we found the climbing fern, and came home laden with pink and white trilliums, and later, yellow lady's-slippers." The herbarium has a few trilliums but no yellow lady's slipper.

Since many wild plants are highly localized and have a brief flowering season, serious collecting requires close observation and persistent wandering. Having accompanied her younger friend on her "woodland walks," Emily Fowler was impressed by the extent of her knowledge: she "knew the wood-lore of the region round about, and could name the haunts and the habits of every wild or garden growth within her reach." How exploratory was she? In Mary Adèle Allen's recollection, the fringed gentian was so rare in the vicinity of Amherst "that we were early taught to leave it." This late-season flower is on page 21 of Dickinson's collection, and in several poems as well. Checking the herbarium against Edward Hitchcock's *Catalogue of Plants . . . in the Vicinity of Amherst College,* which names the localities of less common species, one finds ten of these special plants. They include *Orobanche americana* [now *O. uni-*

---

5. Because Hitchcock wrote nothing by this title, Thomas H. Johnson proposed the poet had in mind his *Catalogue of Plants Growing without Cultivation in the Vicinity of Amherst College.* This work, a list of species, would not be likely to assure anyone, even Emily Dickinson, that plants "lived." A more plausible explanation is that she mistook the author rather than the title and was thinking of Eaton's *Manual of Botany, for North America.*

flora], or cancerroot (it grew on Mount Holyoke, Hitchcock noted); *Verbena augustifolia* (found in South Hadley), and *Rhodora canadensis*. Dickinson also had *Blitum capitatum*, or strawberry blite, one of the few Hitchcock called "Rare."

Clearly, even though Emily may have been given specimens by others, she developed a close firsthand acquaintance with the surrounding countryside. It was as Lincoln said: "the love of native wild flowers is . . . greatly heightened by the habit of seeking them out, and observing them in their peculiar situations."

As for the fear of wandering by herself, years later the poet noted that "when much in the Woods as a little Girl, I was told that the Snake would bite me, that I might pick a poisonous flower,[6] or Goblins kidnap me, but I went along and met no one but Angels, who were far shyer of me, than I could be of them." Eventually, she looked back at this free and fearless outdoor sauntering as a defining activity of her life "when a boy"—a phrase that became indispensable to her after her habits of seclusion were established.[7] It shows up in "A narrow fellow in the grass," her well-known poem on the snake:

> He likes a Boggy Acre
> A Floor too cool for Corn
> Yet when a Boy, and Barefoot –
> I more than once at Noon
> Have passed, I thought, a Whip lash
> Unbraiding in the Sun
> When stooping to secure it
> It wrinkled, and was gone . . .
>
> Fr1096B

---

6. "In collecting flowers, you should be cautious with respect to *poisonous* plants. Such as have five stamens and *one pistil* . . . are usually poisonous." Lincoln, *Familiar Lectures*, 31.

7. Dickinson's earliest approach to this usage, at age twenty-three—"Well – we were all boys once, as Mrs. Partington says"—suggests a connection with Benjamin P. Shillaber's humorous and popular sketches of a New England Mrs. Malaprop.

When her friend Samuel Bowles read this about 1866, he reportedly exclaimed, "How did that girl ever know that a boggy field wasn't good for corn?" Her sister-in-law's apposite reply: "Oh, you forget that was Emily *'when a boy'*!" And in fact the speaker in this tricky poem is *not* male but a woman who was once a boy.

By the time Dickinson could see herself as transsexual (so to speak, of course), her girlhood, like the cardinal flower, had undergone a splitting metamorphosis into the life of the imagination. Only if we keep in mind what the huge childhood herbarium implies—the rich and varied pleasures of roaming the outdoors, searching and finding, alone or with others—can we estimate the cost of that metamorphosis. Eye-opening, it was also blinding, as she suggests in one of her most painful poems:

> *Before I got my eye put out*
> *I liked as well to see –*
> *As other Creatures, that have Eyes*
> *And know no other way –*
>
> *But were it told to me – today –*
> *That I might have the sky*
> *For mine – I tell you that my Heart*
> *Would split, for size of me –*
>
> *The Meadows – mine –*
> *The Mountains – mine –*
> *All Forests – Stintless Stars –*
> *As much of Noon as I could take*
> *Between my finite eyes –*
>
> *The Motions of The Dipping Birds –*
> *The Morning's Amber Road –*
> *For mine – to look at when I liked –*
> *The News would strike me dead –*

So safer Guess —
With just my soul opon the Window pane —
Where other Creatures put their eyes —
Incautious — of the Sun —

Fr336A

As Dickinson gradually restricted herself to her father's house and yard, the plants, birds, insects, and surrounding hills that she had closely observed became increasingly symbolic. They announced the seasons, and the seasons came to be emblems of the phases of psychic existence. In this and other ways, the poet turned from nature and the outdoors to the conservatory of the imagination.

Composition

What is true of Emily's herbarium is truer yet for her early letters and schoolroom essays: she threw herself with such zest into an endeavor governed by standardized expectations that correspondents, schoolmates, and teachers were left in the dust.

The attentiveness to language that Emily had exhibited at two and a half was a lavishly exercised gift for writing by her early teens. The eleven long letters she sent Abiah Root from 1845 to early 1847, the only surviving compositions of the period (it is thanks to Mabel Loomis Todd that we have them), give evidence of a huge delight in the act of expression.

Having a taste for mimicry, the poet-to-be loved to admit other voices into her prose, seemingly on the spur of the moment. Once, at fourteen, as she noted with envy and derision that an older girl was about to complete her preparation to teach, the familiar preceptorial formulas used in recitation suddenly made themselves heard: "[Jane Gridley] has nearly gained the summit and we are plodding along on foot after her. Well said and sufficient this." She loved to purloin the formal dignities of adult speech, then quickly resume a schoolgirl voice. Here she is answering Abiah's request for news:

In the first place, Mrs Jones and Mrs S[amuel Ely] Mack have both
of them a little *daughter*. Very promising *Children* I understand. I dont
doubt if they live they will be ornaments to society. I think they are
both to be considered as Embryos of future usefullness[.] Mrs. Washburn. Mack has now two grand daughters. Isnt she to be envied.

Adopting the plummy complacent tones of a matronly gossip, Emily
veils yet hints at her own more distant feelings. Mrs. Harriet Washburn
Mack, daughter of the Reverend David Parsons, had been married to the
late Reverend Royal Washburn and was now the wife of General (and
Deacon) David Mack. She must have had a stately presence, judging
from the impressive pauses Emily inserted into her name on another occasion: "Mrs! Deacon! Washburn! Mack!"

What Emily had to say about formal correctness points to the social
attitudes underlying this stylistic freedom. "Are the teachers as pleasant
as our old school teachers," she wondered after Abiah left Amherst
Academy. "I expect you have a great many prim, starched up young ladys
there, who I doubt not are perfect models of propriety & good behavior."

But there were times when the girl tried to lose her edgy voice in the
hum of approved phrases and sentiments. After Abiah sent a New Year's
letter full of the usual admonitions, Emily made an attempt to respond
in kind, then gave it up:

Your soliloquy on the year that is past and gone was not unheeded by
me. Would that we might spend the year which is now fleeting so
swiftly by to better advantage than the one which we have not the
power to recall. Now I know you will laugh and say I wonder what
makes Emily so sentimental.

Here she regained her balance. Elsewhere she sometimes lost it, particularly when overcome by florid revival rhetoric:

I hope the golden opportunity is not far hence when my heart will
willingly yield itself to Christ, and that my sins will be all blotted out
of the book of remembrance. Perhaps before the close of the year

now swiftly upon the wing, some one of our number will be summoned to the Judgment Seat above, and I hope we may not be separated when the final decision is made, for how sad would it be for one of our number to go to the dark realms of wo.

The oddity here (and there are similar passages in other letters of the 1840s) is the split between speaker and sentiment. The speaker *says* she is unsaved but her ideas and rhetorical moves are those of a perfectly assured minister, not a struggling soul. Profoundly confused, the passage shows the great danger of growing up too quickly: the girl was open to the most invasive and manipulative practices of the day. And suddenly we realize why an impudent and unredeemable childishness came to be an intermittent feature of Dickinson's free adult voice: she had to go back and become the bad girl she hadn't been.

In poetry, Emily's early tastes were hardly unconventional. She liked to quote from memory Edward Young's *Night Thoughts,* a long, reflective poem in blank verse and her father's favorite: "We take no note of Time, but from its loss." She asked Abiah whether she had seen "a beautiful piece of poetry which has been going through the papers lately? Are we almost there?[8] is the title of it." But she could also be satirical: "I would love to send you a Boquet if I had an opportunity, and you could press it and write under it, The last flowers of summer. Wouldnt it be poetical, and you know that is what young ladys aim to be now a days."

The girl's trip-wire nerves are suggested by an episode Emily Fowler observed. It seems the poet James Russell Lowell "was especially dear to us, and once I saw a passionate fit of crying brought on [in Dickinson], when a tutor of the College [Henry M. Spofford] . . . told us from his eight years of seniority, that 'Byron had a much better style,' " and advised us "to leave Lowell, Motherwell and Emerson alone." The argument must have taken place during Spofford's tutorship from fall 1842

---

8. Set to music, the popular "Are We Almost There?" tells of a girl who dies on her return journey to the home she yearns for:

> Then she talked of her flowers, and she thought of the well
> Where the cool waters dashed o'er the large white stone . . .

to December 1844. Though we may doubt that Emily was reading Emerson at the time, there is no reason to question the fact of her crying. She had a strong will, and to have it overborne by complacent male authority rendered intolerable the sense of weakness.

However, it was prose composition, not poetry, that most interested Emily in her academy years. Like pressed flowers, "papers" were exchanged within her circle of friends, one of the sought-after accolades being "exceedingly witty." She once justified her delay in answering by saying that a hastily composed letter would be "no smarter than anybody else, and you know I hate to be common." Edward had prodded his gifted daughter to be the best little girl in Amherst, and the desire to shine, to stand out and be admired, had become a vital spur. Fifty years later, Daniel T. Fiske still remembered the envy her "strikingly original" compositions aroused.

Amherst Academy stimulated Emily's ambition by turning essay writing into a public contest. "Only think," a girl pupil wrote in 1838, "my name has come first on the composition list." Looking back at Dickinson as "one of the wits of the school," Emily Fowler remembered being impressed by her "irresistible" contributions to *Forest Leaves,* an occasional collection put out by the more talented girls. Each issue was "in script, and was passed around the school, where the contributions were easily recognized from the handwriting, which in Emily's case was very beautiful—small, clear, and finished." Fanny E. Montague, the student Fowler remembered as doing the pen-and-ink drawings for these compilations, attended Amherst Academy in 1841–1842 and then transferred to the Pittsfield Young Ladies' Institute. Thus, Emily may have been as young as ten or eleven when she gained a name for her written compositions.[9] And not just for written, if there is anything in another schoolmate's testimony that she "was always surrounded by a group of girls at recess, to hear her strange and intensely funny stories, invented upon the spot."

9. But this witness tends to garble dates and sequences. Her claim that one of Dickinson's pieces in *Forest Leaves* was "stolen by a roguish editor for the College paper" refers to a prose valentine written in 1850.

In sum, Emily gained a local reputation for the finesse, the unexpectedly droll turns, and the brilliant resourcefulness of her word spinning. That she was well aware of her early eminence is clear from her "gasping" admission while studying for exams—her fear that she would "lose my character" if she didn't answer everything to perfection. But the fear was outweighed by the dawning sense of genius—the realization that her capacities were far above the ordinary.

In her early thirties she recalled this exalting and clarifying discovery in one of her most revelatory poems:

> *It was given to me by the Gods –*
> *When I was a little Girl –*
> *They give us Presents most – you know –*
> *When we are new – and small.*
> *I kept it in my Hand –*
> *I never put it down –*
> *I did not dare to eat – or sleep –*
> *For fear it would be gone –*
> *I heard such words as "Rich" –*
> *When hurrying to school –*
> *From lips at Corners of the Streets –*
> *And wrestled with a smile.*
> *Rich! 'Twas Myself – was rich –*
> *To take the name of Gold –*
> *And Gold to own – in solid Bars –*
> *The Difference – made me bold –*

Fr455

The gold she remembers glorying in recalls her most conspicuous feature, red hair, which she described at age fourteen as "golden tresses." Since the letter containing this phrase says she has "grown tall a good deal," has "altered a good deal," it may be that gold also stands for her dawning womanhood. But most of all, gold is the prodigious inner wealth she now understands is hers. She realizes she has been given something of supreme value that sets her apart from others. "*Thine* is the power" is the message from the gods, and her fellow townsmen standing on the corners know it. She stands out; she is an admired and envied prodigy. The recognition is communal, and, though it does not amount as yet to an authentic calling, it gives the shy and serious (but fun-loving) girl the courage to be bold.

The poem, one of many by Dickinson on moments of bliss, is about her first glorious intimation that she had genius and could take the name of gold if she was daring enough. But how much boldness will a girl need if her religion mandates submission and her loved father believes in the inferiority of women's intellectual powers and has no use for public literary females?

Chapter 9

Death and Friendship

Intimate Communion with Another

"The child's faith is new" (Fr701), a poem Dickinson wrote in her early thirties, when she could feel that her innocence was finally gone, concerns the childish assumption that paradise is attainable in a very mundane world. Behind the poem was her memory of the very great risks she had taken as a girl, when her precocious ability in approved endeavors and her responsiveness to what was set before her as vital and ultimate, especially in evangelical religion, exposed her to major inner trouble. Like Icarus, she aimed for the sun as soon as she could fly. Like his father, Daedalus, she contrived to save herself, preserving her early idealism through substitutes and compensations, postponing the crash till age thirty. Still, even this most resourceful of children was not prepared for her first season of death.

In 1846 Emily confided to a friend that as a younger girl she briefly and mistakenly believed she had found salvation. "I can say that I never enjoyed such perfect peace and happiness," she wrote, "as the short time in which I felt I had found my savior." Looking back, she felt that those "few short moments . . . I would not now exchange for a thousand worlds like this. It was then my greatest pleasure to commune alone with the great God & to feel that he would listen to my prayers."

Little is known about this false conversion other than that Emily's prayers soon ceased to be a spontaneous pleasure and she began avoiding the small prayer circle she had joined. The existence of this group tells us the experience coincided with one of the periodical revivals that shook the First Church under the Reverend Aaron M. Colton. If we knew the year, we might be able to integrate the episode with other aspects of her life as a child. It may be that the friends who "reasoned with me & told me of the danger I was in of grieving away the Holy spirit of God" were members of this circle.

This brief taste of perfect joy, peace, and communion with God had divided results. It established an absolute scale by which to measure all later experience, in that way confirming the child's exalted expectations. But it also made her wary of all solicitations to surrender and of her own quick responsiveness. In 1845 there was a powerful revival in her church that affected many young people and resulted in forty-six confessions of faith that year. This time she stayed away from the daily meetings, fearing she "was so easily excited that I might again be deceived." Many talked to her in private, and she was "almost inclined to yeild."[1] She had no doubt she would be wise to do so: "There is an aching void in my heart which I am convinced the world never can fill. . . . I continually hear Christ saying to me Daughter give me thine heart."

Until about 1850 Dickinson accepted the evangelical system pretty much on its own terms, seeing herself as not only in need of regeneration

---

1. We can gauge the pressure Emily was subjected to from an 1844 book by Heman Humphrey, the president of Amherst College. *Revival Conversations* consists of sample dialogues between a pastor and various types named Inquirer, Dissembler, Caviler, and so forth. A striking feature is the forcefulness with which the pastor overcomes every plea: "The question is not . . . how you feel, but how you *ought* to feel." "Just stop and consider into what a maze of contradictions your deceitful heart is leading you." "You want more time! What if you should die in a fit, before you get home?"

but liable at any moment to die and thus to miss out on heaven, the one thing worth living for. She resembled her father in this, both withholding themselves without excuse from the inner act they believed they had to perform. Growing up on the edge in this way, the girl was not well armed for the deaths that suddenly fell thick and fast on all sides of the Dickinson household.

The Deepening Menace

In 1882, after Dickinson's mother and father were dead, she noted that "no Verse in the Bible has frightened me so much from a Child as 'from him that hath not, shall be taken even that he hath.' Was it because its dark menace deepened our own Door?"

At first glance, these words seem to indicate an immediate fear for the members of her family, an anxiety stemming from her parents' extreme protectiveness. No doubt the girl felt that, yet we should note that the Bible verse could not have applied to the Dickinsons, who suffered no bereavements: none of *them* was "taken." In fact, the verb is "deepened," not "darkened"—a hint that death was outside the home and that it was others' losses that gave Emily a scared sense of living behind a well-fortified door. To look out and see how *catching* death proved was to experience a peculiar fear in one's protected state.

Since Amherst's burial ground was behind the Dickinsons' home on West Street, death deepened the young poet's windows as well as her doors and gates. Once, as she sat writing a friend, she broke her flow of thought to say, "I have just seen a funeral procession go by of a negro baby." Still, the casualness with which she mentioned this and other interments shows they were an aspect of community life for her, something she took for granted much as anyone else. She was not Mark Twain's Emmeline Grangerford, composing a lugubrious tribute whenever anyone died.

But of course some deaths struck nearer than others. On May 19, 1842, Lavinia and Loring Norcross lost their first child, a four-year-old girl, probably in Boston. Since the surviving letters from that spring predate the death, we know nothing about its attendant circumstances. Given the family's close ties to the Dickinsons, however, we can take for granted it was deeply felt on West Street.

At the time, careful attention was paid to last words and acts, especially in orthodox communities like Amherst. In fall 1842, after Emily Fowler's small brother died of a fever, his desolated mother sent a friend a detailed account of his last delirium. The boy had been convinced he "was in a deep well & *always* away from his pleasant home & dear parents." When given a glass of water, he thought it "was a hatchet uplifted to destroy him." At the end, when he was unable to speak and even to "see us," his tortured mother made one last effort to break through: "if Webster loves his mother press her hand." And he was just able to do so. One would like to know whether this striking deathbed story was communicated to young Emily.

"People *always* are dying here," wrote Mary Shepard in September 1843, expressing the strong sense of mortality that oppressed Amherst's inhabitants at the time. But 1843 was nothing compared to the first half of 1844, when a series of deaths made a dramatic impression on the town and precipitated the poet's most serious childhood crisis.

Deborah Fiske, the gifted and vibrant wife of a professor, was remembered as one who greeted children "with a kind remark always." A victim of consumption, she had a "deep and hoarse" cough, weighed seventy-nine pounds by August 1843, and, aware that she was dying, kept her older daughter, Helen [Hunt Jackson], home from school. Anxious about her younger daughter, Ann, who had lost weight from illness, despondency, and loneliness, she counted on giving the nine-year-old a cheerful birthday party on December 25. Instead, she had to send a peremptory last-minute request to Emily Norcross Dickinson: "If convenient to you, Ann may visit Emily and Lavinia this afternoon . . . I had intended to let her invite your daughters and two or three other misses . . . but I am too feeble to [hear? bear?] any noise of playing."

Emily probably attended Mrs. Fiske's funeral on February 21, 1844, and heard the sermon delivered by Heman Humphrey, president of the college. Sharing the general admiration of the deceased, he took as his theme the importance of the "domestic virtues" in wives and mothers. At the end, as was the custom, he solemnly drew attention to the various classes of survivors, particularly "the bereaved children," whose "loss is far greater than they can at present realize." No one is quite so pitiable, he grimly stated, as the child "who has not enjoyed the earliest teaching, as well as caresses of a pious and faithful mother. The loss cannot be repaired." As if to qualify this dark forecast, he invoked the dead woman's spirit as his unseen listener: "I seem at this moment to see her finger upon her lips, warning me that my words should be few, and carefully chosen. I stand before God; in what other invisible presences I know not." Even if Emily missed this tremendous ghostly scene, in which choosing the right words carried so much weight, she could have read the published text after the widower presented it to her mother.

Next came the turn of Harriet W. Fowler, daughter of Noah Webster, best friend of Mrs. Fiske, wife of another professor, and mother of Webster and Emily Fowler. Harriet had also been dwindling from consumption for many years, doing her best to spare her children and make her home cheerful and hospitable. One winter night, as she lay in bed with no lamps lit, she felt her mouth filling with blood. If she got up to spit, she feared, she would have a paroxysm of coughing and wake her husband and children, so she made herself swallow "two or three mouthsful." On February 16, 1844, Mrs. Fowler was taken by sleigh to visit Mrs. Fiske, who exclaimed, "Why, how quick you breathe! Perhaps you will follow me next winter, and I shall be the first to welcome you [in heaven]." They knew this was their last sight of each other, and when the visitor tried to leave, she was called back for "another affectionate farewell." Three days later Mrs. Fiske died. Another six weeks and Mrs. Fowler followed, her suffering reportedly "severe." "Death is doing his work thoroughly in this place," observed Jeremiah Taylor, who dismissed the academy early on the afternoon of April 2 so that those who wished could attend the funeral. Chances are, Emily did and thus heard President Humphrey praise Mrs. Fowler's "sprightly conversation, cultivated manners, and refined sensibility," and also "the ceaseless overflowing of her maternal love." The Last Interview of Mrs. Fowler and Mrs. Fiske would be remembered with admiration.

Ann and Helen Fiske and Emily Fowler were not Emily's closest friends, but it was a fearful thing to see acquaintances lose a mother. The Fowler girl had to withdraw from school in order to take charge of her father's household. When another friend, Luthera Norton, lost her mother the following year, Emily reported that "she seems to feel very lonely, now her mother is dead, and thinks were she only alive it would be all she would ask. I pity her much, for she loved her mother devotedly."

In April came the devastating death. Sophia Holland was Emily's second cousin, a granddaughter of the Lucinda Dickinson who moved to Tennessee after lending Samuel Fowler Dickinson too much money. What little we know about the girls' friendship dates from 1846, two years later, when Emily recalled Sophia as a "friend near my age & with whom my thoughts & her own were the same." We note the resemblance between this perfect communion and what Emily had enjoyed following her conversion, and also that the cousin was two and a half years older. Her death from typhus on April 29 proved utterly traumatic. Emily was allowed to watch "over her bed," but when the dying girl grew delirious the young visitor was excluded on doctor's orders. "It seemed to me I should die too," Emily recalled, "if I could not be permitted to watch over her or even to look at her face."

On the night of April 28, a Sunday, Lucius Boltwood informed a correspondent that "Seneca Holland's daughter is very sick with a brain fever—& it is thought that she will not live till morning." It may have been that night or the next day that Emily prevailed on the doctor to allow one last look. She took off her shoes and quietly stepped to the sickroom, stopping in the doorway. There Sophia

> lay mild & beautiful as in health & her pale features lit up with an unearthly – smile. I looked as long as friends would permit & when they told me I must look no longer I let them lead me away.

The hushed calm, the bystander's rapt gaze, the uncanny and uninterpretable "smile" (the preceding dash evoking the pause in which the writer scans for the right word): this is fifteen-year-old Emily's retrospective narration of *her* first Last Interview. It may lack the mastery of,

say, Walt Whitman's "A March in the Ranks Hard-Prest," where a
marching soldier receives a dying soldier's mysterious "half-smile" from
out of absolute hell, but it nicely anticipates a fundamental aspect of
Dickinson's mature writing—the sense that life's awesome climaxes are
all too likely to prove hauntingly elusive. In her poems and letters, rapt
participants are forever turning into bystanders, their minds heavy with
unfinished business.

Letting herself be led away before she had finished looking, Emily
could neither observe the moment of death nor settle the meaning of
that . . . smile. Recalling the disturbing experience two years later, the
girl brought into play the therapeutic formulas of her era:

> I shed no tear, for my heart was too full to weep, but after she was laid
> in her coffin & I felt I could not call her back again I gave way to a
> fixed melancholy.
>
> I told no one the cause of my grief, though it was gnawing at my
> very heart strings. I was not well & I went to Boston & stayed a
> month & my health improved so that my spirits were better.

In spite of the clichés ("fixed melancholy," "gnawing at my very heart
strings"), this brief account shows how attentive the young writer already
was to the life of feeling. The stiff dignity of her response to trauma
seems particularly impressive. Unlike the popular literature of the time,
she insists on no resolution, no final healing tears. She had not been able
to achieve a saving conversion, and now she does not claim a satisfying
termination of her paralyzing grief. Instead, she simply leaves home for
a month and experiences a gradual lift in "health" and "spirits," so that in
time the inherently uncompletable experience ("I could not call her back
again") can at least be looked at and narrated. Her helpless veracity, quite
unlike President Humphrey's funeral sermons for Mrs. Fiske and Mrs.
Fowler, shows what it means to be injured "Where the Meanings, are"
(Fr320; J258).

But there was one more death to be absorbed in 1844, the most hor-
rifying yet. The letters sent to Emily in Boston, running from May 19 to
June 4, imply she was back in Amherst at the end of June, when Martha

Dwight Strong, the sixty-two-year-old wife of Hezekiah Wright Strong, a prominent man who had often figured in the Dickinson family's annals, killed herself. According to the *Hampshire Gazette,* Mrs. Strong had been both incoherent and depressed of late, frequently declaring "she should soon give up the Ghost." On Sunday, the thirtieth, apparently "quite cheerful," she was left at home while her husband went to church. Unable to find her on his return, he "at last discovered her in a well in the yard," into which she had apparently "thrown herself headlong." The official death notice gives the cause of death as "Suicide. Drowned in a state of mental derangement."

In general, suicides were not considered eligible for heaven. But *was* Mrs. Strong's death a suicide if she wasn't in her right mind? And who is to say the all-powerful God of John Calvin cannot raise up such a person if He so elects?

In a letter Dickinson is thought to have written in June 1877, on the third anniversary of her father's death, she dredged up the memory of a long-ago funeral in this fashion:

> Since my Father's dying, everything sacred enlarged so – it was dim to own – When a few years old – I was taken to a Funeral which I now know was of peculiar distress, and the Clergyman asked "Is the Arm of the Lord shortened that it cannot save?"
>
> He italicized the "cannot." I mistook the accent for a doubt of Immortality and not daring to ask, it besets me still.

After age thirty, Dickinson tended to exaggerate her earlier youthfulness and innocence, sometimes representing her "Little Girl'hood" as having extended into her late twenties. We should not be misled by her "few years old." The clergyman's question fits Mrs. Strong's funeral better than any other of the time. Since she and her husband were members of Amherst's East Church, whose pastor was the Reverend Pomeroy Belden, the funeral would have been an easy ride for the Dickinsons. It may have been this event that the poet was recalling—the fourth death in a row to touch her, all of the dead female and all dying in her fourteenth year. Only after Father's death, when "sacred" things enlarged and "dim" things were recovered, was Dickinson ready to bring this memory up from the Strongs' fearsome well.[2]

That Dickinson *now* knew the funeral had a "peculiar" pain suggests she was not given the full story at the time. Yet she evidently registered the effort made by the officiating minister to be generous as well as just. It is an index of her early preoccupations that she mistook the question as one of strength. What the young listener surmised was that God might be weaker than he was thought to be and that heaven could be a fable—two more burdensome issues not to be carried to Mother or Father and thus necessitating a further increase in her own powers. As she would one day write,

> *I can wade Grief –*
> *Whole Pools of it –*
> *I'm used to that . . .*
>
> Fr312

So Independent She Don't Say a Word

All that is known of Emily's recuperative month-long visit to Lavinia and Loring Norcross in Boston, and also to the William Dickinsons in Worcester, is found in her parents' affectionate messages to her. Saying nothing about her illness and depression, these letters seem determinedly cheerful. Mother mentions David Mack's marriage to Harriet Washburn ("pleasant indeed"), assures her daughter her plants "look finely," and mentions more than once that Emily's friends have been asking after her. In separate letters she twice writes the identical words,

---

2. A draft of a poem also assigned to 1877 begins, "What mystery pervades a well!" and ends with an impressive statement on the unknowability of nature: ". . . those who know her, know her less / The nearer her they get" (Fr1433[A]).

"we are lonely without you," thus communicating both her love and her meager epistolary resources. Vinnie having also been sick, Mrs. Dickinson reports that she is "now able to assist me considerable." Her statement that Vinnie "gets along better without you" than had been expected gives us our first glimpse of the sisters' closeness.

In her last years the poet wrote Charles H. Clark that "your Bond to your Brother reminds me of mine to my Sister – early – earnest – indissoluble." The indissolubility of this bond is nicely expressed by one of Edward's letters to Emily in Boston: "[Vinnie] takes hold very smartly—She is so independent, that she don't say a word about you. She means to brave it out. I hope you will get home safely." Whether or not Lavinia really felt the stoic resolve her father attributed to her, his letter surely reveals his own anxious, intense, but undemonstrative love. Being independent, not saying a word, braving it out: in his mind these were the strategies for overcoming loneliness and separation. They were among Emily's strategies also, though by no means her only ones.

Protective as ever, Edward gave his daughter the type of advice he often pressed on absent family members: "When you come home—be careful, & get out of the cars at *Palmer*—don't fall, Keep hold of something all the time, till you are safely off—lest they should start, & throw you down & run over you." The passage clearly brings out his worried sense of his daughter's vulnerability when traveling by herself. To some, the flatness with which he envisioned a catastrophic possibility may seem ham-handed, especially as sent to a child oppressed by death. But it is also a sign of the clearsightedness he wished to foster.

Another of Father's recommendations—"I want to have you see the Lunatic Hospital, & other interesting places in Worcester"—also catches our eye. Nine years earlier, when her mother went to Boston and Worcester to recover *her* health, he gave the same advice. Did he hope his overwrought females would regain their balance if they inspected the behavior and treatment of the insane? Or did he want wife and daughter to share his interest in enlightened amelioration—the sort of thing animating an essay he wrote in college, "The importance of providing an Asylum for the insane"?

Remarkable Fancies and the "Five"

But it was time and friendship and her own imaginative resources that did the most to bring thirteen-year-old Emily out of her sickness unto death—not stoicism or religion or visits to the Lunatic Hospital in Worcester.

She returned home on a Wednesday in June, arriving in time for the afternoon "Speaking" at Amherst Academy. Revisiting the scene of former triumphs, she climbed to the school's third floor along with the regularly enrolled students. Ascending behind her was someone new, an attractive and sedate girl wearing dandelions in her hair. "I shall never forget that scene," Emily told her eight years later, "nor the very remarkable fancies it gave me then of you."[3] Young Emily herself was remembered as having been "exquisitely neat and careful in her dress," and always with "flowers about her." But the reason the dandelion girl made a lasting impression went deeper than that, given the background of sickness and death: who was this if not the May Queen, rising with all her natural vitality on display and ready to help Emily make a new start?

The girl was Abiah Palmer Root, as Emily learned after "unceremoniously" introducing herself. She came from a hamlet near Springfield called Feeding Hills, where her father was a merchant and Congregational deacon and the family was well regarded. Judging from Abiah's flowery curls and the "romance" she began writing in Amherst, she seems to have been a lively and original child. Not only was it decidedly ambitious for a girl to attempt a novel, but in the Dickinson home, where Edward's views of current fiction grew more and more censorious, such an undertaking would have been quite transgressive. Emily's first letter to this friend pleads for a look at the great romance: "I am in a fever to read it. I expect it will be against my Whig feelings." The advice

---

3. A letter Dickinson wrote about the same time personified the earth in springtime as a woman arrayed in new foliage and flowers: "Then her *hair*, Jennie, perfectly *crowned* with flowers – Oh she'll be a comely maid, by May Day, and she shall be *queen*, if she can!"

that followed her friend's transfer to a girls' school in Springfield—"dont let your free spirit be chained" by the "starched up young ladys there"— says a great deal about both girls. But the advice may have been forgotten: the little that is known of Abiah's later history does not bear out her early and unconventional promise.

"How happy we all were together *that term* we went to Miss Adams," Emily recalled in spring 1845; "I wish it might be so again, but I never expect it" [italics added]. The striking thing about the girls' friendship is that, although it produced a correspondence lasting into their early twenties, nearly ten years, they were originally in close daily contact for well under two school terms.[4] This rapid crystallization suggests how much Emily's hunger for love was stimulated by her private mourning. But it also reveals a lifelong pattern of response—a quickness in attaching herself to others and a fixity in holding on. "She loved with all her might," Emily Fowler recalled, immediately adding, "there was never a touch of the worldling about her." That was the consensual view: impulsive, loyal, generous to the point of improvidence, perhaps naive. Lavinia put it well in saying that, rather than being "withdrawn or exclusive," the poet was "always watching for the rewarding person to come."

In his 1849 novel, *Kavanagh,* Henry Wadsworth Longfellow gave this account of two schoolgirls' close friendship: they "sat together in school; they walked together after school; they told each other their manifold secrets; they wrote long and impassioned letters to each other in the evening; in a word, they were in love with each other." In the Dickinson family copy, the passage is marked twice, once by Emily. She, too, would (repeatedly) "Choose One," as she put it in "The soul selects her own society" (Fr409), yet Longfellow's description does not quite match her friendship with Abiah. The two were less an exclusive pair than members of a congenial group, "the 'five,' " which coalesced in fall

---

4. A family letter of June 4, 1844, shows that Emily was expected home any day. Amherst Academy was then two weeks into its summer session, which began May 22 and ran for eleven weeks. If she did as in 1846, when she sat out a full term after missing the first couple of weeks, she waited to re-enroll till August 28, 1844, the first day of fall term. That was Abiah's last term in Amherst.

1844 under the preceptress Elizabeth C. Adams. The other three were Abby Wood (met in a previous chapter), Harriet Merrill, and Sarah S. Tracy. Once, touching off their distinctive traits, Emily noted that Abby was studious, Harriet was "making fun," and Sarah was "as consistent and calm and lovely as ever"—adjectives partly suggesting why the latter was tagged as "alias Virgil." It was the coming together of this tight yet disparate group following a series of deaths that gave the fall term a special, never-to-be-forgotten flavor for Emily.[5]

The letters in which she tried to perpetuate this short-lived circle have led unwary scholars to suppose it endured for years. In fact, soon after Abiah transferred elsewhere, Harriet and then Sarah also left. The poet's letters to them, mentioned to Abiah, have not been found, yet there is no question but that Emily was by far the most persistent in keeping the connection alive. Unwilling to accept Harriet's obvious lack of interest, she urged Abiah to besiege her with letters—"heap coals of fire opon her head by writing to her constantly until you get an answer." As late as 1847 she was still writing Harriet, harping on "old & I fear, forgotten friends." Why were there no remembrances in Harriet's notes to her grandmother in Amherst? Was there a "mystery" in this silence? Having heard nothing from her "this age," or Sarah either, Emily felt a perplexed pain.[6]

---

5. Meanwhile, it looks as if Emily's mother was excluded from the literate group of women associated with the college. Perhaps her stiffness as a writer kept her from contributing to the notes Mrs. Fiske, Mrs. Fowler, and others were constantly circulating (many of them preserved in the Helen Hunt Jackson Papers at Colorado College and the Emily Fowler Ford and Ford Family Papers at the New York Public Library). In 1843 Mary Shepard, a member of the Boltwood clan, called on Mrs. Dickinson and, finding her "as usual full of plaintive talk," undertook the delicate task of explaining why Hannah Terry, wife of a Hartford judge, "did not now visit her." That Mrs. Terry was the person Mrs. Dickinson had looked up in Boston in 1835 (after calling hours) adds to the general picture of a respectable woman who feels neglected and isolated, and increasingly melancholic.

6. Dickinson's earliest known poem, a valentine from 1850, names a "*Sarah*" and a "*Harriet*." Standard editions identify them as Sarah S. Tracy and Harriet Merrill, even though both had been out of the picture for nearly four years. The poet probably had in mind Sarah Porter Ferry, who helped her mother run a boardinghouse on Amity Street, and Harriet Austin Dickinson, sister of William Cowper and daughter of Reverend Baxter. Harriet attended Amherst Academy in 1848–1849 and became friends with Vinnie.

Also painful was the impact of her friends' conversions on girlhood intimacies. As long as Abiah was still unsaved, Emily could be free and easy with her vagrant fancies. "I have lately come to the conclusion that I am Eve," she wrote soon after her fifteenth birthday. "You know there is no account of her death in the Bible, and why am not I Eve? If you find any statements which you think likely to prove the truth of the case I wish you would send them to me without delay." Although the sprightly tone of this arresting passage is an implicit plea not to pick it to shreds, one can't help wondering what the writer understood as the point of identity. Was it that she felt archetypal and original, or more naturally wayward than others, or essentially parentless? However we interpret this appealing provocation, Abiah was in no mood to play along. Overwhelmed by a revival, she drafted and sent a somber report on her "unsettled" state of mind. Following suit, Emily composed a solemn lament on her former and false conversion, excoriating herself in the best evangelical fashion for her stubborn refusal to submit.

Since Abiah was not yet among the regenerate, Emily was free to bring out her gloomy reflection that, fearful as it was to die, living forever almost seemed worse. "Does not Eternity appear dreadful to you. I often get thinking of it and it seems so dark to me that I almost wish there was no Eternity. To think that we must forever live and never cease to be." Here, we seem to have the dark side of the teasing fantasy about being Eve and living on and on. Had the girl caught a glimpse of something that would occupy her as poet—the undischargeable burdens of vision, consciousness, integrity?

By the time Emily wrote her next letter, in March 1846, she had received the momentous news of Abiah's conversion and carried it to Abby Wood, the two friends doing their best to digest it. Since by now Sarah Tracy had also been saved, Emily and Abby saw themselves, inevitably, as "left." Torn between joy and sorrow, they hoped the revival then under way at the college would result in their own conversions.

There are indications that Abiah now became somewhat preachy in her letters, further eroding the old frolicsomeness. Emily tried to be responsive as well as honest, admitting she was concerned about "the all important subject, to which you have so frequently & so affectionately called my attention in your letters. But . . . I do not feel that I could give up all for Christ." Following Abby's conversion in 1850, Emily sent Abiah an account of their friend's altered appearance, her face seeming "calmer, but full of radiance." Struck by Abby's candor in talking about her feelings, Emily remarked on the contrast between this apparent openness and the furtive conduct of "the lingering *bad* ones," herself included: "*I* slink away, and pause, and ponder, and ponder, and pause." However, such writing was hardly slinking, exemplifying as it did a kind of honesty the regenerate were not prepared to accept. Abiah and Abby's retreat to the safety of standard beliefs and feelings posed a challenge to the poet's expressive drive, helping explain both her sentimental returns to the past and her teasing recklessness.

A sentence Dickinson jotted down in later life reads, "Did we not find (gain) as we lost we should make but a threadbare exhibition after a few years." It was partly because Abiah was found after Sophia had been lost that Emily adhered with such tenacity as this girlhood friend entered the church, adult life, and marriage, leaving less and less to write about. There is an interesting contrast in these letters between the rich growth of the writer's mind and style and her insistence on keeping the past in amber. At times, a correspondence that had its origins in a lifesaving friendship very nearly became a disguise for a relationship gone stale. Not until 1854 was Dickinson prepared to recognize that it was all over. By then, she had new gains to cover this latest loss.

At no time was it harder to deny the obvious than in August 1848, when Abiah unexpectedly showed up at Mount Holyoke's Commencement, then vanished without a word. That Emily hung on after this brush-off gives the measure of what friendship, memory, writing meant to her: "Why did you not come back that day, and tell me what had sealed your lips toward me? . . . if you dont want to be my friend any longer, say so, & I'll try *once* more to blot you from my memory. Tell me very soon, for suspense is intolerable."

The work of communicating thought and feeling was as unstoppable as the soul itself. If Dickinson's fidelity to her select intimates proved a great trial to them and her, that was partly because the responsibilities of consciousness could not be put aside.

Friendship and Conspiracy at Home

Of course, there were other friends. On the perimeter of the "five" were Sabra Palmer, Abiah's cousin in Amherst, and Mary Warner, daughter of a professor of rhetoric at the college. Jane Humphrey, no longer in Amherst, apparently remained in touch, and Eliza Coleman would become one of the poet's dearest friends. The offspring of professional or mercantile providers, these young women were relatively well educated and refined and without the "rough & uncultivated manners" Emily shied away from. She joined parties and excursions but kept her distance, as her parents preferred, from even the safest of organizations. At fifteen, unlike "most of the girls near my age," she did not attend the large gatherings of the "Ladys Sewing Circle," giving as her reason that "Mother thinks it not best for me to go into society so soon." This was in tacit accord with Father's conservative views opposing women's participation in societies.

The society that perhaps meant more to Emily than any other was the one we know least about, that of her siblings at home. Since letters are obviously occasioned by absence, her ordinary domestic intimacies left few written records. When she was away at Boston or Mount Holyoke Seminary, she was repeatedly assured—it made her very "happy"—that " 'they were *so lonely*' " without her. Writing Austin, she quoted what he seems to have said in person, that in her absence home felt "like a funeral." There are a few retrospects from later years, as when she told Higginson that when Austin brought *Kavanagh* home, he "hid it under the piano cover & made signs to her & they read it: her father at last found it & was displeased." The retrospect is consistent with everything we know about the family. But what biography wants is *contemporary* evidence.

We find a faint trace in a book the Dickinsons owned, John Pendleton Kennedy's popular *Swallow Barn, or a Sojourn in the Old Dominion*. Among numerous marginalia is an underlined passage: "Ned pretended to impute all this tediousness to Sunday, which, he remarked, *was always the most difficult day in the week to get through.*" In the margin, in what appears to be Austin's handwriting, we read, "that's a fact." Someone else—Emily, judging by the handwriting—came upon the comment, added an asterisk, and wrote at the bottom, "unless you have some such book as this to read." This exchange was conjecturally assigned to 1844 by Jay Leyda. Whatever the date, the comments nicely evoke the conspiratorial feeling that united Austin and Emily against grown-up severities. The tedium of Sundays was to be a leading topic in her letters to him in the early 1850s.

Our best insights into the children's associated life at home come from Joseph B. Lyman, who briefly lived with them in his boyhood and became a close friend of the poet. His entrance into the family was a consequence of her father's insistence on providing a trusty male protector when he was away overnight. This practice went back at least to 1829, when Samuel Fowler Dickinson, facing an unavoidable absence, asked a student to move in "as *a guard.*" In the late 1830s, when Edward served in the General Court and General Mack occupied the Homestead's west half, the question didn't arise, the General being a militia in himself. But after the Dickinsons moved to their own place, the more Edward got involved in politics the more a household guard was required.[7] In 1845 and 1846 he was elected to the Governor's Council, which was responsible for vetting all pardons, judicial appointments, and treasury warrants. Joining this powerful watchdog group had consequences for Edward's family, among other things introducing Emily to her first governor, George N. Briggs. (After he came to Amherst College's commencements of 1846 and 1847, she answered Abiah's boast of meeting Daniel Webster with the retort, "However you dont know Govr Briggs & I do.") A more important result was her getting to know young Joseph Lyman.

---

7. An odd consequence of all this obsessive guarding was the poet's fondness for a phrase from Psalms 91:11: "For he shall give his angels charge over thee, to keep thee in all thy ways." In the Gospels of Matthew and Luke, the Tempter quotes this verse to Jesus in urging him to leap from a Temple pinnacle. Taking the devil's hint, Dickinson would again and again "give his angels charge," *demanding* that her friends be preserved.

The rule at home, as Edward succinctly put it, was that "Austin cannot well be spared, when I am absent." After the principal of Amherst Academy resigned in March 1846 and the school fell into disarray, the boy wanted to return to Williston Seminary at term's end, March 31—just when the Council would have its hands full of business and his father had to be in Boston. Edward's resourceful resolution of this conflict is spelled out in a letter by sixteen-year-old Joseph, who was also planning to transfer to Easthampton. As of March 12 he was eagerly anticipating the move. Then, writing his older brother on April 7, he had surprising news:

> Since I have been here [in Amherst] to school I have formed accuaintance with one Austin Dickinson son of Hon E Dickinson, College Treasurer, he was intending to go to E[asthampton] at the close of the term but the nature of his fathers business demanded that he should remain at home. As was very natural he felt quite disappoined and said he would like very much to have me remain with him and board in his family untill the commencement of the summer term in E. . . . I have taken up with the kind and advantageous offer as I pay no charges for my board. I am prosecuting my studies with my usual dilligence . . . under the instruction of H[enry] Edwards and during vacation shall recite to Proff Tyler which I consider a great privilege. . . . [A]lthough I study with pleasure I have very pleasant recreations such as riding, gardening, "swinging in the grove" &c.

Council minutes show that Edward was indeed present from March 31 through April 8 and again on April 14–15. And meanwhile his females were safe and his son and son's friend were getting the best possible tutoring: Henry Edwards was the Latin salutatorian in 1847 and William S. Tyler was professor of Greek.

The young man who now entered the Dickinson household for some two months before leaving for Williston was a pleasing, talented, ebullient lad; rather a "scamp," in the eyes of a Yale professor. Energetic and forward-looking, Joseph relished his introduction into the "very improving society" of families like the Dickinsons. He was attractive to girls, and a romance developed between him and Lavinia, with scenes like the following during the next five years:

> She sat in my lap and pulled the pins from her long soft chestnut hair and tied the long silken mass around my neck and kissed me again & again. She was always at my side clinging to my arm and used to have a little red ottoman that she brought & placed close by my chair and laid her book across my lap when she read. Her skin was very soft. Her arms were fat & white and I was very, very happy with her.

There was none of this kittenish love play with the older daughter. Instead, Emily "read German Plays with me and sat close beside me so as to look out words from the same Dictionary." The friendship grew during the young man's years at Yale, 1846–1850, when (unlike Abiah Root) he regularly dropped in on the family, which he thought of as "that charming second home of mine." Occasionally, he boasted of receiving "letters very pleasant from the Dick. girls in Amh. and fr Austin." A decade later, residing in New Orleans, he and "Em" were still in touch. Although their correspondence was interrupted by marriage and the Civil War (Joseph fought for the Confederacy), they made renewed contact after he returned north. He died of smallpox in 1872.

Unlike Abiah, Joseph was changed by friendship with Emily, acquiring a more challenging ideal of what conversation and letter-writing could be. In 1849, when he and his older brother exchanged youthful pronouncements on women's conversational powers, "You are right about ladies' talk," Joseph wrote; "they dont know how." But as he cited the older girls he "flirted a little with last summer," he thought of an exception: "Em. Dickinson is a year younger it is true but older . . . in mind & heart." Even in her teens and well before she was a poet, she stood out for this young man as exceptional.

Proud of his conquests, Joseph wrote about the Dickinson girls with greater frankness to certain male friends and to his fiancée, Laura Baker. A boy who knew the Dickinsons only through Joseph's letters liked to picture him in Amherst "playing—what? 'spooney,' I suppose—with Vinnie, or sitting up late of night to talk with Emily, when less spiritual beings, such as watchful parents, are fast asleep." Distant as it is, this glimpse reinforces one's impressions from elsewhere: that Father and Mother thoroughly indulged their daughters at home, that plump-armed Lavinia was pretty much available, and that "spiritual" Emily was on the whole more fascinating.

After the Civil War Joseph transcribed several excerpts from Emily's letters, apparently revising as he wrote. Most of these date from their maturer acquaintance, but there is one that may go back to the late 1840s. It offers a vivid glimpse of the playful ingenuity with which Austin and Emily whiled away a Sunday at home:

> We had merry talk about them [bumblebees] the other day. Austin wanted me to say what is their music. So he ~~went~~ buzzed like one and I mocked the wee hum they make down in the ~~cayl~~ calix of a holly hock. I'm sure I don't know much about bumble bees tho' I have seen them a hundred times go thump down ~~onto~~ on a ~~clover~~ butter-cup head & never ~~dig~~ come out. But Father came out from the sanctity of his sunday nap and said he was glad to see the little people enjoy themselves.

That Father still saw them as "little" reinforces the suspicion the letter is a product of the late 1840s. It provides a fascinating glimpse of sister and brother at home, enduring another boring Sunday by improvising a humming bumblebee duet. Emily's mimicry of "the wee hum they make down in the calix" says something about what she noticed and thus about *her*. The passage may mark the earliest appearance of the erotic flower-seeking bees that wander through her letters and poems, most famously in "Come slowly – Eden!" where "the fainting Bee,"

> *Reaching late his flower,*
> *Round her chamber hums –*
> *Counts his nectars –*
> *Enters – and is lost in Balms.*
> Fr205

That Emily first imitated this bee's "wee hum" in company with Austin shows how much the (probably) unconscious eroticism of her language and imagery pervaded her ordinary talk. At home with her brother or in school with her girlfriends or in letters to her chosen intimates, young Emily Dickinson expressed her affectionate ardor in what was even then an unusually innocent, unguarded, and unworldly fashion. She was like her sister, who knotted her tresses around sexy young Joseph in order to kiss and keep him, except that Emily made knots with words. Even more than Vinnie, the poet-to-be was unbelievably well guarded and unbelievably exposed.

The Early Daguerreotype

It used to be assumed on no very convincing evidence that Dickinson's early daguerreotype was taken in fall 1847, when she was attending Mount Holyoke and nearly eighteen years old. In fact, as Elizabeth Bernhard argued in 1999, the image probably dates from the previous winter. Beginning December 10, 1846, and running to March 25, 1847, a "Daguerrian Artist" named William C. North advertised his services in Amherst's *Hampshire and Franklin Express*. His arrival made Mrs. Dickinson "very anxious" to secure a copy of a portrait of her father, Joel, who had died the previous May. It now seems likely that she and Emily had their own images recorded at this time, with the same props and pose, though not the same expression.

Knowing that we are looking at the poet during the three and a half months after her sixteenth birthday opens our eyes a little. Her dress, gathered at waist and bodice to accommodate her growth, already seems too tight at neck and wrists. There's a trace of the gawky adolescent, recently stretched out but not yet fully formed, and then we remember she has recently recovered from a long and threatening pulmonary episode, perhaps accounting for her thin cheeks. Chances are (and we have Vinnie's statement to support this), the mature Dickinson looked quite different. We note as well that her naturally curly hair must have been straightened before her session with the "Daguerrian Artist." Small wonder she came to object to the conventions of studio portraits, remarking in July 1862 how "the Quick wore off those things,[8] in a few days."

Having resumed her studies at Amherst Academy, the young woman has the face of someone who is back in the world and ready to take it on again. It can't be said she's pretty, but there is absolutely no flinching—not a trace of deprecation or obliquity or abjectness in that straight and steady gaze. Whatever her thoughts and feelings may be, there is no attempt to make a display of them. That will be the work of the full lips and the long and graceful fingers, nearly ready for plucking.

---

8. Does the plural imply she had undergone the process more than once, and had been satisfied by none of the results? There is no doubt she cherished others' images, owning three portraits of Elizabeth Barrett Browning as of August 1862.

Part Four

1847-1852

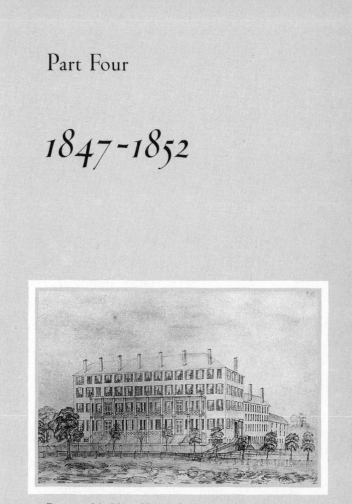

Drawing of the Mount Holyoke Seminary building, May 2, 1844.

Chapter 10

1847–1848: Mount Holyoke Female Seminary

In 1875 a financially secure friend of Susan and Austin Dickinson, Maria Whitney, was offered a teaching position at Vassar College. At the time, Whitney was living in Northampton, in her late father's comfortable home. The main reason she turned the offer down was her unwillingness "after this independent family life to be shut up in such a big institution with such an army of girls."

This statement helps explain why Emily Dickinson's year at Mount Holyoke College in South Hadley, only nine miles south of Amherst, proved such a trial for her. Away from the comforts of home, she slept, studied, recited, attended religious meetings, and ate her meals in a large, four-story brick building; she was one of 235 students and 12 teachers. Her classes were more systematic than at Amherst Academy, and she was obliged to follow a tight daily regimen, with each half-hour accounted for. Everyone rose at six, teachers were friendly but strict, the rules forbade the occasional trip home over Sunday, and there was little privacy. There was also an unrelenting emphasis on conversion. Back home, given Father's views on women and meetings and on the musty church basement, it was easy not to attend prayer sessions during a revival. Here, there was no such margin.

Mount Holyoke toughened Dickinson, who worked hard and did well and at one point became "much interested" in chemistry and physiology. But we should remember that women's higher education was then in its shaky beginnings: her teachers lacked advanced training, did little or no research, did not produce or translate standard texts, and could not assume they were helping to create the subjects they taught. Still in its pioneering phase, female education was badly undermined by the denial of equal access to the professions. Since women were not supposed to lecture, preach to, or in other ways publicly guide the adult world, rhetorical and even literary study lost part of its rationale. Mount Holyoke had nothing like the debating societies that flourished at Yale, where Edward Dickinson's student essays on public policy questions took for granted that positions of leadership were open to him. Since women could not even vote, the focus inevitably shifted from analysis of issues to attention to detail. When Emily studied Alexander Pope's *Essay on Man,* the lessons proved, disappointingly, to be "merely transposition."[1] Aware that something was missing, she complained to her brother (rather airily) that "I dont know anything more about affairs in the world, than if I was in a trance. . . . Has the Mexican war terminated yet & how? Are we beat?" A teacher who shared this uneasiness regretted that "we know little of the political world, in our little community."

What Mount Holyoke then chiefly encouraged was not detached critical judgment but intense commitment: to religion, daily lessons, the

---

1. Defined as follows in Webster's 1844 *American Dictionary:* "In *grammar,* a change of the natural order of words in a sentence. The Latin and Greek languages admit *transposition* without inconvenience, to a much greater extent than the English."

rules. Reading the letters Dickinson sent from school—seven to Austin, three to Abiah Root—it is clear she found the institutional tone less and less congenial as the year passed. The enthusiasm she brought faded so completely she never named a teacher she admired or a new book she was glad she was exposed to. We know of no new friends she kept up with after leaving. In later years she hardly mentioned the place.

Three weeks into the school year, a traveling menagerie staged a show in front of the college. Most of the army of girls stepped outside to see the monkeys and bears. Staying inside, Emily "enjoyed the solitude finely."

An Eager Student

Mount Holyoke's school year began with placement exams designed to weed out the unprepared and assign new students to one of three levels—Junior, Middle, or Senior. Although the exams were made harder than ever in 1847, Emily seems to have breezed through, writing afterward that she "found them about what I had anticipated." Her first six weeks consisted of an accelerated review of Junior courses, following which she and several others entered the Middle level.

The seminary did not yet grant the bachelor's degree, instead awarding a certificate to those who completed their Senior year. Most students, having no need for this piece of paper, attended classes for one year only. Emily was no exception. By the middle of February it was settled—to her great relief—that she would not be coming back: "My good angel only waits to see the tears coming & then whispers, only this year!"

Her roommate was Emily Lavinia Norcross, a first cousin and, like Dickinson's old friend Jane Humphrey, a Senior. Cousin Emily had lost both her parents to consumption, her father in her infancy and her mother, Amanda, in 1836, following a brief second marriage to Charles Stearns, an enterprising Springfield builder. These deaths and remarriage left the girl financially well off under the successive guardianships of her grandfather Joel and her uncle Albert Norcross. At Mount

Holyoke, developing a taste shared with other Norcrosses,[2] she "devoted considerable time to music." Afterward, she taught in Ohio for about a year, though it seems neither she nor Mary Lyon, Mount Holyoke's founder and principal, was quite sure she was "qualified to teach."

In character, Cousin Emily was built along very different lines from the poet. When the seminary was swept by religious fervor in 1846–1847, she sent Hannah Porter a detailed account of her dutiful travail: agonizing over whether to go to a religious meeting, then "burst[ing] into tears," then finding herself able to "give up" and "trust in the Savior"—the act bringing "such a calm as I never before experienced." It was probably because of this conversion as well as the cousinship that she was paired with the unsaved Miss Dickinson, the policy being to assign roommates on the basis of "congeniality of feeling, and a mutual salutary influence." The two seem to have got on well, the poet pronouncing her cousin an "excellent room-mate," one who did "all in her power to make me happy." At the opening of the second term, Dickinson was relieved when Emily Norcross finally showed up, ten days late.

This cousin's presence alleviated but could not cure the terrible homesickness that oppressed Emily. At first, as she admitted to Abiah, "it seemed to me I could not live here. But I am now contented & quite happy, if I can be happy when absent from my dear home & friends." In claiming to be contented, she was not so much voicing her actual feeling as stating her determination. Feeling voiced itself in a different fashion, as when, sitting at her window, she saw her parents approaching and "danced & clapped my hands, & flew to meet them."

Homesickness notwithstanding, Emily was eager and determined to make the best of her situation. Unlike Amherst Academy, Mount Holyoke was obviously on the rise, with a steady annual increase in the number and quality of students. Instead of complaining about meals, she sent Austin the bill of fare for November 2—roast veal, potatoes, squash, apple dumpling, salt, pepper, water—and then triumphantly declared,

---

2. Lavinia Norcross once wrote her sister in Amherst, "I tho't of you to-day in church—How I wished you was here I wanted to have you hear our singing—I almost weep every Sabbath—it is so beautiful—It completely melts me down."

"Is'nt that a dinner fit to set before a King." To Abiah she reported that the teachers (resident in the building) "call on us frequently & urge us to return their calls & when we do, we always receive a cordial welcome." Emily's kitchen duties could not have been easier: "carrying the Knives from the 1st tier of tables at morning & noon & at night washing & wiping the same quantity of Knives." This "domestic work," assigned to each student in order to lower fees, was derided by those who assumed a girls' school should chiefly provide a genteel finishing.

In December, having passed the exam in Euclid "without a failure at any time," Emily began the more appealing courses in chemistry and physiology. Calisthenics, singing, and the piano she practiced daily. In May she took astronomy from Sophia D. Hazen and rhetoric from Mary W. Chapin, briskly informing Abiah that these courses "take me through to the senior studies." That she took no Latin suggests she had already translated at least four books of the Aeneid, one of the require-ments for becoming a Senior.

Two conclusions to be drawn about the poet's studies at Mount Holyoke are that the offerings in science were richer than those in the humanities, and that the curriculum was on the whole not well differ-entiated from that of academies. Most textbooks listed in the seminary catalog—Newman's *Rhetoric*, Hitchcock's *Geology*, Upham's *Mental Philosophy*—Emily had already met with in Amherst. By the late 1840s, Mount Holyoke was still very much a college in the making. A letter she wrote in her third and last term refers to it as a "boarding school." She probably didn't think of it as the pioneering institution it was.

As at Amherst Academy, Emily had to write a composition every two weeks. Clara Newman Turner, a first cousin thirteen years younger, had the impression she was "the idol of the school & its Preceptress, & her appointment for a composition marked a 'Red Letter Day.'" This picture, probably exaggerated, certainly unconfirmed elsewhere, may have originated with Vinnie, who often boasted about her sister's pow-ers. There was no preceptress at Mount Holyoke, and the teacher in charge of the Middle class, Mary C. Whitman, regarded the future poet in a way that fell far short of idolatry.

As the mid-year exams approached, Emily felt a rising dread of failure but hoped, in Father's words, she would "not disgrace" herself. Her attention had been arrested by the spectacle of another daughter's shameful performance:

> A young lady by the name of Beach. left here for home this morning. She could not get through her examinations & was very wild beside. Miss Lyon. said she should write her father, if she did not change her course & as she did not, her father came for her last night. He was an interesting man & seemed to feel very badly that his daughter should be obliged to leave, on account of bad conduct. Perhaps you saw an account some time since, of a carriage. being presented to Henry Clay. by a Mr. Beach. It was the self same.

Henry Clay was a Whig, Edward Dickinson had been a Clay man, and young Emily's Whig feelings were clearly in the ascendant. The striking thing about this, her fullest account of a "wild" girl, is its emphasis on the worthy father's disappointment.

As Emily accustomed herself to the "army of girls," she kept her tie to her independent and fabulously upright and dignified male parent, orthodox in belief though still unsaved, and with a reactionary ideal of "female excellence." The previous year, after Sarah Tracy proved more loyal to her father than to her friends, Emily wrote Abiah, "You know Sarah is an obedient daughter! & she preferred to gratify her father rather than to spend the summer with her friends in Amherst."

One of the questions to be decided was: how would the father Emily took with her, the father in her mind, shape her adjustment to the close-knit female world she had entered?

Hannah Porter and Mount Holyoke's Revivals

As had been the case with Amherst College two decades earlier, the vision that gave birth to Mount Holyoke Female Seminary in 1837 was both religious and educational. Mary Lyon, the original visionary and for eleven years the forceful head of the school, had come from a devout but poorly schooled family. Her great intellectual powers had been stimulated by a few terms at Amherst Academy and other schools, and by friendship with Edward and Orra White Hitchcock. She shared this couple's evangelicalism, and as she taught at or directed various academies, most notably Ipswich Female Seminary, she felt a growing need for an endowed institution that would develop women's minds and turn out an influential corps of wives, teachers, missionaries.

Her dream was conservative and revolutionary alike. When Rufus Anderson, head of the American Board of Commissioners for Foreign Missions, spoke at Mount Holyoke's second anniversary, he assumed the school would carry on the fight to wrest spiritual control from the forces of liberal infidelity. At the same time, believing that women were as responsible as men for converting the world, he decried the "ancient prejudice" that "learning has a tendency to unfit" women for their proper work.

As practical and tireless as she was far-seeing, Mary Lyon was the preeminent force in creating the school, yet it could not have come to life if, like Amherst College, it had not been supported by organized and dedicated evangelicals. Among these was Hannah Porter, founder of the secretive 1827 group that counted several Norcross women among its members, Monson's First Female Praying Circle. This group had fomented the 1829 revival that brought about the conversion of Hannah's husband, Andrew W. Porter. In 1836, under pressure from his wife, Andrew assumed direction of the committee in charge of Mount Holyoke's first building. The following spring, when construction was threatened by the Panic, Hannah sent some confidential information about his finances to Lyon, disclosing that if a certain $5,000 came in, her husband would "advance it for the building." "This information," she added, "you will not let him know you possess." The same sort of tactics would target Emily Dickinson in winter 1848.

On the surface the Porters and Dickinsons had the same Whig and orthodox orientation, but underneath were sharp oppositions. Where Edward insisted that females stay home and that children's health be protected at all costs, Hannah was a total activist, giving more of her time to societies and meetings than to house and family. After her first three children were dead, the one survivor, weakened by scarlet fever and a "heart difficulty," had to work in the Porters' kitchen in the intervals of school. The girl died at age thirteen.

It was never quite clear whether Porter was working with men in common benevolent causes or trying to circumvent and perhaps turn them out of office. According to a disgruntled male observer, a certain candidate became the new minister of Monson's First Church chiefly because his wife was "Mrs. Dea. Porter's *woman*." One reason Porter was so committed to Mount Holyoke was her outrage at misrule by male Jacksonian Democrats:

> I want two or three hundred [added later: "thousand"] Mothers & Teachers educated there [at Mount Holyoke] now training the rising generation—for destruction seems near at hand unless there is more moral principle in the great men of our nation—Can it be our members of Congress would descend to such . . . wickedness as has been the case this session if they had had proper culture in early life.

For Porter as for Lyon, the key step in preparing the next generation's mothers and teachers was to convert them in their youth. In 1849, speaking at Lyon's funeral, Heman Humphrey was amazed the college had had "*eleven* revivals in *twelve* years" and that so few students had remained unsaved. One year "not *one* individual was left without hope, and in another, only *three*." No one at Amherst College, certainly not Humphrey during his years as president, ever approached such results. Elizabeth Alden Green's excellent life of Lyon offers some vivid accounts of the collective mood during Mount Holyoke's annual awakenings—the silence, the students' and teachers' taut earnestness, the spur-of-the-moment prayers of small groups, the girls so overcome they couldn't eat. "Such a room full I never saw," wrote one student after an inquiry meeting, "not a dry eye could be seen."

Such rooms were Porter's element. "I should be most happy to come & stop long enough with you to become personally acquainted with the young converts," she wrote Lyon; "I find it impossible to feel that deep interest in the present work of grace, as when formerly I knew the individuals, had been in your meetings, conversed with enquirers & witnessed the first evidence of sanctified affection."

This passage suggests the nature of Porter's activities during the twelve-day period in 1847–1848 when she moved into Lyon's rooms and assisted with the revival then just beginning. For twelve days she and the seventeen-year-old Dickinson were fellow occupants of the building the older woman had helped finance ten years earlier and in which the younger one now ate, slept, studied, and attended painful collective inquiry sessions.

Without Hope

Mount Holyoke's teachers kept an institutional journal that was reproduced by student copyists and sent around the world to missionary alumnae. According to Susan L. Tolman, the journal keeper for the first two terms of 1847–1848, the school year opened with a ceremony that had become customary. Students were asked to rise, it was ascertained whether they were saved or not, and they were then placed in the appropriate "class" (a word that already resonated for the poet): "I cannot tell you how solemn it was, as one after another class arose. I saw more than one weep as her name was put down '*no hope*.' There is a large class of this character will it be so at the end of the year?" Those who had reason to believe they were saved and could thus profess their faith were "professors." Those who had "a hope" had some basis for thinking they were in preparation for grace. The third group consisted of students who did not yet "have a hope" and were thus "impenitent." This was Dickinson's "class."

Frequent meetings were convened, particularly for those without hope. On October 11 they heard a solemn talk by Lyon, whose purpose was "to help them in seeking the salvation of their souls" and whose strategy was "to describe the different thoughts and feelings of each heart." "You all know," the journal keeper reminded the scattered missionaries, "how strikingly she can do this." On the fourteenth, a teacher met with the impenitent and spent the hour looking up Bible passages bearing upon Human Depravity; "nearly all seemed attentive." On October 18 Lyon spoke to them about "the exceeding hardness of the human heart," pointedly reminding her listeners that even though they *knew* the great Christian truths, they still refused to *feel* them: "Do not you all know, that as sinners, you are condemned, already, do not you know that you are now exposed to God's wrath, that a miserable eternity is before you."

The seminary had scores of rules, such as not "speaking loud in a spaceway," and students were required to submit "notes of Criticism" reporting others' delinquencies. On November 4 Lyon told the assembled students and teachers she

> knew there had been some in past years, and perhaps there were some this year, who would object to this method of correcting many things. If there was any [such dissenter] among the new scholars, she wished her to go home now. . . . She considered it mean for any one to come back here, knowing our regulations small & great and then talk about them and be unwilling to conform to them.

Every student was required to be in cordial agreement with the rules, expunging all private reservations.

Judging from the comprehensive account of life at Mount Holyoke that Emily sent Abiah two days after Lyon's talk, this particular new scholar was bent on full compliance. "Everything is pleasant & happy here." "One thing is certain & that is, that Miss. Lyon & all the teachers, seem to consult our comfort & happiness in everything they do." "Things seem much more like home than I anticipated." But as Emily anticipated her return to Amherst for Thanksgiving, her true feelings declared themselves: "Only to think Abiah, that in 2½ weeks I shall be at my *own dear home* again."

A third of Emily's next long letter to Abiah recalls the Thanksgiving break: her long and anxious wait at a window, the sight of a promising carriage in the distance, how it proved to be Austin, and how she "dashed down stairs." She vividly recalled the rain-filled streamlets running beside the road, the sight of the familiar meetinghouse spire, and "Mother with tears in her eyes." The striking fact is that Emily wrote this narrative almost two months after her short trip home, virtually ignoring recent events. A partial explanation lies in two sentences squeezed in after the letter had been finished and there was no room to elaborate: "There is a great deal of religious interest here and many are flocking to the ark of safety. I have not yet given up to the claims of Christ, but trust I am not entirely thoughtless on so important & serious a subject." The revival was on, in other words, and this time she could not seek refuge at home, except in memory and imagination.

The ordeal began December 19, when the Reverend Pomeroy Belden of Amherst's East Parish, preaching in South Hadley, announced that his church would celebrate Christmas Eve with fasting and prayer. This announcement not only gave Lyon a solution for the problem of Christmas, which the seminary regarded as a pagan or Romish survival and tried to ignore;[3] it presented her with an opportunity to awaken the hardhearted impenitents. Proposing that the seminary follow Belden's lead by making the twenty-fourth a day of prayer and fasting, she inspired the teachers to float the idea in their respective sections and then bring back a general "desire" for the observance.

In 1924 Martha Dickinson Bianchi, the poet's unveracious niece, made the dramatic claim that when Lyon (supposedly) asked the assembled students whether anyone was "so lost" to the meaning of Christmas that she opposed the fast, the one person who rose to her feet was defiant Emily Dickinson. Bianchi's anecdote has some impossible details and was largely discredited ten years later by Sydney R. McLean, who investigated the matter by going back to the Mount Holyoke journal letter. There the question rested until 1960, when Jay Leyda printed a telling excerpt from Clara Newman Turner's unpublished reminiscence, to the effect that Dickinson alone kept her seat when Lyon "asked all those who wanted to be Christians to rise." We can't say what the occasion was or

---

3. As in many New England academies at this time, there was no Christmas vacation. When a student wished teacher Mary C. Whitman a merry Christmas in 1845, "she looked up with surprise, 'Why is to day Christmas?'" In 1847 a teacher reported with satisfaction that she "hardly heard one 'Merry Christmas' this morning." By contrast, when Emily was home she hung a stocking on her bedpost and received "a great many presents" from Santa Claus.

whether the young woman rose to her feet or stayed seated, but she evidently signaled her dissent in some conspicuous way from the coercive proceedings. And meanwhile, as her own letters make clear, she had a painful conviction that she *ought* to "give up & become a Christian."

As the twenty-fourth approached, Lyon had more meetings with "the impenitent," warning that there had never been a fast day at the seminary "when some soul had not been born again." Tension grew, the moment was ripening, and on the evening of the twenty-third Hannah Porter arrived and settled in.

On Christmas Eve, the tightly packed building was "very still" all day. Hours were appointed for group and solitary prayer, a church service, and devotions, and then Lyon had another session "with all the impenitent." Again, she pressed the great truths home, asking all those who wished "to give up their hearts to the influences of the Holy Spirit" to place "a sealed note" in her box. Over fifty notes came in. There was "feeling manifested." One girl "expressed a hope." More meetings ensued, at one of which Porter "made some very excellent remarks." But twenty-five girls in the Middle class were still without hope (indicating that Dickinson was not the only holdout).

During Porter's first four days at the seminary, she did so much praying, preaching, and exhorting that by the twenty-seventh she had "lost her voice." Some of her time had been spent with Dickinson's roommate and with Sarah Jane Anderson, daughter of the head of the American Board of Commissioners for Foreign Missions. Afterward, Sarah recalled the comforting presence of the older woman, "sitting in the rocking chair by my side, and listening to hear what I may have to communicate." In all likelihood, Emily Dickinson came in for similar attentions.

After returning to Monson, Porter was sent reports on her by Cousin Emily and Sarah, and also by the teacher Mary C. Whitman. These letters, still extant, disclose the well-coordinated campaign of which the future poet was the focus.

The first to report was Cousin Emily. Writing on January 11, when the temperature fell to ten below zero and the two roommates "suffered very much" in their cold room, she noted that almost forty impenitents at Lyon's last Sunday meeting felt they had been saved this term. But

> Emily Dickinson appears no different. I hoped I might have good news to write, with regard to her. She says she has no particular objection to becoming a Christian and . . . feels bad when she hears of one and another of her friends who are expressing a hope but still she feels no more interest.

"Feels no interest," a technical phrase, means the young woman had no emotional evidence that could justify a claim of grace. The problem was not one of belief, doubt, or interpretation, since she had the right views and admitted the necessity of regeneration. It was something else, something she didn't or couldn't articulate (at least to her cousin), that was holding her back.

At the end of her letter, Cousin Emily assured Porter that her roommate "intended to write you a note to send in this but did not have time. She wishes me to say that she will do it the next opportunity she has." The message tells us Dickinson was in direct communication with Porter, or at least felt she ought to be. Whether the promised letter was written is not known.

Six days later Sarah sent an update on Amherst's stubborn holdout: "I believe Emilie [L. Norcross] wrote you last week, and probably she told you about her room-mate. She still *appears* unconcerned." Again, the future poet was seen as remote and unreadable, a contrast to the scores of new converts testifying "feeling" and "hope" in standard phrases. How were they seen by *her*? One answer is implicit in her 1865 poem on self-brandishing feelings: "Aloud / Is nothing that is chief" (Fr1057). Another appears in her 1870 statement to Thomas Wentworth Higginson: "Women talk: men are silent: that is why I dread women."

The previous school year, when Dickinson's cousin was assigned an unsaved roommate, she accepted the responsibility with the utmost seriousness: "Perhaps she is to room with me that I may have an opportunity of doing her good. I hope I may not be an injury to her by setting her a bad example." Now that she had another impenitent on her hands, her own gifted cousin, she was once again, in Sarah's words, "anxious lest she . . . bring reproach upon the cause of Christ" as the revival climaxed. Sarah Anderson was even more tightly wound, and as the February exams approached, her "nervous system [was] in such a state" she had to skip them and return home—a repeat performance from 1846–1847. Such was the tense, scrupulous zeal that lapped the future poet on all sides.

On the same day as Sarah's update, the overworked Mary C. Whitman, Lyon's second-in-command, sent Porter a letter making private arrangements for a visit to Monson and offering the latest news on Dickinson. The previous morning, a Sunday, had seen a special meeting of recently converted students, numbering forty-seven in all. "Is it not wonderful, and so silent," exclaimed Whitman. In the evening a solemn meeting was held with seventeen unsaved girls who "felt unusually anxious to choose the service of God that night." This time "Emily Dickinson was among the number." And then the really big news: "I have heard to day of one of those who attended, who thinks she [that is, Dickinson] found the Savior after the meeting." But the rumor was untrue, being sufficiently refuted by her letter to Abiah a few months later regretting she had not "give[n] up and become a Christian."

One wonders whether Dickinson realized the extent to which she was the target of a devout and determined group of women—her roommate and cousin, her friends, her teachers, with Mrs. Porter coordinating the effort and Monson's efficient Female Praying Circle probably doing its part. All this intimate and extremely well-organized pressure shows what was at issue when the poet sat down, *also* on January 17, and composed the letter restaging her Thanksgiving escape two months earlier. Especially touching is the delicacy with which she admits her disillusionment:

> This term is the longest in the year & I would not wish to live it over again, I can assure you. I love this Seminary & all the teachers are

bound strongly to my heart by ties of affection. There are many sweet girls here & dearly do I love some new faces, but I have not yet found the place of a *few* dear ones filled, nor would I wish it to be here.

This sounds like the voice of an outsider who doesn't quite grasp her status, and fails to understand that the manipulative love coming at her from all sides may not be equivalent to the eager human affection she seeks.

In May, after the revival subsided and it was safe to sing another tune, Dickinson excoriated her own hardheartedness: "I have neglected the one thing needful when all were obtaining it, & I may never, never again pass through such a season as was granted us last winter. Abiah, you may be surprised to hear me speak as I do . . . but I am not happy." The underlined phrase comes from Jesus' reproach in Luke 10:41–42: "Martha, Martha, thou art careful and troubled about many things: But one thing is needful: and Mary hath chosen that good part." With the pressure off, the stiff resistance that had preserved the girl's independence could relax. But now there was an interior problem: opaque in the view of others, she saw herself as insincere and double-minded. She admired Abby Wood's apparent simplicity, her stated desire "only . . . to be good," even as she realized this transparency was not for her: "How I wish I could say that with sincerity, but I fear I never can."

How does someone who goes in for essentials and ultimates continue living with herself if she feels she is neglecting the *one thing needful*? Dickinson was becoming a dark storm cloud, with a rising electric potential that would have to declare itself.

A Confidential Rebel

When the long first term, lasting sixteen weeks, finally came to an end on January 20, Emily returned to Amherst for the two-week break. Never before had home and friends felt "so dear," or had her happiness been so marred by an impending departure, now "constantly in my dreams, by night & day." Back in school, she tried to console herself with memories of meals and household fires, "the cheerful voices & the merry laugh," but these vivid images only deepened the present desolation.

She missed the fun of Valentine week, she missed Vinnie, but most of all, judging from her letters to her brother, she missed Austin's free and easy companionship. Now more than ever, she needed him as confidant and encourager and fellow connoisseur of exaggerated stories. Vinnie, a sister reprobate and a sparkling mime, was unfortunately a poor correspondent, like Mother taking little interest in expressing herself on the page; her letters are rife with blots and misspellings and the sketchiest of social notes. Inevitably, it was to Austin that Emily defined her new relationship to Mount Holyoke once the revival cooled.

In February she received a "*welcome* letter" from him while "engrossed in the history of, Sulphuric Acid!!!!!" Her reply smokes with corrosive sarcasm directed at the institutional tone:

> I deliberated for a few moments . . . on the propriety of carrying [his letter] to Miss. Whitman, your friend. The result of my deliberation was a conclusion to open it with moderation, peruse its contents with sobriety becoming my station, & if after a close investigation of its contents I found nothing which savored of rebellion or an unsubdued will, I would lay it away in my folio & forget I had ever received it. Are you not gratified that I am so rapidly gaining correct ideas of female propriety & sedate deportment?

Dickinson's irony shows the same orientation to feminine gentility as three years earlier, when she urged Abiah not to let her "free spirit be chained" by "starched up young ladys," but now she writes with real animosity. With Austin, she feels free to *sound* ungodly, to "savor of" rebellion and an unsubdued will and in the process get off some high-spirited, sulfuric prose. But as her performance ends, she begs him (writing in the margin) "not to show this letter for it is strictly confidential."

All we have of Dickinson's letters to Abby Wood, some of which must have been sent from Mount Holyoke, is Abby's son's response after reading them in 1913: "I see that 'Emily' was very early a rebel!" Judging from extant letters, however, her subversive energies were confined to matters of style, language, attitude: an open and direct challenge was not to be thought of. Referring to those girls who broke the rules by writing Valentine notes, she pointedly declared, "I have not written one nor do I now intend to."

Her caution is evident in her remarks on a question of great interest to her and her brother: whether the imagination should be "governed." When she learned early in the school year that he was reading the *Arabian Nights,* she counseled him in her best starched-up prose to "cultivate your other powers in proportion as you allow Imagination to captivate you." But then she undid her sage advice with a self-conscious pirouette, demanding, "Am not I a very wise *young lady*?" As Austin came out more openly for the imagination, Emily felt more and more disposed to trust her stylistic and projective gifts. Chances are, being home at the time, she heard him read a translated excerpt from Longinus' essay on the sublime at the Amherst College exhibition of April 18. In May she sent him some tongue-in-cheek praise: "I was highly edified with your *imaginative* note to me & think your flights of fancy indeed wonderful at your age!!" The stern advice Lyon issued the day after this letter was written—"of *all* the leading strings . . . in the *world*, the last to follow should be *fancy*"—probably fell on skeptical ears.[4]

Austin's one surviving "imaginative" composition is thought to date from his sister's year at Mount Holyoke. Although the piece is too labored to be of interest in itself, embedded in it are two sentences from a vanished letter—one of Emily's?—that make us instantly sit up. The scene is West Street. Vinnie, Mother, and Austin are spending a quiet evening at home. Outside, a man is heard shouting and dancing, drawing the attention of a crowd. Holding an opened letter, he can read only a brief passage before laughing wildly and stamping his foot, an act producing such a "concussion that the whole firmiment was shaken, the

4. Though remaining silent on Lyon's frequent talks, Dickinson responded with prompt enthusiasm to the Reverend Henry Boynton Smith: "such sermons I never heard in my life. We were all charmed with him, & dreaded to have him close." Mary C. Whitman also admired his "piety and talents."

whole planetary system was deranged, the stars twinkled, and the clouds fell from the heavens strewing the earth with a white feathery substance." The sentences that provoke this studied climax are the ones worth paying attention to. The pronouns hold the key to their meaning. "I" seems to be Emily, "you" Edward, and "she" someone in authority at Mount Holyoke, possibly Whitman or Lyon:

> "I told her you were not afraid of her being too strict with me, and she replied, Tell him I am much obliged to him . . . and when I told her how gratified you were at our early rising she said Tell him that is the only way to make vigorous children."

This passage, first printed in 1955, has not been recognized as composed by Dickinson. If this attribution is correct, what we have here is one of only two extant communications addressed to her father.[5] Judging from Austin's hyperbolic account, Edward opened his daughter's letter as he walked home from the post office, was amused by her account of a frosty exchange with a teacher, and broke into laughter while reading it to his family. The piece records something nowhere else documented—the father's enjoyment of his daughter's point-perfect accuracy in quoting her elders' solemn catch-phrases, his own included.

If the teacher was Lyon, we should note that she was ill, in her last year of life, and more driven and depressed than ever. Before the revival she had begun to ask "of what use" the college was. In April, when the excitement ended and thirty girls were still without hope, her discouragement returned: in no previous school year had the Spirit "tarried so long." Then, in late May, after a Junior passed away saying "she would *gladly* die, if she might be the means of saving *one*," another strenuous effort was made. Lyon explained that Jesus was speaking through the girl and that heaven's gates, having opened, "were now scarcely shut." Everyone was encouraged to "look at the corpse." A meeting was convened for the impenitent. This was their last chance.

---

5. The other, on the back of poem Fr1333 and dating from the time of his death, reads in its entirety, "Dear Father – [large blank space] Emily – "

The letter Emily sent Austin four days after this scary episode makes no mention of it, voicing instead her hardening opposition toward the seminary. Father had written her of his wish to have her and her roommate spend the first Sunday in June in Amherst. When Emily sought Whitman's permission,

> she seemed stunned by my request & could not find utterance to an answer for some time. At length, she said "did you not know it was contrary to the rules of the Seminary to ask to be absent on the Sabbath"?[6] I told her I did not. She then took a Catalogue. from her table & showed me the law in full at the last part of it.
>
> She closed by saying that we could not go & I returned to my room, without farther ado. So you see I shall be deprived of the pleasure of a visit home & you that of seeing me, if I may have the presumption to call it a *pleasure*!! . . . we had better be contented to obey the commands.

In her defense, Dickinson could have said that when the catalog was issued in late April, she had been recuperating at home. As it is, two things stand out in her response—her snapping resentment, and her determined acceptance of "the law."

Another onerous rule involved male visitors. In young Ned Hitchcock's view, the college "was a terribly tabooed place." Boys and men were required to "send our names in to Miss Lyon & then if she thot best we could see the girl, but it must be only in the parlor, & in the presence of a teacher who must be a watch over us both in deed & word." When a family friend arrived with letters for Emily, he found it quite a challenge to get past the female dragons. Amused, she merely reported home that "Bowdoin. had quite an adventure about seeing me, which he will tell you."

---

6. "The young ladies do not make or receive calls on the Sabbath. Neither should they spend a single Sabbath from the Seminary during term time. . . . The excitement of visiting, of meeting friends and of home scenes, will prevent in a great measure the improvement [*sic*]. The place of weekly labors is the most favorable spot for the scenes of the Sabbath." Jane Humphrey, expecting to graduate, was told it would "lower her classification" if she accepted an invitation to the Dickinsons'. Even Rebecca W. Fiske, a teacher, was obliged to decline.

That a number of other girls remained unconverted in 1847–1848 shows that Dickinson was not the only one resisting the college's invasive spiritual practices. In her case, resistance was not a sign of unbelief, since she was intellectually convinced she ought to "give up." Rather, her withholding of herself grew out of her experience with revivals, her ability to trust her feelings and wishes, and her deep attachment to home and to her tall, unsaved, and independent father and brother. As the patriarchal ruler of his household, Edward obviously oppressed his brilliant daughter, especially in his dismissive attitudes toward women's minds. But he also and in spite of everything contrived to place his authority at her disposal. That someone so opaque and powerful should (in Austin's flight of fancy) approve of, laugh at, and enjoy her toughness was simply immense. Indeed, that was the subject of the conversation at the center of Austin's piece: how to "make vigorous children."

In the Porter family, the wife's tenacity and matchless organizational zeal brought about a husband's conversion, helped build the first female college, was saving the world. In the Dickinson family the wife's ineffectual spiritual powers were on display each Communion Sunday as her unredeemed husband had to rise and walk out. The lesson for Emily was the advantage of becoming one's father rather than one's mother. She, too, could hold herself aloof, apart, keeping her feelings to herself instead of "manifesting hope." Thus, following the example and influence of her hard, old-fashioned sire, she stood off the invasive community of devout women led by Lyon and Porter.

The disquieting irony is that on July 19–20, when the poet was in her last term at Mount Holyoke, a small convention at Seneca Falls, New York, initiated the women's rights movement. More than one scholar has wanted to see a connection between this epochal meeting and the great female lyric poet. In the present writer's view, such efforts ignore the bedrock facts of Emily Dickinson's life. Not only was her family extremely conservative on women's issues, but she herself, having resisted the religious brainwashing at Mount Holyoke, was not disposed to see women as an oppressed class or to feel that they must organize themselves in order to free themselves. Dickinson had had enough for one lifetime of "classes" and "circles." Nothing would interest her less than political reform or social activism. Her work in life would be to attempt and achieve an unprecedented imaginative freedom while dwelling in what looks like privileged captivity.

Emilie Led Off in Triumph

The remarkable thing is that she understood home *was* captivity and not the sum of her wishes. That insight became acute after a friend from Amherst, probably Abby Wood or Mary Warner, spent a week with her at school and then spilled the secret Emily had been keeping from her family—her bad cough. It could have been serious: she had had several pulmonary episodes as a girl, the Norcrosses suffered from consumption (not then known to be infectious), and in four years her roommate would die of the disease. Without warning, Austin appeared March 25, 1848, "with orders from head-quarters," meaning Father,

> to bring me home at all events. At first I had recourse to words, & a desperate battle with those weapons was waged for a few moments, between my *sophomore* brother & myself. Finding words of no avail, I next resorted to tears. But woman's tears are of little avail & I am sure mine flowed in vain. As you can imagine, Austin was victorious & poor, defeated I, was led off in triumph.

This account, sent to Abiah, reveals a new and crucial aspect of the poet's sense of identity. Here, father and brother are not only a part of home but members of a superior conquering power, the army of men. Her implicit metaphor, reappearing elsewhere, may have come from a poem she had just read, Alfred Tennyson's *The Princess*, which tells how a female university is undone by a group of determined knights.

Even the signature hints at a subtly reconfigured feminine selfhood. Changing her name for the first time, the writer signed off as "Emilie E. Dickinson," in this way adopting one of the spellings of "my room-mate, Emilie." Had her cousin effected a kind of conversion after all? The poet never used this spelling in legal signatures, but she alternated between it and "y" during the 1850s, "ie" being the dominant form in letters to Austin, her close friend Susan Gilbert, and the Hollands. Its last known use dates from 1860, after which she returned to "y."

Dickinson had good reasons for not wanting to be dragged back to Amherst. She had held her own in spite of the rules and the revival and was doing well in her studies. No doubt she feared she would be forced to miss the rest of the school year, as in 1846. Most of all, she resented the medical humiliation—in public a pitiable spectacle, in private a victim of Father's unrelenting doses.[7] A letter to Abiah tries to explain the inconsistency between her tears and her attachment to home:

> You must not imbibe the idea from what I have said that I do not love home – far from it. But I could not bear to leave teachers & companions before the close of the term and go home to be dosed & receive the physician daily, & take warm drinks & be condoled with . . . by all the old ladies in town. . . . Father is quite a hand to give medicine, especially if it is not desirable to the patient, & I was dosed for about a month after my return home, without any mercy, till at last out of mere pity my cough went away.

"Havnt I given a ludicrous account of going home sick from a boarding school?" wondered Emilie/Emily. The question epitomizes the uneasy and unsimple identity that had crystallized during her year in the army of girls. First, she discovered how vitally she was attached to her dear home in Amherst, and then she put up a fierce, instinctive resistance when compelled to return ahead of time. When she finally came back for good in August, no doubt happily, none of her big questions had been resolved. Mount Holyoke Seminary had not achieved what it was supposed to.

---

7. Three years later, when Austin had one of his bouts of facial "neuralgia," Emily sensibly advised "warmth and rest, cold water and care" as "the best medicines for it." By the 1890s her brother realized the Dickinsons' worries about sickness had been excessive, and he asked Mabel Loomis Todd to edit the "frequent references to the family's ill-health" out of Emily's letters.

Chapter 11

1848–1850: First Drunkenness

Emily's schooling having ended, the question of her future was now more insistent. Since her mother continued to perform much of the household labor, including the baking that eventually became the poet's department, it was a question for which she had sufficient leisure.

She got a taste of one possible future in spring 1850, when Vinnie was attending Ipswich Female Seminary and Mother was invalided with "Acute Neuralgia." Even though Father may have found the "girl or woman who is capable of doing the entire work of a small family," for whom he advertised, the cooking and dishwashing seem to have devolved on Emily for the time being. A letter expressing her feelings about these responsibilities makes clear that until now she had "neglected the culinary arts." She boasted with beginner's pride about the "twin loaves of bread . . . born into the world under my auspices," but she also pitied herself as an enchanted captive out of the *Arabian Nights:* "Would'nt you love to see me in these bonds of great despair, looking around my kitchen, and praying for kind deliverance, and declaring by 'Omar's beard' I never was in such plight. *My* kitchen I think I called it, God forbid that it was, or shall be my own – God keep me from what they call *households*!" One wonders what Abiah, the letter's recipient, thought about this brazen petulance, in which the discontented writer made no effort to come to terms with her probable female destiny.

Unlike Grandmother Sarah, Cousin Emily Lavinia, and various friends, Dickinson probably never gave a thought to teaching as an interim possibility. In August 1848 her friend Jane Humphrey returned to Amherst to become the academy's preceptress for five terms. When Dickinson looked back at this interval, recalling how the two friends sat "in the front door, afternoons after school," what she emphasized was not the need to be serious and defined but the indolent freedom from work—how there would be "some farmer cutting down a tree in the woods, and you and I, sitting there, could hear his sharp ax ring."

With older girls such as Emily Fowler, one of Amherst's most accomplished "belles," Dickinson was on a more equal footing now. When Abiah came back to Amherst for a week in January 1850, Emily got "to know her anew as a splendid girl" and they agreed to resume their letter-writing, which, on the poet's side, sounded some new and restless and at times quite wounding tonalities. On the whole, she was beginning to feel constricted by these two girlfriends: once, informing Abiah what she had been reading, she accused herself of pedantry. No such apologies were needed with Susan Gilbert, bright, ambitious, and with a haughty edge that attracted and punished admirers. Susan would do a great deal to widen Dickinson's horizons.

But Susan did not really enter the picture until the last half of 1850. For the moment, it was a certain group of literary young men who brought about a major expansion in Dickinson's reading and intellectual interests. Amherst College had always offered a variety of public exercises for her to attend in others' company, from the recurring exhibitions, senior levees, and commencement ceremonies to onetime events like the dedication of Appleton Cabinet in 1848 or the library in 1853, but now that Emily was older and her brother an upperclassman, the school became an indispensable resource. Indeed, it was partly owing to Austin's membership in the Alpha Delta Phi fraternity that his Senior year, 1849–1850, had so much zest for her. Most of the students and tutors who called on her and Vinnie prove to have been members of this, the leading "secret society."[1] John Laurens Spencer, one of two college students who joined her and others in an ascent of Mount Holyoke in October 1849, belonged, as did George Henry Gould, the lanky Senior who sent her an invitation to a "*Candy Pulling!!*" the following February—on the back of which, a quarter century later, she drafted a poem about winter's unwished-for approach.

Between Emily and the more devout students, such as William Cowper Dickinson, son of an eminent preacher, one can feel a definite tension. A Valentine this young man composed for her made her bristle, its tone being "a little condescending, & sarcastic . . . a little like an Eagle, stooping to salute a Wren." Another semi-clerical friend was James Parker Kimball, class of 1849, who gave her a copy of Oliver Wendell Holmes's *Poems*. Kimball entered the ministry a few years later (as did William Cowper Dickinson), but well before that Emily twigged him as "our 'Theologian' " and "young 'D.D.' "—Doctor of Divinity. After he angered her in some way, she sent him a sharp letter intended to make him "feel some things." "I only prayed for *pride*," she informed Jane; "I have received yet more; indifference." The obscure quarrel may be related to a note of hers that has been assigned to 1850 on the basis of handwriting:

> With the sincere spite of
> a *Woman*.

---

1. A short list over the years would include, in addition to Spencer and Gould, Samuel Julius Learned, Francis Andrew March, Leonard Humphrey, William Cowper Dickinson, John Milton Emerson, Edward Hitchcock, Jr., George Howland, John Howland Thompson (Austin's Sophomore and Junior roommate), John Elliot Sanford, Brainard Timothy Harrington, Edward Payson Crowell, Henry Vaughan Emmons, John Long Graves. William Gardiner Hammond, a prominent student who called on young townswomen but whose student diary doesn't mention Dickinson, belonged to the rival Psi Upsilon.

The folded paper shows the indentation of a round object attached to a chain, perhaps a medallion or locket. It may be that Dickinson took offense at something Kimball said about women and returned a gift.

Many of those whose company she enjoyed at this time were not conspicuously pious. The preferred social tone shows up in a letter written by her brother when he and Emily were alone at home: "We are anticipating a fine time in the absence of the ancient people [the parents]. Wish you were here to help us laugh—I think there is a chance for our having some company tonight." The letter was sent to Joseph Lyman, a fellow free spirit. Another comrade, Elbridge Gridley Bowdoin, Edward's junior law partner from 1847 to 1855, belonged to the First Parish but not the church proper. Ten years older than Emily and typed as "a confirmed bachelor," the laconic Bowdoin amused her and stimulated her first known effort in verse, a teasing Valentine poem. He also lent her *Jane Eyre,* the riveting and subversive novel by a new but unidentified British writer.

But it was another young attorney, also in his late twenties and equally alert to contemporary literature, who had the greatest impact on the eighteen-year-old woman, doing more to make a poet out of her than all previous teachers combined.

My Tutor

Born in Worcester in 1821, Benjamin Franklin Newton was nine years older than Dickinson and, unlike nearly everyone else in her social orbit, not orthodox. He belonged to Worcester's second Unitarian society, the Church of the Unity, of which Benjamin F. Thomas, the judge who launched his brief legal career, was a charter member. In early nineteenth-century Massachusetts, as George Merriam noted, "a social partition line had run between Orthodox and Liberals." Newton was the first person from the other side of this divide to make a strong impression on Dickinson.

Writing to a stranger after his death, Dickinson explained the relationship by saying he had been "with my Father two years, before going to Worcester – in pursuing his studies, and was much in our family."

Newton's apprenticeship with Dickinson and Bowdoin may have begun about the time she left for Mount Holyoke. Shortly before she returned for her four-day Thanksgiving holiday, she asked Austin whether Newton would be "going away" before she got back. The question suggests she looked forward to seeing him.

In August 1849, as Newton's stay in Amherst was coming to an end, he entered a choice remark in Emily's autograph album:

> All can write autographs, but few paragraphs; for we are mostly no more than *names*. —B. F. Newton

As engaging for its wit as its modesty, the quip hints at the personal qualities that inspired a phrase in the young attorney's obituary: "universally esteemed for his suavity of disposition and high moral integrity."

Dickinson's tribute to her friend, written in early 1854 almost a year after his death and sent to a Unitarian clergyman, characterized him as the formative influence on her mental and spiritual growth:

> I was then but a child, yet I was old enough to admire the strength, and grace, of an intellect far surpassing my own, and it taught me many lessons, for which I thank it humbly, now that it is gone. Mr. Newton became to me a gentle, yet grave Preceptor, teaching me what to read, what authors to admire, what was most grand or beautiful in nature, and that sublimer lesson, a faith in things unseen, and in a life again, nobler, and much more blessed –

At the time it was not unusual for gifted women to voice this sort of sweeping indebtedness to a male mentor. Summing up a minister's influence on the heroine of *Mercy Philbrick's Choice,* Helen Hunt Jackson wrote that "he taught her and trained her, and developed her, patiently, exactingly, and yet tenderly, as if she had been his sister." Dickinson's tribute, full of the same period flavor, was a declaration that Newton had helped her overcome some of the defects of her education. She had passed through the hands of dozens of indoctrinators, but he was the first to combine a friend's gentleness with a master's or minister's gravity. This was not the last time Dickinson acted out an intense admiration for an authoritative man. Hero worship was one of the means by which she reinvented herself.

It is thought that her autobiographical statement of 1862—"When a little Girl, I had a friend, who taught me Immortality – but venturing too near, himself – he never returned"—is another reference to Newton. The misleading words, "little Girl," refer to the same age she earlier characterized as "but a child"—her late teens. As Dickinson aged, this "'Little Girl'hood" of hers (the phrase dates from 1882), seems to have lasted longer and longer in her retrospects, eventually extending to age thirty. As she looked back at young adulthood from the perspective of middle age, what she saw was a childhood persisting beyond its time. It was as if her precocity had landed her in a strange, ungrown-up limbo, from which it took her years to escape.

Her tribute's conclusion may seem off the mark, considering all her previous pastors, teachers, and spiritual counselors had inculcated a "faith in things unseen" and a blessed afterlife for the saved. In fact, her words record a seismic lurch in her sense of things, a shift from Calvinist depravity and discipline to the immanent dignity of life and the validity of human intuition. In this new orientation, faith does not mean "giving up" but bestowing respectful attention on what is "grand or beautiful" in nature and books. The mind has a sovereignty of its own and may be trusted to ascend to what is beyond nature. To move from the orthodox teachings on heaven to this "sublimer" perspective, as taught by Newton, was to enter a radically different register. Unlike "Eternity," which struck fifteen-year-old Emily as "dreadful," the law student's "Immortality" offered a transcendence free of terror.

One reason Newton's lesson sank so deep was that it gave her an exit from the Calvinist evangelicalism she both accepted and resisted—in which state she was blocked, "without hope." Whether he is judged to be cause or catalyst, he stimulated her to reinterpret her rich Puritan endowment, which she eventually transformed into a kind of Romanticism. Her account of his teaching is so full of Wordsworthian echoes one suspects him of recommending this author to her. Certainly, the developmental stages she describes—from enjoyment of nature to an apprehension of the "sublimer" things of the spirit—are in harmony with "Tintern Abbey," where the speaker grows from an unreflecting enjoyment of natural beauty to "a sense sublime / Of something far more deeply interfused." As a letter of 1852 indicates, she was familiar with Wordsworth's "We Are Seven," where a child voices absolute faith in the present-tense existence of dead siblings.

The one book Newton is known to have given Dickinson surely had a liberating effect on her. On January 23, 1850, after he had left Amherst, she informed Jane Humphrey she "had a letter – and Ralph Emerson's Poems – a beautiful copy – from Newton the other day. I should love to read you them both – they are very pleasant to me." At the time Emerson was known chiefly for his challenging lectures and essays. That Newton chose to present his 1847 *Poems,* his first collected verse, suggests both an advanced taste and a sense of Dickinson's needs. "I can write him in about three weeks," she declared, "and I *shall.*"

Included in the volume were such poems as "The Sphinx," "The Problem," "Give All to Love," "Merlin I and II," and "The Humble-Bee." Many of them discard as ephemeral and illusory the laws, distinctions, and boundaries that constitute human reality. Uriel says,

> *"Line in nature is not found;*
> *Unit and universe are round;*
> *In vain produced, all rays return;*
> *Evil will bless, and ice will burn."*
>
> "Uriel"

Other poems make the poet a figure of vast intuitive power, whose Delphic insight penetrates to the heart of creation. Most thrillingly, the new oracle came right out of homely New England, often speaking in the laconic accents of a tough Yankee preacher:

> *The God who made New Hampshire*
> *Taunted the lofty land*
> *With little men.*
>
> "Ode, Inscribed to W. H. Channing"

Emerson's influence on Dickinson, pervasive but hard to pinpoint, was backed up, as George Frisbie Whicher said long ago, with a vast cultural authority. His basic lesson was to trust oneself: all things exist for the creative mind, and no institution or precedent or prohibition is ever binding. He was not afraid to oppose common sense, to be unintelligible, to rest his case on image and metaphor—on "fancy." He would have been anathema at Mount Holyoke. That Dickinson welcomed his poems tells us she was ready for new directions, yet she was by no means alone in this regard: soon after her mention of Newton's gift, Amherst College's literary magazine, *The Indicator,* ran its first piece on Emerson, a review of *Representative Men.* The reviewer disapproved of his "erratic genius and brilliant oddity" and his "complete antagonism" to Christianity, but the last word was: "we always rise from his perusal, with the consciousness that our intellects have been quickened and strengthened by communion with a master-mind."

The value of such communion is made clear by Dickinson's "Strong draughts of their refreshing minds" (Fr770), which says that a drink from another's "Hermetic Mind" enables one to "go elastic" through the desert, like a camel. A later poem treating the same idea shows how elastic the right book can make one:

> He ate and drank the precious Words –
> His Spirit grew robust –
> He knew no more that he was poor,
> Nor that his frame was Dust –
> He danced along the dingy Days
> And this Bequest of Wings
> Was but a Book – What Liberty
> A loosened Spirit brings –

> Fr1593

As is generally the case with Dickinson's verse, this poem is itself "loosened" from particular circumstances, naming neither man nor book and thus achieving an extended applicability. But it should be noted that the man's poverty, weak frame, dingy circumstances, and cheerful spirit are congruent with Newton's basic facts, and also that the poem was written several months after Emerson's death in 1882. His passing called up her last known reference to Newton: "Ralph Waldo Emerson – whose name my Father's Law Student taught me, has touched the secret Spring."

It seems unlikely that Dickinson's correspondence with this "tutor" had a romantic character. If his first letter from Worcester had been as personal as that, she wouldn't have wanted to share it with Jane, or have described it and Emerson's *Poems* as equally "pleasant." Since Dickinson does not say she *may* but rather "can write in about three weeks," it may be that Newton's circumstances, not parental orders, delayed her reply. Her "I *shall*" leaves no doubt as to her eagerness and determination.

What little we know about the correspondence indicates that Newton made clear his high regard for Dickinson. In 1862, after Higginson praised some of her poems, she compared her feelings to those her former "tutor" had aroused:

> Your letter gave no Drunkenness, because I tasted Rum before – Domingo comes but once – yet I have had few pleasures so deep as your opinion, and if I tried to thank you, my tears would block my tongue –
>
> My dying Tutor told me that he would like to live till I had been a poet.

Higginson moved her, but it was Newton who conferred the primal intoxication that no later rum, "Domingo," could possibly match.

Apparently, that was because he was the first to announce her to herself, foretelling her vocation. In the gospel of Luke there is a righteous old man named Simeon who believes he will not die before seeing the Messiah, and who, when the infant Jesus is brought to Jerusalem, says, "Lord, now let thy servant depart in peace." When the dying Newton wrote Dickinson he "would like" to live till she achieved the greatness he foresaw, he was acting out—and altering—this classic recognition scene.

Dickinson's last and somewhat obscure reference to Newton's messages may be read with that in mind. Writing to Higginson in 1876 and perhaps referring to the same letter as before, she said, "My earliest friend wrote me the week before he died 'If I live, I will go to Amherst – if I die, I certainly will.' " In their original context, these words were apparently connected to his prophetic sense of her vocation. Dying from tuberculosis and straightening up his affairs, Newton seems to have sent Dickinson a final statement, reaffirming that he had seen the poet in her and meant to see her crowned with glory. If she won her laurels before he died, he would go to Amherst to observe the coronation. If after, he would still be a witness. He was that convinced of immortality—hers as poet, his as spirit. This seems to have been one of the ways in which, as she later put it, he "taught me Immortality."

No one who receives the attestation of that kind of faith from an admired teacher ever forgets it, or the drunken bliss it inspires. Yet Dickinson's evangelical roots went too deep for her to transform herself into a Romantic of the Wordsworthian or Emersonian type. The early liberalism and serenity and strong masculine entitlement of these two poets were not hers for the taking. Newton gave her a vision of vocation and mastery, but the path would be long, uncertain, and painful, taking her through a wilderness her tutor could not have foreseen.

Reading

The oration Austin delivered at Commencement, "Elements of Our National Literature," hints at the literary concerns that occupied him and touched his sister's thinking. Thanks to him and other young men, a handful of novels had a major impact on the poet during the two years after her schooling ended.

In summer 1849 Henry Wadsworth Longfellow's mellow treatment of New England village life, *Kavanagh,* entered the college and then the Dickinson home, where Emily's brother hid it under the "piano cover" for her. It was a good hiding place: the volume was not only slender but had the gloss of "culture," transforming the region's religious and other characteristic aspects into picturesque genre scenes, rigged out with allusions to European art and a line of poetic (but earnest) commentary. The notice in the July *Indicator* acknowledged the novel's avoidances—"no deep emotion, no great truth"—but found it a charming read. So did Emily, who probably took its quiet local color as Amherst seen *en rose*. One of the bits that stuck with her was the exodus of the Pendexters, "turning their backs" on the parish when a modern, liberal, and culti-vated minister takes charge.

The tiny but emphatic vertical marks Emily made beside the pas-sages she liked are easily distinguishable from Austin's longer and lighter ones. It is instructive to see what caught her eye: the account of Alice and Cecelia's loving friendship (also marked by another); aphorisms on love; expressive passages ("poems that rhymed with the running water"); and, most tellingly, reflections on the work of communicating thought and representing life. The novel's theme, the imperative of *doing*, is ex-emplified by a schoolmaster who never starts the great romance he spends his life planning to write. The suggestion that he is weighed down by knowledge—"too deeply freighted, too much laden by the head"—was marked by Emily, as were passages on inchoate awareness and the role of art in voicing thought.[2]

Was she thinking of the task before her? One of the book's charac-ters is a would-be poet, Hiram Adolphus Hawkins, who has an exalted idea of his merits and whose general tone is "sad, desponding, perhaps slightly morbid." In a letter from 1853, Dickinson associated herself with this poseur: "I wrote to you last week, but thought you would laugh at me, and call me sentimental, so I kept my lofty letter for 'Adolphus Hawkins, Esq.' " At the time she was far from having vindicated New-ton's dying faith in her.

Another novel read in 1849, X. B. Saintine's ingenious and facile *Picciola*, she also applied to herself. An international best-seller, it tells of the inner pilgrimage of the Count de Charney, who loses his faith, be-comes a skeptic, and, after giving himself to various pursuits, joins a pointless conspiracy against Napoleon. He is imprisoned in a fortress

---

2. "It is difficult to know at what moment love begins; it is less difficult to know that it has begun." "That could not be fashioned into words, which was not yet fashioned into thoughts, but was still floating, vague and formless, through the mind." "Many have genius, but, wanting art, are for ever dumb."

named Fenestrella, and the story then becomes one of spiritual recovery during captivity. The agent of redemption is a plant Charney finds growing between two paving stones and which he carefully tends, naming it Picciola, little one. It was probably because the book builds an argument for religion that it was bestowed on Dickinson by William Cowper Dickinson, soon to begin his ministerial studies.

After reading part or all of this clever didactic novel, Dickinson conveyed her thanks:

> I'm a "Fenestrellan captive," if this world *be* "Fenestrella," and within my dungeon yard, up from the silent pavement stones, has come a plant, so frail, & yet so beautiful, I tremble lest it die. Tis the first living thing that has beguiled my solitude, & I take strange delight in its society. It's a mysterious plant, & sometimes I fancy that it whispers pleasant things to me – of freedom – and the future.

Plainly, the book struck a chord. Although Dickinson's life at the time (Valentine season) was hardly solitary, she evidently saw a deep resemblance between Charney's restorative confinement and her own situation. The idea of imprisonment, so central in her later writing, had caught her attention. Still, her present hopes were clearly set on freedom and the future.

A poem she recorded in her manuscript books about 1859 shows close affiliations with her response to Saintine's novel:

> *My nosegays are for Captives –*
> *Dim – long expectant eyes –*
> *Fingers denied the plucking,*
> *Patient till Paradise –*
>
> *To such, if they sh'd whisper*
> *Of morning and the moor –*
> *They bear no other errand,*
> *And I, no other prayer.*

Fr74

Whispering of another world to those deprived of freedom and pleasure, Dickinson's "nosegays" (poems) have the same mission as Charney's Picciola. And like this flower, which dies and is forgotten once his faith is restored, the speaker claims to have no aspirations for herself.

A book that engaged Dickinson's energies much more fully was *Jane Eyre,* lent to her by Elbridge Bowdoin in late 1849, just before she was given Emerson's *Poems.* By this time the novel's pseudonymous author, Currer Bell, had been heatedly condemned by various defenders of right thinking. The British *Quarterly Review* characterized him/her as "a person who, with great mental powers, combines a total ignorance of the habits of society, a great coarseness of taste, and a heathenish doctrine of religion." The book's "great and crying mischief" was that Jane's moral strength was that "of a mere heathen mind which is a law unto itself": she epitomized the "unregenerate and undisciplined spirit." The Connecticut Valley's young readers were more receptive. William Gardiner Hammond's largely admiring review in *The Indicator* sketched the heroine's leading trait as something "like self-reliance . . . a sort of self-concentration—a disposition to . . . look within one's self rather than to the world without for motives and rules of action." A young woman who enjoyed the novel more than she thought she ought to wrote, "I read Jane Eyre and was quite interested in it—I did not see anything so very objectionable in it—I dont know whether it is because I have not right views of propriety or because I did not *appreciate the improper things* in it."

Dickinson's response, preserved in the note she sent when returning the book, is so short and takes so much for granted it is easily misread. Since flowers were out of season, she attached a bouquet of fragrant box leaves. The entire note reads, "If all these leaves were altars, and on every one a prayer that Currer Bell might be saved – and you were God – would you answer it.?" The question, as savvy as it is naive, assumes that Bowdoin is well aware of the novel's improper and heathenish things, and that Currer Bell is unlikely to be saved by a properly orthodox deity. Dickinson asks it because she is already a strong partisan of the controversial book and is groping for some sort of heterodox immortality for the unknown author; Druid-like, she even turns the box leaves into altars. The double punctuation at the end seems to catch her in the act, disguising her risky opinion as a question deferentially presented to a man almost ten years her senior.

The tantalizing question about *Jane Eyre* was the unknown author's sex. In *The Indicator* Hammond expressed certainty that "no woman in all the annals of feminine celebrity ever wrote such a style, terse yet eloquent, and filled with energy bordering sometimes almost on rudeness." One would like to know how Dickinson reacted when it was disclosed in 1851 that this unfeminine and incendiary novel was written by Charlotte Brontë. Several years later, she wrote an elegy on the novelist that not only granted her salvation but made heaven the beneficiary:

> *Oh what an afternoon for Heaven,*
> *When "Bronte" entered there!*
>
> Fr146 (J148)

There is so much one would like to know about Dickinson's encounter with her first major woman's text. Having herself resisted indoctrination at freezing Mount Holyoke, what did she think of Lowood, the Calvinist school for girls (but run by a man)? How did she feel about lordly, romantic Rochester, or dictatorial St. John Rivers, who insists that Jane become his missionary wife, or the diminutive heroine herself, repeatedly defying authoritative men after first obeying them? *Jane Eyre* is full of explosive material that looks like a twisted or idealized account of Dickinson's own experience.

The winter she read the novel she acquired her first and only dog, a Newfoundland. This may have been Father's way of seeing that she was guarded when away from home. By Valentine's Day, 1850, the dog had been given the same name as St. John Rivers's dog, Carlo. Years later, villagers recalled the large animal as the poet's frequent companion on walks and visits.

In the copy of *Jane Eyre* that Charlotte Sewall Eastman gave the poet in 1865, two passages describing the sternly devout Rivers are marked with short penciled lines: "The humanities and amenities of life had no attraction for him—its peaceful enjoyments no charm. Literally, he lived only to aspire." "At the fireside, [he was] too often a cold, cumbrous column, gloomy and out of place." Some believe that Dickinson was thinking of her increasingly remote and dour father. Judith Farr has proposed that in her second and third "Master" drafts she assumed the role of Jane. A letter of the 1870s that abruptly quotes what Rochester says to Jane after she saves him from his burning bed—"I find your Benefits no Burden, Jane"—shows how well the poet knew Brontë's novel and how easily she drew on it.

What might be termed evangelical hermeneutics—the duty of making a personal application of sacred texts—had a profound effect on Dickinson. More than most readers, she seems to have defined herself partly through her books, as when she retooled her dependency on male tutors by appropriating Jane's attitude toward Rochester or the narrator's attachment to Paul Emanuel in Brontë's *Villette* (of which Dickinson owned an 1859 edition). For Dickinson no less than for these Victorian heroines, humble veneration was compatible with great inner strength. Indeed, she exercised that strength as she read, seeking and extracting what she could make her own. She wasn't like *Kavanagh*'s unproductive schoolteacher, sinking beneath the weight of excess knowledge.

Writing

The pleasing stimulus of books got a boost from the social whirl that caught Emily up in December 1849 and January 1850, her first brilliant winter. It seems to have been Austin, "always the leader" in "sugaring parties and such pleasures," as another girl recalled, who touched off the festivities. After spending his vacation plowing through David Hume's multivolume *History of England,* he finally reached the end—"the signal," in his sister's words, "for general uproar." There was a sleigh ride to Deerfield that she described as "a frolic, comprising charades – walking around *indefinitely* – music – conversation – and supper – set in most modern style," following which she returned home at two o'clock and "felt no worse for it the next morning." Then came more parties, tableaux at President Hitchcock's home, "cozy sociables." It was as if Father's rules on late hours and dangerous insobrieties had become inoperative.

Yet, even as Emily launched herself, she was not only living at home but, owing to Vinnie's absence, weighed down as never before by household cares. Newton was gone, and when her best friend, Jane Humphrey, left town, Emily moaned, "I am *alone – all* alone." For the moment her life had become a patchwork of bondage and freedom, of steadiness and giddiness—a fabric stretched with tensions, openings, solicitations. The previous summer Austin had read an exhibition essay titled "Mind developed in Action," and then there were Longfellow's admonitory portraits in *Kavanagh* of a slothful would-be romancer and a foolish would-be poet. Had the time come to *act*?

In February and March 1850 Emily was so busy and absorbed she failed to answer a letter from Jane. Not till April, when a second letter arrived with the news of Jane's father's serious illness, did Emily write. Her excuse was uncharacteristic: "Your *first* words found me far out in the world, crowding, and hurrying, and busying." What she didn't say, not wishing to hurt her friend's feelings, was that much of this activity had taken the form of writing: long bold letters, her first known poem, and a prose Valentine resulting in her first appearance in print. It was a burst of audacious energy, much of it directed to men above her in years or education.

The first of these compositions was sent to Joel Warren Norcross in Boston. About the same age as Newton and Bowdoin, Joel was her youngest uncle on the Norcross side, coming between her and her parents' generations. Though he still boarded with his sister Lavinia in Boston, he had struck out for himself as an importer of fancy goods, making frequent buying trips to Europe and trying to cut a figure. The first Norcross to notice the world of fashion, he impressed some as eccentric, self-important, vain. During a visit to Amherst he gave Emily the impression she would be hearing from him. When he forgot and wrote her father instead, she sent him an extraordinarily vehement mock-reproach.

It began with a dream vision of the world of men going about their work, sailing, tending their flocks, keeping "gay stores" (like Joel). They lived for pleasure and made promises of one kind or another—"and *one* man told a lie to his niece." All were condemned to torment, and when the dreamer ("very much scared") heard them crying for help and "called to see who they were . . . up from the pit *you* spoke!" "Not yet aroused to the truth[?]" she paused to ask, trying to sound like an evangelist with a sinner in his sights.

Taking for granted that her uncle is too hardened to pay heed, she ratchets up the terror with a long and furious denunciation—"You villain without a rival – unparralleled doer of crimes – scoundrel unheard of before"—that culminates in a challenge to a duel and an announcement that "I shall kill you." Enumerating the methods she may use, she threatens chloroform, entering his room and plucking out his heart, stabbing him "while sleeping."

Of course it is all in fun, and before she signs her name ("Emilie – I believe"), she shifts into a familiar news-sending mode ("Amherst is alive with fun this winter"). It would be naive to read her violent language as an expression of rage: her script is as small, neat, and regular as anything she wrote and strikingly out of harmony with her fulminations. Like Austin's hyperbolic fantasies, the letter is a self-conscious exhibition of humor, verbosity, "imagination," running in this instance over fifteen hundred words. Yet her idea of fun is more extreme and unsafe than anything Austin is known to have composed. The scenes of punishment are disturbingly direct. Anyone receiving such a letter would feel uneasy.

In a curious digression, the letter facetiously proposes that a murderer bears no responsibility for his crime. The passage points to a fundamental impetus behind the whole performance—a damaged sense of agency, a frustrating inability to *reach* the world of men that has been disclosing itself. Why does Dickinson's father get a letter when she doesn't? Fizzing with surplus vitality, she has little on which to discharge it except twin loaves of bread. Twelve years later, when Higginson accused her or her poems of being "uncontrolled" and she replied, "I have no Tribunal," she was saying the same thing in a more self-conscious way: operating in a void and free of all rules, how could she *not* go over the top?

Twelve days after writing Joel, she again sounded a note of menace, this time to Jane Humphrey. Divulging how bored she was with her second cousins from Michigan (daughters of Nathan Dickinson), the poet threatened, "now do you ever tell of this – and I will certainly put you into a sleep which you cant wake up from!" Dramatizing her response to Jane's departure, she issued a burst of punitive commands: "put her into States-prison – into the House of Correction – bring out the long lashed whip."

On the whole, though, this confidential letter to a close female friend shows little of the studied violence Dickinson worked up for Joel. Instead, she achieved a rich, spur-of-the-moment self-disclosure surpassing anything she had previously written. At fifteen she had reported herself to Abiah as "gloomy" or "low spirited" or having "unpleasant reflections," but now, going well beyond these normalized formulas, she offered a spot-on account of her moods. "I love to be surly – and muggy – and cross – then I remember you – and feel that I do a kind of justice to you – and myself – which eases my conscience wonderfully." In addition to describing her improper states of mind, she freely indulged them as she wrote, though admonishing herself afterward. Expecting to see Jane before long, she pictured the intervening weeks "with their bony fingers still poking me away – how I *hate* them – and would love to do them harm!" "Oh ugly time – and space," she exclaimed (the same phrase appearing in a letter to Emily Fowler). Aware that such talk was irreligious, she tried to sound contrite: "Is it wicked to talk so Jane – what *can* I say that isn't? Out of a wicked heart cometh wicked words – let us sweep it out – and brush away the cobwebs – and garnish it – and make ready for the Master!" But that kind of housekeeping, literal or figurative, was not to the writer's taste, and before long she was laughing up her sleeve at the Sewing Society's winter program: "now all the poor will be helped – the cold warmed – the warm cooled . . ."

Nineteen-year-old Emily was in a state of eruption, throwing off the rules her elders had pounded into her. But she was not so much the overwhelming central volcano she became in the early 1860s as an irregular tract of geysers, letting off steam in every direction only to clap hand to mouth in feigned apology. The dazzling compositions of early 1850 are those of a young person trying out her voice, her voices, often generating each new statement out of what she has just heard herself say. She lets herself go in the extended and fanciful improvisations that have always amused her various audiences, but now she makes them the vehicle of newly insistent and complicated feelings.

To see the shape of Dickinson's career, we must try to bring these crazy compositions from the winter and spring of 1850 into some sort of focus, and without smoothing away their contradictions and insincerities. A case in point is the letter she sent Abiah six days after writing Jane, and which begins with the solemn assertion "*God* is sitting here, looking into my very soul to see if I think right tho'ts." The writer claims she isn't oppressed by this unblinking surveillance, since "I try to be right and good, and he knows every one of my struggles." But her spiritual effort seems forgotten as she devises an allegorical explanation of how she caught a cold: out for a walk, she met a "little creature" who attached itself to her and followed her home, and who, when she removed her bonnet and shawl, put its arms around her neck and "began to kiss me immoderately, and express so much love, it completely bewildered me." Now it sleeps in her bed and eats out of her plate—meaning, she can't shake her cold.

Is the neutered intimate a version of Emily's own perverse adherence to friends like Abiah? Maybe, but it seems less important to worry out the psychological symbolism than to see that her tale, belonging to the same genre as her brother's concoctions, was meant to amuse, puzzle, scandalize. She was engaging in a defiant and self-conscious play of "imagination," and when she was finished, she impersonated her finger-wagging elders with a hyped-up self-denunciation: "Now my dear friend, let me tell you that these last thoughts are fictions – vain imaginations to lead astray foolish young women. They are flowers of speech, they both *make,* and *tell* deliberate falsehoods, avoid them as the snake." Protesting her complete candor ("Honestly tho' "), she admonishes Abiah to look out for snakes—but only to reverse direction yet again and declare her fondness for "those little green ones that slide around by your shoes in the grass – and make it rustle with their elbows – they are rather my favorites on the whole, but I would'nt influence *you* for the world!"

On the whole, Emily would seem to be the real snake in this, her most serpentine production. Even though this was supposed to be the letter that reestablished a lapsed correspondence, she openly admitted at one point that she couldn't find a suitable topic to write about. Surely there was

> [s]omething besides severe colds, and serpents, and we will try to find *that* something. It cant be a garden [in winter], can it, or a strawberry bed, which rather belongs to a garden – nor it cant be a schoolhouse, nor an Attorney at Law [referring to Newton?]. Oh dear I dont know *what* it is! Love for the absent dont *sound* like it, but try it, and see how it goes.

Following which, on order, she whips up a declaration of love for the absent Abiah: "I miss you very much indeed, think of you at night . . . think of you in the daytime when the cares of the world . . . choke up the love for friends in some of our hearts."

It is easy to be misled by this ironic and artificial declaration of undying love. The letter is a kind of snakebite in words, both professing affection and making a winding and wounding display of unconcern. At the end the writer tried to mend matters by explaining that "I have been introducing you to me in this letter." Conceding its "*want* of *friendly affection*," she signed as "Your very sincere, and *wicked* friend." The effect on Abiah's feelings may be inferred from what she said of a later letter from Emily, which seemed to be written "more affectionately than wont."

Emily was using Abiah's attention as a kind of mirror, trying on a series of deliberately fascinating and bewildering masks. Fittingly enough, the young poet was most in her element during Valentine season, when the Connecticut Valley enjoyed its bland substitute for carnival, and expressions of true and pretended love flew out of every corner. In 1852 the women of Belchertown hosted a Valentine festival that featured oysters and ice cream, and the all-important exchange of messages at a "post office." Emily loved the sport, which stimulated her first known poem and her first and only prose publication. Addressed to a man, each composition was a comic tour de force that seemed to leave the author's real feelings out of the question.

The poem, sent to Bowdoin, her father's thirty-year-old law partner, twitted him for showing no interest in courtship and marriage.[3]

> *all things do go a courting, in earth, or sea, or air,*
> *God hath made nothing single but* thee *in his world so fair!*
> *The* bride, *and then the* bridegroom, *the* two, *and then the* one,
> *Adam, and Eve, his consort, the moon, and then the sun.*

Wherever one looks, there is wooing and mating: the bee courts the flower, the wind the branches, the storm the seashore. Even "the *worm* doth woo the *mortal.*" Bowdoin being the solitary holdout against the universal law, the speaker advises him that six "comely maidens" are sitting in a tree waiting to be plucked. Five of these are named—Sarah, Eliza, Emeline, Harriet, and Susan. The sixth, unnamed, "with *curling hair,*" can only be Emily:

> *approach that tree with caution, then up it boldly climb,*
> *and seize the one thou lovest, nor care for* space, *or* time*!*
> *Then bear her to the greenwood, and build for her a bower,*
> *and give her what she asketh, jewel, or bird, or flower;*
> *and bring the fife, and trumpet, and beat opon the drum –*
> *and bid the world Goodmorrow, and go to glory home!*

Fr1

The poem shows why Dickinson's friends of this period saw her as "full of 'fun' and 'tease,'" and also why this burst of creativity did not

---

3. Bowdoin, a fairly inexpressive man by all accounts, seems to have struck Dickinson as an irresistible target. The following year, having read *Reveries of a Bachelor*, she once again pretended to have the answer to his secret romantic dreams: "*I* know of a shuttle swift – I know of a fairy gift – mat for the 'Lamp of *Life*' – the little Bachelor's wife!!" Judging by the handmade lampmat William Gardiner Hammond received from a young woman four years earlier, this was a conventional gift at the time.

lead to sustained production: the fun was premised on the writer's complete and uncanny absence. Unlike the archaic damsels, who perch in the tree and wait to be seized and mated, the poet offers bold advice in a series of vigorous imperatives: "approach," "climb," "seize," and so forth. "She with *curling hair*," in other words, has nothing in common with Emily-the-writer. The first is defined in terms of appearance, is sexually available, and has no voice, while the second, a witty expert on universal courtship, seems as "solo" as Bowdoin. She can be a poet, in other words, because she is out of the marriage system, thus incidentally obeying the law for literary females as laid down two decades earlier by Father writing as Coelebs.

At some point in the late 1840s or early 1850s, Dickinson asked Emily Fowler if the way people talked, taking "all the clothes off their souls," did not make her "shiver." Although that kind of candor, typical of the recently converted, made her uneasy, she, too, liked to zero in on what she elsewhere called "the timid soul, the blushing, shrinking soul." In order to become the extremely personal, passionate, and complex poet of the 1860s, Dickinson had to cease being the brilliant entertainer and somehow empower that hidden female subject. Yet she never became "confessional," straight autobiographical detail remaining essentially out of place in her verse. In more than one way, she continued to hide.

Her other Valentine composition of 1850 took fun and tease—and female boldness—to a new level. Here, the speaker tells a young man that she seeks a private meeting with him: "I propose, sir, to see you," it doesn't matter where, "at sunrise, or sunset, or the new moon." And not just see: she wants

> a chat sir, or a tete-a-tete, a confab, a mingling of opposite minds . . . I feel sir that we shall agree. We will be David and Jonathan, or Damon and Pythias . . . We will talk over what we have learned in our geographies, and listened to from the pulpit, the press and the Sabbath School.
>
> This is strong language sir, but none the less true. So hurrah for North Carolina, since we are on this point.

The concluding paragraph brings in something the Dickinsons mostly ignored, the radical reform movements of the 1840s:[4]

> But the world is sleeping in ignorance and error, sir, and we must be crowing-cocks, and singing-larks, and a rising sun to awake her; or else we'll pull society up to the roots, and plant it in a different place. We'll build Alms-houses, and transcendental State prisons, and scaffolds – we will blow out the sun, and the moon, and encourage invention. Alpha shall kiss Omega – we will ride up the hill of glory – Hallelujah, all hail!

In scripting this wild fandango, Emily assumed the manic voice of a woman whose head has been turned by her stimulating teachers, and now takes a frenzied interest in the political questions that are for men alone to decide.[5] Instead of waiting to be seized, *this* woman masculinizes herself, not only making overtures to a man but likening the two of them to classic male pairs. The one female role she takes is that of "Judith the heroine," relegating the man to the part of orator. As if to reassure him (Judith had cut off the head of Holofernes), she condescendingly says, "That's what they call a metaphor in our country. Don't be afraid of it, sir, it wont bite." This last word leads to the mention of her dog, Carlo, thus cleverly hinting at her identity.

---

4. Is it owing to the family's conservatism or the accidents of historic preservation that no letter mentions the Northampton Association of Education and Industry? David Mack III (son of the General David Mack, Jr., who bought the Dickinson Homestead) and his wife, Lucy, were resident members of this utopian commune, along with Sojourner Truth and Frederick Douglass. As at the more famous Brook Farm, simplicity and social equality were communal ideals, so that Lucy "scrubbed floors." The Macks left in summer 1845, after David's health broke. Given that he and Edward were Yale classmates and had corresponded, the Dickinsons *must* have known about this social experiment.

5. Conservative writers on women's issues often glanced with alarm at the wild woman speaker who doesn't know her place. As one among thousands of instances, Loring and Lavinia Norcross's pastor invoked the woman who "steps forth to assume the duties of the man" and whose "voice is heard from house to house . . . rising in harsh unnatural tones of denunciation against civil laws and rulers . . . expecting to reform politics and churches, and to put down every real and supposed evil in them, by the right arm of female power."

All in all, if the composition lampoons the energetic female activists of the day, its huge comic energies take it well beyond satire and any imaginable conservatism. Dickinson was finding an outlet, a voice, for her wildness. "Approach that tree with caution," her Valentine poem had advised, "then up it boldly climb." Cautious, she proposed no union other than a mingling of minds. Bold, she ended the prose Valentine with the same rosily dramatic finale as the love poem: "ride up the hill of glory" and "go to glory home!"

Two months later Emily sent Jane Humphrey a teasing confession: "since you left . . . I have dared to do strange things – bold things, and have asked no advice from any – I have heeded beautiful tempters, yet do not think I am wrong." Given the seething letters she had been scribbling and the many blanks in her record, we cannot be certain she was referring only or primarily to her Valentine compositions. Still, the Valentines do meet all specifications, being strange, bold, beautiful, and not at all "wrong." Chances are, Dickinson's veiled confession refers not only to these extravagant overtures to men but to the most daring thing of all—the publication of one of them in Amherst College's literary monthly, *The Indicator.*

Looking back from the 1880s, a Latin professor praised this periodical as unsurpassed "by any generation of students since." Dickinson's prose Valentine appeared in the issue for February 1850, which, by accident or design, was mainly about women in literature. One young male essayist spoke up for Madame de Staël in spite of her "opinions too bitter, and theories too bold, to become a woman's pen." A second argued that Shakespeare's women "trust at once and entirely" and never speculate about fundamentals, there being "no female Hamlets." A third defended the unidentified author, assumed to be a man, of *Jane Eyre* and *Shirley.* Dickinson's piece is found on the last two pages in the small type of the "Editors' Corner," where it is framed by an editorial discussion of how to fill up the issue. An editor whose pseudonym is Van Twiller pronounces her lavish composition the obvious standout among the many "chary" epistles prompted by Valentine's Day. Speculating on her identity, he imagines her fun-loving mouth has no corners and that she is too effervescent to tell "the half of her feelings," and then he appends the standard mathematical initials, Q.E.D., followed by a line of verse explaining how to read them: "Which is the last and most edifying of all." To those who had eyes to see, the anonymous Valentine writer had been exposed.

Van Twiller was Henry Shipley, a senior like Austin and a gifted reprobate who played whist, got drunk on occasion, and did so well in rhetorical exercises the discriminating Hammond judged him to be "a *first-prize* man." Son of a Democratic activist, he went on to edit a series of western newspapers, including the Sacramento *Democratic State Journal.* The professor of Greek characterized him as "one of the most hardened & hopeless & at the same time one of the most talented men of the Senior Class."

Although Emily Fowler called the editor "roguish" and the Valentine "stolen," we cannot rule out the possibility that Shipley or a fellow editor had Dickinson's consent ("I have heeded beautiful tempters"). A more pressing question, in view of her later refusal to publish, concerns the consequences the printing of her gorgeously addlepated piece had for her. Father admired Austin's compositions but literary females were another story, and Madame de Staël was an old bête noire, and if there was one thing he couldn't stand it was a hectoring woman. What business did a daughter of his have putting out such stuff in public when she should be using her time more wisely, especially with Vinnie absent and her mother ill? We may surmise that the poet's first publication earned a paternal reprimand, and that the lesson she drew was that all future writing would have to be conducted more discreetly.

In the April letter to Jane that speaks of strange, bold deeds, Emily wishes she could "confess what *you only* shall know, an experience bitter, and sweet, but the sweet did so beguile me – and life has had an aim – and the world has been too precious for your poor – and striving sister! The winter was all one dream, and the spring has not yet waked me." Was she referring to the consequences of her literary efforts? Her vagueness was deliberate and intended to waken Jane's suspicions:

> What do you weave from all these threads – for I know you hav'nt been idle the while I've been speaking to you, bring it nearer the window, and I will see, it's all wrong unless it has one gold thread in it, a

long, big shining fibre which hides the others – and which will fade away into Heaven while you hold it, and from there come back to me.

We are up against one of the world's great riddle-makers here, one who surely understood that her reader would suspect a romance first of all.

Who was the Valentine's recipient? The universal assumption is that it went to George Henry Gould, a member of *The Indicator*'s editorial staff who was so poor he had to rely on the Charity Fund for college bills. Gould stood six feet eight inches high, had a fine beak of a nose, was a witty writer and public speaker, and became a highly respected minister, though dogged by chronic malaria. He was Alpha Delta Phi (Shipley being Psi Upsilon); he had asked Dickinson to the candy pulling; he is known to have corresponded with her; and unlike Shipley, he shows up in her siblings' social life, appearing in Vinnie's 1851 diary and Austin's 1853 letter drafts. If Gould was the one, as seems likely, we must wonder whether the privacy-loving writer felt betrayed when he let his fellow editor print her communication. Even if she gave her consent, wouldn't she feel exposed by that bold, unblushing Q.E.D.?

Writing Abiah in early May, Emily told how a friend she "love[d] *so* dearly" implored her in the sink room, as she washed the noon dishes, to ride with him in "the sweet-still woods," and how she overcame the "temptation," apparently because of her domestic duties during Mother's continuing illness. In the 1890s Vinnie confided to a few acquaintances that Gould had wanted to marry her sister, and that when Father refused to sanction the match, the couple had a passionate last interview in which she vowed to be faithful till death and wear nothing but white. Even though it would have been in character for Edward to discourage an impoverished suitor with no career as yet, the story has not been taken seriously, for two good reasons: it shows all the marks of a fevered and commonplace imagination, and Dickinson did not adopt perpetual white until the 1860s.

Yet Emily's hesitant refusal to ride with a friend she loved "*so* dearly" does point to a romantic interest, possibly in Gould. Further, her wish to tell Jane "what *you only* shall know" reveals that Austin and Vinnie were mostly in the dark and can't be taken as inside sources in this matter. In school at Ipswich, Vinnie could have had no direct or firsthand knowledge, particularly of the episode in the sink room. Learning about the romance afterward, she would have been likely to give it a conventionally melodramatic cast. The notion of a grand once-in-a-lifetime passion may be dismissed—but not the veiled hints in Emily's letters or the likelihood that the publication of her Valentine had unpleasant consequences for her. "Our father . . . never hindered our friendships *after* we were children" (italics added), Vinnie asserted in 1895, correcting a fictitious account of how Edward spiked Emily's marriage. This interestingly qualified assertion is consistent with a scenario that feels right and reasonable but can't be proven—that Edward took some sort of disciplinary step to arrest his nineteen-year-old daughter's involvement with the impoverished editor who had connived at her exposure in print.[6]

There was definitely something, "an experience bitter, and sweet," as Emily characterized it in April, leaving a dream of "one gold thread." "Nobody *thinks* of the joy, nobody *guesses* it, to all appearance old things are engrossing," she wrote Jane (again showing how little the family knew); "there *now* is nothing old, things are budding, and springing, and singing." In May she was still "dreaming, dreaming a *golden* dream, with eyes all the while wide open," though now it was "almost morning" and she was immersed in humdrum domestic work. The rapture, largely anticipatory, seems to involve the possibility of disappointment or even betrayal: "I hope belief is not wicked, and assurance, and perfect trust. . . . I hope human nature has truth in it." One hears an anti-Calvinist note here, a denial of depravity and a hopeful declaration similar to what she later said she learned from Benjamin Newton—"a faith in things unseen, and in a life again, nobler, and much more blessed." At the same time, her hope seems placed on something less abstract and more personal than that, perhaps on *individual* "human nature."

Some believe her visionary dream was literary; some think it was romantic. It may be that both guesses are correct, mixed in a recipe now

---

6. The fervid stories Mary Lee Hall gathered from Vinnie cannot be reconciled with the latter's statement to Caroline H. Dall that "Emily never had any love disaster." After the poet's death, her sister reportedly confided, "many times when desirable offers of marriage have been made to Emily she has said—I have never seen anyone that I cared for as much as you Vinnie."

lost. Finally, the riddle eludes us, and we are left with the tantalizing images sent to Jane and Abiah, pictures evoking a hope too rich and risky
to be committed to paper—a bright future with one gold thread too
faded for us to see.

No Laughing or Loud Talking

A first-person narrative poem from 1862 begins:

> *It would never be Common – more – I said –*
> *Difference – had begun –*

Convinced that every "bitterness" has ended, the speaker feels her joy
"publish" itself in her eye and on her cheek. With no chariness whatever,
she deals "a word of Gold / To every Creature" she meets. Then, for no
cause given, she undergoes a complete and instantaneous collapse into
her old state of deprivation, and as her attention returns to her sackcloth
hanging on its nail, she wonders what can have happened to her

> *. . . moment of Brocade –*
> *My – drop – of India?*

> Fr388

The poem tells one of Dickinson's most important stories: midnight
at noon, the relapse into despair just when complete fulfillment seems
imminent. Although we can't assume the events of the first half of 1850
inspired *this* midnight-at-noon poem, they seem to fit it well. Going further than ever in her writing and friendships with men, Dickinson was
swamped by the biggest evangelical wave yet, resulting in the conversion
of her sister and father and terminating her first sustained expressive
surge.

Vinnie's change of heart took place during an "awakening" at Ipswich Female Seminary orchestrated by the principal, the Reverend John
P. Cowles. His wife, the matron, had been an associate of Mary Lyon,

and the drill at Ipswich resembled that at Mount Holyoke. According to Jane E. Hitchcock, Vinnie's friend and fellow pupil, the teachers preached daily "about *restraining* our *feelings*," exhorting the girls "to *put on the screws*" and threatening "that if we do it not ourselves, they shall do it for us." Vinnie's first letter to Austin was full of her customary flippancy, but by March resistance had collapsed: "At times, I desire religion above all things, & this world seems small indeed. . . . Does Emilie think of these things at all? Oh! that she might!"

Before this surrender, Vinnie had wondered if Amherst's winter gaieties would provoke "the good people" to "foresee certain destruction." She was right: with February came a period of somber public reflection—in Reverend Colton's phrase, "a season of anxious suspense." Attention focused on the sale of liquor, some college students having been too free or public in their drinking. The question of prohibition was put on the agenda for the annual town meeting, and when March 4 arrived, a huge number of voters assembled. The words that carried the day, spoken by President Hitchcock, were delivered "with an emphasis that fairly choked his utterance": "*better that the college should go down, than that young men should come here to be ruined by drink places.*" Only one or two voters dared oppose the motion. Next morning the "rum resorts" were closed.

With that, a revival began at the college, with the same quiet but powerful scenes as at Yale in 1820 and Mount Holyoke in 1847–1848: heavy attendance at devotional meetings, "no sound of laughing or loud talking," not even "heavy footsteps in the halls." Several professors' children were affected, including Emily's friend Mary Warner. On the last day before spring break, profane Henry Shipley was "hopefully converted." In most years no more than a handful of students joined the college church by profession of faith. This year there was a Sunday on which thirty-two previously unchurched young people, the highest number ever, crowded forward to become members, Shipley among them.[7]

---

7. Shipley's moment of fame came four years later, when, as a newspaper editor, he was horsewhipped by the celebrated dancer Lola Montez for his insinuations on her character. A severe injury caused by a later fall from a horse led to his suicide in a California hotel in November 1859, when he took strychnine and died in agony. The Amherst paper reprinted a report of the tragedy. Dickinson's extant letters do not allude to it.

By then the fervor had spread from college to town, with Emily's only remaining unsaved friends, Abby Wood and Susan Gilbert, undergoing the great and mysterious transformation. "Christ is calling everyone here," she wrote; "all my companions have answered, even my darling Vinnie believes she loves, and trusts him, and I am standing alone in rebellion." The church held its evening meetings in the academy building instead of the dismal basement vestry, which Father might not have entered. Many who once stayed away attended night after night, "proud and hard hearts that had hitherto resisted every call." The packed meetings were "pervaded by a death-stillness, except as broken by sobs that *could* not be wholly suppressed." On Sunday, May 26, Mrs. Fanny H. Boltwood was told by Mrs. Abby Sweetser and Mrs. Phydelia Kellogg (whose house adjoined the Dickinsons') that Edward Dickinson, no less, "had hopefully been converted. He has been long struggling with his feelings." The rumor was true,[8] and in August he and Susan Gilbert and sixty-eight others joined the First Church, Vinnie following in November. We can assume Mother felt great relief and joy, and that Emily was drawn closer to Austin, the only other family member not in the fold.

As was always the case in revivals, the unregenerate were besieged with concerned visitations and letters. After Emily was talked to by Abby and others, perhaps including Vinnie, she confided to Jane that she didn't know "*what* they have found, but *they* think it is something precious. I wonder if it *is*?" She noted how "the eyes of the disobedient look down, and become ashamed," while the saved "seem so very tranquil, and their voices are kind, and gentle, and the tears fill their eyes so often." She asked Jane and Abiah to pray for her conversion—but she also lingered on the "*golden* dream" and her bold strange acts and how thrilled she still felt.

---

8. According to Jay Leyda, a quarter-century later George Gould wrote in his notebook that Edward had been admonished by his pastor, "You want to come to Christ as a *lawyer*—but you must come to him as a *poor sinner.*" One problem with this gossipy story is that it's hard to imagine either participant as divulging it. More troubling, Leyda provides no context for Gould's anecdote and no location for the notebook. Until these are established, the story should be considered apocryphal. In 1930 a relative knew of no "mss or diaries of Gould."

In thinking about this contradiction, we should note that Dickinson was speaking to the converted. How would she have sounded to an un-orthodox friend—Newton, Austin? A recently discovered letter from her brother suggests an answer.

In March or April, Emily Fowler addressed a message of Christian exhortation to Emily and Austin, to which the latter presently replied. The next day Fowler responded with a long letter pleading with him not to be "anxious about your feelings. God may not be working on you by . . . an agonizing conviction of your sinfulness. He may be drawing you by cords of love." Fowler was emphatic: "Do not let this want of 'a sense of sinfulness' be a serious difficulty."

The newly found document, preserved in Emily Fowler Ford's copy of Dickinson's 1890 *Poems*, is the letter from Austin that elicited this ad-vice. In it, he admits he has been a doubter, raising "objections upon al-most every point." But within the last few days religion has begun to seem "more *real*—more *desirable*," mainly because he has been "struck with the lovely traits of character" in those who have been converted. Now he is giving the subject more thought "than all my life before—My great difficulty has been in getting a sense of my sinfulness."

The passage that concerns us comes near the end, where the young man divulges his sister's reaction to Fowler's well-meant interference. Nowhere in the record do we get a more telling glimpse of the poet's im-mediate response to social pressure.

> Your letter is a great prize to me—I have read & reread it many times—Emily I presume, will not answer it—She is rather too wild at present—Vinnie is quite serious—and determined to be a chris-tian—She sends her love to you—If you write another *double* letter—I think it had better be to Vinnie & I—rather than E. [Emily] & I.

That there is a cordial message from Vinnie but nothing from Emily speaks volumes. Instead of exhibiting Austin's compliant spirit, she is "rather too wild at present"—out of control, not amenable to persuasion, not "serious." These disclosures, coming from the brother Emily thought of as her partner in mischief, represent a subtle act of betrayal, a whisper behind her back about how unruly and unreasonable she insists on being.

Austin's description of his sister is consistent with the violent language, mood swings, disguises, and contradictions apparent in her letters that spring, offering an outside take on the raw emotional states that drove that writing. It also offers a handle on her first known message to Fowler, thought to have been written in early 1850. Professing the warmest affection, the poet says she would pay a visit this morning if it weren't for the "wicked snow-storm" (of which four were reported in March 1850). That this may be the letter Austin reported Emily as too wild to undertake is suggested by the odd confessions with which it opens: that she had an undisclosed dream about Fowler the previous night, and that "*me,* and *my spirit* were fighting this morning." Her intent is evidently to appease and disarm, to keep this concerned friend at a distance: writing on a day when a visit is out of the question, she speaks of her turmoil and anger in such a way that Fowler is free to imagine a hopeful religious struggle, *and leave her alone.*

Like the communications sent to Hannah Porter when Dickinson was at Mount Holyoke, Austin's letter reveals how she was managed behind her back by trusted confederates. His recommendation that Fowler not write her raises a central question about her future seclusion: granting that it was self-chosen, was she also pushed in this direction by family pressure? Was she "handled with a Chain" (her phrase in a poem on the treatment of nonconformists, Fr620) just when everyone else was converting and getting serious and closing the rum places and *she* was tasting her first Domingo?

In April, Emily wrote Jane, "How lonely this world is growing, something so desolate creeps over the spirit and we dont know its name, and it wont go away." Several more years and she would be ready to name it: midnight at noon.

Chapter 12

1850–1852: Somebody's Rev-e-ries

As the product of a well-guarded nest, Dickinson had been shielded from many of the social expectations that tyrannize the young, and now took for granted her home's undoubted superiority. Her sister and brother had the same mind-set, all three showing the varieties of independence and dependency, arrogance and narcissism, that such a home engenders. Predictably, they all felt grave misgivings about the onset of adulthood. Vinnie wished "we were all children again & lifes battle not begun," and Austin declared he "would love to be a child always . . . to have a child's pleasure, & a child's freedom from care—a child's father & mother . . . to depend upon." But it was the extravagantly endowed sibling, the one slowly moving toward literary production through a thicket of prohibitions, who had the most trouble growing up. "I wish we were children now," Emily confessed to Austin in 1853; "I wish we were *always* children, how to grow up I dont know."

Some of the Dickinson siblings' least appealing traits resulted from the retention in adulthood of traits and habits characteristic of childhood. Yet the same tendency helps explain the poet's creative freedom from the hidebound rules the adult world took seriously. For good and ill, a kind of retardation in growing up was a vital aspect of her poetic vocation.

Reading and Fancying

To follow what Dickinson read from 1850 to 1852 is to see her moving through a more subdued and inward phase than that of the previous two years, when books like *Jane Eyre* and men like Benjamin Newton, Elbridge Bowdoin, George Gould, and others helped provoke a wild coming-out.[1] For many reasons, ranging from the repressions of her religious and patriarchal culture to her own apparent constitutional frailness, the public world was closed to her, mandating a search for some alternative to open expression and publication. Inevitably, she was drawn to the life of fancy, which essayed the future through imaginative self-projection, not practical effort. Fancy, exquisitely cultivated with close female friends, now became the essential resource.

In her reading, Dickinson tended more than ever to cut out the vivid bits and paste them into her unfolding life. In *David Copperfield* she seized on the famous marriage proposal, "Barkis is very willin'," to characterize her mother's wish for a bonnet resembling Aunt Lavinia's. She applied Mrs. Micawber's staunch fidelity ("I will never desert Micawber") to her own faithfulness in writing Austin. Strangest of all was her use of Hawthorne's *House of the Seven Gables*, where poor old Hepzibah, pathetically loyal to her feeble-minded brother, goes wandering with him through the country until "kind angels took both of them home." To Emily, it "seemed almost a lesson," and when her brother left for Boston, she stood in the wind and pelting drops until he was out of sight, afraid

---

1. However, in 1852 she wrote a Valentine poem for her sister's beau, William Howland, that included the lines, "Mortality is fatal – / Gentility is fine, / Rascality, heroic, / *Insolvency, sublime!*" (Fr2[B]). The sixty-eight-line extravaganza was sent to the *Springfield Republican,* which published the "amusing medley" and invited the unknown author to communicate directly in future—which she didn't.

he might "turn around for a last look at home and I should not be there."
One thing fancy did not promote was levelheaded judgment.

The quantity of mediocre writing she took seriously can be alarming. From 1850 to 1853 she quoted no poem more often, six times, than
Longfellow's wet consolation lyric, "The Rainy Day":

> The day is cold, and dark, and dreary;
> It rains, and the wind is never weary;
> . . . .
>
> Be still, sad heart! and cease repining;
> Behind the clouds is the sun still shining;
> Thy fate is the common fate of all,
> Into each life some rain must fall,
> Some days must be dark and dreary.

Dickinson's citations of the poem suggest she valued the drippy moral
advice as much as the atmospheric melancholy. Of course, not only was
Longfellow the quotable American poet of the day, but "Be still, sad
heart" was one of her own self-exhortations following the events of
spring 1850.

But it is hard to understand why she bothered with *Light in the Valley: A Memorial of Mary Elizabeth Stirling, Who Died at Haddonfield, N.J.,
Jan. 30, 1852,* a long tract heavily overlaid with pious moralizing. Or
with Matilda Anne MacKarness's *"Only,"* shoddy hackwork that drives
home the harmful effects of self-indulgence. In the other work of fiction
by MacKarness that the poet read, *The House on the Rock,* the heroine
learns how to give up "the wild excitement of . . . romantic love" with a
man above her in station (the author was British) and settle for the "calm
and peaceful" life of an unmarried schoolteacher. Naming these books in
a letter to Susan Gilbert, Dickinson admitted "they dont *bewitch* me any.
There are no walks in the wood – no low and earnest voices, no moon-
light, nor stolen love, but pure little lives, loving God, and their parents,
and obeying the laws of the land." One would think that this fine summing up disposed of these severely didactic narratives once and for all,
yet Dickinson also praised them as "sweet and true" and able to "do one

good." Eager to be bewitched, she also took for granted her appetite had no validity.

Dickinson is not known to have met with the new and exciting novels by American women that dominated the market in the 1850s, many of them patterned after *The Wide, Wide World* by Susan Warner: perhaps they were screened out by Amherst's tastemakers. Whatever the explanation, most of the women's books that crossed Dickinson's path at this time came from England and were pitched to the religious trade. In spring 1852 she, Austin, and Susan Gilbert read Lady Georgiana Fullerton's *Ellen Middleton*, a grim life history of a woman whose involvement in a child's accidental drowning gives rise to false guilt and other complications. The author had the sort of Anglo-Catholic mentality that gravitated toward good county society, wise priests, and scenes of painful devotion.[2] Sensing the novel's remoteness from her life, Emily looked forward to discussing it with Susan: "we must find out if some things contained therein are true, and if they are, what you and me are coming to!" The statement suggests she saw her reading as a kind of fieldwork, something experimental.

Another and more appealing British novelist, Dinah Craik, got a much fuller response from Emily, who seems to have paid extremely close attention to the character of Rachel Armstrong, a wronged woman in *The Head of the Family*. Of humble birth, Rachel is drawn to a plausible rogue who reads poems to her, inspires her with a life-changing vision of high culture, marries her in a suspiciously private ceremony, and vanishes after committing her to secrecy. Unaware that she has been in effect seduced and abandoned, she remains tensely, exquisitely, faithful, but with episodes of insanity. Someone asks her if the man who revealed the world of books to her had been her master (meaning teacher). " 'My master?' The proud woman's head was raised, then sunk again humbly, even smilingly. 'Yes, he was my master.' "

---

2. In *Lady-Bird*, a later novel by Fullerton focusing on a well-to-do Catholic circle in Lancashire, the mismated heroine embraces a life of painful service. Reading the book while pursuing Susan, Austin vehemently urged her not to read it, as if fearful it might influence her: " 'Twas to me a story full of only wretchedness & misery . . . of brightest hopes blasted—of mortal lives wasted—of true hearts seperated [*sic*]."

In April 1852, Emily named this novel and *Olive,* Craik's pioneering treatment of the life of a woman artist, as books she planned to read. If she read the latter work, as seems likely, what she found (as in *Jane Eyre*) was a kind of model for her own developing life. The heroine, Olive Rothesay, born with a slightly deformed spine, passes through a Calvinist upbringing (sympathetically presented) and develops "precocious yearnings after the infinite." When she realizes she is likely to remain unmarried, she "has a thought almost like terror. Though fated to live unloved, she could not keep herself from loving." Her solution: "Woman as I am, I will dare all things—endure all things. Let me be an artist!" Craik's distinction was to work out, always *within* the Victorian framework, the steps by which a gifted but handicapped single woman could make herself "into a self-dependent human soul" and claim "life's greatnesses" in place of its "sweetnesses." As we shall see, the novel's key junctures show an arresting congruence with certain phases of Dickinson's life in the late 1850s and early 1860s.

The most immediately inspiring book Dickinson read in her early twenties was *Reveries of a Bachelor* by Ik. Marvel, pseudonym of Donald Grant Mitchell. Published in fall 1850, this cycle of delicate and wistful essays was one of the winter's popular and critical successes; by February 22, when Vinnie finished it, Emily had no doubt devoured it. The book presented the ardent memories and daydreams of a cultivated bachelor, whose life is defined by a succession of unconsummated desires. The pattern is set by the opening three-part reverie on marriage—"Smoke," "Blaze," and "Ashes." In "Smoke" the bachelor thinks of all the reasons not to marry. In "Blaze" his imagination takes fire and he longingly pictures the joys of wedded life. In "Ashes" the burning log he is staring at crumbles and he imagines the illness and death of the wife he might have had and tearfully reaffirms his single state.

The premise of *Reveries* is that, since nothing is as real as "thought and passion," our essential human truth is expressed by our fantasies, not our acts. For Dickinson, the book reinforced the lesson of *Picciola,* transforming the cultivation of sentiment into a very serious business. Austin was so impressed that when he named the books he kept at his side in fall 1851, "Bachelor's Reveries" headed the list. His copy, now at Yale, has several types of vertical lines penciled in the margin. Those made by Emily remind one of her poetic account of a book given her by a friend "Whose Pencil – here and there – / Had notched the place that pleased Him" (Fr640). "Notch" is perfect for the short, neat, emphatic marks she chiseled next to admired passages: "Noon in the country is very still: the birds do not sing: the workmen are not in the field." "The great Now, so quick, so broad, so fleeting, is yours;—in an hour it will belong to the Eternity of the Past." We find the same notch beside a passage contrasting men and women without religion ("A woman without that anchor which they call Faith, is adrift, and a-wreck!"). In February 1852 Dickinson commented on the "exquisite writing" of Marvel's "great" book. It was the first time she is known to have praised a writer's style in this way.

The young woman's enjoyment of *Reveries* was closely tied to her new friendship with Susan Gilbert and the "pleasant musings" they enjoyed together. "If you were only here," wrote Emily, "we would have a 'Reverie' after the form of 'Ik Marvel.'" It would be "just as charming as of that lonely Bachelor, smoking his cigar – and it would be far more profitable as 'Marvel' *only* marvelled, and you and I would *try* to make a little destiny to have for our own." The passage shows how consciously she adapted the cigar-puffing bachelor to her own needs. *Her*, or rather her and Susan's, reveries would not be solitary, resigned, and issueless but companionable and productive, pointing to a possible future. Yet Marvel was on the right track: unlike Lady Fullerton, who crushed desire, he knew how to "interpret these lives of ours." Perhaps that was because he took for granted that daydreams, friendship, and writing flowered together, thus anticipating Dickinson's creative practice of 1859, when poem after poem was sent to Sue. These poems, like her reveries, arose in part from an insistence on making Susan their intimate participant. Yet both were almost certainly hers alone.

One reason Emily turned to Susan was that Abiah Root could no longer be a partner in reveries *à deux*. "You are growing wiser than I am, and nipping in the bud fancies which I let blossom," Emily wrote in late 1850. Leaving Abiah to hug the shore, Emily chose "to buffet the sea – I can count the bitter wrecks here in these pleasant waters, and hear the murmuring winds, but Oh I *love* the *danger!*" Once, after another of

Abiah's abrupt arrivals and departures, Emily voiced her dissatisfaction with these "brief imperfect meetings." Her idea had been that they would "sit together and talk of what we were, and what we *are* and may be – with the shutters *closed,* dear Abiah and the balmiest little breeze stealing in . . . I *love* those little fancies." Perhaps such moments were what grown-up Abiah wished to avoid. In August 1851 and again in January 1852 she repeated her 1848 performance in South Hadley by quietly leaving town, defeating Emily's plan for a heart-to-heart chat. The evasive act did not go unnoticed. As the Dickinson sisters sat with their sewing, Vinnie would "drop her work, and say in much perplexity 'I dont know what to make of Abiah.' " What did friendship mean if it didn't include the sharing of fancies?

Her Little Whip

A year or two after Marvel's follow-up book, *Dream Life: A Fable of the Seasons,* disappointed his admirers, Emily included, her father unloaded some of his antediluvian literary opinions, in the process giving her

> quite a trimming about "Uncle Tom" and "Charles Dickens" and these "modern Literati" who he says are *nothing,* compared to past generations, who flourished when *he was a boy.* Then he said there were "somebody's *rev-e-ries*" he did'nt know whose they were, that he thought were very ridiculous, so I'm quite in disgrace at present.

Instead of contesting these judgments, Emily bethought herself of Austin's haughtiness—"that 'pinnacle' on which you always mount, when anybody insults you." This proved "a comfort," especially now that Father had "made up his mind that its pretty much all *real life.*" "Fathers real life and *mine,*" she wrote, "sometimes come into collision, but as yet, escape unhurt!" For many reasons, a life of not putting fancy to the test, of dignified evasion in the manner of *Picciola* and *Reveries,* was becoming the obvious choice.

When Edward was in one of his dark moods, the Dickinson home lay under a pall and his daughters went on tiptoe, even in their private remarks. After visitors kept him from a lecture, Vinnie wrote in her diary, "Bowdoin, Thompson took supper here. Father is _____ *Wanted* to *hear* Mr [Henry Ward] *Beecher*." Other entries read, "*A Storm arose* in the house" and "Father at home '*Sick*.'" To Austin, Vinnie confided that home had become "a gloomy place" with "very black" clouds. Some of Emily's letters reinforce the impression, yet the pleasure with which she sketched Edward's angularities shows how unoppressed she felt. There was a definite margin of freedom and trust: when an eagerly awaited letter from Austin arrived, Father didn't insist on hearing the parts she preferred not to read aloud. In spite of everything, she was certain home was "a holy thing," a "bit of Eden," and that "nothing of doubt or distrust can enter its blessed portals."

On the whole, Emily was comfortable with her family's sharp contradictions—the warmth and the frigidity, the freedom and the restrictiveness. This was her native briar patch, and no matter how much Father scorned the life of the imagination, she continued to look up to him as preeminent among men. When a fire broke out on the Common, he and the sheriff "took charge" and saved the town. When the Northern Lights appeared, he got everyone's attention with "a violent church bell ringing." When he stepped out with his pantaloons casually tucked in his boots, she didn't "think 'negligé' quite becoming to so mighty a man."

The worst thing Father did was to give the horse "a 'basteing' occasionally." Writing Austin in 1852, Vinnie paused for the late-breaking news: "Oh! dear! Father is killing the horse . . . whipping him because he did'nt look quite '*umble*' enough. . . . Emilie is screaming to the top of her voice. She's so vexed about it." This, the poet's angriest known outburst, shows how disturbed she could be by the infliction of pain. Yet she, too, was fond of a certain punitive ritual. Anticipating Susan's return to Amherst, she described herself as sitting "here with my little whip, cracking the time away, till not an hour is left of it." The whip was her pen, her quick mind, and what she was hurrying was time itself. Missing Austin, she ordered the days to "flee away – 'lest with a whip of *scorpions* I overtake your lingering!'" The dragging weeks, days, hours drove her mad with impatience. "I'll punish *them*," she wrote Jane Humphrey when she was expected; "you know they ought to be whipped."

Her Little Gate Flies Open to See Her Coming Home

Shortly before her twentieth birthday, Dickinson attended an exhibition of the college Eclectic Society. Vinnie, pretty and popular, was escorted by a young man whose oration, "The Past," appears on that evening's printed program. Emily, her mind apparently racing, sat with Ebenezer and Sabra Snell, a staid faculty couple.

As she listened to the young men's speeches, she jotted on her program the passages that caught her ear. From John E. Sanford's oration on the most unsavory figure (to date) in American politics, she copied a bold judgment and a neat antithesis: "Aaron Burr was undoubtedly a remarkable man" and "An avowed rather than disguised rascal." As the evening wore on, it was not ideas as such that she noted but resonant and well-turned passages, some of which touched her private concerns:

> Concentration gives intensity . . .
>
> The brightest luminaries in the "galaxy of human geniuses – "
>
> The majesty of his manhood gone –
>
> He stands like a tree stripped of the foliage of self esteem & torn by the blast of self reproach –
>
> Grateful as the distant echoes of evening bells He hears the voice from behind the vail which
>
> "Pleasant but Mournful to the Soul – "

Back home, she wrote a cryptic memorandum that was later erased, though ineffectively: ". . . This night is long to be remembered. New things have happened. 'The crooked is made straight.' I am confided in by one – and *despised* by an *other*! and another still!" This, Dickinson's only known diarylike record of an event, seems to mark a stage in the crystallization of her odd position in the tightly organized college town. What is striking is that even though she learns she is "despised," she neither registers self-pity nor tries to justify herself. Instead, she builds up the drama of her situation.

A contemporaneous letter confessing she is no longer friends with Abby Wood hints at the identity of one despiser. They took "different views of life," Emily wrote Abiah, and would probably "disagree" if they saw more of one another. Unlike Abby, a woman now, Emily still loved "to be a child." Just how far her fondness for this old friend had "drooped" became apparent at the Sweetsers' annual after-dinner Thanksgiving gathering in 1851, when she left the room as Abby sang.

The record of Emily's social activities during the year and a half following the evening of speeches is exceptionally well documented. On New Year's, 1851, Vinnie was given a diary, and although its minuscule size ruled out much detail (which wouldn't have suited her anyway), her social notes illuminate her sister's daily life. Austin's year in Boston teaching school called forth an all but weekly letter from Emily and many shorter notes from Vinnie. Letters also went to Baltimore, where Susan Gilbert, Emily's last best friend, was making her own experiment of a year's schoolteaching. These two absences caused so much ink to flow that the poet's extant letters from June 1851 through June 1852 make as thick a pile as her first nine years of correspondence. All these (and other) materials permit an assured assessment of the basic direction of her social life, which grew in intensity as it decreased in scope.

The one organized group she belonged to was a reading club, a select literary circle of young unmarried men and women that met on Tuesday and Friday evenings. Vinnie recorded attending eleven times, from March 21 to July 25, the final meeting. That Emily also went, though probably less regularly, we learn from two of her letters to Austin. Once, after a Tuesday gathering that Vinnie "did not enjoy . . . *at all*," Emily Fowler spent a morning at the Dickinson house "reading Shakespeare," possibly to encourage the sisters' attendance. Fowler, an organizer, thought of the group as the "Shakespeare Club." Once, as she recalled decades later, when a young man proposed inking out the bawdy speeches in everyone's copies, Dickinson "took her departure, saying, 'There's nothing wicked in Shakespeare, and if there is I don't want to know it' "—a speech that represents a decidedly ambiguous attack on censorship. This was probably the session Vinnie didn't like *at all*.

Dickinson would not be ready for Shakespeare till the mid-1860s, when she found the treatment of passion in *Antony and Cleopatra* and *Othello* of compelling interest. Prior to that, there is little or no evidence of enthusiasm. Two days after the morning reading with Fowler, she complained that the club "seems lonely – perhaps it weeps for you." The next week she told him that after they finished reading, Fowler's brother put in an appearance "and we broke up with a *dance*," following which the tutors escorted the women home. "We *enjoy that*!" she added—her most emphatic expression of interest. "Pleasant time," says her sister's diary.

A kind of daily telegraph from the mid-nineteenth century to our time, this diary taps out Amherst's mundane social rhythms for us. The chief activity, "calling," absorbed so much of Vinnie's time her parents repeatedly tried to rein her in. Becoming, in Emily's words, "*perter* and *more* pert day by day," she once made an unapproved day trip to Ware with her main beau for the year, William Howland. But Vinnie didn't need to leave Amherst to keep busy and stimulated. In the first eight months of the year, her diary records a total of thirty-five social interactions with Susan Gilbert. Many of these probably involved Emily, particularly when Susan and her sister Martha came calling. For the year as a whole, Vinnie recorded a single quarrel with her sister: "offended Emily [over?] dress."

Omitting a trip to Boston, we know of thirteen times the Dickinson sisters jointly "called," "walked," "went out," "rode," or "rode horseback" (sidesaddle?), or together attended a concert or "Freshman levee" or group excursion to Montague or Holyoke. In only four diary entries do we see Emily stepping out without her sister: on March 5 "Emilie & Austin were from home," on the twenty-fourth "Joseph [Lyman] & Emilie went to walk," on September 8 "Emily rode with Mr Leavitt,"[3]

---

3. Twenty-seven-year-old Thomas H. Leavitt, an accountant and a member of Boston's Bowdoin Street Church, boarded with Matthew F. Wood, Loring Norcross's business partner, at 22 McLean Street, across from the Norcross home.

and on the evening of December 16 she visited the Kelloggs, neighbors to the south. Of course, it wasn't Vinnie's intention to track her sister's movements. After the sugaring expedition to Montague on March 25, she did not bother noting that her friend Joseph Lyman was "with Emily a good deal," as a letter of his reveals. Still, Emily's own letters add surprisingly few outings to the list—the prize speeches by the graduating Seniors, the commencement address on imagination by Henry Ward Beecher, a call one June evening on Susan Gilbert and Emily Fowler. The tally doesn't come to much for a twenty-year-old residing in a socially active village.

The pressure to stay home came from both without and within. After making her summer evening call on Gilbert and Fowler, Emily returned at nine o'clock to find "Father in great agitation at my protracted stay – and mother and Vinnie in tears, for fear that he would kill me." In spite of her comic exaggeration, she found Father's anxieties as infectious as they were insistent. Writing to Jane Humphrey the next year, Emily said that "when some pleasant friend invites me to pass a week with her, I look at my father and mother and Vinnie, and all my friends, and I say no – no, cant leave them, what if they die when I'm gone." Again, notwithstanding the humor, we shouldn't underestimate or dismiss her fear: the paternal worries about eternal separation and what might happen when the women left home had taken effect.

Staying home from group events had in fact become an open preference. For unexplained reasons, she skipped a pleasant excursion to nearby Pelham Springs and a couple of exhibitions. She wrote letter after letter on Sunday mornings or afternoons when her mother, father, and sister were hearing Reverend Colton's sermons, a tiresome ordeal now for her and Austin. "They will all go but me, to the usual meeting-house, to hear the usual sermon; the inclemency of the storm so kindly detaining me; and as I sit here Susie, alone with the winds and you, I have the old *king feeling*." Thanks to her "*slender constitution*," she was excused from attending in bad weather. One beautiful spring day she "bought the privilege" of skipping afternoon meeting by staying in church to Communion.

Emily's view of the social rituals Vinnie loved was that "a constant interchange *wastes tho't* and feeling, and we are then obliged to *repair* and *renew* – there is'nt the *brimfull* feeling"—cousin of the old "*king feeling.*" All the same, she loved seeing the chosen few and thinking about them in their absence; indeed, the point of staying home alone was partly to commune more intensely over a distance. A penciled note sent to Susan decades later sums up this imaginative intensity: "To the faithful Absence is condensed presence – To others, but there *are* no others – " All the same, she was uneasy about her brother's antisocial potential, and when he lived in a boardinghouse in Boston, she and Vinnie urged him to spend time with friends, fearing that isolation would "make an ascetic" of him.

Dickinson could not always count on the self-possession that carries one through embarrassments. One cold March evening, when Father was rheumatic and making a bear of himself in the sitting room, she found herself trapped between his command "not to stand at the door" (owing to drafts[4]) and a male caller's reluctance to step inside. When the contretemps was over, she returned to the kitchen, where Mother and Vinnie were "making most desperate efforts to control themselves." Then two more young men called and she went back to the sitting room and struggled to keep the talk alive as Father stiffly presided. Her trite observation about the weather was greeted with nervous and "*wonderful unanimity,*" and then she came out with the absurd statement that last Sunday's preacher bore a "strong resemblance" to evangelist George Whitefield—of the previous century. "Oh such a look as I got from my rheumatic sire," she wrote her brother. Capping the incongruities, in walked Father's unstylish cousin from Hadley, Thankful Smith, wrapped in "the furs and robes of her ancestors." Emily wanted to "shrink away into primeval nothingness." Not until Father and Thankful retired to the kitchen did she, Vinnie, and the young men enjoy themselves.

---

4. According to Joseph and Laura Lyman's *Philosophy of House-Keeping* (1867), "a column of air that can pass through the key-hole of a door upon a person sitting in a warm room will often lay the foundation of a disease which may result in death."

This account of her embarrassment is full of revelations about the inner workings of the Dickinson household and the domestic sources of Emily's liveliest writing. The half-choked laughter in the kitchen makes audible the nervous accommodations Mother and Vinnie made to the stiff patriarchal back they lived with. This situation encouraged Emily to spin (and of course embroider) her own amusing narratives of such episodes, her writing being fed by the stifled glee of the household women who *couldn't* write. The scene helps explain the poet's fondness for grotesque fun, even at her own expense: for her, good jokes and good writing had to do with a certain *absence* of competent social dignity.

Such considerations shed light on her persistent uneasiness with Emily Fowler. Not only was this older friend said to be "the most beautiful woman who ever went out of Amherst," but she had the public assurance Dickinson lacked. Coached from an early age by her able mother (Noah Webster's daughter), she acquitted herself with aplomb at public exams. When her bosom friend, Olivia Coleman, lay dying in fall 1847, she traveled alone to Princeton to be with her—a mission that would have been beyond Dickinson. Indeed, Fowler rather imposed herself: in 1873, writing George Eliot no less, she let it be known she was a member "by birth and position . . . of what has been playfully called 'the brahmin' caste of New England." One cannot imagine Dickinson making such a boast while approaching an admired eminence.

When Fowler's life took a painful turn, Dickinson felt a deep but complicated pity, telling Austin in fall 1851 that their beautiful friend had never "seemed more sincere." Her family home was breaking up as her brothers matured and left, and her unsympathetic father did not approve of her fiancé, Francis Andrew March, a brilliant Amherst graduate just starting out on Wall Street. That winter March's lungs hemorrhaged and he had to sail south, abandoning his partnership and releasing Emily Fowler from their engagement. Dickinson followed the story with deep interest, informing Austin in February that the sick man had reached "Havana – and writes encouragingly . . . Emily [Fowler] has much to make her sad – I wonder how she endures all her numberless trials." To Fowler, Dickinson overflowed with sympathy and solace, always on the assumption she would keep faith with her menaced lover. In May the poet wanted "very much to hear how Mr M is now . . . it's a good many weeks since I hav[e] known anything of him. . . . I shall pray for him, and for you, and for your home on earth, which will be *next* the one in heaven."[5] The home in heaven comes up in another letter as well: "dont weep, for you will both be so happy, where 'sorrow cannot come.' "

What Dickinson didn't know was that Fowler's father preferred a rival, and that Fowler was not averse. On March 12 this parent sent a warm invitation to Gordon L. Ford, her ex-fiancé's former—and wealthy—partner: "We should *all of us* be glad to see you" (italics added). At month's end the poet innocently noted that Ford was in town and had come calling with Emily. The next year Vinnie could hardly believe it when Fowler chose to forget her recovering ex-fiancé[6] and marry the new man. Dickinson was respectful and congratulatory, but privately she called him "a popinjay."

Beautiful, cultured, poised, saved—one of Mark Twain's Christians holding four aces—Emily Fowler Ford was not the kind of person one would expect Dickinson to warm to. But before the pretense of intimacy ended, no one brought out the poet's precious and unreal side more than she. According to Vinnie's diary, she called on the family at least eighteen times in 1851. Of the poet's ten notes or letters sent locally to her, all but three explain why it is not possible to make a reciprocal visit. Once, presenting her latest excuse, she used a piece of paper only two and a half inches wide to announce her resolve to pay many visits and "stay a long while." The real message would seem to be: anxious avoidance.

The most interesting of these notes must be reproduced in its entirety:

---

5. Years later, to avoid embarrassment, Fowler replaced "M" with "Ford" in the copy she made for the 1894 *Letters*. In 1958 this doctored version entered the Harvard University Press edition of Dickinson's letters, where it was dated spring 1854, consistent with the misrepresentation. The true date is soon after May 10, 1852, when Vinnie noted that Fowler was gone for the summer.

6. March went on to a long and distinguished career as professor of English at Lafayette College. An early proponent of the teaching of Old English and the philological (word-by-word) approach to modern literatures, he became president of the Modern Language Association in 1892, succeeding James Russell Lowell.

Thursday morn

Dear Emily,

I cant come in this morning, because I am so cold, but you will know I am here – ringing the big front door bell, and leaving a note for you.

Oh I *want* to come in, I have a great mind *now* to follow little Jane into your warm sitting room; are you there, dear Emily?

No, I resist temptation, and run away from the door just as fast as my feet will carry me, lest if I once come in, I shall grow so happy, *happy,* that I shall stay there *always,* and never go home at all! You will have read this quite, by the time I reach the office, and you cant think how fast I run!

Aff[ectionately]

Emily

P.S. I have just shot past the corner, and now all the wayside houses, and the little gate flies open to see me coming home!

In this fantastically ingenious concoction, Dickinson describes herself as present within the message, and then as running home while the recipient reads it, finally entering the gate as the postscript is read. Fleet-footed Emily professes a wish to stay, but the speed with which she heads north past the intersection of Main and West Streets reveals her true desire. And then her gate flies open of its own accord to welcome her.

The note was written in ink on a minuscule piece of paper that had been scissored and torn down to size, then folded to make four sides or pages, one of which was reserved for the recipient's name. That the postscript neatly fills the last bit of open space on the third written page shows how perfectly the apparent spontaneity had been worked out in advance.

One guesses what Emily Fowler made of this note from her observation that the poet "was exquisitely neat and careful in her dress." The lesson for biographers is that its deviser was as well defended as the home her parents had created, and that we are going to need all our wits—and more—to get inside that automatic gate.

Glycerine Taken Internally

Vinnie's diary and Emily's letters for 1851 often speak of ailing health and consultations with Dr. John Milton Brewster, who "fussed" over the sisters to no avail. "We work and go out and have company," Emily wrote about the time she and Vinnie were taken to Greenfield for a second professional opinion, "but neither of us are well." Beneath her self-deprecating humor, as when she likened herself to small summer apples or mere "*skin and bones,*" was a detectable anxiety about her thinness. It was decided to seek advice in Boston, and a trip was planned for July. When it was mysteriously canceled at the last minute, she let her brother know how "discouraged" the sisters were about their health and how much they had counted on seeing Aunt Lavinia's homeopath, Dr. William Wesselhoeft.

The trip finally came off in September. There was a brief stop in Worcester to see Uncle William (whose wife, Eliza, had died July 11), followed by two weeks with Loring and Lavinia Norcross. The last time Emily had gone to Boston to shake off a cough and "bad feelings," 1846, she had visited Bunker Hill, the State House, and Mount Auburn Cemetery, where she got her first sight of a modern parklike burial ground. She had taken in concerts, a horticultural exhibition, and a "Chinese Museum"'s thrilling spectacle of two reformed opium addicts ("There is something peculiarly interesting to me in their self *denial*," the fifteen-year-old had noted). Now, showing much less interest in the urban scene, she urged Austin not to make "so many plans for our pleasure and happiness." There were calls paid and received and trips to an ice-cream saloon and a visit to the school where her brother taught, but there is no evidence she accompanied Vinnie to some concerts or a performance of *Othello*. After returning to Amherst, Emily claimed the two of them were "rich in disdain for Bostonians and Boston," but this was a half-truth, as Austin noted: Vinnie had "enjoyed herself, as she always does among strangers," whereas "Emily became confirmed in her opinion of the hollowness & awfulness of the *world*." The one detail she recalled years later was a tree near the Norcross home on McLean Street "whose leaves went topsy-turvy . . . and showed an ashen side," symbolic of "fright."

Wesselhoeft was consulted and his remedy faithfully taken back home, but to no avail. Fortunately, the day before leaving Boston, Vinnie felt sufficiently "indisposed" she sought a second opinion from a regular doctor—"called at Dr Jackson's"—and he prescribed glycerine. This physician has been identified as Dr. James Jackson (1777–1867), a professor of medicine at Harvard and long recognized as far away as Amherst as an expert in "pulmonary difficulties." His basic advice for sufferers from phthisis (tuberculosis) in *Letters to a Young Physician* was to eat well and exercise in the open air; "working in a garden would suit some persons."

As for glycerine, in 1849 the *Boston Medical and Surgical Journal* informed physicians that "this new and elegant article" was "beginning to have a reputation" for treating various skin complaints, and that a Mr. Burnett on Tremont Row carried an especially pure stock. Then a second use for glycerine was found when taken internally: it soothed or suppressed the dry cough caused by consumption. However, the medical journals did not report this use until four years after Vinnie's session with Jackson. One of two inferences is in order: either both sisters had a skin problem or the doctor was prescribing for coughs ahead of standard protocols. The first hypothesis may be dismissed: not only is there no positive evidence, but admiring comments on the poet's fine, unwrinkled skin suggest it wasn't unduly dry. Norbert Hirschhorn is surely right in arguing that, like her Mount Holyoke roommate and so many others (see Appendix 3), Dickinson had pulmonary tuberculosis, two of her symptoms being weight loss and a cough.

That fall, Edward informed Austin that Emily was "better than for *years,* since she returned from Boston," and Vinnie agreed, describing her as "very much improved. She has really grown *fat,* if youll believe it. I am very strict with her & I shouldn't wonder if she should come out bright some time after all." Emily herself found the glycerine so helpful she had her brother refill the prescription again and again over the next two and a half years, often sending him the old "vial" or "bottle." The druggist who filled it was the one recommended by the medical journal.

Although the disease evidently went into remission, Vinnie's prediction proved too rosy. In January 1852, after Abiah left town without a farewell, Emily offered a pathetic inducement for next time by promising to "try to get stout and well before you come again." That she continued to get her vial filled during the next few years suggests that her cough persisted and she remained less than "stout." It would appear that the mysterious wasting disease that killed so many was a constant thorn in her side, and in her mind as well.

Insolvency

Another pressing question is how much the poet knew about Uncle Loring's bankruptcy, a disaster so well covered up it is not mentioned in any extant family letter. We have many reasons for wanting to know: she was closer to Loring's family than to all her other relatives, the proceedings apparently thwarted her summer 1851 trip to Boston, and the vocabulary of insolvency would be unusually salient in her poetry.

As the assessed valuation of Norcross and Wood slowly rose to a modest $10,000, the firm's indebtedness shot up to $67,000, finally persuading the partners to call it quits in 1846. The state's insolvency statute provided for three creditors' meetings followed by a proportional distribution and a discharge from debt. At Norcross and Wood's third meeting, however, some of the biggest creditors opposed settlement, and the partnership muddled on for four years. Then, in early July 1851, it was announced in the *Boston Daily Advertiser* that the fourth meeting would take place on the twenty-second. As Loring readied a petition for the allowance "which the law allows" ($3 per family member) and in other ways prepared for his ordeal, his nieces' visit had to be called off. The first official notice of the meeting was published July 8. Vinnie's diary for July 10 says, "Heavy disappointment this morning *can not* go to Boston cried some." The obscure letter Emily wrote Austin July 13 doesn't make clear whether she was given the reason for the abrupt cancellation.

Because of the trust established by Joel Norcross, Loring's wife's inheritance could not be seized and the family probably lived in comfort, in spite of having to sell their furniture. As a precaution, two weeks before the final creditors' meeting, held January 22, 1852, Lavinia drew up a will leaving her paternal estate in trust for her two daughters. That she made Loring the *sole* trustee, empowering him to manage the estate and appropriate the income, tells us she wished to stand by her besieged husband as well as protect her daughters. It causes a twinge, though, to note that the will is in his hand.

Did anyone talk about Loring's still unsettled bankruptcy during Emily and Vinnie's September visit? Perhaps not, seeing that money problems were not the province of young ladies. After Austin paid the sisters' bills in Boston, Emily followed up her assurance that he would be reimbursed with an apology, knowing he didn't "like to have us ever speak of such things." Even Aunt Lavinia, once so outspoken and indiscreet, had apparently learned not to "speak." Three times in 1852 and 1853 Vinnie complained about her silence to Austin: "What does it mean?" "Tell her I'm quite impatient." "I think its very strange indeed." No answers are forthcoming, but we may surmise the Norcross family was undergoing severe strains and that much was not explained to the Dickinson sisters.

And yet, if Loring's financial mire was kept from the poet, she was obviously too keen and intuitive not to catch wind of it, the result probably being what is usual in such cases—a mystified version of events. Is it only coincidence that, soon after Loring's last session with his creditors in January 1852, Dickinson composed the ebullient line "*Insolvency, sublime!*" (Fr2[B]), which, one can't help noticing, denies the obvious?

With her unparalleled gifts of language and impassioned reverie, Dickinson was mapping out the private domains of the imagination. This was her choice, based in part on an aversion to what Austin called "the hollowness & awfulness of the *world*." But also, she had little choice, the *world* having been closed to her in dozens of ways.

Susan Gilbert

After her death, when the poet's sister-in-law jotted down some notes for a possible essay on her, the second topic on the list was "Affection her strength" (the first being "Flowers love of"). The phrase was exactly right, affection being a source of tremendous personal strength for the poet, a partial solution of the problem of life. Her love was generous, but it was also exacting and uncompromising, the expression of a powerful ego demanding that friendship live up to a high standard. Her sister-in-law understood this well, having been for thirty-five years one of the poet's select intimates. The great irony is that this special lifelong friend—a motherless orphan who grew up to be an exceptionally able, informed, and socially ambitious woman—had much in common with Emily Fowler.

Susan Gilbert was born December 19, 1830, nine days after the poet. The youngest of seven children, she, too, came from established Connecticut Valley forebears: her father's father, Colonel Eliel Gilbert, had owned a tavern (meaning a hotel), was elected six times to the General Court, and was said to have had the first piano in Greenfield. His son Thomas, Susan's father, a lesser version of the Colonel, went for one term to the state legislature and kept a series of taverns in Greenfield, Deerfield, and Amherst. In later years he was remembered as a drunkard and his daughter's social aspirations were sometimes explained as compensating for a sense of family disgrace. One reason not to accept this pat explanation is that Susan had several well-educated and prosperous aunts, uncles, and older brothers to admire and emulate.[7] The poet's sister-in-law may have been arrogant and snobbish, but she was no arriviste.

Because Susan was only six when her consumptive mother died, her mother's face faded from memory as the girl grew up. What didn't fade was the sense of maternal piety—a "silent, though powerful influence," in the words of the orphaned daughter, who cherished the conviction that Harriet Arms Gilbert had been "a *christian*" and that a "happy reunion in Heaven" awaited her converted offspring. All her life Susan

---

7. Her uncle Ebenezer White Arms graduated from Yale and became a successful lawyer in Aurora, New York. Her two older brothers helped found Grand Haven, Michigan, and made fortunes in timber and lake shipping. By 1870 each was worth well over $100,000, and one was a regent of the University of Michigan.

sporadically insisted on certain orthodox prohibitions, her lips suddenly pursing at Sabbath letter-writing or visiting. After attending her first play in Baltimore in 1851, she felt "disgusted with the Theatre." In 1878, seeing *Risks, or, Insure Your Life,* she found "the fun a little too coarse for my taste." She could be quite indignant about low décolletages.

Fully orphaned by her father's death in 1841, she and her next older sister, Martha, were brought up by Sophia Van Vranken, a jovial maternal aunt living in Geneva, New York. Sophia's husband, a graduate of Union College, evidently wanted Susan to develop her mind, as she was sent in 1846–1847 to Amherst Academy, where she took the Classical course (Emily, in her last year, was in the English course). In 1848–1849 and 1849–1850 Susan went on to the best girls' school west of Troy, Utica Female Academy, which boasted a stately Ionic portico and offered instruction in everything from Latin and "Technology" to flower painting and guitar. Unlike Amherst's shaky academy, Utica had a permanent and proven director, Miss Jane E. Kelly, who emphasized teacher training. A sentence Susan or her friend Kate Scott wrote in a textbook they shared—"Send your imagination *out* upon the *wing*"—may catch the tone of Kelly's instruction. But Susan's early letters are less distinguished for qualities of flight than for polish and self-possession. Her great subject was mathematics, she was always concerned with improving her mind, and when an important new book came out, like the translation of Jean Paul's *Titan* in 1862, she would get hold of a copy and wade in. Emily rarely did this.

In 1848, the year the first women's rights convention was held at nearby Seneca Falls, Kelly presented Susan with a copy of Tennyson's curious and often mocking poem about an imaginary university founded by and for women, *The Princess.* The passages the girl chose to mark show how much the position of women was on her mind: "You men have done it: how I hate you all!" and "play the slave to gain the tyranny" and "the woman is the better man." Here and there she underlined key phrases, as in "tricks, which make us <u>toys of men</u>" or "unfurl the maiden banner of <u>our rights</u>." In the end, however, after the university is wrecked by the combined love and guile of men, her marks suggest an acceptance of Tennyson's obviously antifeminist summing-up: "The woman's cause is man's: they rise or sink / Together."

Susan was in her teens when she entered the household of an older married sister, Harriet Cutler, joining sisters Mary and Martha. William, Harriet's husband, was a partner in Amherst's leading mercantile outlet, Sweetser and Cutler, with annual sales of $30,000 in 1843.[8] By all accounts, he was a Bovary-like study in bourgeois respectability—stiff, deliberate, self-satisfied, utterly charmless. Ned Hitchcock never forgot a party at the Cutlers' where the grown-ups sat in the parlor and the children served and William expressed his "impatience at the slowness of my getting the sugar & cream to him!" When the three Dickinson siblings called on the Cutlers on February 27, 1851, Vinnie summed the visit up in one word: "Dreadful!" Once, as Emily sent Austin a report on the Cutlers, she slipped into an imitation of the head of the house: "derive much satisfaction from contemplating my shrewdness – Hope 'Self and wife' will always be so 'uniform' – hope I give no offense." Susan and Martha found it a great trial to be dependent on this man and endure his obsession with feeding fires and adjusting dampers. "I have actually suffocated for the last few days," wrote Martha one spring; "Mr Cutler has the most intense enjoyment in stuffing the stoves and seeing us sweat." Trapped in the furnace, Susan yearned all the more for a home of her own.

In April 1849 the four Gilbert sisters wrote a collective letter to their rich faraway brothers that nicely conveys Susan's exceptional qualities. The three older sisters wrote first, each taking a page or so. Mary said that Martha had once again begun "to *crook*" (slouch). Martha hoped the brothers were pleased with their lamp mat. Harriet talked about home improvements and a local robbery. Following these newsy items, the part composed by eighteen-year-old Susan betrays an obvious wish to stand out: "I can assure you . . . it is not without much agitation, that I attempt a line, after the

---

8. Edward Dickinson was an early informant for the national credit rating agency that in time became Dun and Bradstreet. In 1850, when informants' initials had not yet given way to the safer anonymity of numbers, "E. D." reported that the firm of Luke Sweetser and William and George Cutler "is a no. 1.—money eno."

brilliant effusions of my older sisters." That, along with her name for the Cutler house, "Old Maid's Retreat," shows what sort of teenager she must have been—laceratingly self-conscious, desperate to distinguish herself.

Sister Martha, with her poor posture, was an easier person—gentler, more sympathetic and passive. Even though Susan was the younger of the two, Martha felt she stood "a poor chance following her—everyone seems to think she is the quintessence of perfection." One difference between them was that, while Martha showed no anger, her younger sister was quick to take offense at real or imagined slights; as Dickinson put it years later, "Susan fronts on the Gulf Stream." Ned Hitchcock spent so much time with her at the Cutlers' in 1850 that she badly missed him when he began teaching at Williston Academy: he had been "a great comfort to her of late," "her only true friend." But when he casually addressed a letter to her as "Sue," she was "indignant" at the liberty.

The reason Sue was grateful to Ned was that she had been shattered by a death in the family. On Sunday, July 14, 1850, twenty-five days after giving birth to a daughter in Grand Haven, Michigan, her sister Mary died of "intermittent"—puerperal—fever. Martha had gone west to help nurse her, and since she didn't return until February 1851, Susan had seven months in which to brood over the painful event without her sister's consoling presence. Each Sunday, brutal images of the far-off unseen burial flashed on her "with a painful vividness and reality."

It was in this time of bereavement, with Martha absent, that Emily and Sue became friends. The poet's earliest known message to her, the first of hundreds, dates from the end of February 1851, the day of Martha's long-delayed return to the Cutler home on Amity Street.[9] The letter is affectionate, speaks of kisses, mentions "*sainted* Mary," and in every way assumes a high degree of intimacy. "Dont forget all the little friends who have tried so hard to *be* sisters, when indeed you *were* alone!" writes Emily, obviously thinking of herself. She knows the reunited sisters must be left to themselves after their long separation ("how Sue and

9. Johnson, Leyda, and Hart and Smith mistakenly assign this letter to late 1850 even though Martha had not yet arrived from the West. She does not appear in Vinnie's diary prior to February 27, when the Dickinson siblings called on the Cutlers, an occasion evidently marking Martha's reentry in Amherst's social life.

I will talk," Martha had written) and that her presence would be an "intrusion." But she still intrudes with pen and ink, possessively claiming a small share of the sisters' intimacy and comparing their room to Alice Archer's refuge in Longfellow's *Kavanagh*—"that columbarium [dovecote] lined with warmth, and softness." The comparison suited the writer's home-nurtured fancies, but whether it appealed to the Gilbert sisters, trapped in their brother-in-law's stovelike house, is open to question. And remembering that Sue singled out Ned Hitchcock as "the only one who called on her regularly," we may wonder how she regarded Emily's statement about trying to be a faithful sister.

The sheltered Dickinson siblings did not know what it was to suffer bereavement in their family or to have an insecure footing in the world. Emily and Austin and Susan and Martha were closely involved now, and the entanglements were growing complicated. In December 1850, after a misunderstanding with Susan, Austin was struck by "that unapproachable dignity, that rigid formality," she would abruptly assume. In fall 1851, she let him know how distrustful she was of those not connected "by 'natural ties.' " Insensitive to the disparities in background and outlook, the Dickinsons couldn't help wounding her, and provoking her latent ferocity. Her entry into the family would change it forever.

A Quiet Romance

Before Martha left for Michigan in summer 1850, Austin had not shown a preference for either sister, but once the kinder, gentler one was out of the picture, out for two-thirds of a year, his friendship with the edgy one became transformed. Two weeks after Mary's death, he wrote a note asking Sue to ride with him—ride privately, seeing that she was in mourning. That fall, as the young college graduate conducted a school at Sunderland, a few miles north of Amherst, for one term, the notes and letters multiplied. Presently, he and Sue agreed to signalize their growing closeness by separately and simultaneously eating a chestnut every evening "at the first stroke of the vesper bell." No one knew of this humorous private ritual except, in Austin's words, "the all seeing spirits."

Meanwhile, Vinnie and Emily, feeling neglected, chastised their brother for failing to visit or write. "Come home Naughty Boy!" Emily scolded in a postscript to Vinnie's note, and in a letter of her own reprimanded his neglect and arrogance. After acting like Jupiter, sitting on Mount Olympus and "whittling the lightnings out, and hurling at your relations,"[10] it was time for "Topknot" to lay down his schoolmaster's crown and scepter "and once more a patient child receive reproof." He should also come to the East Hampshire Agricultural Society's first annual Cattle Show—"School masters and Monkeys half price." She ended with a jocular message from Sue, who had apparently just been calling on the Dickinsons: " 'Serve God, and fear the King'! Exit *Sue*!!!" Vaguely echoing Emily's tart advice, Sue's message gave nothing away, least of all the couple's odd digestive celebration of the harvest season.

In November the fall term closed at Sunderland, and Austin returned to Amherst. Continuing to see Sue, he felt a secret and "inward satisfaction" on Thanksgiving when his sisters asked her "family into the circle which had for two or three years been gradually forming." Father fetched her, Austin bided his time as she joined the annual after-dinner gathering at the Sweetsers', and then there was a moment together in the dark—"you know the rest," he wrote her.

The romance was conducted very quietly on both sides. From Geneva, Martha complained about her sister's silence and the lack of news. Since Sue had been seeing Ned Hitchcock when Martha was last in Amherst, Martha naturally connected their names when writing Ned in November. There is no solid evidence that Martha fancied Austin, yet, when the time came for her to return in February, he felt a certain "dread of her," as if some tall explaining, a possible disillusioning, lay ahead. And Emily was also in the dark, not realizing her closest confidants, Sue and Austin, were growing much closer to one another than either could be to her.

---

10. Emily was referring to the hostile letter Austin sent Aunt Elizabeth in fall 1850. Her reply, a fifty-stanza poem completed December 10, complained about his quarrelsome and verbose attempt "to *show me up*" and accused him of wandering in a transcendental fog and surrendering to the power of "*full-orbed* Fancy." The next year, seeking a reconciliation, she promised not "to *insist upon any recollections*, which are not very agreeable."

In good weather Emily liked to talk with Sue on the "broad stone step" where she and Jane Humphrey used to sit. But the developing friendship produced no written traces until June, when Austin left for Boston for another teaching stint. Emily's first letter (composed the day after he left) assured him Sue and Martha were both sorry he had gone. The next communication also failed to distinguish between the sisters: "They miss you very much – they send their 'united loves.' " It looks as if the poet had not been taken into Sue or Austin's confidence, even though she saw "more of Susie than of any other girl."

Suddenly restless, Sue went by herself to New York to visit a friend and attend a Jenny Lind concert. She also began looking for a temporary teaching position, contrary to William Cutler's advice. Her Utica alma mater had a stated policy of providing "suitable testimonials" for former pupils, and presently she landed an appointment at a girls' school in Baltimore. The explanations she offered for this surprising and enterprising move show a typical vagueness and lack of candor (she never explained her choices with any fullness). The job appealed to her "fancy." She supposed she would be "improving [her]self, as well as doing a little good." She was "tired of being so quiet in Amherst." And she wanted the money, mentioned more than once. The chief motives were probably an eagerness to have a go at the larger world and a need to draw back from the entangling Dickinsons.

Mr. and Mrs. Archer's Boarding and Day School for Young Ladies, at 40 Lexington Street and with an enrollment of one hundred thirty, was one of the South's leading female academies. The principal had graduated from West Point; the matron, his wife, was a daughter of Maryland's chief justice; the catalog's two-page list of references was headed by Winfield Scott (the Whig presidential candidate in 1852); and the teaching corps included the harpist Madame Mayre and a "Professor of Dancing." The school's clientele and drawing power are apparent from the 1850 federal census schedule, which lists a Barnard from Mississippi, Poindexters from Louisiana and South Carolina, and two Pennsylvania Sharplesses. After the annual public examination, the local press reported with bland approval that "the analysis of Paradise Lost, and the exercises of the class in Botany, were especially the subject of remark." But there was no Classical course, catalogs said nothing about teacher training, and the science professor also taught penmanship. Compared with the workaday academies of New York and Massachusetts, the school had a conspicuously aristocratic tone. On Sue, the effect was probably to accent her taste for rank and display.

The public institution where Austin was employed could not have been more different. Occupying the second and third stories of a plain brick building, Boston's Endicott School was crammed with nearly four hundred boys and girls, mostly Irish. The young man's job as "usher" (a lower pedagogical rank) seems to have gone unfilled the previous year. Word of the opening must have come from Uncle Loring, who in 1851 was in his first year of service on the Boston School Committee, with an assignment to the Endicott subcommittee. A few months before Austin went to work, the teachers in all six rooms complained that the air was "unsatisfactory to the demands of respiration," being "filled with black dust." A new furnace was approved, but then (after Austin finished his year) it was decided to close the school.

For Austin, classroom teaching was only a temporary job before he committed himself to studying the law. His motives for taking on the children of Massachusetts' often illiterate Irish Catholic population— "the darkened Laddy," as Emily put it, perhaps echoing her brother—are not hard to guess. College graduates often spent a year or two teaching, Austin thought of himself as "fond" of such work, and he saw a public need and felt a sense of duty. But with fifty restless boys in his charge, he found the work more "laborious" than expected, indeed "almost irksome," as he wrote Sue, who taught older girls and was off duty from two in the afternoon.

Writing home, the young man evidently sent an exaggerated account of the disciplinary whippings he administered. His sister's response to these humorously described scenes of punishment was utterly unlike her infuriated protest at Father's "basteing" of a horse. Distinguishing between herself and Mother, who was afraid her son might go too far and injure a boy, Emily wrote Austin she rather hoped he would "kill some – there are so many now, there is no room for the Americans." It was a joke, of course, yet the joke had a serious vein: the Irish were "bad enough in darkness" and she didn't want them to "come to the light," especially through "such a darling medium" as Austin.

This callous nativism seems in line with the program of the American or Know-Nothing Party, which wanted a twenty-one-year waiting period before immigrants could become citizens. Yet we should bear in mind that Emily's father detested this party,[11] and that she herself was already a noncitizen for life. What her violent anti-Irish humor expressed was not a coherent politics but a profound helplessness. As in her harrowing 1850 letter to Joel W. Norcross, she was assuming that nothing she could say or do would take effect. There was a feeling that as long as her brother was away from home, her life and his were at a standstill. She wrote him about the dust falling in his empty room, and how she avoided going there after dark. She wanted to cry at the thought of his missing autumn's grapes. After Father waked her from a dream in which she was about to open a letter from Austin, she spent the day imagining how she would break the seal if one *did* arrive. She feared her brother would suffer from loneliness, or strain his eyes, or that his facial "neuralgia"[12] would worsen. Longing for "this Boston year . . . to perish and flee away, and be forever gone," she sent him the yearning invitation of the Bible's last verse: "the spirit and the bride say *come*."

When she learned he *was* coming for the 1851 Cattle Show, she "put away [her] sewing and [went] out in the yard to think." She may have been cogitating the poem into which her answering letter suddenly bursts, filling the page's remaining free space: "*here* is a little forest whose leaf is ever green, here is a *brighter* garden, where not a frost has been, in its unfading flowers I hear the bright bee hum, prithee, my Brother, into *my* garden come!" One reason she wrote this as prose was that she had no room left for space-eating lines of verse. There was an uncanny and exquisite precision in her act, inviting her brother into her closed space as she neatly filled her paper's boundaries.

---

11. There is no foundation for a scholar's assertion that Austin became "active in the Know-Nothing Party."

12. "At the present day we hear much of a disease called *Neuralgia*," Dr. James Jackson wrote. "This name is applied to any case of severe pain which cannot be traced to inflammation, nor to any organic affection."

To focus on her invitation's innocent eroticism is to miss the larger picture: her life's growing emptiness, her dependence on her tall, superior, active older brother. The more isolated she was, the more she needed him, and vice versa. And the longer he was absent, the more she forgot the impediments between them, particularly his impatience with her play of sentiment. Her first letters after his departure spoke of this, recalling how he "would 'poke fun' at my feelings." Lugubriously evoking their conversations in the barn, she also recalled how scornful he could be: "I suppose I am a fool – you always said I was one." Vinnie seems to have been more tolerant of the sentimentalizing: "every thing goes on at home as usual. Emilie is pensive just now recollections of 'by gones' you know, 'Old un' &c." "Old un" was a pet term for Austin.

This captive fixation was a distinctly Victorian bond, best illustrated by Maggie Tulliver's eager desire to serve her older brother in George Eliot's *The Mill on the Floss*. And just as Maggie's best efforts backfire with the stolid Tom, Emily often overstepped the line. When she sent Austin a flattering report of Father's response to a letter—"applause deafened applause . . . the sun went down in clouds – the moon arose in glory – Alpha Delta, All Hail!"—he said he didn't understand and preferred a "simpler style."[13]

Stung, Emily began her long reply the day the reprimand arrived: "At my old stand again . . . and happy as a queen to know that while I speak those whom I love are listening." She loved being Austin's lifeline home, loved serving up his weekly information and amusement. A passage written when worn out—"you must'nt expect any style. This is truly extempore, Austin – I have no notes in my pocket"—shows how much care she ordinarily took. And her patron was satisfied, mostly, telling Sue that "Emily's letters are to me just about what Mat's are to you—She writes me every week—and always something I like to read."

---

13. This rebuke made an opening for Vinnie, who promptly wrote at greater length than usual: "Emilie has fed you on air so long, that I think a little 'sound common sense' perhaps wouldnt come amiss *Plain english* you *know* such as Father likes." Austin sent Sue a complaint about "a sort of land of Canaan letter" from Emily, who was "too high up to give me any of the monuments on earth."

The great sensation of the day was Jenny Lind, the Swedish soprano. Austin was one of the few not overwhelmed, and when the rest of the family heard her perform her virtuoso repertoire in Northampton— Taubert's "Bird Song," the "Echo Song," "Comin' thro' the Rye"—they too were unimpressed. Emily, responding to "*herself,* and not her music," fancied a longing for home in the singer's eyes. The most interesting object was Edward Dickinson, who held the poet's attention more closely than Lind:

> Father sat all the evening looking *mad,* and *silly,* and yet so much amused you would have *died* a laughing – when the performers bowed, he said "Good evening Sir" – and when they retired, "very well – that will do," it was'nt *sarcasm* exactly, nor it was'nt *disdain,* it was infinitely funnier than either of those virtues, as if old Abraham had come to see the show, and thought it was all very well, but a little excess of *Monkey!*

In Sue's absence, Emily relied a great deal more on Martha Gilbert's quiet companionship. In May 1852 they "had a long, sad talk about [*Sue, and*][14] Michigan, and Life, and our own future, and Mattie cried and I cried, and we had a solemn time." "Michigan" was short for Mary Gilbert Learned's death, observed by Martha, from puerperal fever. "Our own future" meant the young women's chances for love and marriage, sex and death. The next month the two friends had another talk "on the front door stone . . . about life and love, and whispered our childish fancies about such blissful things." Empty as the present was, the future seemed freighted with rapture and danger.

The "childish fancies" passage was sent to Sue. Given the poised and decorous tone of her letters to others, one wonders how she answered Emily's more and more impassioned and confidential manner: "heart-talk blazing on the paper," Marvel's bachelor called it. A phrase sent from Baltimore and quoted by Emily—"*will* you 'love me more if ever you

---

14. Here and elsewhere, words that are bracketed and italicized were erased much later by someone else but are still barely legible.

come home'?"—suggests Sue saw herself as having held back and intended to be more responsive in future. But *could* anyone be sufficiently
responsive to Emily? Even she admitted that " 'eye hath not seen, nor ear
heard, nor can the heart conceive' *my* Susie, whom I love"—*my* Susie
being the imagined one to whom all fancies could be whispered. Except
when Martha was sick, Emily imparted very little news from Amherst
and said nothing about Sue's life in Baltimore, focusing instead on her
own longings and alarms and private symbols. Indeed, she tried to get her
correspondent to write "saintlier, and more like Susie *Spirit*," showing
again that *Emily* Spirit wasn't perfectly suited by the southern mail.

Once, anticipating how Martha and Sue would marry and leave her
behind, Dickinson confessed the mere *"fancy* of ever being so lone" almost made her cry. Then her thoughts turned to death and she let herself imagine that one "of our precious band . . . should pass away." As she
worked out the agonizing scenario, it slipped her mind that her correspondent still wore mourning for a dead sister—that for the real Susie, if
not for Susie *Spirit*, the precious band was already shattered. Emily was
showing the same commanding self-absorption as her brother, who
often proposed to Sue when they were apart that they do the same thing
at exactly the same time: eat a chestnut, read the Amherst paper, and so
forth. These were prosaic versions of what the poet was also aiming at:
sharing, controlling, Sue's inner life.

Ten years later, when Sue had a home, a husband, and a child, and
Emily apparently realized she would always be single, she sent her sister-
in-law a retrospective letter-poem on their opposite fates, "Your riches
taught me poverty" (Fr418A). By that time she had left her " 'Little
Girl'hood" behind and was engaged in a complex and powerful explo-
ration of the tragic life of desire. In the early 1850s, by contrast, many
things conspiring, she let herself dream of a perfect sharing of the life of
fancy with a capable, independent, and imaginative girl. Sue's year-long
absence gave the poet-in-the-making the space to indulge this dream as
she had not done with Abiah Root or Jane Humphrey or Emily Fowler.
When she was supposed to be doing housework, she confessed how she
loved to "hide away from them all; here in dear Susie's bosom." When

others sang a hymn at church, she "made up words and kept singing how I loved you, and you had gone." When Sue wrote about what she had " 'lost and loved' " (parents? sister?), Emily replied, "You wont cry any more, will you, Susie, for my father will be your father, and my home will be your home, and where you go, I will go, and we will lie side by side in the kirkyard." But did it meet Sue's needs to be told to put away her grief and entertain this intense and rather morbid prospect?

When her friend's return was a few weeks away, Emily could no longer put off the question that had been surfacing. Taking a big risk, she proposed that when they were together they have an intimate talk about "those unions . . . by which two lives are one." Did Susie have a "dear fancy, illumining all [her] life"? How did she feel about the act of surrender, from which "we shall not run away . . . but lie still and be happy!" Comparing man to "the mighty sun" and woman to a dependent flower, Emily was bringing out her fear of male sexual dominance and her own potential abjectness. Granted, a bride might be happy for a time, but what if "the man of noon" loses interest in her, and what if she feels she belongs to him forever? Aren't such women doomed to a self-destroying desire?

> They will cry for sunlight, and pine for the burning noon, tho' it scorches them. . . . Oh, Susie, it is dangerous, and it is all too dear, these simple trusting spirits, and the spirits mightier, which we cannot resist! It does so rend me, Susie, the thought of it when it comes, that I tremble lest at sometime I, too, am yielded up.

Emily's terror of being "yielded up," going very deep, was rooted in the extreme power differential between her father and mother, her inner struggle during the revivals that asked her to "give up" everything to the Savior, and her tearful talks with Martha about "Michigan" and what that boded. The fear had been given form by Dinah Craik's *The Head of the Family,* which Emily had mentioned to Sue two months earlier. Drawing impressively on Ovid's story of Clytie's worshipful adoration of the sun god Apollo and her metamorphosis into a flower always turning in his direction, this novel brought Emily's predicament to life in the richly imagined Rachel Armstrong, whose self-transforming love of her deceiver is

> as wild, as daring, as hopeless as Clytie's for the Sun. Until at last the Sun, looking down from his sphere, saw the flower which his beams had wakened into life—saw it, loved it, lifted it up into his heart. And the poor flower would have been content, even if his brightness had scorched it to death, knowing it had lived one hour there.

The flower scorched; the woman abandoned and transformed: the poet had stumbled onto part of her elemental material and was developing it in breathless disclosures to a distant confidante.[15]

Yet the confidante she had been trying to conjure up, Susie *Spirit*, was not the same as Susie *Flesh*, a real human being struggling with difficult conditions. Susie Flesh had to hide the secret courtship from Emily—had to be, not a helpless adoring flower, but a skilled operator looking out for herself. She planned to return to Amherst in July 1852. As the moment of truth approached, Dickinson felt a searing doubt about the reality of her captivating dreams: "will you indeed come home next Saturday, and be my own again, and kiss me as you used to . . . or am I *fancying* so, and dreaming blessed dreams from which the day will wake me? I . . . feel that *now* I must have you – that the expectation . . . makes me feel hot and feverish, and my heart beats so fast." Was it desire that scorched her, or was it the fear of waking up from a seductive reverie? Not knowing, she felt "so funnily" she almost wished "the precious day would'nt come quite so soon, till I could know how to feel, and get my thoughts ready for it." "Why, Susie," she said, "it seems to me as if my absent Lover was coming"—the one desired and feared.

---

15. A central character in the other Craik novel Dickinson may have read that spring, *Olive,* is the unloved wife, Mrs. Rothesay. The novel is partly about rejection—what it is to be "a thing sighed for, snatched, caressed, wearied of, neglected, scorned!"

Part Five

1852 - 1858

> . . . *so you see when you go away, the world looks staringly, and I*
>
> *find I need more vail . . .*

March 12, 1853. Emily Dickinson to Susan Gilbert. Reproduction 156%
original size.

Chapter 13

1852–1854:
A Sheltered Life

It is twelve years since the Dickinsons moved into the large frame house on West Street, and their daily and seasonal routines have thickened into a solid root-mass. Summer and fall, there are peaches, grapes, prizewinning apples, and even figs to be gathered and brought inside. At mealtime, "Graham" bread, made of whole wheat flour and still "smoking" (Emily's word), is carried straight from oven to table. The table itself is moved from the dining room to the warmer sitting room in early November, and soon it is time for New England's annual festival of plenty and careful provisioning and ancestral piety.

Fall is Austin's season. A student at Harvard Law School for three terms, he spends so much time in Amherst he is awarded a degree only after his professors petition on his behalf. When his clothes need washing and mending, he sends them home in a valise, an arrangement insisted on by his mother and sisters, who tuck their finest apples, polished and wrapped, into the clean linen they return. Emily dispatches letter after letter to him, writing with a pencil instead of a pen and always insisting how much she misses him and how she and Father enjoy his uproarious letters. For all that, Father's expression grows so severe his daughters become anxious. One evening, Vinnie tries to amuse him by reading the "spicey" bits from Fanny Fern, the popular madcap columnist who is alternately caustic and demure; Vinnie probably has *Fern Leaves from Fanny's Portfolio* in her hands, the author's first best-seller. Father relaxes, but advises his rushing daughter to pronounce each word fully.

Sometimes Emily is the first one out of bed and downstairs, where she builds and lights the fires and prepares breakfast for the others. In winter these chores would have been performed with little light. If we had been there in the shadows, hearing the clang of cast iron as she threw in the wood and regulated the draft and raised the oven temperature, we would never again think of her as helpless.

Father's Responsibilities

In December 1852 Emily's Brooklyn cousins, the Newmans, lost their father to tuberculosis, their mother having died earlier that year of the disease. The boy named William Dickinson of Worcester as his guardian, but the girls became wards of Edward, the older ones by their own act, the younger ones (Clara and Anna) by order of probate court. In April 1853 he brought all four girls to Amherst with their Irish maid and their father's widowed sister, Hannah Newman Fay. Mrs. Merrill's boardinghouse refused entry to the maid, who had to stay with the Dickinsons till the orphans' new home was ready—the house on the Common that Edward had bought thirteen years earlier from Cousin Nathan.

The Dickinson children did not exactly welcome their pious city cousins. Emily sarcastically remarked that their arrival, along with that of the Sweetser cousins, would "please" Austin, and Vinnie was afraid "the relations will keep close to us as long as we live!" It bothered her to see the orphans "sitting down perfectly passive, waiting Fathers next direction"; it was a "bad thing for him to have that care." Emily's take on the situation was more speculative and self-reflexive, though no less exclusive: "The Newmans seem very pleasant, but they are not *like us*. What makes a few of us so different from others? It's a question I often ask myself."

Inevitably, Mrs. Fay detected the cool, insular temperature and complained about it to Abby Sweetser, who told Harriet Cutler, who told Sue, who carried the ungrateful murmur back to Vinnie. Swelling with outrage, she told Austin she was going to march up to Mrs. Sweetser's and "bring up all past grievances & set them in order before her & see what she'll say for herself . . . her bonnet has bobbed long enough." The manner in which her brother reined in this ferocity speaks volumes about the Dickinson children's sense of entitlement:

> Let the woman talk if it makes her any happier. . . . And that miserable, fretful, old maidish widow [Mrs. Fay], let her alone too. . . . [I]f she barks too loud, & troubles your sleep, tell father & have him inform her her services are no longer needed, and hire some more servicable girl to take charge of those children. We can turn her out of the house any day and she cant say one word.

For Edward, the real problem was Mark Haskell Newman's ill-advised will, with its large and complicated bequests to foreign and domestic missions. More concerned with evangelical soul-saving than with his offspring's worldly interests, Newman left only $25,000, a third of his net worth, to his five orphaned children. Although he provided a second and equal sum for their maintenance and education, they were to get the interest only, the principal reverting to the American Home Missionary Society along with the remainder of his estate. These provisions not only went against Edward's inclination to put one's children first, they saddled him with the conflicting responsibilities of guardian, executor, and trustee. He also had to maintain Newman's partnership agreement for the time being and dispose of his valuable Brooklyn residence, whose large lot, two hundred feet square, ran street to street from Clinton to Vanderbilt Avenue. The estate was more complex than his own, and as an out-of-state attorney he failed to realize that some of the powers granted him by the will were invalid in New York. Quickly selling the Newman house in spring 1853 for $22,000, he learned five years later that he had not provided clear title. To protect himself and the heirs, he had to turn to the Kings County—that is, Brooklyn—Supreme Court (Brooklyn's trial-level court, not an appellate court) to reconstruct the will. In the end, a descendant recalled, the orphans received "a larger allowance for their education" than their father had provided.

A very different set of problems arose in August 1852, when the Reverend Aaron Colton announced his wish to step down from the First Church pulpit. A letter in the papers of the Reverend Samuel C. Bartlett reveals that the poet's father was a key actor in the delicate work of finding the right successor. Bartlett had just returned to New England from Ohio's Western Reserve and was known for his piety, taste, and intelligence; he later became president of Dartmouth College. In September Edward informed him of the opening in Amherst and invited him to pass "a Sabbath with me, at some day not far distant, & preach in our pulpit. You can reply with perfect freedom, & confidence." Treading with care, the attorney added, "I do not feel at liberty to say more, now." Within the family, this cautious formula was already an old story. The previous year, in one of her inimitable mimicries, Emily wrote Austin: "Our church grows interesting, Zion lifts her head – I overhear remarks signifying Jerusalem, I do not feel at liberty to say any more today!"

Meanwhile, the performances of two interim preachers hired by the Supplying Committee caused Edward to erupt in fury. The Reverend Phinehas Cooke, six feet six and over seventy years old, had held pastorates in New Hampshire and was now living in retirement in North Amherst. He was remembered as a commanding presence, friendly, candid, straight-talking, and rigorously orthodox. Once, taking I Corinthians 1:13 as his text ("Is Christ divided?"), he argued that the Bible made the doctrines of depravity and divine election so clear and distinct that no one could possibly question them. Another sermon, preached to a congregation that had just dismissed him, ended with this body blow: "Sinners, while I give you my farewell message, let me tell you, if I find you at the judgment, what you now are, however agonizing your doom, I must say to it, AMEN." The First Church hired Cooke to preach for the first three months of 1853, a duty he performed till March 27, when he became ill; a month later he was dead of influenza. Curiously, this man who had all the right ancestral stuff proved wholly indigestible to Edward, who, Vinnie noted, became "so outraged towards parson Cooke[1] that he would not let Emilie or me go to church all day last Sunday." That Sunday, March 20, happened to be the last day the preacher was physically able to deliver a sermon. Father "prefered" that Mother, too, stay home, but she went anyway and caught the old stalwart's last performance.

Another supply preacher that year provoked a memorable display of derision in the Dickinson home. The Reverend John Henry Martin Leland, son of the previous Amherst College treasurer, was apparently a very poor sermonizer. According to seminary alumni records, his career consisted of brief pastorates in out-of-the-way towns followed by early retirement and "Fire Insurance." In May 1853, dismissed by a congregation in Maine, he returned to Amherst. On the first Sunday in June, Emily informed her brother:

> The rest have gone to meeting, to hear Rev Martin Leland. I listened to him this forenoon in a state of mind very near frenzy. . . . The morning exercises were perfectly ridiculous, and we spent the intermission in mimicking the Preacher. . . . I never heard father so funny. . . . [At church] he didn't dare look at Sue – he said he saw her bonnet coming round our way, and he looked "straight ahead." . . . He says if anyone asks him [what he thinks of the preaching], he shall put his hand to his mouth, and his mouth in the dust, and cry, Unclean – Unclean!!

Father was playing with some verses from Lamentations about the destruction of Jerusalem and the Temple: "He putteth his mouth in the

---

1. Although this person has been identified as the Reverend George Cooke, the parish audit shows that "Ph. Cook" was paid $99 on April 5, 1853. The original March 17 voucher survives, authorizing payment of $109. On it the tough and honest old man wrote, "Error of ten dollars deducted leaving it ninety nine. Phinehas Cooke."

dust" (3:29) and "Depart ye; it is unclean; depart, depart" (4:15).[2] We catch wind here of the weird humor Edward ordinarily chose to suppress.

Such outbursts riveted Emily's attention, in part because Father was the absolute embodiment of sedate public authority. In 1850, his dignity had been lampooned in a mock public program perpetrated by an unknown group of college students. Among the performances listed on the printed document are a snare drum solo by Satan and a song by the "Ambitious Young Ladies of Amherst" (including Emily for her recent "ambitious" publication of a Valentine in *The Indicator*?). The crowd-pleasing finale was to be a "Grand break down from the Treasurer with village accompaniment." The idea is a pleasing one, and we cannot resist picturing the poet's severe father in coat and neckcloth, stiff above the waist as his mad feet stir up the dust. As he dances, he mutteringly laments, "Unclean, unclean!"

Edward headed the search committee that brought in the Reverend Edward S. Dwight as candidate for minister; he won unanimous approval. Dwight had a more refined pulpit manner than his predecessor, the pungent Colton, and he made a fine first impression on George C. Shepard, who described him as "a good looking, pleasanter, social, gentlemanly man." Unlike Phinehas Cooke, Dwight made orthodoxy palatable and up-to-date, striking everyone, even Emily, as an excellent choice. She not only shared the church's anxiety that he might decline its offer, she resumed going to meeting, forenoon and afternoon. "He has preached wonderfully," she wrote Austin; "how I wished you were there."

Although Dickinson often turned to ministers for advice and comfort, Dwight was the last whose preaching she regularly sought out. For a time, she even went to church when she alone occupied the family pew, located close to the front on the right aisle. The letters describing her feelings as she walked toward this conspicuous seat show how much she abhorred the public gaze and required the mediating

2. That such passages were part of the oratorical culture of the day is shown by an 1852 speech in the House of Representatives, in which George T. Davis urged his opponents "to put their hands upon their mouths, and their mouths in the dust, and apologize."

presence of favored intimates. Once, she made a point of arriving five minutes early so as "not to have to go in after all the people had got there." When Vinnie was gone and Sue was missing from the nearby Cutler pew, she felt a queasy exposure to village stares: "How big and broad the aisle seemed . . . as I quaked slowly up – and reached my usual seat! In vain I sought to hide behind your feathers – Susie – feathers and *Bird* had flown, and there I sat, and sighed, and wondered I was scared so, for surely in the whole world was nothing I need to fear – Yet there the Phantom was." Trying to make sense of this panic, she noted that in Sue's absence "the world looks staringly, and I find I need more vail."[3]

By 1860 the Reverend Dwight seems to have fallen out of favor, his wife's health was failing, and it was time to quit. In Shepard's eyes, he had shrunk to a mere tailor's block, "a fine little specimen of a man, with black cravat [and] black coat that sets so well." Nothing in his sermons was ever "said amiss—& nothing to instruct or edify any one—He is a pretty nonentity!" The wrath of this listener (who taught preaching in a seminary) becomes somewhat understandable if one opens Dwight's slender published corpus and listens to his bland, perfectly modulated, and very boring voice. A trustee of Amherst College, he found his true niche—a subordinate one: he served as recording secretary. The only praise he got in William S. Tyler's tepid biographical sketch was for his "neatness, propriety and faithfulness" in keeping minutes.

Emily eventually lost interest in Dwight's preaching and ceased going to meeting, but she remained a loyal friend to him and his wife. Among his leading ideas were the voluntary nature of religious instruction and the separation of church and state. Underneath, unlike Colton and Cooke and Shepard and many other evangelical preachers, the man wasn't confrontational. One reason the poet-in-the-making favored the "pretty nonentity" was that he offered protection—helped weave the intricate "vail" behind which she could feel safe.

---

3. The statement is followed by one of her few epistolary references to marrying: "Frank Pierce thinks I mean *berage* vail, and makes a sprightly plan to import the 'article,' but dear Susie knows what I mean." "Berage" is "marriage," spoken with a head cold.

The Amherst and Belchertown Railroad

Although Dickinson believed in her father's basic rightness and hoped he would prevail, she was not well informed about his many civic, business, and political engagements, which impacted her chiefly through the ongoing labor of entertaining invited clerics, judges, governors, and such. Yet she remained deeply invested in the success of his operations. Hearing that someone had praised a rival as "the finest Lawyer in Amherst," she huffily denounced the opinion as "the apex of human impudence."

On one intriguing question, Emily's reaction in her early twenties to her father's energetic antifeminism, the record is frustratingly blank. In 1853 a former teacher named Prudence W. Eastman sued her husband, a minister, for divorce on grounds of cruelty. Deposed testimony indicated he was harsh and exacting and that she was subject to "convulsive affections of her nerves." Her mother saw bruises, heard her daughter groan behind closed doors, and confirmed that the minister had done what the suit alleged—namely, attempted "forcibly to confine her" at home and in a lunatic asylum. The wife was represented by Rufus Choate, the state's attorney general and leading trial lawyer; the husband, by Edward Dickinson. The *Springfield Republican,* following the trial closely, described Edward's defense as a "vigorous onset" that "carried the war into Africa." Calling a number of witnesses, mainly female, to show she "was at times greatly excited, and would talk very rapidly and shed tears very profusely," he succeeded in construing Prudence's emotional fragility as "insanity" and turning it to her disadvantage. We know Emily was paying close attention to the *Republican* at the time but can only guess where her sympathies lay when the suit was dismissed.

We know a great deal, on the other hand, about her excited reaction to Edward's two big achievements in this period—bringing a railroad to Amherst and getting elected to Congress.

After earlier failures to bring a branch line to Amherst, Edward renewed the struggle in 1850, when a railroad running north from New

London reached nearby Palmer. Since branch lines rarely paid and were hard to finance, it was decided to propose a through line north from Palmer that would pass through Belchertown and Amherst and, terminating at Montague, connect with an existing line. Emily's father, Luke Sweetser, Ithamar Conkey, and others got themselves incorporated as the Amherst and Belchertown Railroad and began raising money. The *Hampshire and Franklin Express* whipped up enthusiasm, the college authorized Treasurer Dickinson to buy fifty shares at $100 each (though some trustees questioned the security of the investment), and local citizens were induced to step forward and back the venture. Opposition arose, part of it from farmers who didn't want their land sliced up,[4] but the promoters were not to be stopped.

In February 1852 a crowd of four hundred assembled in Sweetser's Hall to hear the electrifying news: enough shares had been sold for construction to begin, and the New London, Willimantic, and Palmer Company was going to operate the line. Edward and others made speeches, a cannon was set off, and two days later his son got a note from him in which the boasting was qualified by a dry behind-the-scenes sarcasm:

You will see by the Editor's glorification article in today's 'Express,' that the Am. & Bel. r. road is "a fixed fact." The contract is made— the workmen will be digging, in "Logtown," next week—& we shall see those animating shantees, smoking through an old flour barrel, for a chimney, before many days. . . .

    The two great eras in the history of Amherst, are

        1. The founding of the College.

        2. The building of the rail road.

    We here "set up our Ebenezer."

    HaHa!!!

---

4. When Thomas Hastings of South Amherst took a hostile petition to the Supreme Judicial Court in 1852, the legal team that defeated him, Edward and Conkey, belonged, not by accident, to the railroad's board of directors.

According to I Samuel 7:12, the Ebenezer, or stone of help, was erected to commemorate God's intervention for Israel against the Philistines. In Job 39:24–25 the warhorse "swalloweth the ground . . . [and] saith among the trumpets, Ha, ha."

In the same envelope went a crowing letter from Emily:

> Every body is wide awake, every thing is stirring, the streets are full of people talking cheeringly. . . . The men begin working next week, only think of it, Austin; why I verily believe we shall fall down and worship the first "Son of Erin" that comes, and the first sod he turns will be preserved as an emblem of the struggles and victory of our heroic fathers. Such old fellows as Col' Smith *and his wife,* fold their arms complacently, and say, "well, I declare, we have got it after all" – *got it,* you good for nothings! and so we *have,* in spite of sneers and pities, and insults from all around; and we will *keep* it too, in spite of earth and heaven!

Here, the poet's sympathies seem wholly enlisted on the side of her father, echoing his partisanship and mockery alike. For the moment she, too, sounds like the ha-haing warhorse.

But in summer 1853, when a crowd came up from New London to celebrate the new line's operation, she acted like a bystander, preferring the woods to industrial progress:

> Father was as usual, Chief Marshal of the day, and went marching around the town with New London at his heels like some old Roman General, upon a Triumph Day. . . . Carriages flew like sparks, hither, and thither and yon, and they all said t'was fine. I spose it was – I sat in Prof Tyler's woods and saw the train move off, and then ran home again for fear somebody would see me, or ask me how I did.

The original idea was to build the line in two stages: first the nineteen miles from Palmer to Amherst, then the remainder to Montague. But after the first half proved a financial wash, the second was indefinitely postponed and the road remained a branch line after all. The capital outlay, $290,000, was far out of line with the level of traffic in goods and passengers. One month after the big party, Vinnie reported that Father was "mad with the *whole* New London company, they are very mean & impudent." The *Republican* openly complained about the A&B's unpaid printing bills, and a national credit-rating company noted in its ledgers that the stock paid no dividends and the company could raise money only by finding "sureties for its repayment." Always a backer of local development, Edward provided much of this money, buying $8,100 worth of A&B bonds by the end of 1854. One notes, however, that, unlike the shares bought by Amherst College and others, bonds entail repayment.

In Dickinson's well-known poem about a train, a first-person speaker enjoys observing an iron horse that insists on having its own disruptive way, swallowing ground and water and noisily complaining when squeezed by a rocky cut. Carrying no freight or passengers, as Charles Anderson noted, her train exists to enact its own powerful and mechanical will, in the process offering a spectatorial thrill. In the end, however, as Domhnall Mitchell observes, the locomotive only "*seems* unstoppable":

> *I like to see it lap the Miles –*
> *And lick the Valleys up –*
> *And stop to feed itself at Tanks –*
> *And then – prodigious step*
>
> *Around a Pile of Mountains –*
> *And supercilious peer*
> *In Shanties – by the sides of Roads –*
> *And then a Quarry pare*
>
> *To fit its Ribs*
> *And crawl between*
> *Complaining all the while*
> *In horrid – hooting stanza –*
> *Then chase itself down Hill –*

And neigh like Boanerges –
Then – punctual as a Star
Stop – docile and omnipotent
At its own stable door –

Fr383

The poem nicely represents the huge destabilizing forces of the industrial revolution, not omitting the shanties and blasted bedrock, yet the
conclusion, with its safe return home, has a naive and reassuring pas-
toralism. The poem evokes two opposing aspects of Dickinson's life:
her sympathy with her father's invincible push for a rail link, and her
dependence on the bucolic shelter he provided. Untamable and domestic, omnipotent and docile, she and her locomotive exemplify the
same paradox.

We get the more prosaic truth about Amherst's railroad from Helen
Hunt Jackson's description of a branch line in *Mercy Philbrick's Choice.*
As Jackson's train heads for the village that marks the termination of the
line, the conductor tells the two remaining passengers that the company
originally intended "to connect with the northern roads; but they've
come to a stand-still for want o' funds, an' more'n half the time I don't
carry nobody over this last ten miles. Most o' the people from our town
go the other way, on the river road. It's shorter, an' some cheaper." The
actual A&B must have been a lot duller than the poem suggests. The real
thrill lay elsewhere, in the attempt to harness a supreme and overpower-
ing force. That was partly what Edward and Emily were after, in such
different ways.

Constancy Without Reward

Edward's one term in the U.S. House of Representatives basically ended
his political career, transforming him into a man without a party, side-
lined and frustrated. His brief entrance on the national stage had two
momentous consequences for Dickinson: she met the man, as we shall

see in the next chapter, whom she came to think of as "my dearest earthly friend," and her father's political isolation gave her a way to understand and confront her own destiny.

Not being a career politician whose livelihood depended on getting elected, Edward did not have to adjust to changing views on the bitterly divisive issues associated with slavery. That he detested the peculiar institution seems clear: in his first year at college he argued it was "manifestly unjust for one human being to hold another in bondage," and in 1840 he defended three local blacks who had abducted an eleven-year-old black orphan girl to keep her from being sold into slavery. Yet Edward also detested abolition, believing that a federal prohibition of slavery would violate state sovereignty and undo the Constitution. As he and other conservative Whigs recognized, our founding document, a product of negotiation and compromise, did in fact legitimize slavery. What he and they could not face was that this feature represented a catastrophic original flaw.

Straddling the difficulty in the classic Whig way, Edward opposed the formation of new slave states but brooked no federal interference with state law. Following Daniel Webster, he took his stand on the Compromise of 1850, which gave the South the Fugitive Slave Law in exchange for the admission of California as a free state and some other measures. Abolitionists were furious with Webster, but Massachusetts' old-line Whigs backed him all the way, opening themselves to the charge of compromising with principle. Henceforth, Edward found himself making common cause at times with such pro-slavery men as William C. Fowler (father of Emily Fowler). Some years later, as if to defend himself, he marked the passages in Hinton Helper's *Impending Crisis of the South* that proved Webster's hatred of slavery.

When Edward went to Baltimore in June 1852 to represent his district at the Whig national convention, he dryly wrote home that "the whole world was there, and some from other worlds" but admitted he had found "many old friends" and was enjoying himself. Emily was relieved "to have father at last, among men who sympathize with him, and know what he really is." Home-loving as he was, Emily knew how much he required the masculine strife of politics and principle. The specter of his and others' isolation greatly troubled her.[5]

Webster's support proved too regional to snag the nomination, and the convention chose as its presidential nominee General Winfield Scott, a southerner thought to be antislavery. Resolutely supporting his party, Edward was rewarded in September with the nomination for Massachusetts' 10th Congressional District. But the Whigs were hopelessly divided, the northern wing splintered by a vigorous Free Soil movement, the southern wing defecting to the Democrats. Massachusetts sent a solid Whig phalanx to Congress, including the poet's father, who won by a plurality in a December runoff, but nationwide Scott was crushed and the party fared so poorly it ceased to be a viable political force. Edward would go to the Capitol as part of an isolated remnant, with no chance of making his views prevail.

Emily apparently got word of her father's narrow victory on December 16. The note she wrote Sue the next day seems more elated than dismayed, but her tone is so giddy it is hard to interpret. Her opening sentences announce that she has been stunned, knocked out of her proper sphere: "I regret to inform you that at 3. oclock yesterday [when she heard the news?], my mind came to a stand, and has since then been stationary. . . . By this untoward providence a mental and moral being has been swept ruthlessly from her sphere." Following this, she seems to be doing a series of spot riffs and impersonations, talking bigtime like a victorious male politician: "I see by the Boston papers that *Giddings* is up again – hope you'll arrange with Corwin, and have the North all straight . . . have spoken for 52 cord black walnut." Joshua Giddings and Thomas Corwin were former or present Whigs with abolition tendencies. No matter how much wood was needed for a celebratory bonfire (and Edward's woodpile did sustain a memorable raid), fifty-two cords would obviously be excessive.

---

5. To Austin after his return to Cambridge: "Did'nt you find it very lonely, going back to Mrs Ware's?" To Emily Fowler in Francis A. March's absence: "I fear you will be lonely." To her after her marriage: "Sunday evening your father came in . . . I thought he looked solitary. I thought he had grown old. How lonely he must be – I'm sorry for him." To Mary Haven (wife of an Amherst professor who took a new job in Chicago): "I know you are lonely."

Edward left for Washington in December 1853, when Congress convened for a session lasting eight months. To mark the event, Emily took a sheet of stationery with an embossed Capitol and drew a feathered Indian, captioned "Member from 10th," walking toward the domed hall. Adding a smoking chimney and making some rough pencil strokes to emphasize the curved top, she deftly turned Congress into a wigwam—the rounded northeastern Indian house that Democrats, beginning with Tammany Hall, had made the symbol of their party organization. Given the party's Irish support, the drawing may also allude to shanties and barrel chimneys. Emily was saying that Congress was now a Democratic stronghold, and that the Member from 10th was walking into a fight.

She was also caricaturing her father's small-town roughness and ferocity, something everyone agreed he would have to try to mend. When he sent out cards, Vinnie commented that "he says he dont know much about etiquet but he is trying to learn." Still, the New Englander saw no reason to qualify his supercilious view of Washington: there was "hardly enough of mentality here to hold the place together," he wrote Austin—"a dont-care air which renders every body callous to everything good." Nothing could trump his allegiance to home and community. Having consented to referee a local lawsuit, he returned to Massachusetts in January and again in February to help broker a deal.

It was perhaps during these visits that plans were made for his wife and children to visit Washington that spring, both daughters being at first included. But an exception had to be made for the one who hated traveling, and whose spiky will required delicate handling. As Edward put it to Austin, "I have written home, to have Lavinia come with yr mother & you—& Emily too, if she will—but that I will not insist upon her coming."

This journey, the longest ever taken by Mrs. Dickinson and Vinnie, entailed weeks of anxious sewing and shopping. The letters Emily wrote during these preparations show no regret whatever at missing the grand excursion. Vinnie was in a quandary whether to "leave Emily alone," but then it was decided to bring Susan Gilbert in as companion and Cousin John Long Graves, a student at Amherst College, as guard. Everyone took for granted the twenty-three-year-old woman could not be left by herself.

Seventy-five years later, Graves's elderly daughter recalled for the *Boston Sunday Globe* what her father had told her: "Mr Dickinson's duties as Representative from Amherst often kept him in Washington," and when his women needed "a man to protect them," Graves moved into their house. Sometimes, after being waked up by distant piano playing, he was told by Emily in the morning that she could "improvise better at night." This memory finds confirmation in a letter Emily sent Graves in 1856: "I play the old – odd tunes yet, which used to flit about your head after honest hours – and wake dear Sue, and madden me, with their grief and fun."

Sue's report of the nights on West Street has a different ring. "I forgot to tell you," we read at the end of a letter revealing she has been "blue all day" and longs to see Martha and the Bartletts, "I am keeping house with Emily, while the family are in Washington— We frighten each other to death nearly every night—with that exception, we have very independent times." Implying that the two go their separate ways during the day, the letter conveys little or no pleasure in Emily's companionship. The night-frights are consistent with the youthful terrors Sue recorded in later years,[6] but they seem at odds with the poet's piano-playing enjoyment of her home after dark. It so happens that every letter of Emily's expressing a fear of the dark dates from after her family's move back to the Homestead in 1855.

In Washington, Edward was assigned to a special House committee on the national armories at Springfield and Harper's Ferry. At issue was whether these arms factories and depots should be under military or civilian management. Springfield was in Edward's district, and as he well knew, the issue had been a hot one ever since an army officer took charge in 1842, sacking many mechanics. Curiously, Springfield's lead-

---

6. One of Sue's rough drafts tells of a nighttime descent into a "black cellar." Another, "the most awful night of my life," features bloodcurdling shrieks from a woman sleeping in an adjacent room and "subject to night-mare." After waking her from "the clutches of her horrors," Sue gave up "watching" with the sick.

ing spokesman for civilian control, Charles Stearns, had been Amanda Brown Norcross's second husband. A self-educated master mason, Stearns belonged to a Whig faction that lacked access to the press and other levers of power. Unlike party regulars, he championed the civil liberties of skilled workingmen. His son, a militant abolitionist, would publicize the story of Henry Box Brown, whose hiding place while escaping north became his middle name.

As a young man, Edward had defended the benefits of military academies and favored a militia reform few other state officers would have tolerated: supervision by West Point. Now, ignoring local sentiment, he fought tooth and nail against the resumption of civilian control. Stymied by the Democratic leadership, he visited the Springfield armory on his own, then returned to Washington to announce that the workers were happy and productive, the factory modern and efficient, and the steam engine "the most beautiful piece of machinery that I ever saw."

Edward made these statements on the House floor after his committee had ended its hearings and the chair had tacked the restoration of civilian control onto a regular appropriations bill. Denouncing this move in an indignant one-hour speech, Edward complained of the chair's discourtesy, unfairness, procedural incompetence, and "complete monomania" (making, one notes, yet another accusation of insanity). "There never was a commission authorized by anybody on earth, for the discharge of important duties, which failed so completely." This, Edward's one major speech during his term in the House, raises questions about his effectiveness as legislator. Did he have to be so principled and clearsighted and combative and humiliating? Was it wise to reduce the issue to superlatives and ultimates, to leave no room for conciliation, to trample on local opinion? To answer yes, one would probably have to agree that the real issue was the defense of rightful authority—Edward's "monomania."

But we must not forget that he belonged to a disintegrating minority party, or that in May 1854, soon after his family left Washington, the Kansas-Nebraska Act was approved over the vehement objection of the Massachusetts delegation. Abrogating previous restrictive agreements on slavery in the territories, this measure allowed white settlers to decide whether certain new states would be free or slave. Thomas Dawes Eliot of New Bedford, who had taken his House seat April 17 (becoming Edward's roommate at the National Hotel), vigorously questioned the implicit disenfranchisement of free black settlers. Edward, by contrast, spoke less to the point and more belligerently. When a South Carolinian made an inaccurate remark about Samuel Hoar, one of Massachusetts' distinguished elder statesmen, Edward rose in full bristle. "I do not wish to have my State improperly represented in this matter," announced the warbonneted Member from 10th, adding, "there is not a purer man in the United States than Mr. Hoar." There is no doubt Hoar had been a courageous and principled public servant, yet Edward's angry riposte contributed nothing of substance to the debate.

The morning after the measure passed, a group of northern Whigs gathered in Edward and Eliot's hotel room to talk strategy. "A few still counselled adherence to the Whig party," but most agreed that a new organization was called for—the Republican Party. Under this rubric, Whigs and Free Soilers made common cause in Michigan and elsewhere, but not in Massachusetts, and especially not in the 10th District, where the Whigs who now renominated Edward refused to censure the party's southern wing for backing Kansas-Nebraska.

In his reelection bid, Edward was supported by leading local papers and by Salmon P. Chase, the eminent Free Soil Senator from Ohio. But the state's voters were disturbed, and when the 1854 elections were held an astonishing thing happened. To a man, the Whigs were driven from office, while the mysterious American or Know-Nothing Party took every single state and federal contest it entered in Massachusetts, pulling three times as many votes as the Whigs. Edward was defeated, 7,712 to 2,754. In Amherst he lost by more than two to one; in Pelham, nineteen to one. It was a repeat of what had happened to his father in the congressional race of 1828, and it had the same result: Edward was knocked out of the political arena. The victor was Henry Morris, his own student boarder of twenty-five years earlier. What may have stung most of all was that before taking his seat, Morris was induced to resign by the

Know-Nothing governor-elect, who offered him a judgeship in a deal smelling of backroom chicanery.

The 10th's defeated congressman never recovered. During the heyday of the American Party, he accused it (with nice hyperbole) of "the wickedest . . . political rascalities . . . since the days of Judas Iscariot." By 1860 it was already defunct, yet he continued to detect its spoor in the North's new party and to keep his distance, unwilling to "vote for Know Nothingism . . . by the *name* of Republicanism." When a family friend sent wishes for each of the Dickinsons in 1865, he hoped for "forgetfulness of the past" for Edward. The wish did not come true: the poet's father remained lastingly unreconciled, declaring in 1869 that "since the uprising of the K. N." organization he had ceased to vote by party. By then, no one even remembered the K. N.'s.

Emily Dickinson interpreted her father's insistence on the "high, strong ground" and his resolute political isolation as signs of noble character. Seeing him in this way furnished a model for defining and taking control of her own emerging fate. His fixities authorized her own, and most of all with respect to her life's work. A central and enabling idea in her poetry is that loyalty persists beyond hope of reward. Another is that greatness is tragic and solitary. Another is that you have to be supremely strong. "Be thou faithful unto death," Christ is quoted as saying in Revelation 2:10, "and I will give thee a crown of life." In taking the first part of this command to heart, Dickinson, like Father, spurned the very idea of payment. To publish would be to market her spirit and betray the integrity of her suffering. To qualify her "troth"—her fierce virginal constancy—would be thinkable only

> *When they dislocate my Brain!*
> *Amputate my freckled Bosom!*
> *Make me bearded like a man!*
>
> Fr267 (J1737)

Which is to say, *never!*

A couple of years after Edward's death in 1874, Dickinson boldly corrected Christ's words in Revelation:

> *"Faithful to the end" amended*
> *From the Heavenly clause –*
> *Constancy with a Proviso*
> *Constancy abhors –*
>
> *"Crowns of Life" are servile Prizes*
> *To the stately Heart,*
> *Given for the Giving, solely,*
> *No Emolument.*
>
> Fr1386D

In extolling what she saw as her father's unrewarded constancy, the poet was characterizing a vital aspect of her own vocation.

Of course, there were differences, the most important being that Dickinson wasn't paralyzed by a sense of embittered dignity. Like Dinah Craik's heroic Olive Rothesay, who finds strength in weakness, she had a sense of loving unpaid service that kept her emotionally supple. As she put it about 1864,

> *The Service without Hope –*
> *Is tenderest, I think –*
> *Because 'tis unsustained . . .*
>
> Fr880

A Complicated Engagement

In July 1852 Susan Gilbert and Austin returned to Amherst from their schoolteaching jobs in Baltimore and Boston. Since Emily had no reason now to write to either, we can only surmise how much she knew about their growing intimacy, or how long she maintained her wishful belief in Sue's invulnerability to male gallantry: "If [my heart] is stony, yours is stone, upon stone, for you never yield *any*."

Technically mistaken, these words of Emily's were deeply prophetic, applying to her own "suit" as well as her brother's. That winter, when Sue complained to a friend about the lack of excitement and stimulation in Amherst, her statement that "the girls are all gone Abbie—Jane—and Vinnie" ignored Emily's presence. Overlooked on this occasion, on others she served as a pretext. A note of Austin's outlines a typical ruse: Sue will tell the Cutlers she plans to spend the evening with the Dickinson girls, then, after "a half hour or so with them—I will undertake to accompany you home—& find a carriage tied near by our door which we will avail ourselves of for half an hour or an hour." At the October cattle show, they occupied one end of a table along with Vinnie, Edmund Converse, Joel W. Norcross, and other friends (Emily was absent). Gossip reported the couple as "constantly together," and by early winter, following a "week never to be forgotten," they were secretly engaged, beginning what Austin called a "new life exquisite as a dream."

Becoming more confidential, Sue lent Austin her copy of Elizabeth Barrett Browning's *Prometheus Bound, and Other Poems* (still extant), and he spent a day at home reading "the marked passages." This is the book that printed "Sonnets from the Portuguese," the impassioned cycle of love poems stimulated by Robert Browning's courtship. To read those that Sue marked and wanted Austin to think about is to glimpse the parallels she saw between Barrett Browning's courtship and her own. Beside Sonnet III, which begins, "Unlike are we, unlike, O princely Heart!" we find a heavy mark. Sonnet V, also marked, evidently spoke to Sue's sense of bereavement:

> *I lift my heavy heart up solemnly,*
> *As once Electra her sepulchral urn,*
> *And, looking in thine eyes, I overturn*
> *The ashes at thy feet. Behold and see*
> *What a great heap of grief lay hid in me.*

The one poem marked with double lines, Sonnet XXXV, further describes the torment of leaving grief behind—of turning away from "dead eyes too tender to know change." The poem ends:

Alas, I have grieved so I am hard to love.
Yet love me—wilt thou? Open thine heart wide,
And fold within the wet wings of thy dove.

These love sonnets evoke as nothing else the vectors of Sue's conflicted passion. For the moment, she was a tamed Electra, struggling to forget her mourning and give herself to someone outside her family.

Although the couple's love letters were eventually burned, Austin for some reason preserved the many rough drafts of his side of the correspondence: "O, my God, I am worthy of nothing—Thou has granted me everything—I tremble in my very joy. . . . Can it be that I am dreaming —or is this all real!" When Martha sent congratulations, he replied that he and Sue "love each other—with a strength & a passion . . . mightier than you can guess—mightier than in opium dreams many have conceived of in their imagination—We love each other, Mat, with a love strong—stronger than life itself." For three years Austin kept turning out this sort of thing, a torrent of bloviation that he probably regarded as fine writing, and that never approached what his sister easily dashed off.

In addition to surrendering to a banal imagination, Austin was warding off the dissonances he didn't want to recognize. To Martha, he expressed amazement that such "tall proud, stiff people [as he and Sue], so easily miffed . . . [could] speak words—& look, look, so cold—so bitter, as hardly the deepest hatred could have prompted." This cold hate came to the surface with some regularity, as when he compared himself to the charmed victim of a snake's "deadly embrace": "You *know* Sue . . . where I waited—& shuddered—& sickened—you know the lines [in her letter to him] I read oftenest—that I read slowest." Twice he wrote, then canceled, "serpent." In the end he always came back to his dream of an ideal and oddly literary union: "we'll live just as beautifully as Longfellow's Kavanagh is beautiful."

In February 1853, when Sue left for a month's visit to the Bartletts in New Hampshire, Emily resumed her letter-writing. The first of the series, dated the twenty-fourth, discloses her awareness of the secret engagement and of her new basis with Sue. Making no sign until the letter's end, she abruptly reverts, as if helpless to contain herself any longer, to her confidential manner of the previous spring: "Oh Susie, Susie, I must call out to you in the old, old way – I must say how it seems to me to hear the clock so silently tick all the hours away, and bring me not my gift – my own, my own!" Signing off, she transmits "my" mother's and sister's love but then at once corrects the pronoun, as the betrothal requires: "*thy* mother and thy sister, and the Youth, the Lone Youth, Susie, you know the rest!" These passages, the poet's first recorded response to the engagement, do not exhibit the rage, jealousy, or fragmentation a few scholars believe she felt. Instead, making a conspicuous accommodation, she recalls her "old way" with Sue, signals an acceptance of the altered relationship, and gives final emphasis to Austin as the Lone Youth temporarily left behind in Amherst.[7]

Subsequent letters show the same mix of attitudes. With Sue away, Dickinson confessed she found it "harder to live alone than . . . when you were in Baltimore." But she also made a point of recognizing the affianced couple's preferences: "*Somebody loves you* more – or I were there this evening," she wrote Sue on her return from a trip to New York, and when it was Austin's turn to be gone she informed him she had "taken *your place* [with Sue] Saturday evening . . . but I will give it back to you as soon as you get home. *Get home* dear Austin." She took great pleasure in serving as the facilitating confidante. When her brother left for Harvard Law School on March 5, she addressed some envelopes to Sue for him so that the couple's correspondence could elude surveillance. And when they arranged a secret rendezvous at a Boston hotel, she reveled in

---

7. Years later, the references to Sue in Dickinson's letters to Austin were erased. These tamperings, scrupulously disclosed in *Emily Dickinson's Home* in 1955, have recently been interpreted as an attempt to suppress evidence of the poet's supposed lesbianism. One objection to this line of argument is that she would not be likely to express her homoerotic desire to her brother and rival. Another is that *none* of the many erasures that remain legible are sexual, compromising, or personally embarrassing. "You shall have Vinnie and me [*and somebody dearer than either of us*] to take care of you." "I was very happy last week, [*for we were at Susie's house*(?), or Susie was at our house most all the time, and Susie(?) always makes us happy. Vinnie is down(?) there now*]." The most reasonable inference is that someone meant to obliterate *all* references to Sue, no matter how innocuous. This accords with a statement by Millicent Todd Bingham in 1931. Quoting her mother (Austin's mistress), she said he had been so insistent the 1894 edition of the poet's letters not mention his estranged wife that he " 'himself erased from the manuscripts' " some passages.

the role of go-between. Afterward, parading her maiden-sister sympathy, she told Austin she "did 'drop in at the Revere' [in spirit] a great
many times yesterday. I hope you have been made happy." That Vinnie
sent the same message—"I suppose you are perfectly happy to night
Austin"—reminds us we are dealing with a family's as well as a person's
unusual psychology. Even in romance, the Dickinson children held
hands, so to speak.[8] Informed of the engagement well before their parents, the sisters eagerly welcomed the outsider to the exclusive inner circle. "I love the opportunity," Emily wrote Sue, "to soften the least
asperity in the path which ne'er 'ran smooth.' "

Sue's response to all this participatory fervor was tepid at best. During her month with the Bartletts, Dickinson sent her a poem headed
"Write! Comrade, write!" (Fr3A) and three ardent letters, the second of
which pleaded, "Why dont you write me, Darling? Did I in that quick
[first] letter say anything which grieved you, or made it hard for you to
take your usual pen and trace affection for your bad, sad Emilie?" She
evidently feared she had overstepped the line in that bit about the "old
way" and "my own, my own." In reply, she received one short note—"not
much," as she admitted to Austin. It was left to Vinnie to complain, indignantly, that Sue's silence "made E. very unhappy & me vexed."

A letter of Sue's written immediately after her return to Amherst
hints at her growing anxiety and distress. Feeling "really homesick" for
the Bartletts, she made the remarkable statement that when she pictured
them "the world did'nt seem all hollow, [nor?] suicide as much of a relief
as it does sometimes." Brilliant and adhesive as Emily was, she seems to
have had little real insight into her future sister-in-law's queasy reserves.
The same was true for Austin. When he read Sue's afterthoughts about
their meeting at the Revere Hotel, he was shocked to discover that as
"you sat by my side—& pillowed your head upon my bosom & felt my
arm around your neck & my lips on your cheek & my heart beating in
its great love for you—Even there & then—you were doubting—*doubt-*

---

8. At this stage Austin also "collectivized" the romance. "I *do* love you Mattie," he wrote his future
sister-in-law, "just as well as Emily . . . & you *all* enter into all Sue's & my plans for the future."

ing—questioning if after all you had any love for me." This is the draft that calls Sue a serpent.

In spite of the "great love" the members of this tight and exclusive circle felt for one another, there were striking lapses of sympathy and understanding. When Emily learned from Sue's one note how happy she was in New Hampshire, she used her reply to glance at "the shadows fast stealing" over her own life, in this way both suggesting her premonitions about herself and asking for something like reciprocity. With Austin, too, she was beginning to see that he meant more to her than she to him. Arguing that the Dickinson siblings' difference from "most everyone" made them all the more "dependent on each other for delight" (this being an implicit plea), Emily wondered if he thought "of us as often as we all do of you." The question "troubles me," she confessed. She was right to be uneasy. After reading her brilliant account of a German concert "the evening of Exhibition day," he wrote Sue that Emily hadn't even mentioned the Exhibition; he doubted "she knew there had been one." This inattention to the writing she lavished on him is as striking as his insistence on the idea of her remoteness.

And so she overdid her tending of his romance. When Sue finally put away her mourning for Mary Learned (as in Barrett Browning's sonnet), Emily sent Austin a tempting sketch of her white dress, fawn-colored silk mantilla, and straw hat. And when local gossips got wind of the Revere Hotel assignation, she became so solicitous for his peace of mind she ended up annoying and embarrassing him. On June 9, hoping he wouldn't be troubled by "any remarks," she begged him to let her and a trusty servant "*help a little.*" Four days later she assured Austin "the stories are all still . . . and Susie says she dont care now the least at all for them. They must not trouble you – they are very low – of the earth – they cannot reach our heaven." This naively collective heaven, based on a rejection of coarse imputations, recalls her "lofty" denial two years earlier that there was anything "wicked in Shakespeare."

After Austin scolded his sisters for their interference, Vinnie apologized for both: "We received your notes last evening . . . they made me feel very badly & I hope there will be no more occasion for such ones. I think Emilie & I were in the fault some what. I thought she ought not to say what she did the last morning & tried to prevent it, but she felt you must know it." Emilie's next letter opens on a distinctly downcast note: "Do you want to hear from me, Austin? I'm going to write to you altho' it dont seem much as if you would care to have me. I dont know why exactly, but things look blue, today, and I hardly know what to do, everything looks so strangely." The episode reveals the twenty-two-year-old's distress at overstepping—and without knowing "why exactly"—the bounds of maidenly speech.

The frank erotic passion of Dickinson's mature poetry need not obscure her naïveté as a young woman, when she could not allow sex, something "low" and "of the earth," to have anything to do with the love that found fulfillment in "heaven." Her youthful over-the-top language, surging and transgressing, was the sign of an innocence that was lasting too long.

Chapter 14

1853–1855: News of the Ancient School of True Poets

The Hollands

On June 9, 1853, the day Edward Dickinson marched the New London visitors around Amherst, his daughter became acquainted with her first full-time writer, Dr. Josiah Gilbert Holland, literary editor of the *Springfield Republican* and one of the mid-century's most popular essayists. An unusually direct and engaging man, Holland asked Mrs. Dickinson while calling at West Street whether her daughters could visit him and his family in Springfield. The invitation was taken seriously after he and Elizabeth, his appealing wife, dropped in without warning the next month and had "Champagne for dinner, and a very fine time." He seemed to be in top form, insisting, as Emily told Austin, that "you would be a Judge – there was no help for it – you must certainly be a Judge!" "Splendid visit," echoed Vinnie.

When Abiah Root invited Emily to visit, she was turned down out of hand: "I'm so old fashioned, Darling, that all your friends would stare." All objections vanished with the Hollands, however, and in September 1853 the sisters spent a night at their Springfield home, on the corner of Bliss and Water Streets—Emily's only known trip to a new friend who wasn't a relative. That she and Vinnie returned a year later for a longer stay tells us a major new stimulus had entered the poet's life, initiating one of her closest, longest-lasting, and least understood friendships.

Unlike Dickinson, Holland was not only a preacher at heart but had a sure grasp of mass-market tastes. Whether explaining the wisdom of proverbs or exposing the weakness of the female imagination, he knew how to drive home standard views with the charm and certainty readers wanted, often with a gesture of punitive severity at the end. A polished simplifier, he gained a much bigger following in the Midwest than in Boston or New York. His work "had the immense advantage," summed up a keen obituarist, "of keeping on a plane of thought just above that of a vast multitude of readers." Although Dickinson praised one of his lyric poems, she had little to say about his widely popular books. Yet she instantly responded to his cordial manner, remembering all her life his way of praying on her first visit, "so simple, so believing"—and so unlike her stentorian sire, who, in conducting household prayers, would rasp " 'I say unto you' . . . with a militant Accent that would startle one." Tall, suave, dark-complexioned, and with a "clear tenor voice," Holland presented the poet with familiar elements in a novel combination.

After the first visit, Dickinson wrote to say how much she had been thinking of the couple: "If it wasn't for broad daylight, and cooking-stoves, and roosters, I'm afraid you would have occasion to smile at my letters often, but so sure as 'this mortal' essays immortality, a crow from a neighboring farm-yard dissipates the illusion." She was adapting the statement in I Corinthians 15:53 that "this corruptible [flesh] must put on incorruption, and this mortal must put on immortality." An odd use of a familiar text, her passage shows a complicated self-consciousness about her obsession with heaven, a dominant concern in the correspondences she initiated in the 1850s.

In her letters to the Hollands, Dickinson liked to bring out her desire for a heavenly reunion with them ("if God is willing, we are neighbors then") even as she brandished her irreverence ("Wonder if God is just – presume he is, however, and t'was only a blunder of Matthew's"). What did the editor think about this baffling young woman, always anticipating heaven in spite of being technically "without hope"? And why did *she* snuggle up to his authority, as when, "scared" by an 1854 sermon on "death and judgment" and lapsing into a child's voice, she told the Hollands she "longed to come to you, and tell you all about it, and learn how to be better." Both questions are partly answered if we note how much the doctor made of the distinction between religious fervor and doctrinal correctness. "Christianity, in the form of abstract statement, and in the shape of a creed, has not for me any particular meaning," he would say; "I have to test things through my heart and best feelings." It was this opinion, which sometimes got him into trouble, that made a temporary basis between the crowd-pleasing moralist and the individually questing poet. What she took from him was authorization to go on trusting her feelings. It is an interesting connection, a writer who was merely successful giving courage to one who was primal.

Much shorter than Josiah, Elizabeth seems to have been a classic helpmeet, "a typical womanly woman," pleasing in looks and manner and bent on smoothing the way for her husband. His biographer, looking back from the 1890s, saw their domestic relationship as " 'sweet' " in an old-fashioned way. The same source claimed "he never printed any important book without first reading it to her." The spectacle of "the dark man with the doll-wife," or "the Angel Wife," as Dickinson variously typed them years later, appealed to her on a very deep level. In several poems of the early 1860s, she seems to picture herself in just such a relationship:

> *Forever at His side to walk –*
> *The smaller of the two! . . .*
>
> Fr264

But her attention was fixed less on the doctor, who never became a romantic figure for her, than on his wife seen in relation to him. Then he receded and she became the point of attachment.

A Theology of the Feelings

One of the biggest mistakes we make with Dickinson is to detach her from the religious currents of the 1850s, without which she could not have become herself. Of these, the single most important was the growing tendency within orthodoxy to question the primacy, even the necessity, of a rationally articulated faith. *Was* it so vital, after all, to have correct abstract doctrines? Wasn't there also a true religion of the heart that would do just as well, and which could be expressed "aesthetically" rather than abstractly? Such questions, particularly as worked out by Horace Bushnell and Edwards A. Park, New England's boldest Protestant thinkers, helped make feasible Dickinson's work as poet.

The fundamental text is Bushnell's 1849 *God in Christ*, which challenged the need for dogma by examining the nature of human speech. Impressed by its inexactness and inherent inadequacies, Bushnell argued that language is always approximate, figurative, and paradoxical in handling religious matters. Words are at best "hints, or images"; ultimate truth must be approached through repeated poetic attempts; only the prophet or poet speaks with truly religious accents. Indeed, for Bushnell, the basic Christian idea—the descent of the ineffable into human forms, the incarnation of God in Christ—almost seemed replicated "in every writer, distinguished by mental life." It is the work of writing to "receive a new inbreathing of life and power," and it is "the right of every author, who deserves attention at all, to claim a certain liberty." Bushnell also dared to say that the force of revivalism was "spent" and that a new kind of spiritual life addressed to our aesthetic powers was being born. His views invite comparison with other theories of language and writing that show an antirational impetus: Coleridge, *écriture féminine*, deconstruction.

The year after Bushnell's book appeared, Dickinson applied the idea of an incarnate divine "life" to her own letter writing and quest for perfect friendship: "as these few imperfect words to the full communion of spirits, so this small giddy life to the *better*, the life eternal, and that *we* may live this life, and be filled with this true communion, I shall not cease to pray." By the end of the decade, she could be quite forceful in declaring she did "not respect 'doctrines.'" Her poems sometimes express a kind of Bushnellian relief at the abandonment of propositional analysis, the "easing" turn from theology to art:

> *The Definition of Beauty is*
> *That Definition is none –*
> *Of Heaven, easing Analysis,*
> *Since Heaven and He are One.*
>
> Fr797B

No contemporary thinker came closer than the liberal Trinitarian Bushnell to formulating the linguistic rationale for Dickinson's poetic vocation.[1] Although we can't be certain she read him, he stood out as New England's most eminent theological mind, and his influence was pervasive among the bright young future ministers Dickinson knew in Alpha Delta Phi, including George H. Gould, whose ornate "music of words" drew criticism.

But the most important person in Dickinson's orbit to voice Bushnell's aesthetic vision was his ally in theological warfare, Edwards A. Park, who taught at Andover Theological Seminary and had extremely close ties with Amherst College. Although Park did not go as far as Bushnell in dis-

---

1. Which is partly why some of her poems look like a commentary on Bushnellian thought, particularly "A word made flesh is seldom" (Fr1715), which suggests that *everyone*, not just the poet, apprehends the vital new life that cannot be articulated: "Each one of us has tasted / With ecstasies of stealth . . ."

carding systematic theology, his 1850 essay, "The Theology of the Intellect and That of the Feelings," vigorously argued that abstract propositions could not capture the truths of religion, which can be approximated only by symbol and hyperbole. If the exposition of doctrine gives the impression "the divine government is harsh" or leaves "the sensibilities torpid," then "*somewhere it must be wrong*." Creating a separate space for aesthetic truth, Park insisted on the necessity of "rendering unto poetry the things that are designed for poetry, and unto prose what belongs to prose." An 1857 essay urges the importance of "condensing a world of import" so as to intimate "what 'eye hath not seen, nor ear heard.' "

Putting such ideas into practice, Park became New England's most mesmerizing preacher and lecturer, stunning his listeners with the drama and brilliance of his sermons, his "weird abstraction" in the pulpit, his huge lantern jaw. His students felt "shivers along our whole system of nerves" and wondered if they were hearing "trumpets of angels." "Truly a great preacher," a professor at Amherst College noted; "he is sometimes *tremendous*, in thought and manner."

On November 20, 1853, preaching in Amherst's First Church, Professor Park delivered his famous sermon on Judas. The next morning Dickinson tried to let her brother know what he had missed: "I never heard anything like it, and dont expect to again, till we stand at the great white throne. . . . And when it was all over, and that wonderful man sat down, people stared at each other, and looked as wan and wild, as if they had seen a spirit." Decades later she called this "the loveliest sermon I ever heard."

Given this enthusiasm, she probably attended Park's formal address two days later at the dedication of the new college library. His leading idea was that art and religion were not opposed, as many thought, but intimately affiliated. "Reverence, veneration, awe," he said, should be "complete mental states in which religion and taste meet." He also suggested that Amherst's lovely setting be regarded as the nursery of great poetry and art: "In surveying this rich valley—this amphitheatre of villages, and streams, and noble woods . . . I have often thought that the [residents] . . . were blessed with means of aesthetic culture for which poets and painters have longed." He ended with a prophecy: that "some poet now unborn" would emerge from this landscape and become "known through the world."

You May Think My Desire Strange, Sir

Dickinson's early 1854 letter requesting information about Benjamin Newton's last hours shows another facet of her combined religious-poetic quest. Sent to a leading Unitarian minister, the Reverend Edward Everett Hale, this letter hints at her struggle to devise a nonorthodox "hope" of her own.

When Newton left Edward's law office four years earlier, he moved to Worcester, completed his studies, and became district attorney. Dickinson's two references to him suggest she had not been able to keep in close touch. In summer 1851, having finished a letter to Austin, she added in a larger hand, "*BFN* – is *married*." That she was writing eighteen days after the event tells us she had not been given timely notice of it. Almost two years later, she again added a few last words to a sisterly letter, this time inside the envelope flap: "Love from us all. Monday noon. Oh Austin, Newton is dead. The first of my own friends. Pace." The date was March 28, 1853, five days after Austin and Sue's rendezvous in Boston, when exclusive friendship was much on the poet's mind. In singling Newton out as the first of her own friends, she probably meant her first adult friend not shared with Vinnie or Austin.

After reflecting on Ben's death for the better part of a year, Dickinson dispatched a strange letter to the pastor of his church, Reverend Hale:

> Pardon the liberty Sir, which a stranger takes in addressing you, but I think you may be familiar with the last hours of a Friend. . . . I often have hoped to know if his last hours were cheerful, and if he was willing to die. . . . You may think my desire strange, Sir, but the Dead was dear to me, and I would love to know that he sleeps peacefully. . . . He often talked of God, but I do not know certainly if he was his Father in Heaven – Please Sir, to tell me if he was willing to

die, and if you think him at Home, I should love so much to know
certainly, that he was today in Heaven.

What prompted this shockingly ingenuous query (Did Newton go to
Heaven, Sir, please?) is that he had been a Unitarian, outside the evangelical system. Did he die as he lived, in peace and trust, or did his soul ago-
nize with the foretaste of future torment? Significantly, at the time the
poet sent this question, January 13, 1854, her father was in Washington,
Austin in Cambridge, and Vinnie in Boston. Sue may have been gone as
well. It was two days later that Emily, alone with her fears and fancies,
quaked at "the Phantom" when going to meeting by herself. Her letter has
been explained in terms of the general interest in deathbed scenes, but this
benign cultural explanation misses the point: her fixation on questions of
death and immortality, her desperate search for men who *knew*.

What Dickinson didn't realize was that she had the wrong minister.
Worcester had two Unitarian societies, and though Newton did in fact
belong to Hale's church, it was the pastor of the other one, the Reverend
Alonzo Hill, who attended his deathbed. A specialist in dying and a
meticulous record keeper, Reverend Hill was gradually assembling a curious collection of personal obituaries, in which (as in Danilo Kiš's great
story "The Encyclopedia of the Dead"), he tried to sum up the life of
each person he helped die. His entry for March 24, 1853, reads:

> Benjamin F. Newton Esq Aet 33 [in fact, 32] Consumption He was
> a member of the Church of the Unity, but desired my attendance
> during the last days of his sickness. He was District Attorney & tho
> enfeebled by disease performed the duties of his office with ability &
> success. He rode out the day before his death. He had secured an in-
> surance of $1500 on his life which would have expired on the first of
> May. Buried from the Ch of the Unity.

That the man knew he was insolvent explains his risky last-minute renewal of his life insurance. But his wife still ended up on the poor farm.

The thank-you letter Emily sent in February lacks a salutation but
probably went to Hale, not Hill:

I thank you when you tell me that he was brave, and patient –
and that he dared to die.

I thought he would not fear, because his soul was – valiant – but
that they met, and fought, and that my Brother conquered, and
passed on triumphing, blessed it is to know.

Her response to Hale's expressed wish that she "might have passed an
hour" with Newton is worth noting: "To purchase such an one I would
have offered worlds, had they been mine to bring, but hours like those
are costly, and most too poor to buy."

A few years later, as if uneasy about the naïveté of her initial query,
the poet sent Hale a strange reminder: "Perhaps you forget a Stranger
maid, who several springs ago – asked of a Friend's Eternity, and if in her
simplicity, she still remembers you, and culls for you a Rose, and hopes
upon a purer morn, to pluck you buds serener – please pardon her, and
them." It is an apology for remembering in a world that can be trusted
to forget. If the "buds serener" mean the poems she had begun to make,
the passage (itself iambic) hints at the sequence by which she converted
an obsession with heaven into her work as poet.

Emmons and the Honeybee

The poet's most intriguing literary friendship of the mid-1850s began
half a year after Newton's surprise marriage. If the attorney was a virtual
"elder brother," Henry Vaughan Emmons might be thought of as a fraternal twin, albeit two years younger. He came to Amherst College in
1851 from Hallowell, Maine, where his father, Judge Williams Emmons, a pious and well-educated Websterian Whig, had the same secure
position in the local hierarchy as Edward Dickinson in Amherst.[2] The
young man's mother had been a Vaughan, one of an extraordinarily cul-

---

2. The Emmons home was said to have "an air of state and elegance not surpassed in any of the
old-time mansions of Hallowell." When it burned, a large collection of books and papers were
destroyed, perhaps including some of Dickinson's letters.

tivated family with a private library said to be four-fifths the size of Harvard's. Her father, educated in England by Joseph Priestley, had been private secretary to Lord Shelburne. The boy's other grandfather, the Reverend Nathanael Emmons, had coached Samuel Fowler Dickinson in Calvinist theology in the 1790s. Now, sixty years later, their grandchildren would put their heads together to construct an aesthetic alternative to New England's suddenly decaying orthodoxy.

Henry seems to have been an exceptionally self-defined and learned young man. Entering college as a sophomore after having once run away from home, he broke the mold in a second way by rooming off campus all three years. By February 1852 he and Emily were well enough acquainted that she accompanied "*Sophomore Emmons*" one evening on a ride—"alone," as she emphasized to Austin. To Sue she described him as her "beautiful, new, friend." More rides and walks followed, along with evenings in the Dickinson home, often in the company of his roommate and her cousin John Long Graves. In June, when Vinnie attended the Senior levee, Henry and Emily went for a walk together.

The notes Emily sent Henry over the next two years tell of a friendship that was not so much romantic as intensely literary and "spiritual." Before long, they were exchanging compositions. "Since receiving your beautiful writing," she told him, "I have often desired to thank you thro' a few of my flowers, and arranged the fairest for you." She added, "I have very few today, and they compare but slightly with the immortal blossoms you kindly gathered me, but will you please accept them – the 'Lily of the field' for the blossoms of Paradise, and if 'tis ever mine to gather those which fade not, from the garden we have not seen, you shall have a brighter one than I can find today." Within her guarded and humble forecast (the syntax and diction of which anticipate her last note to Hale) lurked a shy admission of poetic ambition. When Henry replied with a "beautiful acknowledgment," she politely reminded him that "while with pleasure I *lend* you the little manuscript, I shall beg leave to claim it." Her next note was sharper: "Please recollect if you will two little volumes of mine which I thoughtlessly lend [*sic*] you." Behind this anxiety lay memories of 1850, when a Valentine sent to a student editor ended up in the now defunct *Indicator*.

As Emily knew, Henry was also an editor, having recently taken the lead in founding a college literary magazine. In the prospectus he drafted for this venture, the high-minded young man hoped "to counteract the many adverse influences at work in the present college tone" and correct the impression that Amherst lacked "cultivation—literary power." Comparing the school to Yale, he wrote that "the bees are always swarming there—and fill the air with their buzzing clamor—while here they are silently at work making honey."

In its first year of publication, the *Collegiate Magazine* ran eleven of Emmons's labored and earnest essays, all of them clogged with an unusually imagistic prose. Interested in great men and turning points, he was drawn to the Renaissance as a time of lofty aspiration, to the power of the imagination and humane learning. "Power" was a key word for him, but not the power of logic, system, will—the strenuously rational orthodoxy his grandfather Nathanael had epitomized. Rather, it was the power of lambent symbols and images—those bees silently at work.

Two of Emmons's essays help unpack Dickinson's early sense of herself as poet. "Poetry the Voice of Sorrow," published October 1853, proposes that God appoints a select few to "listen to His voice more nearly than other men." These are the poets, who, like Jacob, "wrestle with the angel of sorrow till he leaves a blessing upon them," after which they "bring peace and beauty to common men"; they are the true tribe of Levi. As Emmons worked the idea out, he quoted "A Vision of Poets" by Elizabeth Barrett Browning: "Knowledge by suffering entereth, / And Life is perfected by Death!" These lines (a Victorian commonplace) are heavily marked in Sue's copy of Barrett Browning's collected poetry, acquired in 1853.

As Dickinson moved toward a deeper understanding of herself and her vocation in 1853–1854, "A Vision of Poets" seems to have played a vital role. This thousand-line narrative, variously flat, verbose, and thrilling, sets forth a dream vision of the pantheon of poets—"king-poets" as Barrett Browning calls them, though they include one woman,

Sappho. Where each poet's heart should be, the dreamer sees "a wound instead of it / From whence the blood dropped to their feet." Asked if they are satisfied to pay their heart's blood for their art, they "bent / Their awful brows and said 'Content.' " Over all, the work presents poetry as analogous to Scripture, with poets serving as saints and martyrs, a select group of wounded saviors.

For Dickinson, this view had great appeal and relevance, if only because it suggested a way to deploy the evangelicalism she could not accept in doctrinal form. The solution (following Bushnell and Park) was to aestheticize it—to transform orthodoxy into a drama of which the suffering poet is the central figure. That is the program many of her later poems work out, such as the one that begins, "The Martyr Poets – did not tell – / But wrought their Pang in syllable" (Fr665).

The second essay, "The Words of Rock Rimmon," was prompted by one of the mountain-naming excursions Edward Hitchcock annually staged. This time Emmons made a daring personal application of Barrett Browning's "Vision." On June 6, 1854, a large group of Amherst College students and others ascended a granite knob in Belchertown that was to be known henceforth (but hasn't been) as Rock Rimmon. In the elaborate program, a professor spoke about mountains as "a source of inspiration to much of our finest literature," citing the Psalmist, Greek and Latin poets, Milton, Wordsworth, and Byron. Emmons was master of ceremonies.

Though Dickinson wouldn't have been present, she paid the closest attention to Emmons's dreamy account of what happened afterward during a solitary all-night vigil on the newly named hilltop. In this narrative, published in the *Collegiate Magazine* in July 1854, the gigantic spirits of the Holyoke Range and other peaks approach Rock Rimmon and listen as its Spirit remembers the sacred events associated with certain biblical mountains. The ancient geological upheavals in Massachusetts also had a secret purpose, the Spirit announces: to prepare New England for its errand of saving the world. Then day breaks, and as the sole human observer gazes on the plain below, he feels a "strange earnestness thrilling in my heart." The essay ends with a tercet from "A Vision of Poets":

The golden morning's open flowings,
Did sway the trees to murmurous bowings,
In metric chant of blessed poems.

In Barrett Browning, these lines belong to the climactic moment in which an aspiring poet "journeyed homeward through the wood." In Emmons, they express an ardent youthful dream of joining the ancient school of true poets.

He graduated in August 1854, by which time Commencement had become an old story for Dickinson—the speechmaking, the dusty booths on the Common, the hordes of curious onlookers mixed with returning alumni, many in clerical collars. Now that she was about to lose one of her closest friends, however, the annual event proved unusually packed, painful, and clarifying. Busy as she was with the work of hospitality, she had some private time with Henry, and also with Eliza M. Coleman, who evidently stayed with the Dickinsons. Afterward, as Eliza prepared to leave, she opened Emily's Bible and made a penciled bracket around the eight verses of Psalm 121, which begins, "I will lift up mine eyes unto the hills, from whence cometh my help." As if to memorialize the moment, Eliza wrote in the margin, "E.M.C. 14th Augt 1854." The next day Emily wrote John Graves, "Quite sad it is when friends go, and sad when all are gone, to sit by pensive window, and recollect them."

Contributing to the pensive intensity was Emmons's recently announced engagement to Susan D. Phelps, of Hadley. When the news was imparted to Dickinson, she at once appointed a ride with him so that the two could "speak of *her*." Declaring her heart "full of joy," the poet earnestly "thank[ed] the Father who's given her to you," adding, "My hand trembles." She may have been quoting his recently published paragraph on strong feeling, which says that when "deep emotion chokes the utterance" the soul finds other avenues of expression, such as "the trembling frame."

For Dickinson, a great many things—friendship, loneliness, the wounded heart, poetic ambition, sacred mountains—were coming together in a very tight package. Before leaving, Emmons sent her a literary gift of some kind. Her thank-you and farewell begins, "I find it Friend – I read it – I stop to thank you for it, just as the world is still – I thank you for them all – the pearl, and then the onyx, and then the emerald stone." Though her references are obscure, she was drawing on the opulent imagery of Revelation 21, where the gates of the New Jerusalem are said to be of pearl and the fourth and fifth foundations are adorned with emerald and sardonyx.[3] Perhaps she was likening his gifts to heavenly gems. Continuing:

> My crown, indeed! I do not fear the king, attired in this grandeur.
> Please send me gems again – I have a flower. It looks like them,
>   and for its bright resemblance, receive it.

If Emmons's gems are his essays or poems, that would explain why Dickinson asks for more. In exchange, she sends him a "flower"—another poem?—and ventures for the first time in her surviving correspondence to speak of her crown: thanks to his encouragement, she feels attired, authorized, to meet "the king," an obscure figure that may refer to Barrett Browning's king-poets or the powerful fathers or even Clytie's Apollo. However we interpret this symbol, Dickinson clearly gives the credit for her boldness to Emmons and to the female predecessor she then proceeds to bring in, quoting the same tercet from "A Vision of Poets" but arranging it as prose: "A pleasant journey to you, both in the pathway home, and in the longer way – *Then* 'golden morning's open flowings, *shall* sway the trees to murmurous bowings, in metric chant of blessed poems.' " Paralleling Emmons's journey home with that of the aspiring poet in Barrett Browning, she was declaring her faith in her friend's artistic future.

---

3. The "Gem chapter" (Dickinson's phrase) was familiar to both religious and secular writers, as Rebecca Patterson has shown. Edward Hitchcock had preached on it at Mount Holyoke College in fall 1847. There is no sound basis for reading the first letters of pearl, onyx, and emerald as a coded reference to Poe, who had no provable impact on Dickinson.

Dickinson was too circumspect to speak of her own future. But it seems clear that her friendship with this young man (who would achieve little) had produced a more solemn understanding of what it was to be a poet—a crystallization in her consciousness of self, now more distinct and singled out than ever. She not only felt more confident in her readiness to meet "the king," she *sounded* like Emily Dickinson: imagistic, succinct, enigmatic. Years later, telling Joseph Lyman how she had given up loquacity for concision—a key development for her—she mentioned another gem: "We used to think, Joseph, when I was an unsifted girl and you so scholarly that words were cheap & weak. Now I dont know of anything so mighty. . . . Sometimes I write one, and look at his outlines till he glows as no sapphire."

Writing Sue in late August or September, she gave the impression the last few weeks would have been dull and empty if not for Emmons: "There was much that was sweet Commencement week – much too that was dusty, but my bee gathered many drops of the sweetest and purest honey." It was the same image and idea as in her friend's proposal for a literary magazine, the bees "silently at work making honey." Without pausing, she added, "I had many talks with Emmons, which I will not forget, and a charming farewell ride, before he went away – he stayed more than a week after Commencement was done, and came to see me often. . . . I shall miss Emmons very much."

Like Ben Newton, this young man—her last close student friend— helped call out the poet in Dickinson and then moved out of the way. The difference between these mentors was that Newton, an imposing older brother and Unitarian, presented her with Emerson's hard-to-assimilate poems, whereas Emmons, more of an equal and operating within orthodoxy, brought a viable female model. Together, Emmons and Barrett Browning pointed the way to two major discoveries: how to write from wounded affection, and how to aestheticize the aggressive evangelical tradition and in that way hold her own against it. Solitude and pain could be turned into art. As the poet put it some nine years later in the best of her commemorative lyrics on Barrett Browning, "The Dark – felt beautiful" (Fr627; J593).

Her Amherst Friends Wholly Misinterpret Her

Contributing to the summer's tensions and clarifications was a bitter and probably inevitable quarrel with Sue, who for her part went through a breakdown lasting several months.

Although the Cutlers thought Sue "made [her]self sick" by sewing too much, her own opinion was that a breakdown had been coming on "for a year." As the self-diagnosis hints, the stresses of her engagement had perhaps made her more anxious and obsessive. There was much to be uneasy about: her dependency on the Cutlers, the possessiveness of Austin's and Emily's love, her fiancé's religious doubts, his "man's requirements," and now the need to set a wedding day. Collapsing and taking to her bed, Sue was cared for by a professional nurse and by relations and friends, including Emily, who described her in late July as "suffering much within the last few weeks, from a Nervous Fever." Then, on August 4, two days before the bustle of Commencement week, she was "hurried" out of town by her sister Harriet. A month later she spoke of "weakness in my back" and suspected her hair would fall out. "For pity's sake," she wrote Ned Hitchcock, "don't get *nervous*." Only after six months' rest with maternal relatives in New York and Michigan was she able to go back to Amherst.

This illness brought out Sue's conscientious and censorious sides in high relief. On August 13, she began an epistle by first squaring matters with her high principles: "I never write letters Sabbath night, but it is quite allowable in the present instance I am sure." In December, learning that Mary Bartlett had given birth to a daughter two months earlier, she bristled with asperity and hauteur:

> Great business, I think, to have a feminine accession to the family at the Parsonage and not apprise Aunt Sue personally—I have half a mind not to write you a word and forswear all love for the very juvenile Miss—If I was a witch I do believe I'd glide through the keyhole this minute and pinch her nose with my invisible fingers, for her

Mother's misdemeanors—bad woman—I stood aghast with astonishment, when Julius informed me.

Sue could be extremely resourceful in making others squirm for their
lapses. Here, she sounds exactly like the vengeful fairy godmother overlooked at the christening.

The reason the quarrel between Sue and Emily has been poorly understood is that the poet's two letters speaking of it have been dated after
Sue's removal from Amherst and then placed in reverse order. In all likelihood, the earlier of the two, which begins "Sue – you can go or stay,"
was written shortly before her departure for Geneva. "We differ often
lately," Emily continued, "and this must be the last." A few years earlier,
explaining her cooling friendship with Abby Wood, Emily had written:
"we take different views of life – our thoughts would not dwell together."
Now, losing patience after a series of arguments, she declares the relationship has reached a crisis and that the next step is up to Sue, who
should have no illusions as to the writer's dependency: "You need not
fear to leave me lest I should be alone, for I often part with things I fancy
I have loved, – sometimes to the grave, and sometimes to an oblivion
rather bitterer than death." She marks the rupture by returning an unnamed token of friendship: "It is the lingering emblem of the Heaven I
once dreamed, and though if this is taken, I shall remain alone, and
though in that last day, the Jesus Christ you love, remark he does not
know me – there is a darker spirit will not disown its child."

But then the letter undergoes a surprising transformation. In a gesture that one would not expect from Sue, Emily offers a generous poetic
tribute to her alienated friend:

> *I have a Bird in spring*
> *Which for myself doth sing –*

Although this bird flies away "as the summer nears," the speaker trusts
that it will learn a new melody elsewhere and that "each little discord
here" will be resolved:

> *Then will I not repine,*
> *Knowing that Bird of mine*
> *Though flown*
> *Shall in a distant tree*
> *Bright melody for me*
> *Return.*

Fr4A

The last lines imply that even if Sue does not come back to Amherst, she can still restore the friendship by writing.

Written during the heat of a quarrel, this communication exhibits the hopeful and giving turn ("return") that made a poet out of Emily. Her attachment stretched to the limit, she shifts from a damaged relationship to the larger generalities of art. Although the poem constitutes a "private message" (as Cristanne Miller puts it in another connection), it is "universalized by a double release from private circumstance." The release is simultaneously emotional and artistic, so that what begins as a letter conceding the end of a relationship turns into a poem that foresees a consolatory alternative. We here observe a generative moment in Dickinson's art, which comes into being just as her isolation seems about to triumph. In part a surrogate for the relationships she hasn't been able to realize, her poetry arises as an act of transcendence or resurrection, in a way fulfilling her youthful idea that heaven is necessary in order to complete earth's frustrating friendships.

If Eliza Coleman had learned about the quarrel during her Commencement stay with the Dickinsons, as seems likely, that would help explain her counsel to look to the hills for strength. Staying in touch with the poet, she wrote John Graves that autumn that "*Emilie* too, sends me beautiful letters & each one makes me love her more. I know you appreciate her & I think few of her Amherst friends do. They wholly misinterpret her, I believe." The operative distinction here is between the poet's Amherst friends, among whom Sue was preeminent, and friends from elsewhere (Emmons, Graves, Coleman); the implication is that Sue remains unforgiving. When Dickinson learned that Graves had patched things up with an alienated friend, "tears of happiness came shining in my eyes." She wrote this at a time when her own conciliatory gesture was still unsuccessful.

In late August or September, hearing nothing from her flown bird, Emily tried again. This time she sent an apology laced with humor and not a hint of recrimination: "I was foolish eno' to be vexed at a little thing, and I hope God will forgive me, as he'll have to many times, if he lives long enough." Without specifying the "little thing," she told how her feelings had shifted from resentment to forgiveness: though "much of sorrow has gathered at your name, [so] that ought [i.e., "aught"] but peace was 'tween us, yet I remembered on, and bye and bye the day came." She confided that she had concealed Sue's silence from everyone except Austin and Vinnie, then concluded with a signal that it was her friend's move: "Write if you love, to Emilie."

Sue did write, eventually, from Grand Haven, though it isn't known whether the letter was addressed to Emily or another. Seizing on the news that Sue walked and sewed alone, Emily assured her that "*I* walk and sew alone" as well. This, however, was not a very rich connection, and in her frustration the poet wished she could "paint a portrait which would bring the tears" to her hard-hearted friend: "the scene should be – *solitude,* and the figures – solitude – and the lights and shades, each a solitude." Austin being about to leave for Chicago, she exclaimed: "He will see you, Darling! What I cannot do. Oh *could* I!" Full of irony and exclamation, her thoughts racing, the writer seems to have been less despondent than a hasty reading might suggest. Or perhaps the act of writing picked her up. One thing is clear: she was working her seductive powers of language for all they were worth.

By late January 1855, Emily was indignant. Recalling the front doorstep where she exchanged confidences with her friends, she all but demanded an answer:

> I love you as dearly, Susie, as when love first began, on the step at the front door, and under the Evergreens, and it breaks my heart sometimes, because I do not hear from you. I wrote you many days ago – I wont say many *weeks,* because it will look sadder so, and then I cannot write. . . . I fall asleep in tears, for your dear face, yet not one

word comes back to me from that silent West. If it is finished, tell me, and I will raise the lid to my box of Phantoms, and lay one more love in. . . . Why Susie – think of it – you are my precious Sister, and will be till you die.

Why was no melody returned?

Unbreakable but unreturned affection; thoughts of heaven that wouldn't go away; a father's absoluteness in defeat; art as metaphor and vision; the artist as wounded; the artist as constant; a very private box: the elements of the poet's situation were being assembled.

Chapter 15

1855–1858: Troubles and Riddles

The period from 1855 to 1858, marked by obscure and painful trials, collapses, transformations, ended with Dickinson's long-gestated emergence as a working poet who knew what she was about. The documentation of her life in these years is so slender that some have concluded she had an incapacitating and well-covered-up breakdown, perhaps even a fully psychotic episode. As with other hypotheses that seek to explain this writer, nothing proves quite so useful as gimlet-eyed scrutiny and an insistence on plausible evidence. That she experienced severe and mounting troubles is clear. That she became any less capable of performing her usual functions, domestic and compositional, is not. The sharp reduction in the number of her surviving letters has several explanations: most of her earlier friendships had lapsed; many ongoing or new correspondences were destroyed in their entirety; and with Sue and Austin settling in next door she had no occasion to produce the detailed record of the early 1850s. Most important, her continuing shift from reportorial to lyric modes tended to throw another veil over her life, the thickest one yet. To an extent, she disappeared into her poems, which, in 1858, apparently without telling anyone, she began preserving in small, neatly copied, hand-sewn booklets. Increasingly, her bulletins would come from a place no one we know had seen or visited.

From Washington to Wadsworth

Representative Dickinson and his two daughters checked in at Willard's Hotel in Washington on February 10, 1855—the same day the Gilbert sisters planned to return to Amherst. Just missing Sue in this way made Emily all the more averse to the long trip south, but Father was not to be withstood, it seems. A trip to a city was one of his standing remedies for village doldrums; Emily needed an enlivening shaking-up, as when she went to Boston in 1851; and since Edward was now a lame-duck congressman, this would be her one chance at the sights and society of the nation's capital. But her new and fashionable outfits made her feel like an "embarrassed Peacock."

This note of discomfiture stands out in Emily's letters home to Sue and the Hollands (those to Austin, who stayed behind with Mother, have not survived). Unlike Vinnie, who wore herself out walking with the ladies she met, Emily was glad to be excused from the "gaities" by illness, "tho' at that," she quickly added, "I'm gayer than I was." Feeling that "all is jostle, here – scramble and confusion," she remained within the circuit of her preoccupations, as we see in a family story about her falsely naive reaction to a flaming plum pudding brought on at dinner: "Oh, Sir, may one eat of hell fire with impunity here?" Her dismissal of official and social Washington—"the pomp – the court – the etiquette – they are of the earth – will not enter Heaven"—resembles her equally sweeping judgment of Boston four years earlier. Even when she expressed appreciation of the "many sweet ladies and noble gentlemen [who] have taken us by the hand and smiled upon us pleasantly," her social discernment remained strikingly rudimentary.

Dickinson's only known sightseeing excursion on this trip was by boat to Mount Vernon, then recently opened to the public and exhibiting a weathered and unpainted exterior. She told the Hollands how, after landing, "we reached the tomb of General George Washington, how we paused beside it, and no one spoke a word, then hand in hand, walked on again, not less wise or sad for that marble story; how we went within the door – raised the latch he lifted when he last went home – thank the Ones in Light that he's since passed in through a brighter wicket!" Making allowance for the simple tone she often took with the Hollands, it is dismaying to reflect that this unobserving and insipid prose issued from the pen of a great poet. But Dickinson was as radically out of place in Washington as she would be in the no less chaotic postwar era, when the rising young writers—Mark Twain, Henry James, W. D. Howells—established themselves precisely through travel writing and exact social description. Dickinson's powers became inoperative in the public realm this new generation helped teach the nation to see. In fact, she already thought of herself as "so old fashioned."

Her one account of a new acquaintance seems typical. After Vinnie was introduced in the hotel parlor to an officer named Rufus Saxton, a relation of Sue's, Emily was persuaded to descend in company with her sister. On being introduced (as she told Sue and Martha), "we walked in the hall a long while, talking of you, my Children, vieing with each other in compliment to those we loved so well." Did she realize that Lieutenant Saxton had recently participated in a major expedition through the Missouri and Columbia River drainages . . . and would it have mattered? In every way, including the mild adventure of walking in the hall, the episode reveals the tightly circumscribed boundaries within which she would have to devise some kind of freedom.

What little we know about Dickinson's exposure to Washington society comes mostly from others. On February 19 a woman who had checked into the hotel two weeks earlier, Mrs. James Brown of Alabama, gave the Dickinson sisters an inscribed copy of Elizabeth Stuart Phelps's posthumous volume, *The Last Leaf from Sunny Side*. When Emily met the William G. Bates family, fellow hotel guests from Westfield, Massachusetts, she impressed the daughter, Jeanie, "as a girl with large, warm heart, earnest nature, & delicate tastes, & we soon became friends." In

1890 Vinnie recalled, how accurately one cannot say, that she and her sister "had an adoring love" for Edward's colleague in the House, Thomas Dawes Eliot, looking up to him as "their girlish ideal" of the perfect man. He, too, was staying at Willard's.

After three weeks of Washington, Edward took his daughters to Philadelphia and then went home, leaving Emily and Vinnie to spend at least two weeks with their friend and second cousin, Eliza Coleman, on Nineteenth Street below Chestnut. Hotel life was over now, and the poet was back in the familiar world of private connections: Eliza's father, Lyman, was her old German teacher. Now he ran Philadelphia's Presbyterian Academy, the school of choice for the denomination's local "families of position."

Although the sequence of events will no doubt always be obscure, it is thought Dickinson was taken to the Arch Street Presbyterian Church to hear the Reverend Charles Wadsworth, and that he made such an impression on her she later solicited his counsel and thus initiated one of her most vital friendships. There is no doubt his pulpit oratory had made him the most famous of the city's ministers, the one "the stranger within the gates" went to hear, and that he was well and active in March 1855. It is also certain the poet corresponded with him before he moved to San Francisco in 1862. At his death she variously typed him as "my Philadelphia," "my Clergyman," "my dearest earthly friend," "my Shepherd from 'Little Girl'hood." The relationship was obviously a central one for her. In trying to understand it, we seem to get, if not the key, at least a rough period template from the nineteenth-century life of Emily Brontë that speaks of "the reverent, eager friendship that intellectual girls often give to a man much older than they."

Judging from contemporary reports, Wadsworth's deep bass tones, reserved emotional power, and luminous language, combined with his original exposition of Old School Presbyterian thought, produced an unforgettable effect. He impressed believers and unbelievers alike, including Mark Twain, who heard him in San Francisco and liked his humorous glare. Extremely reclusive, he avoided the members of his congregation and even fellow pastors, letting himself be known only through his preaching, which seemed to emerge from dark internal sources he simultaneously protected and pointed to. "You feel," wrote an admiring colleague, "that behind all he says there must be lying years of conflict and agony, of trials and sorrows, of deep gloom and despondency, of strong cries and tears." Strong, tragic, unknowable: this was how he impressed Dickinson, who, characterizing him decades later as "a 'Man of sorrow,' " recalled this curious scene: "once when he seemed almost overpowered by a spasm of gloom, I said 'You are troubled.' Shivering as he spoke, 'My Life is full of dark secrets,' he said. He never spoke of himself, and encroachment I know would have slain him." According to his eulogist, Wadsworth produced the effect of "a messenger from another world." After his death, reading something by or about him, Dickinson said, "I have had a Letter from another World."

Her care not to encroach reminds us of Thomas Wentworth Higginson's wariness with *her* ("the slightest attempt at direct cross-examination would make her withdraw into her shell; I could only sit still and watch"). But Wadsworth's enigmatic self-presentation was more portentous and tragic than her own, as if he were concealing an old wound too terrible to be looked at. When an alumni officer at Princeton Theological Seminary wanted an update, the minister replied that he had lived "extempore" and "was born without a memory." Apparently, Dickinson saw him only twice after 1855. Other than that "his Life was so shy and his tastes so unknown," she gleaned little about him.

No doubt Wadsworth had his secrets, yet there seems little mystery about the basic outline of his life, beginning with his fractured youth. Born in 1814 near Litchfield, Connecticut, he was the product of prominent and well-to-do forebears, partners in one of the area's slitting mills (for slicing iron bars or plates into squared nail rods). As he once recalled, he "never got whipped for I was a 'Wadsor' and my father was 'Lord of the Manor.' " All such privileges ended in 1830, when father Henry died insolvent and everything he owned down to his clothes had to be sold to pay his debts. Left with no obvious means of support, his widow, Mary Ann, remarried in December 1834, shortly before the final liquidation. She and Charles seem to have been very close.

Leaving Litchfield for upstate New York, the boy attended a variety of schools including the Oneida Institute, a respected manual-labor academy in Whitesboro for intended ministers. After being expelled from Hamilton College for an unauthorized absence, he graduated from Union College, at the time something of a degree mill. By then he had already gained a reputation as a poetic prodigy, his work appearing in respected outlets under the name Sedley. Adept, unforced, conventional, his verse shows traces of orthodox Calvinism, eighteenth-century "graveyard" meditation, and, interestingly, Lord Byron. Like the latter's Childe Harold, Sedley seems weighed down by a gloomy and premature initiation into life's sorrows. He is evidently in exile from New England and oppressed by memories of a vanished Eden and lost family members; his subjects include the night sky, solitude, the 1832 cholera epidemic. One intriguing poem, "To ___ ___ ___," written at age seventeen, probably at the Oneida Institute, says good-bye to a loved woman who has saved him from despair:

> *Lady! I did not, could not deem,*
> *A year ago, that love could fling*
> *The witchings of its rainbow dream*
> *Upon my spirit's drooping wing!*

Having gained a name as a precocious genius, Wadsworth turned to the ministry, used his expressive talents for sermon writing, and gave up poetry. This was his life's pivot: away from the sad and artful backward look and toward the modern practical world and applied religion. "The poet, the creator of these later times," he insisted in 1852, "brings forth, not day dreams, but realities." The steam engine was a "mightier epic than the Paradise Lost," the telegraph "a lovelier and loftier creation of true poetry than . . . Shakespeare's Tempest." In his 1857 Thanksgiving message, "Religious Glorying," a spirited exhortation to be of good cheer in spite of the financial panic, Wadsworth was extremely critical of "the infirmities of the poetic impulse." He quoted from Wordsworth's "Immortality Ode" only to rebuke lyric poetry as such for its unphilosophical and self-indulgent "wild plaint." The next year he denounced "our poetry" as "mystically spasmodic—uttering transcendental nothings, very wild and *very watery*." Whitman remained outside the pale for the minister, but by 1865 he had changed his mind on Wordsworth, quoting his ode with approval.

As preacher, Wadsworth frequently used his poetic gifts to celebrate Anglo-Saxon triumphalism. It wasn't always clear whether he had in mind spiritual or military victory:

> See yonder great Indian city, walled to the skies, battlemented with adamant, swarming with an armed soldiery, arrogant and boastful as if unconquerable and everlasting. But hark! Out of the midnight comes a strange dull sound, at first tremulous, indistinct, distant; yet now drawing nearer, waxing louder—and now you know it—the advance of an armed host; the tramp of marshalled men; the clangor of British steel; the peal of the Highland music; the grand old Saxon war-cry—the challenge of Christian chivalry unto the strength and pride of Heathenism. And now you catch, through the shadows of night, the gleam of bristling armor; the waving of plumes and banners; the march of mighty men. See! they throw up batteries—they advance the lines—they man the trenches—they rush to the assault . . .

His San Francisco congregation, before whom he uttered these stirring and fearsome words, remembered him as "a man of one idea—the pulpit his throne, and he knowing it, endeavoring at all times to fill it with kingly presence." In the eyes of a son, he stood out for "all who knew him as 'a strong man.' " What evidence there is suggests that his "Saxon" force appealed to Dickinson as much as it built up the tension between them.

That she admired the preacher was well enough known to Eudocia Flynt, of Monson, for her to send the poet on January 4, 1858, "Mr Wadsworth Sermon—preached in Phil." The sermon was probably the just published "Religious Glorying," which wrote off lyric poetry as a weak, backward-looking wail.

Dickinson lives for us because she was able to pack grief, gaiety, memory, and so much more in a tight, always fresh, lyric package. The unsettling irony is that when she sought pastoral advice, she turned to a man who went public at an early age with his precocious verse and then found success by repudiating poetry and the past and celebrating the triumph of modern, industrial Protestantism. According to Austin, the poet "reached out eagerly, fervently even, toward anybody who kindled the spark." Even though we know next to nothing about her relationship with her chosen shepherd, "born <u>without</u> <u>a memory</u>," it seems obvious it can't have been an easy one for her.

Austin Converts

In May 1853 Edward Dickinson was apprised of Austin and Sue's secret engagement. The next time church let out in the evening, he proudly escorted his daughter-in-law-elect to the Cutler house, delighting Emily with the thought of all the turning bonnets ("I thought the folks would stare"). There was an instant rapport between Sue and Father, who felt, as Emily put it, that "she appreciates him, better than most anybody else." Sue adored his severe, upright manhood, his stylish horsemanship in particular, "sitting very erect, reins taut," compelling the animal to hold its head as high as his own. To catch the Squire (as he, too, was now known) driving Amherst's quiet, unpaved streets in his 1851 carriage was to see on display all his expertness, discipline, pride.

Austin also presented himself well, striking others as a "smart" or "fine" fellow. After the engagement was made public, Sue described him in a letter to her brother Dwight as "strong, manly, resolute—understands human-nature and will take care of me." But the one point at which she expressed any real fervor was in connection with the "long-cherished wish of my heart to have a home where my brothers and sisters can come." Austin she spoke of merely as "the man I love well enough to marry." This lukewarmness calls to mind her enthusiasm for singleness and sisterhood in Tennyson's *Princess,* and her lingering eye for Ned Hitchcock, now teaching at Williston Seminary.[1] But what chiefly troubled her was Austin himself—his basic inner quality.

After all, how manly and resolute was he? Still "poor and young," with his fortune to make, did he measure up to his father or her brothers? Once, sounding like the much-indulged boy he was, Austin assured Martha Gilbert that "the world is very wide & Fortune very kind & fears & doubts are for the [weaker?] & the wicked," as if an orphan's vigilance were a mark of weakness. In winter 1854–1855 he traveled west to look for business openings, mainly in Chicago, it seems, where John Thompson, his college roommate, was launching a legal career. Whether there was any real testing of fortune isn't known. The feeler led to nothing.

John Cody has cogently argued that Sue's doubts about her fiancé gave her "the upper hand." From time to time Austin was overcome by a fear "like the wasting Simoon . . . [P]erhaps I shall not be able to [illegible] you happy—perhaps I shall not satisfy you." When she confided that the "mere relation of wife" left her with "gloomy thoughts," he made the possibly tactical concession that their union need not be physical: "can I not say that you may live just exactly as you are happiest in living . . . as you please *just like a girl always* if so you are happiest—that I will ask nothing of you take nothing from you—you are not the happier in giving me" (italics added). He was especially concerned to assure her that their first year of marriage need not be "a year of 'fearful unhappiness.' "

In religious matters, Austin also gave away a great deal. When Sue opposed his attending a Unitarian church in Cambridge, he stopped going. When she voiced her suspicion he would "turn away from [her let-

---

1. Nine months and a day after Ned married Mary Judson on November 30, 1853, she gave birth. When the couple showed up in Amherst with their baby, Emily sent a report to Sue in Michigan:

> I called upon Mary – she appears very sweetly, and the baby is quite becoming to her. . . . Mary inquired for you with a good deal of warmth, and wanted to send her love when I wrote. Susie – had that been you – well-well I must stop, *Sister*. Things *have* wagged, dear Susie, and they're wagging still.

Imagining what Sue's life would have been if *she* had married Ned and had that baby, Emily showily suppresses her improper train of thought. The passage shows her fondness for touching on delicate matters and tracing alternative or phantom lives. The "wagging" things are (surely) tongues, talking about months and pregnancy.

ter] to live on . . . indifferently to the great truths of religion," he earnestly promised (at much greater length than this) "to think more seriously on the subject." And so he did, apparently reading the religious literature she pressed on him, such as *The Christian Life Social and Individual* by Peter Bayne. Inscribed "Austin—from Sue," this book opens with a prefatory scuttling of the notion that "evangelical religion . . . comports ill with solidity and compass of intellect" and ends with one of the recipient's bow ties pressed between the pages. His one courtship letter preserved with Sue's papers gushes over her saving role: "Oh the mystery—the mystery of love! it affects me all the more, that it has not been my wont to *believe* in *realities*—I never *felt* anything *real* before. . . . Perhaps God has chosen this way to bring a naturally pure, honest, inquiring soul from the deep darkness of such infidelity into the marvelous light of the real."

And thus it came about that the poet's last ally ceased resisting. In late 1855, listening to an afternoon sermon at the First Church, Austin was struck by the closing words, apparently "choose now." Several weeks later he rose at an evening service and made a confession of belief that was deemed sound enough to admit him to full membership on January 6. He proved to be the only new member to join by profession of faith for all of 1856. Most converts were saved during revivals and joined in groups. Austin came in alone, saved, one might say, by Sue.

If his confession followed the lines of the draft statement preserved with his papers, it opened with the curious (and unspontaneous) admission that "my own voice . . . as I speak almost startles me. It seems . . . as though some other must be speaking in me." Recalling his legal training, he characterized himself as a witness who had given false testimony and now wished to amend it. Formerly, he had said that religion was "a delusion, the bible a fable, life an enigma," and that if God "had desired to reveal himself to us, he would have done so in a way we could not have mistaken." Now, he was sure the Bible was "*no* fable, that the law of love which it commands could have originated in no human breast." Saying nothing about sin, guilt, or doctrines, he assured his listeners that Christianity was "the happiest brightest, most joyous thing" the heart could know.

Austin had a loud, flat, carrying voice that was said to "blat."[2] If Emily was there to hear him, his self-important peroration must have left a bitter aftertaste. Like Prince Hal repudiating Falstaff, her brother not only renounced the candid irreverence he had shared with his sister but, addressing the unsaved with his usual assurance, advised them that God is *full* of love for you" and that they too should "choose while you may— tonight you may." Tonight God "will make the darkness in you light." And then came the old familiar threat: "the words I have now spoken may one day come back like words of fire to burn upon your soul."

Betrayal had been the subject of Edwards A. Park's sermon two years earlier, a dramatic treatment of the friendship of Judas and Jesus. Two decades later, Emily remembered it as "the loveliest sermon I ever heard." What stayed with her was "the disappointment of Jesus . . . It was told like a mortal story of intimate young men. I suppose no surprise we can ever have will be so sick as that."

Five years after Austin's confession of faith, Emily ended a letter to a Unitarian friend with a series of wacky excuses for not relaying the usual messages of love. Vinnie, asleep, had gone to "meet tomorrow." Mother was out "sweeping up a leaf." As for Austin, he "would send his [love] – but he dont live here – now – He married – and went East." The passage mystifies, not only because Austin and Sue's house was west of the Dickinson Homestead but because the marriage was by now old news. The explanation may be that Austin "went East" by getting religion, and that long after the event Dickinson's sense of fraternal abandonment was apt to revive. Her strange present tense ("I do not know of you, a long while – I remember you – several times") nicely conveys memory's timeless limbo, where nothing ever terminates or gets resolved.

"The Babies we *were are* buried," the poet wrote Abiah, "and their shadows are plodding on." Among her rare gifts was the capacity to sense where those old and shadowy selves (which Wadsworth fled) were heading. Another was the ability to give herself to her friends without sacrificing her independence and integrity. In her earlier pleas to her

---

2. Years later, when Captain J. L. Skinner went fishing, he got a humiliating public tongue-lashing from Austin that was "blat[t]ed out in his rough way loud enough to be heard half a mile."

brother to come into her garden, to return to Amherst, to think of home as heaven, she was asking him to stay with her always in the land of memory and childhood. Of course he could not do this, but was it necessary to publicly betray her?

Perhaps it was, given his own self-betrayal—his light and easy conversion for his fiancée's sake. His sister's solitude, as the next few years would teach her, was now much deeper.

Father Moves

In 1851, when the Dickinson Mansion was owned and occupied by the aging David Mack, Emily was relieved her family did not "come home as we used, to this old castle," which she pictured as full of specters, echoes, mold. Having lived there until she was nine, she associated the house with an ancestral past she had no interest in revisiting.

In 1855, a year after Mack died, his son Samuel, living in Cincinnati, had to raise money quickly to cover the debts of a failed business partner for whom he had endorsed. One of Amherst's most desirable residential properties now came on the market, catching the eye of several potential buyers, among them Judge Seth Terry of Hartford. But it was already too late: on April 20, the Amherst newspaper disclosed that "the Hon. Edward Dickinson, whose father, Samuel F. Dickinson, formerly owned the place," had purchased it. He gave $6,000 for house and land, a great bargain according to the disgusted Mrs. Terry, who declared the seller had "no judgment & is wasting all his Father left him." Along with the two-and-a-half-acre home lot, Edward acquired the eleven-acre "meadow" across the road. This field had been reduced in size a few years earlier, when Mack sold the easternmost third to the A&B Railroad for tracks, depot, and factory sites.

There is no mystery as to Edward's motives in buying the place his father had built and lost. In addition to securing possession of one of Amherst's finest houses, he was publicly redeeming his father's loss of property and prestige, salving his own recent reelection defeat, and publishing his success in the world. Advertising for a mason skilled in stonework, brick, and plaster, to whom he promised six months' employment, Edward set in motion a major and expensive remodeling, rumored to cost more than $5,000. It was at this time that the house substantially assumed its present size and configuration: a square cupola was built; the west wing was replaced with a porch; the rear ell was also demolished, and replaced with a large two-story service ell, including a kitchen; and an attached greenhouse (since destroyed) was built on the southeast. The latter structure, probably designed for the two Emilys, eventually became the younger one's special domain. "We shall be in our new house soon," the poet predicted in mid-October; "they are papering now."

A couple of weeks after snagging the old family place, Edward induced his son to give up the thought of moving west by offering to make him full partner and build a house for him and Sue. This marked the end of Edward's partnership with Elbridge G. Bowdoin, who, "owing to ill health," it was said, left for Iowa and settled there. The new house was to go up adjacent to the Homestead on what Edward had once called the neighborhood's "best building lot." Over the years he had pieced it together as if preparing for this very moment. Indeed, his realm was being consolidated everywhere: at church, where Austin bought a pew across from his family on the right aisle's power row, and in the cemetery, where Edward arranged for the removal of someone else's infant from what was now the Dickinson family plot. Setting himself against the usual American patterns of dispersal, Edward was creating a walled patriarchy—a project bearing comparison with Emily's dream of gathering her friends and going " 'no more out.' "

Informing her brother about these exciting plans, Sue addressed the tensions between Austin and herself with typical firmness and aplomb:

> Austin's Father has over-ruled all objections to our remaining here [in Amherst] and tho' it has been something of a sacrifice for Austin's spirit and rather of a struggle with his pre-conceived ideas, I feel satisfied that in the end it will be best. . . . [W]e have decided to defer our marriage till another Spring and *that* will give me no more time than I shall need, to prepare for housekeeping. . . . Won't I be proud

to get you an oyster supper some cold night? Don't speak of it—it makes me too happy.

Picturing herself as about to fulfill her longstanding dream of re-creating the Gilberts' broken home, she presents Austin as the one who has made the accommodating sacrifices. This portrayal seems accurate enough except for her claim that "we" have decided to put off the wedding; in fact, her fiancé had opposed further postponements. At bottom, though, he shared her belief that a rare dream was about to come true: "*what* a home you & I shall make, Sue—Did anyone else ever dream of such a home?"

The house was paid for by Edward, who retained ownership, but his son was in charge of design. An elevation sent by one of Sue's wealthy brothers prompted Austin to announce he didn't "like handsome houses—home-ly houses are my kind, rather plain, [ample?] comfortable looking suggesting repose wealth and yet independence of wealth." Still, intrigued by Dwight's "brilliant" plan, he was willing to consider "an angle or two better than has yet been done in G.R. [Grand Rapids] domestic architecture." It isn't known whether the house as built, an up-to-date Italianate villa with a flat-roofed tower, wide porch, and "angles"[3] galore, was based on the Michigan design. The local builder, William Fenno Pratt of Northampton, no doubt contributed many ideas. Construction got under way the winter Austin joined the church. The first named house in Amherst, it was called the Evergreens after his interest in tree planting and landscaping. Considerable attention was given to compositional effect, from the smooth stone-colored siding and bright green shutters to the select rhododendrons scattered under the trees.

In November 1855 the Dickinsons moved back to the Homestead, leaving for good their West Street house, its well-tended garden, orchard, and grapevine arbor, and the stand of pines—the *old* evergreens, planted by Austin. This was Edward's moment: his father's catastrophe had been wiped out, his son and daughter-in-law would soon be in their

---

3. In the Italianate villa, the intended effect of "superior comfort or refinement" was achieved partly by making the kitchen less conspicuous than in traditional New England houses. Sue and Austin put theirs in an older preexisting house hidden behind and joined to the new and larger structure. Undergoing restoration at present, the Evergreens is open to the public on a limited basis.

model home next door, and everyone was safely churched and bound for heaven, except Emily. But the move brought confusion or collapse to her and Mother.

The poet's one account of this move dwells on her feelings of dizziness and fragmentation. Remembering the Hollands' early visit to the Dickinsons' former parlor, she felt the memory take on "a *spectral* air," with the participants turning to "phantoms" and vanishing. Indeed, she felt that she herself had been "lost in the *mêlée*" on moving day, and that the few wits she retained were "so badly shattered that repair is useless – and still I can't help laughing at my own catastrophe." Recalling the hackneyed proverb that home is where the heart is, she offered a sturdy correction: "I think it is where the *house* is, and the adjacent buildings." Which was tantamount to saying, beneath the insouciance, that her own heart wasn't in the new house.

That said, the determined gaiety ceased and she spoke of the real trouble: "But, my dear Mrs. Holland, I have another story, and lay my laughter all away. . . . Mother has been an invalid since we came *home*, . . . lies upon the lounge, or sits in her easy chair. I don't know what her sickness is, for I am but a simple child, and frightened at myself." Not only did the two Emilys take little pleasure at returning to what the younger one rightly termed "our father's house," but the older one's oddly timed collapse caused the poet to take fright at *herself*, fearing her own "machinery [would] get slightly out of gear" and that someone might have to "stop the wheel."

The letter was an extremely complicated performance, throwing any number of veils over the writer's confusion and worry. But it made no attempt to conceal the link between Mother's collapse and Emily's panic, both inexplicable. The mother's and daughter's time of troubles had begun.

Breakdowns and Collapses

Dickinson's sketchy account of her mother's inability, reluctance, or refusal to leave her chair pretty much sums up what we know about her long-lasting collapse. Indeed, two years would pass before any of the poet's few extant letters from this period mention it again. Writing a professor's wife in summer 1858, she said she would pay a call if she could leave "home, or mother. I do not go out at all, lest father will come and miss me, or miss some little act, which I might forget, should I run away – Mother is much as usual. I know not what to hope of her. Please remember Vinnie and I, for we are perplexed often." As was always the case during Mrs. Dickinson's illnesses, the poet's domestic responsibilities had become much heavier. Yet the passage has a strategic opacity, providing no information about Mother's symptoms and not making clear which parent actually obliged the daughter to stay home. The odd parallel between Mother's not leaving her chair and Emily's not going out leaves us wondering how much the daughter truly wished to "run away."

Some forty years later, when Vinnie wanted to set a reviewer straight regarding her sister's seclusion, she said: "Our mother had a period of invalidism, and one of her daughters must be constantly at home; Emily chose this part and, finding the life with her books and nature so congenial, continued to live it." Although this version of events oversimplifies the considerations that induced the poet to stay home, and also her feelings about this, it does look as if Mother's illness reinforced a tendency.

Outside the family, we find as few contemporary references to Mrs. Dickinson's invalidism as within it. The most revealing comes from Jane Hitchcock, detailing the news of September 1856: "Eliza Coleman is visiting Emily & Vinnie at present, while they are housekeepers; for Mrs. D's health is poor & she is at the water-cure in N. Hampton." Water cures, in vogue from the 1840s, specialized in applications of hot and cold towels and were prescribed for a variety of physical and nervous disorders. In 1864 Northampton's reputation as an up-to-date hydropathic center would attract young Henry James for a few months. As long as Emily Norcross Dickinson was a patient there, Emily and Vinnie automatically became dual housekeepers, charged with running a large house still somewhat new to them. The stressed sisters were probably glad to have Eliza on hand.

At the end of 1857, a friend in Cincinnati was "gratified to hear of any improvement in Mrs Dickinson's health." In August 1859 she ascended Mount Holyoke with her husband, Vinnie, and Charlotte Sewall Eastman, probably riding in a horse-drawn rig most of the way. That winter she was able to visit Mary Shepard, who promptly reported that "among the callers, we have had—was *Mrs.* Edward Dickinson, last Thursday P.M. appearing as well, as *4 years* ago—when last she was here." The next morning Shepard sent her caller a note that all but rustles with stiff millinery proprieties: "Will Mrs. Dickinson be kind enough to lend me her winter Bonnet, to look at; & keep through the day? And if she recollect the quantity of silk, in it, please to mention it." That this flattering trifle was preserved among the recipient's few letters says something about her life's social bareness.

In later years, daughter-in-law Sue, with her keen sense of social punctilio, often presided over weddings and funerals, receptions and excursions. Her great difficulty in planning her own wedding on July 1, 1856, was that Amherst's two locations were each unsuitable: Austin's house lay under a pall of invalidism, and the Cutler house was ruled by an intolerable paterfamilias. Her decision to have the ceremony performed in Geneva, at the home of Aunt Sophia Van Vranken, seems sensible enough, yet it met with strong opposition in Amherst, causing, in Sue's words, "great shaking among the old plans, and thawing of fancy's frost works." She didn't specify the bearing of these metaphors, which point to Austin and Emily among others: Austin always planning the couple's perfect future, Emily often fancying intensities of friendship.[4] Sue's two extant wedding letters do not mention the Dickinsons, referring only to Gilbert brothers and sisters and "a *very few* of our special friends." The omission seems odd, even allowing that Mrs. Dickinson's incapacity would have kept Emily and Vinnie from traveling to Geneva. It almost looks as if Sue began wedded life with a symbolic act of exclusion.

As to the nature of Mrs. Dickinson's trouble, clearly more serious

---

4. Sue's only note to Dickinson commenting on a poem speaks of a stanza's "ghostly shimmer" and how she always wants to "go to the fire and get warm after thinking of it." She could almost be describing "fancy's frost works."

than her recurring "neuralgia," we might note the fatigue and depression that overcame her sister Lavinia in the early days of her marriage: "I do not go out a great deal it tires me to walk or makes my back ache. . . . A great deal of the time I look very pale the truth is I feel as tho every thing was a burden." The arresting detail—that Emily Norcross Dickinson collapsed after moving back to the house she had occupied in the early years of her own marriage—invites us to think about the hidden life of old feelings and the conditions under which they revive. Recalling the insecure domestic arrangements of her early married years, her drivenness as a housekeeper, her inexpressiveness, and the many deaths in her own family, we may wonder if her old and unresolved emotional issues had resurfaced. Did the grief she hadn't been free to entertain in her hard-pressed younger days now return, leaving her too tired to want to do anything? Did it worsen her malaise to have a haughty, highly literate, and socially expert daughter-in-law living next door? Why is it that none of Sue's writings have anything to say about her mother-in-law?

Another event that undoubtedly weighed on Mrs. Dickinson was the financial collapse of sister Lavinia's husband. At first, with the resolution of Norcross and Wood's bankruptcy in 1852, Loring seemed to land on his feet. He continued serving on the Boston School Committee, and when Sarah Vaill Norcross drew up her will with Edward Dickinson's advice, she made Loring an executor; he was still seen as solid enough for that.[5] Then came 1854, a year of "great commercial depression and disaster" for commission merchants. Loring kept creditors at bay by writing and endorsing six- or nine-month drafts payable to himself, but when the rubber money bounced he was taken to court. For four years beginning in 1855, the city of Boston assessed his taxable property at zero. The city directory for 1856 does not even give a business address for him.

Capping that, however, was the painful family lawsuit in which the failed merchant was unsuccessfully represented by Edward Dickinson. Since 1846, Loring and his brother Albert had been trustees of the part

---

5. Written in Edward's hand and signed on July 1, 1853, at the end of Sarah's week-long visit, this will was witnessed by him, Vinnie, and Emily.

of Joel Norcross's estate that went to William O. Norcross's children. In 1849, eager to invest trust funds in a promising ten-acre parcel in Newark, New Jersey (where William resided), the brothers sought legal sanction to invest out of state. The petition, drawn up rather sloppily by Edward, was dismissed. Loring and Albert then bought the land anyway, spending $3,000 of what should have been their own money.

It was Loring's one smart investment, and five years later, when the property was sold for $7,000, he and Albert regarded the profit as their own. Seeing things differently, the heirs brought suit in January 1857, accusing the trustees of retaining trust income for "their own personal and private use." The Hampden County Probate Court agreed and ordered them to pay the profit over to the trust fund. Appealing to the Supreme Judicial Court, the brothers maintained through their attorney—Edward—that the money they invested had been their own. But Edward couldn't make the argument stick, and in its April 1858 term Massachusetts' highest court handed Loring the worst of his humiliations. From now on, whatever the true merits of his and Albert's position, it would look as if they had tried to defraud their first cousin's children.

This seems to have been the only legal fight among Joel's heirs, still a very tight clan. It must have had a wrenching effect on Emily Norcross Dickinson, given her closeness to Lavinia and, at least formerly, to William. Never before or since, one guesses, did she take a greater interest in Edward's law work or share with him a more rankling defeat. But one only guesses: no extant family letter mentions the suit.

Loring's sorry financial and legal record helps explain why his daughters, Louisa and Frances, did not allow the poet's first editor to see her letters to them, instead making excerpts and then destroying the originals: they were shielding their *own* privacy as well as their cousin's. Their sensitivity about their family's past offers a key to some of the poet's remarks, such as her curious 1863 eulogy of their deceased father: "the meek mild gentleman who thought no harm but peace toward all." Writing against a background of invidious comment, she was saying (to those in the know) that the harm Loring did was not deliberate and did not reflect on his fairness and kindliness. On this delicate matter, Dickinson apparently took the same line as her family.

Does Edward's defense of Loring and Albert imply that he saw the Newman estate as available for his own use, given his large real estate and building commitments? One scholar has argued that he dipped into this trust fund in 1857 and thus "augmented the Dickinsons at the expense of the Newmans." The accusation has three serious flaws: it is based on an error in reading Edward's inventories; there is no other producible evidence; and at no time did the Newman heirs or their husbands register dissatisfaction with his oversight of their affairs.

It's pointless to charge Edward with criminal peculation. When the *Boston Courier* floated his name for governor, the argument was that his administration would be free of "the corrupting influences from which we now suffer." In 1858 the national credit rating agency considered him and his son to be "Perf[ectly] Reliab[le] men of m[ean]s do a lar[ge] bus[iness]." The poet's sense of her father's incorruptibility was the communal perception.

Still, the man was every inch a Yankee, capable of shaving ethics if not the law. In March 1856 he sold the Nathan Dickinson place to his brother William for $6,000 and then, acting as Newman trustee, bought it back at the same figure. In effect he was unloading his own property on the trust account he managed, using William as intermediary. The obvious question is whether the price was a fair one. One answers it by noting that he paid the same amount, $6,000, for the Dickinson Homestead and meadow but that the valuation of these properties on Amherst's tax rolls was far from equal, the Newman place being assessed at $3,200 and the Dickinson place (*before* improvements) at $5,600. Even allowing for the vagaries of assessment, Edward clearly drove a much harder bargain with the Newman estate than Samuel E. Mack had driven with him. There is no getting around it: he turned a very sweet deal by selling to himself as trustee.

An even more ambiguous transaction lurks in the shadows of one of Emily's most mysterious and important letters. When the panic year of 1857 put an end to what a newspaper called the "mania for railroad building," the Amherst and Belchertown line went into financial collapse. The road survived, but only after being reorganized with a capital of $85,000, less than a third of the original investment; the stockholders seem to have been the big losers. The bondholders, on the other hand, of whom the poet's father was one, were able to buy the line and protect their interests. Fronting for them was none other than William Dickinson, who acted as receiver at a critical moment. This obscure transaction was a major event in the lives of Amherst's citizen-investors, yet the town's only paper, the *Hampshire and Franklin Express* (controlled by Edward and the railroad clique), did not provide a clear explanation of the reorganization or so much as mention William's name.[6]

The pattern running through these varied events—Mother's perplexing illness, Loring's failure, Norcross versus Norcross, the Panic, the A&B fiasco—was one of collapse and cover-up, of trouble too deep-seated to be examined in the light of day. That was how the world looked from the Dickinson mansion's second floor as 1858 dawned. The consequence: for Amherst, a major revival with numerous conversions; for Emily, a final and decisive acceptance of a vocation.

Great Awakenings

Because there seem to be no extant Dickinson letters for all of 1857, it is sometimes thought she had a breakdown that left her unable to write. Yet she is known to have been in touch with a friend in New Orleans, Joseph Lyman, whose correspondence that spring and summer speaks of letters received from Emily and Vinnie. On May 24, 1857, short of paper, he expanded an envelope that had just come from Emily and used it to write his fiancée. Visible on the outside are two blurry postmarks, May 16, the posting date, and May 24, the day the New Orleans post office processed the letter. Also visible are Joseph's name and address in Dickinson's large,

---

6. This cover-up has persisted in Dickinson biography in the repeated claim that Amherst College never lost a penny during Edward's treasurership. In fact, as a former president, Stanley King, long ago disclosed, the school lost a third of its investment in the line its treasurer had promoted, and was "fortunate" to lose no more.

flowing, confident-looking hand. Chances are, some other correspondents, such as Eliza Coleman, also heard from her that year.

Which is not to say she wasn't oppressed by her mother's breakdown and the other collapses and failures. The line dividing this world from the next, always present in her letters, became painfully salient in 1856 and 1858. Recalling the West Street parlor where she and Elizabeth Holland had met, she wrote, "We shall sit in a parlor 'not made with hands' unless we are very careful!" Reminding John Long Graves of "the crumbling wall that divides us from Mr Sweetser" (the Dickinsons' neighbor to the north), she jumped to other evidences of mortality: old flowers, last year's crickets, "*wings* half gone to dust." "We, too, are flying – fading," she moralized, adding (a glance at her poems?), "To live, and die, and mount again in triumphant body . . . is no schoolboy's theme!" Such thoughts became so obtrusive that in February 1858 Lyman complained to his fiancée: "Emily Dickinson I did like very much and do still. But she is rather morbid & unnatural."

This, the one contemporary account of her state of mind, coincides with the breaking out of a revival so intense and widespread it was given a name lifted from the era of George Whitefield: the Great Awakening. Edward Hitchcock had witnessed many such stirrings, but this one had a more "universal and thoroughly subduing power" than anything he had seen. At the nightly meetings in Henry Ward Beecher's church in Brooklyn, everyone "laughed and cried by turns, and hardly knew which to do most," having "got over the old shame connected with tears." At Philadelphia's Arch Street Church, Charles Wadsworth declared that "since Christ came, there have been but three revival seasons comparable with the present; the old Pentecost, in the first century, the Reformation in the sixteenth, and the great Awakening in the eighteenth." When news of the commotion reached France, Henry and William James's father took it as a sign of an "immense spiritual revolution" in America.

In Amherst, the excitement began in winter and ran into spring, bringing a total of twenty-four new members into the First Church by confession of faith. There can be little doubt Emily came in for special attention as the only family member still unconverted, or that her sense of pariahhood grew more acute. Thanking Mary Haven in early 1859 for an "*unmerited* remembrance," she added, " 'Grace' – the saints would call it. Careless girls like me, cannot testify."

It may have been this revival that spurred her to write Charles Wadsworth. Or perhaps, as Leyda guessed, she sought his counsel earlier, when her mother collapsed. Whatever the occasion, the minister found her appeal as obscure as it was anguished:

> My Dear Miss Dickenson
>
> 　I am distressed beyond measure at your note, received this moment,—I can only imagine the affliction which has befallen, or is now befalling you. . . .
>
> 　I am very, very anxious to learn more definitely of your trial— and though I have no right to intrude upon your sorrows yet I beg you to write me, though it be but a word.
>
> 　　　　　　　　　　　　　In great haste
> 　　　　　　　　　Sincerely and most affectionately <u>Yours</u>—

Wadsworth clearly intended to show his disturbed correspondent she had his complete attention. But did his pressing concern and last underlined word stir an unintended thought?

Although scholars have varied widely in dating this note, some putting it as late as 1877, it cannot have been written after spring 1862, when Wadsworth resigned his Arch Street pulpit: the monogrammed paper is identical to that of another extant letter of his dated "Arch St Dec 19" and sent to someone else. His misspelling of the poet's name, together with his ignorance as to the nature of her trouble, suggests the message dates from the beginning of their correspondence.

Why was this note alone preserved out of the correspondence? Of all the explanations that come to mind, one stands out: it marked a significant new departure in a developing relationship. Arriving in a time of distress, it held out an open ear and a warm heart—a promise of understanding.

"I Stagger as I Write"

Austin's conversion, Mother's and Uncle Loring's persistent collapses, the Norcross suit, the railroad, the revival, and the appeal to Wadsworth help us make sense of two enigmatic documents from Dickinson's hand, probably dating from the spring and summer of 1858: a draft of a note to someone she calls "Master" and a letter to Joseph A. Sweetser. "Much has occurred, dear Uncle," she reminds the latter, "so much – that I stagger as I write." And there we have it: a series of outer events accompanying an inner crisis, which manifests itself in a style too disturbed to make matters clear to strangers not in the know, namely us.

The note to Master, prompted by news of his[7] poor health, begins by disclosing that she has had another bad winter:

> I am ill – but grieving more that you are ill, I make my stronger hand work long eno' to tell you – I thought perhaps you were in Heaven, and when you spoke again, it seemed quite sweet, and wonderful, and surprised me so – I wish that you were well.

Evidently intending to produce a clean letter, Dickinson realized as she wrote that revision would be necessary and proceeded to introduce several interlineations. Did she go on to make a final copy and post it? Although the sense of urgency in her last words—"Will you tell me, please to tell me, soon as you are well"—shows she had cause to do so, we cannot say for sure any more than we can identify the recipient. The letter is tender and solicitous, including the recipient among those she loves ("I

---

7. I think it unlikely this person was a woman. In none of Dickinson's letters can "master" be shown to have a female referent. She spoke of Leonard Humphrey as her "Master" after reading *Jane Eyre*, where this is Jane's habitual term of address for Rochester. In Dinah Craik's *The Head of the Family*, read two years later, Rachel Armstrong regards the man who has awakened her mind as her "master"; see above, page 248. In four of Dickinson's seven poems containing the word, gendered language shows that this figure is male (Fr75, Fr133, Fr185, Fr764). In the other three (Fr395, Fr427, Fr697), the diction does not specify sex; perhaps it was taken for granted. In Fr395, "Sue," erased, is on the back of the sheet.

would that all I love, should be weak no more"), but it is not exactly a love letter. And we detect signs of a disconnect: her "flowers" (poems?) seem to have left him mystified, and there is another point on which she must briskly correct him: "Listen again, Master – I did not tell you that today had been the Sabbath Day." These misunderstandings, along with the man's geographical distance, may bring Wadsworth to mind but cannot be taken as serious evidence he was the one.

In the draft Dickinson says that the spring has inspired her with an intense desire to communicate what she sees of nature and beyond: "Indeed it is God's house – and these are gates of Heaven, and to and fro, the angels go, with their sweet postillions – I wish that I were great, like Mr – Michael Angelo, and could paint for you." The last sentence, her clearest hint yet of artistic aspiration, also has her earliest known use of "great" in relation to herself. How to be great and true as a painter of what she experiences has become a provoking torment, an outgrowth of the sweet pains of letter writing. There is a warm connection here between friendship and ambition.

The other letter, to Sweetser, also involves both a current trouble and the larger torment of artistic representation. Out of the distressing events that cause her to "stagger as I write," Dickinson focuses on one that has persisted through the change of seasons: "Summers of bloom – and months of frost, and days of jingling bells – yet all the while this hand upon our fireside. Today has been so glad without, and yet so grieved within – so jolly, shone the sun – and now the moon comes stealing, and yet it makes none glad." The hand that chilled the fireside was probably Mother's perplexing illness, now going on its third summer, but other troubles may have contributed to the dismal mood: the railroad mess was worsening, and Edward had just lost the Norcross suit.

Turning to the immediate season, as in the "Master" draft, Dickinson wishes she could communicate what she sees and hears but refrains from making the attempt:

> There is a smiling summer here, which causes birds to sing, and sets the bees in motion.

Strange blooms arise on many stalks, and trees receive their tenants.

I would you saw what I can see, and imbibed this music. The day went down, long time ago, and still a simple Choir bear the canto on.

The reference was to the sound of crickets or cicadas in trees. Dickinson knew that Sweetser, residing at 17 East Twenty-fourth Street in New York, couldn't hear this "Choir," which, as the next sentence hints, had become a symbol for her own ability to function in darkness and depression: "I dont know who it is, that sings, nor *did* I, would I tell!" Her emphatic obscurity marks the affiliation between her act of writing and the night's dark music.

Letters that fall to Sue and the Hollands proclaim the same reticence: "I shall never tell!" and "I shall not tell how short time is." A recently discovered note from Dickinson's last years shows how deep her identification with crickets went: "I am too rustic to know if reply to your lovely courtesy is authorized, but the Crickets are too unseen to be censured and their sable homage disturbs none."

Why did the poet's message from the night go to Uncle Joseph rather than, say, his wife, Catharine? As a commission merchant who had weathered the recent business panic, he would have known about Loring's failure and the great railroad trouble and thus how to read her opening words, "Much has occurred." At the same time, he was her most literary uncle, writing polished anniversary poems to his wife and from 1855 to 1858 funding Amherst College's first ongoing oratorical and literary prizes. The Sweetser awards in English composition were bestowed on June 29, 1858, and the "Sweetser Prize Declamation" took place on August 9, during Commencement Week. Her letter may anticipate her uncle's arrival for one of these events.

Knowing that Sweetser was a devotee of fine writing helps explain Dickinson's access of self-consciousness at her letter's end: "I hardly know what I have said – my words put all their feathers on – and fluttered here and there." She was admitting that her letter was a performance before a keenly judging eye, and also that one could easily say too much in a time of troubles and cover-ups. Hand in hand with her desire to announce herself as a writer went a self-protective secrecy. "I shall never tell!"

The First Manuscript Book

In 1858, apparently in summer, Dickinson undertook what R. W. Franklin terms "a major stocktaking, . . . a sifting and winnowing of her entire corpus." Reviewing the poems she had written in the distant and recent past even as she continued to compose new ones, she set about making clean copies of her work on good stationery. Entering several poems on each sheet, which came folded from the factory, she filled four sheets and bound them into a little booklet with needle and thread, stabbing near the fold. In this, she followed a practice like her father's years before, when he preserved his (messier) college compositions by sewing their pages together.

Unlike Edward, who didn't bother retranscribing, Emily assembled her manuscript books or fascicles with the same neat care as she had her herbarium a dozen years earlier. And just as the schoolgirl endeavor proved exceptionally ambitious, the forty fascicles and ten unthreaded "sets" she created from 1858 through 1865 eventually held some eight hundred poems. One difference was that the girlhood assemblage was open to others' inspection but the adult one was definitely not: until after her death, no one realized how carefully she had recorded her poems or how many there were. Where the herbarium was designed to exhibit as well as preserve, the manuscript books were a private hoard, or a secret garden of work done, or a thing put through for its own inherent excellence. Or so we guess, not having one explicit statement as to what the massive project meant to her.

Although Dickinson sent hundreds of poems to friends, she revealed to no one, not Sue, not even Vinnie, the existence of these books, which remained strictly behind the "vail." Did she foresee their eventual discovery and publication? When Thomas Wentworth Higginson cautioned that her work was not ready to go before the world, she emphatically assured him that publication was "foreign to my thought."

Apparently sharing the conservative view that feminine self-respect was not compatible with public life,[8] she reportedly asked Helen Hunt Jackson how she could bear to "print a piece of your soul." The question was in accord with Edward Dickinson's pronouncements on publishing females in his Coelebs essays.

"On this wondrous sea" (Fr3), a poem Dickinson copied on her first fascicle sheet, had been sent to Sue in 1853. Other poems, particularly those that echo her earlier letters, may also have been several years old. "I had a guinea golden," complaining of a friend's silence—

> *Grant that repentance solemn*
> *May seize opon his mind –*
> *And he no consolation*
> *Beneath the sun may find*
>
> Fr12

—reminds us of her 1850 assault on Joel W. Norcross. Of the sixteen poems Franklin believes were transcribed "about summer 1858," seven seem designed to introduce gifts, mainly flowers. Secretive as Dickinson was in creating her booklets, individual poems remained a vital part of the commerce of friendship.

Compared to the disturbed letters to Master and Sweetser, the first fascicle seems infinitely more serene, "affirmative," at least on the surface. As in 1854, when Dickinson's poem about her troubled relations with Sue, "I have a bird in spring," showed an equability absent from the letter leading up to it, these poems seem designed to contain or cover up distress, not get it out: *not* telling remained part of the impetus. A case in point is the "exultant" treatment of one of Dickinson's pressing subjects, the transition from death to heaven:

---

8. In 1858 the poet and columnist Mary Clemmer Ames was struck by a refined woman's shocked reaction to a theatre placard for Julia Deane Hayne: "How utterly lost to every fine feeling of womanhood a woman must be, before she will thus allow her name to be published in the public street!" Ames explained this repulsion as "the spontaneous utterance of one whose life had been as carefully guarded as that of an exotic flower."

Adrift! A little boat adrift!
And night is coming down!
Will no one guide a little boat
Unto the nearest town?

So sailors say – on yesterday –
Just as the dusk was brown
One little boat gave up its strife
And gurgled down and down.

So angels say – on yesterday –
Just as the dawn was red
One little boat – o'erspent with gales –
Retrimmed its masts – redecked its sails –
And shot – exultant on!

                                        Fr6

The basic metrical pattern, often called ballad meter or (in hymnals) common meter, alternates between four- and three-stress lines. In the last stanza, lines four and five break free of the pattern, thus imitating the boat's shooting on—the release from mortal limits. In this way as in others, Dickinson directs attention to the moment of transition from mortal life to immortality. But the poem "gives up its strife" a little too easily: the anguish and tragedy that set it in motion are so neatly reversed we might not guess the author was struggling to devise a nonorthodox "hope" of her own. Like many other lyrics in the first manuscript book, this one is a clever performance that neatly wraps up matters still at issue for the writer. It gives too knowing and willful an answer to her riddle.

Since Dickinson destroyed preliminary drafts after making her final copies, the compositional and biographical origins of this and most other works remain obscure. For all the poems in her forty fascicles, there is only one mysteriously surviving rough draft, from summer 1858. Happily, it is a riddling poem rather less obvious than its companions:

> *If those I loved were lost,*
> *the crier's voice would tell me –*
> *If those I loved were found,*
> *the bells of Ghent would ring,*
> *Did those I loved repose,*
> *the Daisy would impel me –*
> *Philip when bewildered –*
> *bore his riddle in –*
>
>   Fr20A

As Johnson pointed out, the enigmatic last couplet has to do with the tragically ignominious death of Philip van Artevelde, the title character in a verse drama owned by Austin. Unlike the speaker, whose questions about life and death receive an easy public answer, Philip keeps his riddle and meditates on it.

This unique rough draft, penciled onto a tiny folded paper, fills the free space without spilling over and thus makes visible the poet's fantastic "regard for boundaries," as Franklin calls it. The draft suggests that from the beginning she had the poem well in mind except for the last couplet, which originally read: "Philip questioned eager / I, my riddle bring." In this version, with its confusing second "I," the final line may be read as if in quotation marks. That is, eagerly questioned, Philip merely says he brings his riddle with him and that it must be let stand. The poem is contrapuntal, the conclusion implying that the big questions are less easily disposed of than the first part—and Dickinson's other early poems—would have it.

It is not that we have a "breakthrough" (a tiresome notion) in this early and happily preserved draft, but rather that, as we follow the poet's swift act of writing, we see her stumble and hesitate precisely at the critical point. When Austin faced the imperative to choose now, he chose conversion, then stood up in church and "blat[t]ed" out his new, consoling, and convenient truths. Emily went on to choose, not affirmation, as in "Adrift! A little boat adrift!" but mystery. "If those I loved were lost" predicts what lies ahead for her as she, like Philip, learns how to bear her riddle in, and in, and in.

Part Six

1858-1865

I could not have defined the Change -

Conversion of the Mind

Like Sanctifying in the Soul -

Is witnessed - not explained -

About 1863. Fr627, stanza 6. Reproduction 124% original size.

Chapter 16

1858–1860: Nothing's Small!

As if the Boston Norcrosses did not have their share of trouble, Aunt Lavinia began to die in the winter of 1858–1859, her state such that Vinnie had to leave home and help get her through her "invalid winter," as Emily called it. Vinnie was gone for months, from before Christmas to the middle of spring, and, as Emily's letters make clear, was badly missed, not just for sewing and housekeeping but as companion, informant, arbiter.

The older sister had become highly dependent on the knowing and somewhat bossy younger one. But the relationship eludes easy categorizing, if only because Emily's comments on it date mainly from Vinnie's absences, when the writer was apt to stress her sisterly need. She herself was amazed the lack of intellectual sympathy didn't count for more. As she said in a brilliant passage to Joseph Lyman, "It is so weird and so vastly mysterious, [Vinnie] sleeps by my side . . . and the tie is quite vital; yet if we had come up for the first time from two wells where we had hitherto been bred her astonishment would not be greater at some things I say." This intimate alienation persuaded the poet "that space & time are things of the body & have little or nothing to do with our Selves. My Country is Truth. Vinnie lives much of the time in the State of Regret. I like Truth—it sets free is a free Democracy." The passage catches the paradox of the poet's familial basis: a dependency that sets free.

Emily's sister-in-law served to mobilize her powers in a very different way. If Vinnie lived in the State of Regret, Sue ruled a wide empire of Literature, Religion, the Best Society, with a heavily contested border with Truth. As Mrs. Dickinson's slow recovery released her daughters from domestic servitude, Sue and Austin's next-door home became a focus of Emily's social and literary life, introducing her to new people, books, and ideas and drawing poem after poem from her. From 1858 to 1861 this enriched social scene was a powerful stimulus, both qualifying and reinforcing the isolation of her well. It was the old story, more tormenting than ever: a tantalizing combination of nearness and distance; a quick responsiveness that cannot find reciprocity. And so we get a creative outburst of unprecedented brilliance and intensity.

A Poet and the Life Next Door

Austin seemed in no doubt his and Sue's union had a rare perfection. On their second Christmas, he gave her *The Angel in the House: The Betrothal*, Coventry Patmore's smarmy narrative poem about an idealized Victorian courtship. In his presentation inscription, he drew a parallel between the male protagonist's wooing of Honoria, the youngest of three daughters, and their own courtship: "Some one has been watching us, Sue." His wife, the youngest of four, read the book attentively and marked admired passages with her usual lines and X's. When she reached the statement that woman can redeem man only by initially withholding her sexual favors, she made her first double lines, suggesting emphatic agreement:

Knowing he cannot choose but pay,
How has she cheapen'd paradise;
How given for nought her priceless gift,
How spoil'd the bread and spill'd the wine,
Which, spent with due, respective thrift,
Had made brutes men and men divine.

Thirty years later, writing Emily's obituary and wishing to emphasize her exquisite domesticity, Sue quoted the last three words of Patmore's description of the refined home shared by Honoria and her sisters:

A tent pitched in a world not right
It seem'd, whose inmates, every one,
On tranquil faces bore the light
Of duties beautifully done.

At the time the obituarist's own tent had been irreparably torn.

Keenly aware of the risks of childbearing, Sue also seems to have held a censorious view of sexuality.[1] Since she and Austin were married five years before their first child was born, the question arises whether their union was a chaste one for a time, as Austin had promised. A letter sent him by his friend Samuel Bowles after the latter's wife gave birth to a stillborn infant suggests an ongoing conversation about sex and offspring: "I do not pray your exemption from such risks: they are fearful, but . . . they have their uses. Greener grows the grass where the fire has burned." Another early letter from the same friend touches on the question of fertility with mixed jocularity and delicacy. Hoping for "blessings on both your houses" (Evergreens and Homestead), Bowles added, "I'd liked to have written another word with a b, as the prattle of my babies reaches my ears,—but prudence & propriety came in time to stay the

---

1. Decades later, as if to justify Austin's infidelity, his mistress recorded his complaints about Sue. Second on the list was "Entire disappointment in all so-called married life." Surviving letters make it doubtful that this disillusionment set in before the mid-1860s.

impulse." Again, the censored "b" word, which must be *baby*, hints at the issues the two men canvassed.

By now, Austin's feelings about babies were fairly snarled by accommodations and rationalizations, or so one surmises from a defensive outburst Jane Hitchcock reported in a December 1860 letter to brother Ned in Europe:

> I told [Austin] you missed the children, & he exclaimed that if he had three children he believed it would cause him to start for Europe immediately & stay as long as he could. I ventured to suggest that he was not capable of judging of the feelings of a Father, & he intimated that he considered himself fortunate in being so.

Sue would have been three or four months pregnant at the time of this conversation. Evidently, her husband had not been informed that he was about to experience "the feelings of a Father."

A further irony is that he already had children. In fall 1858 the Newman orphanage had been broken up and Mrs. Fay sent packing, the older daughters leaving Amherst and the two younger ones, Clara and Anna, fourteen and twelve, moving into the Evergreens. Since Edward continued to be the girls' legal guardian, the new arrangement was not a true adoption. Still, it endured for nine years in spite of real friction between wards and caretakers. As for the one Newman boy, a document filed in Brooklyn places him in Philadelphia, married to a woman named Mary who couldn't sign her name and had to make $\overset{\text{her}}{\underset{\text{mark}}{+}}$.

What evidence there is of Austin and Emily's relations in 1858–1860 suggests a kind of closing down. One of her letters speaks of "calling upon him" Sunday afternoon—an oddly formal phrase. When Sue went to Geneva to visit Martha (married since 1857 to a thriving dry-goods retailer), the letter that came from Emily assumed a classic Yankee dryness in reporting that "Austin supped with us. 'Appears well.'" This laconic distance seems just the opposite of her eager participation in the courtship.

A month later, Austin was not at all well, having contracted typhoid fever at a time when Frazar Stearns, son of the college president, was "very sick" with the disease and the town was ravaged by an epidemic of scarlet fever. The fatalities included eight-year-old Harriet Matthews, daughter of the Dickinsons' handyman. Presently Emily sent a wildly ebullient letter to the Hollands dramatizing her own giddy readiness to die:

> Good-night! I can't stay any longer in a world of death. Austin is ill of fever. I buried my garden last week – our man, Dick, lost a little girl through the scarlet fever. I thought perhaps that *you* were dead, and not knowing the sexton's address, interrogate the daisies. Ah! dainty – dainty Death! Ah! democratic Death! Grasping the proudest zinnia from my purple garden, – then deep to his bosom calling the serf's child!

Readers are shocked by Dickinson's equating "the serf's child" with her frost-killed flowers.[2] In thinking about this apparent heartlessness, we shouldn't forget how often epidemics have inspired a strained and humorous dance of death, with all sense of scale abandoned. Was it because so many were dying that she gave such hurried treatment to Austin's life-threatening fever, or did her lack of concern reflect a doctor's opinion that he was "better"? Whatever the explanation, she failed to convey the gravity of his illness, which lingered into January "as a neuralgic presence."

If Emily depended less on Austin now, she clutched as much as ever her at times unresponsive sister-in-law. In spite of the vigorously pressed claim that this was a close and fully mutual relationship, Dickinson regularly gave voice to a feeling of neglect. Her letter to Geneva opens with a familiar lament about Sue's silence: "I hav'nt any paper, dear, but faith continues firm." This typical sentence not only has an iambic regularity but, if broken after "dear," would form two lines in common meter. It

---

2. In 1863, on the other hand, writing to Louisa and Frances Norcross, Dickinson spoke tenderly of Matthews's grief for his girl. Then again, when President Garfield was shot two decades later, she flippantly equated flowers and people: "Vinnie lost her Sultans too – it was 'Guiteau' year – Presidents and Sultans were alike doomed."

was the poet's old refrain with silent friends, starting with Harriet Merrill in 1845.

About the time Sue returned from Geneva, Emily composed a poetic tribute based on the contrast between her two sisterly bonds. Unlike
much-loved Vinnie, who

> . . . *came the road that I came* –
> *And wore my last year's gown* –

Sue entered as a deeply attaching foreigner:

> *She did not sing as we did* –
> *It was a different tune* –
> *Herself to her a music*
> *As Bumble bee of June.*

The speaker has no difficulty admitting her continuing dependency on
this self-sufficing stranger:

> *Today is far from Childhood* –
> *But up and down the hills*
> *I held her hand the tighter* –
> *Which shortened all the miles* –

Now, even though Sue has become one of the Dickinsons, she seems
distinct, absorbed by her separate past and interior life:

> *And still her hum*
> *The years among,*
> *Deceives the Butterfly;*
> *Still in her Eye*
> *The Violets lie*
> *Mouldered this many May.*

Is Austin the butterfly that persistently misreads the alien hum? Do the "mouldered" violets in Sue's eye refer back to her sister Mary, dying in the springtime of life but still unforgotten? One thing seems clear: the stranger's self-contained and unchanging nature appeals to the speaker, who has also given up the temporal for the eternal, though in a different fashion:

> *I spilt the dew –*
> *But took the morn;*
> *I chose this single star*
> *From out the wide night's numbers –*
> *Sue – forevermore!*[3]

Fr5A

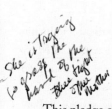

She is trying to grasp the hand of the Blue fight other

This pledge of allegiance is at least as striking for what it doesn't say as for what it does. Whether Sue is regarded as a bee humming to herself or as a worshipped astral being, she seems beyond understanding. There is no easy or tangible reciprocity; the hand Emily grips does not necessarily grip back. And just as the poem doesn't clarify Sue's remote mentality, neither does it explore the speaker's adhesiveness, which remains unchanging, fixed, beyond psychology. One sister is given, and then a second and very different sister is given, and she too is tightly held. But the two sisterly bonds are not the same, the second being as abstract as it is invigorating.

Although few of Dickinson's poems from 1858 to 1860 are explicitly about Sue, the three or four that are, a special group, all take for granted a certain absence or distance. Their theme is not precisely intimacy (however defined) but the desire for intimacy. In the earliest of the group, "I often passed the village," an unnamed speaker addresses "Dollie" (the Gilberts' pet name for Sue) from the cemetery. Having reached

---

3. Decades later, as shown in the facsimile edition of Emily's manuscript books, an unknown hand, possibly Austin's, made a laborious effort to obliterate the poem.

the village earlier than expected, this speaker—the first of Dickinson's voices from the grave—assures Dollie of its soothing and restful nature and then extends an invitation:

> Trust the loving promise
> Underneath the mould,
> Cry "it's I," "take Dollie,"
> And I will enfold!
>
> Fr41

The "I" that will enfold or embrace is not death but a patient and loving human spirit "underneath" decay. Even if we identify this spirit as Mary Gilbert Learned, the lost sister who waits for Sue, we must also leave room for Emily, who in 1852 made the impassioned declaration that "we will lie side by side in the kirkyard." This yearning forecast, sent to Baltimore, exhibits the same basic elements as the poem: a great distance, a great sorrow, and a tireless love waiting to erase both.

Another strategy for erasing the gap is seen in a poem from 1859 that stresses the disparities in scale between Sue and Emily, enabling the latter to be the former's humble client:

> Her breast is fit for pearls,
> But I was not a "Diver" –
> Her brow is fit for thrones
> But I have not a crest.
> Her heart is fit for home –
> I – a Sparrow – build there
> Sweet of twigs and twine
> My perennial nest.
>
> Fr121A

This nest-seeking speaker diminishes herself so drastically that anything like reciprocity becomes unimaginable.

A poem sent to Sue about the same time hints at the impact of her social and intellectual command. Here, as a typically "low" speaker

Portraits of the Dickinson family
by Otis A. Bullard, early 1840.

Edward Dickinson

Emily Norcross Dickinson

Emily, age nine; Austin, ten; Lavinia, nearly
seven.

All known mechanically reproduced images of the poet.

The silhouette from age fourteen shows the bulge below her lower lip, evident in other members of her family on both sides.

Taken soon after her sixteenth birthday, following an extended period of illness, by William C. North.

The newly discovered albumen print of an earlier daguerreotype. Acquired by Philip F. Gura in 2000 and believed by him and the author to represent Dickinson. See pp. 419–21 and Appendix 1.

Parents, brother, and sister.

Mother, undoubtedly taken at the same time as the image to the left.

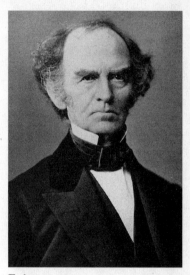

Father

Austin. "I think of that 'pinnacle' on which you always mount, when anybody insults you." ED

Lavinia, "*perter* and *more* pert day by day." ED

Some paternal uncles and aunts.

Lucretia Dickinson Bullard

Asa Bullard, editor of the widely distributed *Sabbath School Visiter.*

William Dickinson: "He always had an opinion . . ."

Samuel Fowler Dickinson, Jr.

Catharine Dickinson Sweetser, Emily's favorite paternal aunt.

Elizabeth Dickinson Currier, "the only male relative on the female side." ED

"The Newmans seem very pleasant, but they are not *like us* . . ." ED

Mary Dickinson Newman, Edward's favorite sister, married a successful bookseller and lived in Brooklyn. The family portrait dates from shortly before her and her husband's death from consumption in 1852.

Clara and Anna, the two youngest Newman orphans, lived next door to the poet, in the Evergreens, from 1858 to 1868 or 1869.

Relatives on the maternal, Norcross, side.

The poet's two maternal uncles who were photographed.

William O. Norcross was on the winning side of a family lawsuit against Loring Norcross, represented by the poet's father.

Joel W. Norcross, a successful importer of "fancy goods," was sent one of the poet's most vehement letters.

Joel Norcross, of Monson, the poet's prosperous maternal grandfather. Age and artist unknown.

The poet's relations were particularly close with Loring and Lavinia
Norcross and their daughters, Louisa and Frances.

Loring

Lavinia and daughter Louisa

Frances in her mid-teens. Twenty years later, as she acted in a play at Concord, Lidian Emerson, Ralph Waldo's widow, whispered to her daughter, Ellen, "Isn't she modest and sweet?"

School; a teacher; a friend made at school.

Amherst Academy. On the third story was a "real nice hall, & arched roof, . . . for the speaking of Wednesday afternoon." Edward Hitchcock, Jr.

Caroline Dutch Hunt taught both the poet and her mother.

Abiah Root, with whom the poet became close friends in 1844, during a term at school.

Youthful friends.

Joseph B. Lyman looked up German words with Emily.

Henry Vaughan Emmons. "The poets . . . wrestle with the angel of sorrow till he leaves a blessing upon them . . ." Emmons, "Poetry the Voice of Sorrow"

Susan Gilbert.
I have a Bird in spring
Which for myself doth sing —
ED (Fr4)

Martha Gilbert. "We had a long, sad talk . . . and Mattie cried and I cried, and we had a solemn time." ED

Men whose preaching made a powerful impression on Dickinson.

The Reverend Aaron M. Colton, pastor of the First Church in Amherst, 1840-1853.

Professor Edwards A. Park. "He is sometimes *tremendous* . . ." Henry Boynton Smith

Dickinson is thought to have heard the Reverend Charles Wadsworth in Philadelphia in 1855. "The very appearance of the man in the pulpit shows his abhorrence of claptrap." George Burrowes. Photograph by F. Gutekunst.

Elizabeth Holland and Samuel Bowles were among the correspondents Dickinson most confided in.

Elizabeth Holland, the poet's "Little Sister."

Samuel Bowles. "We shall never settle the woman question so long as we . . . divide them off as the Shakers do in their meetings." Review of Dr. Holland's *Miss Gilbert's Career.*

Mary Bowles, compared by her husband, Samuel, to a porcupine.

Some of Dickinson's most vital correspondences
were with people she saw little of.

Thomas Wentworth Higginson, the
Brahmin radical who was selected by
Dickinson as her "preceptor."

Maria Whitney taught German and
French at Smith College.
How well I knew Her not
ED (Fr813A)

Sarah Tuckerman, wife of the
Amherst College botanist, received
many messages from Dickinson but
never saw her.

The Dickinson Compound.

The poet's home. The two windows on the upper left, her bedroom. On the far right, her conservatory.

The Evergreens, an "Italianate villa" built in 1856 for Austin and Susan Dickinson.

Ned Dickinson, age thirteen.

Mattie Dickinson. "That's the Little Girl
I always meant to be, but wasn't . . ." ED

Susan Dickinson holding Gib, her
third child.

Gib died of typhoid fever in October
1883.

eeply affected by family events next door,
ever went there.

Austin Dickinson

Mrs. Mabel Loomis Todd, half Austin's age, became his mistress in December 1883.

Susan Dickinson in old age.

In her last years Dickinson became romantically attached to Judge Otis Phillips Lord.

"He was strong in his intellect, strong in his emotions, strong in his friendships, strong in his dislikes and prejudices, strong in thought, and strong in language."
Marcus Morton, Chief Justice of the Supreme Judicial Court of Massachusetts

It may have been a stroke that prompted Lord's retirement from the Supreme Judicial Court in December 1882.

works at a problem in mathematics (Sue's forte), she finds her powers abruptly baffled:

> Low at my problem bending –
> Another *problem comes* –
> *Larger than mine – Serener* –
> *Involving statelier sums* –
> *I check my busy pencil* –
> *My Ciphers steal away* –
> *Wherefore my baffled fingers*
> *Thine extremity?*
>
> Fr99A

In one sense, however, the "statelier" presence next door did not inhibit the writer's busy pencil, which in 1859 recorded at least thirteen additional poems concerned with low, meek, or humble states of being.[4]

Although some have postulated a nonhierarchical equality between the sisters-in-law, the poems dealing with this relationship are marked on one side by desire, on the other by distance, highness, aloofness. The asymmetry helped stimulate Dickinson's growing productivity, with poem after poem going next door to the Evergreens—by Franklin's count, nine or ten in 1858, twenty-one in 1859, twenty in 1860. Poems were given to other friends in these years, but Sue remained the primary recipient. We cannot know whether Emily would have been as copious

---

4. | Delayed till she had ceased to know | Fr67 |
    | So bashful when I spied her! | Fr70 |
    | Went up a year this evening! | Fr72 |
    | One dignity delays for all | Fr77 |
    | I hide myself within my flower | Fr80 |
    | She bore it till the simple veins | Fr81 |
    | We should not mind so small a flower | Fr82 |
    | On such a night, or such a night | Fr84 |
    | In rags mysterious as these | Fr102 |
    | In lands I never saw – they say | Fr108 |
    | So from the mould | Fr110 |
    | Ambition cannot find him | Fr115 |
    | A poor – torn heart – a tattered heart | Fr125 |

a writer without her sister-in-law, but it seems beyond question that Sue's elusive presence proved endlessly stimulating.

It is also clear that Sue admired Emily's poetry and that this appreciation meant a great deal. Did the sister-in-law offer useful criticism? Her 1861 critique of "Safe in their alabaster chambers" spurred the poet to draft alternative versions of a stanza that failed to please, and then to enter them in a manuscript book. Inferring that what Sue did once she must have done many times, Martha Nell Smith has elevated her into a full literary collaborator in a "poetry workshop." The theory has won adherents but has also met widespread skepticism, if only because induction requires more than one example. In the next chapter we will look at the exchange over the "alabaster" poem. For now, it is enough to say that Sue seems to have been a constantly available audience—alert, intelligent, tasteful, nodding approval, often silent. Not even her daughter, Martha, who treasured the documentary record and made a great point of her mother and aunt's closeness (there were private motives for stressing this), could provide more than the one instance of criticism offered. As creator, Emily was basically on her own.

Fittingly, a poem sent next door in 1860 expresses a strong sense of discipline and privation:

> *A little bread, a crust – a crumb,*
> *A little trust, a Demijohn –*
> *Can keep the soul alive –*
> *Not portly – mind!*
> *But breathing – warm –*
> *Conscious . . .*

Likening her position to that of soldiers under fire or Napoleon on the eve of crowning himself Emperor, Dickinson seems to regard her life as one whose terms require a high degree of courage, commitment, discipline, honor:

> *A brief campaign of sting and sweet,*
> *Is plenty! is enough! . . .*

Fr135A

Her military language, conspicuous in her poetry even before the Civil War, reminds us of what she had in common with Major Edward Dickinson. For her, however, the military stood less for male combativeness than for a resolute attitude in private life. It was linked to a sense of deprivation, northernness, apartness.

What made Sue's distant nearness so powerful a stimulant was that it fit a basic rule of life for Dickinson: always seeking intimacy and finding it withheld. The pattern shows up not only in her friendships but in her orientation to nature and religion. The naive fixation on heaven that was so central in Protestant America, and which she had recklessly taken to heart without experiencing a conversion, had generated a pressing quest for the absolute *within* the mundane. This perennially expected rush is one of the things that gives her poems on bees, sunsets, and the seasons their Dickinsonian cachet:

the God / the sacred / within

> *A something in a summer's Day*
> *As slow her flambeaux burn away*
> *Which solemnizes me.*
>
> *A something in a summer's noon –*
> *A depth – an Azure – a perfume –*
> *Transcending extasy.*

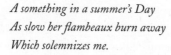

the divine & feminine was missing

6/e life was out of balance

The last line was not hyperbole. Ecstasy comes with fulfillment, but what moved Dickinson was expectation: not rowing in Eden, but the thought of rowing in Eden. A later stanza of this poem describes the action of nature's fingers on the responsive heart:

> *The wizard fingers never rest –*
> *The purple brook within the breast*
> *Still chafes its narrow bed –*

Fr104

Sexual, yes, but so much more than sexual, this constant chafing that results in a poetry of increasing power, daring, mastery. The poetry of arousal, it is the product of the single heart lying in its narrow bed and dreaming of a final escape from itself.

Another poem sent to Sue conveys the poet's energetic readiness:

> *I never hear the word 'Escape'*
> *Without a quicker blood!*
> *A sudden expectation!*
> *A flying attitude!*
>
> *I never hear of prisons broad*
> *By soldiers battered down –*
> *But I tug, childish, at my bars –*
> *Only to fail again!*
>
> Fr144A

How did someone apparently writing from her own quick blood avoid the narrow egotism so blatant in Austin or Vinnie? Dickinson's success in this regard may be related to her "childish" female voice. Issuing from a position assumed to be powerless, this voice does not command or moralize in the fashion of so many Victorian voices, even Whitman's. It is a noncitizen's voice, disenfranchised and always aware of its lack of standing in debate or the arts of persuasion. All it can do is resort to the personal, the perceptual, the divine, often in the first person and with an implicit acknowledgment of its disabilities and "lowness."

Yet Dickinson was rarely as direct or confessional as she seemed. Among all the distances in her poetry, one of the most crucial was the distance from herself. Growing up in a culture that saw nature and human experience as hieroglyphs of heaven, she early acquired the art of rendering exemplary her own life—turning it into story or drama. Such transformations were more imperious yet less egotistical than Austin's attempt to see his marriage as a version of *Kavanagh* or *The Angel in the House.*

One of the poems that illustrates all these distances, "Our lives are Swiss," speaks not of "me" but "us." Sent to Sue in late 1859, this splendid work reminds us of the writer's captive spectatorship in winter, her bedroom looking south to the Mount Holyoke Range and west to the curtained windows of the Italianate villa next door. Yet to limit the poem to these perspectives would be to kill it, a brilliant transformative power having already operated on the writer's perceptual experience:

> *Our lives are Swiss –*
> *So still – so cool –*
> *Till some odd afternoon*
> *The Alps neglect their curtains*
> *And we look further on.*
> Italy *stands the other side.*
> *While like a guard between –*
> *The solemn Alps –*
> *The siren Alps*
> *Forever intervene –*
>
> Fr129A

This is work of a very high order, bringing together an intense lyric brio with an expansive cartographic abstraction. The poem spoke to Sue, and at the same time it placed its maker on a stage not limited by place or time.

As of 1860, Dickinson was not yet ready to really explore the finality of that "forever intervene." Only in a few poems—most of them sent to Sue—did she draw out the tragic potential of her material. In one of these, we see her fusing her basic concerns—pleasure and denial, struggle and defeat, distance and comprehension—then bringing them down to a single heartbreaking point:

> *Success is counted sweetest*
> *By those who ne'er succeed.*
> *To comprehend a nectar*
> *Requires sorest need –*
> *Not one of all the purple Host*
> *Who took the flag today*
> *Can tell the definition so Clear of Victory –*

As he defeated – dying –
On whose forbidden Ear
The distant strains of triumph
Burst agonized and Clear –

Fr112A

This rightly famous poem, distilled with such mastery from its maker's experience, doesn't have the first-person speaker that became so essential in her tragic poetry of the early 1860s. That was what would come next: putting a female "I" back in that clear and agonizing perspective.

Condor Kate

The reverse of Emily Norcross Dickinson, Sue relished being a hostess and opening the Evergreens to a succession of prominent literary and political visitors. Those she entertained over the years included Ralph Waldo Emerson, Bret Harte, Wendell Phillips, and Anna Dickinson, the pioneering woman orator during and after the Civil War. After failing to snag a visiting English lion, Charles Kingsley, in 1874, she felt a lifelong regret. Although her home was not a true literary salon, it almost functioned as one for the poet next door, in the process offering useful stimulation.[5] If Sue had not been there to mediate the social and literary world for Emily, introducing her to a few people, providing a setting for lively talk, lending issues of the *Atlantic Monthly*, the poetry would almost certainly be less interesting.

Of course, the Evergreens was not the poet's only door on society. In September 1858 she was the first to call on a bride new to Amherst, Mrs. Mary Allen, and she continued to play a marginal part in the social round, once making a visit to the Aaron Warners that so exhausted her

---

5. It was partly because Sewall and Leyda owed a great deal to Millicent Todd Bingham that they softpedaled Sue's importance for the poet. Anxious to restore her centrality, a more recent group of scholars, Martha Nell Smith and Ellen Louise Hart, has stressed personal erotics. Both factions radically simplify the complex social and literary functions Sue performed for ED.

she begged off a planned musical evening next door. Yet avoidance was by now so well established that in the winter of 1859–1860 she pointedly reminded cousin Louisa she was one of the few "from whom I do not run away!" It isn't known whether she saw Emerson when he put up at Sue and Austin's in December 1857 (and if she didn't whether she excluded herself or wasn't invited). She was probably in Cambridge when he came a second time in 1865.

One of the few guests she met and made friends with was Catharine Scott Turner, young, beautiful, and, like Sue from 1850 to 1853, dressed in mourning. Raised in Cooperstown, New York, Kate had attended Utica Female Seminary with Sue, both signing the same copy of Kames's *Elements of Criticism.* In 1855 she married a doctor whose tuberculosis was so advanced a local diarist thought he looked "dreadfully" and felt "so sorry for him and also poor Kate." A year and a half later the man was dead, aged twenty-six.

In January 1859 the young widow came to the Evergreens for a visit that lasted till February 18; she would return for two more extended stays in October 1861 and January 1863. Decades later she reminisced about her nights at the Evergreens as if they were the best she had known: "Those celestial evenings in the Library—the blazing *wood* fire—*Emily*—*Austin,*—the music—the rampant fun—the inextinguishable laughter, the uproarious spirits of our chosen—our most congenial circle." She vividly remembered "Emily with her dog, & Lantern! often at the piano playing weird & beautiful melodies, all from her own inspiration, oh! she was a choice spirit." The first exclamation point marks Kate's recollection of the time the revels lasted so far into the night Emily's father suddenly appeared with a lantern to take his reckless daughter home. The next morning, her high spirits undiminished, she took her revenge by snipping from his modern reprint of *The New England Primer* a woodcut of a youth fleeing a demon. She sent this next door, explaining that the youth stood for her and the pursuing "Reptile" for her "more immediate friends, and connections"—meaning of course her overprotective father.

Far more humiliating was the night she and Kate made fools of themselves in front of Reuben A. Chapman, a dignified family friend about to step up to Massachusetts' Supreme Judicial Court. Remembered as having "great respect for existing institutions," Chapman was a conservative on abolition, and as a good Calvinist felt a "special dislike" for "alterations of old and familiar hymns." At home, he was always "serene and unruffled," and fond of reading serious theology. As Emily later explained to Elizabeth Holland, she was spending the evening with Sue and Kate ("as I often do") when "some one rang the bell and I ran, as is my custom." Kate ran with her, and as they stood behind a door "clinging fast like culprit mice," they heard the Judge's voice. "Since the dead might have heard us scamper," Emily proposed they return, but before they could act they were exposed to view. Although she "gasped a brief apology," the sense of disgrace did not subside, especially after she was reproached by Austin. Drafting a full apology, she sent it to Elizabeth for her to approve and then forward. "Mr. Chapman is my friend," Emily explained: he "talks of my books with me."

After Kate was back in Cooperstown, Emily sent her a note recalling the pleasures of their congenial group. Until now, the only "girls" she had missed had been named Sue, Eliza, and Martha. Now, a new candidate knocking at her door, she pretends to speak for the other women in the coterie: "Go Home! We don't take Katies here!" Then, abruptly changing her mind but continuing the game ("Stay! My heart votes for you"), she grills the applicant on her qualifications for the exclusive sisterhood: "Dare you dwell in the *East* where we dwell? Are you afraid of the sun? When you hear the new violet sucking her way among the sods, shall you be *resolute*? All *we* are *strangers* . . . And Pilgrims! . . . and *Soldiers*." The letter offers another take on Dickinson's sense of a special calling, as sensuous and playful as it is austere and spiritual. Enclosing a single rose, meant to be "worn upon the breast," she concluded with a statement of attachment: "So I rise, wearing her – so I sleep, holding, – Sleep at last with her fast in my hand and wake bearing my flower.'"

Dickinson's three later letters to Kate were equally direct, intense, impassioned, humorous. Referring to her widowhood as something the two of them had not discussed, the poet stated that she had also seen dear ones buried and flowers blooming on their graves: "I, too in Daisy mounds possess hid treasure – therefore I guard you more." Speaking quite lyrically of those who have lost their loved ones ("through the snow go many loving feet parted by 'Alps' how brief from Vineyards and the Sun!"), she echoed her poem on how "The siren Alps – Forever intervene." Composed the previous winter, this poem pictorialized the icy blockages the letters fervently tried to melt.

Who could keep pace with someone always writing, playing, joking at this white heat? "You cease indeed to talk," Emily wrote in her second letter, only to proclaim her determined faithfulness to the new friend. The next letter, from summer 1860, begins by spurning Kate's excuse for being so remiss a correspondent: "The prettiest of pleas, dear, but with a Lynx like me quite unavailable." No one could possibly keep up with—or elude—Emily.

Emily-the-lynx's unrelenting pursuit is apparent in the teasing lines that accompanied a pair of garters she knit for her new friend:

> When Katie walks, this Simple pair accompany her side,
> When Katie runs unwearied they follow on the road,
> When Katie kneels, their loving hands still clasp her pious knee –
> Ah! Katie! Smile at Fortune, with two so knit to thee!

Fr49[A.1]

Attractive and flirtatious, Kate was also a serious Episcopalian. Her first husband had been extremely devout, and when she went to Europe in 1872–1873 with the second one (also dying), she faithfully observed the ecclesiastical calendar and gave her mind to sermons and works of devotion. Dickinson knew all about the pious attitude. Mischievously clasping the pious knee, she was not about to leave it to its devoirs.

Samuel Bowles

Another person who entered Dickinson's life by way of the Evergreens was Samuel Bowles, the influential owner and editor-in-chief of the *Springfield Republican* and possibly her most dynamic, volatile, and fascinating male friend. A relaxed intimate of Sue and Austin's, he was known to their children as Uncle Sam. For Emily, he remained either Mr. Bowles or (in a much later letter to Maria Whitney) "that Arabian presence." It wasn't love, or love exactly, but whatever it was it brought out some of her most intense writing.

Sue's draft essay about her prominent guests, "Annals of the Evergreens," names Samuel as the first important visitor to "our newly married home." He had come to Amherst in the company of a "~~lady~~ friend" to "report the result of some agricultural experiments on an estate near us, for the 'Springfield Republican.' " Though Sue tended to move dates back in time and inflate mundane facts (she wrote "farm" first, then substituted "estate"), the event she recalled was in fact well documented by the newspaper she named, which had a weekly "Farm and Garden" feature and gave extensive coverage to horse fairs and fall cattle shows. On June 30, 1858, on the large North Amherst farm of Levi D. Cowles, there was a competitive demonstration of some experimental machines designed to replace scythes. The next day the *Republican* ran a story on the well-attended contest—"Trial of Mowing Machines in Amherst." This was the event that brought Samuel to Sue and Austin's home and into the poet's world.[6]

Two years earlier, Edward had taken the lead in developing the First Church's basement into an agricultural hall. The Dickinsons not only shared Bowles's interest in agricultural progress, but wintered their stock on hay from their own field, easily visible from the poet's south window. A letter she sent Bowles the following year introduces the topic of haying with the abruptness that bespeaks a shared reference: "The men are mowing the second Hay. The cocks are smaller than the first, and spicier."

Both Samuel and his wife, Mary, were Unitarians, with liberal views on religious and social questions. Eagerly responsive, Dickinson made sure the couple realized from the outset that she spurned her pastor's teaching that "we are a 'Worm' " (Natural Depravity) and took no interest in " 'Cephas and Apollos' " (leaders of doctrinal schools in I

---

6. That Bowles entered the poet's life after the generally received date of her first "Master" draft, spring 1858, proves he could not have been Master.

Corinthians 1:12). When Mary gave her a book by the controversial Theodore Parker, she replied, "I heard that he was 'poison.' Then I like poison very well." The book is thought to have been *The Two Christmas Celebrations*, which explains in Parker's downright fashion that Jesus was not the Savior but "a good man with a genius for religion," and that after his death his true history was lost to sight, "overgrown with a great mass of fictions."

Handsome, energetic, still in his early thirties, Bowles was very much a man on the rise. With his flair for what was new, daring, and controversial, he was turning the *Republican* into one of the nation's most progressive and influential newspapers. Before the Whig collapse of 1854, the paper backed Edward Dickinson and other conservatives. Afterward, it generally supported the Republican Party but retained a lively interest in independent challenges. It was thanks to Bowles that the paper exemplified "that rare type of journalism, which, placing the public welfare above private interests and party affiliations, is ready to risk popular antipathy and even financial losses to support causes it deems just."

But the man was canny as well as conscientious, making frequent calls on leading politicians in Boston, New York, and Washington, then using his paper to push breaking developments.[7] In August 1861, for example, the *Republican* floated the idea of a needed shake-up in Lincoln's war cabinet. The next day George Ashmun wrote Nathaniel P. Banks to put him in the picture: "A free conversation with Mr Bowles led to his Editorials of yesterday. . . . They were intended rather to prepare for the breaking of the ice—than to break it." Ashmun had presided at the Republican National Convention that nominated Lincoln. Banks had been Speaker of the House and, for three terms, governor of Massachusetts. Another sign of how powerful Bowles was is that fifty years after his death he was remembered as one of a small group who "from private stations largely governed Massachusetts."

The editor could not get on a train without meeting or making an

---

7. One of his grandchildren was Chester Bowles, the foreign-policy maven whose vision of Southeast Asian economic development was ignored by President John F. Kennedy and his cold warriors.

acquaintance, and this unreserved openness showed up in his writing, which was always straining to sum up everything to date as rapidly as possible. Like Dickinson, he took liberties with standard English. Unlike her, he was so graphic, breezy, and current his newspaper gained a reputation for "slang." He could be a thrilling companion for alert single women conscious of being denied a man's entrée to the world. When Maria Whitney accompanied him to Washington in 1872, she was amazed by his "hosts of friends" and the "glimpses behind the scenes of political life & strife." The poet also responded to Bowles with startling intensity, but she filtered out the politics that excited Whitney. When Governor Banks stayed at the Homestead for the 1860 Commencement, Dickinson's only known reaction to the visit, sent to Sue with thanks for an extra loaf of bread, was: "Wish Pope to Rome – that's all."

The 163 letters that Samuel is known to have written Austin and Sue from 1858 to 1877, his last full year, suggest they may have been his best friends. He and Austin shared a commitment to Amherst College, art collecting, and an up-to-date style of ease and privacy. Both disdained stuffy bores. "How are you, grease spot?" begins one of Samuel's letters. Another ends in sardonic exhaustion: "Are you going to keep a livery stable? Do you, & I will open a nursery, & vegetable garden. Then we shall live." That he had missed out on the education Austin received seems to have strengthened his sense of attachment, as Sewall perceived. Tied to a wife whose withdrawn and prickly tendencies were aggravated by chronic asthma, Samuel more than once took his marital troubles to the Evergreens. Four years into the friendship, he began calling Sue by her first name, going on to discuss such delicate matters as his temptation to infidelity (rarely yielded to). He saw her as a masterful and fascinating woman, one of the "aristocrats," the "Queen of Pelham."

That Sue and Austin were more conservative than the editor made little difference. He clearly needed this couple, needed to see them at regular intervals and keep them posted on his dizzy life. Perhaps they helped him manage the enormous centrifugal forces always about to tear him apart. Certainly, he depended far less on Emily, who is spoken of only eleven times in the voluminous correspondence.

Accompanied by Mary, Samuel made another visit to the Evergreens in late 1858, when Austin was still feeling the effects of typhoid fever. On January 2, dashing off a New Year's greeting to this new friend, the editor said he had written him "a dozen imaginary letters since we 'visited you in affliction.'" He also invited either "of the girls from the paternal mansion" to come to Springfield. The offer reflects the same etiquette that prompted the Hollands to invite the Dickinson sisters after Elizabeth's first visit in 1853. At that time Emily went with Vinnie. Now, with her sister in Boston, she no doubt declined.

The poet's connection with the Hollands had quickly defined itself as mainly with Elizabeth, but with the Bowleses she aimed at separate relationships. For three years she tried to make contact with Mary, sending the stolid woman some of her most confidential, ingenious, and moving productions, many of which presented the writer as quite powerless. In late 1859, stressing how "little dominion" she had, Emily sent Mary not a flower but "my heart; a little one, sunburnt, half broken sometimes, yet close as the spaniel, to its friends." About the same time, declaring her "childish hope to gather all I love together," she begged for a written expression of affection: "perhaps you could write a letter, saying how much you would like to [visit]." In her next communication her cheek was "red with shame because I write so often."

An early poem sent this unresponsive acquaintance compares the poet's feeling of rejection to Christ's:

> *"They have not chosen me," he said,*
> *"But I have chosen them."*
> *Brave – Broken hearted statement –*
> *Uttered in Bethleem!*
>
> *I could not have told it,*
> *But since Jesus dared –*
> *Sovreign! Know a Daisy*
> *Thy dishonor shared!*

> Fr87A

Another ingenious poem, this one wrapped around a pencil stub, was probably meant for Mary, not her husband:

> If it had no pencil,
> Would it try mine –
> Worn – now – and dull – *sweet*,
> Writing much to thee.
> If it had no word –
> Would it make the Daisy,
> Most as big as I was –
> When it plucked me?
>
> Fr184

In spite of this persistence, it was clear from the start that Samuel was the one who counted for Emily. On February 4, 1859, he ended a letter to Austin with his first remembrance for her: "let there be something over for the sister of the other house who never forgets my spiritual longings." The passage marks his sly recognition of her double "spirituality"—her constant interest in heaven and her care to serve him the "spirits" she knew he relished (mostly sherry and homemade currant and berry wines).

Friendship entered a new phase following Mary's traumatic May 15 stillbirth. Answering the poet's as well as Sue and Austin's consolatory messages, Samuel wrote that "Emily's beautiful thought" (which does not survive) had been "well appreciated." This was the first time he used her Christian name, yet he didn't thank her directly, relying instead on the Evergreens to relay the message. Perhaps it was already obvious that her social life had to be mediated by others. When he showed up at the Dickinson compound, it was the Evergreens he headed for, not the Homestead. Only after his arrival—and then not invariably—did Sue step next door and announce him. Once, when Emily was too late to present her flower and wine (and poem?), she lamented, "I did not know you were going so soon – Oh my tardy feet!" During his tour of Europe in 1862, she touched on her chronic remoteness with a far-fetched comparison: tracing his movements through the newspaper's meager ship news was almost like his "ringing at the door, when Sue says you will call." It takes a second look at this resolutely cheerful statement for its implications to sink in.

The stillbirth had been Mary's second in a row. That summer, hoping to overcome her depression, Samuel took her on a restorative jaunt whose itinerary included Amherst. Afterward, writing her one letter to both husband and wife (though thinking of him as her real audience), Emily hoped "your tour was bright, and gladdened Mrs Bowles." Taking for granted the new attachment would bring a degree of pain, she was "sorry you came, because you went away. Hereafter, I will pick no Rose, lest it fade or prick me." The paradox, a typical one for the writer, was borne out by Mary's persistent refusal to write, though she did send flowers, a book, other gifts.

Comparing a yellow and purple sunset to " 'Jerusalem,' " Emily added, "I think Jerusalem must be like Sue's Drawing Room, when we are talking and laughing there, and you and Mrs Bowles are by."[8] With this seemingly recherché comparison, the writer was alluding to her conversation with Bowles about the Bible's next-to-last chapter, Revelation 21, which lists the twelve gems that are to adorn the New Jerusalem's twelve foundations. Two decades later, condoling with Mary after the editor's death, Dickinson recalled this very talk: "When purples come on Pelham, in the afternoon we say 'Mr. Bowles's colors.' I spoke to him once of his Gem chapter, and the beautiful eyes rose till they were out of reach of mine."

September 6, 1859, the Bowleses' eleventh anniversary, was probably the occasion for Emily's gift of a flower and a riddling poem:

> *If* she *had been the Mistletoe*
> *And I had been the Rose –*
> *How gay opon your table*
> *My velvet life to Close –*
> *Since I am of the Druid –*

8. In the 1894 edition of Dickinson's letters, this sentence was dropped, as were all other references to Austin's wife.

And she is of the dew –
I'll deck Tradition's buttonhole
And send the Rose to you.

Fr60A

Wife Mary is the rose, and friend Emily the mistletoe—weird, more Druid than Christian, and emphatically not "of the dew." Boldly imagining what it would be like to trade places with the wife, thus ending life on "your" table, the poet makes doubly clear how offbeat she is. But in the end she consents to follow tradition, sending the flower that stands for love.

The first communication Dickinson received from Bowles seems to have been the pamphlet on Hadley's bicentennial that printed her father's toast to New England's errand into the wilderness. In her thank-you letter she ignored the celebration, dwelling instead on personal and spiritual topics. Anxious about Mary's health, she voiced her chronic fear lest "in such a porcelain life . . . one stumble upon one's hopes in a pile of broken crockery." As if to ward off a smile at her morbid preoccupation with the loss of friends, she added, "My friends are my 'estate.' Forgive me then the avarice to hoard them!"

It was the old song. Every rose had its thorn. Friends were made to be lost. Intimacy created loneliness. "We want to see you, Mr Bowles," she said, "but spare you the rehearsal of 'familiar truths.' "

Practicing Titanic Opera

After 1860, we have only one letter signed "Emilie." Her abandonment of this spelling, picked up at Mount Holyoke, was a sign her " 'Little Girl'hood" was finally coming to an end.

A complicating element in the poet's friendship with Bowles was his liberalism on women's issues and his support of women's writing. Well ahead of current opinion, the editor realized about 1860 that women's civic freedoms and functions had to be drastically enlarged, if only for the good of society. His progressivism seems to have made Dickinson all the more sensitive about her "small," "oldfashioned," fugitive side. He is the only known recipient for the defensive "Perhaps you think me *stooping!*" (Fr273A). She was well aware how little she had in common with the modern women Bowles admired: Maria Whitney, who would teach French and German at Smith College; Lucia Gilbert Runkle,[9] a writer for the *New York Tribune*.

On women's issues, there were far-reaching differences between Bowles and his literary editor, Josiah Holland, who owned a fourth of the *Republican* and was thus free to impose his opinions. His belittling unsigned essay, "Women in Literature" (1858), worked out the familiar idea that, because men express principles and women fancies, "the genuine classics of every language [are] the work of men and not of women." *Jane Eyre* and *Aurora Leigh* "set the world in a flutter" for a time, but that was because woman's true ministry is "ephemeral"—not to create "the permanent treasures of literature" but to give the multitude its daily bread. Holland remained a determined voice against female suffrage. After the Civil War, in his lecture "The Woman Question," he went so far as to oppose the legislative reforms that gave wives "independent control" of their property. Given Dickinson's friendship with both him and Bowles, we would very much like to know how their opposite views on issues related to her emerging vocation played into her explosive development. The absence of datable letters from her to the Hollands between 1860 and 1865 darkens the question.

Unlike Holland, Bowles not only venerated Elizabeth Barrett Browning's *Aurora Leigh* but discovered, published, and promoted several local women writers. There was an antagonism between the two editors, "an unseen bar," as Holland put it in April 1860 as he began detaching himself from the newspaper. Tellingly, he was replaced with Fidelia Hayward Cooke, a widow whose poetry and fiction the paper had been publishing and who remained the new literary editor for about

---

9. Bowles's letters to Runkle, whom he once called "the one best woman journalist in America," are in the Samuel Bowles Papers at Yale. On the back of one, someone, probably his son Samuel III, listed six impressive women he was friends with: Mrs. Runkle, Rose Kingsley, Mrs. [Mary Clemmer] Ames, Emily Dickinson, Mrs. Beasley, Sue Dickinson.

six years. Cooke was probably the author of "When Should *We* Write" (italics added), the 1860 editorial on women's "literature of misery" that has been widely attributed to Bowles. She was remembered as "the second woman in the world" who worked as an "editor on the staff of an influential daily newspaper" (the first being Margaret Fuller).[10]

Once, apparently in early 1861 when the Bowleses were out of town, Cooke opened an envelope from Amherst and found Dickinson's "A feather from the whippowil" (Fr208A). She forwarded it to her boss with a note on the back: "Enclosed in this was a sprig of white pine, which I have carefully preserved." Three inferences seem in order. The literary editor knew enough about Dickinson to assume the poem was a private communication, not a submission. Bowles would not have authorized her to open the poet's notes if he had reason to think they might be embarrassing. And Cooke may have seen other and more personal messages in Bowles's absence.

The most prolific and outspoken of the women writers he brought forward was Mary Clemmer Ames. In August 1859 the paper published her effusive poem about the Bowleses' five-year-old daughter:

> *And Mamie comes to breakfast with morning glories crowned,*
> *A band of purple bell-cups around her forehead bound . . .*
> *A wondrous world of prophecy within our darling's eyes.*

Mediocre as this was, it was duly noted by Dickinson, perhaps because of the Bowles family's nearly contemporaneous visit to Amherst. That winter she assured Mary Bowles that "traditions of 'Memes' [Mamie's] eyes . . . are handed down," and some two years later, in a passage that is hopelessly obscure if the allusion is missed, she promised to catch a butterfly if Mamie would "build him a House in her 'Morning-Glory.' " Dickinson probably read the New England women poets who appeared

---

10. Some readers seem to make Dickinson the standard-bearer for a creative manuscript-based female culture writing in resistance to a standardized male print-based culture. The proponents of this view have not been aware that a woman ran the *Republican*'s literary department during the period of the poet's greatest productivity.

in the *Republican*, but it seems unlikely she (or Bowles[11]) had an exalted opinion of their merits, particularly as compared with Barrett Browning, the leading female Victorian poet, or the Brontë sisters, whose poems she at one point owned. The contemporary women writers who meant the most to her were, evidently, all British.

Dickinson's copy of *Aurora Leigh* was issued the same year, 1859, that she and Bowles had their talk about Revelation's "Gem chapter." The topic was undoubtedly inspired by the incandescent conclusion of Barrett Browning's poem, where the triumphant Aurora looks at the dawn for her blind lover and sees

> *The first foundations of that new, near Day*
> *Which should be builded out of heaven to God.*
>
> (9:955–56)

She then enumerates the sequence of colors, which, identical with the Bible's gems, herald the approaching millennium:

> *"Jasper first," I said,*
> *"And second, sapphire; third, chalcedony;*
> *The rest in order, – last, an amethyst."*
>
> (9:962–64)

Bowles knew these lines so well he could quote them from memory.

Once, in 1851, using a scratchy pen for her weekly letter to Austin, Emily had written, "I am in a hurry – this pen is too slow for me – 'it hath done what it could.' " She was picking up the familiar tag from Mark 14:8, where Jesus, defending a woman who has anointed him, declares, "She hath done what she could." The words had become proverbial, being regularly trotted out to exhort women to be satisfied with the subordinate services best suited to them. Emily gave the phrase a nicely

---

11. A confidential note to Sue and Austin indicates Ames's position in Samuel's regard: "I enclose a fresh letter from Mrs Ames—very like her, indeed. Please burn it, & forget it." There is no reason to think he discarded any of Emily's communications.

ironic turn, of course, but she was still very far from seeing how a female
pen could aspire to greatness. Her encounter a few years later with Barrett Browning's ambitious statement, "A Vision of Poets," may have been
crucial and defining, but this work had nothing to say about female experience and artistic ambition. Not until 1859 were Dickinson's eyes
opened, owing in large part to *Aurora Leigh,* which was seen as making
good a new set of claims for women's imaginative powers. That was one
of the thrilling messages in Aurora's gemmed dawn.

The main reason *Aurora Leigh* made a lasting impression on Dickinson and so many other mid-century readers (though not on Holland) is
that it was a new thing under the sun—a female epic tracing the growth
of a woman writer and dealing with women's special burdens and capacities. Brought up by an aunt who leads a "cage-bird life" (1:305)—the
phrase was marked by Dickinson—Aurora, the heroine, attains a pierc-
ing understanding of women's usual social function:

> *The works of women are symbolical.*
> *We sew, sew, prick our fingers, dull our sight,*
> *Producing what? A pair of slippers, sir,*
> *To put on when you're weary – or a stool*
> *To tumble over and vex you . . .*
>
> (1:456–60)

This insight into women's symbolic service (we recall the lamp mat Dickinson gave Elbridge Bowdoin) is also marked in her copy.

About 1863 Dickinson composed a poem that reconsidered her
original reaction to Barrett Browning:

> *I think I was enchanted*
> *When first a sombre Girl –*
> *I read that Foreign Lady . . .*

Describing her response as one of bewildered hilarity, the speaker sees
Browning as the witch or magician whose writings effected a transfor-

mation in perception. Under her spell, the enchanted aspirant found that small things were now outsized:

> The Bees – became as Butterflies –
> The Butterflies – as Swans –
> Approached – and spurned the narrow Grass –
> And just the meanest Tunes
>
> That Nature murmured to herself
> To keep herself in Cheer –
> I took for Giants – practising
> Titanic Opera . . .

Fr627

Though the poem credits "that Foreign lady" for the release and expansion that came with Dickinson's newly claimed poetic vocation, Barrett Browning was less the agent than the exemplar of the inspiring realization that a woman could be a power, a giant, in the world of thought. Greatness had become thinkable, especially with the *Republican's* disclosure (also in August 1859) that George Eliot, the author of *Adam Bede,* was in fact a Miss Marian Evans of Coventry, England. In *Aurora Leigh's* words,

> And truly, I reiterate, nothing's small!
> No lily-muffled hum of a summer-bee,
> But finds some coupling with the spinning stars;
> No pebble at your foot, but proves a sphere.

(7:813–16)

In Sue's copy, there are two kinds of marks beside the first couplet: the long wavy line Sue typically made in the 1850s, and a pair of short, neat parallel lines. In these tiny strokes (but nothing's small!) we have a trace of that heady "Conversion of the Mind" in the poet's tribute to Barrett Browning.

For anyone growing up in the Dickinson family, the idea of female greatness defied the basic order of things. Emily's earliest surviving letter appropriating this idea (the letter has been carelessly misdated by editors) was sent about December 1859 to Loring and Lavinia Norcross's daughter Louisa, then nearly eighteen. It recalls a conversation in which

> you and I in the dining room decided to be distinguished. It's a great thing to be "great" Loo, and you and I might tug for a life, and never accomplish it, but no one can stop our looking on, and you know some cannot sing, but the orchard is full of birds and we all can listen. What if we learn ourselves some day!

This conversation took place on an "October morning" when their families were out driving. That was two months after the talk with Bowles about the gem chapter.

After making this warily hedged confession of poetic ambition, Dickinson wrote, "Do you still attend Fanny Kemble." This was the actress who had left her southern slaveholding husband and was making a career reading Shakespeare's plays, first in the United States and eventually in England, where she became a friend of Henry James. The previous winter Kemble had performed in New York, where her reading of *Othello* earned a rave notice in Mary Clemmer Ames's New York letter to the *Republican:* "the genius of the tragedy was revealed, and glorified by the genius of the reader. Fanny Kemble is unreservedly great. And when a woman stands before the world as an artist, with what delight . . . I say, 'She is great.'" Was this trenchant opinion noted in Amherst? Kemble opened in Boston's Tremont Temple the next winter, offering a "course" of twelve plays from December 9, 1859, to January 7, 1860. These are the boundary dates for the letter to Louisa, which, significantly, records Dickinson's dissent from the Homestead's reigning authority: "Aaron Burr and father think [Kemble] an 'animal' but I fear zoölogy has few such instances. I have heard many notedly *bad* readers, and a fine one would be almost a fairy surprise." ("Aaron Burr" was probably Aaron Warner, Amherst College's retired professor of rhetoric.)

"Fairy" was not the word Kemble's admirers used to describe her powerful readings, yet the passage shows how Dickinson, moving from her great distance with the times, was beginning to take a stand, however privately and delicately ("I fear"). Her growing courage came in part from a sense of solidarity with champions like Barrett Browning and Kemble. But though she felt the stirrings of ambition, stepping out before the public was another matter entirely.

Nothing would have been easier for Dickinson than to find a publishing outlet. Given Bowles's friendship and encouragement of women writers, the *Republican* would have been open to her, especially with Cooke as literary editor. The paper's tastes were far from hidebound: Bowles was always confronting barriers and crossing boundaries and seeking a vital new woman's voice. In spite of Dickinson's "Druid" nature, her work was eminently publishable—subject to the usual editorial adjustments, of course. Nothing of hers showed up in the paper after she met the Hollands in 1853, but on August 2, 1858, one month after Bowles's trip to Amherst for the mowing machine contest, "Nobody knows this little rose" (Fr11) appeared in print, with the explanatory heading: "To Mrs. _____, with a Rose. [Surreptitiously communicated to The Republican.]" Clearly, someone other than the author had submitted it.[12]

It is not the case that Dickinson was denied an outlet, or that her work was deemed too "modern" or "incorrect" or "daring" to be published in her time. As Karen Dandurand and Joanne Dobson have shown, many conservative nineteenth-century Americans continued to hold the old idea that the best sort of writing circulates in private. Recognizing how special Dickinson's work was, those who received her poems often shared them with equally fascinated friends. This seems to be how Dickinson

---

12. Three possible recipients are the "~~lady~~ friend" who came with Samuel to the mowing machine trial, Mary Bowles, and Sue, whose obituary of Dickinson uses "surreptitiously" in connection with the unauthorized release of her work. There is no firm evidence that Dickinson sanctioned the appearance of any of the ten poems published in her lifetime. Disdain for payment ("Publication – is the Auction / Of the Mind of Man") can't have been the motive for withholding her work from the *Republican,* since, as Bowles admitted, the paper "never paid for poems."

In one of history's endless twists, the private circulation of manuscripts among privileged upper-class readers is now seen by some of Dickinson's readers as a politically radical act.

wanted to be read. Certainly, it was in line with her father's views on feminine decorum, her brother's uneasiness about her "wild" side, and her own profound shrinking from the public gaze. It would have been unthinkable for her to give up the protection and privacy she required. To that extent, her very being was at odds with Bowles's enlightened advocacy of a greater public role for women. And yet she was, emphatically, staking everything on a bold claim to greatness.

Not surprisingly, Bowles was the one who, whether on purpose or not, called this contradiction to her attention. In fall 1860 he was given an advance copy of Holland's latest attack on literary women, *Miss Gilbert's Career*. The novel's heroine, a young woman from western New England who is determined to "have a career," writes two novels that capture the public's attention. Acquiring the fame she has dreamed of, Miss Gilbert finds herself more and more dissatisfied. No acceptable marriage proposals arrive, and when curious strangers stare at her she feels violated. It isn't long before her "woman's nature, kept so long in abeyance, asserts itself! How ambition fades away, and love of freedom dies in the desire for bondage!" In the end, rightly choosing servitude and renouncing writing, the heroine "gladly laid down her proud self-reliance, and found her womanhood."

On October 10, three days before this book went on sale, Bowles's full-page unsigned review appeared in the *Tri-Weekly Republican*. Devoting most of his space to praise of Holland's realistic local color, illustrated with long extracts, Bowles reserved the meat of his remarks for the final paragraph, which took direct issue with the novel's "mission or moral." Noting that "a mere career" also leaves men unfulfilled, he squarely attacked the prevailing idea that woman's work was distinct from man's work: "we shall never get on to the millennium by parcelling out the labor of life in this way."

Dickinson had never shown the slightest interest in any available career, in spite of mild encouragement from Sarah Vaill Norcross, her step-grandmother, who bequeathed two books to her by or about pioneering women educators. Years later, when the editor Thomas Niles solicited her work, she attached to her refusal a poem contrasting humble independence with professional life:

How happy is the little Stone
That rambles in the Road alone
And does'nt care about Careers . . .

Fr1570E

In the last half of 1860, probably in August or October, Bowles and Dickinson had a disagreement on an issue involving "women." Afterward, she was so disturbed she sent an apology that stands as one of her most revealing performances.

Sunday night

Dear Mr Bowles.

I am much ashamed. I misbehaved tonight. I would like to sit in the dust. I fear I am your little friend no more, but Mrs Jim Crow.

I am sorry I smiled at women.

Indeed, I revere holy ones, like Mrs Fry and Miss Nightingale. I will never be giddy again. Pray forgive me now: Respect little Bob o' Lincoln again!

My friends are a very few. I can count them opon my fingers, and besides, have fingers to spare.

I am gay to see you – because you come so scarcely, else I had been graver.

Good night, God will forgive me – Will you please to *try*?

Emily.

It looks as if Samuel had brought out his belief that women should become more prominent in public life and Emily had scoffed at the notion. Now, backpedaling, she insists on her reverence for devoted philanthropists like Florence Nightingale and prison reformer Elizabeth Fry, who could be seen as selfless, "holy." It isn't known how Samuel reacted to her explanation. Clearly, the views her letter implies were more old-fashioned than his.

But the letter's most striking quality is its humble and needy self-denigration—its literal self-blackening. Afraid she has forfeited her friend's respect, Emily pretends he sees her as the female version of the stock blackface role many whites found comic. Exaggerating her unacceptableness in this fashion, she tries to simultaneously appeal to his humor and appease his disdain, basing her case not on justice but a strategy of conciliation that stresses her unworthiness and smallness. Just as God will forgive, so Bowles must condescend to overlook her naughtiness, mainly because she has so few friends and cannot do without him. And so she puts on blackface, presenting herself as a pariah and scapegrace in order to get back into master's good graces.

In substance, rhetoric, and style, this letter seems light-years removed from the bold self-assertion implicit in *Aurora Leigh* and in Kemble's readings of Shakespeare. Bowles had brought to the surface the profound contradictions in Dickinson's history and character. The episode stands as a portent of what lay ahead for the tortured writer: a deeper isolation, a more ferocious and even masochistic self-abasement, a terror of coming apart. It also affords a glimpse of what lay beneath her superb poem written about this time:

> *A* wounded *Deer – leaps highest –*
> *I've heard the Hunter tell –*
> *'Tis but the extasy of death –*
> *And then the Brake is still!*
>
> *The* smitten *Rock that gushes!*
> *The* trampled *Steel that springs!*
> *A Cheek is always redder*
> *Just where the Hectic stings!*
>
> *Mirth is the mail of Anguish –*
> *In which it cautious Arm,*
> *Lest Anybody spy the blood*
> *And "you're hurt" exclaim!*

Fr181B

These are among the few lines in English whose compressed and pulsating energies bear comparison with William Blake's "The Tyger." Agonized and unconfessional (the very point), the poem is infinitely suggestive as to what that ungainly mirth of Mrs. Jim Crow was all about. "The *trampled* Steel that springs!"

"The *smitten* Rock that gushes!" According to Exodus 17:6, Moses brought forth water for the Israelites in Sinai by striking a rock with his rod. That rod was on Dickinson now, and the one pressing question was whether blood or literature would flow.

"Meanwhile the jocular jailkeepers crow
Sing us a Ziong Ballad of woe
Chanties of Zionville, how do they go!"

Chapter 17

1860–1862: Carrying and Singing the Heart's Heavy Freight

Lavinia Norcross was known to be "failing *very* rapidly," but Emily was still caught off guard when she died of consumption in April 1860, aged forty-eight. Vinnie had gone to help, and the sister who stayed home couldn't believe it when letters arrived reporting "what Aunt Lavinia said 'just before she died.'" There had been no nearer death in the family, and Emily would "sob and cry till I can hardly see my way 'round the house."

The effort to absorb this event brought the poet even closer to her aunt's daughters, Louisa and Frances:[1] "I know you both better than I

---

1. Dickinson scholars prefer "Louise" to "Louisa," often referring to her as Loo and to Frances as Fanny, the pet names the poet is assumed to have used. In fact, Louisa was the correct legal name, and, judging by Frances's transcripts of the poet's letters, Emily variously addressed them as Fan or Fanny, Lou, Loo, Loulie, Loolie, or Louisa (with an "a").

did," she wrote that September. A consolatory poem sent to them, " 'Mama' never forgets her birds," affirmed the dead mother's (and Emily's) ongoing care of the sisters:

> If either of her "sparrows fall",
> She "notices" above.
>
> Fr130

The allusion was to Jesus' comforting statement, "Are not two sparrows sold for a farthing? and one of them shall not fall on the ground without your Father." Her substitution of "mama" as the providential agent reveals a growing inclination to replace paternalistic authority with a specifically feminine sensibility. There was a new and tougher tenderness, a feeling that the heart that loves had better be dogged, self-reliant, armed for trouble.

Two years later, when Aunt Lamira, the wife of Joel W. Norcross, died in a New York hotel at age twenty-nine, also of consumption and also leaving two children, the poet sent her husband a strong, finely calibrated letter of consolation. In the past, she and Vinnie had been put off by Joel's egotism and emotional remoteness. Now, taking a firm line, she reminded him of his parental responsibilities and pointedly hoped "we shall be more mindful of each other, for just her sake – learning a quicker tenderness." It was not religion but the dead woman's spirit that mandated this duty. Indeed, rather than extend the usual consolatory pieties, Dickinson wondered if the songbirds "know Heaven better than me – down here – so far away." To her, it looked as if Lamira had been "snatched."

The sinister word also shows up in a fragment about an unbroken family or couple: "They're so happy you know. That makes it doubtful. Heaven hunts round for those that find itself below [i.e., find heaven below], and then it snatches." This was sent to Frances and Louisa, who had begun to receive the poet's darkest thoughts: "Seeing pain one can't relieve makes a demon of one. . . . Heaven is so cold!" Thinking of Myra's "young face in the dark" made Emily wish she could explain "the anguish in the world. I wish one could be sure the suffering had a loving side." Was there no final and absolute comfort after all? That such doubts were imparted to a motherless twenty-year-old shows the degree of candor and equality the relationship assumed.

When Loring died in January 1863, leaving Louisa and Frances fully orphaned, the poet began the first of two warm letters with a declaration of support and solidarity: "What shall I tell these darlings except that my father and mother are half their father and mother, and my home half theirs, whenever and for as long as they will." Leaving many things implicit—the guttering failure of Loring's life, the burdens his daughters would have to shoulder—Emily spoke of how "tired" (depressed?) he had been since Lavinia's death and how happy the reunited couple must be. Her basic move was to offer the comforts of sympathy: she let her cousins know how their various friends in Amherst grieved for them, and "because I cannot pray" proceeded to "sing," likening the dead to birds that fly south and the bereaved to "birds that stay / The shiverers round farmers' doors" (Fr528[A]). Written in mid-winter, the poem tried to lift Louisa and fifteen-year-old Frances out of the particulars of their situation, yet not deny their grief. "Be sure you don't doubt about the sparrow," she wrote,[2] but it was human love, not faith in divine providence, that prompted the thought.

Lavinia had placed the large estate she had from her father in trust for her daughters, but she let Loring manage it as he saw fit. Thanks to his chronic bad judgment, her decision in this matter proved a costly one for Louisa and Frances. Three months before his death, acting as trustee, he invested $17,500 in a house and double lot on Boston's recently developed Chester Square. About the same time, the opening of the Back Bay caused a stampede out of the South End, leaving his daughters to dispose of the property the following June for $12,000. At his death, Loring owed his wife's estate $11,200, of which no more than $2,400 could be found (his debts were five times his assets). Still, mama's prov-

---

2. In a passage that was dropped from the 1894 edition of this letter and has never seen print, the poet informed her cousins that "Austin, whom Lou and Fanny might not think so thoughtful, tells how their mother and father were all the relatives he had who cared for him, a boy, and such as he could do for their little girls, would be gladly done. – says 'Lou and Fanny are alone' with a lower tone, and Vinnie and I reply 'no.' Sweet that some know better."

idential arrangements enabled her sparrows to live comfortably on some modest real-estate investments in Lynn.

The truly fearful question, not mentioned in extant letters, was "the evils" of first-cousin marriages such as Loring and Lavinia's. From the early 1850s, the public was advised in newspapers read by the poet that half the offspring of first-cousin marriage "will be deaf, dumb, blind or imbecile." It isn't known how Emily reacted to such brutal forecasts, or whether they had any impact on the Norcross sisters' decision not to marry. But it seems likely the suspicious regard cast on the children of first cousins only enhanced Frances and Louisa's appeal to Emily, who, a Druid in 1859, had become "the only Kangaroo among the Beauty" by 1862, the year she called Fan and Loulie her "little brothers." It was surely a comfort to be a little freakish, a little outside the pale, with them. That she seemed more "natural and spontaneous" with them than with others was noted in the 1894 edition of her letters.

Of all the Homestead's guests, the "dearest to us, as children," re-called Martha, the Evergreens' second child, were the Norcross sisters. Frances, "a great favorite with both houses," was "bright and charming, ready to play with us, and full of fun." Lou, equally playful, had a quieter and quainter appeal. Small, dainty, fanciful, impractical, she told the children she would come up some spring as a daffodil. She was "a spell-binder," with a "serious softness contradicted by the fun dancing in her eyes." She had ideas about the private lives of birds—"the probability" of a hummingbird "at home like other fathers." In the eyes of this young observer, "Cousin Lou was more like Aunt Emily than anybody."

Yet the orphaned cousins, products of a shattered home, had a worldly competence not possible for Emily, with her protective father and retiring habits. After Lamira's death, Louisa went to Lynn to tend Joel's children and run the household. The next summer, Vinnie being away, Emily begged her cousins to help "cut the cake . . . and chirp to those trustees." She was thinking of her great annual ordeal, the trea-surer's reception during Commencement week. "If you should fail me," she wrote, "my little life would fail of itself." Another pleading letter compared Commencement to "some vast anthropopic bear, ordained to eat me up." Still, as was the case with the poet's other friendships, the dependencies were mutual, complex, and not easily summed up. She often referred to her cousins as her "children" and "little girls," lavishing a kind of mothering on them that seems to have been gratifying for all concerned.

That all three were readers greatly enriched the friendship. When Emily needed books, Fanny found them for her in Lafayette Burnham's selection of "antique and modern books" on Boylston Street. Heading the other direction were poems, seventy-one at a minimum, in which Emily "sang" to her cousins. There were also oral performances, as Louisa recalled in 1904 in a letter to the *Woman's Journal,* a suffragist magazine. Defending the dignity of domestic labor, she remembered how "Emily Dickinson wrote most emphatic things in the pantry, so cool and quiet, while she skimmed the milk; because I sat on the footstool behind the door, in delight, as she read them to me. The blinds were closed, but through the green slats she saw all those fascinating ups and downs going on outside that she wrote about." It adds to the value of this firsthand testimony to know that our witness not only heard Fanny Kemble but acted in private theatricals (see Chapter 18). Since neither Sue nor her daughter ever described such readings, it appears Aunt Lavinia's girls knew Emily in ways no one else did.

What kind of oral rendition did the poet give of her work? A little-known 1895 essay drawing on Vinnie's authority suggests an answer:

> Emily was herself a most charming reader. It was done with great
> simplicity and naturalness, with an earnest desire to express the exact
> conception of the author, without any thought of herself, or the im-
> pression her reading was sure to make.

This account goes against two influential interpretations of Dickinson's art: that it lacked an oral dimension, and that it was high camp performance.

A common past can be a powerful bond for those who live into changing times. One of Emily's letters to Frances and Louisa smiles at Reverend Joseph Vaill (Grandma Norcross's brother) and his down-home pronunciation of "Lorin' and Laviny." Following the death of Barrett Browning in June 1861 and the publication of an article on George Sand in November, Dickinson wrote: "Your letters are real, just the tangled road children walked before you. . . . That Mrs. Browning fainted, we need not read *Aurora Leigh* to know, when she lived with her English aunt; and 'George Sand' 'must make no noise in her grandmother's bed-room.' Poor children! Women, now, queens, now!" Although we don't know what the cousins had complained of, the poet evidently intended a soothing parallel between their troubles and the hard early years of Barrett Browning and George Sand. Emily, of course, had had an unusually quiet, confined, rule-bound girlhood. Did the three cousins explore their pasts together? Emily would come out against all forms of childhood discipline, and when a Society for the Prevention of Cruelty to Children was organized in Concord in the 1880s, Louisa was a charter member.

As for religion, Louisa and Frances were also trudging the long road out of Calvinism. Both had grown up in Boston's militantly evangelical Bowdoin Street Church,[3] but Louisa's conversion at age seventeen took a very different form from her mother's tormented self-confinement. The committee that questioned her about her spiritual experience noted she did "not remember any particular time when she gave herself to Christ," and her confession of faith said nothing about a sense of sin. Moving to Cambridge after Loring's death, she and Frances joined the evangelical Prospect Street Church[4] in January 1865. The affiliation didn't hold, and when the sisters settled in Concord in the 1870s, they became active in the extremely liberal First Parish, whose most famous member was Ralph Waldo Emerson. Their withdrawal from orthodoxy surely added to the common ground already shared with Dickinson.

Those who believe the Civil War had no impact on the poet haven't

---

3. Built of large granite blocks and topped with battlements, this church, still intact after years of neglect, makes visible the fighting evangelicalism that erected it. When its first minister, the Reverend Lyman Beecher, resigned, it was to run the Cincinnati seminary that hired Dickinson's grandfather.

4. The Reverend William A. Stearns was pastor of this church before becoming president of Amherst College in 1854. Today the stately edifice bears the name Igreja Presbiteriana Cristo Rei.

read her Norcross correspondence. When President Stearns's admired son, Frazar, was killed in March 1862, she sent her cousins a vivid report of the local anguish. Several weeks later, condoling with Uncle Joel on his wife's death, she wrote, "So many brave – have died, this year – it dont seem lonely – as it did – before Battle begun." At year's end, extending this line of thought, she let her cousins know how the terrible conflict was entering her life:

> Sorrow seems more general than it did, and not the estate of a few persons, since the war began; and if the anguish of others helped one with one's own, now would be many medicines. . . . I noticed that Robert Browning had made another poem, and was astonished – till I remembered that I, myself, in my smaller way, sang off charnel steps. Every day life feels mightier, and what we have the power to be, more stupendous.[5]

This important passage reveals the intricate linkage between the poet's creative ordeal and the spectacle of wartime anguish and heroism. Bereavement had always been a defining experience for her, most recently with the deaths of aunts Lavinia and Lamira. The war multiplied and generalized her sense of mortal risk and large issues and a nearness to ultimates. Now, as she accomplished the greatness she and Louisa had anticipated in October 1859, she saw that her new powers had something to do with the national ordeal. It was as if her own fundamentals had been endorsed.

Sequestered though she was, Dickinson was very much a part of the society of her time. To detach her from the war is to miss seeing how her poetry of the early 1860s, a great and classic descent into a personal inferno, was made possible by the staggering disaster in the distance.

---

5. Dated 1864? by Johnson, this letter, L298, was correctly moved to December 1862 by Leyda, who found an announcement in the *Republican* of a new poem by Robert Browning. Getting the date right is crucial: it shows that, on the eve of her most productive year, 1863, the poet made the connection between the war and her growing powers.

The Poet and the Civil War

As the North moved toward Abraham Lincoln and the South toward secession, Edward Dickinson continued to flirt with the small Constitutional Unionist Party. Headed by John Bell of Tennessee and Edward Everett of Massachusetts, this party tried to cool the sectional conflict by simply reaffirming the Union and the Constitution. When the "Belleveretts," as they were derisively called, held a "union meeting" in December 1859, Edward, one of many vice presidents, contributed a letter rebuking the intemperate public tone both North and South and recommending compromise and harmony. In 1860, Massachusetts' Unionists chose him as their candidate for lieutenant governor. Although he at once declined (Henry Morris, the man who whipped him in 1854, was on the ticket), the Belleverett newspapers were still running his name above their editorial columns ten days later. Writing to Frances in Boston, Emily asked her to "give my respects to the 'Bell and Everett party' if she passes that organization on her way to school? I hear they wish to make me Lieutenant-Governor's daughter. Were they cats I would pull their tails, but as they are only patriots, I must forego the bliss." Her odd mixture of disdain and respect resembles her father's mixed signals. At the polls Amherst's voters chose Lincoln over Bell, 405 to 26. When hostilities commenced, the Unionists were seen as the party of appeasement.

The next year, in an effort to unite all factions under a common war banner, the state Republicans also made Edward their nominee for lieutenant governor. Now was the time, some thought, for him to stop sulking in his tent and come to the aid of his country. Instead, keeping his distance and his principles, he wrote a long public letter that repudiated "the immediate and universal emancipation of slaves," on grounds of states' rights. This stiff-necked Whiggishness brought an immediate public denunciation from "Warrington," the *Republican*'s Boston columnist. Contrasting the poet's father to Edward Everett, who consented to join the cause, "Warrington" wrote that "the difference between him and

Mr Dickinson is the difference between a patriot and a partisan, a liberal and a bigot, a man and a mouse." It was a bitter moment.

Yet, even as Edward kept clear of all parties, he vigorously backed the northern war effort, offering bounties to volunteers and sending fire-breathing letters of support to the leaders with whom he refused to act. To Senator Charles Sumner, a radical abolitionist in the eyes of old-line Whigs, he dispatched a heated statement condemning not just the South but the spectrum of northern political opinion: "This infernal rebellion which must soon be put down forever! & forever!! will so shake up the extremes of conservatism & radicalism, that true views of our Republican Institutions will be widespread, and enduring! & our gov't be exorcised of the unclean devils who have made their 'dens' in our very Council Chambers!" This intemperate prediction, as utopian as it is incoherent, hardly accords with Edward's earlier defense of moderation. After listening to one of these diatribes in 1864, George Shepard noted privately that he seemed to forget he had "always been in action a *conservative* or a pro slavery man." Still, the poet's father sometimes realized how he struck others. An 1868 letter to Sumner ends, "Excuse my croaking."

Emily's position relative to the war was as oblique and conflicted as her father's. Once, she looked forward to watering geraniums in the winter when Sue and Vinnie, with their more martial feelings, would "have gone to the War." Unlike many patriotic women, she refused to help make bandages. As she put it in 1861, she could not "weave Blankets, or Boots," and thus would "have no winter this year – on account of the soldiers." Remote from the physical and emotional dangers combatants faced, she sounded her odd brittle note when a Yankee on his way to war stopped to request a nosegay: "I suppose he thought we kept an Aquarium."

In February and March 1864, as Karen Dandurand discovered, three of her poems appeared in *Drum Beat,* a short-run Brooklyn paper designed to raise money for medical care for Union soldiers; in April, "Success is counted sweetest" came out in the *Brooklyn Daily Union.* Since the first of these papers was edited by an Amherst College trustee and occasional guest at the Evergreens, the Reverend Richard Salter Storrs,

Jr., it has been thought that he may have secured Emily's work by going through Sue. Another good possibility is Sue's friend in Brooklyn, Gertrude Vanderbilt, a publishing writer who helped organize sanitary fairs in New York. Whoever the persuader was, Dandurand believes the *Drum Beat* poems were not submitted "surreptitiously," like some other Dickinson poems published in her lifetime, but appeared with her consent.

Perhaps, but letters from Samuel Bowles tell a different story. A facility called Soldiers' Rest had been established in Springfield to care for the many sick and wounded combatants passing through the city. When a money-raising fair was organized in December 1864 to pay for expenses, Samuel asked Austin three times, apparently without success, to lend some paintings for the art exhibit. About the same time, drumming up contributions for a short-run sheet to be sold at the fair, the editor wrote Sue: "Speaking of writing, do you & Emily give us some gems for the 'Springfield Musket', & then come to the Fair." The publication he named was a literary miscellany in the form of a newspaper, issued in four numbers over the duration of the fair. This appeal also failed: it was as hard to get the poet to join the war as it was to overcome the standoffishness of her father and brother.

And yet, like them, she was deeply engaged by the spectacle of victory, defeat, and death, often expressing thoughts others left silent. A few months before Frazar Stearns was killed, she hoped "that ruddy face won't be brought home frozen." When a professor's widow lost the second of her sons, she spoke feelingly of the woman's collapse and pictured the young man's ghost "riding tonight in the mad wind – back to the village burying-ground where he never dreamed of sleeping: Ah! the dreamless sleep!" After Bowles was back from Europe in fall 1862, Dickinson informed him that "we used to tell each other, when you were from America – how failure in a Battle – were easier – and you here." From this, we surmise she shared the North's dismay after the Second Battle of Bull Run, in August.

The few poems that explicitly touch on the war, such as "When I was small, a woman died" (Fr518) or "It feels a shame to be alive" (Fr524), were inspired by fatalities. "It dont sound so terrible quite as it did"

(Fr384) may have been suggested by Stearns's death. Fascicle 23, from late 1862, contains two dramatizations of an emphatic willingness to die: in "Wolfe demanded during dying" (Fr482) the fatally wounded opposing generals in the eighteenth-century battle for Quebec find it "easy" and "sweet" to die for their cause, and in "He fought like those who've nought to lose" (Fr480B) a combatant with no "further Use" for life emerges unharmed, unlike his fallen comrades. The Civil War offered Dickinson a stark symbolic theater, a place of ultimate terror and exultation in which mundane life was forgotten and there was both everything and nothing to lose. War gave her a powerful vehicle with which to parse her own extremity.

Whether deliberately or not, the poem Dickinson sandwiched between the two last-mentioned works is her one first-person poem about fame:

> *Fame of Myself, to justify,*
> *All other Plaudit be*
> *Superfluous – An Incense*
> *Beyond Nescessity –*
>
> *Fame of Myself to lack – Although*
> *My Name be else supreme –*
> *This were an Honor honorless –*
> *A futile Diadem –*
>
> Fr481

Others' praise could neither justify her self-approval ("Fame of Myself") nor compensate for its absence. Enclosed by two poems about an honorable performance in battle, these lines, apparently shown to no one, underline what Dickinson's work as a whole all but proclaims: she wasn't driven by a quest for recognition. Rather, her writing was the expression of a hard existential fight that could not be shirked, and for which no attitude was quite so fitting as a gay tragic irony. Knowing that others were also fighting counted for a great deal.

& Send 2 Sunsets

Apotheosis

It has long been understood that Dickinson's productivity climaxed in the first half of the 1860s. Thomas Johnson believed she composed 86 poems in 1861, 366 in 1862, 141 in 1863, and 174 in 1864. R. W. Franklin's more recent tally yields 88 poems in 1861, 227 in 1862, 295 in 1863, and 98 in 1864. Although these later figures are more trustworthy, they should still be taken as mere estimates of her astonishing output. On some days she must have produced more than one poem, perhaps many more. "I send Two Sunsets," begins a lighthearted boast from 1863 about her fecundity:

> *Day and I – in competition ran –*
> *I finished Two – and several Stars –*
> *While He – was making One –*
>
> Fr557B

But we remind ourselves that this is not a diary entry and that we know almost nothing about the daily originating matrix of the writer's work. We have no rough drafts of poems from the early 1860s, no notebooks, no authorial memoirs telling us how the writing connected with the events of life. A few poems can be dated exactly and most of the rest with a fair approximation, and of course we learn something by seeing how some of them are bedded in letters. Yet it often happens that the poems that speak of the most vital of private experiences were preserved in the manuscript books only, giving us virtually no context.

Only a few of Dickinson's early first-person poems—"I never lost as much but twice" (Fr39), "Heart! We will forget him" (Fr64)—seem to tell stories about the writer. Around 1860, poems of this type become much more abundant, sometimes placing a first-person experience in the present, sometimes in the past, but generally implying a passionate inquiry into the writer's peculiar destiny. In "I was the slightest in the house," the speaker reflects on her modesty and sense of privacy: "I could not bear to live – aloud – / The Racket shamed me so" (Fr473). In "I had been hungry all the years," she imagines approaching a loaded table after long starvation, but only to feel "ill – and odd" (Fr439). In another, she looks back on her earlier life as one of chronic and vital deprivation: "It would have starved a Gnat – / To live so small as I" (Fr444). Full as they are of exaggerated and fabulistic elements, these dramatic first-person retrospects articulate a very real personal effort—that "tug for a life" that Dickinson spoke of to Louisa Norcross in late 1859.

In these colorful autobiographies, Dickinson assumed the mask of fiction in order to tease out her essentials. In "The Malay took the pearl" (Fr451), a noble speaker contrasts his timidity with the desperate bold-ness of a dark-skinned rival, who dives and wins the prize: "The Negro never knew / I – wooed it – too." Drawing on an article in *Harper's Monthly* with illustrations of dark-skinned pearl divers, the poem gives us its maker's ongoing meditation on aspiration and singleness ("I spilt the dew," "by birth a Bachelor"). But how far do we go in fitting the story this poem tells to the facts of her life? Those who make Austin the Malay, Sue the jewel, and Emily the earl who might have dived for her seem at once too literal and too allegorical, and too unwilling to grant the poet her pro-jective liberties. She was also the triumphant Malay, after all. The "as if" idea, explicit in many poems—"As if some little Arctic flower" (Fr177), "As if the sea should part" (Fr720), "As if a Goblin with a Guage" (line 10, Fr425)—was surely taken for granted in many more.

But there is still personal reference; if the poems' fables change, their emotional core does not; they are always welling up from a massive cen-tral volcano, like the lava flows on Mars. "I dwell in possibility," which seems to be about the undisciplined fancy, the imagination set free from the conditions of life, announces its true subject in its final words: "The spreading wide my narrow Hands / To gather Paradise" (Fr466). That subject is, first and last, desire, and when the topic shifts to heaven, that is because it is the only place where earth's broken conversations can be completed. Emily had worked it out at age twenty: "Dont you think . . . these brief imperfect meetings have a tale to tell . . . whose site is in the skies."

By 1862, the poet was pushing this germinal idea very far indeed:

✻
> *Heaven is so far of the Mind*
> *That were the Mind dissolved –*
> *The Site – of it – by Architect*
> *Could not again be proved –*
>
> *'Tis Vast – as our Capacity –*
> *As fair – as our idea –*
> *To Him of adequate desire*
> *No further 'tis, than Here.*

Fr413

"So far" carries the sense of *to that extent,* though without excluding the idea of distance. Like "I dwell in possibility," the poem says that just *because* paradise is something dreamed by the mind, it is within reach of anyone whose desire is adequate. Beginning with the infinite, Dickinson returns to its generative source—the soul trapped in a body trapped in empty space.

Many poems—"He forgot and I remembered" (Fr232), "I showed her hights she never saw" (Fr346)—treat the same questions we hear in letter after letter: Why don't you write, why is so-and-so silent, do I alone remember, have I offended, won't you forgive, won't you write? When Vinnie summed up a basic pattern of her sister's life—the loss of friends ("cut to the heart when death robbed her again and again")—the statement would have been even truer if "neglect" were paired with "death." In a poem probably sent to Bowles, Dickinson seems to try to control her affectionate nature:

✻
> *What shall I do – it whimpers so –*
> *This little Hound within the Heart*
> *All day and night with bark and start –*

Fr237A

In an even more extreme poem, she is a crucified lovebird lavishing her last blood-soaked melody on the man who has given her the death-thrust:

> *Stab the Bird – that built in your bosom –*
> *Oh, could you catch her last Refrain –*
> *Bubble! "forgive" – "Some better" – Bubble!*
> *"Carol for Him – when I am gone"!*
>
> Fr309 (J238)

The final couplet exhibits the songbird's oozing heart, each "Bubble!" representing the bloody froth that mingles with her last words (in quotes). Like Jesus' "forgive them for they know not what they do," the dying "Refrain" seeks what is best for the murderer. This shocking poem goes way beyond the bounds of good taste and proper self-respect. But how does someone living in "possibility" draw the line?

The idea of extreme pain, appearing in a few poems in 1859, became one of Dickinson's major subjects in the early 1860s. Of the twenty-one instances of the word "hurt" in her poems (noun or verb), every single one occurs between 1860 and 1863. The apparatus of torture—"gimblets" (Fr242), "metallic grin" (Fr243), "A Weight with Needles" (Fr294)—now becomes almost routine, along with references to Jesus' betrayal and crucifixion, generally linked to the speaker's own passion. In a fascicle poem possibly dating from spring 1861, the speaker emphasizes the immediacy of her pain, felt in the act of writing:

> *I shall know why – when Time is over –*
> *And I have ceased to wonder why –*
> *Christ will explain each separate anguish*
> *In the fair schoolroom of the sky –*
>
> *He will tell me what "Peter" promised –*
> *And I – for wonder at his woe –*
> *I shall forget the drop of anguish*
> *That scalds me now – that scalds me now!*
>
> Fr215

Peter promised to stand by his Master in his hour of trial, then denied knowing him. What the speaker hopes is that when she gets to heaven and Christ tells her of the agony of his abandonment, she will at last be able to stop thinking about her own. Wishing for nothing so much as the cessation of her anguish, Dickinson does not much look like a masochist in this poem.

In 1862, after the pain had receded, Dickinson wrote in retrospect about

> *. . . the Prayer*
> *I knew so perfect – yesterday –*
> *That scalding one – Sabacthini –*
> *Recited fluent – here –*
>
> Fr283C (J313)

"Lama sabachthini"—"Why hast thou forsaken me?"—were Jesus' last words on the cross. The poem, sent to Louisa and Frances (apparently between their parents' deaths), justifies pain in the orthodox way, as beneficial for the soul. This was the argument in the Wadsworth sermon sent to Dickinson in 1858: "Character is the creature of development and discipline. It depends quite as much upon experience of pain, as of pleasure."

Be that as it may (and Dickinson does seem to have taken the idea to heart), her most impressive treatments of suffering—"I like a look of agony" (Fr339), "I felt a funeral in my brain" (Fr340), "After great pain a formal feeling comes" (Fr372)—offer no such justification. We note as well that these three poems, entered about 1862 in manuscript books 16 and 18, aren't known to have been shown to anyone.

"Wife"

Many of the pain poems from 1861 and 1862 join a large group dealing with a first-person speaker's attachment to an unnamed man, variously addressed or spoken of as "Master," "Signor," "Sir," "Caviler," "he," "him," or "you." One of the things that makes this cycle of love lyrics so remarkable is the fullness of voice it gives to frustrated desire and energetic fantasizing. At times, as in "Again his voice is at the door" (Fr274) or the commemorative "One year ago jots what?" (Fr301, early 1862?), the speaker seems to be dwelling on a past event. At other times she expresses a desire to be with him again, either for eternity—"Forever at his side to walk" (Fr264)—or just an hour—"What would I give to see his face?" (Fr266). Invariably, the distances between them are impassable, as in "Ah, moon and star!" where she ends by admitting "He – is more than a firmament – from me" (Fr262). In spite of this, she reaffirms her faithfulness again and again, as in another lunar poem likening the absent lover to the moon and herself to the responsive tides:

> Oh, Signor, Thine, the Amber Hand –
> And mine – the distant Sea –
> Obedient to the least command
> Thine eye impose on me –
>
> Fr387 (J429)

A favorite fantasy is that of an eventual heavenly reunion, as in "Fitter to see him I may be" (Fr834). In some of the poems that develop this thought, she speaks of herself as his waiting betrothed, or even "wife."

The relationship this group of erotic poems had to the external events of Dickinson's life remains an unsolved problem. A few readers have proposed, in spite of the gendered nouns and pronouns, that the lover was a woman. Others, making a hard-and-fast rule of the poet's statement that her lyric "I" is a "supposed person," read the marriage poems as essentially fictive. Still others evade the problem by reading them as "texts" existing in no universe but their own. These solutions, deriving from various fixed positions, serve to disinfect her work of its manifest if elusive autobiographical content.

Another possibility is that Dickinson was out of her mind, unable to draw the line between fantasy and reality. In 1852, in the first of several passages about her "insanity," she wrote Sue that "in thinking of those I love, my reason is all gone from me, and I do fear sometimes that I must make a hospital for the hopelessly insane." Ignoring the playful exaggeration of such passages, a few scholars have taken her at her word, most

notably John Cody, who sees an incapacitating psychotic episode following Austin and Sue's marriage: "Emily's ego was like an opal, rent by fis-
sures and fractures, brittle, never coalescing into a unity, reflecting first
this, then that fracture-surface." One reason to be wary of this (admit-
tedly impressive) image and the accompanying diagnosis is the difficulty
of reconciling such fragmentation with the integrative resourcefulness of
the poet's work. Another is that not one document from her many literate and outspoken contemporaries speaks of her as crazy.

Edward Dickinson, always so quick to raise the specter of "insanity"
or "monomania," becomes a key witness here. As a college student, he
had urged that insanity be considered a disease and asylums established
for its victims. In the following decades he promoted the Worcester hospital for the insane, and in 1859 he was appointed trustee of the newly
established State Lunatic Hospital at Northampton, which he would
later praise as a "safe & valuable & desirable retreat." When Pliny Earle
took charge of this institution in 1864,[6] he recognized Edward's interest
and expertness by sending him a book on the Parish will case in New
York, which turned on the legal competence of a wealthy victim of
apoplexy. By this time, Hampshire County had had its own famous will
case, in which the heirs of Oliver Smith of Hatfield challenged his phil-
anthropic bequests by claiming that one of his witnesses had been insane. Heard in Northampton, the appeal pitted Rufus Choate against
Daniel Webster; a transcript was published by James W. Boyden, an
Amherst attorney. All in all, Emily's father was extremely well posted on
the legal risks in using signatories who were mentally unsound, or could
be deemed such. Nevertheless, on six occasions between April 1859 and
November 1862 (see Appendix 4), he asked Emily to witness his real estate transactions. The inference is that he assumed she was of sound
mind and able to withstand legal scrutiny.

---

6. Edward's letters to Earle give evidence of a continuing and enlightened concern. In 1868 he
was "pleased with . . . the happy results of experiments, upon diseased bodies & minds." After
reading Earle's medical school lectures on mental illness, he deprecated the "erroneous
views . . . entertained by the community" and looked forward to the day when "Insanity [would
be] generally recognised as a *disease*."

That the love poems were a response to an actual and painful relationship with a man seems the only plausible way to take them. Yet even as we scour them for news of the poet's life, we must keep in mind her predilection for fiction, fantasy, secrecy. She may or may not have had a special "Box – / In which his letters grew" (Fr292), but there probably was a correspondence. Several poems, such as "Doubt me! My dim companion!" (Fr332), seem to react to messages received in the present or past, in this instance questioning her constancy. Closely related are those poems, such as "Civilization spurns the leopard!" in which she defends herself against reproach: "This was the Leopard's nature – Signor – / Need – a keeper – frown?" (Fr276).[7] Again and again, there are hints of tension, disagreement, and struggle, often a pained sense of having offended.

A few poems seem to recall a face-to-face meeting in which "I groped opon his breast" (Fr349), or a conversation in which

> You said it hurt you – most –
> Mine – was an Acorn's Breast –
> And could not know how fondness grew
> In Shaggier Vest –

Coming up with a belated retort, she corrects his arrogance by saying that if he had looked into her heart he would have seen "A Giant – eye to eye with you" (Fr301). The intense reconstructive energies at work in this and other poems show that, while there may indeed have been some sort of talk, embrace, or parting scene, something leaving a sharp-edged trace, biographers must exercise great caution in reading these narratives.

The most suggestive, "There came a day at summer's full," makes the Lord's Supper (to which the speaker is finally admitted) the metaphor for an intense farewell scene in which nothing is said and everything is

---

7. The allusion is to Jeremiah 13:23, "Can the Ethiopian change his skin, or the leopard his spots?" and the corresponding hymn in *Watts and Select:* "Let the wild leopards of the wood / Put off the spots that nature gives. . . ."

changed. At the end, as the speaker and the other person part, she feels they have sealed a compact that can be fulfilled only in heaven:

> *And so – when all the time had failed –*
> *Without external sound –*
> *Each – bound the other's Crucifix –*
> *We gave no other bond –*
>
> *Sufficient troth – that we shall rise –*
> *Deposed – at length – the Grave –*
> *To that New Marriage –*
> *Justified – through Calvaries of Love!*
>
> Fr325C

The date of the earliest known version of this poem, January 1862, would be consistent with a parting during the summer of 1860 or 1861.

Among the poems that scout the suggestion that the speaker could be unfaithful to her tacit pledge is "Me change! Me alter!" (Fr281), also about 1862. In another, the speaker insists that her " 'Wife's' Affection" can change only when her mind and sex are surgically tampered with. She begins in white-hot outrage at what seems to be someone's advice or prediction:

> *Rearrange a "Wife's" Affection!*
> *When they dislocate my Brain!*
> *Amputate my freckled Bosom!*
> *Make me bearded like a man!*
>
> *Blush, my spirit, in thy Fastness –*
> *Blush, my unacknowledged clay –*
> *Seven years of troth have taught thee*
> *More than Wifehood ever may!*
>
> *Love that never leaped its socket –*
> *Trust intrenched in narrow pain –*

> *Constancy thro' fire – awarded –*
> *Anguish – bare of anodyne!*
>
> *Burden – borne so far triumphant –*
> *None suspect me of the crown,*
> *For I wear the "Thorns" till Sunset –*
> *Then – my Diadem put on.*
>
> *Big my Secret but it's* bandaged –
> *It will never get away*
> *Till the Day its Weary Keeper*
> *Leads it through the Grave to thee.*
>
> Fr267

In this remarkable poem, recorded on the same sheet as "What would I give to see his face?" (Fr266) but later destroyed by a family member (though not before being copied by an assistant of Mabel Loomis Todd), Dickinson used an emphatically physical vocabulary to establish her passion. Her freckled breasts and blushing flesh ("clay") culminate in the daring fifth stanza, where the betrothed speaker, seduced and abandoned, big with her secret, finally leads it as a small child to a heavenly reunion with her lover. The poem dates from the same period as "There came a day at summer's full"; both offer similar constructions of a relationship that is to involve no more face-to-face meetings. Franklin puts "Rearrange a 'wife's' affection" in late 1861. If we move it to early 1862 and take the seven years literally—two big ifs—the originating event (heavily fantasized) could be assigned to March 1855, when Dickinson was in Philadelphia.

In this work Dickinson presents herself as figuratively ravished, possessed, owned, with the implication that her tragic victimhood is also her glory—that she has transformed a shameful private burden into a crown. The trick in "getting" the poem is to sense how it plays with the poet's reality. We can assume she was too well informed to see herself as literally betrothed or seduced: in 1853 she heard about a breach-of-promise suit from Vinnie; in 1860 her father successfully defended a man in another such case all the way to the Supreme Judicial Court; in August 1861 it was reported in the Amherst paper that the unmarried daughter of a "prominent and respectable citizen" of Greenfield gave birth while her family attended church. A lawyer's daughter with a gossipy sister heard enough about such events to be able to devise a truth-telling fiction of her own, especially if she had been deeply impressed, as Dickinson was, by Dinah Craik's *Head of the Family*. Tricked into becoming a "wife," Craik's Rachel Armstrong makes herself into a great actress precisely by remaining painfully faithful to the "master" who has trifled with her. Her story forms a partial but fascinating parallel with Dickinson's "wife" poems.[8]

In "Many a phrase has the English language," the poet speaks of one persistent phrase

> *Breaking in bright Orthography*
> *On my simple sleep –*
> *Thundering its Prospective –*
> *Till I stir, and weep –*

Abruptly turning to the speaker who has violated her peace, she ends with this plea:

> *Not for the Sorrow, done me –*
> *But the push of Joy –*
> *Say it again, Saxon!*
> *Hush – Only to me!*

Fr333

---

8. In her distinguished study of twentieth-century women writers, *Writing beyond the Ending*, Rachel Blau DuPlessis suggests that nineteenth-century narratives about women contained two opposite strands, quest versus love, and that the standard ending subordinated the former to the latter. Dickinson clearly "wrote beyond the ending," like more modern writers, yet, for her as for Rachel Armstrong, quest was saturated with desire, and erotic love led to wildness rather than to social order.

Just what the phrase is that must be spoken to her alone, in a whisper, the poem does not say, of course. No one else is to know it. "None suspect me of the crown."

In the manuscript books "Saxon" is marked with a + for an alternative word or words, presumably consisting of two syllables, with the accent on the first. But no word or phrase appears. It is as if something stopped her from entering it.

One thinks of another poem, also thought to be from early 1862, beginning:

> *I got so I could hear his name –*
> *Without – Tremendous gain –*
> *That Stop-sensation – on my Soul . . .*
>
> Fr292

Master

The links between Dickinson's love poems and her second and third drafts to "Master" are as problematic as they are obvious. These drafts have been assigned by Franklin to 1861, on the basis of paper and handwriting. The one that is in pencil, an excruciating letter of apology, begins "Oh! did I offend it – Did'nt it want me to tell it the truth, Daisy – Daisy – offend it." The other, in ink and not so rough a draft, might have been mailed if Dickinson hadn't introduced revisions after she began, thus necessitating another copy. This letter also begins by reacting to something the unknown correspondent has written. Evidently, the poet has been blindsided:

Master.

If you saw a bullet hit a Bird – and he told you he was'nt shot – you might weep at his courtesy, but you would certainly doubt his word –

One drop more from the gash that stains your Daisy's bosom –
then would you *believe*?

Even apart from the wounded and bleeding bird, or the writer's agonized perception that Master cannot accept her as she is, or her insistence on her truth and fidelity, the drafts echo the poems in countless
ways. The desire is frank and fully voiced: "I want to see you more – Sir
– than all I wish for in this world – and the wish – altered a little – will
be my only one – for the skies." She tells him that when she asked him
for "Redemption," he gave her "something else" that caused her to forget
the request. "I did'nt tell you for a long time," she added in a passage
later canceled, "but I knew you had altered me." Recalling his farewell in
the draft Franklin dates early 1861, she says she "never flinched thro' that
awful parting – but held her life so tight he should not see the wound."

Readers are shocked by the openness and direness of her need. If you
could "come to New England," the writer cajoles, "would you come to
Amherst – Would you like to come – Master?" Presenting herself as beg-
ging at his knee, she implores him to make a special place for her in his
life:

> Master – open your life wide, and take me in forever, I will never be
> tired – I will never be noisy when you want to be still – I will be ~~glad~~
> ~~as the~~ your best little girl – nobody else will see me, but you – but that
> is enough.

What she seeks is not marriage (clearly out of reach) but some sort of private, nonphysical union, which no one else need ever know about and in
which she will always be the best little girl anyone could possibly wish for.

Paradoxically, Dickinson makes this infantile proposition with an
energetic fullness of expression that is nothing less than . . . masterly.
And even as she revels in her humble " 'Little Girl'hood," she flouts the
usual feminine rule by making her desire fully visible. *She* is wooer and
seducer here, putting out a line of talk designed to overcome the other's
reluctance. At one point, imagining their sexes reversed—"if I had the

Beard on my cheek – like you[9] – and you – had Daisy's petals – and you cared so for me – what would become of you?"—she conjures up the erotic charge between his scratchy beard and her smooth petals precisely by reversing them: *as if* becoming a vehicle for *what is*. In spite of such displacements, the drafts attain a kind of ultimate in the direct expression of desire and agony.

Although the writer calls herself "Daisy," as a sign of her commonness and lowness, she knows very well she is also a volcano. Replying to her correspondent's complaint that she has not told him everything, she writes, "Vesuvius dont talk – Etna – dont – one of them – said a syllable – a thousand years ago, and Pompeii heard it, and hid forever." Taking for granted that much must remain unsaid, she still dares, like Vesuvius, a "syllable."

To date, there is only one candidate who matches what we infer about the unknown correspondent. The Reverend Charles Wadsworth didn't reside in New England, occasionally traveled there, offered "Redemption" as a minister of the Gospel, and, as shown by the derisive treatment of poetry in his sermons, would have been seriously at odds with Dickinson. We know they exchanged letters before spring 1862 and that she took a special interest in him. Also, like Master in the following passage, Wadsworth was married, a Presbyterian, and (in her phrase from twenty years later) a "Man of sorrow":

> [I]f I can never forget that I am not with you – and that sorrow and frost are nearer than I – if I wish with a might I cannot repress – that mine were the Queen's place – the love of the – Plantagenet is my only apology[.] – To come nearer than Presbyteries – and nearer than the new coat – that the Tailor made – the prank of the Heart at play on the Heart – in holy Holiday – is forbidden me.

---

9. The phrase "like you," one of many interlineated additions, makes explicit the recipient's gender and thus stands in the way of those who would like Master to be female. Martha Nell Smith has conducted something of a scorched-earth attack on these two words, calling them "redundant," declaring the handwriting comes from a "much different time," even suggesting they are a fraudulent interpolation "by whomever." I have examined the manuscript and can see no basis for the last two claims.

"The Queen's place" is the wife's place; "the Plantagenet," an elegant substitution for king, Lord, or Master. Confessing her wish that she could have married him, Dickinson embeds it in a long "if" clause, tacitly conceding satisfaction is out of reach. That Wadsworth was happily married by no means rules him out, since the poet takes for granted her love is not returned, and that all she can possibly get are the meager pleasures she puts in for—walking with him in the Dickinson meadow for an hour, being his secret best little girl for the rest of life.

The Master drafts quote a sentence from one of his letters, " 'Tell you [that is, him] of the want.' " (It was standard practice to adjust pronouns for correct reference.) The sentence recalls Wadsworth's solicitous concern in his one surviving note to her: "I am very, very anxious to learn more definitely of your trial. . . . I beg you to write me, though it be but a word."

Following Wadsworth's death in 1882, the letters Dickinson sent his friend James Dickson Clark twice brought up an early visit the minister had paid her. In one of these passages, she remembered noticing the mourning on his hat: " 'Some one has died' I said. 'Yes' – he said, 'his Mother.' 'Did you love her,' I asked. He replied with his deep 'Yes.' " Mary Ann Wadsworth Hannahs died September 29 or October 1, 1859, age sixty-four. Very likely her son would still be wearing black the following summer, though possibly not in 1861.

In the other recollection, Dickinson said Wadsworth had spoken of "calling upon you, or perhaps remaining a brief time at your Home in Northampton." James Clark belonged to an extremely close Connecticut Valley family that had shifted to Brooklyn without cutting local roots. Never marrying, James and his one sibling, Charles H. (in some ways they resembled the Dickinson sisters), resided for years at a stretch with their father, an early, prominent, and successful member of the New York Stock Exchange. One or both brothers liked to summer at the old family place in Northampton, where, by a happy chance, the 1860 town directory has a listing for Charles H. on Elm Street, site of the five-acre Clark homestead. Sold to Smith College in 1889, Clark House still stands, though much remodeled. If Wadsworth put up here, as Dickinson understood, it would have been an easy hour's ride to his remarkable and as yet unseen Amherst correspondent.

Like Wadsworth, with his background in western Connecticut and upstate New York, his honorary doctorate from New York University, and his transcontinental jump in 1862, the Clarks operated in far-reaching and cosmopolitan networks. The father, also called Charles, had started out in business in Philadelphia and Charleston before arriving on Wall Street. At the same time (again like the minister and indeed the poet), the Clarks were members in good standing of a very private Protestant patriciate, living in comfort, performing their duties no matter what, and accustomed to the discreet exercise of weighty responsibilities. Charles Clark was an elder in Brooklyn's Second Presbyterian Church (Old School—Wadsworth's affiliation) and actively supported its programs, "looking after the wanderers" and "visiting the sick and indigent." He was also remembered for showing up at his office on Wall Street in the blizzard of 1888, at age eighty-three. When the family's last survivor, Charles H., a bookkeeper, died in a New York hotel in 1915, also in his eighties, he bequeathed everything to the longtime family housekeeper, Jessie Ferguson, with the request that she be buried in the Clarks' plot in Northampton. Since she was dead by that time, the entire estate went to an orphanage, a home for needy women, and similar charities. *The New York Times* ran a story on this unusual will that failed to note the deceased's link to Dickinson, then at the low point of her posthumous reputation.

One of the poet's memorable encounters occurred when James, the other brother, showed up at the Dickinson mansion: "I could scarcely have believed, the Morning you called with Mr Brownell," she wrote some two decades later, "that I should eventually speak with you, and you only, with the exception of my Sister, of my dearest earthly friend." Whatever the purpose of Clark and Brownell's call, it must have taken place between 1858 and 1863, when the two men conducted a private school in Brooklyn. Even though this seems to have been the poet's only face-to-face meeting with the teacher, it was to have a crucial sequel: after Wadsworth's death, a posthumous collection of his sermons was sent to her by James, an act resulting in extended correspondence with both brothers. James evidently knew—from the minister?—how vital this Dickinson connection was. Like Charles H., both knew how to guard the confidentiality of clients, parishioners, and trusting female friends.[10]

As Albert J. Gelpi concluded many years ago, "Wadsworth would seem the unquestionable choice for Master." That seems truer than ever, yet the evidence remains so circumstantial and conjectural it is wisest to hold back. In principle, there could have been another man, someone for whom we have no surviving documentary evidence, leaving Wadsworth to play the role of pastoral adviser. Still, there are enough clues pointing to the minister that he is the one we will consider as occasion offers.

I Am So Far from Land

There was a man, probably a minister; he was married and in other ways out of reach and unsuitable; his feelings for her had little in common with hers for him; she knew little about him and began to project her powerful desires and fantasies on him; their correspondence became increasingly troubling for her; they met, perhaps in 1860, perhaps only once, parting in a way that may have looked quite ordinary to a bystander; and in the poems she wrote afterward she returned again and again to this impossible relationship, developing its latent elements in fantastic ways.

Whether or not Wadsworth was the man, this romantic crisis was the necessary and climactic phase of Dickinson's long-delayed maturity and of the huge demands she made on intimates. This was the event that forced her to think about the satisfactions she could reasonably expect in

---

10. If the newly discovered photograph of "Emily Dickinson" (reproduced on page 2 of the photo section) is authenticated, as I predict it will be, its history may look something like this: sent by Dickinson to Wadsworth shortly before he left for California in 1862; entrusted before or after his death in 1882 to his friends the Clarks; discreetly kept for the next third of a century by Charles H., who couldn't reveal its existence for fear of the inevitable gossip about the minister and the poet; and finally falling between the cracks when this faithful friend died with "no near relatives" to care for his personal effects.

life and the compensatory goals she might plausibly achieve. By 1863, when she wrote in passing of "the Heart I former wore" (Fr757), she had come to regard the crisis as her life's transforming event.

What made her trouble all the more painful and defining was that Samuel Bowles and Susan Dickinson were caught up in their own crises in 1861 and couldn't afford the attention and understanding the poet demanded. Triply abandoned, she had no choice but to work matters out on her own terms, in writing.

Soon after November 7, 1860, when Mary Bowles was delivered of her third unviable child in a row, she received a strange and moving letter of sympathy:

> Don't cry, dear Mary. Let us do that for you, because you are too tired now. We don't know how dark it is, but if you are at sea, perhaps when we say that we are there, you won't be as afraid.
>
> The waves are very big, but every one that covers you, covers us, too.

Emily had gone through nothing resembling Mary's ordeal, yet the letter spoke with authority, in part because its author was drawing on a new sense of the solidarity of female pain. "Are the children women, and the women thinking it will soon be afternoon?" she had asked Elizabeth Holland in 1859; "We will help each other bear our unique burdens." Now, helping Mary, she wrote as one who had reason to feel she was in the same deep water as other women.

The lost-at-sea image had by this time acquired a special resonance. In fall 1859, the poet informed Kate Scott, probably ironically, that she was "pleasantly located in the deep sea." When Susan D. Phelps, for a time the fiancée of Henry Vaughan Emmons, was in difficulty, Emily sent her a note based on Isaiah 43:2: "When thou goest through the Waters, I will go with thee." Now, going with Mary, she offered not a life rope but a vivid image of being swamped by waves in darkness, a shared desperation. Was she remembering that Mary's Aunt Laura Dwight Childe had gone down in 1854 with the *Arctic,* one of the great transatlantic packets? So dramatic and unforgettable was this shipwreck that it showed up in Henry James's 1913 memoir, *A Small Boy and Others*. The *Republican* ran a graphic series about the launching of spars, the final mad rush for boats, and similar horrors. The casualty figures were brutal: as the captain and sixty-two crew members saved themselves, over two hundred passengers were abandoned and drowned, including every woman and child on board. The Amherst paper drew attention to the death of Mrs. Childe and her daughter. It brought the tragedy even closer to home that Emily's Aunt Catharine had made a transatlantic crossing on the ship one year earlier. When Emily wrote Mary that every wave "that covers you, covers us, too," the words were thick with recent history.

As Dickinson drifted out to sea in the winter of 1860–1861, she suffered her usual seasonal (consumptive?) symptoms—a "cough as big as a thimble," "a Tomahawk in my side." Samuel appears to have sent a get-well message early in the year, judging by her somber and enigmatic way of taking issue with his genial optimism:

> You spoke of the "East." I have thought about it this winter.
> Dont you think you and I should be shrewder, to take the *Mountain Road*?
> That *Bareheaded life* – under the grass – worries one like a Wasp.

Despite the obscurities, it is evident she was troubled by the thought of death. Samuel was always talking up a warm and fuzzy and very Victorian faith that everything would be better, even his own deteriorating back, stomach, head. His letters to Austin and Sue were full of exhorting and reaffirming mantras: "We are full of Faith & Hope," "wait in Patience & Faith," "Faith I find grows larger & richer with me as I myself grow more powerless." The well-known poem that opens Emily's wasp-note was surely a riposte to this tireless uplift:

> *"Faith" is a fine invention*
> *When Gentlemen can* see –
> *But* Microscopes *are prudent*
> *In an Emergency.*
>
> Fr202A

What Dickinson wanted from Bowles was the kind of sympathy that took her and her extremity seriously. In early 1861, in her strongest plea yet, she sent him a dramatic narrative poem that combined the lost-at-sea image with a life-and-death struggle between two survivors of a shipwreck. It is a repetition of the *Arctic,* with the man (it seems) abandoning the woman:

> *Two swimmers wrestled on the spar*
> *Until the morning sun –*
> *When One turned, smiling, to the land –*
> *Oh God! the other One!*
> *The stray ships – passing, spied a face*
> *Opon the waters borne,*
> *With eyes, in death, still begging – raised,*   ✶
> *And hands – beseeching – thrown!*

Fr227A

Dickinson's statement introducing this powerful poem—"I cant explain it, Mr Bowles"—suggests it concerned a matter she dared not otherwise elucidate. It has been applied to her life in many ways, but the obvious connection is with her worsening relations with Master, who, the poem hints, has abandoned her at sea. Since it was out of the question to expose the details to Samuel, she sent an image of pleading desolation, hoping, perhaps, to stimulate the sympathy *she* had offered Mary.

The closest she came to telling him her secret was in the ecstatic poem also (apparently) dating from spring 1861:

> *Title divine – is mine!*
> *The Wife – without the Sign!*
> *Acute Degree – conferred on me –*
> *Empress of Calvary! . . .*

Fr194A

The poem intimates that though she is not truly wedded and has thus not known the highly mystified "swoon / God sends us Women," she *has* accomplished her unique and painful destiny and can now perform an ironic imitation of true wives, who have the right to say " 'My husband.' " At the end she went out of her way to emphasize the confidentiality of her disclosures: "*Heres* – what I had to 'tell you' – You will tell no other? Honor – is its own pawn."

If Dickinson wanted Bowles to somehow appreciate her "unique burden"—her painful sense of being lastingly, transformingly, bound to a man not her husband—her message fell far short of explicitness. He may have taken her obscure confession in the way that most people would, drawing the wrong inference about her "purity." Certainly, her tone in correcting him could not have been more lofty:

> If you doubted my Snow – for a moment – you never will – again
> – I know –
> Because I could not say it – I fixed it in the Verse – for you to
> read – when your thought wavers, for such a foot as mine –[11]

The poem she attached, opposing fixedness to wavering, compared the faith of martyrs, their "everlasting troth," to the magnetic needle that always points north (Fr187B; J792).

Responsive as Bowles was, he was not the ideal receiver for Dickinson's impassioned but cloudy self-disclosures. In fall 1861, meeting William and Henry James's newly married cousin, Catharine James Prince, he left a vivid record of his impression of the unstable woman: "The wife is fascinating, or can be, most assuredly. She quite impressed me

---

11. Lurking in the shadows of this exchange is an unsigned essay published on the *Republican*'s editorial page on June 1. Titled "Over the Border," it concerned the attraction felt by some "conscientious people" to the "border land between virtue and vice." There is the good woman, for instance, who "explores *with curious foot* [italics added] every inch of that debateable ground from which her more prudent sisters timidly retreat . . . prepar[ing] her household eggs and coffee in the hot ashes of the smouldering crater." Bowles admired the essay and informed Austin it was by Fidelia H. Cooke, his new literary editor: "she touches inner life very deeply & shrewdly." We know from the manuscript of "A feather from the whippowil" that Cooke was authorized to open the poet's letters during Bowles's absences, of which there were several in early 1861. One wonders why he called the essay to Austin's attention, and whether it was prompted in part by Dickinson's confidences, and (most important) what she herself made of it.

with evidences of genius; but there is a wild unsettled look about her that would frighten most men." He had heard that Rebecca Harding Davis's novel *Margret Howth* was "powerful, weird, but 'unhealthy.'" Samuel wanted women to be steady, reliable, and up-to-date, and not to rear up with nerves and vagaries.[12] Absorbed in his paper, the political scene, and the suddenly explosive Civil War, which he described in April as this "new world of action & thoughts, that the rest of us are talking about daily," the man simply couldn't afford the time and patience Emily required.

About the time she realized that Samuel could not be the strong and sympathetic male friend she needed, he was laid low by a physical collapse that completely altered their basis with each other. Terribly afraid for him, she wondered if another of her cherished friends was going to be "snatched." Yet she also drew strength from his trouble, and just when she needed it.

His crisis began in February 1861 as he drove by sleigh from Amherst to Springfield during a heavy snow. He had to get out from time to time, and the result was "a violent attack of sciatica" and a series of forced absences from his paper's editorial office, regardless of wartime pressures. In early June, as a Northampton paper reported, he spent several days recuperating "in town and vicinity"—mainly Greenfield, it seems. Later that month he toured the Berkshire Hills and in July the White Mountains. In September, back from a health trip to Saratoga, his back "doubled up on me with a vengeance" and he "fairly cried with pain & disappointment," though still managing a joke about "boils & bowels & sciatica." Finally, on October 16, with his wife nearing the fearsome end of yet another pregnancy, he had no choice but to try Dr. Denniston's Northampton water cure for a month or two. Once there, even though his "bent back & crippled leg tether[ed him] as closely as a young calf," Samuel gallantly managed a ride to the Evergreens, apologizing afterward for having been so "*stooped.*"

---

12. After an accident with a runaway horse, Samuel wrote Austin that "the feminine element predominated in that animal." Aware that he and Mary could supply "all the nerves & fidgets necessary" behind the dashboard, he demanded "calmness & good sense in front."

Emily's many letters touching on this affliction are hard to date, inconsistent, and charged with intense feeling. In one she tells Samuel she prays "to 'Alla' " for his health; in another, she both reminds him she hasn't learned to pray and assures him she often carries her friends' pains to the Virgin Mary. Fearing the worst for him, she nevertheless kept her distance during one of his visits because "something troubled me – and I knew you needed light – and air." Both explanations ring true, even the second, however fantastical: she knew how exhausting she could be. When Thomas Wentworth Higginson called on her in 1870, he was struck that she "often thought me *tired.*"

One of many reasons Samuel can't be Master is that Emily's messages repeatedly press others' claims on him. With Master she pleaded her own case, but with Bowles she positioned herself within an anxious and admiring group, showing little possessiveness. Once, telling him how she, Sue, and Vinnie had talked about him, she mimicked a recording secretary's report: "We voted to remember you." When she again refused to see him in late 1862, her stated reason was: "I gave my part that [Vinnie and Austin] might have the more." This, too, rings true, showing that she (rightly) assumed she did not come first with this choice family friend.

All the same, Dickinson wanted Bowles to see her as his special and devoted well-wisher, and to realize that her sympathy was boundless and entirely at his disposal. Associating him with Mr. Swiveller in *The Old Curiosity Shop,* she cast herself as the tiny scullery maid who works and eats in a miserable basement kitchen. After Swiveller teaches this servant to play cribbage, renames her the Marchioness, and in other ways shows an interest, she runs away from her tyrannical mistress to nurse him through a three-week illness. "It grieves me till I cannot speak, that you are suffering," Emily told Samuel in a letter offering dainty remedies and signed " 'Marchioness.' " It "grieve[d]" her a second time when he left the nearby water cure for New York's Brevoort Hotel, where he could scarcely walk the two blocks to Broadway. She was grieved most of all by his 1861 Christmas gifts, which included a photo of himself that made him look, in Sue's words, "paler, and thinner, than when you were here." Emily's thank-you note was choked with emotion: "You are thoughtful so many times, you grieve me *always* – *now*. The old words are *numb* – and there *a'nt* any *new* ones." She said she would explain her reaction to the picture on his next visit to Amherst, though she wasn't sure she could:

> *But the Heart with the heaviest freight on –*
> *Does'nt – always – move –*
>
> Fr193A (J688)

A letter written about the same time to the Reverend Edward S. Dwight, whose wife had recently died, helps clarify these intensities of grief and sympathy: "I do not ask if you are 'better' – because split lives – never 'get well' – but the love of friends – sometimes helps the Staggering – when the Heart has on its great freight." This somber insight into personal loss was contemporaneous with "There came a day at summer's full," about a final parting of her own. She was writing from personal and painful experience, staggering like Bowles and Dwight under a heavy weight she couldn't risk explaining, no matter how close she felt to these male friends.

What she was reaching for was a way to make her "unique burden" serve great and generous ends. One reason Bowles's photo grieved her was that it seemed to reveal how he had been consuming himself for his friends. Like the spectacle of wartime sorrow, the photo further stimulated her drive to make herself larger than she was—"more stupendous," more primal. The more the editor suffered, the more determined she was to live up to what she perceived as *his* level.

There is a recurring image in her letters to Bowles—the brimming cup, the lashes holding their tear—that suggests her incommunicable emotional surplus. Her feelings were so far in excess of any conceivable relationship or social context that they could not possibly be discharged; but they had to be. One of the ways she resolved this torment was to make her private agony the point of departure for a generalized treatment of human desire as such. Another was to simply *seize* the power she didn't have, as when, in her most muscular treatment of the lost-at-sea material, she assured her suffering friend:

> *Should you but fail at – Sea –*
> *In sight of me –*[13]
> *Or doomed lie –*
> *Next Sun – to die –*
> *Or rap – at Paradise – unheard –*
> *I'd harass God –*
> *Until He let you in!*
>
>   Fr275

Some may wish to dismiss this poem, surely not one of Dickinson's best, as pointlessly hypothetical and vaunting. It would be wiser to take it as exercise, *practice,* by which the tiny "Marchioness" lifted herself into power, boldness, creativity. If she could save Mr. Bowles, she would appropriate not only his range and command but God's as well. Dickinson belonged to that select group who find their way to supreme mastery by being as generous as they are daring and egotistical.

A Birth

As Bowles brought all this to the surface, Sue brought something else by a very different route.

By now the Evergreens' interior life had become a world in itself. Unlike the Homestead, where space was defined by stately dimensions and heavy Empire furniture, Sue and Austin's smaller rooms aimed at an up-to-date jewel-box effect—an exhibition of privacy and comfort organized around high-definition kitsch, including a statuette of Cupid

---

13. The previous summer, the *Republican* ran a tribute to Barrett Browning that told how she had watched a boat carrying her loved brother go "down in a tranquil sea." Bowles pronounced the unsigned piece, which Cooke had written, "very good."

and Psyche in rapturous embrace. Like Samuel, Austin had become an habitué of New York's leading galleries, yearning for pieces he couldn't afford yet feeling (in Sue's words) "he *must* have them." This itch became so well known that Mary Clemmer Ames slyly glanced at it in one of her New York letters to the *Republican:* "There are at least two pairs of eyes in Amherst . . . which would gaze delighted on Ginoux's latest and greatest picture, 'Indian Summer.' " Régis Gignoux, a landscapist specializing in snow scenes, was a great favorite at the Evergreens.

So far, neither spouse showed signs of disenchantment with the other. When Austin gave Sue an ivory hairpin in the shape of a lamb, she had never been "so pleased with a gift." Surviving letters express the usual attention and affection, as when he offers to fetch whatever "you want" from Boston or calls her "My dear old girl." Samuel's one mention of discord in a letter to Sue—"You quarrel with Austin in color & in rhythm"—dates from much later, 1875.

As the end of Sue's pregnancy drew near in June 1861, the thirty-year-old wife and her husband came under heavy stress, to judge from Samuel's many concerned letters. On June 8, a Saturday, going to Greenfield for the weekend, he saw Austin in Northampton, was told of some alarming development with Sue, and took away an impression of dire trouble. Three days later he wrote that "the memory of your face Saturday is ever present with me." When he belatedly shared Austin's ominous news, whatever it was, with Mary, she became so "nervous & anxious" she might have gone forthwith to the Evergreens if a reassuring note hadn't arrived. Meanwhile, Emily heard from Austin "Saturday morning – that [Samuel was] not so well" and did her best to encourage her friend: "Wont you decide soon – to be the strong man we first knew?"

Incapacitated as he was by his pinched sciatic nerve, Samuel sent a steady stream of letters expressing his anxiety about Sue and guying Austin for trying to learn (in a bad pun) "infantry tactics." On Monday, June 17, setting off on another desperate restorative trip, the editor made a brief unplanned stop at the Evergreens. Sue was only two days away from giving birth, yet the visitor's bread-and-butter note suggests she was able to manage some of the duties of hospitality. When news of her successful delivery on June 19 reached him in North Adams, he sent a long letter expressing his relief and assuring the couple that all their worry and agony would be repaid "ten-fold."

One of the most troubling aspects of this childbirth was its implication of an obscure female doom among the Gilbert sisters. It was on another June 19 eleven years earlier that Mary Gilbert Learned had given birth to her first child, only to die a few weeks later of puerperal fever. A second bad omen was that on June 14, 1861, five days before Sue's labor, sister Martha lost *her* first and (as yet) only child. Even before these uncanny and frightening coincidences, Sue's sense of Gilbert family unity had been acute. That summer, poor bereft Martha came for a visit but found it "almost broke [her] heart" to see the new mother and her baby in bed. When Samuel drove to Amherst from Denniston's water cure, Sue was so full of "tearful remi[ni]scences & forebodings" about her stricken sister that Martha promptly showed up in the sympathetic editor's "morning dreams." Reports of Sue's crying are extremely rare. She seems to have feared for her sister's life, and perhaps her own. To be a Gilbert and a mother was to risk terrifying troubles.

Provisionally called Jacky, the baby wasn't given a proper name (Edward, soon shortened to Ned) until he was half a year old. He proved inordinately difficult, not only crying night and day but raising doubts as to his normality and survival. Austin's "infantry tactics" did not begin to meet the challenge, and by October the stressed father was looking "thin & pale." For Samuel, the explanation was obvious: "the summer campaign with your new life has evidently borne hard on you both." This was the battle summer of 1861, when the North was not prevailing and everyone in the poet's circle seemed to be losing ground.

Four months after the birth, a nurse playfully hoped Austin had "left the *corner far* behind," presumably the corner from illness to recovery. It was a household phrase: "Now we will turn the corner," the poet wrote in 1871. But the new father's complaint was as persistent as it was debilitating and depressing, and the following spring Samuel could only hope he was "not so pathetic & sad as when I last saw, & . . ." The rest of the letter is torn away, perhaps because of what came next.

The baby's first nurse was a former slave whom the Bowleses and

Dickinsons knew as Aunt Abbe, Abba, Abby, or Abbie. Born in 1800, she had been a personal maid in Savannah and at Dungeness, the large Sea Island estate of General Nathanael Greene. During her extensive travels with her mistress, Louisa Greene Shaw, Aboo (as she was then known) had resided for several years in France, where she learned the language and "frequently" saw Lafayette, a friend of Louisa's father; she picked up other languages as well. When her mistress drafted her will in 1829, she tried to assure her slave's future by requiring a nephew to provide a "mat house" and quarterly stipend. It didn't work, and by 1850 the cosmopolitan but illiterate Aboo was living in an industrial section of Springfield known as Indian Orchard and supporting herself as an itinerant lady's nurse. The Bowleses lined her up for Sue by persuading her to leave another's employ.

At first, Sue was charmed with the spectacle of her "gay-turbaned nurse, sauntering over the grounds with baby . . . his long white robe flowing effectively over her [scanter?] draperies." But as the exotic appeal faded, the employer decided that Aunt Abbie's "evolution" wasn't up to the job of tending a crying baby night and day. Caught "sound asleep with the priceless baby in her lap," the aging nurse was, in Sue's euphemistic phrase, "gently . . . transferred . . . to her home in S____."

Abbie's successor—her name appears to be Cerinthia Inghram in Sue's difficult script—was a tough, egalitarian Yankee from the vicinity of Amherst. Nothing bothered Inghram, who could rock a baby for hours with one foot while reading the *New-York Observer*, a national conservative religious weekly. Hardy enough to ignore the constant crying, she also refused to act the part of a servant, demanding "cowcumbers and pie for breakfast," questioning her employer about the cost of furniture, and urging home remedies like goldthread (*Coptis groenlandica*). When she quit, she declared "in fierce tones there was something radically wrong with the baby—his head was too large—his crying unnatural she never had seen nothing like him." Informed of Inghram's misdemeanors, Samuel wrote in late September that "these long weeks of that nurse must have prepared [Sue] for Heaven, if anything will." Soon after, on his first visit from the water cure, he was relieved to see her looking "so well after 'suffering so many things from so many' nurses."

The third nurse, Maggie (Conroy?) of Hartford, apparently arriving in October, was an immediate success. When she left the following spring, a new arrangement was worked out about which we know nothing beyond Samuel's approving comment: "You are going through a revolution, indeed—losing Maggie, & putting Jacky away in one way to draw him nearer in others. I foreshadowed as much, when I saw you last. It is well, necessary for you." It sounds as if the baby was being weaned.

As this complicated domestic ordeal worked itself out at the Evergreens, Emily Dickinson was sinking deeper into her own troubles and intensities and learning how to write her way out of them. She was probably acquainted with the first and third nurses, judging from the polite letters they sent after leaving the Evergreens. Shaw's dictated letter asked to be remembered "with all respect to Mrs. Dickinson & the ladies—I dont forget their kind remembrances to me, all of them," and Maggie sent "compliments to . . . Miss Aunt Vinie Miss Aunt emily" and others. Apart from these courteous expressions, we have nothing to connect the poet to the domestic drama next door.

Nothing, that is, beyond the strange poem of June 19 or soon thereafter expressing great wariness about the newborn baby:

> Is it true, dear Sue?
> Are there two?
> I should'nt like to come
> For fear of joggling Him!
> If you could shut him up
> In a Coffee Cup,
> Or tie him to a pin
> Till I got in –
> Or make him fast
> To "Toby's" fist –
> Hist! Whist! I'd come!

Fr189

The poem is bizarre in so many ways, whether thinking of the mother as dividing into two, or imagining the baby as a minuscule and fearful

squirmer, or proposing such cruel uses for coffee cup, pin, and Toby the
cat's paw. It isn't clear what, if anything, these features tell us about the
writer's notions of childbirth and babies. Perhaps very little: one could
easily go too far in interpreting this little impromptu, which never got
into the manuscript books. But one thing seems obvious: the poem is an
excuse for not going next door. Although two lines end with "come," the
message is one of distance and disconnection. In an age when it was assumed that maiden sisters and sisters-in-law helped out, the first thing
Emily said was that she would not get involved.

The split that opened in summer 1861 between Emily and Sue resembles what often happens to first-time parents and their childless
adult friends. In this case, however, the wedge was driven with great
force from each side. With all her troubles, the inexperienced mother
was as little inclined to humor Emily as Emily was to help with Jacky.
The poet loved and identified with children, but babies were another
story. As she said years later, "I know but little of Little Ones, but love
them very softly." Very softly indeed: her congratulatory note following
Mary Bowles's safe delivery at the Brevoort begins: "Can you leave *your*
flower long enough – just to look at *mine*? Which is the prettiest?" If this
suggests she saw her friends' babies as rivals, the next letter offers amusing confirmation: "Could you leave 'Charlie' – long enough? Have you
time for *me*? . . . Dont love him so well – you know – as to forget us – We
shall wish he was'nt *there* – if you do." Remembering Mary's three preceding stillbirths, we can sense why the woman, apparently quite judgmental, wouldn't answer this needy and extremely cheeky voice.

Dickinson's poems from the early sixties often express a keen sense
of exclusion. One from late 1861 begins:

> *Why – do they shut me out of Heaven?*
> *Did I sing – too loud?*

As in the Master draft that offers to be his "best little girl," the poem's
small, insistent voice promises to be perfectly quiet, if only they will
open to "the little Hand":

> *Would'nt the Angels try me –*
> *Just – once – more –*
> *Just – see – if I troubled them –*
> *But dont – shut the door!*

Fr268

Another poem along these lines was sent to Sue in 1861[14]:

> *Could I – then – shut the door –*
> *Lest my beseeching face – at last –*
> *Rejected – be – of Her?*

Fr188

A serious breach in friendship, it lasted into the fall. Emily couldn't appreciate the pressure Sue was under, and Sue had no time for Emily or anyone else: the narrative she wrote decades later about her search for a nurse dwells on her own fatigue and worry and ignores husband, in-laws, friends. For the poet, it was a repeat of how she had been treated by Master. With the baby crying, and Austin in a funk, and Sue contending with him and Jacky and Cerinthia Inghram, and Samuel making one trip after another to escape his terrible sciatica, Dickinson came to understand her position in the world as never before.

The following April, in her second letter to Higginson, the poet said she "had a terror – since September – I could tell to none – and so I sing, as the Boy does by the Burying Ground – because I am afraid." The enigmatic statement has been explained chiefly in two ways: that she had early symptoms of her eye trouble of 1864 and 1865 and feared she was going blind, and that she felt deserted when she learned that Wadsworth would accept the pastorate at San Francisco's Calvary Presbyterian Church. Under scrutiny, neither explanation holds up. There is no real evidence of eye trouble in 1861, and no reason to think this would be a problem she could "tell to none." As for the minister, it is true that Cal-

---

14. Two closely related poems—" 'Tis true – They shut me in the cold" (Fr658), "They won't frown always – some sweet day" (Fr923)—have been assigned to 1863 and 1865.

vary's previous pastor resigned on September 23, after his refusal to back the Union precipitated a riot, yet it was not till December 9 that the congregation voted to call Wadsworth, and even then his acceptance was delayed for months. News of his imminent move to California may have deepened but cannot have precipitated her crisis. There was no discrete event: Dickinson felt deserted by *everyone* who was dearest and could understand her, and on whom she most depended.

The terror since September, a profound and systemic and ongoing state lasting through the winter, was the thing Dickinson had been booked to fall into. It may have begun with a moment when "the meaning goes out of things," as she put it in one of her jottings, but its essence was a recognition of something permanent: the disconnection between her heart's absolutism and the realities of life. Painful and transforming, it brought a final sense of isolation, abandonment, rejection. Her troubles with Master had helped her understand her "unique burden" as a woman, and now there was Sue's apparent uninterest. To be forgotten by her selected ones—" 'They have not chosen me,' he said, / 'But I have chosen them' " (Fr87A)—had always been the great and primary fear.

The one extant note from Sue to Emily relating mainly to personal matters seems to have been written at the end of summer 1861, in September or October:

> I have intended to write you Emily to-day but the quiet has not been mine—I send you this, lest I should seem to have turned away from a kiss—
> If you have suffered this past Summer—I am sorry—[for] *I*
> Emily bear a sorrow that I never uncover—If a nightingale sings with her breast against a thorn, why not *we*?[15] When I can, I shall write—
>   Sue

15. The letter is scissored through twice, making three horizontal pieces. The idea was to delete the middle piece, everything from "for *I* Emily bear a sorrow" to "why not *we*?" leaving the impression that the top and bottom fragments comprised the entire letter. The placement of "for," however, frustrated this scheme. When the tamperer—Austin?—realized the top and bottom pieces could not be made to fit, he gave up his foolish effort.

An apology for ignoring Emily, the note confirms that her summer had been a painful one, and that Sue had been too distracted to answer her notes and poems. Perhaps the reason she did not disclose her special sorrow to her unmarried sister-in-law was that it involved marriage, sexuality, and motherhood. Going into labor on the birthday of a dead sister's child, five days after the death of another sister's child, Sue had cause to see herself as entering the common doom of maternal anguish. Her tearful conversation with Bowles that fall—their first since June 17—shows how distraught she was.

Although Sue did not spell out her trouble or invite Emily to be more confidential about her own suffering, she still defined a common ground: shared female lyricism growing out of private female pain. Her emphatic solidarity—"why not *we*?"—undoubtedly meant a great deal to the poet and may explain why this one note was preserved: it affirmed a connection at a time of loneliness and despair. The following April, when the poet said she sang because of the terror she "could tell to none," she was virtually echoing her sister-in-law's "sorrow that I never uncover."

We hear other echoes in a slightly later poem written for Sue:

> For largest Woman's Heart I knew –
> 'Tis little I can do –
> And yet the largest Woman's Heart
> Could hold an Arrow – too –
> And so, instructed by my own,
> I tenderer, turn me to.

> Fr542A

This looks like a chastened affirmation of the ground shared by these two very different women. Just *because* each heart held its own arrow, there was a place for tender gestures, however "little." It was a restatement of what Sue had said.

A major consequence of this "turn" toward each other was the well-known exchange over "Safe in their alabaster chambers." First composed about 1859, this poem presents the buried dead as sleeping in hermetic isolation till the moment of resurrection:

Safe in their Alabaster Chambers –
Untouched by morning
And untouched by noon –
Sleep the meek members of the Resurrection –
Rafter of satin,
And Roof of stone.

Light laughs the breeze
In her Castle above them –
Babbles the Bee in a stolid Ear,
Pipe the sweet Birds in ignorant cadence –
Ah, what sagacity perished here!

                                      Fr124B

The range of interpretation this has spurred matches the differing ideas about the sleep of the dead in Dickinson's time. The 1844 funeral sermon for Deborah Fiske gives the orthodox view: "We would not disturb her repose, for we believe she sleeps in Jesus, and that in the morning of the resurrection, he will awake her." Preferring an active immortality, in early 1859 Higginson scoffed at a popular hymn about "the pious dead" and "soft their sleeping bed." Dickinson herself, uniting the passive and the active, imagined the dead Adams boy riding the wind "back to the village burying-ground where he never dreamed of sleeping: Ah! the dreamless sleep!" That was on December 31, 1861.

When Sue expressed her dissatisfaction with stanza 2, which contrasts the activity of high summer to the immaculately sealed dead, Emily drafted a replacement and sent it next door: "Perhaps this verse would please you better."

Grand go the Years – in the Crescent – above them –
Worlds scoop their Arcs –
And Firmaments – row –
Diadems – drop – and Doges – surrender –
Soundless as dots – on a Disc of snow –

                                      Fr124C

Dropping her too frequent bees and birds, the poet introduced a sublime perspective that utterly changed the scale. In the first version the dead are sealed away from nature's pleasing bustle and music, but in the second they lie still while time itself cycles above them, grand and irrelevant. What does the spinning zodiac or the fall of kingdoms and republics—the passing universe, in other words—mean to those waiting for the resurrection? The last line, with its sudden plunge into *their* perspective, gives the answer: it is all as hushed and insubstantial as dots dropping "on a Disc of snow."

But the splendid new stanza was not to Sue's taste:

> I am not suited dear Emily with the second verse—It is remarkable as the chain lightening that blinds us hot nights in the Southern sky but it does not go with the ghostly shimmer of the first verse as well as the other one. . . . You never made a peer for that verse, and I *guess* you[r] kingdom does'nt hold one—I always go to the fire and get warm after thinking of it, but I never *can* again.

She added, as if in explanation or apology, "Susan is tired making *bibs* for her bird—her ring-dove. . . ."

Johnson's placement of this exchange in summer 1861 seems most unlikely, while Franklin's date, "about 1861," is needlessly vague. Everything points to winter: "Disc of snow" replacing a summer scene, Sue's warming herself at a fire, the baby's fat "ring-dove" neck crease now that he had put on some weight,[16] and the bib making that preceded weaning. Winter's rule is even more emphatic in the third and fourth versions of the second stanza that Emily went on to draft. Even the chain lightning, normally suggestive of summer, points in this instance to December 1861 or January 1862: writing to Samuel on Christmas night, Sue was so full of "Summer visions" she had "but to open the door to see the hot lightning in the southwest." Her note to Emily must have been roughly contemporaneous with this letter.

---

16. In 1864 Emily asked Sue to "kiss little Ned in the seam in the neck, entirely for Me."

The reason for getting the chronology straight is that it helps explain the existence, meaning, and tone of this unique critical exchange, in which a friendly and conciliatory tone accompanies underlying differences. It was because of the recent breach that each was making a special effort—Sue to offer detailed comment, Emily to accept and consider it. But they still failed to agree. Not only did Sue not care for the replacement stanza, but she compared it to something that "blinds us" and had the temerity to predict the poet would never equal the first stanza (surely not *that* good). On the whole, her comment foregrounds the delicate connoisseurship of her own sensibility. Emily's reply—"Your praise is good – to me – because I *know* it *knows* – and *suppose* it *means*"—suggests she didn't quite see the bearing of Sue's shivery response but was willing to take it on faith. *Her* comment is one more expression of loyalty to Sue's hidden essence, as opposed to her appearance or action.

What do we make of the fact that Sue and Emily's only known discussion of a poem concerns this particular one, and that the exchange took place after a period of alienation? From one point of view, the dialogue shows an uncanny symbolic aspect, as if the two living women were themselves hermetically sealed, and that *that* was what they were really talking about. Emily had refused to help with Jacky, and Sue had dismissed the old and exhausted Aboo, apparently without a qualm. The question of what sisterhood amounted to had often come up for the poet, as when, in 1854–1855, her future sister-in-law failed to write from the "silent West": "Why Susie – think of it – you are my precious Sister, and will be till you die, and will be still, when Austin and Vinnie and Mat, and you and I are marble – and life has forgotten us!" There, in prophetic clarity, we have the marbled dead of "Safe in their alabaster chambers."

Emily remembered and used Sue's images of the lightning and the cold. In 1862 she wrote a poem in which the speaker, a passive connoisseur of painting, music, and poetry, wonders what it would be like "Had I the Art to stun myself / With Bolts – of Melody!" (Fr348). And when Higginson visited, she told him that if a book "makes my whole body so cold no fire ever can warm me I know *that* is poetry." Protected as she was, it can't be said that the poet lived safe in alabaster: she was always gathering and spinning. ✓

Her reply to Sue's critique concluded by offering a glimpse of the pride and ambition she had previously confided to Louisa and Frances Norcross: "Could I make you and Austin – proud – sometime – a great way off – 'twould give me taller feet." That "great way off" has a nice ambiguity. Was she anticipating the distant time when her fame would burst on the couple, or was she signaling her determination to keep her brother and sister-in-law at a distance from her act of creating?

The two women stubbornly adhered to their differing judgments of "Safe in their alabaster chambers." When Sue arranged for publication in the *Republican*, she sent the original babbling-bee version. And when Emily sought Thomas Wentworth Higginson's opinion of her work one month later, she submitted the Disc of snow.

The poet's preparatory years were behind her: the ordeal of being Dickinson had been transformed into a vocation wholly her own. Sinking deep into essential troubles, finding that who she was and what she suffered could be made the basis of an art, she had begun to wield her "stupendous" powers. Of course she would have to remain "a great way off" while doing her work, but there were advantages to that. Now it was time to get an opinion from an informed reader representing the literary world at large.

Chapter 18

1862–1865:
The Fighting Years

Oceans Between Her Friends and Her

In faraway San Francisco, the members of Calvary Presbyterian Church had voted on December 9 to call the Reverend Charles Wadsworth as their next pastor. Although they probably had reason to think he would accept the offer, he didn't do so until mid-March, partly, it seems, because of hostile letters he received from opposing members. Released from Philadelphia's Arch Street Church on April 3, he set sail for Panama on May 1 with his wife and two children, crossing the isthmus by train and then embarking on a second ship for San Francisco. He reached the raw young city on May 26 and the following Sunday began preaching the Gospel.

Prior to Wadsworth's departure, Dickinson may have asked Samuel
Bowles to do the same favor for her the Hollands did years later: address
and mail her letters to Philadelphia. A January letter to Bowles beginning, "Are you willing? I am so far from Land – To offer *you* the cup – it
might some Sabbath come *my* turn," may have requested him to direct a
sealed message for the minister. The implication was that she was so at
sea she had to have Wadsworth's counsel—and could someday return
the favor to Bowles. She appealed to him again in early March, not
knowing he was off to Washington and New York. Learning of her mistake, she explained to his wife that she had "sent Mr Bowles – a little
note – last Saturday morning – asking him – to do an errand for me."
Extremely anxious, she brought all her diplomacy and ingenuity to bear
on the editor's wife:

> Now – Mary – I fear he did not get it – and *you* tried to do the errand
> for me – and it troubled you – *Did* it? Will you tell me? Just say with
> your pencil – "it did'nt tire me – Emily" – and then – I shall be sure.

Knowing how stern and disapproving Mary could be, Emily simply had
to find out whether she was too "troubled" to render the dubious-
looking service her husband apparently performed (and even he had
questioned her "Snow"). Desperately uneasy, she went down on her
knees before the unresponsive woman: "You wont forget my little note –
tomorrow – in the mail – It will be the *first one* – you ever wrote me – in
your life – and yet – was I the little friend – a *long time? Was* I – Mary?"

Presently, Dickinson thought of an expedient for disguising her for-
warding requests. In late March, apparently sending yet another to
Bowles, she took the precaution of substituting her brother's name for
her own in case her letter was opened by the wrong person: "Will you be
kind to *Austin* – again? And would you be kinder than sometimes – and
put the name – on – too." Conceivably, one of these requests could have
involved the newly found photograph of "Emily Dickinson."

What Wadsworth's departure meant to Dickinson is suggested by
her second letter to Thomas Wentworth Higginson, postmarked April

28 and summing up her education. After her first tutor died, "my Lexicon – was my only companion – Then I found one more – but he was not
contented I be his scholar – so he left the Land." It is of little importance
that Wadsworth wouldn't sail for a few more days: once his departure
was definite, she was already abandoned. For a homebound New Englander, San Francisco was inconceivably remote, whether one thought
of it as on the far side of an unexplored continent or two oceans away via
the Panama route. One of her most powerful and despairing poems, "I
cannot live with you" (Fr706), speaks of her lover as one that "served
Heaven" and was now "Oceans" away. Years later, she informed Higginson that, although he hadn't known it, he had "saved my Life."

That Bowles also sailed that same April only added to her sense of
desertion. By now the man's many afflictions—sciatica, headache, indi-
gestion, sleeplessness—had forced him to delegate most of his editorial
work at the *Republican*. Hoping to relax yet stay abreast of fast-breaking
events, he made an exhausting series of trips to the centers of power,
worrying all the while that his staff would "run the machine wrong." In
Emily's eyes, Samuel was undone by working too hard and being too
alive: "Vitality costs itself." Taking a harsher view, Frederick Law Olmsted believed he had "a diseased nervous impulse to activity of the brain."
This "mental intemperance" had become so habitual that now the editor
imagined he was "trying to rest, when you are really trying to beat the
devil round the stump." One of the reasons Dickinson responded so
powerfully to the driven Bowles was that she could see her own hyper-
energetic states in him.

By the time Bowles was persuaded to take the usual remedy for
American exhaustion, a trip to Europe, he was too broken down to go to
Amherst to say good-bye. Nor was Sue quite ready to entertain him now
that nurse Maggie's departure had resulted in "upturning & disorder" at
the Evergreens. But the baby's weaning left the mother free to travel
once again, and so Samuel invited Sue and Austin to dinner, "to stay till
4 o'clock train." This was obviously the right arrangement—best for
everyone except stay-at-home Emily, who promptly got off one of her
most abject letters: " 'Mr Bowles – not coming'! *Would*'nt you, *tomorrow*
– and this be but a *bad Dream*. . . . *Please* do not take our *spring* – away –

since you blot Summer – out!" Pretending that Sue and Vinnie shared her predicament, she said, "We cannot *count* our tears . . . they drop so fast – and the Black eye – and the Blue eye – and a Brown – I know – hold their lashes full." Although in the end she plaintively allowed that "Part" of the family would "go to see you," she concluded with another display of childish need: "I must do my Good night, in *crayon* – I *meant* to – in Red." As in her Jim Crow letter, brown-eyed Emily was making the most of her helpless side.

On April 5, Sue and Austin went to Springfield to bid their suffering friend farewell. Afterward, regretting that his sorry condition had made the visit "too dreary," he thanked them for showing their affection and concern. His sentence acknowledging the messages they brought spoke of Edward's "kind & rich note, & Emily's, considerate attentions & full words." Could he have been referring to her "hold-their-lashes-full" moan?

Soon after Samuel sailed on April 9, Emily sent a letter of sympathy to Mary: "When the Best is gone – I know that other things are not of consequence – The Heart wants what it wants." Aware that Mary's eyebrows might be going up, she immediately explained: "You wonder why I write – so – Because I cannot help – I like to have you know some care – so when your life gets faint for its other life – you can lean on us – We wont break, Mary. We look very small – but the Reed can carry weight." As in the earlier consolatory note following Mary's stillbirth, Emily was hinting at her own woman troubles, her own separation pains: "Not to see what we love, is very terrible – and talking – does'nt ease it. . . . The Eyes and Hair, we chose – are all there are – to us." This was a way of talking about the man who sailed away from *her*.

For once, Mary replied, as Emily informed Samuel in the first of her two transatlantic letters to him. Vaguely hoping "those Foreign people are kind," the poet asked two easy favors of him: take note of whatever was said about Mrs. Browning, and when he visited her grave in Florence "put one hand on the Head, for me – her unmentioned Mourner." She was afraid Amherst would look "smaller" when seen from abroad, and in fact Samuel was wrestling with the contrasts: "Paris to Amherst! I wonder if the towns ever would understand each other." Oppressed by

the impossibility of communicating his initiations, he feared that between him and Mary "a wall was building up . . . of beauty & life & experience." More aware now of his own barbarisms, he confessed to Sue
that "you always thought too well of me at your house; & I have ever
been expecting the bubble would burst."

The letter from Samuel that anticipates his visit to Florence "& Mrs
Browning's grave" is silent about Amherst's "unmentioned Mourner."
And it was only after finishing another letter that he scribbled along one
edge, "When next you write, tell Emily to give me one of her little gems!
How does she do this summer!" The passage seems to glance at her pre-
vious summer's troubles, yet it also allows a public heartiness to do duty
for friendly intimacy. Apparently, this was his only message to her from
Europe.

How appreciative was he of her "gems"? A lament on the torture of
being an invalid tourist—"to see the nectar close to lips, parching of
thirst, & yet have to turn away"—seems to echo a poem he is not otherwise known to have seen:

> I bring an unaccustomed wine
> To lips long parching
> Next to mine,
> And summon them to drink. . . .

The next time the speaker looks in, the sufferer is dead:

> The lips I w'd have cooled, alas,
> Are so superfluous Cold. . . .
>
> Fr126

The serving of wine or cordials had been a frequent topic in the messages Samuel received from his loyal "Marchioness," who was always offering to restore him. The poem, however, comes closer to the truth of
his and Emily's relationship: there was little either could do to relieve the
other's "parching."

After the editor came home in November, his friendship with Sue
and Austin flourished as never before. In 1863 he sent them at least

twenty-nine letters; in 1864, twenty-three. As if trying to ventilate every corner of his life, he wrote about his attachment to Maria Whitney, his troubles with his sickly and antisocial wife, his belief in marital fidelity. With the poet, on the other hand, the threshold of intimacy seemed to be raised higher than ever. When the returned traveler showed up in Amherst after Thanksgiving, Emily wouldn't see him. Excusing her absence in a brief note, she followed up with a letter in which, while admitting that Vinnie and Austin had "upbraided" her, she claimed the loftiest of motives: "They did not know I gave my part that they might have the more." She knew how precarious his health was and that the Evergreens was his preferred second home, but there was still something evasive and uncandid in her apology, especially when she hoped to see him "often"—a clear case of protesting too much.

That was in late November or early December, 1862. In early January, annoyed by Maria Whitney's interest in the work of the philanthropist Charles Loring Brace, Bowles grumbled that "the vagaries of fine womanhood are as strange as the tides, or _____." (Did the blank stand for "menses"?) Four days later, to Austin, he dashed off what looks like a riposte to Dickinson's nonappearance:

> To the [Newman] girls & all hearty thought.—Vinnie ditto.—& to the Queen Recluse my especial sympathy—that she has "overcome the world."— Is it really true that they sing "old hundred" & China [a hymn tune] perpetually, in heaven—ask her; and are dandelions, asphodels, or *Maiden's vows* the standard flowers of the ethereal?

This irreverent treatment of Dickinson's queenly withdrawal and obsession with heaven would not have upset someone with her keen humor, but there was an unforgettable shock in that emphatic—and public—"*Maiden's vows.*" Two years earlier she had sent Bowles an ecstatic announcement of her excruciating "marriage"—"Title divine – is mine! / The Wife – without the Sign!" Insisting the matter be regarded as strictly confidential, she added, "You will tell no other? Honor – is its own pawn" (Fr194A). Now, playing with her trust, he all but dangled the great secret in front of the brother whose sympathetic understanding she no longer took for granted. That scoffing "*Maiden's vows*" carried the suggestion that her fervent and private attachment to Wadsworth was some sort of virgin fancy, a product of inexperience. Could this be the case? Had she caught a wink in transit from one man to another? *"Ask her."*

When Bowles visited Annie Fields, whose Boston apartment was at the center of New England's literary culture (her husband ran Ticknor & Fields), she felt that, talented as he was, the editor was altogether too slapdash—too given to "careless writing and careless thinking." This offhand and superficial nature, colliding with Dickinson's mandarin sensibility, had now (as he had feared) burst the bubble. Because of the misdating of key documents, it hasn't been understood that between late 1862 and 1874 she sent him no personal letters and few poems. One or two of the latter seem effusive enough, but the appearance is misleading: the relationship had been irreparably damaged, adding another betrayal to Emily's experience and initiating a twelve-year hiatus in friendship.

Of the five or six poems Bowles received in the years immediately following his unfortunate message, the earliest, from 1863, offers a reproach for withholding a small, unstated favor:

> *Just once – Oh Least Request –*
> *Could Adamant refuse*
> *So small a Grace –*
> *So scanty put –*
> *Such agonizing terms?*
>
> *Would not a God of Flint*
> *Be conscious of a Sigh*
> *As down His Heaven dropt remote –*
> *"Just Once" – Sweet Deity?*

                                            Fr478B

In 1861 Dickinson had sent Bowles a poem on God's parsimony, "Victory comes late" (Fr195A). Building on that line of thought, the present work was an oblique but impassioned protest at her friend's failure to honor her tortured confidence. If even the flinty Calvinist Jehovah could respect the agony in her "Least Request" for understanding and secrecy, why couldn't Bowles?

In the second half of 1863 she sent him a stanza fantasizing the generosity that would have lavished everything on him:

> Just to be Rich –
> To waste my Guinea
> On so Broad a Heart –
> Just to be Poor –
> For Barefoot Pleasure
> You – Sir – Shut me out –
>
> Fr635B (J523)

In the last line the man's abrupt rejection dramatically wipes out the pleasure the speaker anticipates from her eager service.

Early in 1864 Dickinson sent a poem in which nature and God are said to know her so thoroughly they impress her as the quasi-legal "Executors / Of an identity." "Yet," the speaker adds, drawing an implicit contrast with human perfidy, "neither – told – that I could learn." With nature and God—if not with Bowles—"My secret" has remained "secure" (Fr803A; J835).

The animus these poems express seems unmistakable once one grasps how Bowles had forfeited Dickinson's trust. Her openness with him was conditioned on an absolute matching opacity—that thick, protective "vail" she could not do without. "Good to hide, and hear 'em hunt!" begins a poem of 1865, which then goes on to speak of the even greater fun of revealing oneself to the "rare Ear / Not too dull" (Fr945). But where was that special undulled ear?

Another poem from 1865 (this one also sent to no one) gives a dramatic rendition of the terror of exposure:

> To my quick ear the Leaves – conferred –
> The Bushes – they were Bells –
> I could not find a Privacy
> From Nature's sentinels –

> *In Cave if I presumed to hide*
> *The Walls – begun to tell –*
> *Creation seemed a mighty Crack –*
> *To make me visible –*

> Fr912

Since these lines deal with a fundamental aspect of Dickinson's vulnerable and self-protective identity, they should not be read as a specific comment on Bowles's careless betrayal. But they help explain why his "telling" disqualified him as the one rare ear and sharpened her fear of becoming "visible."

On his side, Bowles's letters to Austin and Sue began to register an uneasy sense of Dickinson's alienation. "I have been in a savage, turbulent state for some time," he wrote in May 1863, "indulging in a sort of chronic disgust at everything & everybody—I guess a good deal as Emily feels." It was a kind of apology, a rough effort to reestablish contact with someone he hadn't been hearing from. He concluded with a jocular message: "Tell Emily I am here, in the old place. 'Can you not watch one hour??[']" Quoting Jesus' reproach to his sleeping disciples in Gethsemane, he was playing on *her* identification with the abandoned Savior. And in fact she *had* promised just before his blunder that if he somehow alienated his "other friends – 'twould please me to remain."

But Bowles no longer had the key to Dickinson's attention. As she said in a poem entered in a fascicle about autumn 1862,

> *The Soul selects her own Society –*
> *Then – shuts the Door – . . .*

> *I've known her – from an ample nation –*
> *Choose One –*
> *Then – close the Valves of her attention –*
> *Like Stone –*

> Fr409A

In June 1863, as if shrugging off her offended hauteur, Samuel praised two women from Boston as "not brilliant, nor morbid, as American women are,—but cheery & pleasant." In December, however, making one of the bruised confessions that punctuate his letters to the Evergreens, he wrote: "I see my friends falling away around me, withdrawing in disappointment, in unrealized idealism, in breaking expectation." Two months later, in a brilliant self-analysis, he described himself as "a suggestion, rather than a realization, & elusive & spasmodic & fragmentary; but no more to others than to myself. And it tires me more than they."[1]

Bowles's driving personality and many troubles—overwork, terrible health, an unhappy marriage, a scattered life—go far to explain his nagging sense of failure. Did it make it worse that Dickinson slammed shut on him—"Like Stone"—the valves of her attention? Neither of these extraordinary people could begin to figure out the other: the editor torn open by his reckless embrace of modern multiplicity; the poet taking a high dive into the absolute only to plunge deep into the terrors of herself.

Higginson

The April that removed Wadsworth and Bowles brought a new *Atlantic Monthly* with a striking lead article by Thomas Wentworth Higginson, "A Letter to a Young Contributor." Full of witty practical advice for would-be writers, Higginson's essay held up a high literary standard even while opening the gates to women and immigrants. He liked the hospitality of American English to foreign imports, the superiority of written to spoken language, the basic "mystery of words," which can

---

1. A poem sent to Sue in 1863, signed "Springfield," almost seems to concede Bowles's failure in life: "Ungained – it may be / By a Life's low Venture" (Fr724A). His biographer saw him as paying too heavy a price for his will to power: "To command success, to win full expression and achievement for all the powers within him, to conquer disease, to hold Death himself at bay . . . this was his ceaseless effort."

contain "years of crowded passion." Warning that a newspaperman's "mental alertness is bought at a severe price," he urged aspiring writers not to rush into print; they should live "nobly," for eternity. Fifteen years later, Dickinson quoted from memory one of the essay's keenest sentences: "Such being the Majesty of the Art you presume to practice, you can at least take time before dishonoring it." Did the author of this piece possess the one rare ear? "I read your Chapters in the Atlantic," Dickinson explained in her second letter to him, "and experienced honor for you."

Like Ralph Waldo Emerson and Edward Everett Hale, Higginson was an ex-minister who had quit the pulpit for freer modes of action and expression. A radical abolitionist, he had repeatedly engaged in direct and illegal resistance, as when he led a crowd of armed Bostonians that tried to save the freedom-seeking Anthony Burns from the slavecatchers and federal marshals. He also provided financial backing for John Brown's assault on the federal arms depot at Harper's Ferry. "What fascinates us," he wrote in his essay on the seventeenth-century Frenchwoman known as Mademoiselle, "is simply her daring, that inborn fire of the blood to which danger is its own exceeding great reward." Like Edward Dickinson, Higginson appropriated his Puritan ancestors' nononsense boldness in the ongoing fight for justice and truth. Unlike Edward, he valued civil rights more than law and order.

During the four years following his resignation of his Free Church pastorate in Worcester, where he still resided, Higginson had been so successful in his new career as writer and lecturer that he already seemed to be speaking for the upper reaches of the literary establishment. At ease with Boston's literary and political elites, this radical Brahmin understood what would and wouldn't go down, yet he also valued passion and freedom and the open-air life, knew how not to interrupt, and answered his mail. His fine *Atlantic Monthly* essays were attracting so much interest he began to be spoken of as a major new writer. In early 1862 Sue tried to acquire his photograph.

An admirer of Thoreau, Higginson had been turning out a series of delicate nature essays that paid close attention to New England's seasonal changes and flowering plants. "My Out-Door Study," in the September 1861 *Atlantic*, posed the kind of question—had the world's art and literature done anything "towards describing one summer day?"—that could engage Dickinson's energies. The essay's answer was even more invigorating: we are "no nearer to it than to the blue sky which is its dome; our words are shot up against it like arrows, and fall back helpless." As Sewall surmised, the poet undoubtedly saw Higginson's exquisite nature writing "as a firm bond between them." One of the first poems she sent him rose to his challenge by proposing to tell "how the Sun rose" (Fr204B; J318).

Further qualifying Higginson as "tutor" was his advocacy of women's rights. His sardonically titled "Ought Women to Learn the Alphabet?" was an indignant plea for equal education: "We deny woman her fair share of training, of encouragement, of remuneration, and then talk fine nonsense about her instincts and intuitions." If she has failed to match man's achievements, that is because the "pathway of education has been obstructed for her." Higginson's explanation for this unfair treatment—"sheer contempt for the supposed intellectual inferiority of woman"—neatly sums up Edward Dickinson's insistence as a young man that women's mental powers were unequal to men's.

On April 15, with Bowles at sea and Wadsworth preparing to embark, Edward's thirty-one-year-old daughter took the initiative of sending four poems and a note to busy Higginson: "Are you too deeply occupied, to say if my Verse is alive?" It was the central heart-pounding question, stated politely and with full permission to say no. Twice she used the word "honor," in the second instance repeating what she had said the year before to Bowles: "That you will not betray me – it is needless to ask – since Honor is its own pawn." Leaving her note unsigned, she enclosed a smaller envelope containing her name on a card—a box in a box, so to speak, with herself deep inside. Everything was in ink except for her name, written in pencil.

As one might have guessed from all this heavy veiling, the poems she sent did not include any autobiographical narratives. Along with "I'll tell you how the sun rose," there was a treatment of the frustrating pursuit of happiness, "The nearest dream recedes unrealized" (Fr304B). A third and more challenging poem based on stringing beads—"We play at

Paste – / Till qualified, for Pearl"—was about childhood's end, the stepped growth from dull earthbound play to divine action. Proposing that we learn "*Gem*-tactics / Practising *Sands*" (Fr282A), the poem bounced off the rage for calisthenics as exemplified in Higginson's recent essay, "*Gym*nastics" [italics added]. The fourth was "Safe in their alabaster chambers"—not the version Sue preferred but the visionary one in which worlds collapse "Soundless as Dots, / On a Disc of Snow" (Fr124F). Ignoring her sister-in-law in a second way, Dickinson said she needed outside criticism but had "none to ask." This would seem to be another strike against the theory of a shared poetry "workshop."

Subsequent letters usually carried Dickinson's signature, but her envelopes bear witness to another kind of concealment. How she did it isn't known, but after April 15 every 1862 letter to Higginson for which an envelope survives was posted in nearby Palmer, not Amherst. Her three 1866 envelopes bear a Hadley postmark, and her one 1867 letter was mailed from Middletown, Connecticut, Eliza Coleman Dudley's home. After her initial approach, in other words, she didn't post a single letter to Higginson from her town. Was she afraid the postmaster, Lucius M. Boltwood, would see the well-known name in her writing and make a remark? All we can say is that she seems to have been extremely anxious to shield the correspondence from public view.

Although Higginson's letters were destroyed, some of his comments, advice, and questions can be inferred from Dickinson's replies. He began by performing some sort of "surgery," as she called it, on her submissions, for which she thanked him. His second letter, on the other hand, must have bestowed some very high praise for her to write, "I have had few pleasures so deep as your opinion, and if I tried to thank you, my tears would block my tongue." When he advised (as in "A Letter to a Young Contributor") that she "delay 'to publish'," she announced that print was as foreign an element to her as the sky to a fish—"as Firmament to Fin." She undoubtedly meant this, yet we should not be misled by the apparent modesty: the next sentence audaciously proposes that "If fame belonged to me, I could not escape her." As with patrician political candidates in the early republic, honor would have to find her, not vice versa.

Convinced by Higginson's initial critique that he was prepared to take her seriously, Dickinson responded with a series of unparalleled self-disclosures. Again and again she made it clear her writing emerged from dread and ecstasy: she sang "as the Boy does by the Burying Ground – because I am afraid"; her observation of nature made her tremble, producing "a palsy . . . the Verses just relieve"; if her lines had a " 'spasmodic' " gait, that was because "I am in danger – Sir." She confessed her "terror – since September" and dared to submit the very personal and suggestive "There came a day at summer's full," which tells how a scene of separation marks the start of a probationary lifelong "troth" and final heavenly "Marriage" (Fr325D). Her fourth letter carried the weighty personal poem, "Your riches taught me poverty" (Fr418B), and the tragic "Success is counted sweetest" (Fr112D). She was exhibiting her profound paradoxes, desires, abysses—the void from which creation rose—to a man she hadn't met.

All the same, she warned him about the fictional distancing that belonged to her sense of lyric form: "When I state myself, as the Representative of the Verse – it does not mean – me – but a supposed person." This, her one remark about the status of her first-person speakers, seems to dissolve any linkage between them and herself. In fact, her poems transform her experience in many ways. Sometimes her speakers voice her private situation (aspects of it) frankly and directly. Sometimes they are the actors of her favorite fantasies, fictions, projections. Often they represent a generalized human subject. Interpreters who take the declaration as an all-purpose passport into her work tend to divorce text from person, and also to elide the question her statement must surely prompt: What if *it* is part fiction? What if she wished to shield herself from too-direct readings of "There came a day at summer's full" or "Your riches taught me poverty"? It is well to keep in mind the sequence of pleasures in "Good to hide and hear 'em hunt!"—one, hiding; two, self-disclosure (optional). Another poem beginning "I hide myself within my flower" (Fr80) surely gives us the right premise: that she herself is concealed within many of her "supposed persons." The corollary, of course, is that we mustn't presume to find her every time. This is her game, after all.

Inevitably, the letters to Higginson enacted the poet's fondness for self-dramatization. She gave heavy stress to her solitariness, naming as her only real companions the hills, the sundown, and her dog, Carlo. When her new mentor chided her for " 'shunning Men and Women'," she retorted that people "talk of Hallowed things, aloud – and embarrass my Dog." She spoke of a brother and sister but said nothing about her sister-in-law. Her mother didn't "care for Thought," and although her father bought books for her, he begged her "not to read them – because he fears they joggle the Mind." About her family as a group, her first point was that they were "religious" and she wasn't.

These claims should not be taken at face value, yet they offer powerful insights into her conception of her situation. The isolation she claimed was by no means wholly fictive: she *was* the only family member who hadn't joined the First Church, and there was much about her that the others, even Vinnie, didn't know, beginning with the manuscript books. When Austin read the 1891 *Atlantic* essay in which Higginson excerpted and commented on her letters, he reacted like an all-knowing older brother, according to his mistress: "as to the 'innocent and confiding' nature of them, Austin smiles. He says Emily definitely posed in those letters, he knows her thoroughly, through and through, as no one else ever did." It is true her brother knew her in ways we do not, but it is also the case that we know some poems and letters and relationships better than he. The fraternal view had its blind spots, like the paternal condescension toward the female mind.[2] These familial male superiorities help explain many things, including the poet's quest for authoritative "tutors" and "masters" outside her home.

Of course, Dickinson threw dust in her advisor's eyes. There is little evidence that for "Prose" she went to Ruskin or Thomas Browne, both of whom just happened to be cited in "A Letter to a Young Contributor." But her statement that she hadn't read Whitman because she was "told that he was disgraceful" sounds plausible. The Outsetting Bard was not

---

2. In Richard B. Sewall's biography, Austin's assessment is accorded a centrality it doesn't merit. It had first been cited by his lover's daughter, Millicent Todd Bingham, who worked closely with Sewall and gave him access to many valuable materials not previously made public. He ended up absorbing Austin's perspective on Sue and, more important, on Emily's "posing," which became one of Sewall's leading themes. Few things can be so dangerous for biographical objectivity as the sense of privileged access.

seen as homosexual so much as simply and flagrantly indecent. Under Holland, the *Republican* loudly objected to him, running a review under the terse and witty headline, " 'Leaves of Grass'—Smut in Them."

Regarding another daring American writer of the time, Dickinson told Higginson she had "read Miss [Harriet] Prescott's 'Circumstance,' but it followed me, in the Dark – so I avoided her." According to Sue, however, writing in 1903, the poet reacted enthusiastically to this sensational story: "This is the only thing I ever saw in my life I did not think I could have written myself. You stand nearer the world than I do. Send me everything she writes." The article containing this supposed quotation, which doesn't sound like Dickinson, was written in Rome, probably without access to the original note. Chances are, the letter to Higginson gives the more trustworthy account of Dickinson's final opinion of Prescott. Certainly, a number of poems express a low estimate of sensation novels:

> No Romance sold unto
> Could so enthrall a Man
> As the perusal of
> His Individual One –
> 'Tis Fiction's – to dilute to Plausibility
> Our *Novel* . . .
>
> Fr590A

This was sent to Sue about 1863, when Prescott was already starting to fade.

The critical surgery Higginson tried to perform on Dickinson seems to have been sadly conventional. His later essay on her considers the poem, "Your riches taught me poverty," which ends:

> Its far – far Treasure to surmise –
> And estimate the Pearl –
> That slipped my simple fingers through –
> While just a Girl at school!
>
> Fr418B

Here, wrote her frustrated adviser, was

> manifest that defiance of form, never through carelessness, and never
> precisely from whim, which so marked her. The slightest change in
> the order of words—thus, "While yet at school, a girl"—would have
> given her a rhyme for this last line; but no; she was intent upon her
> thought, and it would not have satisfied her to make the change.

The passage nicely catches the exasperated patience that led Higginson
to call her "wayward," and accuse her of confessing minor infractions
while saying nothing about major ones.

Yet it will not do simply to smile at Higginson's insistence on exact
rhyme, standard punctuation, correct grammar, titles, and the like. His
sense of poetic form may seem rigidly time-bound, but he shouldn't be
underestimated. He not only brought the poet before the world in the
first edition of her poems, he still embodies the sympathetic bafflement
and even dismay of more sophisticated readers. No critic who admires
everything in Dickinson can be relied on, having renounced that
birthright of independent judgment we honor her for exercising. Norman Talbot, one of her shrewdest admirers, has nicely characterized
"that curious tilt of naivety, elusiveness, stubbornness and impudence"
that both attracts and grates on readers.

But it goes deeper than that. Approaching Higginson soon after
Wadsworth, Bowles, and her sister-in-law had all proved inadequate,
Dickinson wanted a hand in moving from the "zeroes" of her life to
"phosphorus," from depression and desertion to incandescent mastery.
Higginson's job was to help her learn the self-control she needed now
that her " 'Little Girl'hood" was at last behind her. Holding no illusions
about her preparation at Amherst Academy and Mount Holyoke, she
admitted she "went to school – but in your manner of the phrase – had
no education." In August 1862 she ceased sending earlier poems to concentrate on more recently composed ones: "Are these more orderly?"
Perhaps some were written with her new preceptor partly in mind. "I
had no Monarch in my life," she confessed, showing how ambivalent she

felt about her singleness and independence, "and cannot rule myself, and when I try to organize – my little Force explodes – and leaves me bare and charred." And yet she *was* engaged in a massive "organizing," recording poems in manuscript books and burning the rough drafts she had accumulated.

In late 1862 Higginson was asked by Brigadier General Rufus Saxton to take charge of the first regiment of ex-slaves. Saxton (the army officer Dickinson met in Washington in 1855) was now military governor of captured southern territory. Accepting a challenge most white officers would have scorned, Higginson soon found himself on a Sea Island off the coast of South Carolina. Writing to him there but saying nothing about his work with black troops (her letters never mention his radical politics), the poet said that war felt like "an oblique place," that she too had "an 'Island.'" If you could, "with honor, avoid Death," she would be much obliged. Mischievously, she signed herself "Your Gnome," then added a postscript hoping his recent essay, "The Procession of the Flowers," would not prove a bad omen. It was another example of her gallows humor, "off charnel steps."

Friendships with Women

The Friendships of Women, a genial volume brought out in 1868 by a Bostonian named William R. Alger, drew on European and American literature and history to characterize the patterns of women's closest relationships. Alger's longest chapter was on Platonic love between women and men. His next longest, "Pairs of Female Friends," was about women's passionate but Platonic same-sex bonds. The topic was in the air.

On July 10, 1862, Eudocia Converse Flynt, wife of Emily's mother's first cousin, came to Amherst for Commencement and the Dickinson reception. Flynt's diary shows she met Governor John Andrew, the Hollands, and the Lords, and thoroughly enjoyed herself. Back home in Monson, she got an unexpected note:

You and I, did'nt finish talking. Have you room for the sequel,
in your Vase?

> *All the letters I could*
> *write,*
> *Were not fair as this –*
> *Syllables of velvet –*
> *Sentences of Plush –*
> *Depths of Ruby, undrained –*
> *Hid, Lip, for Thee,*
> *Play it were a*
> *Humming Bird*
> *And sipped just*
> *Me –*

> > > Emily –[3]

> > > > Fr380A

As in the poem "My river runs to thee," sent the previous year to Mary
Bowles and concluding, "*Say* – Sea – / Take *Me*!" (Fr219C), the writer
almost seemed to be offering herself as an erotic treat to a woman who
was several years older, not especially close, and married. The poems appear to invite an affectionate union, but in their original context they
posed an enigmatic challenge to any conceivable response. They offered
no recognizable social categories, only metaphors of union drawn from
nature. How does one answer such an intense and unsocialized invitation? Flynt's diary entry—"Had a letter from Emily Dickinson!!!!"—
suggests she was floored by this attempt to "finish talking." "Finish" was
the right word: there could be no reply.

Dickinson showed a more practical affection to cousins Clara and
Anna Newman, whose footing in the Evergreens was becoming increasingly uncomfortable. Instead of acting as mother to the orphans, Sue used
them as substitutes for the nurses she no longer hired. A surviving letter

---

3. Dickinson's manuscript, whose lineation is here reproduced, shows that she gave "Me" its own
line even though she had sufficient room between "just" and the edge of the page.

from sixteen-year-old Anna gives a full report on Ned's daily activities while Sue was visiting Gertrude Vanderbilt in Flatbush. More often, the boy's care was assigned to Clara, against her will. Petty insults and punishments were visited on the sisters, as when they were forced to "study an entire evening seated in a lighted bay window with the shades up."

Clara's interest in Charles H. Sweetser (or his in her) presented a special problem. Austin was so opposed to this talented but flighty young journalist, who graduated from Amherst College in 1862, that Bowles came to the young man's defense: "I do *not* understand what you say about Sweetser. I do not find him out yet." Still, Bowles agreed the young man should not "have either of your girls. They surely must do better." Receiving little sympathy or love at home, Clara confided in Emily at a certain "trysting-place" on the Homestead's back staircase. When the time came for the girl's rigorous all-day entrance examination at Amherst's newly established high school, the poet was full of comfort and reassurance.

The poet's friendship with Kate Turner, Sue's schoolmate from Cooperstown, was in abeyance when the *Republican* reported that much of the town had been destroyed by fire. The story ran April 12, 1862, three days after Bowles sailed and three days before the first letter to Higginson. "Katie is doubtless in *ashes*," Emily thought, or so she claimed in answering Kate's letter about the disaster. But the real comfort lay elsewhere, in knowing she hadn't been dropped: "Thank you Katie, it *was* relief, you had'nt spoke so long, I got a bad whim." Once again, a friend's unresponsive silence had given rise to dark fears. "So tired, Katie," Emily abruptly wrote at letter's end. The next year the beautiful widow returned to the Evergreens, but there is no evidence that she and Emily polished their rusty connection. Like so many others, Kate remained Sue's friend more than Emily's.

About the time Bowles reached Paris, his friend Maria Whitney made that first "call on Mrs [Susan] Dickinson that I have been wanting to pay, so long," in the process bringing a new element into the Dickinson compound. Born the same year as the poet and growing up in a well-to-do Northampton family, Whitney was a robust, well-traveled, cultivated woman, with an interest in foreign languages and social progress. She had many strong family ties and a lively sense of order and duty, and as she passed through her thirties her skilled help was requisitioned for others' illnesses and childbirths. Twice she moved in with the Bowleses to assist in medical or household emergencies, in all giving about a year to the family; her feelings for Samuel were warm and worshipful. At intervals she was depressed by a sense of unattached homelessness—"my otherwise empty life," as she put it, with "its great wants & deficiencies." Not long before her visit to Sue, she spent a year in New York teaching impoverished German girls. Now, having returned for the time being to her banker-father's Northampton home, she looked forward to "occasional walks to Amherst" as fall came on.

When Whitney reported on her new social resource to Samuel, the favorable verdict was relayed back to the Evergreens: "She writes enthusiastically of you all, & of your pleasant home. Her enthusiasm about Austin fairly makes me jealous. . . . He is a 'sly dog,' isn't he? Yet everybody thinks he is such an open, frank fellow!" The letter omitted all mention of Emily, who probably didn't make contact with the new recruit. For the rest of the decade, in fact, no extant letter by either woman so much as alludes to the other. It appears the connection didn't take hold until Samuel's death in 1878, when Emily, knowing Maria loved him, had the necessary basis for some of her best letters.

From early on, however, Maria was sent poems written expressly for her. The first has been assigned to fall 1862, when she was making her seven-mile treks (each way) to Amherst. Probably sent next door to the Evergreens during one of these visits, the poem presents a typical excuse:

> A Charm invests a face
> Imperfectly beheld –
> The Lady dare not lift her Vail –
> For fear it be dispelled –
> But peers beyond her mesh –
> And wishes – and denies –
> Lest interview – annul a want –
> That Image – satisfies –

Fr430A

Demonstrating how much anxious thought was being given to the visitor, the poem contrived to satisfy the requirements of politeness without lifting the "Vail." The same was true of the second lyric, "But little carmine hath her face" (Fr566A), from 1863, which accompanied a flower intended to "exhibit" the poet's love; this may also have been sent next door. Both works drew their force from their creator's invisibility.

The third poem, "How well I knew her not," has been obscured by the claim that it was occasioned by the death of Maria's sister, Sarah Learned, in July 1864. This is highly improbable: Maria was in California on that date, Emily was in Cambridgeport, she isn't known to have sent her work across the continent, and the fourth line mentions a grief "Next door." The actual train of events began in summer 1863, when the Whitneys were extremely anxious about Maria's sister living in San Francisco, Elizabeth Putnam, pregnant, in poor health, and with six children to bring up. Maria was preparing to travel west to offer assistance when a telegram arrived saying her sister had "died June 23d. Maria not needed." "Almost overcome," Maria felt depleted and purposeless after her "busy days . . . made full of delight by the thought of going to be with Lizzie after so many years of cruel separation"; she doubted she would ever "have another such friend." That winter, changing her mind, she resolved to go to California after all and look after the Putnam children for two or three years. When Austin went to Northampton to say good-bye shortly before her February 13 sailing, he thought it felt like "the next thing to a funeral."

With him, perhaps, went Emily's poem, which said good-bye in a strange, oblique, yet honest fashion:

> How well I knew Her not
> Whom not to know – has been
> A Bounty in prospective – now
> Next door to mine, the pain –

Fr813A

A hesitant bystander, Emily had been looking forward to the day she would get to know Maria, the "Bounty in prospective." Now, she confronts the likelihood that this undeveloped friendship that has been occupying her ("How well I knew Her not") will not materialize. Maria's painful bereavement is "Next door" in two senses: it is in nearby Northampton, and it is a far more tragic version of Emily's loss of a potential intimate. A decade later the poet would express the idea more lucidly to Sue: "To lose what we never owned might seem an eccentric Bereavement but Presumption has its Affliction as actually as Claim." The idea (not so very far-fetched if you live in anticipation) was eventually molded into a nice paradox: "the parting of those that never met."

The three Whitney poems' sense of next-doorness shows up in other lyrics prompted by events that touched Dickinson through the Evergreens. In March 1864 Sue's Flatbush friend, Gertrude Vanderbilt, was shot in the intestines while trying to protect a servant from a stalker; she wasn't expected to survive. Bowles immediately forwarded the *Brooklyn Eagle*'s account of the brutality along with his own stunned reaction: "It is all horrible, & tears, & tortures, & sets all fundamental ideas afloat." When the victim astonished everyone by living, Henry Ward Beecher apparently called her the "visible evidence of the spiritual life." "A sort of 'Second Coming,' eh?" wrote Bowles. But Dickinson wasn't surprised, having "believed" all along in Vanderbilt's survival. The resulting poem, "To this world she returned," picking up Bowles's idea, articulated the wounded woman's—and the poet's—odd position in the world, both in and out:

> . . . *hesitating, half of Dust –*
> *And half of Day, the Bride.*
>
> Fr815A (J830)

When Vanderbilt came to Amherst in the last half of June, Dickinson was in Cambridge and thus couldn't have seen her. Nevertheless, this and three other poems were eventually sent to her—more instances of verse standing in for contact.

On March 18, 1865, Harriet Gilbert Cutler died, only forty-four and with children at home—"in the midst of her usefulness," as the obituary put it. In a year when Amherst's sixty-one other deaths were all assigned a standard cause in the town's vital records, Harriet's entry says only, "Unknown, 24 days." The effect of this unexplained death on Sue, who had now lost two of her three sisters, was a protracted illness or breakdown. Assuming she would soon recover, the Bowleses were "surprised & shocked" to learn six weeks later that her life had been in question. "It touches the realities of existence," Samuel wrote Austin, "to have those close to us so prostrated, so tentative as to going or staying." In mid-May the editor was still hoping her "long days of sickness & trial" would terminate in a "speedy convalescence."

That spring Emily sent her sister-in-law a consolatory stanza asserting an unshakable faith in her survival as well as in Harriet's immortality:

> Unable are the Loved – to die –
> For Love is immortality –
> Nay – it is Deity –
>
> Fr951A

More impressive is the impassioned note in which the poet insisted she be allowed to die, or give way to despair, before Sue:

> You must let me go first, Sue, because I live in the Sea always and know the Road.
> I would have drowned twice to save you sinking, dear, If I could only have covered your Eyes so you would'nt have seen the Water.

Forced to leave home for eye treatment about two weeks after Harriet's death, Emily must have been terribly anxious for her sister-in-law. The bland get-well message sent through Vinnie some weeks later—"Is Sue still improving? Give her love from us all, and how much we talk of her"—tells us the crisis had passed.

Another tragic Gilbert family death took place November 3, when

Martha Gilbert Smith once again lost her only child, this time a two-year-old named Susan. "The redoubtable God!" exclaimed Emily to Elizabeth Holland; "I notice where Death has been introduced, he frequently calls, making it desirable to forestall his advances." A poem describes the huge grief the girl left behind as the "Andes – in the Bosoms where / She had begun to lie" (Fr897C). Another 1865 poem, telling how two yearly cycles end in death during the season of fullness, may commemorate this child:

> *Two full Autumns for the Squirrel*
> *Bounteous prepared –*
> *Nature, Had'st thou not a Berry*
> *For thy wandering Bird?*
>
> Fr950 (J846)

These poems exhibit the tenderness that Dickinson distilled with such mastery, but they scarcely hint at the power of two others that dramatize the grieved laying out of a female corpse. The earlier of the two, from summer 1861, contemplates a worn-out housewife whose death permits the bystander to at last

> *Stroke the cool forehead – hot so often –*
> *Lift – if you care – the listless hair –*
> *Handle the adamantine fingers*
> *Never a thimble – more – shall wear –*
>
> Fr238 (J187)

In the later poem, from 1863, which seems to involve a young girl, we are commanded to close her eyes, stroke her cheeks, steal one last kiss, and adjust (and drop tears on) her feet, all in an incantatory Victorian ritual of helpless physical love:

> *These – saw Visions –*
> *Latch them softly –*
> *These – held Dimples –*

> *Smooth them slow –*
> *This – addressed departing accents –*
> *Quick – Sweet Mouth – to miss thee so – . . .*
> *These – adjust – that ran to meet Us –*
> *Pearl – for stocking – Pearl for Shoe – . . .*
>
> Fr769

Ironically, these supremely tactile and moving funerary poems cannot be linked to real—touchable—people. It looks as if all that wonderful stroking was not a product of experience.

Poems to Sue

Sue, who received a total of seventy-three poems from 1863 through 1865 (Franklin's count), continued to hear from Emily more than anyone else. With a few exceptions, chiefly the tender "For largest woman's heart I knew" (Fr542A) and "I could not drink it, Sue" (Fr816A), these poems do not chronicle a relationship marked by episodes, changing feelings, and so forth. Instead, the few lyrics that comment on the friendship, such as "To love thee year by year" (Fr618[A]), mostly restate the poet's unchanging affection and devotion. Often, there is an implication of distance, as in "An hour is a sea" (Fr898) and "So set its sun in thee" (Fr940A). One intricate poem, which also went to Higginson and the Norcross cousins, imagines the pleasure of merely looking forward to a single glance at the recipient. The work probably dates from Dickinson's stay in Cambridge for eye treatments:

> *The luxury to apprehend*
> *The luxury 'twould be*
> *To look at thee a single time . . .*
>
> Fr819B

It would be naive to take these many lyric messages as signs of daily intimacy.

The most substantial of the group addresses a majestically aloof peak that spurns sunsets and the speaker alike:

> *Ah, Teneriffe!*
> *Retreating Mountain! . . .*
>
> *Still – Clad in your Mail of ices –*
> *Thigh of Granite – and thew – of Steel –*
> *Heedless – alike – of pomp – or parting*
>
> *Ah, Teneriffe!*
> *I'm kneeling – still –*
>
> Fr752A

A classic treatment of haughty unresponsiveness versus humble, admiring, undying love, this poem wasn't sent to anyone but Sue.

In subject matter, the verse sent next door in this period continued to deal with sunsets, the seasons, the future, immortality, and so forth. But the most frequent theme, a new one, was the independent or autonomous soul, the focus of at least nine poems Sue received in 1863–1865. Many of these are marked by the gnomic astringency that was becoming more salient in Dickinson's work. One begins, "Reverse cannot befall that fine Prosperity / Whose sources are interior" (Fr565[A]). In other poems also, the opening couplet tells the basic story: "The Soul's Superior instants / Occur to Her – alone" (Fr630A); "there is a June when Corn is cut, / whose option is within" (Fr811A).[4] At times this ideal self-containment suggests that ordinary social contact is a diversion that may be dispensed with:

---

4. Autonomy also has the sinister potential of ultimate self-betrayal:

> *The Soul unto itself*
> *Is an imperial friend –*
> *Or the most agonizing Spy*
> *An Enemy – could send . . .*
> Fr579B

> *The Soul that hath a Guest*
> *Doth seldom go abroad –*
> *Diviner Crowd at Home –*
> *Obliterate the need – . . .*
>
> Fr592A

Like Sue, the poet was, in addition to being many warmer things, a cold and majestic Teneriffe. She had to be (of course) to create an original and independent oeuvre.

If Dickinson's many poems on autonomy are somewhere near the center of her work, the most revealing may be those that reflect on the *history* of her self-reliance. One of these traces her tough self-containment back to the fearful hopes she used to entertain:

> *When I hoped, I feared –*
> *Since I hoped I dared*
> *Everywhere alone*
> *As a church remain –*
> *Spectre cannot harm*
> *Serpent cannot charm*
> *He is Prince of Harm*
> *Who hath suffered him –*
>
> Fr594B

"Since I hoped" seems to mean "since I ceased hoping." Like a magic rune devised to neutralize "Harm," these lines have the flavor of a wizard's hermetic immunity. More impressive, however, is a poem from 1864 that proudly tells how the speaker overcame her troubles precisely by cultivating them:

> *On the Bleakness of my Lot*
> *Bloom I strove to raise –*
> *Late – My Garden of a Rock*
> *Yielded Grape – and Maise –*

> *Soil of Flint, if steady tilled*
> *Will refund the Hand –*
> *Seed of Palm, by Lybian Sun*
> *Fructified in Sand –*
>
> Fr862B

The desert imagery, perfectly appropriate, reveals Dickinson's awareness that her poetic flowers could not have been cultivated in the domestic plots worked by happily married women. Only the more impersonal second stanza was sent to Sue.

Another crop-growing poem speaks both of what she hoarded and what she sent others:

> *The Products of my Farm are these*
> *Sufficient for my Own*
> *And here and there a Benefit*
> *Unto a Neighbor's Bin . . .*
>
> Fr1036

The implication (and these lines were also not sent to Sue) is that Dickinson's ultimate purpose in writing was something other than communication.

A poem that *was* dispatched next door sketches a dismissive picture of flutteringly responsive female gossip:

> *The Leaves like Women interchange*
> *Exclusive Confidence –*
> *Somewhat of nods and somewhat*
> *Portentous inference –*
>
> *The Parties in both cases*
> *Enjoining secrecy –*
> *Inviolable compact*
> *To notoriety.*
>
> Fr1098A

About 1865 Sue was trusted with a version of the poem unwisely confided to Samuel, "Title divine is mine," whose speaker calls herself "The Wife without the Sign" and toys with the phrase " 'My Husband' " (Fr194B). (In that case, one notes, it was a man who couldn't keep the secret.) The gift implies a high degree of trust in Sue's discretion and raises the important question whether the sisters-in-law discussed the poem's private meaning.

In 1924, a decade after Sue's death, her daughter Martha Bianchi published the sensational claim that Aunt Emily had "met [her] fate" on a visit to Philadelphia, where she and a married man fell in love but agreed to renounce one another. The story was supposedly imparted as "a confidence to her Sister Sue," who "sacredly guarded [it] . . . till death." These melodramatic disclosures were met with so much skepticism and outright scorn that Bianchi was driven to amplify them in 1932. Now it appeared the man had been a clergyman and that many others besides Sue were possessed of the story—Austin, Vinnie, Martha Gilbert Smith, an Amherst College trustee's wife, and various relatives. What this list of informants chiefly reveals is that Dickinson's family shared a secret understanding about her, confided no doubt with the "nod" she understood so well. Martha's story is too heavily salted with "portentous inference" to be swallowed whole, yet she *was* close enough to her mother that there could have been a factual basis. The trouble with rumor is that it can have a grain of truth.

How the Mountain Rose

If the more than six hundred poems that Dickinson wrote in 1863, 1864, and 1865 are read against those of 1861 (an experiment made possible by the new variorum edition's refined dating), certain directional tendencies stand out with such clarity it is unlikely her work can ever again be seen as somehow not developing—not building on her experience. Proportionally, we find an increase in the number of poems on abstract themes and a corresponding decrease in the number of first-person narratives (though she of course continued to produce these). The voicing of present, extreme, and exclamatory feeling—"the drop of anguish / That scalds me now" (Fr215)—more or less disappears, its place being taken by a story line in which the speaker gives a respectful account of what she has achieved. These various developments are beautifully summed up by the poem, "Further in summer than the birds" (Fr895), in which the restful drone of stasis succeeds clamorous anticipation.

Of course, many things did not change. In a poem from 1863—"Alter! When the hills do" (Fr755B)—the speaker indignantly denies she could possibly be unfaithful to the man she loves. Sending the first stanza to Sue, Dickinson withheld the second, whose "Sir" identifies the imagined recipient's sex. In another poem that would dispel her lover's doubts of her constancy, she imagines the river of death rising to her feet, breast, and mouth, and last of all her "searching eyes," which, to the very end, remain "quick – with Thee!" (Fr631). "Quick" has all its meanings here, "fast," "darting," "energetic," "pregnant," all focused on the second-person singular pronoun toward which the bravura ending builds. The point the poem makes seems valid: the poet's eyes *were* fixed on her lover, whose remote and perpetually retouched image helped direct her huge energies. His face played a role in her artistic life similar to the idea of heaven, being the perfect but absent good that spurred her to rise above an enslaving reality. The secretly cherished "relationship" was the fantasy that helped her devise a very real and powerful freedom.[5]

A poem from 1865 in which Dickinson offers to sacrifice herself as proof of her devotion to her "Sceptic Thomas" (the doubting Disciple) touches on her inexhaustible fertility:

> Split the Lark – and you'll find the Music –
> Bulb after Bulb, in Silver rolled –

---

5. In Dinah Craik's *Olive*, the heroine feels degraded when she realizes that "unwooed, unrequited, she has dared to love" a certain minister. Then she boldly resolves not to disown her feelings: "Though a world lay between us, my spirit shall follow him all his life long. Distance shall be nothing—years nothing! . . . And then, after death, I shall await him in the land of souls." Keeping the arrow in her heart, the "virgin martyr" makes art "the chief interest and enjoyment of her life," works hard and achieves success. This was not so far removed from Dickinson's story.

Scantily dealt to the Summer Morning
Saved for your Ear, when Lutes be old – . . .

Fr905

Eager to demonstrate her truth, Emily-the-lark, the ultimate female, imagines her disbelieving lover splitting open her heart and there beholding her countless lyrics in the form of immature bulbs. These, the eggs of poems, would have been his alone if he hadn't killed his bird to prove her loyalty. "Bulb after Bulb, in Silver rolled": was she thinking of the manuscript books she "[s]cantily dealt" to others' eyes, a single poem at a time, often only a stanza? Was there a dream of "saving" everything for a select pair of ears?

Like her father, who isolated himself by his loyalty to Whig federalism, Emily was evidently bent on playing out the heart's unswerving pledges. Poem after poem looks forward to a final reunion with the unseen lover: "Fitter to see him I may be" (Fr834), "Each scar I'll keep for him" (Fr920), "My worthiness is all my doubt" (Fr791). In the last of these, what chiefly weighs on the speaker's "thronging Mind" is the fear she might be inadequate for "His beloved Need." Playing a sustaining role in her personal and poetry-writing economy, the anticipated reunion becomes, as one poem concedes, an addictive drug:

The Stimulus, beyond the Grave
His Countenance to see
Supports me like imperial Drams
Afforded Day by Day.

Fr1001

Another poem's speaker says she has nothing to do pending the last reunion but "sing"—the one activity that overcomes present darkness and approximates future "telling":

I sing to use the Waiting,
My Bonnet but to tie

> *And shut the Door unto my House*
> *No more to do have I*
>
> *Till His best step approaching*
> *We journey to the Day*
> *And tell each other how We sung*
> *To keep the Dark away.*

Fr955

None of her post-1855 messages to Sue anticipate such a scene.

A necessary aspect of these poems (here we observe the same rule as in those sent Sue) is her separation from the man. This distance is sometimes intangible, as in "I had not minded walls" (1863), where the speaker says that mere physical barriers could not have deterred her. Even if the universe were one solid rock and she "heard his silver Call" on the opposite side (as Jane heard Rochester), she would tunnel through, but as things stand she is stopped by "A filament – a law" (Fr554). In many poems written after 1862, however, the distance seems as much spatial as anything. In "I've none to tell me to but thee," the speaker, addressing one who has moved "Beyond my Boundary," imagines how she would react if their situations were reversed and *she* had "ebbed" from *him* "On some unanswering Shore" (Fr929). In "The spry arms of the wind," she wishes she could be blown to "an adjoining Zone" to perform a brief errand:

> *To ascertain the House*
> *And if the soul's within*
> *And hold the Wick of mine to it*
> *To light, and then return –*

Fr802

That is, she would like to locate the faraway person, verify he is still alive, and by this brief contact relight her benighted spirit.

Another charged poem considers two widely separated persons who are united only by the same daily cycle of light and dark:

The Noon unwinds Her Blue
Till One Breadth cover Two –
Remotest – still – . . .

The Midnight's Dusky Arms
Clasp Hemispheres, and Homes
And so
Opon her Bosom – One
And One opon Her Hem –
Both lie –

Fr765 (J710)

The two people are not merely apart but "Remotest." One sleeps on the bosom and the other on the hem, meaning perhaps that when it is midnight for one it is dusk or dawn for the other, or that they sleep within the continent and on its edge respectively, or that one lies in the heart of passion and the other . . . doesn't. The poem's eroticism lies in its wistfully compensatory effort to pull one huge hemispheric cover over two widely parted bodies.

Another poem, whose coyly postponed last word identifies the recipient's gender, opens with the decisive statement that "Where Thou art – that – is Home – / Cashmere – or Calvary – the same." Cashmere is soft pleasure, Calvary torture, yet they would be equally welcome if the speaker could only be with the man. As it is, their relationship is one of absence and negatives, dooming her to a kind of hell:

Where Thou art not – is Wo –
Tho' Bands of Spices – row –
What Thou dost not – Despair –
Tho' Gabriel – praise me – Sir –

Fr749

Although the last line hints at Dickinson's satisfying awareness of her achievement as an artist, the realization does not allay her despair, or so the speaker says.

A poem entered in the manuscript books in fall 1862, "I envy seas whereon he rides," is, like others cited here, consistent with the facts of Wadsworth's trip to San Francisco. The speaker envies all the objects associated with his journey and new home—sparrows nesting under the eaves, flies on windowpanes. Wishing she could "be Noon to Him," she ends by acknowledging the interdiction of her desire, on pain of punishment—

> *Lest noon in everlasting night –*
> *Drop Gabriel – and me –*
>
> Fr368

Generally, as in the preceding poem, the archangel Gabriel is beyond the ravages of fortune. Here, perhaps identified with Wadsworth (on account of religious function and magnificent voice), he is as much at risk as Dickinson.

A closely related poem was recorded in the manuscript books about a year after the minister's move west. Largely ignored by critics and biographers, it merits quoting in its entirety:

> *I could die – to know –*
> *'Tis a trifling knowledge –*
> *News-Boys salute the Door –*
> *Carts – joggle by –*
> *Morning's bold face – stares in the window –*
> *Were but mine – the Charter of the least Fly –*
>
> *Houses hunch the House*
> *With their Brick shoulders –*
> *Coals – from a Rolling Load – rattle – how – near –*
> *To the very Square – His foot is passing –*
> *Possibly, this moment –*
> *While I – dream – Here –*
>
> Fr537

The door, the window, the house: at the focus of this reverie stands the man's supposed domicile. Dickinson conjures up an ordinary city scene with newsboys, traffic, closely built brick houses, and a load of coal noisily rolling down on the pavement just as he, or rather his foot, passes. In her huge lyric oeuvre, this seems to be the one approximation of what was not yet known as realism, the vivid evocation of a gritty workaday scene. Introduced as "trifling," the well-drawn picture captures the urban chaos, uses the dumped load of coal to bring eye and ear down to street level in preparation for that approaching foot, then frames the whole by returning to the poet's act of imagining, now felt as remote and idle: "While I – dream – Here"—"Here" also being the page itself. With surprising ease, she carries off a kind of writing not in her usual line.

More characteristically, she continued to write about extreme states: mental anguish, despair, the self as bomb or volcano, the fear that one may be coming apart. No other American writer of her time explored with equal sensitivity and mastery the experience of fragmentation. "I felt a cleaving in my mind" (Fr867), "Finding is the first act" (Fr910), and "Crumbling is not an instant's act" (Fr1010) are among the poems describing from varying angles the ego's unraveling. Significantly, these works were composed in a period, not of collapse, but reconstruction.

An affiliated group attends to the way the mind protects itself by means of a selective inattention:

> There is a pain – so utter –
> It swallows substance up –
> Then covers the Abyss with Trance –
> So Memory can step
> Around – across – opon it –
> As One within a Swoon –
> Goes safely – where an open eye –
> Would drop Him – Bone by Bone –

Fr515

Based on the conventional idea of the sleepwalker's instinctive avoidance of danger, the poem proposes that our minds shield our disasters and abysses from us so that we can successfully negotiate them, stepping around, across, and eventually on. The beautiful tentativeness of movement captures both the indirectness and persistence of Dickinson's creative act, always devising a way to function and always returning to essential troubles. The poem elucidates her answer to Higginson's charge that her gait was "spasmodic": "I am in danger – Sir." Yet her danger is not what we should remember so much as her hard-won balance.

In early 1865, looking back at her path, she wrote:

> I stepped from Plank to Plank
> A slow and cautious way
> The Stars about my Head I felt
> About my Feet the Sea –
>
> I knew not but the next
> Would be my final inch –
> This gave me that precarious Gait
> Some call Experience –

Fr926

These lines exemplify a type of first-person retrospection that became more frequent as the North gradually prevailed in the Civil War: the proud declaration that the speaker has fought through. The essential story in this group is that she has survived starvation, shipwreck, and imprisonment, including the prison of innocence. One of the most suggestive of these dramatizations, "Let us play yesterday," tells how, thanks to her lover, she escaped her prolonged and tormenting girlhood. Like a hatchling chick who wouldn't leave its shell, she had dreamed there must be more to life yet persisted in trying to satisfy her yearnings with her "Lexicon." Then her tutor/lover cracked her isolation:

> Still at the Egg-life –
> Chafing the Shell –

Friend do it this way - that is,
whatever you do in life,
do the very best you can
with both your heart and mind.

And if you do it that way,
the Power of The Universe
will come to your assistance,
if your heart and mind are in Unity.

When one sits in the Hoop of The People,
one must be responsible because
All of Creation is related.
And the hurt of one is the hurt of all.
And the honor of one is the honor of all.
And whatever we do effects everything in the universe.

If you do it that way - that is,
if you truly join your heart and mind
as One - whatever you ask for,
that's the Way It's Going to Be.

Lakota Instructions for Living
passed down from White Buffalo Calf Woman

in you consider supporting the ...

...ose who have such little power in their lives? As the poem above sta...
...of one is the hurt of all. With your care and generosity, we can bring
...and who are often treated dishonorably. Along with the imperative f...
...rience the depth of wisdom to be gained from within these cultures th...
...e land for centuries.

...ll over the world, in 18 countries, Medical Mission Sisters are persist...
...ence to those who are most in need. We are developing meaningful, ...
...tionships and providing healthcare, advocacy and hope to thousands o...
...dren. Thank you for joining us in our passion to be a healing presence...

Gratefully in Christ,

S. Patricia

Sister Patricia A. Lo...

...: We are pleased to include a brochure, *Precious Earth Precious Peo...
...edical Mission Sisters' work with the indigenous people of Peru and th...

... S.: As you prepare to file your taxes thi...

The fool's
gold

> *When you troubled the Ellipse –*
> *And the Bird fell –*
>
> Fr754

Having experienced the sky, the speaker now knows how painful it would be to "resume the Shell" and hopes her liberty won't be taken from her.

Again and again Dickinson recorded how she had taken control of her ordained victimhood, turning deficits to assets. In "God gave a Loaf to every Bird – / But just a Crumb – to Me," she tells how she converted deprivation into a state of wealth that makes her "Sovereign of them all" (Fr748B). In another work, one of the few in iambic pentameter, she presents herself as an encouraging case of recovery from disaster:

> *If any sink, assure that this, now standing –*
> *Failed like Themselves – and conscious that it rose –*
> *Grew by the Fact, and not the Understanding*
> *How Weakness passed – or Force – arose – . . .*
>
> Fr616

As humble as they are proud, these lines offer an impressive statement on the obscure process by which "Force" is regained—a process that eludes understanding yet requires thought and effort to make it work. To stand after sinking: Dickinson had done that no less than the mortally wounded Gertrude Vanderbilt.

The most revealing poems may be those that make the connection between psychic recovery and the work of writing. "God made a little gentian," entered in the manuscript books about spring 1863, a year after Wadsworth's departure and a few months after Bowles's humiliating betrayal, concerns a flower that wants and fails to be a rose. Laughed at by "all the Summer," the fringed gentian blooms only after other flowers are killed by autumn's frost: "There rose a Purple Creature – / That ravished all the Hill." Dickinson ends her story of this royal but painful triumph by asking, "Creator – Shall I – bloom?" (Fr520).

Such poems, anticipating production, are outnumbered by those that look back and assess it. Of these, one of the most arresting treats her poetry writing as a kind of self-therapy. She begins by addressing the special person she misses:

> *Severer Service of myself*
> *I hastened to demand*
> *To fill the awful Vacuum*
> *Your life had left behind –*
>
> *I worried Nature with my Wheels*
> *When Hers had ceased to run –*
> *When she had put away Her Work*
> *My own had just begun –*
>
> *I strove to weary Brain and Bone –*
> *To harass to fatigue*
> *The glittering Retinue of nerves –*
> *Vitality to clog . . .*

Nothing else written by Dickinson so vividly evokes her lamplit bedroom, laborious nights, and disciplined effort to quiet her "nerves." Not stopping there, however, the poem goes on to admit the failure of her program: "Affliction would not be appeased" and she remains in "Darkness." The lesson the last stanza draws is that essential problems are not to be remedied:

> *No Drug for Consciousness – can be –*
> *Alternative to die*
> *Is Nature's only Pharmacy*
> *For Being's Malady –*
>
> Fr887

The poem is so honest and tough we must be careful not to take it as the "real" story of Dickinson's life in writing. As always, her full truth was more complicated; certainly, she herself gave other explanations for her drive to expression.[6] Still, "Severer service of myself" does suggest a motive for her phenomenal production even as it tells us not to make the therapeutic perspective our primary one. As those astringent last lines warn, psychology, the "Retinue of nerves," was not what she was ultimately concerned with.

This and other survival narratives are closely allied to the many poems on the soul's sovereignty that were given to Sue. Also related are various meditations on what might be called the power of growth. "Through the Dark Sod – as Education – / The Lily passes sure" (Fr559B) was sent to Louisa and Frances Norcross, perhaps about 1863, a dark time for the newly orphaned cousins. That year there were other poems about the mysterious push upward:

> The Mountains – grow unnoticed –
> Their Purple figures rise
> Without attempt – Exhaustion –
> Assistance – or Applause – . . .
>
> Fr768

The subject here is in part the poet's own creative effort and achievement: the second line restates the gentian poem's "There rose a Purple Creature"; the fourth reminds us that Dickinson's private monument building did not depend on others' advice or approval. Manuscript book 37, also from 1863, repeatedly considers the inherent dignity of things that act independently: "You taught me waiting with myself" (Fr774),

---

6. In the same manuscript book, for instance, "It is a lonesome glee" has this to say about solitary birdsong:

> Delight without a Cause –
> Arrestless as invisible –
> A Matter of the Skies.
>
> Fr873

Here, the motive for lyric expression has nothing to do with pain, release, discipline.

"Life and death and giants" (Fr777), "Four trees upon a solitary acre" (Fr778), and "Growth of man like growth of nature." The last of these, a major statement, welds the idea of autonomy to vocation:

> Each – its difficult Ideal
> Must achieve – Itself –
> Through the solitary prowess
> Of a Silent Life –
>
> Effort – is the sole condition –
> Patience of Itself –
> Patience of opposing forces –
> And intact Belief –
>
> Looking on – is the Department
> Of its Audience –
> But Transaction – is assisted
> By no Countenance –
>
> Fr790

The poem states what no reader of Dickinson must ever forget. To date, as far as we know, no one, not Bowles, not Higginson, not Susan Dickinson, had "countenanced"—seen, approved of—very much of her best work.

In 1864 we begin to see poems registering a sense that the struggles of youth and early maturity are over. In "The admirations and contempts of time," death's approach

> Reorganizes Estimate
> And what We saw not
> We distinguish clear –
> And mostly – see not
> What We saw before – . . .
>
> Fr830

Another poem, contrasting "plan for Noon and plan for Night" (the last word may mean blindness as well as the end of life), says that while

The Foot opon the Earth
At Distance, and Achievement, strains,
The Foot opon the Grave
Makes effort at Conclusion . . .

Fr1075 (J960)

From the beginning, Dickinson's poetry was animated by a conviction that the world is a symbolic theater that directs our minds toward the infinite but that we generally misinterpret. The idea had stayed with her, but now she applied it to her experience, not her prospects. In "What twigs we held by," she exclaims at the inadequacy of the people and things we clutch in "Life's swift River," in our effort at self-preservation. Only at the end, as we "pause before a further plunge," is it apparent how flimsy are the attachments that have held us. Was she thinking of her fixation on Master, less necessary now and beginning to recede? Shifting the metaphor (as usual), the poem concludes:

How scant, by everlasting Light
The Discs that satisfied our sight –
How dimmer than a Saturn's Bar
The Things esteemed, for Things that are!

Fr1046

This was said with a ripe authority Dickinson hadn't earned in her younger and shallower judgments of the world's "hollowness." It is another sign of her incomparable resourcefulness that she could say what she had already said and speak more richly than ever. She was a writer whose material could not be used up: who even in looking back kept moving forward.

The Only Woe That Ever Made Me Tremble

Dickinson's productivity seems even more heroic in view of the disabling eye complaint that showed up in September 1863. From late April to

November 21 in 1864, and again from April 1 to October in 1865, she underwent prolonged treatment at the hands of Boston's leading ophthalmologist, Dr. Henry Willard Williams. During these two extended periods, she lived with her cousins Louisa and Frances Norcross in the Cambridge boardinghouse to which they had recently moved.

There is no record of Williams's diagnosis, and of his treatment all we know is that the sessions at his office were "painful" and that Dickinson was told to avoid bright light and close work. She had to let her cousins mend her stockings, and, worse, not look "at the Spring." Mabel Loomis Todd was told she spent "part of the time in darkness." The patient's own account of her symptoms was written in Amherst between her two courses of treatment, after Louisa insisted on a report:

> The eyes are as with you, sometimes easy, sometimes sad. I think they are not worse, nor do I think them better than when I came home.
>
> The snow light offends them, and the house is bright . . . Vinnie [is] good to me, but "cannot see why I don't get well." This makes me think I am long sick, and this takes the ache to my eyes.

Although Dickinson regretted her inability to help with the housework, what chiefly oppressed and frightened was the interdiction on reading, as she later informed Joseph Lyman:

> Some years ago I had a woe, the only one that ever made me tremble. It was a shutting out of all the dearest ones of time, the strongest friends of the soul – BOOKS. The Medical man said . . . "down, thoughts, & plunge into her soul." He might as well have said, "Eyes be blind," "heart be still." So I had eight weary months of Siberia.

Dr. Williams's office was in his new brownstone house on Arlington Street, on the site now occupied by the Ritz-Carlton Hotel. The books he wrote shortly before and after seeing Dickinson—*A Practical Guide to the Study of the Diseases of the Eye* (1862) and *Recent Advances in Ophthalmic Science* (1866)—reveal an easy familiarity with recent European inventions, procedures, experiments. They also indicate how concerned he was to alleviate pain and facilitate recovery. He sounds gentle and reassuring, and in fact the poet took note of his delicate excuse for wiping her cheeks—for "caution of my Hat." All the same, Williams was very much the man in charge: an editorial by him in *The Boston Medical and Surgical Journal* forcefully argued that women's "physical organization," especially "*during a portion of every month,* disqualifies them" from the medical professions.

Dickinson's daguerreotype, together with her sensitivity to light in 1864–1865, has prompted some scholars to diagnose her trouble as exotropia—divergent, "wall-eyed" vision. A more likely diagnosis, proposed by Norbert Hirschhorn and Polly Longsworth, is anterior uveitis: what used to be called rheumatic iritis. According to Williams's *Practical Guide,* the pain caused by this disease "is of an aching character and deep-seated . . . often severe, sometimes agonizing," capable of returning "with increased severity at evening, or in the night, after a comparatively tranquil day." His observation that "large anodynes are often ineffectual to procure sleep" brings to mind the early 1864 poem whose speaker labors into the night to wear out the "glittering Retinue of nerves" (Fr887). Another symptom is "intolerance of light." Happily, if the disease is caught in time and properly treated, the prognosis is "almost always . . . favorable"—not the case with exotropia. As Dickinson noted, the doctor was "enthusiastic, about my getting well."

It so happens that during her second course of treatment, one of Williams's medical students took notes of his lecture on rheumatic iritis on April 27, 1865. The first recommendation was "Atropine 4 grs to 1 oz once or twice a day, or oftener, or a stronger solution." After listing other remedies, the notetaker wrote, "No mercury," assuring us that at least on this occasion the poet escaped poisoning. Atropine was an old and standard agent, derived from belladonna. In addition to being used to dilate the pupil, thus increasing the eye's sensitivity to light, the drug was known to prevent or break down "adhesions between the iris and lens in iritis." Williams's *Practical Guide* stressed the gradualness of recovery and the need for continuous monitoring. The patient "should be cautious, at least for some months, in regard to exposure to glare of light from the snow or from light surfaces." The poet's statement that her eyes were bothered by "snow light . . . and the house is bright" almost sounds like an echo of her doctor's advice.

Dickinson's living arrangements in downtown Cambridge, or Cambridgeport, as the city's commercial and administrative quarter was known, provided her first extended experience of ordinary urban life. Since the boardinghouse was at 86 (later 124) Austin Street, only one short block from the central business district, there must have been considerably more bustle, noise, and dust than she was used to. Her neighbors, spanning the usual middle-class occupations, included a grocer, an apothecary, a livery stable operator, and a customhouse appraiser. A block or so up the nearest cross street was the Prospect Street Church, which Louisa and Frances joined in January 1865. Somewhat farther, at 24 Centre Street, resided Asa and Lucretia Dickinson Bullard, and with them Catharine Newman, a schoolteacher. In nearby Lynn was Uncle Joel W. Norcross, now retired.

A presentation inscription in the poet's copy of *Jane Eyre* tells us she was probably visited by Charlotte Sewall Eastman on September 20, 1865. "How are your eyes my dear Emily," asks a letter from Eastman seven years later. Yet Cambridgeport opened few or no social vistas for Dickinson, and in fact it is impossible to picture her joining others on the Austin Street veranda on hot summer evenings (though she complained about mosquitoes). She noted for Vinnie's sake that bonnets were giving way to straw hats, but in general the events she deemed newsworthy—Clara and Anna Newman's unexpected visit, the arrival of Joel's eight-year-old daughter, Anna, the blooming of certain plants—disclose an attention riveted on the indoors. A new couple's arrival merited notice because of the threat to privacy: "I do little but fly, yet always find a nest."

As for Bowles, two contemporaneous letters to Austin and Sue speak of trips to Boston without raising the question of looking up Emily. When he mentioned her and her illness, it was only in connection with family members, as when he wrote from California in summer 1865 and wished for "health & happiness for Sue; eyes for Emily; patience & a love of a bonnet for Vinnie. . . ."

Dickinson's statement that "Mrs Bangs and her Daughter [are] very kind" tells us she got on amicably with the landladies, Eunice and Louise Bangs, and their Irish-born servant, Margaret Tripper. Since Eunice's husband, a bookkeeper, didn't own the house and had no Cambridge real estate or taxable assets, it would appear the family took boarders to supplement a tight income. For the daughter, Louise, who never married, this was to be a lifelong occupation: fifty years after her death, a Cambridge resident remembered a respectable Sparks Street house she had run. In all likelihood, Dickinson's accommodations in 1864 and 1865 were more than adequate. Her cousins were not so impecunious, after all, as to have to settle for an undusted, door-banging boardinghouse.

Most of what we know about the poet's life at this time comes from her messages to Vinnie, packed with questions and information about the ongoing life at home and in Cambridgeport. The first in the series, evidently responding to Vinnie's demand for news, explains why Emily hasn't written, assures her sister of her love, and (as Samuel would do) recommends patience. Like Martha in the Bible, Vinnie was needlessly "troubled about things," such as the loose mortar left in the yard by brick masons: "don't work too hard, picking up after Chimneys" Emily urged; "The Grass will cover it all up." Along with the mundane advice, we see a great deal of tender familiarity, and also a running assumption that Vinnie won't require any lofty composition: "Much love for both Houses, from the Girls and me – Is the Lettuce ripe –" When it was time to return home by train, it was Vinnie who received the peremptory order that didn't need explaining: "You will get me at Palmer – yourself – Let no one beside, come." There is no evidence any poems were sent to her.

The letters to Sue, by contrast, are highly wrought literary objects, enameled, glittering, succinct to the point of obscurity. Assuming an exalted or even transcendent grasp, these charged messages anticipate the many oracular aphorisms the poet sent next door in her last two decades. Soon after May 19, 1864, when Hawthorne died during a trip away from his home in Concord (twenty miles west of Cambridge), she wrote, "Our beautiful Neighbor 'moved' in May – It leaves an Unimportance." When a gift from the Evergreens apparently went astray, she thanked her sister-in-law anyway and assured her she wouldn't "mind [that is, miss] the Gloves – I knew it was the Bell, and not the Noon, that failed." This seems to mean that she knew Sue's love (the noon) was there even if its sensory reminder (the bell—that is, the gloves) didn't materialize. "To believe – is enough, and the right of supposing." The basic idea, a faith in essence not evidence, comes up again and again, as in this enigmatic passage rejecting an offered gift or wish:[7] "Take back that 'Bee' and 'Buttercup' – I have no Field for them [in downtown Cambridge?], though for the Woman whom I prefer, Here is Festival – When my Hands are cut, Her fingers will be found inside." The dramatic concluding image identifies Sue as the animating presence in Emily's writing. However generous and exaggerated, this declaration had a core of truth: Vinnie could never have aroused the energetic writing that Sue provoked. The poet's flights required a basis outside her birth family, who would have smiled at her "posing," her "excess of *Monkey*." Like the fantasied lover oceans away, the fantasied intimate in the house next door stimulated Dickinson to convert her kind of isolation into productive creativity.

If Vinnie and Sue shared letters, they would have noticed each was singled out as the favorite. "It would be best to see you," Sue was assured several months after Vinnie was told, "I miss you most." The apparent insincerity is another trace of Dickinson's compartmentalizations. For Sue, there were endless assurances of devotion in a union involving little direct contact and few tangible signs; for Vinnie, simple reminders of a familiar interdependency. It was the difference between sacred and ordinary love.

No matter whom she addressed, Dickinson spoke of herself as living in exile, prison, destitution, wilderness. In "Let us play yesterday," she had revelled in her belated escape from the "Egg-life," but now, forced back into the shell, she told Vinnie she was "discouraged" and ominously

---

7. Curiously, Dickinson often let her friends know she didn't need their gifts, such as "the little Bat" (alpenstock?) Bowles brought back from Europe.

recalled Byron's Prisoner of Chillon, who "did not know Liberty when it came, and asked to go back to Jail." With Sue, reverting to the lost-at-sea image, she began a letter with the free-standing phrase, "At Centre of the Sea," and concluded with an image of unending darkness: "Should I turn in my long night I should murmur 'Sue'?" The script, not very neat, suggests she was writing in crepuscular light. There is no doubt this was one of her grimmest periods.

In her one letter to Higginson from Cambridge, Dickinson presented herself as living amid ultimates:

> *The only News I know*
> *Is Bulletins all day*
> *From Immortality.*
>
> Fr820B

Throughout, her emphasis was on compensatory powers. The doctor has "taken away my Pen," she writes in pencil. He won't let her go home, "yet I work in my Prison, and make Guests for myself." She could bring neither the mountains nor Carlo, who "would die, in Jail, . . . so I brought but the Gods." With her extraordinary retention (never sending the same poem twice to the same person), she obviously remembered informing Higginson two years earlier that her companions were a dog, the hills, and the sundown. The last of these, the subject of so many poems, was no doubt one of her portable gods. Even in Cambridge, even with photophobic eyes, one could look at the sundown.

As for those guests Dickinson made for herself, one reason for thinking she continued composing in Cambridge and then brought her rough drafts home at the end of her treatment is that a huge number of perfect copies in ink—her unstitched "sets"—have been assigned to early and late 1865. It says something about her basic impetus that few of these poems involve her current ordeal. The only one that speaks of her uprooting in the present tense, "Away from home are they and I" (Fr807A, from 1864), links her exile to that of the recently orphaned and relocated Norcross sisters. They and she, emigrants in "a Metropolis of

Homes," are all trying to acquire "The Habit of a Foreign Sky." Conspicuous by its rarity, the poem reminds us how rarely she made her verse a vehicle for comment on passing troubles.

Another answer to how she got through all that dead time lies in Louisa and Frances Norcross's love of drama. Several years earlier, when Fanny Kemble gave public readings of twelve of Shakespeare's plays in Boston, Louisa was there for at least part of the series, and in the 1880s, when she and her sister lived in Concord, they took part in the Frolic Club's all-female theatricals. Once, as Frances joined a chorus of "sorrowing Israelites" from the Book of Ruth, Emerson's widow whispered, "Isn't she modest and sweet?" On another evening Louisa was so delicious in a comic role that Emerson's daughter Ellen named her as one of the evening's two "great actors."

Certain at age twenty that Shakespeare could write nothing "wicked," Dickinson had to do a great deal of growing up before he could become an invigorating presence for her. As late as 1863, in her only poem mentioning him, she insisted that "Drama's Vitallest Expression" is found in the human heart and ordinary events, not in formal tragedies, which "Perish in the Recitation" (Fr776).[8] Now, apparently listening to Louisa and Frances's own recitations, she seems to have had her ears opened, and to have left Cambridge with a voracious desire to read for herself. As she confided to Joseph Lyman, "going home I flew to the shelves and devoured the luscious passages. I thought I should tear the leaves out as I turned them. Then I settled down to a willingness for all the rest to go but William Shakespeare." Writing Louisa, she described an oral performance in a location where she would not be overheard or interrupted: "I read a few words since I came home – John Talbot's parting with his son, and Margaret's with Suffolk. I read them in the garret, and the rafters wept." This interest in *1 Henry VI*, suggests that the Austin Street readings had gone well beyond the standard plays. The matter seems clinched by two later remarks. To Higginson: "When

8. Two years earlier Bowles voiced the same idea after seeing Charlotte Cushman play Romeo: "real tragedies are so [illegible] in life that the stage ones, however well done, do not impress my soul."

I lost the use of my Eyes it was a comfort to think there were so few real *books* that I could easily find some one to read me all of them." To Louisa Norcross: "This little sheet of paper has lain for several years in my Shakespeare, and though it is blotted and antiquated is endeared by its resting-place."

Among the plays Louisa may have heard Fanny Kemble read was *Antony and Cleopatra,* on December 16, 1859. We lack the connecting links, but it is clear that by the time the poet returned to Amherst in fall 1864 she was well prepared:

> How my blood bounded! Shakespeare was the first; Antony & Cleopatra where Enobarbus laments the amorous lapse of his master. Here is the ring of it – "heart that in the scuffles of great fights hath burst the buckle on his breast"
>
> Then I thought why ~~touch~~ clasp any hand but this, give me ever to drink of this wine.

he sustaining attraction pull + the arts 8

No play meant more to Dickinson or was quoted more often. As Judith Farr has shown, she saw aspects of herself in the great-hearted voluptuary who renounces the world for what his heart says is better than it. Associating Cleopatra with her sister-in-law, the poet neatly marked two speeches in Sue's expensive edition of Shakespeare: "Age cannot wither her" and "Egypt, thou knew'st too well, / My heart was to thy rudder tied." In a note sent next door in the 1880s, Emily restated her near-but-distant relation to Sue by taking the part of the captivated Roman: "Susan's Calls are like Antony's Supper – 'And pays his Heart for what his Eyes eat, only.'" Her identification with the buckle-bursting soldier went very deep, incorporating her sense of herself as fighter and lover, boldly daring to forfeit everything.

Was it during her second summer in Cambridge, living by her ears and not her eyes, that she composed the elegiac meditation "Further in summer than the birds"? Written originally in seven stanzas, the poem was reconceived by early 1866, when the last five stanzas, discursive and unfocused, were replaced with two infinitely tauter ones. Dickinson had always been fascinated by detached sounds—an ax ringing in the woods, wind swishing through foliage, crickets stridulating everywhere. By August, when songbirds have fallen silent, cricket song has become the ubiquitous but scarcely noticed background. Now that the poet was in her mid-thirties, it was time to reach for the meaning of this quiet, constant sound:

> Further in Summer than the Birds
> Pathetic from the Grass
> A minor Nation celebrates
> Its unobtrusive Mass.
>
> No Ordinance be seen
> So gradual the Grace
> A pensive Custom it becomes
> Enlarging Loneliness.
>
> Antiquest[9] felt at Noon
> When August burning low
> Arise this spectral Canticle
> Repose to typify
>
> Remit as yet no Grace
> No Furrow on the Glow
> Yet a Druidic Difference
> Enhances Nature now

Fr895D

The poem is as unemphatic as the crickets, with nothing dramatic or painful happening, no distracting scratch, no "Furrow on the Glow." As

---

9. Dickinson's first version of line 9 had another unusual superlative: " 'Tis Audiblest, at Dusk." The next version used a comparative, "Antiquer felt at Noon," which was then amended with an *st* written over the *r*. She evidently wanted the superlative of "antique," perhaps to convey the classic and the age-old, two qualities she had long associated with cricket song. In August 1854, writing John L. Graves after Commencement was over and Amherst had quieted, she compared a merry woman friend to a honeybee "among more antique insects."

the summer noon blazes, the pacified listener sinks into the pensive background drone. Some songs propose to release us from loneliness; this song merely enlarges it. This is all there is, this is all there is: that is what the crickets say. It is the chant of acceptance, not Christian but Druid, leaving behind a keener sense of nature and solitude, a recognition that everything is different from what one thought and hoped, and that one has already begun to live with that.

The war was over. The time had come for repose.

Part Seven

1866-1886

How everlasting are the Lips

Known only to the Dew –

These are the Brides of permanence –

Supplanting me and you.

About 1873. Fr1299, stanza 2. Reproduction 78% original size.

Chapter 19

1866–1870: Repose

When the large dog that had been Dickinson's companion for sixteen years expired in the winter of 1865–1866, Thomas Wentworth Higginson received a death notice pared to the minimum:

> Carlo died –
>> E. Dickinson
> Would you instruct me now?

She was not asking for consolation but for a critique of the enclosed "Further in summer than the birds," which seems to have perplexed the recipient: the manuscript still has his penciled "Insect-Sounds?" His letter of reply must have said something about the elusiveness of poem and author alike, as her following communication opened with a flat denial: "Whom my Dog understood could not elude others." Still, the next time she sent the poem out, seventeen years later, she condescended to give the reader a helping hand by calling it "My Cricket."

Carlo's death marked the end of something for Dickinson, who in summer 1866 admitted to Higginson, "I explore but little since my mute

Confederate [died]." Immortality was still "the Flood subject" for her, but for the time being she was content to stay on shore, which she had been told "was the safest place for a Finless Mind." In another letter from 1866, she spoke of her "slowness," asked her preceptor to be patient with her, and transcribed lines composed three years earlier:

> *Except the smaller size*
> *No lives are round –*
> *These – hurry to a sphere*
> *And show and end –*
> *The larger – slower grow*
> *And later hang –*
> *The Summers of Hesperides*
> *Are long.*
>
> Fr606C

Consonant with Higginson's advice to young writers to be less precipitous in publishing, the poem was also a statement about Dickinson's creative production. She evidently knew she was not one of "the smaller size," an early-summer fruit that ripens and drops, but a late-summer apple, a keeper, one of the golden pomes guarded by the daughters of Hesperus. For the first time in her writing life, she signed herself, simply, "Dickinson."

Beginning in 1858, the poet's heroic production had been driven in part by the working-out of inner matters. Eighteen sixty-five, the last year she kept up her blistering pace, resulted in more than two hundred poems recorded on the unsewn sheafs termed sets. During the next five years, no longer assembling these, she composed only about seventy poems—less than in any one of the previous five years. There were fewer letters as well. This abruptly reduced activity has been read, reasonably enough, as a sign of dormancy or even exhaustion. Also, as Aífe Murray has pointed out, the four-year period in which the Dickinsons were without steady domestic help neatly coincides with the poet's lessened productivity. But that is not to say the slowdown wasn't deliberate—a version of the dignified seasonal repose of "Except the smaller size" and "Further in summer than the birds."

Remarkably, of the seven poems written in the first person singular from 1866 through 1869, only one has a speaker engaged in reviewing the past: "I noticed People disappeared / When but a little child – " (Fr1154). And as the full text makes clear, the "I" of this poem is not so much a version of the writer as a generalized observer reflecting on how death is disguised. For four years, in other words, Dickinson does not seem to have produced a single first-person poem recapitulating or reflecting on her past. The writer who had lavished herself on acts of memory, exploring her history, her singularity, her starved triumphs, her hard-won mastery, had for the time being stopped trying to tell her story.

Of course, there are poems without an "I" that evidently concern the writer's identity and history. From 1867, one of her most slenderly documented years, we have a composition reminiscent of the tough boasts of 1864 and 1865: "There is a strength in proving that it can be borne." The concluding lines, which combine Jesus' walking on water with the need to "fight," hint at Dickinson's sense of embattled achievement:

> *The ship might be of satin had it not to fight –*
> *To walk on seas requires cedar Feet*
>
> Fr1133

Another poem touches on the satisfactions of autonomy and victory over circumstance:

> *There is another Loneliness*
> *That many die without – [;]*
> *Not want of friend occasions it*
> *Or circumstance of Lot*
>
> *But nature, sometimes, sometimes thought [;]*
> *And whoso it befall*
> *Be richer than could be revealed*
> *By mortal numeral –*
>
> Fr1138A

That is, there exists a rare and rich type of loneliness, one that does not stem from social or other deprivations but rather from native endowment or personal "thought." Perhaps, in her case, the poet considered "thought" the right explanation. That, at any rate, was the view taken by Vinnie, who had begun to take a signal pride in her sister. Once, specifying the distinct contribution of each family member, she wrote that Emily "had to think—she was the only one of us who had that to do."

About 1871, when Dickinson was reengaged in her vocation after her five-year quiescence, she wrote a poem that looks like an indirect summation of her desperate struggle in the early 1860s. The opening line may refer to Henry Thoreau, whom she had come to admire.

> 'Twas fighting for his Life he was –
> That sort accomplish well –
> The Ordnance of Vitality
> Is frugal of its Ball.
>
> It aims once – kills once – conquers once –
> There is no second War
> In that Campaign inscrutable
> Of the Interior.

Fr1230

These lines suggest how Dickinson looked back on her beset years, when she was driven in self-defense to perfect her "aim" and accomplish something once and for all. They form an intriguing contrast to the more famous "My life had stood a loaded gun," from 1863, in which the speaker also kills as often as she shoots:

> None stir the second time –
> On whom I lay a Yellow Eye –

Dickinson *was* the gun in the earlier work—a hint of the extent to which her existence had been subsumed in "fight." In the later and freer

So full of the arts to express > the thought; the feeling; the truth
1866–1870: Repose
to get down to the truth, the rockbed of truth
501

work, by contrast, she is able to consider another's effort and to gener-
alize about the nature of the battle. Before, she was caught up in the
idea of living for and serving a master. Now she understands the basic
issue as fighting for one's own life. In 1863 the story lacked a resolution
(and in fact many readers have been dissatisfied with the way the poem
ends):

> *For I have but the power to kill,*
> *Without – the power to die –*
>
> Fr764

In 1871 the result was more definitive: "That sort accomplish well."
These contrasts attest to what Dickinson had achieved in the intervening years: a relaxed sense of security, a mature and detached perspective
on herself.

That seems to be the basic story of 1865–1870, a period in which
Dickinson slowly circled back on herself from higher ground. It was a
process of reaching out and enlargement in which a number of people
figured in complex ways.

Servants

A few months before Carlo's death, the Dickinsons lost the household
servant, Margaret O'Bryan, the same age as Austin, on whom they had
depended for some nine years. On October 18, 1865, she got married in
working-class Holyoke's Catholic church. Two weeks later, when the
poet's brother returned from a visit to the Smiths in Geneva, where Sue
and Ned were staying on, he let his "dear Spouse" know how the hunt for
Margaret's replacement had gone: "No girl at the other house yet—consequence—depression."

Chances are, the complaints he heard came from Vinnie, Mother, or
Father, not Emily, who pointedly made light of minor troubles. Once,
when Margaret was still present and objected to furnace heat in early Oc-

tober, Emily agreed to "dwell in my bonnet and suffer comfortably."[1] It had been her job to dry the dishes as Margaret washed. Doing the washing herself now, she "winced at her loss" but quickly accepted the new domestic order: "to all except anguish, the mind soon adjusts." Apparently, Margaret was a very large woman. The first time Samuel Bowles called after her departure, according to Vinnie, the front door was opened ("strange as that may seem") by Emily. "Where is your Colossus?" asked the visitor. "She has rode," said the poet, not missing a beat.

It was not until 1869 that the Dickinsons finally reeled in a permanent successor for Margaret. In the interim the laundry was probably done by washerwomen and some of the sewing by seamstresses, but the Dickinson women had to shoulder more of the basic housekeeping work than they had been accustomed to. In the new division of labor, baking and dessert making seem to have fallen to the poet, so that, deeply sequestered as she already was, she now gave even more of her time to the family. Just as in 1856–1858, when Mother's invalidism furnished another reason not to leave home, the new work detail in kitchen, pantry, and sink room reduced social contacts and writing alike.

"The art of making perfect bread," in the opinion of Emily's old friend Joseph Lyman and his wife, Laura, who together brought out a comprehensive domestic manual in 1867, *The Philosophy of House-Keeping*, "outweighs every other domestic merit." Dickinson became so expert at this art, in Clara Newman's memory, that her father "prefered" (translation: demanded) bread from her hands alone. Even after Margaret's successor had settled in, the poet still made "all the bread," as Higginson noted in 1870, "for her father only likes hers."

The longest chapter in *The Philosophy of House-Keeping* was on "Cakes, Desserts, and Delicacies"—all Dickinson specialties. Her gingerbread was so successful both Sue and Elizabeth Holland secured the recipe: 4 cups flour, ½ cup butter, ½ cup cream, a tablespoon of ginger, a

ik a monk - Maşet Breel mākes [handwritten marginalia]

---

1. However, following these words came a complaint suppressed in the 1894 and all later editions of her letters: "Father didn't go to Northampton, the omnibus meeting was postponed, so I have to roast meat and vegetables much against my will."

teaspoon of soda, and salt, with molasses for sweetening. At a time when a proper cake was understood to be "winy and spicy and fruity," hers were no exception. Her famous recipe for black cake, which included cloves, nutmeg, cinnamon, and five pounds of raisins, was probably designed for her father's annual Commencement reception. When she told Higginson, "& people must have puddings," he noted that she spoke "*very* dreamily, as if they were comets." It was a hot August day, and her visitor may not have known how much stirring at a cast-iron stove a pudding involved.

In February 1869 the Dickinsons' long search for steady domestic help came to a successful conclusion. Margaret Maher ("Maggie"), born in Tipperary and employed by Lucius M. and Clarinda Boltwood, had accompanied them on their move to Hartford. When Maggie's father died and her brother-in-law Thomas Kelley lost an arm in a bad fall, she rejoined her family in Amherst, taking temporary jobs and intending to eventually return to Hartford or go to a brother in California. But one of her short-term employers was Edward Dickinson, and, judging from the young woman's letters to Mrs. Boltwood, he was not about to let this faithful and devoted servant work for anyone else. Even when Maggie went to Palmer "to get the girl that worket for them before me," the Dickinsons "would not take her." Maggie found them kindly enough, but their home felt strange to her and she had too much time on her hands: "there is one grate trouble that I have not half enough of work so that I must play with the cats to Plase Miss Vinny." She insisted she would "do as I like when I will get a chance without giving much notice," but when she tried to quit, "Mr D" made her feel the Dickinsons would "be very angry with us all so we will wait for a nother time."

Another time never arrived. Maggie's California brother wrote Edward he wished her to stay in Amherst "for the Preasant," and her sister "would not give me any consent" to go to Hartford. For thirty years Maher worked for the Dickinsons as housekeeper, cook, and maid, at a salary (in the 1890s) of $3 a week. Her afternoons she spent with her family, but she slept at the Homestead. Humble and honest, loyal, eager to serve, she committed herself to a lifelong relationship defined partly by the labor market and partly by family ties and Irish and Yankee ideas of class, subservience, and patronage.

The mix of close affection and inequality can make a modern reader uncomfortable, as when, in a letter to Louisa, Emily associated Maggie and a hired man with draft animals and pets:

> Tim is washing Dick's [the horse's] feet, and talking to him now and then in an intimate way. Poor fellow, how he warmed when I gave him your message! The red reached clear to his beard, he was so gratified; and Maggie stood as still for hers as a puss for patting. The hearts of these poor people lie so unconcealed you bare them with a smile.

Over the years Maher became a strong and indispensable presence and Dickinson's relationship with her deepened and intensified, but it was always *de haut en bas*. Those who would like to democratize the poet should give some thought to how she might have patronized their forebears. And those who see nothing but class privilege should keep in mind that she was a noncitizen by force of custom and law, that many doors were closed to her, and that she left behind more good hard work than any of us.

One of the things we most want to know about Emily the poem-and breadmaker is her private recipe for mixing the high and the low. In relation to her era's male authorities and institutions, she often presented herself as childish and subservient, or childish and disobedient. But she also had a way of pulling down the mighty, as when she ridiculed an excessively dignified judge by appealing to the Father of all: "Complacency! My Father! in such a world as this, when we must all stand barefoot before thy jasper doors!"

Going barefoot (figuratively) was one of the strategies by which the poet defined herself in relation to society and strove for an unmediated relation to nature and spirit. But she also remained a member in good standing of New England's Protestant patriciate. Footfree and classy, she imported her odd social position into an artistry that struck many of her Brahmin contemporaries as flagrantly careless.

And Masters

Edward Dickinson was the last man in Amherst who was deemed to be a "squire," a role that mixed property, privilege, and responsibility in a way that was starting to look archaic.

As a man of property, he continued to be an active shareholder in the Hampden Cotton Manufacturing Company, now going into decline. He also remained invested in the private, toll-charging Sunderland Bridge, on one occasion refusing to accommodate a customer who demanded special terms for a four-horse team pulling ties: "The owners have some rights, and for one, I shall execute them, if any man undertakes to rule over us." In 1868 he and his son moved their prosperous law firm into "a very pleasant office" in Palmer's Block, the site of his first office forty years earlier. The postwar years saw a healthy growth in his net worth: $28,700 in 1866, $32,600 in 1867, $47,800 in 1868. No longer quite so prominent in the First Church, he continued to take a keen interest in the Northampton Lunatic Asylum.

Edward's biggest achievement for the decade was to help bring Massachusetts Agricultural College to Amherst. In securing this, the town's second college (today it is the University of Massachusetts at Amherst), the local citizenry had to pledge the large sum of $50,000 in order to get the charter. Following in the old squire's footsteps, Edward played a major role in pushing things through and quashing opposition. When a bitter fight broke out over the campus layout, he was an active behind-the-scenes operator, going "to see the Governor" and keeping in touch with the landscape consultant Frederick Law Olmsted.

Father's distinctive voice comes through loud and clear in two letters of the time. On Christmas 1868, after Samuel Bowles's attack on a crooked financier landed the editor in jail for a night, Edward weighed in with voluminous dignity: "I would rather have borne your name, on that night in Ludlow St. jail, and have been one of the troops of friends who made New York ring with the recital of your wrongs, and the execration of the robber & thief . . . than to have owned the mines of Potosi." Although Emily never engaged in just this sort of grandstand rhetoric, her writing shows a similar fondness for sententious peroration. The following year, she, too, made the old Bolivian silver mines at Potosí a symbol of supreme value:

> Potosi never to be spent
> But hoarded in the mind [:]
> What Misers wring their hands tonight
> For Indies in the Ground!
>
> Fr1162 (J1117)

As the meter indicates, she moved the accent forward on PoTOsi.

The second letter was prompted by Governor Alexander H. Bullock's farewell address to the legislature. Singling out what he regarded as the chief executive's most honorable acts, Edward praised him for nominating Judge Benjamin F. Thomas (who had left the Republican Party during the war), for sustaining the majesty of the law by hanging "Murderer Green," and for making a legislative committee "appointed to insult the Governor . . . [feel] like whipped Spaniels." Edward's hope that the political will of President-elect Grant would be as fearless as "his military courage" shows he still looked forward to the day when firm authority would put an end to the slack compromises of democratic rule.

Although Edward and Austin often worked in tandem, as when they got Samuel Bowles onto the board of trustees of Amherst College in spite of his Unitarianism, Austin did not seek public office or make a name for himself outside Amherst. He helped run the town, but his real interests often proved aesthetic: instead of helping to found colleges and railroads like his grandfather and father, he specialized in architecture, interior decorating, landscaping. He guided the building program at Amherst College, and he also played a key role in the First Church's move from the old wooden meetinghouse near College Hill to a new, stylish, and expensive granite sanctuary on Main Street. Judging from parish records and other sources, the poet's brother had a hand in the two contingent commitments that overcame the embattled opposition to this move: only if a new edifice was built would the Reverend Jonathan L. Jenkins accept a call; and only if it was built on Main Street would Henry F. Hills, the owner of a palm-leaf hat factory, contribute his thousands. Designed by the architect George Hawthorne, the church went up on the old Montague place across from the Evergreens, its tall spire and massive grace and stained-glass windows announcing that Amherst, the Dickinson quarter especially, was a place of distinction. It isn't known whether Emily ever crossed the street to look inside. According to Vinnie, she crept to the Evergreens' hemlock hedge one night and peered through.

Unlike his father and grandfathers, who worked hard for their local standing, Austin pretty much took privilege for granted. In him, the Dickinson determination devolved into the sort of haughtiness that sees pleasure as its due and solaces itself with vengeful fantasy when balked. When the Agricultural College's enemies happened to win a round, he wrote Sue that if he could "come suddenly upon the managers against us felicitating . . . I'd make a rattling among" them. When a Boston gallery tried his patience, he looked forward to the time when they would "fairly *cry out* down there for me to come and take anything I please at my own price. They've tormented and tantalized me long enough." Austin's way of coping with the modern world was to turn his home and his town into a charming manorial park, out of which he gazed with the cold disdain we see in his photographs. The man's bitter superiority was a distant kin of his sister's veiled mastery.

Bitter superiority

Dust and Dew

In her long and well-informed obituary of the poet, Sue attributed the occasional publication of her verse to friends whose admiration "would turn love to larceny." One of these loving thefts took place on Valentine's Day, 1866. The criminal was undoubtedly Sue herself:

The Snake

A narrow fellow in the grass
Occasionally rides;

> *You may have met him – did you not?*
> *His notice instant is . . .*

Since Dickinson had let Higginson understand she "did not print," she
feared he would consider her "ostensible," untruthful, if the poem was
picked up by other papers and he happened to see it. Explaining that it
was "robbed of me," she singled out for objection the inserted question
mark, which forced a pause between the "third and fourth" lines and thus
undid the effect she evidently wanted—the abrupt shock of encounter.

> *You may have met Him – did you not*
> *His notice sudden is . . .*
>
> Fr1096B

This letter offers her only known comment on the unauthorized publication of her work. Her tacit acceptance of the newspaper's conventional
line divisions suggests she did not regard her manuscript's spilled-over
lines as essential to the poem's meaning. What she resented was the tam-
pering with content, the act of theft, and the publicity. Years later, a
woman who had grown up in Amherst remembered hearing Sue confess, probably referring to this poem, that its appearance "nearly caused
a breach in the close friendship of the two."

In September Samuel and Mary Bowles arranged for a nurse to go
to the Evergreens "as desired," and two months later, on the night of November 29, Sue gave birth to the second of her three children, a girl.
Named Martha after her aunt in Geneva, she showed the same drive for
dominance and self-expression as her mother and father. At about age
three, she was characterized by the poet as "stern and lovely – literary,
they tell me – a graduate of Mother Goose and otherwise ambitious."

Dickinson's messages to Sue continued to profess an undying love—
"Busy missing you" and "Susan's idolator keeps a Shrine for Susan"—and
to work out new variations on the idea that distance insures closeness.
Although most of the notes and poems are so uncontextualized it is impossible to say how they contributed to the ongoing relationship, there
are two buoyant and newsy letters written while Sue was summering on

The spiritual "frost"
Overtaking human civilization
1866–1870: Repose   509

the coast or visiting her sister in Geneva. In one of these, Emily reports she "Dreamed of your meeting Tennyson in Ticknor and Fields – Where the Treasure is, there the Brain is also." The dream tells us how occupied she was with Sue, and how exalted a sense she had of her sister-in-law's literary stature.

Some of the poems sent to Sue in this period seem to express a grimmer mood than usual. "I cannot meet the spring unmoved" (Fr1122) regards the season as a time for mixed feelings and hesitation rather than renewal. Another poem opposing seasonal expectations declares that Thanksgiving can be honestly celebrated only by those who feel "no sharp subtraction / From the early Sum"—who haven't surrendered dear ones to "an Acre or a Caption" (Fr1110B). This surprisingly bitter statement, composed in late 1865 and sent next door about 1867, calls to mind the many Gilbert family deaths that Sue would have remembered.

Dickinson's most wrathful lyric, from about 1866, narrates a fight to preserve a flower from frost—the sort of effort she often wrote about in connection with garden and conservatory. In this poem, however, the frost is so snakelike, aggressive, and persistent and the speaker has such a high stake in the outcome, that it is clear that larger issues are involved. The narrator is one of a group that has struggled to save the doomed flower by taking it "to Sea – / To mountain – to the Sun." As the frost came nearer, "we wedged" ourselves

> *Himself and her between –*
> *Yet easy as the narrow Snake*
> *He forked his way along*
>
> *Till all her helpless beauty bent*
> *And then our wrath begun –*
> *We hunted him to his Ravine*
> *We chased him to his Den –*
>
> *We hated Death and hated Life*
> *And nowhere was to go – . . .*
>
> Fr1130C (J1136)

The probable explanation of this unusually agitated response, so different from the chilled awe of "Zero at the Bone," is that the poem reacts
to the death of Susan D. Phelps, a friend about whom almost nothing is
known. The friendship went back to 1854, when Phelps, of an old
Hadley family, became engaged to Henry Vaughan Emmons. In the intervening years, as the engagement was broken and the young woman
succumbed to a serious illness, her connection with the poet seems to
have deepened. On December 1, 1865, the day before she died, her
brother noted in his journal that she had been "very sick for some days
under Dr. Bonney's care Today Dr Fiske was sent for . . . but gave no
hope." Her death was reported in the *Republican* and other papers on
December 5, the date of her funeral. It was probably the memory of this
day that led Dickinson, five years later, to inscribe "December 5th" at the
head of her copies of two important poems, one of which begins,

> *The Days that we can spare*
> *Are those a Function die*
> *Or Friend or Nature . . .*
> Fr1229C

Phelps was thirty-eight at the time of her death, the cause of which was
not recorded. Her memorial window in Amherst's Grace Episcopal
Church, dating from 1866, shows a crown of thorns captioned "My soul
waiteth for the Lord," and a crown of victory: "Till the day break and the
shadows flee away."

About 1867 the poet sent Sue a somber reflection on the sounds of
crickets and cicadas:

> *The murmuring of Bees, has ceased*
> *But murmuring of some*
> *Posterior, prophetic,*
> *Has simultaneous come.*

These, the year's "lower metres," are

The Revelations of the Book
Whose Genesis was June . . .

Now, they suggest, not repose exactly, as in "Further in summer than the birds," but a steady process of mutual detachment and alienation. What the poet is finally left with, "As Accent fades to interval / With separating Friends," are her own thoughts, now "More intimate . . . / Than Persons" (Fr1142B). It is the same idea as in one of the "December 5th" poems, "A wind that rose through not a leaf" (Fr1216C), which celebrates a certain kind of self-communing self-sufficiency.

After 1865, according to Bowles's friend and biographer, the editor often showed signs of "heavy shadows" on his inner life, a "deep heart-hunger." Once, he sent Sue a vivid warning against the lassitude and isolation into which he felt himself sinking:

> Don't you of all people grow faint & weary, & feel life & friends wearing away. Better go out & hang yourself, as I would, if I dared. There is nothing so sad as such living death; to feel your power gone, the charms fade away; the trees grow bare, & the dead leaves rustle hollow around & on you; others take your place, do your work, win your friends,—& you still cumber the ground. It is to come back, after death, & see how little you are missed.

Anxious about Sue's recurring prostrations, in 1868 he tried to flatter her out of depression, declaring that "Life should not be dreary or barren to such as you." But his letters, less frequent now, tended to dwell on the loss of freshness: "How are you? Last I heard Austin had a bad cold. Has he thawed? Tell a fellow. And the mother—and the babies—& the sisters, & all—, Speak & break the thick silence." A lament of his in 1869 about "great passages of silence" found an echo in a poem sent to Sue about 1870, "Great streets of silence led away" (Fr1166B). It was as Emily had said (getting things exactly right): "Accent fades to interval / With separating Friends."

Judging from the remnants of the poet's correspondence with

Louisa and Frances, there were few cold intervals with them. In 1867, as Martha Ackmann has surmised, the cousins went to stay with sickly Eliza Coleman Dudley in Middletown, Connecticut, while her husband went to Europe. On July 2, with no male guard in the house, a man was discovered under a bed: the classic threat. The news got into the *Hartford Courant* and soon made its way to Amherst, eliciting a fearful and sympathetic letter: "Oh, Loo, why were the children sent too faint to stand alone. Every hour is anxious now, and heaven protect the lamb, who shared her fleece, with a timider, even Emily." The children sent as guards were the Norcrosses and the lamb was Eliza, who had shared her fleece with Emily by shielding her "from publicity" during Commencement receptions.

A Norcross family letter from 1868 noting that Louisa was "unusually well" suggests her health had been uncertain. It was apparently in that year that Dickinson wrote to express "grief and surprise" at an emergency and offer her best encouragement: "Not a flake assaults my birds but it freezes me. Comfort, little creatures – whatever befall us, this world is but this world. Think of that great courageous place we have never seen!" It was her customary and effective strategy: gathering strength precisely from what was beyond experience.

In spring 1869, on a visit to the Dickinsons, Louisa sat outside and gathered a petticoat for Mrs. Dickinson while the hired man, Horace Church, was in a tree, grafting scions and "ogling" (Emily's word) the visitor. That fall, when her cousin's troubles had cleared up, the poet rejoiced "that my wren can rise and touch the sky again. We all have moments with the dust, but the dew is given." Again, one notes the emphatic resiliency.

The spirited letters sent to Elizabeth Holland in 1865 and 1866 offer further evidence that Emily wasn't held down by the low spirits that depressed Sue and Samuel. She couldn't "stop smiling" when Father discovered to his chagrin that his steelyard had been giving him an unfair advantage, or when her second cousin Perez Cowan, a senior at Amherst, revealed that Elizabeth would be present to back her up at the annual reception. Elizabeth had a cheerful and elastic personality, and

Emily's letters to her are full of ecstatic springtime dispatches: "The Wind blows gay today and the Jays bark like Blue Terriers," or again, "I hear today for the first the river in the tree." Still, as was the case in many other relationships, the poet's great affection for this friend was to some extent a product of distance:

> After you went, a low wind warbled through the house like a spacious bird, making it high but lonely. When you had gone the love came. I supposed it would. The supper of the heart is when the guest has gone.
>
> Shame is so intrinsic in a strong affection. . . .

Comparing this to the poet's early letters to Abiah Root, Jane Humphrey, and Sue Gilbert, we see how much her understanding of human intimacy had matured. The old, seductive dream of perfect union with another had been left far behind.

Once, after Elizabeth made the mistake of sending a joint letter to the Dickinson sisters, she received a brisk reproof:

> Sister,
>
> A mutual plum is not a plum. I was too respectful to take the pulp and do not like a stone.
>
> Send no union letters. The soul must go by Death alone, so, it must by life, if it is a soul.
>
> If a committee – no matter . . .

The implication is that some of us—but not the writer, and not Elizabeth—are merely aggregated entities.

Nothing made the poet's toughness stand out in high relief like the religious platitudes she had grown up with. Perez Cowan, a descendant of the Dickinsons who moved to Tennessee in the 1820s, was converted at fourteen and before entering the ministry impressed a college classmate as "one of the sweetest natures that I ever met . . . a paragon of refinement, demeanor, morality, and religious devotion." After the sister closest to him in age, Nannie Cowan Meem, died of a "wasting" disease, Perez sent Dickinson a statement of his faith in the hereafter. Presently, the poet registered her tart dissent:

> You speak with so much trust of that which only trust can prove,
> it makes me feel away, as if my English mates spoke sudden in Italian.
> It grieves me that you speak of Death with so much expecta-
> tion. . . . Dying is a wild Night and a new Road.

Knowing how "hard" and unconsolatory her words were, she wished she could soften them in direct speech: "We bruise each other less in talking than in writing." But she still sent the letter.

A poem recorded slightly later conveys Dickinson's repugnance for dogmatic certainty and axiomatic truth:

> *Experiment escorts us last –*
> *His pungent company*
> *Will not allow an Axiom*
> *An Opportunity –*
>
> Fr1181

We never know what awaits us at the "last": in one respect at least, Dickinson had gone back to the Calvinism of her flinty ancestors, who insisted that no one could possibly know ahead of time who would be let into heaven by their unfathomable deity.

A Quite Rugged Woman in White

From the dying Violetta of *La Traviata* to various white-appareled avatars in popular American culture, the frail, poetic female saint was a major nineteenth-century type—in some men's eyes. Joseph Lyman had two friends he associated with this pure, retiring ideal, Araminta Wharton of Nashville and Emily Dickinson of Amherst, neither of whom, he felt sure, would ever marry. At some point between his return North in

September 1863 and his death from smallpox in January 1872, he renewed his acquaintance with Dickinson, now much more reclusive than
when he last saw her in 1851. Afterward, he made their interview, what
could pass for one, the basis of an impressionistic portrait, followed by a
series of excerpts from Dickinson's letters. An experienced journalist,
Lyman apparently had some sort of article in mind. The plan was to
catch the reader's attention with a dramatic entrance:

Emily

"Things are not what they seem"

NIGHT IN MIDSUMMER

A Library dimly lighted, ~~five~~ three mignonettes in a little stand.
Enter a spirit clad in white, figure so draped as to be misty[,] face
moist, translucent alabaster, forehead firmer as of statuary marble.
Eyes once bright hazel now melted & fused so as to be two, dreamy,
wondering wells of expression, eyes that see no forms but gla[n]ce
swiftly ~~& at once~~ to the core of all things—hands small, firm, deft
but utterly ~~discharged~~ emancipated from all ~~fleshly~~ clasping[s?] of
perishable things, very firm strong little hands absolutely under control of the brain, types of quite rugged health. Mouth made for nothing & used for nothing but uttering choice speech, rare ~~words~~
thoughts, glittering starry misty ~~words~~ figures, winged words.

This description is so dematerialized and "misty" (mouth not used for
eating?) that doubts as to its accuracy inevitably arise. Many years after
it was committed to paper, the poet's death prompted Lyman's widow to
drop a breezy note on one of his old associates: "I was just 'bursting' with
a letter when that notice of Emily Dickinson's death came, but I said
'No, I *wont* write till he does'. . . . You didn't see Emily, did you? Mr.
Lyman didn't really see her, tho' he talked with her." This more or less
confirms that her husband's portrayal was not strictly based on observation, being in part a fanciful spirit-sketch the public could be expected to
recognize and appreciate.

But the white attire, something all Emily-watchers made a point of specifying, seems to be accurate. From the Bible to popular culture, the absence of color was a symbol of sinlessness, spirituality, renunciation. Exactly when the poet began wearing white year-round isn't known. In December 1860, as if putting a stop to rumor, she pointedly asked Louisa Norcross to "tell 'the public' that at present I wear a brown dress." But in early 1862 she recorded a poem that speaks of a vocation for white as a sign of singleness and dedication:

> *A solemn thing – it was – I said –*
> *A Woman – white – to be –*
> *And wear – if God should count me fit –*
> *Her blameless mystery –*

Fr307

Dickinson's one surviving article of clothing is a white cotton dress thought to have been sewn circa 1878–1882. Of the type known as a house dress or wrapper and designed for daily life at home, the garment has a loosely fitted waist, round collar, cuffs, and a pocket; the fabric is a patterned dimity. With its tucks and gores and edge lacing and mother-of-pearl buttons (in front), the dress looks ornate to modern eyes but was ordinary and unpretentious as compared to Gilded Age fashions, which were form-fitting and expensive and involved exacting procedures for sewing, wearing, and maintaining. Whatever Dickinson's purpose in adopting simple white wear, there were good practical reasons for sticking to it: no corsets or expensive dressmakers were required, and one could forget about dyes fading or running.[2] (Once, when the poet added her sister's shoes and bonnet to the wash "to have them nice when she got home," Margaret O'Bryan "accused Vinnie of calicoes"—figured cottons. Evidently, the color had run.)

A fastidious upper-middle-class woman who preferred to wear

---

2. Another way to save and simplify was to move to Italy, as Charlotte Sewall Eastman did for twelve years; from there she wrote Emily and Vinnie in 1872: "I hear so much of the trouble of living and the extravagance of it and of the horrors of servants. . . . Crowds come abroad to be rid of those evils."

white wrappers might understandably be averse to receiving well-dressed callers. To the extent that Dickinson abandoned fashion, in other words, she would have had yet another reason to elude the public gaze. As early as 1867, if a Mack family member's reminiscence can be trusted, Dickinson had begun to talk to certain visitors from the other side of a door "which stood ajar." Similarly, the local undertaker remembered "Miss Emily" as "coyally greeting me from behind the *bannister* but never seeing me." Some such practice would explain how Lyman, going up to Massachusetts with his friend Alfred B. Crandell (also in publishing), could talk to the poet but not "really see her."

Although Dr. Williams wanted Dickinson to have a follow-up exam in May 1866, her eyes were well enough in late 1865 for her to make final copies in ink of thirty-nine poems; by March her father decided she could do without the checkup. Since she never again spoke of her eyes as troubling her, even in writing Elizabeth Holland, whose visual problems led to the surgical removal of an eye in 1872, there is little basis for suspecting an ongoing, let alone a permanent, impairment.

Was Dickinson's health as "rugged" as Lyman said? In spring 1868, her father informed a brother-in-law that "we are having bad colds," adding eleven days later that, "with the exception of colds, we are quite well." That seems to have been shortly before Emily wrote Sue, "I have not tasted Spring – Should there be other Aprils, We will perhaps dine." Once, writing her cousins, she spoke of "physical weakness" and said she was "in bed to-day – a curious place for me." In late 1869 she thanked Louisa "for recollecting my weakness. I am not so well as to forget I was ever ill, but better and working. I suppose we must all 'ail till evening.'" It may have been the following May that, speaking of herself in the third person, she told Louisa that "your remembrance of her is very sweetly touching. She is so weak and lonely." (The last sentence, transcribed for Mabel Loomis Todd, was later suppressed, and has until now not seen print.) That summer, however, the poet was well enough to invite Higginson to Amherst. All in all, though the evidence is vague and conflicting, Dickinson's health looks somewhat less than "rugged" in 1866–1870, though not as threatening as her sister-in-law's (as reflected in Samuel's letters).

During the entire five-year period, there is only one poem that sounds the accent of a self-sacrificial invalid. Making herself "fit" for the sake of others, the poet turns the word into a verb to capture the sense of "fight":

> *I fit for them – I seek the Dark*
> *Till I am thorough fit.*
> *The labor is a sober one*
> *With this sufficient Sweet*
>
> *That abstinence of mine produce*
> *A purer food for them . . .*
>
>   Fr1129

Written in pencil and thus harder to date than manuscripts in ink, these lines have been conjecturally assigned to 1866. If composed earlier, during the compulsory avoidance of light in 1864 and 1865, they may have been prompted by the provisional discipline of inactivity. We recall Dickinson's excuse for not seeing Bowles in late 1862: "I gave my part that they might have the more."

Yet most of the poems and letters from this period show a robust interest in life and a continuing effort at compact and energetic expression. Once, when Vinnie was gone and the poet had the housekeeping, she sent Sue one of her liveliest self-portraits: "I am so hurried with Parents that I run all Day with my tongue abroad, like a Summer Dog." When Sue went to the coast in 1866, not long after the publication of *Cape Cod,* Emily expressed her enthusiasm for her latest idol by asking, "Was the Sea cordial? Kiss him for Thoreau." When a new acquaintance happened to quote Thoreau,[3] she "hastened to press her visitor's hand as she said, 'From this time we are acquainted.' " If the visitor, like the teller of this anecdote, was Ellen E. Dickinson (a first cousin's bride), the meeting probably occurred in September 1869. Hidden as she was and rela-

---

3. In 1881 a series of fires elicited this flash of wit: "The fire-bells are oftener now, almost, than the church-bells. Thoreau would wonder which did the most harm."

tively quiescent, Dickinson was emphatically not in retreat from life. What Lyman may have meant by "rugged health" was her obvious and amazing vitality. Maybe that was why he headed his sketch, "Things are not what they seem."

Others

Dickinson's impetus came not only from "nature" or "thought," as she said in "There is another loneliness" (Fr1138), but from her various friends, some old, some new. This aspect of her life is nicely summed up by her advice to Perez Cowan, mourning for his sister: "I am glad you are working. Others are anodyne. You remembered Clara." Perez's painkiller was his remembering to send best wishes for Clara Newman, who had recently married and escaped the Evergreens, taking Anna with her. ("Marm D____ [Sue] will have to wait on her own children," said tart Mary Bowles.) A complex dynamic was moving to the center of the poet's existence as her obsession with the "one" receded and she turned to others precisely on the basis of her accepted singularity. More than ever now, she entered others' lives only as someone utterly different from them.

In late 1865, at the end of her productive period, Dickinson had composed a postmortem on an experience she did not specify:

> *Ashes denote that Fire was –*
> *Revere the Grayest Pile*
> *For the Departed Creature's sake*
> *That hovered there awhile . . .*
>
> Fr1097

Three or four years later, a breath blowing over those ashes, she realized they were not dead after all:

> *The smouldering embers blush –*
> *Oh Heart within the Coal*

> *Hast thou survived so many years?*
> *The smouldering embers smile —*
>
> *Soft stirs the news of Light*
> *The stolid seconds glow*
> *This requisite has Fire that lasts*
> *It must at first be true —*

Fr1143

This, the one openly erotic poem of these years, harks back to the earlier poems expressing a fixed interest in a man who has left the speaker's orbit. The manuscript, a rough draft in pencil, has been assigned to "about 1868." In April 1869 the *Philadelphia Inquirer* reported that Charles Wadsworth had accepted a call from one of that city's churches. He and his family sailed from San Francisco for Panama on June 30,[4] and on July 24 *The New York Times* reported their arrival. If the news ("news of Light") reached Dickinson, possibly through the Hollands or the Dudleys, "The smouldering embers blush" may be the response, saying what she had said so often in the privacy of her manuscript books: *her* fire was undying.

Another poem on renewal, addressed to "Mr Bowles," may have been written after the editor spent the night at the Evergreens in June 1870:

> *He is alive, this morning —*
> *He is alive — and awake —*
> *Birds are resuming for Him —*
> *Blossoms — dress for His sake . . .*

But the fresh summer concert ends in discord and paralysis:

---

4. Announcing Wadsworth's departure at the head of its "Religious Intelligence," the indiscreet San Francisco *Daily Morning Call* disclosed that he was "suffering from nervous debility." This is the only known public comment on the psychic fractures one senses in the man.

> ... *Me – Only –*
> *Motion, and am dumb.*
>
> Fr1173

As this miserable conclusion virtually predicts, the poem, though addressed to Bowles, apparently remained with the poet's papers. She was not yet able to resume singing to this former friend.

Instead, her most enlivening and productive encounter was with the male friend she had not yet met. By war's end, Higginson had settled in Newport, Rhode Island, which happened to lack a convenient rail link with Amherst. In 1868, he wrote Edward Tuckerman, the Amherst College botanist, that he "dreamed of coming to Amherst, to see you & my unseen correspondent Emily Dickinson." The following spring Higginson strongly urged her to come to Boston to meetings of either the Radical Club or the Woman's Club, the two leading intellectual societies open to her sex. The former—advanced, sometimes erudite—met once a month. The latter, founded the previous year, was identified with the highbrow New England wing of the suffrage movement. Higginson was determined to draw Dickinson out and at last make contact. "You see I am in earnest," he wrote.

It is a mark of Dickinson's honesty that, in turning him down, she did not cite her health or some other presentable excuse, but instead wrote: "Could it please your convenience to come so far as Amherst I should be very glad, but I do not cross my Father's ground to any House or town." No other passage so clearly establishes the link between her sense of spatial limits and the perimeter established by Edward Dickinson. She was saying more emphatically and definitively what she had already twice hinted at with Higginson: "I must omit Boston. Father prefers so. He likes me to travel with him but objects that I visit." "Father objects because he is in the habit of me."

Her strong refusal is one of only six instances in Dickinson's lifetime of correspondence where we can compare a letter of hers to the letter she was answering. Higginson didn't see how she could live alone and yet originate such rare thoughts. Her reply had an aphoristic finality: "You noticed my dwelling alone – To an Emigrant, Country is idle except it be his own." He spoke of the "strange power" of her letters and poems. She responded with her odd interpretation of Matthew 6:13, that the Power included the Kingdom and the Glory. He said he wished to assure himself that she was "real" and mentioned a mutual acquaintance, a woman, who couldn't "tell me much." She said her life could be of no interest to others and denied anyone's authority to speak for her: "My life has been too simple and stern to embarrass any. 'Seen of Angels'[5] scarcely my responsibility." He: "you only enshroud yourself in this fiery mist & I cannot reach you." She: "I am sure that you speak the truth, because the noble do, but your letters always surprise me."

To be sure, her remarks were not meant to be direct replies, especially when she told him, "You were not aware that you saved my Life. To thank you in person has been since then one of my few requests." Just as Dickinson sometimes rejected others' gifts, she found it no easy matter acknowledging what she felt were her debts. A stanza sent to Sue says,

> Gratitude – is not the mention
> Of a Tenderness,
> But its still appreciation
> Out of Plumb of Speech –
>
> Fr1120B

The task of acknowledging what she owed Higginson would prove tense and delicate.

In August 1870 he finally found time to go to Amherst. But first, there was a misunderstanding and another wild carom of a response. Under the impression he was to come a day earlier, Dickinson prepared herself for an arrival that failed to materialize. The result, her visitor amusedly informed his wife, was that she "dreamed all night of *you* (not me)." What made this dreaming all the more striking was that the poet had known of his wife only through a passing reference in a three-year-

---

5. The allusion is to I Timothy 3:16, which says that "God was manifest in the flesh, justified in the Spirit, seen of angels . . ."

old article of his. This was not the first time that wifehood, a packed subject, had risen to the surface in connection with a new and married male friend. One of the first poems sent to Bowles had toyed with the idea of trading places with his wife: "If *she* had been the Mistletoe / And I had been the Rose" (Fr60A).

The visitor's wife, Mary Channing Higginson, permanently confined, suffered from what was called "relaxation or softening of the muscles" and may have been multiple sclerosis. She was pungent and judgmental to the point of being disagreeable, her wit being "of the keenest, and her humor peculiarly her own." Realizing how much her isolation told on her (this helps explain Higginson's reaction to Dickinson's seclusion), her husband tried to be a window on the world for her, giving her his fresh impressions of people and events. That is why, tired as he was on the night of August 16, 1870, he made a point of sending a full report of his two sessions with the poet, whom he had seen in the afternoon and evening and who had exhausted him.

The Dickinsons' home reminded him of the households depicted by the 1860s' most transgressive novelist, Elizabeth Stoddard, whose loosely organized families consist of striking individualists, among them Cassandra Morgeson, the most sexually adventurous heroine of the period.

In the entry hall he heard a "step like a pattering child's & in glided a little plain woman with two smooth bands of reddish hair . . . in a very plain & exquisitely clean white pique & a blue net worsted shawl." He was looking for what his wife would notice. Twice he used the word "childlike." His hostess presented him with two day lilies as her "introduction," then, asking him to "[f]orgive me if I am frightened; I never see strangers & hardly know what I say," she began talking. She talked "continuously" but "deferentially—sometimes stopping to ask me to talk instead of her"—and then resuming. Comparing her to other seemingly uninhibited naifs, such as Louisa May Alcott's often fatuous father, he judged her to be "thoroughly ingenuous & simple." Although he doubted his wife would care for her, he considered much of what she said "wise." Her parting speech—"Gratitude is the only secret that cannot reveal itself"—tells us she hadn't been able to express what she felt she owed him for having "saved my Life." As he walked away, he carried the photograph she had given him of Barrett Browning's grave, a gift that probably meant more to the hostess than to the visitor.

The next day Higginson recorded as many of Dickinson's dicta as he could recollect: "Is it oblivion or absorption when things pass from our minds?" "I never knew how to tell time by the clock till I was 15. My father thought he had taught me but I did not understand & I was afraid to say I did not & afraid to ask any one else lest he should know." What she said about Edward in letters and in person undoubtedly influenced Higginson's first impression of the sixty-seven-year-old man, who struck the visitor as "thin dry & speechless—I saw what her life has been." Soon after, venturing a distinction—"Her father was not severe I should think but remote"—he tried to capture the distances he sensed.

Only after the train had carried him into Vermont and New Hampshire did Higginson record his relief. "I never was with any one who drained my nerve power so much. Without touching her, she drew from me.[6] I am glad not to live near her." Decades later, in a final attempt to sum up his impression, he availed himself of a newer psychological vocabulary: "The impression undoubtedly made on me was that of an excess of tension, and of something abnormal."

It would be a mistake to react to this as Austin might, with a smile. Higginson had a more extensive acquaintance with New England's literary, intellectual, and radical circles than anyone else who tried to describe the poet. He had known all kinds, was liberal and tolerant, and had the occasion and the patience to make a timely memorandum. His thumbnail sketch of Emily Dickinson, the most detailed and vivid on record, is probably the most truthful we will ever have. We should listen to him when he says, with relief, "I am glad not to live near her." And we should think about Sue, trapped next to this powerhouse for thirty years.

---

6. Before Bram Stoker, vampirism was linked to women at least as much as to men and had another kind of sexual valence. In Rebecca Harding Davis's preachy "The Wife's Story," published in the *Atlantic Monthly* of July 1864, a dissatisfied wife has a dream in which the attempted fulfillment of her operatic ambitions results in the death of her husband, seen with a drop of blood on his neck. The man's first wife, an opium addict, had been a "foul vampire" who "sucked his youth away."

Chapter 20

1870–1878: Wisdom That Won't Go Stale

Poems of Retrospection

The year Dickinson turned forty marked the end of her four-year recessional and the start of a long and level period of compositional activity. Without approaching the output of her fighting years, she averaged thirty-five poems annually in the 1870s, dropping to twenty-three the year her mother broke a hip.

From 1871 to 1875, resuming her practice of 1865, Dickinson made clean copies of her poetry on folded sets of stationery. This self-editing, however, was more selective and sporadic than the systematic preservation of 1858–1865, when she preserved the vast preponderance of her work in manuscript books and sets. In the seventies the proportions were reversed, two-thirds of her poems never being collected. Many were sent to friends or kept in clean copies, but most joined a large accumulation of drafts penciled on scraps of stationery, notepaper, or wrapping paper, on discarded letters, envelopes, Commencement programs for Massachusetts Agricultural College, advertising circulars, and the like. Among these are the only known copies of a few of her best-known creations, such as "Tell all the truth but tell it slant" (Fr1263), along with a quantity of inferior work, some of it sketchy, repetitive, obscure. Like other explosively original writers, Dickinson couldn't avoid a certain loss of energy and freshness. At times, going back to ideas she had previously explored, she failed to really reenter and revivify them. Still, she hadn't lost her fantastic alertness.

About 1872 Dickinson composed some lines on a state of mind that would have seemed quite improbable ten years earlier:

> *A Stagnant pleasure like a Pool*
> *That lets its Rushes grow*
> *Until they heedless tumble in*
> *And make the Water slow*
>
> *Impeding navigation bright*
> *Of Shadows going down*
> *Yet even this shall rouse itself*
> *When Freshets come along –*
>
> Fr1258

Whatever it is that clogs the poet's quick responsiveness, which used to allow heaven's shadows to come down through her fresh waters, she is confident that spring's freshets will restore movement and transparency. Neither accepting nor lamenting the present dullness, the poem reaffirms the anticipatory attitude at the center of Dickinson's work.

We hear the accents of lament, however, in another poem concerned with slowness of response:

> *Oh Shadow on the Grass!*
> *Art thou a step or not?*

> *Go make thee fair, my Candidate –*
> *My nominated Heart!*
>
> *Oh Shadow on the Grass!*
> *While I delayed to dress*[1]
> *Some other thou did'st consecrate –*
> *Oh unelected Face!*
>
> Fr1237A

Is it a particular human step that might be approaching, or does the shadow stand for the poetic truth that awaits the prepared heart? Whatever the answer, the speaker's lethargy in dressing or guessing proves irremediable.

But this was Dickinson's only truly regretful poem of the 1870s. In her best work, she managed to express her visionary ardor without forgetting or ignoring her accumulated experience. A case in point is her fabulous riddle on desire and union, which again features the two-stanza, eight-line structure that was so integral to her art:

> *The Sea said "Come" to the Brook –*
> *The Brook said "Let me grow" –*
> *The Sea said "then you will be a Sea –*
> *I want a Brook – Come now"!*
>
> *The Sea said "Go" to the Sea –*
> *The Sea said "I am he*
> *You cherished" – "Learned Waters –*
> *Wisdom is stale – to Me" –*
>
> Fr1275C

The union the sea desires is consummated between stanzas. As the dialogue resumes, the brook has lost its freshness and appeal along with its

---

1. Alternative: *guess.*

identity, and thus the final exchange can only be between sea and sea (the middle speech coming from the former brook). What begins in desire ends in disillusionment, tautology, boredom—someone talking to himself. There is a dazzling gnomic finality here, a simplicity that knows it needn't bother with fancy language. Dickinson was saying what she had often said—without distance and dissatisfaction there can be no life, energy, desire—but saying it in a way that was anything but stale.

About 1873 she sent Higginson another eight-line treatment of consciousness and desire, accompanied by some leaves:

> *Dominion lasts until obtained –*
> *Possession just as long –*
> *But these – endowing as they flit*
> *Eternally belong.*
>
> *How everlasting are the Lips*
> *Known only to the Dew –*
> *These are the Brides of permanence –*
> *Supplanting me and you.*
>
> Fr1299

Though the opening lines resist comprehension, they simply carry the poet's basic paradox one step further. If the pleasures of power and possession are essentially anticipatory, "Dominion," achieved only as the mind looks forward, will always vanish at the moment of consummation. What that means is that enjoyment lasts (reversing the received idea) only "*until* obtained." Since the leaves are not subject to the laws of consciousness, they get what we humans only dream of: immediate contact with freshness, "the Dew." Engaged in an eternal kiss, they know the permanent bliss we vainly arrogate to ourselves, in this way "Supplanting me and you." The last line is exquisite, with that participially embedded "plant" and the direct address that brings in the reader only to forbid him. The poem isn't known to have gone to anyone besides Higginson. She didn't even retain a copy.

These treatments of staleness and freshness have much to say about

Dickinson's sense of herself and the point she had reached. Even more revealing are the first-person retrospections she began composing for the first time since 1865.[2] One of these, on her survival, sees her history as a special case not to be explained, and for which she takes no credit:

> Somehow myself survived the Night
> And entered with the Day –
> That it be saved the Saved suffice
> Without the Formula –
>
> Henceforth I take my living place
> As one commuted led –
> A Candidate for Morning Chance
> But dated with the Dead.

Fr1209

The speaker feels like Lazarus raised from the tomb, or Gertrude Vanderbilt. Yet she doesn't claim to have recovered her youth, and in fact the poem lacks the abandon of earlier work.

Another treatment of her inner history seems to make light of old dreams and disappointments:

> I worked for chaff and earning Wheat
> Was haughty and betrayed . . .

---

2. Other instances of the type that are not discussed here:

"This slow day moved along"	Fr1198	1871
"My triumph lasted till the drums"	Fr1212	"
"Frigid and sweet her parting face"	Fr1231	"
"The stars are old that stood for me"	Fr1242	1872
"Had I not seen the sun"	Fr1249	"
"Through what transports of patience"	Fr1265	"
"I thought that nature was enough"	Fr1269	"
"While I was fearing it – it came"	Fr1317	1874
"My heart ran so to thee"	Fr1331	"
"Let me not mar that perfect dream"	Fr1361	1875
"I sued the news yet feared the news"	Fr1391	1876
"Of their peculiar light"	Fr1396	"

> *I tasted Wheat and hated Chaff*
> *And thanked the ample friend –*
> *Wisdom is more becoming viewed*
> *At distance than at hand.*
>
> Fr1217

In the last two lines, we learn what the brook should have said in reply to the sea's invitation to "Come now!" "Art thou the thing I wanted?" begins another poem, as if confronted by an eligible lover or a case of gratified desire. The answer, trenchant and amusing, suggests that the author, now in her early forties, saw herself as beyond all that:

> *Begone – my Tooth has grown –*
> *Supply the minor Palate*
> *That has not starved so long . . .*
>
> Fr1311A

But erotic love was not that dismissable. About 1871, recalling her dormant attachment to her distant lover, the poet once again felt that she could give almost anything to have the "right" to be with this person, whose "Magic," operating passively (without his active will), had awakened her:

> *Somewhere opon the general Earth*
> *Itself exist Today –*
> *The Magic passive but extant*
> *That consecrated me –*
>
> *Indifferent Seasons doubtless play*
> *Where I for right to be –*
> *Would pay each Atom that I am*
> *But Immortality –*
>
> *Reserving that but just to prove*
> *Another Date of Thee –*

> *Oh God of Width, do not for us*
> *Curtail Eternity!*
>
> Fr1226

The last lines' sudden prayer, acknowledging the deity's fondness for huge expanses of space and time, shows a sudden anxiety about eternity: what if God proves stingy there?

This is the last roughly datable work in which Dickinson seems to anticipate a heavenly reunion with her lover. In all her other first-person retrospective poems of the 1870s, she drew a firm line between past and present, as if to take a stand on the gains of maturity. In one of the most revealing of these backward glances, she reflected on her combined misery and heroism of the early 1860s:

> *I should not dare to be so sad*
> *So many Years again –*
> *A Load is first impossible*
> *When we have put it down –*
>
> *The Superhuman then withdraws*
> *And we who never saw*
> *The Giant at the other side*
> *Begin to perish now.*
>
> Fr1233

"Sad" may be the simplest and least pretentious of words she could have chosen for the "secret sorrow" that had formerly obsessed her. What she now sees is that that sadness was willed or chosen—was something she *dared* to feel, and which called up a strength that in retrospect looks superhuman. For this she takes no credit, however, supposing that the unseen giant who helped her carry the load must have come from "the other side."

Long after her death, the poet's niece recalled that Austin "never liked and would not even hear those of her poems sent over to my mother that were sad or suggested anything of the kind." Not only that, but as the niece grew up she was steered away from "solitude and intro-spection. . . . There were to be no more solitary poets in his family." Such memories disclose the kinds of fraternal censorship to which the poet had to accommodate herself. It *did* take courage—and distance—to be sad.

Poems About Memory

In 1870 Thomas Wentworth Higginson wrote two essays for *The Woman's Journal* (the organ of the American Woman Suffrage Organi-zation), "The Door Unlatched" and "The Gate Unlatched." The first of these began with the story about the Irishman who paid the priests to get his brother out of purgatory. When he asked about his brother's progress and was told that the praying "had got the door unlatched," he put "the rest of the money in his pocket, remarking that if Tim was the boy he used to be he would do the rest himself." Higginson's point was that the door to women's freedom was "plainly unlatching," and that the great reform was now inevitable. Even Dr. Holland's novels, "written ex-pressly to demolish it, helped it." Some months later Dickinson asked the author about an article of his, something "about a 'Latch.'" When Higginson failed to make the connection, she tried again in a letter that may not have been sent: "Is there a magazine called the 'Woman's Jour-nal'? I think it was said to be in that – a Gate, or Door, or Latch."

Nothing conveys a better sense of the stage Dickinson had reached than her poems on memory featuring gates, doors, and latches that *must* be kept closed. As if answering Higginson's challenge, she came back to the topic again and again in the first half of the 1870s.[3] Frequently draw-ing on the machinery of Gothic romance, her poems treat memory as a

---

3. Poems on memory not discussed here include:

"Its hour with itself"	Fr1211	1871
"The past is such a curious creature"	Fr1273	1872
"When memory is full"	Fr1301	1873
"September's baccalaureate"	Fr1313	"
"That sacred closet when you sweep"	Fr1385	1875

place best avoided—a long-abandoned house, a closet that had better not be dusted or swept, a cellar not to be opened lest something "in its Fathoms" be roused to pursuit:

> Remembrance has a Rear and Front.
> 'Tis something like a House –
> It has a Garret also
> For Refuse and the Mouse –
>
> Besides the deepest Cellar
> That ever Mason laid –
> Look to it by its Fathoms
> Ourselves be not pursued –

Fr1234D

The single most dramatic treatment of this material, "I years had been from home," recorded in 1862, shows the speaker approaching a former domicile with a pressing question:

> My Business – just a Life I left –
> Was such – still dwelling there?

Fr440A

She stands at the door for several stanzas, on the verge of knocking and entering but paralyzed to act, grasping the latch "With trembling Care" lest the door spring open and she be left "in the Floor." In the end she turns and flees "gasping," her question unanswered. Ten years later, when Dickinson was writing her cycle of poems about the fearsome house of memory, she opened the manuscript book containing this narrative and revised it—the only pre-1865 poem she is thought to have reworked in 1872. Clearly, the time had come, if not to face the past, at least to think about the mind's avoidance of it.

In one of her finest treatments of this topic, as amusing as it is penetrating, Dickinson imagined the world of nature watching with dismay as the human mind flees from itself:

> *To flee from memory*
> *Had we the Wings*
> *Many would fly[.]*
> *Inured to slower things[,]*
> *Birds with dismay*
> *Would scan the mighty Van*
> *Of men escaping*
> *From the mind of man*
>
> Fr1343

Consciousness, here, can function only by resorting to the most undig-
nified of evasions.

Just as Dickinson did not import the literal detail of her experience
into her lyrics, so her memory-poems of the earlier 1870s refrain from
examining her past. That is their point: not to exorcise the mind's ghosts
but to evoke their haunting presence. The reverse of confessional or confrontational, the poems deal with questions of identity as such—its internal divisions, its continuity over time, its sense of a spectral shadow
self, its need for concealment.

Still, we are free to probe Dickinson's memory-poems for what they
suggest about *her*. What does it mean that memory is so often a "house,"
and that the threatening rooms are associated with storage and rubbish,[4]
and that the idea of not entering, or escaping, is always coming up? Does
this material have something to do with the strict spatial limits Father
seemed to mandate, or with the fact that her memories were divided between two houses? It was seven years after leaving West (now Pleasant)
Street, where Emily lived from age nine to twenty-five, that she composed "I years had been from home." If that is in some sense the house
of the poem (and her West Street letters often mention the steps and
front door, a favored place), the poem would seem to involve her uneasy

---

4. Years later, MacGregor Jenkins, son of the nearby minister, recalled how his neighbors got rid
of their trash: "each spring there was dug on the Edward Dickinson place a huge hole, and into
it the winter's accumulation of rubbish was dumped."

feelings about her pre-crisis self. Something about her " 'Little Girl'-hood" had become very hard to face.

The 1852 note in which Emily sprints back home and the front gate opens of itself in welcome makes an arresting contrast with the 1862 poem, in which she fears the door might swing and pull her in. The difference can be interpreted in many ways, but one thing it suggests is that she had lost her intact identity, acquiring in its place a grown-up's sense of being at large in the world and unsimple in character. The ominous cellars and closets, bulging from the inside with very bad news, were what that eager and friendly gate had turned into—what it *had* to turn into for Emily to mature. There was a further step, of course, but it would have to wait until Father died and she became accustomed to his absence.

Meanwhile, a poem of about 1874 that revisits an old question—why don't they answer?—throws further light on her uneasy sense of who she was:

> *Whether they have forgotten*
> *Or are forgetting now*
> *Or never remembered –*
> *Safer not to know –*
>
> *Miseries of conjecture*
> *Are a softer wo*
> *Than a Fact of Iron*
> *Hardened with I know –*

> Fr1334

Not surprisingly, the occasional reappearance of early friends became one of the torments of the poet's later years. When Emily Fowler Ford summered in Amherst in 1882 after a long absence, the poet apparently refused to see her. In 1873, when Abby Wood Bliss took a leave from her missionary and educational work in Syria, she found that Emily "had become the village mystery, inaccessible to all but an elect few, who were admitted to the sanctuary with appropriate preliminaries and ceremonies."

Unwilling to treat "her old crony as a Sibyl," Abby insisted on being "received on the old basis." The poem that is thought to record the occasion offers a distinctly unsibylline report of a chastening social exchange. Here, ignoring the snow "Flake" in Abby's hair, the hostess politely lies that she hasn't changed, whereupon the honest guest says that Emily *has* aged and advises her to accept time's " 'pillage / For the progress' sake' " (Fr1304B). It took a savvy old friend to bring Dickinson down to earth.

A third visitor, the former Catharine Scott Turner, now Anthon, didn't know how to do this. It was probably in 1877 that the poet composed a tearful excuse for not seeing her:

> I shall not murmur if at last
> The ones I loved below
> Permission have to understand
> For what I shunned them so –
> Divulging it would rest my Heart
> But it would ravage theirs –
> Why, Katie, Treason has a Voice –
> But mine – dispels – in Tears.
>
> Fr1429

Treason is voluble, full of excuses and reassurances, but Emily, still inwardly faithful, dare not speak lest the explanation of her avoidance "ravage" her friends. At the end of time, if all things are made plain and her motives are disclosed, she will not "murmur." Until then, her voice "dispels – in Tears."

These lines, apparently unsent, do not explain Dickinson's avoidance so much as they defend it, in this respect resembling her treatments of memory. Another poem on the same sheet of paper—"We shun because we prize her face" (Fr1430)—seems even less forthcoming. The closest thing we have to an explanation is an undatable poem that seems to justify the refusal to see Kate (the lines survive only in Sue's later copy):

> That she forgot me was the least[;]
> I felt it second pain[.]

> *That I was worthy to forget*
> *Was most I thought upon[.]*
>
> *Faithful was all that I could boast*
> *But Constancy became*
> *To her, by her innominate*
> *A something like a shame*

Fr1716

The poet's constant love, arousing a kind of shame in the other woman, made Emily feel quite "worthy to forget"—which could mean either worthy to be forgotten or inapt to remember. It was the old feeling, summed up in a note sent to Sue in 1873 asking whether anything had as much pathos as "that simple statement 'Not that we loved him but that he loved us'?"

Among all the rubbish thrown into the pit that memory dared not peer into was love unreturned and a life unlived . . . not to mention what lay at the bottom of the Strongs' well.

Village Life on Her Terms

In one of the soundest insights into Dickinson's remote yet far from in-active social life in the 1870s, Theodora Ward wrote, "It was a return after twenty years to a fuller participation in the life of the village, but on terms that she could control." More imperious than ever, the poet turned most visitors away, saw a few by appointment, and always prescribed certain rituals that abolished both the casualness and the stupid conventionalities of ordinary social encounters. Within these limits, she was remembered as indescribably direct, fresh, fascinating, her terms being as generous as they were nonnegotiable.

In 1930 Austin Baxter Keep recalled an encounter involving his aunts Mary Taylor Dickinson and Harriet Austin Dickinson while they were summering in Amherst in 1876. One day they decided to call on their old friend Vinnie. "As they reached the eastern gate of the garden they espied

Emily, all in white, among her flowers. At first, like everyone else, Aunt Mary whispered, 'Oh, there's Emily; now we can get a good look at her'; but almost at once realizing such unfairness she banged the gate, and—presto! she was gone." Soon after, the poet sent the pair an "exquisite note," implying, Keep believed, that she was " 'on' to the situation."

At church the following February, a young woman who went on to a musical career sang a setting of Psalm 23 that made a solemn impression on Vinnie. Emily must have wanted to hear for herself, for on a warm June evening several months later Nora Green and her sister Clara and a brother came to the Dickinson drawing room for a private performance. Although no one was in sight, the Greens guessed they were meant to go ahead and sing, which they did.[5] Afterward, "a light clapping of hands . . . floated down the staircase, and Miss Lavinia came to tell us that Emily would see us—my sister and myself—in the library." When they entered the dimly lit room, "a tiny figure in white darted to greet us, grasped our hands and told us of her pleasure in hearing us." She said she knew their voices and laughs, also their brother's whistle, and that she used to play the piano; she herself spoke with "the breathless voice of a child." Did she also (her niece alone described this habit) catch "her breath that quickest way of hers"? As she stood and talked, Clara was "chiefly aware of a pair of great, dark eyes set in a small, pale, delicately chiseled face, and a little body, quaint, simple as a child and wholly unaffected." That was the only time that Clara, then twenty-one or twenty-two years old, saw the poet.

In 1882 or 1883, William T. Mather, a college freshman from directly across Main Street, came to the Dickinsons' back door with a message for Vinnie. After he knocked, he "heard someone very quietly turning the key in the lock." Seeing Vinnie approach from the garden, he delivered his message, then "teased her a bit about being taken for a burglar. Evidently Miss Emily was listening for she appeared at the door with many apologies and we had a brief but very pleasant chat. All in white with her reddish hair with its net and tassels she made an unusual

---

5. Dickinson also liked to listen from another room to skilled pianists, such as Fred Bliss (Abby's son), and Mrs. Adelaide Dole.

picture." Millicent Todd Bingham, six years old when Dickinson died, also remembered "a brown silk net in which her auburn hair was held, with a brown silk tassel behind each ear."

Once, when a daughter of Elizabeth Holland appeared at the Commencement reception, Dickinson asked her to return the next morning. The visitor, perhaps fourteen years old, was received in a dark utility hallway in the rear of the house and was asked whether she would prefer a rose or a glass of wine. Over sixty years later, Annie Holland Howe remembered her hostess as being "very unusual." "Her voice, her looks, and her whole personality, made an impression on me that is still very vivid."

This dark hallway, known in the family as the Northwest Passage, was a nondescript space between the public front rooms and those where food was stored and prepared. Because it had five doorways, one of which opened to an unlit staircase, it offered multiple possibilities for "access or escape," as Martha Bianchi cannily put it. According to her, when Emily spotted Sue on her way from the Evergreens, she often sought a hurried meeting in this passageway. Martha conveys the impression these get-togethers tended to be interrupted by other family members, who naturally invited Sue into the more presentable front rooms.

To judge from Emily's follow-up letters ("Our parting was somewhat interspersed"), her farewells to intimates often failed to go as planned. Once, after Elizabeth Holland left, she wrote, "The Parting I tried to smuggle resulted in quite a Mob at last! The Fence is the only Sanctuary. That no one invades because no one suspects it." Like the Northwest Passage, the "Fence" must have been another private trysting place, one of the shared secrets Dickinson was fond of evoking, as in this coy (and metrical) passage to Holland about night and darkness:

> The Sun came out when you were gone.
> I chid him for delay –
> He said we had not needed him. Oh prying Sun!

Was she referring to the endearments preceding her friend's early-morning departure? If so, instead of simply recalling the tender moment, she created a curtained scene of intimacy. In this seductive game, the prying sun played as vital a role as the outsiders always breaking in on her staged partings.

Few of the locals who exchanged messages with her during her last fifteen years ever laid eyes on her. Among these unseeing correspondents was Adelaide Hills, who lived in New York and summered in the spacious house east of the Dickinsons', and whose husband ran the mercantile side of the family's palm-leaf hat factory. Others included Olive Stearns, wife of the college president; Abigail Cooper, whose son became Austin's law-partner; and cultivated Sarah Tuckerman, who lived in Amherst's first stone house. The Coopers were "inveterate readers," and Tuckerman's husband, the college botanist, was an expert in lichens. The pleasant college town was attracting a variety of literate and specialized people, making it that much easier for the poet to stay in touch through the written word. Judging from extant notes, she felt a special affinity for Sarah Tuckerman, accomplished, attractive, well-off, whose parties Sue remembered for their "remoteness from Life's ordinary Method."

This phrase aptly describes the scores of polished and ingenious notes the poet sent these women, whether to convey thanks, or condole with, or congratulate, or to accompany flowers or fruit. A note to Tuckerman says, in its entirety: "I fear my congratulation, like repentance according to Calvin, is too late to be plausible, but might there not be an exception, were the delight or the penitence found to be durable?" Read individually or in the mass, these messages imply a rarefied sense of social accountability. They present themselves as tender and original expressions of affectionate consideration, but they may also be read as compensatory substitutes for a denied presence, outdoing all competitors in the field of refined feminine interchange. After Vinnie relayed a message from Adelaide Hills, then in New York, Emily pulled all the stops: "To be remembered is next to being loved, and to be loved is Heaven, and is this quite Earth?" Yet she had little in common with Hills, who didn't mix with the college crowd and whose letters bespeak an ordinary mind: "it seemed real nice to see a little of your handwriting again—& so like you are the words." The reason this wasn't destroyed with other letters is that a charming plain-language poem, "Dear March – Come in" (Fr1320), was scribbled on the back.

That two-thirds of Dickinson's surviving notes and letters date from her last sixteen years tells us how active her social and expressive impulses were within her well-regulated seclusion. These numbers tell us something else as well—that her messages were seen as worth preserving. Their lapidary brilliance was recognized and appreciated, and all the more if they eluded comprehension and had to be scrutinized, deciphered, discussed, before being stored away. A legend was building.

But there was an unmistakable doubleness in the role Emily played in Amherst's social commerce. On one hand, she was so expert in conveying refined affection that her refusal to join in person could not be chalked up to unconcern. But she also took a caustic private view of the saccharine rituals the whole business depended on. Once, as she and her niece listened from the upstairs hall to Vinnie's "lady-callers" say goodbye, she stage-whispered, "Hear them kiss! – the traitors!" A letter to Maria Whitney mentioning a similar scene juxtaposes the poet's opposing attitudes without reconciling them: "How precious to hear you ring at the door and Vinnie ushering you to those melodious moments of which friends are composed – This also is fiction." The last word dryly undoes the preceding sentence without so much as a warning "but," yet the first sentence still gushes (though sounding rather wicked now), "How precious."

Although Dickinson showed no inclination to leave her upstairs listening post when celebrities appeared, she sometimes made contact in her own way. In May 1880, Frances Hodgson Burnett, a recent success with a novel about the Lancashire coal mines, made a brief stop at Austin and Sue's. At lunch, as she remembered years later, "a strange wonderful little poem lying on a bed of exquisite heartsease in a box" was brought to her.

Heading the list of the new people in Dickinson's life were Sarah Jenkins and her husband, the Reverend Jonathan Jenkins, whose appointment Austin had engineered in 1867. Jonathan lived well and attracted influential backers, impressing a general as having a "distinctly

aristocratic personality" and being "one of the most congenial companions that ever graced a table." His wife was remembered for her "beautiful
intonation and a scrupulous precision of language." The new parsonage
was just across Main Street from the Evergreens, and for a time Sarah
and Sue became (in the words of a female parishioner not in the inner
circle) quite "inseperable [sic], much to the disgust of various parties." A
memoir by a Jenkins son describes his parents as always dropping in on
Austin and Sue and raising loud gales of laughter, with Emily pictured
somewhat vaguely as hovering on the foursome's "perimeter." When Sue
visited her sister in Geneva in 1869, Emily "humbly tr[ied] to fill your
place at the Minister's, so faint a competition, it only makes them smile."
What this may mean is that she was writing to them more frequently. It
isn't likely that she crossed the street to the parsonage.

It was perhaps under the new minister's guidance that Edward did
some serious reading in theology, becoming so engaged that in 1870 his
daughter said he "only reads on Sunday – he reads *lonely* & *rigorous*
books." The one revival during Jenkins' ten-year pastorate came in 1873,
helped on by a visiting evangelist. Observing the daily prayer meetings
from her second-story lookout, Dickinson enjoyed watching a pious, ro-
tund, and fancifully dressed neighbor, Abby Sweetser, "roll out in crape
every morning" on her shortcut through the Dickinson compound. The
poet's seventy-year-old father, reacting more solemnly, drafted and
signed a sacred pledge: "I hereby give myself to God. Edward Dickinson
May 1. 1873." Uneasy about his scoffing daughter, he asked Jenkins to
have a pastoral interview with her. In an awkward spot, the minister
must have deployed all his suavity in approaching his dauntingly independent parishioner, and then assuring the anxious parent afterward his
daughter was "sound." What did she make of the episode? Her statement three years later that she talked "with *Father's* Clergyman once"
(italics added) suggests she was aware of the backstage prompting. It
also shows how little she saw of the minister.

Sue's daughter had a vivid memory of the snowy evenings when the
hired man would bring a pail of milk from the Mansion and a small box
with an edible treat and a note or poem from Aunt Emily. Chances are,
some of these, such as "Had this one day not been" (Fr1281) or "Birth-

day of but a single pang" (Fr1541), were occasioned by Sue's December 19 birthdays, which were made much of. In 1875, when Sue gave birth at age forty-four to her third child, Gilbert, the poet's message was much more self-assured and helpful than in 1861: "Emily and all that she has are at Sue's service, if of any comfort to Baby – Will send Maggie, if you will accept her."

In general, the poems that comment on the friendship between the sisters-in-law show far less neediness than in the past. No longer complaining about neglect,[6] the poet was more dignified in her summations of the friendship's permanent features, expressing herself in tones ranging from respectful to adulatory:

> To own a Susan of my own
> Is of itself a Bliss –
> Whatever Realm I forfeit, Lord,
> Continue me in this!
>
> Fr1436, ca. 1877

At the same time, Dickinson continued to stress the near-yet-remote aspect, the most striking example being the one poem she entered into a set and then later tried to destroy:

> Now I knew I lost her –
> Not that she was gone –
> But Remoteness travelled
> On her Face and Tongue.
>
> Alien, though adjoining
> As a Foreign Race . . .
>
> Fr1274A, ca. 1872

---

6. There is no evidence "The most pathetic thing I do / Is play I hear from you" (Fr1345) was sent to Sue or that she was "Goliah," as one critic proposes. The poem was written about 1874, the year Edward died and two years before the earliest attested date for the resumption of Dickinson's correspondence with Wadsworth, who, like Goliath, was seen "as 'a strong man.'"

The fifth line points to Sue, and so does the poem's last word, "Idolatry."

The definitive treatment of Sue as unknowable alien is found in a version of a poem on the mystery of wells in which her first name is substituted for the original word, "nature":

> But Susan is a stranger yet —
> The ones who cite her most
> Have never scaled her Haunted House
> Nor compromised her Ghost —
>
> To pity those who know her not
> Is helped by the regret
> That those who know her know her less
> The nearer her they get —
>
> Fr1433C, ca. 1877 (J1400)

The haunted house that had come to stand for memory is in this instance Sue herself, who resists intimacy and rebuffs those who want to know her. Was Emily thinking of herself or someone else recently antagonized by Sue—Sarah Jenkins, say, who, as gossip had it, was thought to be "pretty thoroughly disgusted with the patronizing and the flattery and the hollowness"?

Emily's letters to Louisa and Frances Norcross in this period show how far she was from regarding them as "a Foreign Race," even during the two or so years they spent in Milwaukee. Living with John and Eliza Dudley, the Norcrosses passed through one of their most painful times, ending with Eliza's death from tuberculosis in June 1871, her husband's marriage to Marion V. Churchill (a strikingly progressive journalist and poet[7] half his age), and the sisters' bruised return to Massachusetts in 1872. They resided in Boston's Berkeley Hotel for about a year, then set-

---

7. From Churchill Dudley's "Midsummer Night" (1878):

> . . . Rock is fluent; ice is wine;
> Mighty nerve-lines, telegraphic,
> Pour your heart-beat into mine . . .

tled in nearby Concord, where they joined the liberal First Parish and made many friends, including Ellen Emerson (Ralph Waldo's daughter) and the clubbable bachelor, James L. Whitney. After James's sister, Maria, passed a day with the Norcrosses in 1875, Dickinson was glad to hear they "loved Miss Whitney on knowing her nearer." She savored her cousins' social pleasures as much as she had grieved with them over earlier troubles. There is never a hint of reproach, even when the subject is the poet's distance from the world: "Sisters, I hear robins a great way off, and wagons a great way off, and rivers a great way off, and all appear to be hurrying somewhere undisclosed to me. Remoteness is the founder of sweetness." The passage recalls a neighbor's memory of her "habit of standing in rapt attention as if she were listening to something very faint and far off."

When others broke in upon this epicure of faraway sweetness, she was apt to unsheathe her claws. In 1872 Louisa and Frances were informed that a certain Miss P____, apparently seeking poems for a benevolent cause,

> request[ed] me to aid the world by my chirrup more. Perhaps she stated it as my duty, I don't distinctly remember, and always burn such letters. . . . I replied declining. She did not write to me again – she might have been offended, or perhaps is extricating humanity from some hopeless ditch.

Johnson conjectured that the request came from Elizabeth Stuart Phelps, whose latest radical novel, *Hedged In* (1870), had confronted the social ban on impoverished unwed mothers. Another possibility would be the editor and activist Elizabeth Peabody. Whoever it was, the poet's shortness with her is of a piece with her derision in 1850 for the Sewing Society's winter program: "now all the poor will be helped – the cold warmed – the warm cooled . . ."

This tartness and lack of sympathy are not the whole story. When Maggie Maher's brother died in a mine accident in 1880, Dickinson used all her tact to organize some comfort: "If the little cousins would give her a note – she does not know I ask it – I think it would help her begin, that bleeding beginning that every mourner knows." Earlier that year, when "an Indian Woman with gay Baskets and a dazzling Baby" appeared at the kitchen door, instead of locking it Emily engaged the stranger in talk, asking what the infant liked. "To step" was the answer, whereupon the poet led the unsteady toddler on a short walk: "she leaned on Clover Walls and they fell, and dropped her – With jargon sweeter than a Bell, she grappled Buttercups – and they sank together." After observing and sharing this direct encounter with nature, Dickinson recalled a line by Henry Vaughan, "My Days that are at best but dim and hoary." Maggie and the baby stirred penetrating thoughts about others and herself. There was no aloof classifying.

Among Children

Few aspects of Dickinson's social life seem quite so defining as her entrance into the world of children, and so easy to misread. Writing by one count sixty or so poems with a child persona, refusing to leave her father's house, and impressing those who met her with her "smallness" or "uninhibited" manner or "breathless childlike voice," she evidently had a conspicuous childishness. At the same time, her determination, independence of mind, power of abstraction, and constant letter-writing suffice to show how much of an adult she must have been.

What we know of her dealings with children is largely owing to one person, MacGregor Jenkins, who brought out a short article in 1891, "A Child's Recollection of Emily Dickinson," expanded forty years later into a memoir, *Emily Dickinson: Friend and Neighbor.* Born in Amherst in April 1869, Mac, as he was called, joined the pack of neighborhood children who played in the Dickinson compound and thus casually observed the poet tending her potted flowers on a rug spread for the purpose just outside the back door. The pack was headed by Martha Dickinson and Sally Jenkins, both several years older than Mac and with whom he struggled to keep up. From across the street came Alice Mather, whose father taught Greek at Amherst

College and whose mother was waging a losing battle against tuberculosis. The children's raucous noise was tolerated, but there was one rule they were obliged to keep in mind and which, when forgotten, was sure to bring down a distant, stentorian order: "Boy, shut that gate." Nothing quelled Mac quite so much as Austin's commanding voice. Not that it was angry: "it was the enormous volume of it and the tone of authority."

Oddly enough, the idea of starvation was a regular feature of the children's games, especially Gypsy and Pirate.[8] In the middle of Gypsy, a signal would come from the Mansion, and then a basket began its slow descent from a second-story window. Mac could never decide whether the poet's "care and deliberation were part of the game or whether they were to avoid attracting Maggie's vigilant attention." Without interrupting their play (a point the memoir insists on), the children stealthily made their way to the basket and removed the "gummy" gingerbread cakes it usually contained. Given the prominence of emotional starvation in Dickinson's earlier poetry—"I had been hungry all the years" (Fr439), "It would have starved a gnat" (Fr444), both from 1862—it would seem the game comported with her fantasies as well as the children's. Their fictions connected; they were playing the same game. As she wrote to her cousins in Concord, "Good times are always mutual; that is what makes good times."

"Aunt Emily stood for *indulgence*" was how Mattie put it. In Mac's memory, she was always offering support to the neighborhood children, often in the third person: "Emily will see that you are supplied. Emily will see that you are not blamed." She wasn't one of them, yet she was on their side against the adult order, especially when defying Maggie by raiding the pantry for cookies or doughnuts. She greatly appealed to children, yet they watched her closely and did not take liberties, realizing she was "a creature made of a little different material." Lavinia be-

---

8. In a letter to brother Ned, nine-year-old Mattie named some other games she enjoyed: "hide and seek was the first game Wolf Battle of Bunker hill and theif followed till Horace [Church, the handyman] forbade the apples flying any longer."

came Vinnie, but Emily was always Miss Emily. It was an honor to be asked to help water her conservatory plants, or assist her in the kitchen, or deliver her notes.

Never moody, she was invariably buoyant, "joyous." But if someone unfamiliar approached, she just vanished, closing the door behind her and giving no excuses or explanations afterward. Once, in the pantry, she said (not speaking in the third person, apparently), "if the butcher boy should come now, I would jump into the flour barrel." The statement shows how absolute and unapologetic she was about her hiding from the world, and also how she discriminated between working-class juveniles and the neighborhood's children of privilege.

Once, when little Gilbert was in kindergarten and boasted about a beautiful white calf that proved to be imaginary, his teacher reprimanded him for the sin of lying and made him cry. Sue tried to convince the benighted woman of the validity of the imagination, but Aunt Emily, as her niece recalled, was too indignant for reasoning and "besought them one and all to come to *her*, she would show them! The white calf was grazing up in her attic at that very moment!" A note she drafted for the wounded boy to take to his teacher had a poem on "The vanity . . . / Of Industry and Morals" (Fr1547B) and pointedly contrasted the punitive Jonathan Edwards with Jesus.

Curiosity was growing about this hidden woman, hidden like the white calf, and her niece was often pumped for information. The line she was to take had no ambiguity whatever: "It was impressed on my brother and myself as early as I can remember, by both our parents, that Aunt Emily was not to be a subject of discussion with outsiders." In 1850 Austin had advised Emily Fowler that his sister was too "wild" to answer a letter and recommended she not be addressed in the next one. By the 1870s, that protective impulse had become a comprehensive policy, with all impudent inquiries stared down or dismissed.

The policy amounted to a blanket endorsement of Dickinson's seclusion. Among her later correspondents, the only ones who urged her to publish or get out into the world or otherwise change her way of life—Thomas Wentworth Higginson, Helen Hunt Jackson, Thomas

Niles, Otis Phillips Lord—were people she had not come to know through the Evergreens. With Austin and Sue and their friends, the rule was to humor, protect, and isolate.

How did Edward feel about his daughter's reclusiveness? Bianchi's surmise that her solitary life "must have been a blow to his worldly pride" probably comes close to the mark. Father had an old and cherished ideal of female excellence, and in 1872, moved by a eulogy of Eliza Bancroft Davis, he dusted it off. Sister of the historian George Bancroft, and widow of a respected senator, Davis had distinguished herself both publicly and privately, as Alexander H. Bullock pointed out in a column-long tribute in Worcester's leading newspaper. Bullock emphasized

> the value of such a person, presiding modestly through half a century over the social life around her, among organized associations and private circles, . . . awakening the public spirit to worthy objects and making them attractive by her own poetic enthusiasm, . . . inspiring women with just conceptions of the higher methods of living.

After reading this description of an exemplary woman leader, Edward wrote to express his hearty agreement with Bullock's "picture of her powers, & virtues & graces & solid accomplishments. . . . You deserve the thanks of the Community, for bringing before us . . . all that entered into the constitution of an almost perfect woman." The letter ends with a plaintive "O, for more such."

As a trustee of Amherst College, Bullock had attempted the previous year to establish a scholarship for both sexes, thus implicitly opening the school to women. His tribute to Mrs. Davis embodied a progressive ideal of which Edward must have been aware when he voiced his agreement. Still, there was another and deeper layer in the man. Two years later, when the Committee on Woman Suffrage held an open hearing in the State House, with such speakers as Julia Ward Howe, author of "Battle Hymn of the Republic," Edward stepped in to listen. He heard women on both sides, he wrote Austin,

some sentimental, some belligerent, some fist shakers—some
scolds—and was disgusted with the class of females which gathered
there—I hope we shall soon have a chance at the subject, & begin to
clear off the scum—they dont expect to get what they ask, this year,
[but] . . . to agitate & agitate, till they find a legislature weak enough
to report in their favor.

Edward's intemperate disgust at the "class of females" speaking in
the forum makes clear how far he was from Bullock's more enlightened
attitudes. Resolved to quash the movement for women's rights, he evidently held the same views he had first worked out in his 1827 Coelebs
papers. This fixity helps us understand why his daughter could not assume an ordinary adult female role consistent with the exercise of her
genius and why she made common cause with the neighborhood children. Yet to think of her as a victim is to exaggerate Edward's control and
belittle her ingenuity. Accepting, embracing, her exclusion from the
public world, she redefined it as the freedom to do and to be whatever
she chose at home. Her way of living with Father was to create a private
domain of friendship, thought, and art he could not enter. What this
meant, however, was that certain doors could not be opened as long as he
lived.

There is a family story, told by Vinnie to Mabel Loomis Todd, that
epitomizes the poet's mastery of closed space. One Sunday during the
nine years of Margaret O'Bryan's service (ending in 1865), Edward was

more than usually determined that Emily should go to church, and
she was especially determined that she would not. He commanded,
she begged off, until they were both weary. She saw there was no further use to talk, so she suddenly disappeared. No one could tell where
she was. They hunted high and low, & went to church without her.
Coming home, she was still unseen, & they began to get very much
worried, particularly her stern father. . . . Some hours after, Emily
was discovered calmly rocking in a chair placed in the cellar bulk-
head, where she had made old Margaret lock her in, before church.

Being Serious with Higginson

After Higginson's visit in August 1870, Dickinson pictured him as the infusing pulse and herself as the passive receptacle: "The Vein cannot thank the Artery – but her solemn indebtedness to him, even the stolidest admit." It is a startling image, suggesting just how invigorating his influence was at this time. Though it doesn't explain why she got back to work after her five-year rest, there is no question but that his respectful attention gave her a new self-consciousness about her vocation. Ironically, this solemnity proved something of a distraction.

A few years earlier she had told him, "Your opinion gives me a serious feeling. I would like to be what you deem me." This is a dangerous attitude for a writer, especially one who, as we see from Dickinson's October 1870 letter to her mentor, has been given high praise: "I was much refreshed by your strong Letter – [new paragraph] Thank you for Greatness – I will have deserved it in a longer time!" The first half of this letter, very different from her usual sequences of observations, offers a sustained treatment of the riddle of immortality. Quoting Jesus and Tennyson in support of the proposition that life should be founded on what cannot be proven, Dickinson almost seems to have intended a brief essay. Was she deserving her "greatness"—trying out some new idea of a poet's serious duties? Perhaps the reason she didn't send the letter (found among her papers) was that she knew she was somehow off her turf.

Dickinson's ambition was becoming more open—as she understood open. After reading Helen Hunt's *Verses* in 1871, she sent Higginson her opinions of the poets of the day. She hadn't read Joaquin Miller because she "could not care about him." She generously pronounced Hunt's poems "stronger than any written by Women since Mrs. Browning, with the exception of Mrs Lewes [George Eliot]." She ended with a statement in which her sententious manner attained a serene and ultimate pomposity: "While Shakespeare remains Literature is firm." Perhaps one reason Dickinson had little skill in making reasoned relative judgments is that she didn't quite enter dialogue. If enthusiasm and dismissal are to be the two responses to writing, there won't be much need for practical criticism, a highly social craft. What is the point of discussing solid achievement if one believes that "truth like Ancestor's Brocades can stand alone"? The image is a telling one, replacing truth-seeking talk with solitary ramrod formality and dignity.

Among the serious and responsible poems Dickinson sent Higginson was a statement on the harmful effect of orthodox indoctrination on the capacity for belief:

> *Who were "the Father and the Son"*
> *We pondered when a child*
> *And what had they to do with us . . .*

Speaking partly for herself and partly for the mid-nineteenth-century generation that had discarded its authoritarian childhood faith, she argued that this collective emancipation from terror had a crippling result:

> *. . . we believe*
> *But once – entirely –*
> *Belief, it does not fit so well*
> *When altered frequently.*

But Dickinson refused to let the poem end in agnostic hesitation, turning instead to a glorious unearned possibility:

> *We blush – that Heaven if we achieve –*
> *Event ineffable –*
> *We shall have shunned until ashamed*
> *To own the Miracle –*
>
>   Fr1280[B], ca. 1873

Another poem sent to Higginson pulls up at the same terminus: although the heaven we once hoped for may be "Untenable to Logic," it is still "possibly the one" (Fr1279D). For an evangelical turned romantic, it was difficult not to reaffirm some version of the old faith.

When Higginson came to Amherst on December 3, 1873, to give a lecture, he had his second and last encounter with the poet. Several months later, bestowing on him her most resonant honorific, she wrote, "Twice, you have gone – Master," then added, "Would you but once come." This enigmatic wish, so open to clumsy misinterpretation, arose both from the frustration she found in most encounters and the apparent emptiness of this one. Her visitor didn't mention it in his diary and in time forgot it, while for her part the long and ambitious poem she sent him afterward correctly predicted that this was their last meeting:

> *Because that you are going*
> *And never coming back . . .*

Reaching for the paradox of their relationship, she observed that, although he was "Existence" itself to her, he himself somehow "forgot to live."[9] But the piece was by and large an unimpressive gathering of previously worked-out conceits, such as the old idea that Heaven would be insufficient "Unless in my Redeemer's Face / I recognize your own." The poem ended by looking forward to an eventual reunion with select friends, when God "will refund us finally / Our confiscated Gods" (Fr1314C). This was one of the few works sent to Higginson that struck him as too weak to merit publication in a selected edition. His judgment was sound: compared to her despairing meditation of 1863, "I cannot live with you" (Fr706), the poem seems turgid and unfelt. Perhaps it came down to the fact that she had adjusted to her life's painful lacks. Higginson wasn't "Master," she didn't need him in that way, and it finally made little sense not to deal with him on the basis of her hard-won literary independence.

On his side, Higginson was tempted to take the view favored by his wife, Mary, and his sisters that the poet was "partially cracked." A letter to the sisters quotes Dickinson:

---

9. Helen Hunt was critical of Higginson's deferentiality: "He steps too softly—knocks like a baby at the door, & then opens it only a quarter of the way & comes in edgewise!"

She says, "there is always one thing to be grateful for – that one is one's self & not somebody else"[10] but Mary thinks this is singularly out of place in E.D.'s case. She (E.D.) glided in, in white, bearing a Daphne odora for me, & said under her breath, "How long are you going to stay." I'm afraid Mary's other remark "Oh why do the insane so cling to you?" still holds.

Keeping his high opinion of Dickinson's work, he made an effort to say the right things in his New Year's message: "certainly I enjoyed being with you. Each time we seem to come together as old & tried friends; and I certainly feel that I have known you long & well." Is the double "certainly" a tip-off to the reservations he was striving to overcome? Gently inviting her into the open, he ended by recommending the "ruddy hues of life" and speaking of Helen Hunt's enjoyment of healthy Colorado.

Dickinson's reply shows that even though she continued to venerate Higginson, she sensed the limits of his usefulness for her. Complimentary and affectionate, she still let him know that his brief visit, his "flitting Coming," had been succeeded by the solitary "Awe" that constituted her true home. Asking a rather depersonalizing question at the end of her letter—"Was it you that came?"—she answered by appending the second half of one of her most astringent and uncompromising poems. (Her letters often incorporated fragments only of her poems.) Yes, Higginson came and flitted, but another wind came and stayed—

> *A Wind that woke a lone Delight*
> *Like Separation's Swell –*
> *Restored in Arctic confidence*
> *To the Invisible.*
>
> Fr1216D (J1259)

---

10. Higginson probably missed her point, which, judging from her poems, may have involved her autonomy, powers of resistance, or special isolation (as in "There is another loneliness," Fr1138).

So far from introducing the poet to the ruddy hues of life, the visit restored her to a confident delight in her own wintry climate. Invisible, back in the Arctic, and glad to be there, she seems to have realized she could not be Higginson's kind of writer, and that the social, serious, responsible voice he called up in her was less vital than this cold high "Wind that rose."

Helen Hunt Jackson

It was thanks to Higginson, however, that Dickinson made useful contact with someone she had known as a girl and who was as unlike her as it was possible to be: Helen Hunt.

Hunt had grown up in Amherst, a daughter of Professor Nathan Fiske and his consumptive wife, Deborah, whose death in 1844 had been part of the series that disturbed Emily at age thirteen. The two girls had lived some distance apart, attended different schools, and had little to do with one another. Helen, a tomboy remembered as "tough & hardy" and quite disposed to "wrestle or fight," left Amherst for good after her father's death and married an engineer in the U.S. Army. When the couple attended a Dickinson reception, probably in 1860, Major Hunt impressed the poet by observing that her dog "understood gravitation." He was killed in a military accident in 1863, and when his widow's last surviving child died in 1865, she moved to Newport, Rhode Island, and took lodgings in the same boardinghouse as Higginson. Eager to support herself by her pen, she was encouraged and advised by him, and before long her energetic talents resulted in a steady output of popular work. Insisting on anonymity, she brought out her poems as H.H. and her stories as "Saxe Holm." A novel, *Mercy Philbrick's Choice,* inaugurated the successful No Name Series published by Roberts Brothers of Boston.[11] Crediting Higginson for her success, she called him "my mentor—my teacher—the one man to whom & to whose style, I chiefly owe what little I have done in lit-

11. Many of the volumes in this teasingly anonymous series were by women. The most popular was the novel *Kismet,* by Julia Constance Fletcher.

erature." Dickinson was by no means the only woman writer who went to him for literary counsel.

As a professional writer, Hunt made deliberate use of what she called her "impudence" and "audacious subjectivity." In the eyes of Emily Fowler Ford, she was "a woman of genius and quick vivid impressions without convictions on any subject." When *Mercy Philbrick* came out, Hunt twisted arms to make sure the *Atlantic Monthly* would not assign its influential review to the rising young international novelist whose scalpel was always sharpest on New England's women writers: "If Henry James does it, M.P.C. will be . . . badly handled. . . . I really think Hatty Preston might do it. It wouldn't take her two hours." The pressure worked and Preston's praise of the book's "beautiful literary workmanship" duly appeared in the *Atlantic*. Set in a western New England village modeled on Amherst, the narrative concerned a woman poet whose "choice" was not to remarry. Locally, it was rumored that Dickinson had helped write the novel, and also the Saxe Holm stories—early examples of the inflated and unreal tales always being told about her.

Higginson started things off by showing Dickinson's poems to his fellow boarder (probably allowing her to make copies for a manuscript volume), and then, in 1869, telling the poet there was a lady in Newport who "once knew you but could [not] tell me much." A correspondence began the next year, when Hunt spent a working summer and fall in Bethlehem, New Hampshire. In August 1873, seeking a healthy place to recuperate, she came to Amherst on the strength of Dickinson's assurance that a lodging house the Norcrosses favored would not be insalutary. When it proved both damp and "close & stifling," Hunt experienced a "disastrous" relapse and fled, ending up in Colorado Springs and marrying William S. Jackson, a banker and railroad man. She returned to New England for long autumn sojourns but spent little time in Amherst. Her depiction of Penfield in *Mercy Philbrick* suggests her view of the girlhood village where her consumptive mother had died—poky, old-fashioned, poorly laid out, dark.

Hunt's 1875 marriage to Jackson elicited from this dull and backward place an electric congratulatory note, which reads in its entirety:

Have I a word but Joy?

E. Dickinson

Who fleeing from the Spring
The Spring avenging fling
To Dooms of Balm –

In this three-line segment of a poem twice as long (Fr1368B), line one may be construed as the direct object of "fling." Helen's history of bereavement, illness, and travel for health's sake forms the background. Compelled to run away from spring (life, vitality, happiness), she has been flung back into the thick of it by this second marriage. If she is doomed, as once seemed the case, it is not to suffering but to a soothing and odorous "Balm." As in other late poems by Dickinson, heaven proves unavoidable.

But "Who" refers to more than Hunt Jackson. Since the word immediately follows "E. Dickinson," it appears that she too is flung from grief into ecstasy. Do the lines incorporate a memory of the wasting depression that sent her to Boston in spring 1844, when Helen lost her mother? Did the poet see the same rebound to joy in her and her friend's utterly different lives?

Whatever the answer, the lines mystified Helen, who rashly sent them back for an explanation: "I do wish I knew just what 'dooms' you meant, though!" No answer was forthcoming, and in March 1876 she wrote again, insisting with her usual bluntness that the poem was "mine—not yours—and be honest." Just as bluntly, she came out with the declaration that "You are a great poet—and it is a wrong to the day you live in, that you will not sing aloud. When you are what men call dead, you will be sorry you were so stingy."

Others had said this, beginning with the two "Editors of Journals" (Samuel Bowles? Fidelia H. Cooke?) who sought the poet's work in the winter of 1861–1862 and, rebuffed, called her "penurious." But it is unlikely that anyone, even Higginson, who also unleashed the word "great," had been quite so categorical. In 1875 he gave a talk on Dickinson and another woman writer ("Two Unknown Poetesses") at the influential New England Woman's Club, reading some lyrics and finding that their "strange power excited much interest." But he was also reported to have said that her work "reminded him of skeleton leaves so pretty but *too delicate*,—not strong enough to publish." Emily Fowler Ford took the same view, and so did Josiah Holland, who called the poems "too ethereal" (the kiss of death) for the mass-market *Scribner's Magazine* he now edited. It took pushy Helen Jackson to hammer out their great vigor.

And Helen would not back off. In August 1876, sending Emily a circular on Roberts Brothers's projected No Name volume of contemporary verse, she offered to make submissions in her hand: "Surely, in the shelter of such *double* anonymousness . . . you need not shrink. I want to see some of your verses in print. Unless you forbid me, I will send some that I have. May I?" Two months later, passing through Amherst, she renewed her plea face to face. She also had the temerity to tell the poet she looked unwell and to scold her for "living away from the sunlight." It was what Higginson thought but hardly dared say.

Unable to field Jackson's importunities, Dickinson asked the useful Higginson for a note saying he "thought me unfit." But he seemed to miss the point, leaving the poet to deal on her own with her aggressive friend, who presently sent a clever follow-up. First, she apologized for her roughness and directness: "Your [hand] felt [l]ike such a wisp in mine that you frigh[tened] me. I felt [li]ke a [gr]eat ox [tal]king to a wh[ite] moth, and beg[ging] it to come and [eat] grass with me [to] see if it could not turn itself into beef! How stupid." But then she returned to the charge, expressing a preference for the "simplest" [translation: earliest] poems and arguing on the basis of enjoyment and reciprocity: "You say you find great pleasure in reading my verses. Let somebody somewhere whom you do not know have the same pleasure in reading yours." The appeal had an effect, though not the one Jackson intended: writing to Higginson soon after, Dickinson delicately upbraided *him* for withholding *his* writing even though it was "sought by others."

As the 1878 publication date approached, Jackson kept up the pressure, reducing her requests from "some" to "one or two" poems and finally to one in particular, which she promised to submit in her own hand to ensure anonymity. Making it impossible to say no—"I ask it as a personal favor"—she finally extracted the poem she wanted, probably with the author's reluctant consent.

When *A Masque of Poets* was issued in late 1878, Dickinson's "Success is counted sweetest," written nineteen years earlier, occupied a conspicuous place at the end of the volume's shorter poems. The editor-in-chief, Thomas Niles, a promoter of women's writing, thanked her for the contribution, "which for want of a known sponsor Mr Emerson has generally had to father." No doubt she was gratified by the high estimate of her work, but did it rankle to have the credit go to another?

Perhaps not. When Sue recognized the published lines and mentioned them to Dickinson, thus unveiling her, she went "so white" her sister-in-law regretted having spoken. This strong and instantaneous reaction suggests there was more to her refusal to publish than a fastidious objection to the regularities of print or to the sprucings up of editors, as is often asserted.

Death Away from Home

In March 1871 Samuel Bowles discovered that Edward Dickinson had been "quite feeble all winter, a sort of breaking-down with dyspepsia" and was now "hardly to be recognized in his old character." For Emily, who had to live with "his lonesome face all day" while assuming he would die, the winter's "terror . . . made a little creature of me, who thought myself so bold." That fall, the Amherst paper paid proper honors in a long story on Edward that stressed his civic contributions. Typed as "a gentleman of the elder school," he was also said to be (was there a question?) "by no means a fogy."

When Edward tried to resign as treasurer of Amherst College in July 1872, the surprised trustees persuaded him to stay on until a successor could be chosen. The search was complicated by the presence of a candidate whose dynastic qualifications outweighed his personal achievements, and by a trustee who pulled every available string for his friend's sake—Austin Dickinson and Samuel Bowles. Once, after two rivals had been eliminated, Samuel sent Austin the inside information and advised a tactical pause: "This is confidential. I guess we can let the pullets set for a little while now." In December 1873, the new treasurer was finally selected at a long and divisive trustees' meeting in a Springfield hotel, after which, at two A.M., Bowles once again violated confidentiality by dashing off a play-by-play report for the successful applicant: "a dramatic performance—long & somewhat doubtful—but we pulled through . . ." Taking over, Austin found the records in such chaos a bookkeeper had to be hired. Overall, however, the son proved less effective than his father in building and maintaining high-level contacts. Once, yielding too much to the heirs of David Sears (a bigtime Boston contributor), he overstepped his limited authority in a way that had to be corrected decades later by the Supreme Judicial Court.

Ironically, as Edward stepped down from the treasurership, he was persuaded to take on a more arduous job. For twenty years, the Commonwealth of Massachusetts had been underwriting the expensive Hoosac Tunnel, designed to give Boston a direct rail link to Albany and points west. Also weighing on local voters was the completion of the Massachusetts Central Railroad, which was to pass through Amherst; the town had pledged $100,000 for the project. When this investment was threatened by the Panic of 1873, Amherst's political operatives felt they had to send "our very best man" to the General Court to protect their interests. That May, Edward had given himself to God. Now, giving himself once again to his community and its economic development, he accepted the nomination. Easily elected to the state's lower house, he was ballyhooed by the conservative *Boston Journal* as one of the Connecticut Valley's long lineage of "River Gods."

Although the Panic seems to have been on Emily's mind, her only surviving comment on her father's election, sent to the Norcrosses, was distant and noncommittal: "I see by the paper that father spends the winter with you." But she clearly felt sorry for him, seventy-one years old and so reluctant to leave home he asked Austin (not her) to write every day. In January he was duly appointed to the ten-member joint committee on the Hoosac Tunnel. His rooms were in the nearby Tremont House.

It was in the middle of that month, on Saturday, January 17, that

Emily's New York uncle, Joseph A. Sweetser, slipped on the ice while entering the Brooklyn ferry and hurt his right temple badly enough that by the following Tuesday the resulting headache was "very severe." In his mid-sixties, Sweetser lived with his wife, Catharine, in the Madison Square Hotel. On Wednesday night, as was "his invariable habit," he stepped out to attend regular services at the Madison Square Presbyterian Church, of which he was "a most consistent and useful member." After he failed to return, the family placed a description in the *New York Herald*'s widely read personals: "5 feet 11 inches . . . right eye discolored by a recent fall."[12] It was feared his head injury had affected his mind and he had "done himself violence."

Although a Mulberry Street detective was hired and a $250 reward offered, nothing was ever heard of the old man. But a spot-on poem came from Amherst saying that death was not the most painful of blows:

> There marauds a sorer Robber –
> Silence . . .
>
> Fr1315 (J1296)

That the head of one's family should leave home and not be seen or heard from again: what greater terror was there?

From time to time Father returned from Boston. Once, Emily reported him "ill at home." On April 29, the ground being covered with fresh snow, he went to the barn in his slippers to get some grain for birds huddling by the kitchen door. During a June legislative recess, a light was seen in his office at night. His last afternoon at home, a Sunday apparently, was spent in his daughter's company: "He seemed peculiarly pleased as I oftenest stayed with myself, and remarked as the Afternoon withdrew, he 'would like it to not end.' " "Almost embarrassed" by this indirect expression of love, she proposed he take a walk with Austin. On Monday, June 15, she woke him for the early train.

---

12. A sampling of other personals from January 25: "Pokie and Ida—Have returned, will meet you at same place Tuesday evening next, same time." "Neapolitaine—Live forever, O Queen! Have I found favor in thy sight? Shylock." "Mary—Waited an hour. You won't fool me again. 'T.' "

The next morning Edward addressed the House on an aspect of the railroad question. It was hot, and as he spoke he "felt faint" and had to sit down. The House adjourning, he walked the quarter-mile to Tremont House, where, according to one account, he dined and then experienced an "apoplectic attack"—a stroke. According to his family's version of events, he began packing for home, and when the doctor who had been sent for arrived, he diagnosed "apoplexy, and proceeded to give him opium or morphine, a drug which had always been poison to him." One reason the Dickinsons favored this story was that it placed the onus on a bumbling physician. But Edward's attempt to pack for home tells us he was already in big trouble and knew it. Unconscious most of the afternoon, he died about six P.M.

Emily was at supper when Austin walked in with a telegram from Boston. As she wrote a few weeks later, she instantly saw "by his face we were all lost." Father was "very sick," and Austin and Vinnie must start at once for Boston, even though the last train had gone. But before the horses were harnessed, word arrived he was dead.

Three days later a simple funeral was held in the Mansion's packed entrance hall, with ranks of settees on the front lawn for the overflow. Eight-year-old Mattie was stunned by the intensity of her father's grief. Vinnie formed part of the "mourning circle," but Emily stayed in her room with the door cracked open.

She also could not and did not attend the memorial service on June 28, when the First Church was filled with laurel and other flowers and the Reverend Jenkins delivered a sermon comparing Edward to Samuel, Israel's last combined prophet-and-judge. The parallel, an apt one, brought together two strong defenders of a faith, a people, and a locality. It was Samuel who erected the boundary-marking "Ebenezer" after a victory over the Philistines, an act Edward invoked after crushing the opposition to Amherst's railroad: "We here 'set up our Ebenezer.' "

The *Springfield Republican*'s long obituary, undoubtedly by Bowles, praised Edward for having "in these days of cowardly conformity . . . *the courage of his convictions*." He was an anachronism in another way as well, being "a Puritan out of time for kinship and appreciation." His great failing was that "he did not understand himself."

It is a tribute to Edward's candor that his memorialists felt they should bring up his faults. Jenkins, too, had a reproach—that he had "so carefully, and may I say, so unwisely, concealed" his gentle nature. Was that because he had "the Puritan notion that sentiment betrayed weakness, or was it his training in that elder school whose primal precept was repression?" To these conjectures, each fairly generic, we add that, like Samuel, prophet and judge, Edward had seen himself as a bulwark for family, community, and college, all of which he spent his life protecting against endless threats: his father's financial collapse, assaults on the Constitution, the corruption of the times. He had chosen to marry a "timid" woman who would need his protection, and his two daughters depended on his manly firmness. That was how he understood his place in the world.

Yet he died intestate. With anyone else, one would assume this was inadvertent, caused by delay or avoidance. With Edward, however, we have a fanatically anxious caretaker who cast annual balance sheets, bought large life insurance policies from 1851 on, and demanded constant assurance when away from home that no one was slipping on the ice or catching scarlet fever or being crushed by railroad cars. In all probability, the reason he did not write a will was that he did not intend to do so. A will would have involved an inventory and a distribution supervised by a probate judge in accordance with state law, all of which would trespass on the privacy of the Dickinson compound ("Boy, shut that gate"). One of the most painful cases in Edward's legal career had involved judicial restrictions on Loring Norcross's handling of trust funds created by a will. A will would not be needed, however, if there was an understanding with Austin that the old arrangement should be continued—that the Mansion's helpless females should be guarded in perpetuity by Edward's son and partner. Indeed, since the Evergreens had not been deeded to Austin and there was no fence between it and the Mansion, the two entities were legally and physically one.

It is not known for certain how the poet's father regarded women's property rights, but there were certainly many men who opposed the reform legislation on this issue. Among them was Dr. Holland, who declared about 1866 that "it is doubtful whether the laws which give the wife the independent control of her property, and thus establish separate pecuniary interests in the family, have done more good than harm." We remember how Lavinia Norcross gave Loring a free hand with her large trust estate.

In Edward's case, the key document is Austin's petition to administer the deceased's estate, a standard printed form with the blanks filled in and the administrator's, Austin's, signature affixed. At the bottom, in the space reserved for "the parties interested in the foregoing Petition" to declare their consent, a consequential act, we read the signed names of Emily Norcross Dickinson, Lavinia, and Emily, in that order. The date was August 3, 1874. Presumably, the application was granted by the judge of probate. And that was it: for the next twenty years Austin did nothing to settle the estate by dividing it among the heirs. A statement filed by Vinnie after his death in 1895 declares that he did not even keep separate accounts for the individual heirs or the two households. The sisters' economic dependency on their brother is hinted at by the friend of Vinnie who wrote (no doubt exaggerating) that she "never had one cent of money."[13] It was by *not* making a will that Edward gave Austin the means to take protective custody of his mother and sisters without anyone's interference.

A defect in this arrangement was that it depended on Austin's continuing to live. In fall 1876, when he was confined for months with "malarial effects," neighbor Amelia Tyler noted that Sue and Vinnie were "hardly on speaking terms. It seems there has never been any division of the Fathers property and Vinnie is really full of trouble— For the sake of his Mother and sisters I hope Austin will live." Austin did live, but the Evergreens inevitably assumed a patronizing attitude toward the dependent Mansion. Two years later Tyler told her son that the Mathers felt "very sorry for Miss Vinney. Mrs Austin rides it rough shod over her— Prof M. says Ned. D____ grows lordly and cynical." Ned's attitude to-

---

13. In 1876, in one of her rare allusions to family finances, the poet warned her fifteen-year-old nephew she would have to retrench on that year's Christmas gifts: "Santa Claus' Bridge blew off, obliging him to be frugal." Edward had owned about $3,000 in Sunderland Bridge shares. When the bridge was wrecked on December 9, 1876, by gale winds, Austin undoubtedly realized he must expect assessments instead of dividends, and passed the word next door.

ward the queer and impractical aunts next door comes out clearly in his letters to his sister, Martha, as when, three years after the poet's death, he confided: "Our surviving Aunt is boring Mother, while I write, what a pity it is that she isn't interesting." When Martha's poems began appearing in the 1890s, he assured her that Aunt Emily's verse looks "very wraith like, and impossible beside her stronger, and saner niece's."[14]

The striking anomaly in Austin's petition to administer his father's estate is that Emily Norcross Dickinson did not sign for herself. Her "signature" was entered by Vinnie, presumably with Austin's approval. Since the poet was the last to sign, she must have noticed the forgery, which sums up as nothing else her family's no-nonsense view of legal protocol and helpless females. When Emily Fowler Ford's father died and she discovered that his will gave preferential treatment to her brothers, she expressed bitter disillusionment. Compared to Ford, with her modern filial and financial attitudes, Dickinson looks flatly archaic. She not only voiced no bad memories but signed her consent allowing the benevolent despotism under which she lived to pass from father to son. If, like Vinnie, she had second thoughts about the estate arrangements, there is no record of them. As a matter of fact, the year Edward died she composed a poem in which a king's realm proves *more* loyal to him after he "relegates" it by dying:

> From his slim Palace in the Dust
> He relegates the Realm,
> More loyal for the exody
> That has befallen him.

Fr1339

That would seem to be how she felt about the transfer of custody—her own, as it were.

---

14. Bianchi would later claim that she and her brother had appreciated their aunt's poetry—had "shared the certainty" and "importance of what she was doing upstairs." Her own verse sometimes looks like a meretricious version of Dickinson's: "The spurnèd bough reveals the path / Her bird has flown; as unaware / A gentle sense of aftermath,— / Renunciation fills the air" ("Indian Summer," 1897).

Living Without a Father

The first time Mattie saw Aunt Emily after the funeral, there were "a few choking words," then "uncontrollable" tears. At night, going upstairs, the poet realized she had associated Father's door—that image again—with "safety." Her statement that he was "quenched so causelessly" suggests she accepted the theory that the opium was to blame. "His Heart was pure and terrible," she wrote Higginson, referring to the severe integrity and self-containment and locked-up affection, "and I think no other like it exists." Friends received a poem idealizing his stoicism: "To his simplicity / To die was little fate" (Fr1387B).

A bulwark was gone, and because it was part of her mind as well as her daily life, her grief was profound and persistent. She could not stop thinking about "Father's lonely Life and his lonelier Death," or "resist the grief to expect" him. Two years later, during a summer hotter than when he died, she dreamed about him "every night, always a different dream, and forget what I am doing daytimes, wondering where he is. Without any body, I keep thinking. What kind can that be?" Her niece never forgot "her husky whisper, 'Where is he? Emily will find him!' " This mysterious promise is partially explained by a remark she made about him and a deceased friend a few years later: "To seek to be nobler for their sakes, is all that remains – and our only Plot for discovering them." A poem addressed to a professor of mathematics who died young[15] says the same thing: "Brother of Ophir / Bright Adieu – / Honor, the shortest route / To you" (Fr1462C). Living up to Father's absoluteness would be the one sure way to "find him."

The last books Edward gave his daughter were George Eliot's *The Legend of Jubal and Other Poems* and a life of Theodore Parker, the radical Unitarian firebrand—choices that show he respected her interests,

---

15. Two years after Professor Root's death, Helen Jameson, a neighbor of the Dickinsons, learned that Martha Cushing, Sarah Tuckerman's unmarried sister, had not been seen for some time and was thought to have "shut herself up as Emily Dickinson has." Jameson's regret that there should be "two lovelorn damsels in the same town, shunning the world & devoting themselves to their grief," shows how the town understood Dickinson's seclusion.

however remote from his own. A year and a half after his death, still "unwilling to open" the volumes, she offered them to Higginson. This unexplained avoidance calls to mind her treatments of the dangers of memory and also a mysterious poem of 1874, "Knock with tremor" (Fr1333), which urges extreme caution in approaching the door of certain "Caesars." Certain awe-inspiring doors *must* stay closed.

The most powerful of Dickinson's commemorative tributes to her father draws on this strong sense of what is hidden. Her inspiration was an ingenious Decoration Day poem by Higginson that appeared in *Scribner's* June 1874, the month Edward died, and that began by posing an ancient question: who among the dead is worthiest of commemoration? "Comrades! in what soldier-grave / Sleeps the bravest of the brave?" Placing his flowers at an ungarlanded plot, in which were buried

> *Youth and beauty, dauntless will,*
> *Dreams that life could ne'er fulfill,*

the speaker reveals in the last stanza that it is a woman's grave: *she* was bravest. After reading this, Dickinson wrote Higginson to express her appreciation of his "beautiful thought." A month later, Edward having died, she asked, "was it not prophetic? It has assisted that Pause of Space which I call 'Father.'" Again, the strange phrase suggests how Edward demarcated space for her.

Three years later, rereading "Decoration," Dickinson devised her own answer to the question of honoring the unknown great:

> Lay this Laurel on the one
> Triumphed and remained unknown –
> Laurel – fell your futile Tree –
> Such a Victor could not be –
> Lay this Laurel on the one
> Too intrinsic for Renown –
> Laurel – vail your deathless Tree –
> Him you chasten – that is he –

Fr1428B

The poem comes clear as soon as one notices the counterpoint of voices, the second sharply dissenting from the first. In lines 1–2 and 5–6, voice number one addresses itself to the Higginsonian task of honoring some-one who is worthy but unknown. In lines 3–4 and 7–8, voice number two, making an aggressive rebuke, twice denies the point of this project. The second time, moderating its tone and replacing "fell" with "vail" and "futile" with "deathless," the dissenting voice instructs the laurel that any public display would be unseemly in this, the ultimate case, where glory denied is itself the mark of highest merit. For Emily, this was the basic and bitter paradox of Father's life, devoted to the public good and termi-nating in loneliness. Her poem rules out the possibility of public honors for him yet sees his kind of honor as transcendent and absolute: him you chasten, *that* is he. The rule held for her, too, of course, in her deeper ob-scurity.[16]

The letter to Higginson that incorporates the second stanza appears to mark the end of Dickinson's mourning and the lifting of one of her heaviest veils. Written in a summer dusk three years after Edward's death, this letter begins by saying the tired day is resting her cheek on the hill "like a child." "Nature confides now," and so does the unusually relaxed writer, who goes on to speak of a new sense of peace and free-dom: "Summer is so kind I had hoped you might come. Since my Fa-ther's dying, everything sacred enlarged so – it was dim to own." She then brings up for the first and only time the unusually distressing fu-neral from her girlhood at which she misunderstood the officiating min-ister's rhetorical question—"Is the Arm of the Lord shortened that it cannot save?" As argued earlier, this sentence was probably uttered at the funeral of Martha Dwight Strong, who killed herself in June 1844 by plunging into a well soon after Emily's return from a recuperative stay in Boston. That was exactly thirty years before Edward died.

"Since my Father's dying, everything sacred enlarged so – it was dim

16. Questions remain about the poem's private significance. Was Dickinson recalling paternal acts that weren't publicized and remain unknown? Is this the place to factor in James W. Boyden and the enormous and unexplained financial losses he caused Edward in the early 1860s? Was the poet saying that something accruing to Father's honor would always have to remain secret?

to own." We do not know what she saw as she looked back at her life, which had also, in a way, been dropped "Into the purple well" (Fr307), as one of her early dedicatory poems put it. But it seems evident that the gate, the door, the latch was no longer locked. After 1877 there were no more poems about the sealed house of memory. Instead, we have "No Passenger was known to flee / Who lodged a night in Memory..." (Fr1451A). Father's dying had made possible a fresh seeing and owning of dim things.

"Emily, You Damned Rascal"

Knowing how devastated Emily Norcross Dickinson was by her husband's death, Samuel Bowles sent a box of flowers for her first widowed Thanksgiving, an excruciating ordeal. From now on, without a man in the house, the three Dickinson women celebrated the holiday with Austin and Sue. One year, the thing to be thankful for was that "Mother didn't cry much."

The deadliest calendar day was the anniversary of Father's death, which the poet twice dated not June 16 but the day before, when he left home for the last time. Her mother seems to have made the same mistake: on June 15, 1875, she suffered a stroke that produced a partial lateral paralysis and an impaired memory (the forged signature dates from earlier). From now on, she often failed to understand why Edward did not come home at night, or how Emily could go to bed without waiting up for him. "Home is so far from Home," Emily lamented, troubled less by Mother's physical demands than by the constant need to ease her worries with palliative lies. Once the poet admitted she had "known little of Literature since my Father died." But she still found time to produce it. "You asked me if I wrote now? I have no other Playmate," she assured Higginson in 1877. However, the next summer Mother fell and broke a hip and became permanently bedridden, requiring even more care. That year Dickinson made half as many playmates as the previous year.

At Edward's funeral, Bowles was the only person out of the family to talk to her. The eleven-year freeze was over, and she resumed writing and, on at least one other occasion, seeing him. Twice her first letter skirted the question of her long silence: "You spoke of not liking to be forgotten. . . . Treason never knew you." Claiming she had been faithful in spite of appearances, she nonetheless avoided the first person and employed a strategic negative: "treason never knew you" rather than "I was always loyal." Her unease shows up in her opening words: "I should think you would have few Letters for your own are so noble that they make men afraid – and sweet as your Approbation is – it is had in fear – lest your depth convict us." If not an apology, this was an admission of the discomfort she felt with him.

Now that she was in touch, it wasn't long before her letters became exuberant: "We miss your vivid Face and the besetting Accents, you bring from your Numidian Haunts." This was her new tone with him, making him a romantic and captivating "Arabian" or a perennial source of life others depended on. The extravagant dependency, however, was less for herself than for others. It wasn't "I miss" but "we miss," even more than in the old days.

Eighteen seventy-five was a terrible year for Bowles. A major lawsuit eroded his health, he became estranged from his brother, and Maria Whitney left for Paris to prepare for her new teaching duties at Smith College; "M's going really oppresses me," he confided. Feeling alone and old, he suspected he would "soon be dried up & exhibited in the College Museum—not with bird tracks over me, but with traces of great grief at the cruelty & desertion of what used to be called 'lovely woman.'"

By 1877 he was visibly in ruins. In late June, exerting himself to attend Commencement and the installation of President Julius H. Seelye (whose appointment he had opposed), he came to Amherst. Stepping into the Mansion, he sent his card up to Emily asking to see her. When a negative came down, it was the last straw. In the story Vinnie told years later to Gertrude M. Graves, Samuel "went to the foot of the stairs and called in a loud and insistent tone, 'Emily, you wretch! No more of this nonsense! I've traveled all the way from Springfield to see you. Come down at once.'" To her sister's surprise, Emily did come down and was "brilliant" and "fascinating." In Bianchi's version, Samuel called her "ras-

cal," not "wretch." The actual phrase, as Johnson deduced from the conclusion of the poet's next and last letter to him ("Your 'Rascal,' [P.S.] I
washed the Adjective"), was undoubtedly "You damned rascal." It makes
a good story, yet it seems likely the failing man was bruised by that initial refusal. A week later, anticipating the next trustees' meeting in
Amherst, he wrote the Evergreens: "I don't mean to [come], if I can help
it—that is, if I can get up courage enough to 'cut' you all dead for once."
It sounds as if he felt used, taken for granted.

For Emily, the interview had a sweeter aftertaste. A few months before Samuel's visit, William S. Robinson, the *Republican*'s Boston correspondent with the pen name Warrington, had died, but not before
entering a serene state that removed all doubts of an afterlife. On the
verge of death, the correspondent not only saw how "this world is but the
anteroom to the life beyond" but observed crowds of "heavenly visi-
tants." As Samuel's talk with Emily drew to an end, he told her of these
"revelations of immortality," then just published. As soon as her friend
left (Emily informed him afterward), she returned to "the Room . . . to
confirm your presence," then drafted a response to the visit and to Warrington's supposed revelations. Tellingly, it was to the effect that the afterlife meant little or nothing to her apart from her present ties to close
friends:

> *I have no Life but this – . . .*
> *Nor tie to Earths to come,*
> *Nor Action new*
> *Except through this Extent*
> *The love of you.*
>
> Fr1432B

Elsewhere, she titled this "a Word to a Friend." That it was a word of
good-bye gives us the necessary perspective on the last four words, both
more and less than a romantic declaration. The tacit implication is that
it was time to be generous and final.

The editor's own gallant follow-up to the visit was preserved in his
stenographer's original shorthand and published in George Merriam's

biography as "written to a woman friend." This is the only letter we have from Bowles to Dickinson.

> It was very sweet to see you at last. I hope I may oftener come
> face to face with you. I have little spare strength or time for writing
> and so testifying to my remembrance, and you are very good to like
> me so much and to say such sweet and encouraging things to me. . . .

He added that Warrington's visions were "greatly impressive to me. Here is the record. You may like to read it, even from an enemy." The "record" was the relevant segment of *"Warrington" Pen-Portraits*. The Boston correspondent had been an "enemy" ever since his 1861 attack on Edward ("fossil," "bigot," "mouse") for declining the Republican nomination for lieutenant governor. Who knew better than Bowles that Dickinsons never forgot a slight?

Higginson was sent the same poem as Bowles, but with a material substitution in the last line: "realm" in place of "love," which would have been out of keeping. The new word was exactly right now that the vast space left by Major Dickinson was partly filled by Colonel Higginson. In 1876 he received more letters from her than during the previous five years, or than went to Bowles from 1874 on. If she needed authorization not to publish "when troubled by entreaty," it was to Higginson she appealed. When he returned from abroad in 1878, she said, "I missed yourself and Mr Bowles, and without a Father, seemed even vaster than before." When Mary Higginson's health worsened, Dickinson sent her Emerson's *Representative Men,* calling it "a little Granite Book you can lean upon." It was this phrase and gift (whose title neatly captures her need of male bulwarks) that drew Higginson's often quoted remark about "my partially cracked poetess."

Since Dickinson's letters to Charles Wadsworth were apparently burned, we cannot know the new terms of their relationship. But it is clear that by fall 1876 she was once again in touch with her Philadelphia "Shepherd," reaching him now by way of the Hollands, who addressed her envelopes and mailed them from New York. In writing other correspondents, she sometimes asked Luke Sweetser and George Montague,[17] old and trusted neighbors, to perform this service; once she asked Maggie Maher. If the practice was designed to secure a legible script, the main purpose was undoubtedly to shield her exchanges from prying eyes. It was the Hollands' understanding that she sought their help with Wadsworth to elude "the scrutiny of a village postmaster," and also that she wasn't sending real "love letters," which would have "betrayed their confidence." Still, one notes that, while local address writers sufficed for other correspondences, this one was hidden from everyone in town. One of the few things we know about Dickinson's relationship with Wadsworth is that she took extreme measures to keep it secret. A letter to Elizabeth Holland alluding to her special help thanks her for "beloved Acts, both revealed and covert."

The most erotic poem composed by Dickinson between 1870 and 1878 has been assigned to the same year, 1876, for which we have the first evidence of her renewed correspondence with Wadsworth:

> *Long Years apart – can make no*
> *Breach a second cannot fill –*
> *Who says the Absence of a Witch*
> *Invalidates his spell?*[18]
>
> *The embers of a Thousand Years*
> *Uncovered by the Hand*
> *That fondled them when they were Fire*
> *Will stir and understand*

Fr1405

---

17. The gentle preciosity of a note from Montague (preserved because of a poem drafted on the back) evokes the cocoon in which Dickinson lived: "Cousin Emily will please forgive me.— I have made a blemish . . . on *two* of her Envelopes, & have substituted two of mine. . . . If they will do, I shall be glad."

18. Franklin's edition does not make clear that after Dickinson drafted her original version of the first stanza, she jotted down an alternative for lines 3–4 (used above) *before* entering the rest of the poem.

The eye-catching detail, the man witch, exemplifies Dickinson's free hand with the gendered specificities we make so hard and fast. Her witch is a wizard whose spells are permanent, who covers the fire he has lit and then a thousand years later uncovers it.

"Uncovered by the Hand." Prior to Wadsworth's death, the poet's surviving letters have only one comment on him. Writing the Hollands after their trip to the Philadelphia Centennial, Dickinson offered to send them the minister's Thanksgiving message, "God's Culture": "The Sermon you failed to hear, I can lend you – though Legerdemain is unconveyed." What she meant was that the printed text could not convey the drama of Wadsworth's voice and delivery. But her diction is thinking of a magician's hand, not a speaking voice.

Again and again, the slender evidence as to the identity of the man Dickinson loved points to Wadsworth. Every other known candidate of either sex can be ruled out; he never is. Yet he is never confirmed. The probable explanation is that the love was on her side only, it was a question of feeling and imagination more than action, she covered her tracks well, and the intensely private Wadsworth was equally careful. Also, her family shielded her—and then whispered among themselves about that married Philadelphia clergyman. His children, one of whom was a minister and another the Philadelphia coroner, undoubtedly did everything in their power to protect their father's reputation, especially after Martha Bianchi went public in 1924 with her foolish version of the story.[19]

Dickinson's letters to Wadsworth from 1876 on probably had nothing resembling the tragic neediness of her Master drafts. Certainly, her posthumous queries to his friends, the Clark brothers, do not suggest a grand passion. Transgressive as she was, by her late forties the poet was a mature and disciplined woman with a vast experience in managing epistolary friendships. For all her talk about magic and revolution and

---

19. George F. Whicher's amusing report of an interview with the last surviving and very dignified child, Dr. William S. Wadsworth, appeared in *The Nation* in 1949. At the end of the conversation, expressing himself much less guardedly than at first, the doctor assured Whicher his father would not have been "unduly impressed by a hysterical young woman's ravings." The outburst may or may not reflect the minister's feelings about Dickinson in the early 1860s, but it speaks volumes about the family's resentment of the way the relationship had been construed.

ecstasy, she may have felt there would be no sweeping changes in her life; perhaps she didn't want any. Extrapolating from her letters to Bowles and Higginson, we may surmise she approached Wadsworth as a select counselor and friend, and that no heavy appeals, confrontations, misunderstandings resulted.

But romance wasn't done with her. On December 10, 1877, in Salem, Elizabeth Farley Lord, wife of a good friend of the Dickinsons, died of cancer. It was the poet's forty-seventh birthday and there was to be an immense consequence for her.

Chapter 21

1878–1884: Late Adventures in Friendship and Love

Readers put off by Emily Dickinson's class privileges should not forget that she was far more exposed to pain and disease than most of us. One October night in 1877, after Lizzie Mather was taken for a drive by Austin, a vessel burst in this consumptive neighbor's lungs and she drowned in her own blood, her family hearing her thumpings on the floor. Would we be tough enough to send the bereaved husband the message that came from across the street? "When you have strength to remember that Dying dispels nothing which was firm before, you have avenged sorrow."

Two months later, when Vinnie came down with a complaint a neighbor called "dropsical," and Emily and Maggie had to spend most of their time nursing her as well as the bedridden, memory-impaired, and much complaining mother, the poet wrote her friend Elizabeth Holland: "This is Night – now – but we are not dreaming." Events took a toll on Dickinson but never qualified her inimitable and noble mischief. Even in her last two and a half years, enfeebled by illness and a series of deaths, her voice never sounded old or defeated. How many writers, getting on in years, have complained so little? It was a question of temperament, of course, but there were also huge outlays of attention, finely calibrated effort, energetic compensation. Because these had become second nature, what looks from a distance like effortless coasting was almost certainly more costly.

A Tender Permission

When Maria Whitney returned from Paris in fall 1877, ready to begin teaching at Smith, she found Samuel Bowles "shockingly changed . . . feeble to the last degree & with a distressing cough." At last he seemed willing to take care of himself, but she feared it was too late, and it was. In December, after he nearly died, his devoted female friends rallied around him. Sue strenuously advised electricity—"I *know* what I am saying, having known of remarkable cures"—eliciting the doctor's frank counsel that "we must give him up." Mary Clemmer Ames composed a tribute to the "prostrate King" lying "with broken lance," and Maria went back and forth between Northampton and Springfield and kept Amherst posted. Dickinson's first letter to "Miss Whitney" acknowledges her "delicate kindness" during "these acuter days."[1] On January 16, 1878, officially from apoplexy, unofficially from "too close application" to work, the editor died. He was fifty-one.

It is clear from Dickinson's several postmortems both how much she

---

1. All editions of Dickinson's letters beginning with that of 1894 omit the middle paragraph of this letter: "To every heart adjoining his, Springfield must be first, and sweetest of unappeased hope is his convalescence."

mourned and how much her mourning was on behalf of others. To her devastated sister-in-law, she sent a sharp aperçu on the man's chronic unfinishedness: "His nature was Future – He had not yet lived." It was the same thing she had spotted in busy Higginson, who "forgot to live." The consolatory notes she sent Mary Bowles show a graduated allowance for her prickliness. At first, Emily praised the widow's generosity for accepting her messages: "Sorrow almost resents love, it is so inflamed." But in the third note, written several months later when grief was less sore, Mary was tactfully admonished to make a self-improving use of her husband's death: "The time will be long till you see him, dear, but it will be short, for have we not each our heart to dress – heavenly as his?" The poet was recommending something like the self-regulatory discipline she herself practiced.

Of all the people Dickinson wrote to about Bowles, her most impassioned remarks went to Maria Whitney, who for many years had been extremely close to the editor, once addressing him as "my dearest friend." This attachment, of great interest to the poet and thus something we must try to see clearly, has been distorted by Dickinson scholars, who assume that Whitney was a frequent or constant member of Bowles's household[2] and possibly his mistress. In fact, she lived with the family for little more than a year: three months in 1863 in a New York hotel, with Samuel showing up on Sundays; a few brief intervals in 1867; and from September 1867 to April 1868. These caretaking stints coincided with two of Mary's births, which added to the nursing and managerial headaches. Worst of all, Mary proved as resentful as she was helpless by contributing to a scandalous rumor in spring 1868 about her

---

2. Whitney lived in California in 1864–1866, taught in Cambridge 1868–1869, resided in Germany 1869–1871 (both studying and chaperoning Sally Bowles), conducted a private class for Northampton girls 1872–1874, studied French in Paris 1875–1876 and then returned for five months in 1877. During her intervals in Northampton, she clipped excerpts for the *Republican*, saw to the remodeling of the family home, helped care for a sister who had typhoid fever in 1873–1874, and did much more besides. She should not be seen as "a supervisory companion and housekeeper for the Bowleses during Mary's pregnancies and depressions in the sixties and early seventies."

husband and Maria, who was alarmed and embittered; she had an extremely punctilious sense of duty. The tale must have reached Amherst, for ten years later, when Emily heard that Mary Bowles had spoken of Maria "with peculiar love," she instantly passed it on, hoping her friend would find it "sweet" to know that "long fidelity in ungracious soil [Mary] was not wholly squandered." Among other things, the letter illustrates Emily's permanent effort to bolster Maria's faith in life.

Yet it is true that Maria loved Samuel, and also that his letters to her, full of talk about literature and religion and politics, are in every way more alive than those to his wife. Underneath the idealism and intellectuality that cemented this friendship lay a rich tangle of emotions. Samuel had an ego that demanded perfect loyalty from women, and was not above exploiting Maria's devotion to secure her care of his wife and children. He resented it when her enthusiasms took her out of his reach, as when she aided Charles Loring Brace or went to New Haven to tend a brother's children. On her side, though she obviously had a life of her own, there was no man who compared with Samuel; certainly, none with his command, charm, brilliance. The unofficial nature of their relationship, along with the fact that his last illness coincided with the beginning of her anxious work at Smith College, made the strain of "keeping up" (her phrase) during his last weeks all but intolerable. A numbed remark to a sister-in-law hints at her unvoiced anguish: "It all seems still utterly incomprehensible, impossible to me; my mind utterly fails to grasp the idea. I only know something dreadful has happened & that I have got to go on, with the sky all gone out of my life."

During the sixteen years of Sue and Austin's friendship with Maria, Emily had made no significant overtures toward her; there is no evidence they met. Now Maria's skylessness gave her the opening she needed. It was probably in January or February 1878 that the poet sent one of those messages she alone could write:

> I have thought of you often since the darkness – though we cannot assist Another's night – . . .
> I hope you may remember me, as I shall always mingle you with

our Mr Bowles – Affection gropes through drifts of Awe, for his tropic door –

I hope you have the power of Hope . . .

It was a typical combination of boldness and delicacy. Taking for granted Maria's private rights as mourner, Emily dared to connect, "mingle," her with Samuel, even imagining a wintry groping for his "tropic door." At the same time, respecting Maria's privacy, she refrained from thrusting any standard consolatory sentiments on her.

To "hope you may remember me" was a politely ambiguous way of asking for a reply. When it came, Emily made explicit the basis on which the friendship would move forward: "Your touching suggestion that those who loved Mr Bowles – be more closely each other's, is a tender permission." Since Maria's part in the ensuing correspondence is lost, we don't know how it played out for her, or what this active, well-traveled, and very correct and reserved woman thought of the poet. Emily is never mentioned in her family correspondence from 1862 through 1887 or in her five surviving notes to Sue (one of which unsentimentally recalls "Sam's last struggle for life"). But it is clear from the poet's seventeen complete or fragmentary letters to Maria that she used the latter's "tender permission" as an authorization to make their friend a kind of glowing focus: "You will be with us while he is with us and that will be while we are ourselves – for Consciousness is the only Home of which we *now* know." Here, "Consciousness" almost looks like a private cult in which the two votaries can worship side by side at that "tropic door."

Early in the correspondence Emily sent Maria the editor's last communication, probably the one on Warrington: "I lend you the last I knew – of the One who taught us of you – to whom we instinctively confide you – The Crucifix requires no glove." That strange final sentence says that anguish does away with the need for formality, the implication being that in this case the widow may be ignored and the letter trusted to Maria, who has special rights on the basis of love and grief. There are only four letters to her that do not mention or allude to the editor. Six years after his death, when Whitney had ceased mourning, the subject remained fresh for the poet, who wrote that she "dreamed Saturday Night of precious Mr Bowles – One glance of his would light a World."[3]

Dickinson had many reasons for returning so obsessively to precious Mr. Bowles, among which was that he gave her something to say (and a way to relate) to a woman with whom she had little in common. He also afforded an occasion for reflections on memory and desire, and, more personally, for the fraught topic of secret devotion. Once, hinting at an attachment of her own, Dickinson brought out her old idea of the moment of reunion in heaven: "I fear we shall care very little for the technical Resurrection, when to behold the one face that to us comprised it – is too much for us and I dare not think of the voraciousness of that only gaze and its only return." But her basic purpose was advisory, not confessional – to offer the consolation of human contact and relieve the aridities of Whitney's life: "though we are each – unknown – to ourself – and each other – 'tis not what well conferred it, the dying soldier asks – it is only the water."

Whitney came to Amherst twice in 1880: in late March, when she was looking forward to a summer away from Northampton, and on July 31, as she made her farewell calls before sailing to Germany (she had resigned her position at Smith in May). On one of these visits, she saw the Dickinson sisters. Afterward, Emily wrote that the caller had spoken "very sweetly to both of us and your sewing and recollecting is a haunting picture." "Recollecting" meant Samuel, of course, at whose image the poet all but smacked her lips: "One sweet sweet more – One liquid more – of that Arabian presence!" She said nothing about Maria's professional life—her teaching, her study of languages—subjects never brought up in letters to this correspondent. In her closest reference to the upcoming move, Emily noted that the distant sound of the Northampton bell

---

3. Todd's 1894 edition of Dickinson's letters gave Johnson his text for most of the Whitney correspondence. After he went to print, the manuscripts of eight of these letters came to light, four of which—letters 537, 539, 591, 948—have passages on Bowles excised in accordance with Whitney's wishes. Todd printed the last of these, on Bowles's light-giving glance, as a detached and unidentified fragment. The same year, "The Lightbearer," a stained-glass window dedicated to Samuel and Mary Bowles, was installed in Springfield's Church of the Unity. Designed by Edward Emerson Simmons and fabricated in the Tiffany Studios, it is on permanent exhibit at the George Walter Vincent Smith Art Museum in Springfield.

would no longer mean "Miss Whitney is going to Church." She repeated "sweet" or "sweetly" five times. That this is the one letter responding to Whitney's presence is another hint that Dickinson was at her best when she was *not* seeing her friends.[4]

A letter reacting to Whitney's absence makes a telling contrast. On May 13, 1882, in unrelated illnesses, her brother Josiah lost his wife and a married daughter, the latter leaving a baby girl. In a fit of generous zeal, fifty-one-year-old Maria offered to care for the infant, a job that required her to leave Germany and give up her study of Old Norse. Even though she and Josiah had never gotten on, she joined him in Cambridge and, devoting herself to the baby, tried to "reform" its "habits" and cope with her brother's silent ungraciousness. By the following May, exhausted and embittered by her unsuccessful effort to act as mother, she was taking "morbid views of things" and performing her duties with a hard-bitten exactness. Earlier, she had hoped to visit Amherst when the apples were blossoming. Now, all she could do, it seems, was to send an account of her hard winter.

This ordeal was what Dickinson had in mind when she wrote her "absent friend," probably in May 1883. Alluding to Jesus' statement that the lilies of the field neither toil nor spin, yet "Solomon in all his glory was not arrayed like one of these," she announced that the sight of this flower made her want to disrobe—and "were I sure no one saw me, I might make those advances of which in after life I should repent." She empathized with Maria's pained "fondness for the little life so mysteriously committed to your care" and trusted the experience would be of value: "the early spiritual influences about a child are more hallowing than we know." Where Whitney tried to break the baby's nightly dependence on its wet nurse, Dickinson took an indulgent view of children's "ravenousness of fondness," asking, "Is there not a sweet wolf within us that

---

4. In the winter of 1882–1883, declining to see a young professor of rhetoric, she said she had "no grace to talk, and my own Words so chill and burn me, that the temperature of Other Minds is too new an Awe."

5. The question follows an appealing anecdote about Dickinson's seven-year-old nephew that is missing from all editions of the letters: "Austin's little Gilbert burst in today, 'Oh Aunt Emily, I want something.' 'What shall it be?' I said with a kiss. 'Oh, everything,' he answered."

demands its food?"[5] If the poet had little practical experience in tending a baby, she still knew how to amuse, stroke, stretch an exhausted caretaker. That was part of her work now: easing distant trouble.

Energetic, competent, learned, responsible, Whitney took on the world as few women of her time dared. One of the results was the nagging sense of homelessness and unfulfillment she tried to assuage in her nursing stints. Another was the stiffly carapaced look evident in her photographs. Did Dickinson see her as unduly expert and armored? Possibly, judging from a poem sent to her that speaks of an unarmored kind of wisdom:

> *Our ignorance our Cuirass is –*
> *We wear Mortality*
> *As lightly as an Option Gown*
> *Till asked to take it off – . . .*
>
> Fr1481B (J1462)

When an autumn frost killed Emily's plants, she wrote Maria with seeming casualness how they "went into camp last night, their tender armor insufficient for the crafty nights."

"I feel Barefoot all over as the Boys say," Emily had jotted down in that unusually relaxed summer of 1877. Undressing and cheerful simplicity and not taking morbid views: these were the topics that had risen to the surface in her correspondence with Maria. An exchange founded on Samuel's memory had acquired an impetus based on the two women's actual relationship. "I am glad you accept rest," Emily wrote a few months after the failed experiment in mothering; "Too many disdain it." Then came flat disagreement on another issue: "You speak of 'disillusion.' That is one of the few subjects on which I am an infidel."

Although the letters to Whitney remind us now and then of the morbid Dickinson of legend, they mostly tell of her high spirits in her late forties and fifties. Having lived past the end of her excruciating story (adapting Rachel Blau DuPlessis's useful title), she became a hidden presence in others' lives by means of her letters and poems. It says something about her that she chose to get involved with a formidable stranger like Whitney. It was a risky assumption of responsibility—not Whitney's kind but just as fearless.

Judge Lord and the Wildest Word in the Language

It is that happy freedom and fearlessness that we see in Dickinson's astounding love letters to Otis Phillips Lord, an elderly judge on Massachusetts' Supreme Judicial Court. These letters, or rather drafts of letters (the distinction is crucial and the source of much controversy), raise the presumption that, whatever her earlier experience, she had the thrill of mutual love with a man.

Born in 1812 and thus closer to Edward's generation than her own, Lord may have been the single most intimidating person on her impressive short list of friends. At his death, the tributes from attorneys emphasized his principled severity and fearsome courtroom presence. "His dynamite was all in his eye," said one lawyer, adding (as if the stipulation was necessary) that his name would never be equivalent to "murder." "No one who met him," said another, "could fail to feel his force, his strength, his grip." Once, cross-examining, his "sudden and powerful mental grip" made a nervous witness faint. His oral powers were spoken of with awe—his gift for succinct clarity, his sly and deadly humor.

An old-line Whig like Edward Dickinson, Lord had been speaker of the Massachusetts House in 1854. After his party's rout that fall, he kept insisting (again like Edward) that "the great heart of Massachusetts is Whig to the core." At the 1855 Whig state convention, he gave a rousing speech defying all compromises: "To-day we are Whig, and we are not anything else. (Laughter and applause.) We have no outsiders to catch to-day; we have no baits to throw to any gudgeons. We stand to-day Whigs upon Whig principles, and we stand there or we fall. (Cheers and cries of 'good—good.')" In July 1862, giving a Commencement address at Amherst College, by then heavily Republican, he blamed the war on "the uneasy men, in all parts of the country" and defended the Bell-Everett program: "the Union as it was and the Constitution as it is." That meant defeating the rebels without compromising their property rights in slaves. Appointed to the Commonwealth's highest court, he was the subject of frequent complaint for harshness and partiality. When Henry Ward Beecher was tried for adultery, Lord examined the minister's self-defense with his steeltrap mind and came out with a ferocious brief for his guilt and hypocrisy. Filling four columns in the *Republican* (which backed the analysis), it must have been seen by Emily.

In private life, Lord was said to be "one of the kindest and most genial of men." His gift for chiseled utterance made him a good talker, "piquant and racy," though only with intimates and kindred spirits. At the Evergreens, according to Sue, he "never seem[ed] to coalesce." Once at dinner, however, when Austin was ill and Vinnie was leading him on and the talk turned to New England's hymns, he made himself "more stiff and erect behind his old-fashioned silk stock" and recited the whole of Isaac Watts's grimmest song:

> *My thoughts on awful subjects roll,*
> *Damnation and the dead;*
> *What horrors seize the guilty soul,*
> *Upon a dying bed.*
>
> *Lingering about these mortal shores,*
> *She makes a long delay;*
> *Till, like a flood with rapid force,*
> *Death sweeps the wretch away.*
>
> *Then, swift and dreadful she descends*
> *Down to the fiery coast;*
> *Amongst abominable fiends,*
> *Herself a frightened ghost . . .*

The response, Sue remembered, was "nervous laughter."[6]

---

6. Vinnie topped this with a comic rendition of another hymn by Watts:

> *Broad is the road that leads to death,*
> *And thousands walk together there:*
> *But wisdom shows a narrow path,*
> *With here and there a traveller . . .*

The judge had a memory for images of being swept away. After his death, when Mary C. Farley drowned in Walden Pond, Dickinson recalled how much he savored the phrase, "an envious sliver broke," from Gertrude's narration of Ophelia's drowning.

Like Dickinson, Lord had the old-fashioned idea that literature was to be cultivated in private with one's friends. His 1871 memoir of Asahel Huntington contains a surprisingly detailed account of the man's close friendship with a "gifted poetess," Hannah Flagg Gould, who lived with her father and whose humorous epitaphs were "distinguished by delicacy and purity of sentiment and by exemplary correctness of versification." James Guthrie has conjectured that some of Dickinson's humorous poems, beginning with "The judge is like the owl" (Fr728) of 1863, may have been sent to Lord, who came to Amherst for college functions or when holding court in Northampton; he was class of 1832.

The first solid evidence of friendship with Dickinson dates from 1872 or 1873: an envelope addressed to her by Lord on which she drafted a poem (Fr1265). In 1873, when Sue was at the seaside near Salem, the poet sent "Love for . . . the dear Lords." From about 1874, on the back of Fr1337, we have her draft of a note to his niece, Abby Farley. In October 1875, a year after Edward's death, the Lords spent a week in Amherst and the poet and her mother made their wills, no doubt with the Judge's legal advice; his wife, Elizabeth, was a witness. His recitation of the hymn probably took place during Austin's malarial illness of fall 1876. The following January, anxious Vinnie sent him a query about the wrecked Sunderland Bridge. In reply, he said he knew nothing about the matter, was too "jaded" for anything but solitaire, and often thought "of you & of Emily, whose last note gave me a good deal of uneasiness, for knowing how entirely unselfish she is, and how unwilling to disclose any ailment, I fear that she has been more ill, than she has told me. I hope you will tell me particularly about her." Not realizing his wife had cancer, he spoke of her "rheumatism or neuralgia" and asked once again for "*full* accounts of the health of *each* of you." Clearly, he was not only in touch with the poet before Elizabeth Lord's death on December 10, 1877, but anxious about her well-being.

Exactly when this friendship turned into a late-life romance is diffi-

cult to say. After the poet's death, in obedience to her wishes, Vinnie
burned the lifetime of letters she had received, presumably including
those from Lord; apparently her letters to him were also destroyed. However, not only did she retain versions of what she sent her lover, but in the
1890s a number of these were given to Mabel Loomis Todd by Austin,
with what motives we can only guess. Some of these are fragmentary
rough drafts. Others are fair copies, with scissored deletions that tell of a
deliberate act of selective preservation, the implication being that what
we have is what we were *meant* to have. The four fair copies that can be
dated all come from 1882: April 30–May 1, May 14, November 11, and
December 3. Although Johnson and Leyda assigned the earliest manuscripts to 1878, that is probably too early, especially for the amorous fragment that refers to spring (letter 563). It seems impossible this could have
been written a few months after Elizabeth Lord died.

What evidence there is points to a later date for the affair's beginning. Some months after Charles Wadsworth's death in April 1882,
Emily wrote Elizabeth Holland, "It sometimes seems as if special
Months gave and took away – August has brought the most to me –
April – robbed me most."[7] Eighteen eighty is the first year after Elizabeth Lord's death in which Otis is known to have visited Amherst in
August, staying from the twenty-third to the thirtieth, longer than any
other visit. Accompanied by some Farley in-laws, he and his entourage
were referred to by Austin as "the Lords." The poet used the same designation in a contemporaneous letter that has been incorrectly dated by
editors. In early September, writing Aunt Catharine Sweetser, she was
profuse with apology and explanation: "I designed to write you, immediately, but the Lords came as you went, and Judge Lord was my father's
closest friend, so I shared my moments with them till they left us last
Monday; then seeing directly after, the death of your loved Dr. A____, I
felt you might like to be alone." Otis left Amherst on Monday, August
30, 1880. The next day the pastor emeritus of Catharine's Madison
Square Church, the Reverend Doctor William Adams, died. The day

7. Her friend Sophia Holland died in April 1844, and it was in April 1862 that she learned
Wadsworth and Bowles would sail.

after that his death notice appeared in the *Republican*. Ignoring for now the effect of Otis and Edward's friendship on Dickinson's susceptibility, one notes both the chapter-and-verse detail and the strained implausibility of her excuse for not writing. It does look as if she was trying to pull the wool over her aunt's eyes.

On September 23, less than a month later—the shortest known interval between the judge's visits—he was back in town. This time, according to Austin's diary, the Farley nieces were squired here and there by Ned, leaving Otis free and unaccounted for from the twenty-fourth to the twenty-sixth.

It was in 1880, according to Sue, that Otis presented Emily with a costly and discriminating gift, a marbled Shakespeare concordance. No earlier gifts from him are known.[8]

The letter to Lord that Johnson and Leyda each placed first in the series looks like an early confession of love:

> My lovely Salem smiles at me – I seek his Face so often – but I have done with guises –
> I confess that I love him – I rejoice that I love him – I thank the maker of Heaven and Earth – that gave him me to love – The Exaltation floods me – I cannot find my channel – the Creek turns Sea – at thought of thee . . .

Further on, in a rough draft of the same letter:

> . . . waking for your sake on Day made magical with you before I went to Sleep – what pretty phrase – we went to sleep as if it were a Country – let us make it one – we could/will make it one, my native Land – my Darling come oh be a patriot now . . . Oh nation of the soul Thou hast thy freedom now

---

8. Two poems possibly associated with Lord—"I thought the train would never come" (Fr1473) and "Oh, honey of an hour" (Fr1477)—are assigned to 1878 without explanation by Franklin. The first of these seems linked to a later, regretful poem that speaks of a train's departure—"The summer that we did not prize" (Fr1622)—and was composed on the back of a letter draft to Lord.

The (apparently) unguarded rapture of such passages has elicited some curious reactions from the poet's scholarly handlers. When Millicent Todd Bingham made them known in 1954, she solemnly quoted God's warning to Moses at the burning bush: "Put off thy shoes from off thy feet, for the place whereon thou standest is holy ground." More recently, in an essay edition that asks us to regard the manuscript fragments as aesthetic objects and refrain from "imagining a plot," Marta L. Werner announces, "My work initiates a break . . . by proposing that the most powerful 'revelations' of the drafts . . . are not biographical but, rather, *textual*."

Werner's facsimiles have much to tell us about Dickinson's writing habits—her use of scraps of paper, the difference between her rough hand and her record-keeping hand. But most readers will surely feel that the real interest of these fragments, plot or no plot, lies in their disclosures about Dickinson's erotic fervor and her relations with Lord. Like some of her youthful letters, they have a kind of unleashed, over-the-top playfulness now that the "soul" is in its native country. This freedom, rooted in a sense of intimacy, expresses itself in a copious and seemingly uninhibited play of language. The poet was writing to a highly literate man, and the pleasures she enjoyed were in part those of a shared imaginative and linguistic romp—what she had called in a tormented letter to Master two decades earlier "the prank of the Heart at play on the Heart." A wordless relationship would have been no fun at all. Sometimes she "almost feared Language was done between us."

In spite of the joy of surrendering her brook to his sea, Dickinson was neither willing to merge nor "done with guises." Her drafts show she had learned the lesson of desire and distance and did not contemplate any real yielding: "Dont you know you are happiest while I withhold and not confer – dont you know that 'No' is the wildest word we consign to Language? [new paragraph] You do, for you know all things."[9] *Did* Otis

---

9. Whoever preserved the manuscript containing these important words wanted them and nothing else: the paper has been scissored top and bottom. If Austin made the cuts before turning this and other Lord manuscripts over to Todd, a motive is deducible from something his daughter remembered—his "morbid horror of his sister Emily being thought to have been 'disappointed' in love."

know, and if so, how did he like it? It may be that Emily's "no" *was* too wild for him, as when she both confessed her desire and insisted on her freedom: "I am but a restive sleeper and often should journey from your Arms through the happy Night, but you will lift me back, wont you, for only there I ask to be." Here, in a single breath, she dares to speak of *their* shared nights and *her* vagrant proclivities. She also appears to assume that "no" is not "no" but a basis for additional play, intimacy, confession. Of course, we can't be sure the letter was actually sent.[10]

As for what Lord wanted from her, the manuscript fragments point two ways. To judge from a fair copy that speaks of a stile she "will not let you cross – but it is all yours, and when it is right I will lift the Bars, and lay you in the Moss," he may have pressed for some kind of erotic satisfaction. Her self-defense—"It is Anguish . . . to let you leave me, hungry, but you ask the divine Crust and that would doom the Bread"—echoes a passage from Coventry Patmore's *Angel in the House,* heavily marked by Sue, in which a woman who yields too soon is said to have "spoil'd the bread and spill'd the wine."

Alternatively, after Dickinson was released by her mother's death on November 14, 1882, Lord apparently asked her to marry him. On December 3 the poet dwelled on the nuances of his mild and considerate proposal:

> You said with loved timidity in asking me to your dear Home, you would "try not to make it unpleasant" – so delicate a diffidence, how beautiful to see! I do not think a Girl Extant has so divine a Modesty –

---

10. In the fair copy of April 30, 1882, Dickinson mentioned having recently "been in your Bosom." This, like her reference to Lord's "Arms," calls to mind Sue's statement, reported by Todd, that the Dickinson sisters "have not, either of them, any idea of morality. . . . I went in there one day, and in the drawing room I found Emily reclining in the arms of a man." Leyda plausibly dated this speech September 1882. But Todd's failure to report it till 1931, fifty years later, calls its accuracy into question.

Dickinson's earlier "Wild nights – Wild nights!" (Fr269), ends with the wish "Might I but moor – Tonight – / In thee!" Though some readers take this as an image of penetration, it probably signified enclosure in an embrace, a powerful Victorian image. In Dinah Craik's *Head of the Family,* the hero "longed to take her and hide her in his bosom"—and he finally does.

> You even call me to your Breast with apology! Of what must my
> poor Heart be made?

This interesting passage not only suggests that the poet cowed the bluff
old judge but shows how avidly she reflected on this, even speculating
(with him) as to how intimidating she was.

The basic understanding the lovers reached seems to have been literary: to write each other every Sunday. A fragment beginning "Tuesday is a deeply depressed Day" traces the poet's stages of anticipation
through the week. Another, prompted by his missing his assignment,
blames her "Naughty one" for making "the bright week noxious." Curiously, there is an independent report of the old man's effort to keep
up his end of things. On April 8, 1883, a Sunday, his niece Abby Farley informed Ned Dickinson that "Uncle Lord is writing in the next
room a letter for the 'Mansion' such a sweet one—I suppose." Abby's
view of the business was openly scornful: "A letter has just arrived from
your neighbor containing sweet flowers, for 'dear Otis' I suppose.
What a lot of humbug there is in this world." Since Otis had substantial property and no children, it was in this niece's interest to thwart a
second marriage. Decades later, old and bitter, she reportedly said of
Dickinson: "Little hussy—didn't I know her? I should say I did. Loose
morals. She was crazy about men. Even tried to get Judge Lord. Insane, too."

Among her ruses for concealing the correspondence, Dickinson had
George Montague address and Thomas Kelley (Maggie's brother-in-
law) post her letters. In May 1882, when the judge was falsely reported
to be near death, Tom thoughtfully appeared and the poet "ran to his
Blue Jacket and let my Heart break there." Another time, she seems to
have informed her lover that a long letter hidden under her clothes had
aroused suspicion by adding to her bulk. In reply, Lord called her
"Jumbo," a name with which she delightedly toyed before promising to
switch stationery: "Tim's suspicions however will be allayed, for I have
thinner Paper, which can elude the very Elect." These evasive maneuvers
may have been designed to protect the judge (from niece Abby?) as well
as herself. Once, she dreamed a statue was made of him after his death

and that when she was asked to "unvail" it she refused. Her explanation: "what I had not done in Life I would not in death."[11]

This dream reaction to her lover's death has less to do with grief than with disrobing and privacy and her intermittent fear of being "too frank." Of course, the romance became known. At the poet's funeral, Vinnie laid "two heliotropes by her hand 'to take to Judge Lord.' " On Lord's side, his Kimball relations knew enough that when a descendant read Bingham's *Revelation* seventy years later, she suddenly realized that her mother, born in 1871, had always spoken of Cousin Otis as Emily Dickinson's friend and never as Edward Dickinson's.

Whether or not Otis was Edward's best friend, as Emily claimed, it is significant that she saw her lover in that light. Each man was an old-fashioned and unbending Whig lawyer who could be identified with the very idea of law, thus making possible some complicated games involving obedience and defiance. The "best little girl in Amherst" delighted in setting Lord up as an embodiment of the right to punish, then daring him to become her accomplice in a lawless frolic. A roughed-out poem in one of her drafts to him declares

> *How fleet – how indiscreet an one –*[12]
> *how always wrong is Love –*
> *The joyful little Deity*
> *We are not scourged to serve –*
>
> Fr1557, ca. 1881

The reverse of masochistic, this poem is about how *not* to be whipped for being "always wrong." Otis was the perfect lover, standing for dignity and order even while being a supple version of Edward (who "never

---

11. This is the poet's only known dream in which the dreamer chooses and acts. For her other accounts of dreams, all very brief, see letters 16, 60, 62, 175, 304, 320. She often mentioned dreaming "about" someone, as in letters 32, 342a, 471, 585, 907. A letter to Whitney, quoted above, mentions a dream about Bowles.

12. The ungainly "an one" was correct usage, appearing in one of Dickinson's letters, Henry Shipley's introduction to her prose valentine in *The Indicator,* and Dinah Craik's *Olive* ("Is such an one as I likely to marry?").

played"). "Papa has still many Closets," she twitted the Judge, "that Love has never ransacked." After his death, she described him as an unstable union of "Calvary and May"—lawgiving Jehovah and troublemaking Cupid. The last of the strong, authoritative men in her life, he had little in common with the "aesthetic" type, much talked of in the 1880s, or with a class she derided as "Manikins"—professors.

Emily proved surprisingly expert in handling her dominating lover, as if this was a relationship she had trained for. The two of them evidently had a glorious time writing and embracing, she made no commitments, and though she was grieved by his death on March 13, 1884, she wasn't shattered. Had his last illnesses and impairments reduced his appeal? After his retirement from the bench in December 1882, as a colleague diplomatically noted, the judge's "mind, brooding over doubts and dangers, might have grown morbid in what some of his friends regarded as prejudices, and his utterances . . . more emphatic and severe."

Dickinson's decision not to marry Lord has been seen as another sign she lacked the "capacity to enjoy personal exchange and closeness and then to let go." Because of all the ambiguities in the relationship, it seems unwise to be quite so categorical in summing up. Indeed, it may be that what the poet did her last time around was precisely to have a good time and then let go. Her suitor's feelings can only be imagined, yet we should remember that, as his literary friend put it, "Good times are always mutual; that is what makes good times." Chances are, Lord enjoyed himself.

Of one thing we can be certain: it would have been a disaster if Emily Dickinson had given up her life for the crusty old man and his implacable niece.

Resolution

One of the things the Reverend Charles Wadsworth brought back to Philadelphia from San Francisco was "an affection of the throat [that] hindered his enunciation" and was perhaps related to the "nervous debility" a California paper mentioned. The trouble was persistent enough that at his funeral a mysterious "diminution of the powers of the organs of speech" was blamed for his reduced effectiveness. In the *Philadelphia Inquirer*'s long obituary, however, we read that he preached "in improved health and with growing popularity" after his installation at the Clinton Street Immanuel Church in 1879.

The next summer—the same one, in all probability, that saw the beginning of Dickinson's romance with Judge Lord—Wadsworth came to Amherst and saw her for the second and last time. She was tending her flowers when he rang, evidently assuming he would not be turned away. Vinnie heard him speaking to Maggie and said, "the Gentleman with the deep voice wants to see you, Emily." In her "glad surprise," she asked why he hadn't notified her in advance, to which he replied that he had come on impulse, "stepped from my Pulpit to the Train." The answer, an odd one, suggests that a partial recovery of his powers of speech may have influenced his decision to come and see her. In her two accounts of the visit, nothing is said about a vocal impediment.

But he gave her to understand he was "liable at any time to die." Two years later, having contracted pneumonia, the minister was advised that his condition was terminal and he should prepare for death. "I have no preparations to make," was the reply; "they have been made." He died early in the morning on April 1, 1882.

The last words of Wadsworth's sermon the previous Sunday— "going home, going home"—were publicized in an article that evidently reached Dickinson. In April 1886, a few weeks before her own death, as she wrote her last known letter mentioning the minister, she twice repeated these words, placing them in quotation marks. The recipient was one of his closest friends. "Excuse me for the Voice, this moment immortal," her letter concludes.

It is a curious fact that although Dickinson wrote about Wadsworth to none of her correspondents except Elizabeth Holland prior to his death, afterward she made a point of telling several men how vital this friendship had been to her. In a letter to Higginson she called the minister her "closest earthly friend," but without naming him. To Lord, she sent a reminder that "My lovely Salem" did not enjoy exclusive rights in her: "it has been an April of meaning to me – I have been in your Bosom

– My Philadelphia has passed from Earth, and . . . Ralph Waldo Emerson . . . has touched the secret Spring."

The one acquaintance Dickinson shared with Wadsworth was the man she had briefly met some two decades earlier, James Dickson Clark, a person (luckily) "of warm and generous affections." Suffering from a spinal complaint, Clark had been living since the early 1870s with his father and brother on Degraw Street, Brooklyn, from which he sent her a volume of Wadsworth's sermons, in press at the time of his death. If she read them, she would have found a defense of the "old-fashioned doctrinal preaching" she disliked, along with some ardent dramatizations of release and rapture: "[They] feel the immortality beating within them, and burst from these poor limits of sense and sin, and soar! soar! soar! to the everlasting glory." During her ensuing correspondence with Clark, Dickinson sought more information about the man who had been at once a stranger and her dearest earthly friend. In the process, she accomplished what she had done with Maria Whitney following Samuel Bowles's death: transformed the termination of one connection into a basis for another. By now, her social world was so thinly populated that each death was catastrophic.

After Clark died in June 1883, Dickinson exclaimed (in a passage deleted from her edited letters), "The Friend and then the Friend's Friend! what an entire loss!" Turning to his brother Charles, she wrote him fifteen times in her last three years, without ever meeting him. Wadsworth was still the focus: her memories of him, his problems with his children, why he once compared the poet to his son Willie. To read these letters is to get a shocking sense of the tenuity of the poet's link to the man who had meant so much to her. Indeed, to read is to follow her in the act of creating further tenuous links with the Friend's Friends.

The Clark correspondence makes clear that Wadsworth *was* central for Dickinson. One letter anticipates his "assist[ing] me in another World." Another dares to call him "my 'Heavenly Father.'" Neither, however, brings up that old conceit of the separated lovers' first mutual gaze in heaven, and nowhere do we find expressions of grief like those elicited by her father's death. Yet, whatever her feelings about the minister (and they do seem to have moderated), we would not expect her to explore the end of her most private relationship anywhere but in her poetry.

In fact, she seems to have done so, in a poem that opens with the death of someone toward whom her life has been pointed:

> *I did not reach Thee*
> *But my feet slip nearer every day*
> *Three Rivers and a Hill to cross*
> *One Desert and a Sea*
> *I shall not count the journey one*
> *When I am telling thee*

Succeeding stanzas recount the journey's hardships. The speaker does not characterize the person she has tried to reach, though she does mention a waiting and helpful "Right hand." Just as in some poems from the early sixties on the remote lover, "telling" is what she looks forward to. At the end, urging her feet to "step merry," she wades into the final sea:

> *The waters murmur new*
> *Three rivers and the Hill are passed*
> *Two deserts and the Sea!*
> *Now Death usurps my Premium*
> *And gets the look at Thee —*
>
> Fr1708

Clearly a major summing-up, the poem gains significance from a companion piece written in 1863, the year after Wadsworth's trip to California. Here, too, Dickinson seems to fantasize a far western trek as her essential inner act:

> *I cross till I am weary*
> *A Mountain — in my mind —*
> *More Mountains — then a Sea —*
> *More Seas — And then*
> *A Desert — find —*

> *And my Horizon blocks*
> *With steady – drifting – Grains . . .*
>
> Fr666

Persisting, she "shout[s]" her feet forward by promising them "the Whole of Heaven / The instant that we meet."

Adding to the power of these strange matching allegories—the earlier one hopeful, the other frustrated—is the parallel with Moses' disappointment following the Exodus and before the entry into Canaan. In 1855, the year after Emily's friend, Henry V. Emmons, presided over a local mountain-naming expedition and then wrote about it in an essay she quoted back at him, the Amherst College library acquired *The Sacred Mountains* by J. T. Headley. In the chapter on Mount Pisgah we find what looks like Dickinson's raw material:

> The sea had been passed—the murmurs of the people borne with—
> the long weary desert travelled over—forty years of the prime of life
> exhausted, to secure one single object, and then [Moses] died with
> that object unreached. . . .

Unfortunately, since "I did not reach thee" is preserved in Sue's handwriting only and thus isn't datable, we can't be certain it was occasioned by Wadsworth's death. We can only recall what Bianchi has told us, namely, that Emily confided her love of him to Sue, and Sue kept the secret. These apparent facts may explain why "I did not reach thee" was entrusted to the sister-in-law, and why she eventually destroyed the manuscript after copying the poem: there may have been a telltale accompanying message.

Two years after Wadsworth's death came that of Judge Lord, in March 1884. Mentioning it to Elizabeth Holland, the Norcross cousins, Catharine Sweetser, and Charles H. Clark, Dickinson generally identified him as "another friend" she had lost; to Sweetser, she described him as "our latest Lost." Throughout, her point was not that she had incurred a once-in-a-lifetime loss but that this was the last of a series that left her frighteningly bereft. "[H]ow to repair my shattered ranks," she wrote

Clark, "is a besetting pain." Nowhere does she give the impression of a *unique* termination. This is not to deny her grief, but, rather, to pay attention to how she understood and represented it. In a poem incorporated in one of these letters, she is a robin searching for "The Birds she lost" (Fr1632). In another, "Each that we lose takes part of us," she is a waning moon who will soon be "summoned by the tides" (Fr1634). The ocean, often present in her verse, takes on a powerful undertow now. "Rest and water are most we want," she wrote her cousins. To Sarah Tuckerman she sent a compelling evocation of the desire to be floated away, as on wings:

> *How slow the Wind – how slow the Sea –*
> *how late their Feathers be!*
>
> Fr1607, ca. 1883

What had happened to her sense of an unbreakable attachment to one man and one man only—that strongly gripped idea in her work of the early 1860s? Putting the question more manageably: how had this idea been modified once Lord declared himself? An answer flashes into view in one of her last letters to him, one that seems to dawdle in a sleepy and undirected monologue, almost a fugue—a way of writing she fell into with no other correspondent. The date was November 11, 1882.

> Please Excuse the wandering writing. Sleeplessness makes my Pencil stumble. Affection clogs it – too. Our Life together was long forgiveness on your part toward me. The trespass of my rustic Love upon your Realms of Ermine, only a Sovereign could forgive. I never knelt to other. The Spirit never twice alike, but every time another – that other more divine. Oh – had I found it sooner! Yet Tenderness has not a Date – it comes – and overwhelms.[13]

---

13. This draft, which Johnson mistakenly spliced to one from April 30 and May 1, 1882, can be dated by the statement that "Mrs Dr Stearns called to know if we didnt think it very shocking for Butler to 'liken himself to his Redeemer.'" On November 7, 1882, Benjamin F. Butler, an outspoken maverick running as a Democrat, was elected governor of Massachusetts after six unsuccessful tries. His victory speech, based on an Old Testament passage Christians apply to Jesus, began, "Fellow citizens—To quote a few words from the Scriptures, the stone that the

Voicing an old regret ("Oh – had I found") that she at once overcomes ("Yet Tenderness"), this passage gives the poet's last thoughts on her experience of erotic love. In the act of denying she knelt to another, she seems to recall that in fact she *had*, whereupon she introduces a modification: "The Spirit never twice alike . . ." That is, with each new loved one, love is different and better. Love itself is single and all-powerful, but now it can embrace more than one person—a heretical notion in the early 1860s. As she warned Lord, she was "but a restive sleeper and often should journey from your Arms."

Erotically, Dickinson had achieved not just an "inner" but a very real and tough freedom. It had been gained in the course of her fighting years, which disciplined her fixation on an out-of-reach man and hugely expanded her personal and imaginative powers. One of her strangest poems, written about 1872 or 1873, when the fight was won and her correspondence with Wadsworth had yet to resume (Lord being even deeper in the wings), registers her "bleak exultation" at her achievement:

> Through what transports of Patience
> I reached the stolid Bliss
> To breathe my Blank without thee
> Attest me this and this – . . .

> Fr1265

Glancing at "this and this" without identifying them (bundles of letters? her manuscript books? parts of her body?), the speaker asks these things to vouch for what she has attained, namely, a dulled ability to get through her vacuous life "without thee." Having reached a perfect and pointless equilibrium, she sums it up in a series of bitter oxymorons. Her only transports are those of waiting, not having. Her only bliss is stolid. Instead of living her life with him, she breathes her blank without him.

---

builders rejected, the same has become the head of the column. (Great laughter and applause.)" Both the *Springfield Republican* and the *Amherst Record* noted these words. Butler's support of women's suffrage and agrarian issues had already made him anathema to conservative Republicans. Dickinson's opinion of him isn't known, but she obviously didn't share Stearns's outrage at the speech. Her uncle, William Dickinson, was a fervent Butlerite.

Not her usual mood, this was nevertheless one of the ways she felt before
her fling with the Judge.

A poem composed about 1882, after the romance had ripened, begins with the statement, "I groped for him before I knew" (Fr1585). Is
it a trace of that groping that the poem just looked at, "Through what
transports of patience," was drafted on an envelope Lord had addressed to her? After his death, in a confiding letter to the Norcrosses,
Dickinson came back to the question of how her passion for him related to the fierce exclusiveness of first love. "Till the first friend dies,
we think ecstasy impersonal, but then discover that he was the cup
from which we drank it, itself as yet unknown." The phrases dovetail:
"before I knew"; "as yet unknown." Hostile Abby Farley called her
"crazy about men." A better way to put it is that her romance with the
judge brought her old and frustrating fixation on Master to a satisfactory emotional resolution. Among her discoveries in Lord's bosom
(her nearest approach to erotic pleasure?) was the difference between
love and the man. Learning this lesson after her obsession with a single "atom" had moderated, she (mostly) let drop her fantasy of the mutual gaze in heaven and tried to get some solid facts about Wadsworth
from the Clarks.

After 1882, if editors' dates are correct, there were only one or two
more treatments of love. Leaving the subject for good, Dickinson composed the following definitive work of retrospection, with "Chum" and
"Playmate" in the plural:

> My Wars are laid away in Books –
> I have one Battle more –
> A Foe whom I have never seen
> But oft has scanned me o'er –
> And hesitated me between
> And others at my side,
> But chose the best – Neglecting me – till
> All the rest have died –
> How sweet if I am not forgot

By Chums that passed away –
Since Playmates at threescore and ten
Are such a scarcity –

Fr1579

Love—its pain, its play—had been completed, turned into art, and laid away in the poet's secret homemade manuscript books.

Chapter 22

1880–1886: Exquisite Containment

For the other inhabitants of the Dickinson compound, some very hard lines had been drawn and the wars were just beginning. Terminally alienated from Sue, Austin fell in love in 1882 with Mabel Loomis Todd, a young faculty wife who ardently returned his feelings. The next year brought the tragic death of Gib, Austin and Sue's youngest child, born in their middle age and a family favorite. Emily, in her fifties and deeply attached to all members of her family, had no choice but to deal with these and other troubles. How she did so tells us a great deal about her sense of family and her conception of her place in the world during her last years.

The family troubles had long-lasting consequences for the publication and reception of Dickinson's writing. In 1890, four years after she died, a selection of her poems was published to wide acclaim. More compilations followed, including a two-volume edition of letters. All were edited by Austin's lover, with Vinnie's encouragement and Higginson's strategic assistance; all took editorial liberties with what the poet had written. After Sue's death in 1913, her daughter, Martha, passionately loyal to her mother, brought out a selection of the poems Emily had sent next door, followed by the first extended biographical account, *The Life and Letters of Emily Dickinson* (1924); eight years later came *Emily Dickinson Face to Face* (1932). Martha was determined to wipe Mrs. Todd out of the record, reclaim Aunt Emily for the family, take the royalties, and vindicate Sue, the spurned wife and tragic mother who had lost both her sons (Ned having died in 1898 of cardiac troubles). Not surprisingly, these books present a sanitized account of Sue's marriage and an idealized picture of her relationship with the genius next door. They are also full of incidental "facts" that cannot be relied on.

And yet Bianchi had been positioned as no one else, and much of what she passed on—Dickinson's absorbed reading of books in the family circle, her "pet gesture of bravado," her twisting an imaginary key in her door and saying, "It's just a turn – and freedom, Matty"—seems to grant us an access no one else could have matched. No one conveyed better than this "imperial Girl," as Emily called her, the poet's love of games, jokes, fiction, secrecy, rule-breaking, and general roguishness. Looking back as an old woman, Bianchi grasped the fine self-command Dickinson had won by her fifties: "The fret of temporal servitudes did not exist for her. There was an exquisite self-containment about her from her very relinquishment of all part in outward event." This assessment catches the independence of spirit that distinguished the poet from grim Austin and harried Vinnie.

So complete was Dickinson's containment that the sense of achievement she expressed in so many poems does not seem to have issued in any open boasts. In general, writers who attain an assured mastery expect a matching public acknowledgment. They leave a collected edition; they make a sly nod at the pantheon to show where their urn might best be placed. Dickinson not only made little or no effort to clean up and organize the poems she continued to write, but failed to take steps to ensure that her work would reach readers at large. Quite the contrary, she exacted promises from Vinnie and Maggie that they would burn her papers, possibly including her manuscript books and ungathered verse. No doubt this was largely owing to her continued aversion to all forms of public exposure. But why do none of her letters comment on her achievement? Is this silence to be explained as humility, carelessness, some kind of disillusionment? Didn't she know how good she was? That may be what we want to know most of all.

One way to try to find out is to follow her interest in two writers who were in some sense her peers, George Eliot and Emily Brontë. Dickinson idolized both, but underneath she had a keen sense of affiliation and a greedy curiosity about personal history. After seeing the announcement of George Eliot's death in 1880, she could not get "[t]he look of the words as they lay in the print" out of her mind. Regretting that the novelist lacked the "gift of belief which her greatness denied her," the poet made a guess at her story: "perhaps having no childhood, she lost her way to the early trust, and no later came." In 1882 the editor Thomas Niles assured Dickinson that George Eliot's second husband had "not abandoned" his projected biography of her. The next year, when Mathilde Blind's *George Eliot* and Agnes Mary F. Robinson's *Emily Brontë* had their American debut, the poet promptly waded in, reacting in ways that hint at her own sense of achievement.

From Blind's *George Eliot*, Dickinson got a picture of Marian Evans's youthful solemnity, awkwardness, and inner solitude; her painful troubles with father and brother; her early rejection of Evangelicalism. The book presented her as coming "into the world fully developed, like a second Minerva," yet insisted that her "intellectual vigor did not exclude the susceptibilities and weaknesses of a peculiarly feminine organization." Getting a much richer picture of what she did and didn't share with the Englishwoman, Dickinson wrote Niles (dropping the male pseudonym): "The Life of Marian Evans had much I never knew – a Doom of Fruit without the Bloom, like the Niger Fig." This fruitful "Doom" recalls the "Dooms of Balm" (Fr1368B) of Helen Hunt's marriage. Incorporated in the letter was a poem on the compensatory fecundity that makes something of nothing, an idea that fits Evans's active life less well than Dickinson's:

Her Losses make our Gains ashamed.
She bore Life's empty Pack
As gallantly as if the East
Were swinging at her Back –

So far the speaker sounds like an abashed admirer who lacks the power to create, but in the second stanza we see that she, too, is a load bearer and honey maker and thus understands Evans's secret:

Life's empty Pack is heaviest,
As every Porter knows –
In vain to punish Honey –
It only sweeter grows –

Fr1602B

Clearly, the poet felt some sort of parity with the novelist.

Robinson's biography, read within a month of publication, confirmed Dickinson's previous image of "gigantic Emily Brontë, of whom her Charlotte said 'Full of ruth for others, on herself she had no mercy.' " Intuitive and highly dramatic, the book was rife with details, insights, claims that must have connected: Brontë's motherlessness, attachment to home, elusiveness with strangers; her powers of self-disciplined labor; her housewifely skills; her indulgence of Branwell; her thorny brilliance; her upright purity but also her bold treatment of passion. There was the large dog she loved, the Calvinism she both abandoned and transformed, the uncanny imaginative power that transmuted "the miriest earth of common life." "If the butcher's boy came to the kitchen door she would be off like a bird." "Kindness and thought for others were part of the nature of this unsocial, rugged woman. . . . She made the bread; and her bread was famous in Haworth." What was this if not a distorted image of Amherst's poet? Writing Elizabeth Holland, Dickinson pronounced the book "more electric far than anything since 'Jane Eyre.' " Calling Brontë the "Napoleon of the Cross!" she grounded the writer's grandeur in the mastery of pain and insisted Elizabeth read the book, bad eye or not. "It is so strange a Strength, I must have you possess it."

Nothing Dickinson ever read was recommended with more force than this biography, which effectively validated her idea of power based in weakness. Still, we can only surmise what the book said to her about her own strange strength as poet, a point on which she was silent. The electric new possession was to be shared, not hugged in private. True greatness, as in "Lay this laurel on the one" (Fr1428), made no claims for itself. On itself—and on us readers and biographers—it had no mercy.

Family Life in the Dickinson Compound

At the Mansion, with Father gone and Mother incapacitated by her stroke and broken hip, everything was in the hands of the three Dickinson siblings, the indoor servant Maggie Maher, and the hired men who brought in the hay and cared for the animals, orchard, and lawn. Austin oversaw the outside work and took charge of major projects, such as the installation of running water in 1880. Indoors, following in Emily Norcross Dickinson's steps, Vinnie tried to see to everything. Her friend and neighbor, Mariette Jameson, had never seen "a daughter so devoted." In Emily's words, Mother needed only to "sigh" before being tended by the "brave – faithful – and punctual" Vinnie. One summer night, when half downtown Amherst went up in the worst of the town's many fires, she came to her sister's room "soft as a moccasin" and said, "Dont be afraid, Emily, it is only the 4th of July." Emily's senses told her that was a lie, but she played along, allowing her sister to shield her from the outside world. When Elizabeth Holland's coded disclosure of a daughter's pregnancy wasn't understood, it was Vinnie who "picked the Sub rosas, and handed them" to the poet.

From all sides, and especially her own scribbled, headlong notes, one gets the impression Vinnie was in a constant mad rush—"under terrific headway," as her sister put it. In the election year of 1880 she was "far more hurried than Presidential Candidates . . . *they* have only the care of the Union, but Vinnie the Universe." As for Austin, though he was more self-possessed, he too seemed always busy and burdened. Unable to accept Clara Newman Turner's invitation to Norwich on account of his many engagements, he asked her to pity him as "a man with an expensive family relying on his daily labor for the delights of life." When he did find time to visit, she pressed some forceful advice on him: "*Don't take life so hard.*"

One of the signal differences between the poet and her siblings was her gift for drawing back in reflective abstraction, reacting from a position of leisure and plenitude and then resting on her playful constructions. Her enjoyment of this internal margin owed a great deal to the family's assumption of responsibility for her. Still, she not only continued to do various chores in pantry, kitchen, and sink room but also helped look after her bedridden mother. In the hot and humid early September of 1880, when the temperature rose to 100, that meant constant tending: "to read to her – to fan her – to tell her 'Health would come Tomorrow,' and make the Counterfeit look real – to explain *why* 'the Grasshopper is a Burden'" often used up the entire day (the grasshopper comes from Ecclesiastes). Yet, instead of resenting the demands on her time, Emily felt real tenderness for "Mother's dear little wants"—this from the daughter who ten years earlier "never had a mother."

The old blockage between mother and daughter was dissolving. Now that Emily Norcross Dickinson had been compelled to give up her lifelong housekeeping cares, she seemed to become, in the poet's phrase, "a larger mother" than before. In spite of her serious disabilities, she took a new interest in others, as when, anxious about the Hollands, she said she wished she could "take them both in my Arms and carry them." The poet was astonished. This was her own self-originating strength—her assumption of imaginative power from the depths of incapacity. There must be common ground after all.

Mrs. Dickinson died November 14, 1882. Five weeks later the poet sent a mellow summing-up to Elizabeth Holland: "We were never intimate . . . while she was our Mother – but Mines in the same Ground meet by tunneling and when she became our Child, the Affection came." The passage exemplifies the poet's skill at finding rapprochements outside the usual patterns. Still, her grief was less intense than after Father's death, and few poems resulted. The one that grazed Mother's reality most closely says, unremarkably, that the "lowliest career" gets the same funerary pageantry as the most "exalted" (Fr1594C; J1626).

The troubles next door were more consequential. Since May 1874, when young Ned had a serious bout of "rheumatism," there had been much anxiety about his heart. This sharpened to fear on the February night in 1877 when the fifteen-year-old boy had the first of the grand mal epileptic seizures that dogged him from then on. Poorly understood, the attack inspired a doctor to issue a warning about his heart and caused the family to feel "intensely excited," as a professor's wife noted. From then on, at irregular intervals, as Austin's diary records, he would be waked in the night "by a jarring sound, as if the house was shaking," or, a month later, "by a sound as of some wagon passing—and a feeling that something was wrong—and by some exclamation from Sue," following which he would rush upstairs and find his son in convulsions, often groaning and breathing with "great effort." In March 1883, the young man was "sick with rheumatism and most everything else," Austin noted, and "occupying most of the family in his care and amusement." Acute rheumatism was synonymous with rheumatic fever, according to a standard medical dictionary of that year, with 50 percent of cases showing cardiac complications. Bianchi never forgot the night (she put it in summer 1883 but her date is suspect) when her brother had "an acute attack of rheumatism, affecting his heart" and she found the poet standing outside a window after midnight: " 'Is he better?—oh, is he better?' she whispered."

Bianchi was mistaken in her claim that Dickinson never again crossed the lawn, yet it seems the case that for long periods she had little direct contact with the Evergreens. For all of 1880, her brother's diary mentions a single visit to the "two sits at other house." After Christmas 1882—a season when he would be expected to drop by—the poet noted that "Austin seldom calls. . . . He visits rarely as Gabriel." Bianchi's first book on her aunt has a photo of a "path just wide enough for two who love" joining the Dickinson houses, with the implication it was worn by Sue and Emily. Some scholars take this seriously, and yet it is obvious the path must have been worn by others, and for various purposes. Face-to-face meetings were so infrequent that when Sue gave Disraeli's latest novel, *Endymion,* as a Christmas gift in 1880, she inscribed it, "Emily—Whom not seeing I still love." Anyone who tackles this panoramic roman à clef, based on an inside knowledge of English politics and society, will wonder why such a gift was chosen, and what it says about the sisters-in-law's relationship. However well the book suited Sue's social aspirations,[1] nothing seems less calculated to appeal to Emily.

Perhaps one reason some of the poet's later notes to her sister-in-law pose an extreme challenge to interpretation is that the relationship had become one of words, not acts. About 1878 she wrote, "Susan knows she is a Siren – and that at a word from her, Emily would forfeit Righteousness." This would have the ring of passion if it weren't for the hyperbolic wit and the accompanying apology: "Please excuse the grossness of this morning – I was for a moment disarmed." We don't know what happened, yet it looks as if the statement of devotion was partly compensatory, making up for an act of avoidance. "Remember, Dear," Emily wrote in January 1884, "an unfaltering *Yes* is my only reply to your utmost question." Again, the statement was occasioned by an inability to satisfy a request, at a time when Sue was in mourning and Emily incapacitated by illness. Sue's part was to "know," to "remember." Emily's part was to reaffirm a union based on commitment, not contact: an *essential* love. Instead of reflecting a relationship that existed in daily life, her messages would seem to be the constitutive agency creating it. As the poet put it, "The tie between us is very fine, but a Hair never dissolves." In 1883–1884, when Sue was in the depths and Emily exerted herself to encourage her, one message wished she "had something vital for Susan, but Susan feeds herself." A poem accompanying this says that, whereas "Declaiming" waters impress no one, still waters (meaning Sue)

> *Are so for that most fatal cause*
> *In Nature – they are full –*
>
> Fr1638B (J1595)

---

1. In 1903, traveling in Europe with Sue, Martha married Captain Alexander E. Bianchi, supposedly of the Imperial Horse Guard of St. Petersburg. The captain accompanied his bride to America, ran through her money, cooled his heels in a New York jail, and vanished. After this costly misadventure, Martha took a keen interest in the royalties to be made from her aunt.

The implication is that Sue wasn't answering Emily's bracing messages because she was too full of trouble to do so.

By this time the air next door *was* lethal. As Mattie and Ned grew increasingly alienated by their father's grim moods, he went to his diary to complain about the parties staged by them and Sue—"an evening carouse" at the Orient Hotel, "a riot in the house till 10 1/2." On Ned's twenty-first birthday, the "wild tear and revel" lasted till one A.M., with "one dancer jamming right through a register." The diarist's usual tone in noting such events was one of sardonic detachment. He wished he had a quiet room in New York to "drown all thought of Amherst." In October 1882, when a Gilbert family wedding emptied the house of Sue and Mattie for three weeks, he wrote a gushing rhapsody on peace and quiet—the "utterly utter sweetness and smoothness of Life . . . since Tuesday" (Tuesday being the day his women departed). Then he mailed it to Michigan so they could see for themselves how relieved he was to be rid of them.

By a happy chance, one of Dickinson's drafts to Lord not only notes Austin's dismay when his wife and daughter returned on November 10 but puts on record her own lack of involvement: "The Wanderers came [home] last Night – Austin says they are brown as Berries and as noisy as Chipmunks,[2] and feels his solitude much invaded, as far as I can learn. These dislocations of privacy among the *Privateers* amuse me very much." Evidently, the poet was not inclined to enter into Austin's situation. Yet she felt enough sympathy to add, "but 'the Heart knoweth its own' Whim." Her attitude, one of tolerant and exculpatory amusement, seems to forestall any harsh judgments of her surly brother, except as her toying with "privacy" calls up a word meaning "pirate." This way of judging, based on spectatorship and wordplay, hints at an anarchic frame of mind not much concerned with social or moral ramifications. As Higginson guessed, the Dickinsons *did* go their separate ways. Which is precisely what the draft justifies: her brother's freedom to follow his "whim"; hers not to take sides.

---

2. Mabel Loomis Todd's diary for that day notes that "Mattie & her mother were very very full of life" after getting home.

But sides were what had formed next door. In late summer 1881, a lively young woman, Mabel Loomis Todd, wife of the newly appointed astronomy teacher at Amherst College, moved to town. Born the year Sue and Austin were married, Todd was a trained singer, pianist, and painter of flowers. She was habituated to city life, handled parasol and fan to charming effect, liked distinguished older men, loved being the center of attraction, and had a shapely figure, lovely hair, very large eyes. One of her diary entries reads, "Every moment was lovely of this perfect day—& David [her husband] loves me so—& everybody else likes & loves & admires me." Doing as she had done with Sarah Jenkins, Sue recruited this promising addition to Amherst society by asking her to the Evergreens. "Wore my thinnest white dress," says Mabel's diary; "I like her *so* much." The newcomer was asked to play and sing at musicales, had long confidential talks and rides with Sue (who "understands me completely"), and was charmed to learn of "the *Myth*" next door, the reclusive genius whose "strange poems" Sue read to her. Her first assessment—"They are full of power"—probably reflects Sue's own admiration. One evening, as the new faculty wife sang next door at the Mansion, "the rare, mysterious Emily listened in the quiet darkness."

The family had such distinction and ease, Mr. Dickinson in particular, so "dignified & strong and a little odd." He seemed to take a special interest, there were walks and drives, the chemistry was right, and on September 11, 1882, a day after Emily had listened to Mabel in the darkness, she and Austin spoke their love face to face on a quiet walk, and then declared it over and over in an impassioned and now famous exchange of letters. Ardent and unreserved, Mabel had a "premonition" they would soon be able to express their love fully. Austin, writing with the mature strength he had not known how to command three decades earlier in courting Sue, never complained, accused, placated. In all respects it seemed a perfect union. Even David proved compliant. There was only one problem: Sue.

The affair had all the elements: ecstasy, an alternating stealth and brazenness, the spurned wife's developing suspicion. Terrified by Sue's icy formality, Mabel, with Austin's approval, sought and found an ally, an unwitting one, in Vinnie. In early 1883 Austin blustered that "Conventionalism is for those not strong enough to be laws for themselves."[3] In June he had a "blow out" with Sue, and in July he promised Mabel to "straighten the matter out before the summer is over, or smash the machine." That fall the couple began to make use of the Mansion as a kind of safe house, having their first intercourse there in December. They also used the Todds' house.

Years passed before Mabel's daughter, Millicent, could admit how disturbed she was by Mr. Dickinson's presence in her early life. Why was that tall, unsmiling man always going into Mama's bedroom and locking the door behind him? What did it mean when Mama was overheard murmuring "My King" to him? In his own home, Austin was more silent and detached than ever, exercising what he called his "supreme independence." That, not smashing the machine, was his real strategy, leaving an impossible situation unresolved. Sue's strategy, drawing on her grief, sickness, and betrayal, was to make sure the children took her side. Writing Mattie in December 1884, she was not just the bereaved but the martyred wife: "I carry very heavy burdens, so heavy that I sometimes feel that you and Ned will be left ere very long without any one but each other, to tell all your griefs to—My soul is heavy much of the time and *hope* lies far behind me." The tacit implication was that Ned and Mattie were already fatherless. The spurned wife was not without weapons on the domestic front.

Outside the family, Austin's best cards were his standing in the community, his intimidating dignity, and his stony refusal to explain or justify. When Mabel took out a loan from a local bank, he brazenly cosigned. To enable her and her husband to build a house, he carved a lot from the Dickinson meadow and somehow got his wife to sign the deed. It became an open secret that he was alienated from Sue and drawn to Mabel, but it was left to others to define the connection. Of course there was gossip, but it is a mistake to assume the liaison was generally under-

---

3. Two years later, when William Dean Howells brought out his most ambitious novel to date, *The Rise of Silas Lapham*, Austin read the serial version. When he reached the July 1885 installment, where the rough-hewn paint magnate turns down a dirty financial offer that would save him from bankruptcy, the reader "was so disgusted with it I would like to have thrown it at Howells' head."

stood to be sexual and condoned as such; there is simply no solid evidence of this from the 1880s. What is obvious but inconvenient is easily denied, and what was less convenient in conservative nineteenth-century Amherst than that the town's leading citizen was having an affair with Mrs. Todd? By 1889 the couple had been intimate for five years. That March Doc Hitchcock pressed Austin to take action against a disorderly lodging house used by students, in which, it was said, "one of the females of the house did sleep with one of the male occupants, & he not her husband either." It seems unthinkable that Austin's old friend could have written this if he had realized the truth.[4]

In her later years Dickinson often defended acts of theft and stolen love. A poem from about 1882 benignantly glances (in an alternate phrase) at "The happy guilt of boy and girl" (Fr1583[B]). But at that point Austin and Mabel weren't "guilty," and in any case, Dickinson, like Emerson, was less lawless than a first acquaintance suggests. When a stableman named Dennis Scannell got drunk, she feared "for the rectitude of the Barn" and sent Ned a tattling warning that ends, "Love for the Police." How deeply law and limits were engrained in her is evident from her riff on Simonides' epigram on the Spartans killed at Thermopylae (of which William Lisle Bowles's translation reads, "Go tell the Spartans, thou that passeth by, / That here, obedient to their laws, we lie"). Dickinson asks if the defenders were motivated by "a Lure – a Longing?" only to deny that psychological explanations like these can explain absolute commitments:

> Oh Nature – none of this –
> To Law – said Sweet Thermopylae
> I give my dying Kiss –
>
> Fr1584 (about 1882) (J1554)

---

4. James's novel *The Ambassadors,* written about a decade later, is premised precisely on a cultivated New Englander's capacity for denial. Unable to accept the fact of young Chad Newsome's affair with an aristocratic Frenchwoman, Lambert Strether persists in believing "such a high fine friendship . . . can't be vulgar or coarse" (Chapter 15), until he encounters the couple enjoying an overnight holiday in the country.

Do we call this erotic sublimation, or do we say that the erotic has come to stand for something more ultimate? Not to dwell on the matter, it appears that Dickinson was a voluptuary of the "Law" as much as of the word "No," and that she was bound to each of these in ways her marriage-fracturing lawyer-brother wasn't.

The question stands, did she *know* it was adultery? In the winter of 1882–1883, when Sue became suspicious, the lovers turned to the Mansion for a refuge. Mabel, friends with Vinnie, was told by Austin to address him at her post office box, where he collected the mail. In mid-March, Emily commented on the frequency of his visits: "my Brother is with us so often each Day, we almost forget that he ever passed to a wedded Home." Does this suggest she knew of the marital rift next door? Very likely: that summer she addressed Mabel as "Brother and Sister's dear friend," apparently excluding Sue; she used the same formula in 1885, when Sue could not possibly have been the sisterly friend. Twice that summer Austin informed his lover he was seeing "Vin and Em more than I did—and you are the constant theme." But there were limits to Austin's confidences. The same year, charmed by one of Mabel's letters, her lover wrote that he would like to "let Emily read it sometime, when it comes right, that she may know of what stuff you are." Sympathetic as Emily was, she was not, in her brother's opinion, ready for the truth. We remember how the news of a Holland family pregnancy went past her. In sum, it seems unlikely she could have been aware of, let alone complicit in (as some assert), the physical side of the affair.

How we answer the question has consequences for how we read her messages to Sue. One of the most arresting of these says, "With the exception of Shakespeare, you have told me of more knowledge than any one living – To say that sincerely is strange praise –" The note survives only in Martha's facsimile and in photostats, which show a tear across the paper below the last words. Martha's motive in publicizing a note comparing her mother to Shakespeare is obvious. The real questions are: was there more to the note, and what do the two sentences mean? The first seems to imply that Sue has again contributed something substantial to Emily's stock of knowledge, but the second does not so much thank her for this as admit that it is strange to do so sincerely. Was Emily being magnanimous in acknowledging what Sue had disclosed? Was the information sufficiently disillusioning that the poet's acknowledgment was "strange praise"?

In Emily's many warm messages to Sue, there is never a hint of criticism of Austin or, for that matter, Mabel. Sue's exclusiveness and vindictiveness made many enemies, including Vinnie, who sided with Austin against her, but Emily seems to have remained unpolarized, contriving to side with but not against. If this achievement was made possible by a habit of withdrawal, it also reflected an irenic temperament and largeness of spirit. Living among the most intimate and irreparable of betrayals, ruptures, hatreds, she found a way to live peaceably, nonviolently, with feuding camps. That was one of the benefits of "exquisite self-containment."

Gib's Death

More devastating than Austin's infidelity was the death of his and Sue's third child, Thomas Gilbert, barely eight years old. Conceived after Ned's heart trouble had declared itself, Gib, as he was called, was a charming and intelligent boy whose "fascinating ways" and "witty little sayings" won everyone. The product of his parents' middle age, he was not only the last best hope for the family lineage under the Dickinson name but the one child affectionately attached to both father and mother.

In fall 1883 Gib contracted typhoid fever. He was tended night and day by his increasingly exhausted parents, but to no avail. The day he died, October 5, a camping outfit was unknowingly mailed to him from Duluth by a cousin. A large tent had been pitched in the yard for him and his playmates that summer; his boyhood adventures had just begun. According to Vinnie, Austin looked "like death." "God help all you poor broken hearted ones," wrote Sue's sister Martha, who felt sorriest for the father; she kept seeing his "pale face."

For the one and only time, Austin's meticulously kept diary goes blank, for nearly two months. Then, on December 13, two weeks after it resumes, we find the first instance of the double lines signifying his and Mabel's sexual unions, ===. Austin was alive again, but for the bereaved mother death had to be dealt with in other ways. A letter received from Geneva indicates how Sue must have described her sense of desolation: "Your days are like mine," wrote the now widowed Martha Smith; "I go to bed nearly every night so tired and lonely." According to Sue's daughter, she "would see no one, would not even be driven through the village for more than a year." The grief for dead Gilbert family members that she had tried to give up when she married now returned for good.

But the suffering next door may have been worse. A family letter by Mariette Jameson, the postmaster's wife, reveals that Dickinson "went over to Austin's with Maggie the night Gilbert died, the first time she had been in the house for 15 years—and the odor from the disinfectants used, sickened her so that she was obliged to go home about 3. A M—and vomited—went to bed and has been feeble ever since, with a terrible pain in the back of her head." A letter from Vinnie confirms that her sister went next door and "received a nervous shock the night Gilbert died & was alarmingly ill for weeks." Jameson had the impression that "sympathy for Austin" was retarding her recovery. Three months after the event, Vinnie informed a former pastor and his wife that Emily had been "very frail since Gilbert died & I'me constantly anxious about her." All these reports seem reliable, yet Emily's own notes and letters reacting to Gib's death command so much strength they remind us of what Charlotte Brontë had said about her sister Emily (words quoted by Dickinson in 1881): "Full of ruth for others, on herself she had no mercy."

The poet's response to this tragedy did not exactly conform to orthodox Christian teaching as exemplified by Wadsworth's sermons. "God's Culture" proclaimed that "to the eye of Faith, nothing is fairer than the death of young children." "Death is not destruction! Death is not even decay! Death is HARVESTING!" Similarly, "Ministrations to Angels" (also in her possession), pictured a family that was desolated by the loss of its beloved "idol," then offered a corrective vision based on metaphor and fervent exhortation: "Had you known it, a crowned creature from eternity had crossed your threshold on a mission of heavenly love, to teach you priceless lessons." Like Wadsworth's sermons, the first of Dickinson's consolatory letters to Sue insisted—and with even greater fervor—that tragedy was triumph. But she altered the program by making no reference to God and interpreting Gib's death as his own transcendent achievement:

> Gilbert rejoiced in Secrets –
> His Life was panting with them . . .
> No crescent was this Creature – He traveled from the Full –
> Such soar, but never set . . .
> Without a speculation, our little Ajax spans the whole . . .

Ajax was a classical hero known for his strength. Like him, the poet was struggling mightily to see her nephew as a figure of unique daring and wisdom, a master of ultimate secrets. Her vision seems consciously "pagan," a term she elsewhere applied to herself. She agreed with Wadsworth that it was imperative to convert tragedy into victory—that all the resources of language must be harnessed to this end. The difference was that, where the minister's language rested on Scripture and orthodox theology, the poet's language rested (if that is the word) on itself.

Later messages, as intense, absolute, and final as anything the poet sent her sister-in-law, were clearly meant to lift up and encourage. One of the most moving considers the spirit's resilience—the way a sense of life and openness comes back after the suffocation of despair:

> Hopelessness in its first Film has not leave to last – That would close the Spirit. . . .
> Intimacy with Mystery, after great Space, will usurp its place –

From this, building on the idea of space, Dickinson tendered an image of human greatness finding its way in a world without meaning or direction: "Moving on in the Dark like Loaded Boats at Night, though there is no Course, there is Boundlessness." To this, she added a poem on the unknowability of heaven,

> *Whose rumor's Gate was shut so tight*
> *Before my Beam[5] was sown,*
> *Not even a Prognostic's push*
> *Could make a Dent thereon –*

Once again, Dickinson was standing at the closed door that was so intrinsic to her mind and art. Her two other 1883 poems that incorporate these lines conclude with them, giving the emphasis to her unsuccessful push at the limits of mortal knowledge. Here, however, she has Gib break through, leaving his mourning family to follow as they can:

> *The World that thou hast opened*
> *Shuts for thee,*
> *But not alone,*
> *We all have followed thee –*

The poem ends with a glance at the vanished explorer's temporary abode on earth—and at his tent pitched in the Dickinson compound:

> *The Tent is listening,*
> *But the Troops are gone![6]*
>
>   Fr1625 (J1584)

Dickinson wrote Elizabeth Holland that the boy's last words were "open the Door, they are waiting for me." Choosing to interpret the delirious speech as visionary, she added: "*Who* were waiting for him, all we possess we would give to know – Anguish at last opened it, and he ran to the little Grave at his Grandparents' feet – All this and more, though *is* there more? More than Love and Death? Then tell me its name!" Tortured as this is, the feeling is by no means raw or artless, with

---

5. Mind, in other versions. Fr1616A, Fr1627B.

6. On his birthday two months earlier, as Martha later recalled, Gib "had a party with drums and cocked hats, horns, a procession that marched over toward the Mansion and around the garden beds—all the neighbors cheering and Aunt Emily waving applause from the window."

the dramatic picture of the boy's running to join his grandparents. Yet even this degree of questioning is absent from the letters to Sue, for whom the poet obviously felt she had to be strong.

The severe illnesses and prostrations that overcame Sue in the next two years gave Emily an additional motive for encouraging her. In summer 1884 there was the curious episode of "poison trouble," as Sue called it, which her daughter blamed on "white dogwood" (poison sumac). In an update on symptoms, the sufferer informed Mattie in August that "my face has troubled me hardly at all, and my hands tolerably quiet. Ned gave me a drive this morning and reminded me it had been ten days since I had been out." In December, Sue again brought up her precarious health ("Your letters have made me nearly sick") to quiet her daughter's complaints about her difficulties at Miss Porter's School in Farmington, Connecticut; soon after, as we have seen, she unloaded her premonitions of death on the girl. At some point she incurred shingles and influenza, and also a prescription of arsenic, with Ned categorically advising his sister she "must never write such a letter home again, for it has made Mother almost sick." A convalescent letter begins, "I am up dear Mopsy [Mattie] with a wrapper on and hope not to undress before four P.M. I have just been down stairs and walked about the rooms. Saw Papa a moment and as I am very shaky I have come back to my hospital [her room]." There is a hint of Austin's coldness here, and how it affected her. His 1884 diary does not even mention her many illnesses. Instead, on December 19, her birthday, he visited the "other house" and had some === in the evening. By contrast, Emily let Sue know that "every Day" she inquired of the stableman, Stephen Sullivan, "if you seem weary." She also reminded the invalid of her son's loving concern. Clearly, the poet understood and tried to satisfy her sister-in-law's need of sympathy.

One of the most difficult messages Dickinson sent next door in 1884 or 1885 has drawn much interest in recent years. If placed against the background of marital trouble, bereavement, sickness, and depression (and also the missionary zeal that led Sue to take charge of a Sunday School in working-class Dwight, or "Logtown"), it looks like a culminating exhortation to be of good cheer:

Morning might come by Accident – Sister –
Night comes by Event –
To believe the final line of the Card would foreclose Faith –
Faith is *Doubt*.
        Sister –

Show me Eternity, and I will show you Memory –
Both in one package lain
And lifted back again –

Be Sue, while I am Emily –
Be next, what you have ever been, Infinity –

                                        Fr1658

As in her letter to grieving Perez Cowan many years earlier, the poet was contesting the kind of belief that claims sure knowledge of ultimate things. If heaven and all the rest were down pat ahead of time, our faith would be "foreclosed" and our minds shackled. It is our ignorance that enlivens us and makes possible our greatness. Underscoring her gravity (and her sympathy) with a second "Sister," she adds a poem that does away with the distinction between the sacred and the human. What you call eternity, it challengingly declares, is what I call memory, both equally belonging to our infinitude. "The past is not a package one can lay away," Dickinson had said a year or two earlier, summing up her final orientation to memory. The last lines urge Sue to be herself—noble, not relying on a petty faith, not complaining. For consolation, she should reflect that when she eventually escapes Night and finds Morning, she will be no more infinite than she has always been.

Like many of the poet's messages to others, this one looks back at a relationship from a vantage point outside daily life. She had repeatedly written "off charnel steps." With Sue, she had again and again drawn back in order to sum up their close yet distant friendship. But 1884–1885 was *the* time for ultimate statements of encouragement.

Yet Dickinson was by this time so frail that such efforts were extremely costly. Instead of writing from a position of weakness (as Sue did to Mattie, her future champion), she drew prodigally on the strength she increasingly lacked. Her wars weren't laid away in books after all: again and again she was driven to assert the priority of freshness and possibility over powerlessness, tragedy, death. It was partly because of this great effort, as was later realized, that her terminal decline began with Gib's shattering death. "Not to outgrow Genesis, is a sweet monition" says a note to a minister's wife from 1885 or 1886, meaning, perhaps, that we should not leave innocence and give in to experience.

When Sarah Tuckerman's husband died in March 1886, the poet sent a note exclaiming, "How ecstatic! How infinite! Says the blissful voice, not yet a voice, but a vision, 'I will not let thee go, except I bless thee.'" She was quoting from the story in Genesis 32:24–32 of Jacob's wrestling through the night with a supernatural being thought to be an angel. At dawn, not knowing whom he has been fighting, Jacob says, "I will not let thee go, except thou bless me,"[7] only to find he has been wrestling—has in fact prevailed against—the Almighty, who then both blesses and wounds: blesses by changing Jacob's name to Israel, wounds by touching the inside of his thigh and giving him a permanent limp. As if it were not enough to wrestle the deity, Dickinson audaciously reversed the relative position of God and man: "except *I* bless *thee*." The switch in pronouns was apparently not a slip. The spring she died, she ended her last letter to Higginson with the same reversal: "Audacity of Bliss, said Jacob to the Angel 'I will not let thee go except I bless thee' – Pugilist and Poet, Jacob was correct –"

The other thing she added to the story, the word "poet," shows how well she understood that her lyric vocation was a function of her essential lifelong struggle. Yielding to the nature of things no more than she had "given up" to the Savior during the revivals of her youth, she asserted her own powers of "pagan" ecstasy and sublime thought. She had been a fundamental rule-breaker, and now, in her last defiant paradox, she declared that *that* was what had made her "correct."

---

7. Twice before, Dickinson turned to this story, first about 1860 in "A little over Jordan" (Fr145). About 1879 she carefully wrote on good stationery, "'Let me go for the Day breaketh,'" later using the reverse to draft "'Secrets' is a daily word" (Fr1494).

It would be melodramatic to see Dickinson as some sort of God-defying Captain Ahab, who had nothing to do with "Bliss," but she did insist on reinterpreting, transcending, what she had been handed by her father, her religion, her culture. As the end approached, she saw herself as having triumphed, like Jacob. It would be hard to disagree. Both won their match. Yet there is a singular difference in that, where Jacob was given an obvious limp, Dickinson hid her own deep wound behind a gated partition, a "vail." Nowhere in her writings did she admit that the limits imposed on her did any serious or fundamental damage. Instead, mustering all the Dickinson determination in her effort to make "No" the wildest word in the language, she devoted her incomparable resources to a kind of virgin closed-door mastery.

That is the other difference between her and Jacob, who had wives and sons and daughters and whose new name became that of a people. Jacob/Israel was a patriarch for whom the blessing and the wound were distinct and separate. Dickinson was a single woman who simultaneously obeyed and defied the patriarchal order, and for whom the blessing and the wound became one and the same. What that seems to mean for us is that her great genius is not to be distinguished from her madness. *No, not her madness — the madness of her society out-of-balance*

An Adjourning Heart

The physician who chiefly attended Dickinson, Dr. Orvis F. Bigelow, gave the cause of death as "Bright's Disease" and its duration as two and a half years—since Gib's death. If we go to Bigelow's copy of Richard Quain's *Dictionary of Medicine* (1883), we find "Bright's Diseases" listed as a plural and designating three different kidney disorders: inflammatory, waxy, cirrhotic. That the doctor failed to indicate which of these it was raises a question about the accuracy of his diagnosis.

There are other reasons for doubting it. Of the sixty-nine deaths in Amherst in 1886, five were attributed to Bright's disease and one each to uraemia and "disease of kidneys." These numbers seem suspiciously high when compared to those from other towns in Massachusetts. Of the 90 deaths in Easthampton in 1886, or the 133 in Ware, or the 48 in Lexington, not one was blamed on Bright's disease. Medford had 140 deaths, only two of them from this cause. We may reasonably ask if kidney disease had become a catch-all category for Dr. Bigelow.

More material reasons for not accepting the official cause of death have been adduced by Dr. Norbert Hirschhorn and Polly Longsworth, who note that Dickinson's youthful and unblemished appearance, often commented on, is inconsistent with the signs of uremic poisoning—yellow skin, itching, an unpleasant odor. The true cause of death, they argue, was severe primary hypertension, a diagnosis not available in 1886. This explanation seems consistent with the known facts in the case: the stress under which the poet lived; the emotional effects of her bereavements; the state of medical science at the time; and the record of symptoms in her last two and a half years, thinking particularly of her bouts of fainting and final stroke.

After Bowles died, the poet wrote Higginson that a friend's death reminds you "you could not begin again, because there was no World." For someone who depended on the exchange of scripted messages with choice friends, the world began to feel bafflingly depleted as death succeeded death. Doing her best to fight back, Dickinson claimed that "Death cannot Plunder half so fast as Fervor can re-earn," referring, perhaps, to new friendships with Whitney and the Clarks. But sooner or later she had to admit that even her powers were insufficient. "The Dyings have been too deep for me," she said in fall 1884, "and before I could raise my Heart from one, another has come."

This was her way of explaining her sudden collapse that summer. On June 14, making a cake with Maggie, she "saw a great darkness coming" and, fainting, remained unconscious till late at night. Austin described the episode as "a singular attack of dizziness &c." Coming to, as she informed her cousins two months later, the earliest she felt able to write, she found her brother "and Vinnie and a strange physician bending over me." Then came "weeks of faintness," during which she "gave the others much alarm."

The one poem she is known to have sent during this period speaks of resignation at the prospect of death: "Not Sickness stains the

Brave, / . . . But an adjourning Heart" (Fr1661). Another time, remembering Gib, she abruptly broke off a letter as if sensing trouble: "But it is growing damp and I must go in. Memory's fog is rising." There is no evidence her doctors mentioned Bright's disease to her. Instead, she was told she was suffering "revenge of the nerves," the same formula she had been given following her nephew's death. Uninterested as she was in medical science ("I do not know the Names of Sickness"), she seems to have accepted this explanation, writing Helen Jackson that September that "Nervous prostration" had kept her sedentary.

On October 12, a Sunday, Austin belatedly discovered that his sister was having another strange and alarming episode. As he recorded in his diary, he

> went over to the other house about 5 and found Vin had been working over Emily, who had had another bad turn—since 3 o'clock alone, no one coming to help her, or within call.
>
> Got her onto the lounge with Stephen's help and sent for Maggie.

Sue's letter to Mattie the next day didn't mention the crisis. Her one report came nine days later after her brother Dwight, on a visit from Michigan, talked to the patient: "Aunt Emily saw Uncle last evening & he said was [*sic*] quite rational." This confirms both that the poet's mind had been wandering and that Sue was not in close touch. As for Vinnie, she was so on edge that three months later she felt anxious whenever Emily was "out of my sight—lest some new danger overcome her."[8] Across the street, Mariette Jameson had the impression that Emily's survival "a year longer than we supposed possible" was owing to "her sister's watchfulness and loving care."

This sense of lurking danger doesn't show up in Dickinson's many

---

8. Dr. Bigelow supposedly complained that the only way he was allowed to examine Dickinson was by watching her "walk by the open door of a room in which I was seated." One obvious problem with this much-loved story is that a patient who is often unconscious can easily be examined. Another is that Leyda, who first recorded it, failed to identify his source (his interview of Bigelow's descendants in the 1950s?). The story should probably not be taken seriously.

notes and letters from 1885. Apparently unworried, she had little to say about her health and, unlike her sister-in-law, who lived into her eighties, didn't solicit sympathy. Continuing to take an interest in others' lives, she commiserated with her friends' sorrows and thanked them for the photographs of children she hadn't seen. When Jackson died of cancer, she assured the bereaved husband that "Helen of Troy will die, but Helen of Colorado, never." To Bowles's son, she wrote, "Take all away from me, but leave me Ecstasy."

On November 30, 1885, her feebleness and other (undescribed) symptoms were so alarming her brother canceled a trip to Boston. For the next few months the poet was confined to bed and Vinnie redoubled her surveillance. On January 19 she and Austin had a serious talk about their sister. Occasionally he took Vinnie's place by her bed for an hour or so. His diary for March 18 reads in part, "at other house [Mansion] till 6, ══ perfect. Ev[en]ing sat an hour with Emily."

In spring, feeling better, Dickinson sent a last burst of letters, some much longer than usual. Telling the Norcrosses she had "lain in my bed since November," she likened her recovery to the flowering of the arbutus in early spring. Writing Charles H. Clark in early April, she asked after Wadsworth's children and said she was beginning "to roam in my room a little, an hour at a time." Clark's reply, partly about his father, eighty-one years old and still vigorous, brought the response, "Fear makes us all martial." She probably meant fear for others, not for herself. This was her closest reference to the fear of dying.

In the end, nothing was as thick as Norcross blood, or as compressed as her final communication to Frances and Louisa:

> Little Cousins,
> Called back.
> Emily.

She was alluding to Hugh Conway's popular *Called Back,* read a year or so earlier. This clever, spellbinding novel, which she had found a "haunting story," " 'greatly impressive to me,' " conjoined two of the decade's topical interests—the telepathic powers of the mind and international conspiratorial anarchism. Early in the story, the blind narrator stumbles on the scene of a fatal stabbing and hears a terrible, muffled moaning. After regaining his sight, he weds a beautiful but apathetic woman who seems to have no past, the marriage being one in name only. Disclosures accumulate, and when the couple revisit the scene of the crime in a sensational chapter titled "Called Back," the woman recovers her memory of her brother's murder, which flashes on the narrator in every last detail each time he touches her hand. Her psychological recovery now begins, but is not completed until the narrator makes a journey into Siberia's vividly described prison system and finds and talks to the murderer.

This was the book from which Dickinson, as usual taking only what she needed, extracted her succinct and ambiguous exit line. Had she been briefly called back to earth after approaching the other world? Or was she about to be called back to the infinite after an unknowing and frustrating term on earth? All we know is that her riddling was as strong and lighthearted as ever.

On the morning of May 13, after supervising the setting out of rhododendrons and azaleas and before leaving for his office, Austin learned from Vinnie that Emily was "feeling poorly." He decided to stay within call. According to his diary, his sister "seemed to go off into a stark unconscious state towards ten—and at this writing 6 P.M. has not come out of it. Dr Bigelow has been with her most of the afternoon." Perhaps the doctor was the source for the *Republican*'s report that she was "stricken with apoplexy" (had a stroke) that morning.

The next day Austin noted that his sister's stertorous breathing had gone on for a full day: "Emily is no better—has been in this heavy breathing and perfectly unconscious since middle of yesterday afternoon." Mabel's diary describes him as "terribly oppressed." The "heavy breathing" went on for another day, and when it finally stopped he was shattered. His record for May 15 reads:

It was settled before morning broke that Emily would not wake again this side.

The day was awful   She ceased to breathe that terrible breathing just before the [afternoon] whistle sounded for six.

Mrs Montague and Mrs Jameson were sitting with Vin.

I was nearby.

May 16 is blank. Vinnie, too, was said to be "utterly bereft."

Taking charge, Sue composed for the *Republican* a long and discriminating obituary that explained Dickinson's reclusiveness by "her sensitive nature" and dwelled on her fineness of mind and character. She arranged for Eunice R. Powell to prepare a white flannel robe and dress the body, which was embalmed by the local mortician, Ellery Strickland. He was surprised the deceased was "so young-looking, her reddish, bronze hair without a silver thread." Mariette Jameson, given a private viewing by Vinnie, felt that "Miss Emily . . . looked more like her brother than her sister, with a wealth of auburn hair and a very spirituelle face."

The funeral, held in the Mansion's library, was simple and short. The new minister, Reverend George S. Dickerman, read a passage from I Corinthians 15 that Dickinson herself had quoted: "For this corruptible must put on incorruption, and this mortal must put on immortality." Higginson, present for the occasion, said as if in rejoinder that the poet "never seemed to have put [immortality] off." Then he read "No Coward Soul Is Mine," the defiant poem by Emily Brontë that had been a favorite with her ("Vain are the thousand creeds / That move men's hearts"). Viewing the body, he, too, thought the face "a wondrous restoration of youth—she is 54 [in fact, 55] & looked 30, not a gray hair or wrinkle." Mabel Loomis Todd attended with her husband, as did Mattie, of course, but Sue's presence is nowhere recorded, even though she had planned the funeral. Mrs. Jameson hoped that "matters [would] be a little more friendly" between Sue and Vinnie.

The four honorary pallbearers—the president of Amherst College, Doc Hitchcock, John Jameson, and Dwight Hills—carried the coffin out the back door, and then Thomas Kelley and Dennis Scannell and Stephen Sullivan and Pat Ward and two others who had worked for the

Dickinsons bore it crosslots to the cemetery, their path a token of respect for the deceased's love of privacy. It was a beautiful spring day, with flowers everywhere. The Todds joined in the procession.

Going through Emily's things, Vinnie did as requested and destroyed her sister's lifetime accumulation of letters, an act she later regretted, but the huge and surprising cache of poems in small sewn bundles seemed too precious to burn. Resolving to get them published, she turned them over to Sue to select and edit. Sue's idea, however, was to print, not publish: believing that "for all of us women not fame but 'Love and home and certainty are best,'" she dreamed of a privately circulated collection of poems and letters. But after two years she had so little to show for her work that Vinnie turned to Mabel Loomis Todd, enlisting her as copyist. The more Todd worked, the more impressed and dedicated she became. She and Vinnie prevailed on Higginson to lend his support and know-how, and by November 1890 a selection of Dickinson's work was ready for the late-nineteenth-century market. Todd contacted William Dean Howells, whose prestige, interest in New England manners, and long track record of welcoming brilliant newcomers made him a useful ally. He replied, "When you showed me Miss Dickinson's poems, I did not half know how good they were. Will you kindly look over this review . . ." Appearing in *Harper's Monthly*, Howells's discerning assessment issued in the conclusion that "if nothing else had come out of our life but this strange poetry we should feel that in the work of Emily Dickinson America, or New England rather, had made a distinctive addition to the literature of the world." Most reviewers felt the same, and *Poems by Emily Dickinson* quickly ran through several editions.

When Austin and Vinnie died in 1895 and 1899, the two deadly rivals and their daughters—Sue and Martha Dickinson Bianchi, Mabel and Millicent Todd Bingham—ended up with large quantities of manuscripts, which were brought out in a series of publications extending past the middle of the twentieth century. Bianchi had the more stifling effect on publication and interpretation, but Todd and Bingham also did their part to manage the legacy. The consequences of the poet's refusal to disseminate her work in a faithful and orderly fashion are still very much with us.

Something with an unheard-of brilliance and purity had come to an end, and something public, derivative, and dependent on a world of stumbling readers had begun. We may suspect the poet would have seen her lasting fame as a contemptible substitute for the limitlessness and perfection she had spent her life thinking about. But it doesn't look as if we are going to find out.

DICKINSON FAMILY CHART

with Gunn, Montague, Smith, Graves,
Cowan, and Newman connections

(many family members not shown)

Capt. Nathaniel Gunn

Jemima Gunn
(ca. 1749–1832)
m (1778)
Zebina Montague
(1754–1809)

Hannah Montague
(b. 1752)
m Nathaniel Gunn

Richard Montague
(1729–1794)
m Lucy Cooley
(ca. 1730–1795)

Nathan Dickinson, Jr.
(1735–1825)
m (1) Esther Fowler
(ca. 1740–1803)
m (2) the widow
Jerusha Dickinson
Blodgett
(d. 1818 or 1822)

Rev. Timothy
Dickinson (1761–1813)

Perez Dickinson
(1763–1813)
m (1) Ruth Dickinson
(d. 1798)
m (2) Lucinda Foster
(1782–1855)

Ezekiel Dickinson
(1765–1833)
m Perley Gunn
(1774–1836)

Esther Dickinson

Thankful Dickinson

Irene Dickinson
(1770–1849)
m Luke Montague
(1766–1818)

Samuel Fowler
Dickinson (1775–1838)
m Lucretia Gunn
(1775–1840)

Anna Dickinson
(1780–1867)
m Oliver Smith
(1769–1851)

Clarissa Gunn
(1779–1850)
m (1834) the widower
Kingsley Underwood,
of Enfield (1770–1849)

Hannah Gunn
(1783–1860)
m Jesse Whitmore
(d. 1856 in Sunderland)

Fanny Gunn
(1792/93–1876)
m Horatio Graves,
of Sunderland
(1788–1867)

Fanny Dickinson
(ca. 1794–Aug. 24, 1844)
m Seneca Holland (1790–1871)

Sophia Holland
(1828–1844)

Nancy Dickinson
(ca. 1806–1846)
m Prof. Joseph Estabrook

Appleton Dickinson
(ca. 1808–1829)

Lucinda Dickinson (1811–1849)
m James H. Cowan (1801–1871)

Perez Dickinson (1813–1901)

Nancy (Nannie) Cowan
(1841–June 21, 1869)
m Capt. John G. Meem, Jr.

Perez Dickinson Cowan
(1843–1923)
m Margaret E. Rhea

Margaret McClung
Cowan (1876–1879)

Eleanor Rhea Cowan
(b. 1885)

Nathan Dickinson
(1799–1861)
m Mary Ann Taylor
(1807–1878)

Mary Ann Dickinson
(1829–1902)

Sarah Jane Dickinson
(1829–1904)
m Darwin L. Gillett,
of Westfield (1823–1901)

George Montague (1804–1893)
m Mary A. Parsons (b. 1812)

Harriet Montague (1808–1895)

Zebina Montague (1810–1881)

William Austin Dickinson
(1829–1895)
m (1856) Susan (Sue)
Huntington Gilbert
(1830–1913)

Edward (Ned)
Dickinson (1861–1898)

Martha (Mattie)
Dickinson (1866–1943)
m (1903)
Alexander D. Bianchi

Thomas Gilbert (Gib)
Dickinson (1875–1883)

Edward Dickinson (1803–1874)
m Emily Norcross (1804–1882)

William Dickinson (1804–1887)
m (1) Eliza Hawley
(d. July 31, 1851)
m (2) Mary L. Whittier

Emily Elizabeth Dickinson,
poet (1830–1886)

Lavinia (Vinnie) Norcross
Dickinson (1833–1899)

William Hawley Dickinson
(1832–1883)
m Ellen E. Pike

Lucretia Dickinson (1806–1885)
m Asa Bullard (1804–1888)

Mary Dickinson
(1809–Mar. 30, 1852)
m Mark Haskell Newman
(1806–Dec. 21, 1852)

Samuel Fowler Dickinson, Jr.
(b. 1811)
m Susan Witherspoon Cook

Catharine Dickinson
(1814–1895)
m Joseph A. Sweetser
(1809–disappeared 1874)

Timothy Dickinson (b. 1816)
m (1838) Hannah Montague
Dickinson (b. 1814)

Frederick Dickinson (b. 1819)
m Mary L. Richardson

Elizabeth Dickinson (1823–86)
m (1866) Augustus N. Currier

Mark Haskell Newman
(b. 1833)
m Mary

Catherine D. Newman
(1836–1868)
m (1865) George A.
Tewkesbury

Sarah Phillips Newman
(1838–1909)
m (1868) J. Anson Bates

Clarissa (Clara) B. Newman
(1844–1920)
m (Oct. 14, 1869) Sidney
Turner (d. 1891)

Anna Dodge Newman
(1846–1887)
m (June 3, 1874) George H.
Carleton

Clara Newman
Carleton
(b. Mar. 21, 1876)
m George E. Pearl

Albert G. Carleton
(b. Dec. 21, 1877)

Thankful Smith (1807–1889)

Oliver Eastman Smith
(1815–1883?)

John Long Graves (1831–1915)
m (1858)
Fanny Greenleaf Britton

Gertrude Montague Graves
(b. 1863)

Louise Britton Graves
(b. 1867)

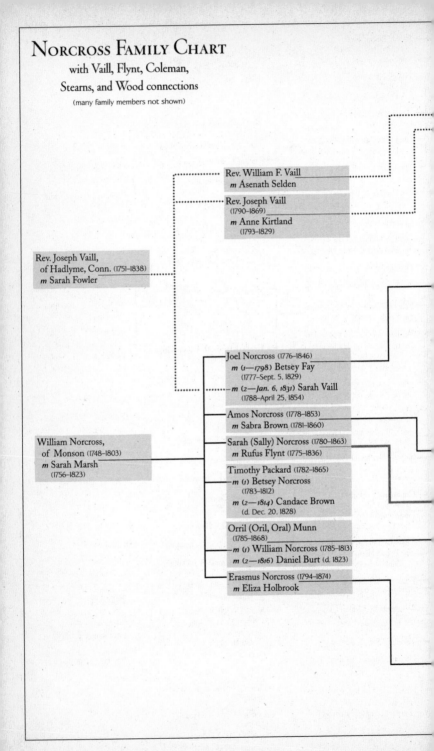

NORCROSS FAMILY CHART

with Vaill, Flynt, Coleman,
Stearns, and Wood connections

(many family members not shown)

Rev. William F. Vaill
m Asenath Selden

Rev. Joseph Vaill
(1790–1869)
m Anne Kirtland
(1793–1829)

Rev. Joseph Vaill,
of Hadlyme, Conn. (1751–1838)
m Sarah Fowler

Joel Norcross (1776–1846)
m (*1*—*1798*) Betsey Fay
(1777–Sept. 5, 1829)
m (*2*—*Jan. 6, 1831*) Sarah Vaill
(1788–April 25, 1854)

Amos Norcross (1778–1853)
m Sabra Brown (1781–1860)

Sarah (Sally) Norcross (1780–1863)
m Rufus Flynt (1775–1836)

Timothy Packard (1782–1865)
m (*1*) Betsey Norcross
(1783–1812)
m (*2*—*1814*) Candace Brown
(d. Dec. 20, 1828)

William Norcross,
of Monson (1748–1803)
m Sarah Marsh
(1756–1823)

Orril (Oril, Oral) Munn
(1785–1868)
m (*1*) William Norcross (1785–1813)
m (*2*—*1816*) Daniel Burt (d. 1823)

Erasmus Norcross (1794–1874)
m Eliza Holbrook

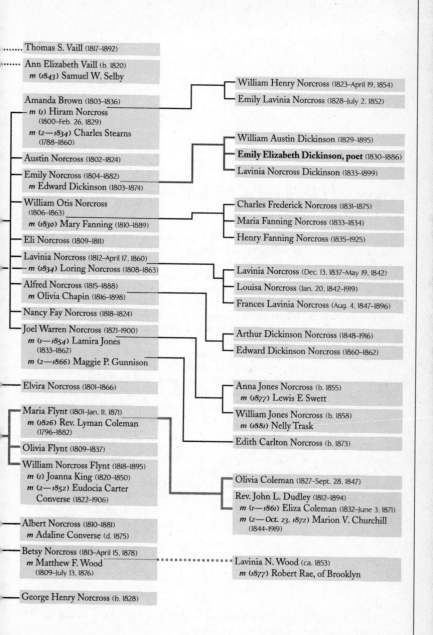

Thomas S. Vaill (1817–1892)

Ann Elizabeth Vaill (b. 1820)
m (*1843*) Samuel W. Selby

Amanda Brown (1803–1836)
— *m* (*1*) Hiram Norcross
(1800–Feb. 26, 1829)
m (*2—1834*) Charles Stearns
(1788–1860)

Austin Norcross (1802–1824)

Emily Norcross (1804–1882)
m Edward Dickinson (1803–1874)

William Otis Norcross
(1806–1863)
m (*1830*) Mary Fanning (1810–1889)

Eli Norcross (1809–1811)

Lavinia Norcross (1812–April 17, 1860)
— *m* (*1834*) Loring Norcross (1808–1863)

Alfred Norcross (1815–1888)
m Olivia Chapin (1816–1898)

Nancy Fay Norcross (1818–1824)

Joel Warren Norcross (1821–1900)
m (*1—1854*) Lamira Jones
(1833–1862)
m (*2—1866*) Maggie P. Gunnison

Elvira Norcross (1801–1866)

Maria Flynt (1801–Jan. 11, 1871)
m (*1826*) Rev. Lyman Coleman
(1796–1882)

Olivia Flynt (1809–1837)

William Norcross Flynt (1818–1895)
m (*1*) Joanna King (1820–1850)
m (*2—1852*) Eudocia Carter
Converse (1822–1906)

Albert Norcross (1810–1881)
m Adaline Converse (d. 1875)

Betsy Norcross (1813–April 15, 1878)
m Matthew F. Wood
(1809–July 13, 1876)

George Henry Norcross (b. 1828)

William Henry Norcross (1823–April 19, 1854)

Emily Lavinia Norcross (1828–July 2, 1852)

William Austin Dickinson (1829–1895)

Emily Elizabeth Dickinson, poet (1830–1886)

Lavinia Norcross Dickinson (1833–1899)

Charles Frederick Norcross (1831–1875)

Maria Fanning Norcross (1833–1834)

Henry Fanning Norcross (1835–1925)

Lavinia Norcross (Dec. 13, 1837–May 19, 1842)

Louisa Norcross (Jan. 20, 1842–1919)

Frances Lavinia Norcross (Aug. 4, 1847–1896)

Arthur Dickinson Norcross (1848–1916)

Edward Dickinson Norcross (1860–1862)

Anna Jones Norcross (b. 1855)
m (*1877*) Lewis E Swett

William Jones Norcross (b. 1858)
m (*1881*) Nelly Trask

Edith Carlton Norcross (b. 1873)

Olivia Coleman (1827–Sept. 28, 1847)

Rev. John L. Dudley (1812–1894)
m (*1—1861*) Eliza Coleman (1832–June 3, 1871)
m (*2— Oct. 23, 1872*) Marion V. Churchill
(1844–1919)

Lavinia N. Wood (ca. 1853)
m (*1877*) Robert Rae, of Brooklyn

Appendix 1

A Second Photograph of Emily Dickinson?

In 2000 a dealer in bulk photographs offered for sale on eBay a photographic portrait of a woman identified on the back as Emily Dickinson. Neither the seller, Janos Novomeszky, nor the dealer from whom he acquired the job lot containing the photo, Stephen White of Los Angeles, was aware that only a single known image of the poet existed. This offering of uncertain provenance was noticed by a professor of American literature and culture at the University of North Carolina at Chapel Hill, Philip F. Gura, who was able to purchase the portrait for $481.[1] It is reproduced on page 2 of the photo section.

The print is a product of the albumen process, popular from the 1860s to the end of the century and often employed to make copies of earlier daguerreotypes (which, having no negatives, were necessarily unique). At the time the print was made, the preexisting daguerreotype may have been tarnished or otherwise damaged. Alternatively, the lack of detail at the bottom may be an effect of duplication, caused by reflected light.

On the back of the print are several penciled marks and captions, none of which appears to be of recent origin. In the lower middle is a large penciled 4, suggesting, perhaps, that this was either the fourth attempt to make an adequate print or the fourth copy of a successful print. Also in pencil, across the bottom right-hand quadrant is a heavily obscured inscription consisting of a few cursive words beginning with a "Q" or "D" and a barely discernible date, 1886. The writing seems to have been overlaid with several swipes of glue. Perhaps the portrait was placed in an album.

A third inscription has been penciled at the top. Obviously intending to record the sitter's identity and year of death, an unknown scribe wrote:

Emily Dickinson—
died
[D?]ec 1886

---

1. "A New Kodak Moment with Emily Dickinson," *New Yorker*, 5-22-2000, p. 30. I am grateful to Professor Gura for information and suggestions.

Some have read the problematic letter as a lower-case "r," thus making the word an abbreviation for "received." Others have proposed that the three-letter word stands for "December," which is of course not the right month for the poet, who died in May. Neither reading explains the odd placement of "died," which, in the original, looks squeezed between the first and third lines. The correct account is probably as follows: immediately after setting down the name, the unknown writer, intending the standard abbreviation for "deceased," wrote "Dec 1886." Then, realizing either that the capital "D" was not well formed or that the letters could be construed as referring to a month, he or she tried to clear up the ambiguity by writing "died" in the space above and between the last two words—the spot where most people would insert a clarification. That the month of her death was not recorded suggests the writer did not know it or did not consider it important; years may have elapsed since she died. What *was* important was to note who this was.

In the initial publicity concerning the image, it was dated about 1865 and the sitter was said to be carrying eyeglasses on a lanyard. In fact, the fashion elements date from twelve or fifteen years earlier, and what was conjectured to be glasses is probably a brooch. Joan Severa, author of *Dressed for the Photographer,* places the dress style in the late 1840s and the hair style as late as the early 1850s. In Nancy Rexford's view, the jacket-style bodice, the collar of the chemisette, and the undersleeves are characteristic of the early 1850s.[2] If these dates are approximately right, and the daguerreotypist's session took place in, say, 1853 at the latest, one may reasonably ask whether the sitter is too old for a woman in her early twenties. The question prompts another: is dress style a dependable clue for someone who conceived herself to be flagrantly behind the times? In 1854 Dickinson assured Abiah Root, "I'm so old fashioned, Darling, that all your friends would stare."[3]

Another insistent question for those used to the familiar image of the poet is whether the new one *looks* like her. Two physical anthropologists consulted by Professor Gura, Nicholas P. Herrmann and Dr. Richard L. Jantz, have used digital scans to compare the morphological features of the two images. After rotating the new image, and scaling it to the same "inter-pupil distance," they find a good match in mandibular height (chin to lips) and other features. Herrmann and Jantz conclude that the two photos "exhibit a consistent pattern and relationship between the identified cranial landmarks and gross morphological features."[4] They are unable to prove that the two photos are *not* of the same person—something that in most cases is easy to demonstrate.

As shown in Chapter 9, the familiar daguerreotype records the poet's appearance soon after her sixteenth birthday and a long period of illness. She also seems to have undergone a spurt of growth, to judge from the tight and ill-fitting dress. Her sister and niece were so dissatisfied with this image they both tried to alter it. To their eyes, the picture that has come to stand for the poet conveyed a blatantly misleading idea of her.

Following Emily's trip to Boston in fall 1851, her sister, Lavinia, noted that her health and spirits were so improved she had grown "quite fat." Equally concerned about her loss of weight, which could be seen as a symptom of consumption, the poet faithfully took Dr. James Jackson's prescription and did her best to acquire and retain a healthy appearance. If she had a second daguerreotype made, we would expect it to date from a period of relative good health. A sleeker, plumper look would not be surprising.[5]

---

2. Joan Severa to Philip F. Gura, 5-8-2000, e-mail; Nancy Rexford to Gura, 8-29-2000, e-mail.
3. *Let* 299.
4. Nicholas P. Herrmann, M.A., and Richard L. Jantz, Ph.D., to Philip F. Gura, 10-21-2000.
5. *Home* 174; "Root" 31. See Chap. 12, pp. 261–63.

In July 1853, some time after Edward Dickinson had a studio portrait taken, Emily wrote her brother in Cambridge, "I hope to send father's Daguerreotype before you come." That fall, uneasy about her parent's excessive solemnity, she confided to Austin her wish that Father "would 'look more cheerful' – I think the Artist was right." This shared memory of a daguerrian artist's remark suggests she could have been present at the session and thus have had her own image taken. The early photos of Austin that aren't mentioned in the epistolary record remind us (once again) how sporadic and selective the surviving documentation is. Emily could easily have had a session with an "Artist" like Jeremiah D. Wells, Northampton's leading daguerreotypist,[6] without the record ever mentioning it.

When Thomas Wentworth Higginson requested her portrait in 1862, she replied:

> Could you believe me – without? I had no portrait, now, but am small, like the Wren. . . .
> It often alarms Father – He says Death might occur, and he has Molds of all the rest – but has no Mold of me, but I noticed the Quick wore off those things, in a few days, and forestall the dishonor. . . .[7]

Does the emphatic "now," enclosed in commas, suggest that until recently she *did* have a photo? Could she have had one taken unknown to Edward, as when she visited Philadelphia in March 1855 (with a new outfit)? Tellingly, the phrase that follows "Mold of me" happens to be in the plural—"those things," as if she had endured the photographic process more than once. As for "the Quick" wearing off, she could have been referring not only to the artificiality of a formal pose or the embarrassing immaturity of one's earlier look, but to a daguerreotype's tarnishing.

Higginson's request shows there was nothing improper in a married man's asking for her portrait. If Dickinson had sent hers to Wadsworth a few months earlier—sent it through Samuel Bowles shortly before the minister left Philadelphia for San Francisco—that could elucidate both her emphatic "now" and the excruciating tone of her March 1862 letter to Mary Bowles. Realizing too late that Samuel had left for Washington, Emily was in agony lest Mary open the letter and find herself "troubled" by the solicited "errand."[8]

Any plausible case for the authenticity of the albumen print must show how it could have failed to surface in the early 1890s, when Mabel Loomis Todd conducted a dogged search for letters and for a portrait suitable for reproduction. As it happens, the hypothesis that the original daguerreotype was sent to Wadsworth not only explains why the image vanished from sight but directs fresh attention to a relevant and arresting passage in the poet's letters to his good friends, James D. and Charles H. Clark.

Willis Buckingham's collection of reviews of Dickinson's first posthumous books reprints a pointed speculation from a Philadelphia newspaper about her unknown lover: "Mrs. Todd has told us that Miss Dickinson was not 'disappointed in love,' but these poems reveal that she thought much of love, and worshipped an ideal lover; some will

---

6. *Let* 262, 269; Chris Steele & Ronald Polito, *A Directory of Massachusetts Photographers 1839–1900* (Camden, Maine: Picton, 1993).

7. *Let* 411.

8. *Let* 396.

think she loved a man."[9] There were obvious reasons why first Wadsworth and then his survivors and friends had to be on guard against the inevitable gossip about him and Dickinson. This persisting caution can be felt in a letter of hers to James D. Clark following the minister's death. After reflecting on Wadsworth's "Grandeur" and gloom and quoting some of his darker remarks, she says:

> Thank you for the Face – which I fear it fatigued you too much to seek –
> and for the monition, tho' to disclose a grief of his I could not surmise –
> Your sweet attempt to repair the irreparable, I must also remember.[10]

The first paragraph tells us that Clark had secured a portrait of Wadsworth for the poet, and suggests that his family, in sending it, enjoined secrecy. The second can be read, quite thrillingly, as a reference to her own hard-to-copy photograph, recently dispatched from Philadelphia. It would make sense for the Wadsworths to send both portraits at the same time, and for Clark and then Dickinson to mention them together. Informed of Clark's attempt to secure a passable reproduction, she "must also remember"—acknowledge—his "sweet" and flattering interest in preserving her own image.

Of the two Clark brothers, it was Charles H., a bookkeeper, who seems to have been Wadsworth's particular friend. After James died in 1883, Charles took over the task of corresponding with the poet, who sent him fifteen letters in her last three years. When her sister asked to have them returned years later,[11] he carefully keyed envelopes to letters and even made penciled transcripts of two of them. Never marrying, outliving all close relatives, Charles was in his seventies by the time he moved back to Massachusetts in the early twentieth century, residing first in Greenfield and then in Longmeadow, both of which, like Northampton, border the Connecticut River. At his death in New York's McAlpin Hotel in 1915, he was eighty-two, with no one to leave his money to. "In excess of $30,000," according to a story in *The New York Times*, the entire estate went to charities in Northampton, Brooklyn, and New York.[12]

The "4" on the back of the newly discovered print resembles the number as formed by James D. Clark,[13] but the hand that wrote the inscription at the top remains unidentified. It is not that of Charles H. Clark or Edith Wadsworth, the minister's daughter.

9. Buckingham 473.

10. *Let* 745.

11. Charles H. Clark to Lavinia Dickinson, 1-14-1892, ED Todd315 A.

12. *Springfield Union* 3-18-1915; *New York Times* 4-10-1915.

13. See James D. Clark to Jonathan Pearson, 4-17-1882, Schaffer Library Special Collections, Union College.

Appendix 2

Standing Buildings Associated with Emily Dickinson

Massachusetts

AMHERST

280 Main Street. Dickinson Homestead. The poet's home, 1830–1840 and 1855–1886.

214 Main Street. "The Evergreens," home of Austin and Susan Dickinson, built 1856.

165 Main Street. First Congregational Church, built 1868.

17 Seelye Street. Parsonage, first occupied by Reverend Jonathan and Sarah Jenkins.

229 Main Street. House of Professor Richard H. and Lizzie Mather.

360 Main Street. Leonard M. Hills house.

390 Main Street. Henry M. and Adelaide Hills house.

81 Lessey Street. Luke and Abby Sweetser house.

Railroad Street. Train station, built about 1853.

90 Spring Street. "The Dell," Mabel Loomis Todd house, originally located south of the street and facing the opposite direction.

East side of the Common. Grace Episcopal Church. The first window on the south is a memorial to Susan D. Phelps.

Corner of South Pleasant Street and Routes 9 and 16. First Congregational Church, 1828–1868. Now College Hall.

Building immediately south of College Hall. Morgan Hall, dedicated as college library, 1853.

175 South Pleasant Street. College president's house, built 1834.

227 South Pleasant Street. Nelson sisters' house and school (probably *not* attended by Dickinson).

249 South Pleasant Street. Helen Fiske Hunt Jackson's childhood home.

271 South Pleasant Street. Edward Hitchcock house.

North College, Amherst College. Erected 1822–1823.

Johnson Chapel, Amherst College. Erected 1826–1827.

College Admissions Office. Judge John Dickinson house.

58 Woodside Street. James W. Boyden house, moved in 1937 from original site south of John Dickinson house.[1]

67 Amity Street. Strong family house, now Amherst Historical Museum, containing the Mabel Loomis Todd Room.

BOSTON

35 Bowdoin Street. Formerly the church of Loring and Lavinia Norcross, now St. John the Evangelist.

CAMBRIDGE

99 Prospect Street. Formerly the Congregational Church Louisa and Frances Norcross joined in 1865, now Igreja Presbiteriana Cristo Rei.

CONCORD

92 Sudbury Road. The Edward Bulkeley House, built in the seventeenth century. Bought by Louisa and Frances Norcross in 1888 and occupied until 1908.[2]

MONSON

15 Mechanic Street. Phoebe Hinsdale Brown house.

12 Cushman Street. William Norcross Cottage, built about 1773. Original Norcross family home.

14 Cushman Street. Norcross Tavern, built 1780–1785. Later Joel and Betsey Fay Norcross's first house. The poet's mother grew up here.

125 Main Street. Joel and Sarah Vaill Norcross's house from 1837.

NORTHAMPTON

50 Elm Street. Clark House, Smith College. Homestead of Charles Clark, kept after he moved to Brooklyn and used as a summer home by his sons, Charles H. and James D.[3]

New York

GENEVA

512 South Main Street. Home of Martha Gilbert Smith and John Williams Smith.

108 William Street. Sophia and William Van Vranken house, where Austin Dickinson and Susan Gilbert were married.

---

1. *Hampshire Gazette* 6-8-1937.

2. Middlesex Co. RD 1878:145, 1879:563; Concord Historical Commission, "Survey of Historical and Architectural Resources" (Concord, 1994) vol. 3, #117, Concord Free Public Library.

3. Hampshire Co. RD 249:189, 425:305; *SR* 3-18-1915; Eleanor Terry Lincoln and John Abel Pinto, *This, the House We Live in: The Smith College Campus from 1871 to 1982* (Northampton: Smith College, 1983) 50.

Appendix 3

Deaths from Consumption (Tuberculosis)

In 1850, according to the *Boston Medical and Surgical Journal* (later the *New England Journal of Medicine*), 22 percent of the deaths in Massachusetts were caused by consumption. An 1854 article in this journal admitted that "not a single advance, of real value," had been made in the treatment of this disease, "beyond the employment of cod-liver oil."[1]

The following lists some of the people in Dickinson's world whose death was attributed to this insidious scourge. AVR stands for Amherst Vital Records, on microfilm at the Jones Library.

YEAR OF DEATH		AGE
1829	Hiram Norcross	28[2]
1836	Amanda Brown Norcross Stearns	33[3]
1837	Harriet Arms Gilbert (Sue's mother)	44 or 45[4]
1840	Lucretia Gunn Dickinson	64[5]
1844	Deborah W. V. Fiske	38 AVR
1844	Harriet Webster Fowler	46 AVR
1844	Fanny D. Holland (Sophia Holland's mother)	50 AVR
1844	Elizabeth W. Parsons (wife of Rev. David)	55 AVR
1847	Olivia M. Coleman	19
1848	Jacob Holt	26 AVR
1851	Abby Haskell (*Let* 189, 197)	19 AVR
1852	Emily Lavinia Norcross	24
1852	Mary Dickinson Newman	43

---

1. Review of *Ninth Report of Births, Marriages and Deaths, in Massachusetts*, in *Boston Medical and Surgical Journal* 45 (1–21-1852) 515; "Pulmonary Consumption," *Boston Medical and Surgical Journal* 50 (2-8-1854) 44.

2. Bernhard 375.

3. Leyda 1:1xvi.

4. Smith 309.

5. *Desc* 206; END's Bible.

YEAR OF DEATH		AGE
1852	Mark Haskell Newman	46
1853	Benjamin Franklin Newton	32
1857	Eliza O. T. Boyden	36[6]
1857	Dr. Campbell Ladd Turner	26
1860	Martha P. Snell	24 AVR
1860	Lavinia Norcross Norcross	48
1861 (Sept. 8)	Caroline P. Dutch Hunt	61 or 62 AVR
1861 (Sept. 11)	Lucy Waterman Dwight (Rev. Dwight's wife)[7]	38 or 39
1862	Lamira Jones Norcross	29[8]
1863	William O. Norcross	56[9]
1866	Chester E. Dickinson (Bela's son: *Let* 509)	17[10]
1869	Sarah D. Hunt (Caroline Hunt's daughter)	32 AVR
1871	Maria Flynt Coleman	69[11]
1871	Eliza Coleman Dudley	39
1871	Mary Maher	20 AVR
1877	Lizzie Carmichael Mather	41
1882	Ethel Stearns (*Let* 742)	17[12]
1882	Mary E. Donohue (*Let* 753)	16[13]

6. MVR-Deaths 112:1.

7. Leyda 2:33.

8. MVR-Deaths 156:226; Joel W. Norcross, "The History and Genealogy of the Norcross Family," 1:126, NEHGS.

9. Genealogical records assembled by Priscilla Chatfield.

10. AVR; *Desc* 483; Amherst directories for 1869 and 1873.

11. Leyda 2:159, 166.

12. Alfred E. Stearns, *An Amherst Boyhood* (Amherst: The College, 1946) 47–48.

13. AVR; 1870 federal census, Amherst, family 281.

Appendix 4

Emily Dickinson's Legal Signatures

This list identifies the known legal instruments signed by the poet, invariably with her middle initial, E. Except for items seven, twenty, and twenty-one, the instruments convey property from her parents to a buyer, with the poet signing as a witness to the transaction. Most of these conveyances survive only as official copies by a county register of deeds (RD) in Michigan and Massachusetts, and thus do not show actual signatures. The six original documents are marked with an asterisk. The dates are those on which the instruments were signed.

The "signature" on the only known copy of Dickinson's will, deposited at the Houghton Library (fms Am 1118.4 [L32]), does not include her middle initial and is not in her handwriting. Like the rest of the document, it seems to be in the hand of her aging neighbor Luke Sweetser. For a facsimile, see *World* 112. I have found no evidence the will went through probate.

1.	9-1-1843	Lapeer Co., MI, RD E:509
2.	8-24-1848	Hampshire Co., MA, RD 126:59
3.	4-16-1851	Ottawa Co., MI, RD E:21 (Austin also a witness)
4.	6-13-1851	Sale of church pew, Hampshire Co., MA, RD 139:431.
5.	12-8-1851	Ottawa Co., MI, RD E:537–58 (Lavinia also a witness)
6.	*1-12-1852	Sale of land in Watertown, MA, Bianchi Coll.
7.	*7-1-1853	Will of Sarah Vaill Norcross, Hampden Co., MA, Probate Court, Case 8351 (Edward and Lavinia also witnesses)
8.	8-1-1853	Ottawa Co., MI, RD G:182–83
9.	11-1-1855	Hampshire Co., MA, RD 239:119
10.	4-5-1859	Lapeer Co., MI, RD P:578
11.	6-3-1859	Hampshire Co., MA, RD 187:254 (Austin also a witness)
12.	4-13-1860	Hampshire Co., MA, RD 247:31 (Austin also a witness)
13.	5-1-1860	Hampshire Co., MA, RD 194:353
14.	*7-1-1861	Sale of farm in Pelham to Austin, Bianchi Coll.
15.	*11-22-1862	Sale of one acre of Dickinson meadow to Mary L. Hitchcock, Doc Hitch, oversize 5:11
16.	2-18-1863	Hampshire Co., MA, RD 210:155 (Austin also a witness)

17.   6-25-1863   Hampshire Co., MA, RD 214:221 (Austin also a witness)
18.   8-15-1863   Hampshire Co., MA, RD 214:130
19.   12-3-1863   Lapeer Co., MI, RD U:387
20.   *8-3-1874   Austin's petition to be appointed administrator of Edward's estate (photocopy), Hampshire Co., MA, Registry of Probate 192:6.
21.   *5-1-1875   Sale by Emily Norcross Dickinson and her children of a strip of the Dickinson meadow adjoining the Hitchcock place to Mary L. Hitchcock, Doc Hitch, oversize 5:11. This was the only deed the poet signed as a principal rather than as a witness.

Appendix 5

Summary of Corrected Dates of Letters

	DATE IN JOHNSON	CORRECT DATE	JUSTIFICATION
L38	about Dec 1850	just before 2-27-1851	above, p. 268
L143	11-23-1853?	just before 11-25-1852	p. 692
L161	spring 1854	soon after 5-10-1852	p. 259
L173	about 1854	shortly before 8-4-1854	pp. 323, 701–2
L180	10-16-1855	10-17-1855	Leyda 1:336
L185	early Aug 1856?	early Aug 1858?	p. 707
L189	about June 1858	summer 1859	Him 2; pp. 709, 710
L193	late Aug 1858?	last half of Aug 1859	pp. 709, 710
L196	about Dec 1858	ca Dec 1859	Him 9; *Var* 1575
L199	about 1-4-1859	between 12-9-1859 and 1-7-1860 (12-29-1859?)	pp. 388, 712
L205	early Apr 1859	Sept–Oct 1859	Him 2; p. 710
L216	1860?	soon after 11-7-1860	pp. 422, 717
L219	about 1860	about spring 1861	*Var* 251
L220	about 1860	early 1861	*Var* 1575
L230	early March 1861?	between Oct 1879 and summer 1883	pp. 673–74
L234 ("Your letters are all real")	1861?	late Oct or early Nov 1861	Leyda 2:37
L250	early 1862	spring 1861	*Var* 1275
L251	early 1862	spring or early summer 1861	*Var* 1275; p. 717
L252	early 1862	ca Christmas 1861	p. 717
L264	late May 1862	May or June 1863?	p. 713
L267	mid-July 1862	mid-July 1863?	p. 713
L283	about 1863	about 1862	*Var* 302
L298	1864?	late Dec? 1862	Leyda 2:72

	DATE IN JOHNSON	CORRECT DATE	JUSTIFICATION
L299	about 1864	May? 1861	Leyda 2:28
L300	about 1864	soon after 6-8-1861	Leyda 2:28; p. 718
L317	spring 1866?	soon after 4-12-1862	*Imagery* 25, 27; p. 461
L322	1866?	soon after attempted robbery of 7-2-1867	Leyda 2:124; Ackmann 229; p. 512
L442	summer 1875	May 1875	pp. 545, 729
L465	about 1876	soon after Thanksgiving 1874	p. 569
L478	late Oct 1876?	Sept 4, 5, or 6, 1880	pp. 587–88, 734
L526	Christmas 1877	between Dec 9 and 25, 1876	p. 564
L559, L560, L561, L562 (see Werner 287)	about 1878	after Aug 1880?	pp. 587–88
L563	about 1878	spring 1881?	pp. 587–88
L591	early 1879?	early 1878?	p. 732
L600	about 1879	after Aug 1880?	pp. 587–88
L643	about June 1880	early Apr or early Aug 1880	pp. 581, 733
L750 (second half, beginning "Door either")	4–30–1882	11-11-1882	pp. 598–99, 610, 736
L888	early 1884	soon after 4-8-1884	WAD's diary for 4-8-1884

Acknowledgments

The libraries with the most abundant and useful materials for the biographer of Emily Dickinson are the Amherst College Archives and Special Collections Library, the Rare Books Department at the Boston Public Library, Brown University's John Hay Library, the Congregational Library in Boston, the Houghton Library at Harvard University, the Jones Library in Amherst, the Mount Holyoke College Archives and Special Collections Library, the Manuscripts and Archives Division of the New York Public Library, and the Yale University Library, including Manuscripts and Archives and the Beinecke Rare Books and Manuscripts Library. To the directors and staff of these institutions, I am profoundly in debt for access to their collections.

Among the many persons I must thank, I wish to single out those librarians whose patience and resourcefulness in dealing with my endless queries have placed them in a very special category: Patricia J. Albright; Mark N. Brown; Daria D'Arienzo and John Lancaster; Sylvia De Santis; Ellen H. Fladger and Betty Allen; Susan Halpert, Jennie Rathbun, Emily Walhout, and Roger Stoddard; Thomas Knoles; Dan Lombardo, Jessica Teters, Peter Nelson, and Kate Boyle; Grace Makepeace (much lamented); Ralph Melnick and Rick Teller; Mariam Touba; and Harold F. Worthley.

The libraries, historical societies, and legal depositories that have proved particularly helpful include the following: Amherst Town Clerk; Andover Historical Society, Mass.; Franklin Trask Library Special Collections, Andover Newton Theological School (Diana Yount); Archives and Records Preservation, Supreme Judicial Court, New Court House, Boston (Elizabeth Bouvier); Baker Library's Historical Collections Department, Harvard Business School; Historical Society of Berks Co., Pa. (Barbara Gill); Berkshire Athenaeum, Mass. (Ruth T. Degenhardt); Boston Public Library; Bowdoin College Special Collections (Susan Ravdin); Burton Historical Collection, Detroit Public Library (John W. Gibson); California State Library (Sibylle Zemitis); Calvary Presbyterian Church, San Francisco (Joe Beyer); Cambridge City Library; Colorado College Special Collections (Virginia R. Kiefer); Concord Free Public Library (Leslie Perrin Wilson); Connecticut State Library; Dartmouth College Library (Philip N. Cronenwett); Duke University Special Collections; Emma Willard School Library, Troy, N.Y. (Barbara Wiley); Enoch Pratt Free Library; Essex County Registry of Deeds, Newark, N.J.; Essex Registry of Deeds, So. Dist., Salem, Mass.; Forbes Library, Northampton, Mass.; Francis A. Countway Library of Medicine; Geneva Historical Society, Geneva, N.Y. (Jennifer L. Walton); Georgia Historical Society (Jessica Burke); Greenfield City Library, Mass.; Hampden County Registry of Deeds (Donald E. Ashe) and Probate Court, Springfield, Mass.; Hampshire County Registry of Deeds (Patricia A. Plaza) and Registry of Probate, Northampton, Mass.; Harvard Law School Special Collections (David R. Warrington);

Hobart and William Smith Colleges, Archives (Charlotte Hegyi); Historic Deerfield (Shirley Majewski); Historic Northampton; Historical Society of Pennsylvania; Hubbard Free Library, Hallowell, Me.; Huntington Library; Ipswich Public Library, Mass. (Genevieve Picard); Lafayette College Special Collections (Diane Windham Shaw); Lapeer County Registry of Deeds, Mich. (Ann Stier); Lehigh University Special Collections (Philip A. Metzger); Library of Congress, Manuscripts (Michael J. Klein); Lilly Library, University of Indiana (Lisa Browar); Litchfield Historical Society, Conn. (Tess Riesmeyer); Lynn Historical Society, Mass. (Diane Shephard); Macomb County Historical Society, Mich. (Betty Lou Morris); Marblehead Historical Society (Karen Mac Innis); Maryland Historical Society (Francis P. O'Neill); Massachusetts Archives; Massachusetts State Library; Massachusetts Historical Society; Middlesex County Registry of Probate, Cambridge, Mass.; Milwaukee County Historical Society; Mississippi Department of Archives & History; Monson Free Library and Reading Room Association; Monson Historical Society; Monson Town Clerk; National Archives (Wayne DeCesar, Mary Frances Morrow, Fred J. Romanski, Joseph Schwarz); New England Historic Genealogical Society; New York Botanical Garden; New-York Historical Society; New York State Historical Association, Cooperstown, N.Y.; New York University, Archives (Kate Senft); North-Prospect United Church of Christ, Cambridge, Mass.; Oneida County Historical Society, Utica, N.Y.; Onondaga Historical Association, Syracuse, N.Y. (Judy E. Haven); Ottawa County Registry of Deeds, Mich.; Free Library of Philadelphia; Polytechnic University Archives, Brooklyn, N.Y. (Heather Walters); Presbyterian Historical Society, Philadelphia (Kenneth J. Ross, Susan J. Flack); Princeton Theological Seminary Library (William O. Harris); Probate Court, District of Litchfield, Conn.; Pusey Library, Harvard University; Radcliffe College Archives; Romeo District Library, Mich. (Beth Martin); Rutherford B. Hayes Presidential Center; Sacramento Public Library, Calif. (Ruth Ellis); Smith College Archives (Aimee E. Brown) and Rare Book Room; Southwick Historical Society, Mass. (Patricia Odiorne); Springfield Library and Museums (Margaret Humberston, Liz S. Ziegler); Stone House Museum, Belchertown, Mass. (Doris Dickinson); Suffolk County Registry of Deeds, Boston, Mass.; University of Massachusetts—Amherst, Special Collections and Archives (Linda Seidman); University of South Carolina, Special Collections; University of Virginia, Special Collections; Utica Public Library, N.Y.; Wendell Town Clerk, Mass.; Westfield Athenaeum, Westfield, Mass. (Ann Tumavicus); Williams College Archives (Sylvia Kennick Brown).

For help with access to materials, I owe a huge debt to Jim Elmborg and Kent Miller, and the Interlibrary Loan services of the University of Kansas and Washington State University.

Others who have helped me in the quest include Melvin E. Bleich (*Romeo Observer*), Claire Dempsey, Cindy Dickinson (Dickinson Homestead), Sam Ellenport (Harcourt Bindery), Gregory Farmer (Martha Dickinson Bianchi Trust), Eliza Habegger, Robert Lord Keyes, Russell M. Lane, Deane Lee, Sue Lorraine, Dorothy Russell, James Seaver, James Avery Smith, Sumner Webber, and C. Conrad Wright.

Several holders of primary materials have graciously made available their texts and images: John and Priscilla Chatfield, Roger L. Gregg, Philip F. Gura, Mary C. Pearl, Jane S. Scott, Cynthia Smith, Alice V. Yarick, and Emily Dickinson V. Resteghini.

Dickinson scholars who have fielded queries and opened intellectual doors include R. W. Franklin, Benjamin Lease, Carolyn S. Moran, Marianne Noble, Hiroko Uno, Jane Donahue Eberwein, and Rowena Revis Jones. To Elizabeth Bernhard and Domhnall Mitchell I am lastingly indebted for a series of unforgettably stimulating conversations and written exchanges, for the warmest hospitality, and for reading and candidly criticizing certain chapters.

Early versions of chapter segments appeared in the *New England Quarterly* ("Evangel") and *ESQ: A Journal of the American Renaissance* ("Lost Homes"), and also in a paper presented at the 1999 conference of the Emily Dickinson International Society. Fellowship support came from the National Endowment for the Humanities.

Finally, for help too varied, informed, and indispensable to be spelled out here (or anywhere), I want to thank my agent, Nat Sobel; my incomparable editor, Bob Loomis; and my expert and painstaking copy editors, Jolanta Benal and Vincent La Scala.

For poems whose first lines are not given, the following table will convert Franklin's numbers to those assigned by Johnson.

Franklin	Johnson
2	3
3	4
215	193
242	244
243	286
292	293
294	264
301	296
348	505
425	414
523	606
528	335
620	435
631	537
724	680
757	646
887	786
897	991
1057	662
1110	814
1230	1188
1265	1153
1279	1293
1304	1267
1337	1507
1368	1337
1422	1404
1547	1522
1583	1553
1616	1588
1627	1576
1632	1606

Abbreviations

All sound scholarship on Emily Dickinson rests on a vast amount of laborious and even heroic work by distinguished predecessors, chief among whom are Mabel Loomis Todd, George Frisbie Whicher, Millicent Todd Bingham, Thomas H. Johnson, Theodora Ward, Jay Leyda, Richard B. Sewall, and R. W. Franklin. Occupying a special niche on the short list is Martha Dickinson Bianchi, in spite of questions about her veracity and care. If I had space to acknowledge in detail what I have learned from these and later workers, certain names—particularly that of Leyda, a matchlessly resourceful explorer—would flood my notes. As it is, in those cases where I have gone to primary sources, I cite them without mentioning the scholarly forebears who pointed me toward them.

As a further space-saving measure, abbreviations have been adopted for a number of persons, libraries, named papers and collections, designated manuscripts, and publications.

PERSONS

AOT	Amelia O. Tyler, 1819–1904
CDS	Catharine Dickinson Sweetser, 1814–1895
CW	Charles Wadsworth, 1814–1882
DWVF	Deborah W. Vinal Fiske, 1805 or 1806–1844
EBW	Elizabeth Wooster Baldwin Whitney, 1824–1912
EdD	Edward Dickinson, 1803–1874
ED	Emily Dickinson, 1830–1886
EDC	Elizabeth Dickinson Currier, 1823–1886
EFF	Emily Fowler Ford, 1826–1893
EH Jr	Edward Hitchcock, Jr. (Ned), 1828–1911
ELN	Emily Lavinia Norcross, 1828–1852
END	Emily Norcross Dickinson, 1804–1882
FHB	Frances H. Boltwood, 1807–1881
FN	Frances Lavinia Norcross, 1847–1896
HHJ	Helen Fiske Hunt Jackson, 1830–1885
HP	Hannah Porter, 1797–1869
HVE	Henry Vaughan Emmons, 1832–1912
JAS	Joseph A. Sweetser, 1809–1874?
JFJ	John Franklin Jameson, 1859–1937
JGH	Josiah Gilbert Holland, 1819–1881
JL	Joseph B. Lyman, 1829–1872

JN	Joel Norcross, 1776–1846
LDB	Lucretia Dickinson Bullard, 1806–1885
LGD	Lucretia Gunn Dickinson, 1775–1840
LMB	Lucius Manlius Boltwood, 1825–1905
LNN	Lavinia Norcross Norcross, 1812–1860
Lord	Otis Phillips Lord, 1812–1884
Loring	Loring Norcross, 1808–1863
MCW	Mary C. Whitman, 1809–1875
MDB	Martha Dickinson Bianchi (Mattie), 1866–1943
MDN	Mary Dickinson Newman, 1809–1852
MGS	Martha Gilbert Smith, 1827 or 1828–1895
MLB	Mary Learned Bartlett, 1824–1893
MLT	Mabel Loomis Todd, 1856–1932
MTB	Millicent Todd Bingham, 1880–1968
MW	Maria Whitney, 1830–1910
Ned	Edward Dickinson, 1861–1898
SB	Samuel Bowles, 1826–1878
SCB	Samuel Colcord Bartlett, 1817–1898
SFD	Samuel Fowler Dickinson, 1775–1838
SFD Jr	Samuel Fowler Dickinson, Jr., 1811–1886
SJL	Samuel J. Learned, 1823–1892
Sue	Susan Huntington Gilbert Dickinson, 1830–1913
SVN	Sarah Vaill Norcross, 1788–1854
TDG	Thomas Dwight Gilbert, 1815–1894
TWH	Thomas Wentworth Higginson, 1823–1911
Vin	Lavinia Norcross Dickinson (Vinnie), 1833–1899
WAD	William Austin Dickinson (Austin), 1829–1895
WDW	William Dwight Whitney, 1827–1894
WON	William Otis Norcross, 1806–1863

FREQUENTLY CITED LIBRARIES AND OTHER DEPOSITORIES

A	Amherst College Library, Archives and Special Collections
AAS	American Antiquarian Society, Worcester, Massachusetts
BPL	Boston Public Library/Rare Books Department
C	Special Collections, Tutt Library, Colorado College, Colorado Springs, Colorado
CL	Congregational Library, Boston
D	Special Collections, Dartmouth College Library
H	Houghton Library, Harvard University. Citations followed by this letter only, with no shelf mark, are to the Dickinson Family Papers, bMS Am 1118.95.[1]
J	Jones Library, Amherst, Massachusetts

---

1. The Houghton Library's reclassification of the Dickinson Family Papers was still in process when this book was completed, making it impossible to give box and folder numbers for cited manuscripts.

LC	Library of Congress
M	Monson Free Library, Monson, Massachusetts
MA Arch	Massachusetts Archives at Columbia Point, Boston
MH	Mount Holyoke College Archives and Special Collections
MHS	Massachusetts Historical Society, Boston
NEHGS	New England Historic Genealogical Society, Boston
NYPL	New York Public Library, Fifth Avenue and 42nd Street, New York City
P	Presbyterian Historical Society, Philadelphia
PTS	Library of Princeton Theological Seminary, Princeton, New Jersey
RD	Registry of Deeds
RP	Registry of Probate
Y-BRBL	Beinecke Rare Book and Manuscript Library, Yale University Library
Y-MSSA	Manuscripts and Archives, Yale University Library

PAPERS OR COLLECTIONS CITED MOST FREQUENTLY

Alumnae	Alumnae Biographical File, MH
Ames Papers	Mary Clemmer Ames Papers, Rutherford B. Hayes Presidential Center, Fremont, Ohio
Amh Coll Ch	Records of the Church of Christ in Amherst College, A
Andover Alumni	Alumni Files, Andover Theological Seminary Archives, Franklin Trask Library, Andover Newton Theological School, Newton, Massachusetts
AP Papers	Andrew Porter Papers, MH
Bianchi Coll	Martha Dickinson Bianchi Papers, John Hay Library, Brown University
Bolt	MS/Boltwood Family Papers, Burton Historical Collection, Detroit Public Library
Bowd St Ch	Records of the Bowdoin Street Church, Boston, CL
Bullock Papers	Alexander H. Bullock Papers, AAS
CT Headstone	Connecticut Headstone Inscriptions: Charles R. Hale Collection, Connecticut State Library
CT Misc	Connecticut Miscellaneous Manuscripts Collection, Y-MSSA
Doc Hitch	Edward (AC 1849) and Mary Judson Hitchcock Family Papers, A
Dun	R. G. Dun & Co. Collection, Baker Library, Harvard Business School
Earle Papers	Pliny Earle Papers, AAS
EDR	Dickinson family books, Emily Dickinson Room, Houghton Library, Harvard University
EFF Papers	Emily Fowler Ford Papers, Manuscripts and Archives Division, NYPL
Emerson	Emerson, Ellen, to Edith Forbes (transcriptions). Emerson Family Papers, bMS Am 1280.235, box 30, vols. 13–14, H
FF Papers	Ford Family Papers, Manuscripts and Archives Division, NYPL
GLF Papers	Gordon L. Ford Papers, Manuscripts and Archives Division, NYPL
HHJ Papers	Helen Hunt Jackson Papers, C

Hills Papers	Hills Family Papers, A
Jameson Papers	J. Franklin Jameson Papers, LC
JGH Papers	Josiah Gilbert Holland Papers, Manuscripts and Archives Division, NYPL
Lyman Papers	Lyman Family Papers, Y-MSSA
MCW Papers	Mary C. Whitman Papers, MH
ML Coll	Mary Lyon Collection, MH
MLT Papers	Mabel Loomis Todd Papers, Y-MSSA
Monson Ch	Records of the First Church of Monson, Monson, Massachusetts (documents at church; microfilm at M)
MTB Papers	Millicent Todd Bingham Papers, Y-MSSA
MVR	Massachusetts Vital Records (microfilm at NEHGS)
Olmsted Papers	Frederick Law Olmsted Papers, LC
SB Let	Letters of Samuel Bowles to Austin and/or Susan Dickinson, bMS Am 1118.8, H
SB Papers	Samuel Bowles Papers, Y-MSSA
SCB Papers	Samuel Colcord Bartlett Papers, D
Seelye Papers	Julius H. Seelye Papers, A
Summit	Summit or Mountain House Registers, Historic Northampton, Northampton, Massachusetts
Sumner Papers	Charles Sumner Papers, bMS Am 1, H
Taggard Papers	Genevieve Taggard Papers, Manuscripts and Archives Division, NYPL
Tyler Papers	William Seymour Tyler Papers, A
WDW Papers	William Dwight Whitney Family Papers, Y-MSSA
Willard Papers	Emma Willard Family Papers, A

ABBREVIATIONS OF PUBLICATIONS AND SEPARATE MANUSCRIPTS

Ackmann	Ackmann, Martha. "The Matrilineage of Emily Dickinson." Ph.D. dissertation: University of Massachusetts, Amherst, 1988.
Address	Dickinson, Samuel Fowler. *An Address Delivered at Northampton, before the Hampshire, Hampden and Franklin, Agricultural Society, October 27, 1831.* Amherst: Adams, 1831.
Allen	Allen, Mary Adèle. *Around a Village Green: Sketches of Life in Amherst.* Northampton, Mass.: Kraushar Press, 1939.
Amh Acad	Tuckerman, Frederick. *Amherst Academy: A New England School of the Past 1814–1861.* Amherst: Trustees, 1929.
Amh Rec	*Amherst Record* (newspaper, 1868–).
Andover	*General Catalogue of the Theological Seminary Andover Massachusetts 1808–1908.* Boston: Thomas Todd, Printer, 1909.
"Annals"	Dickinson, Susan Huntington Gilbert. "Annals of the Evergreens." H.
Austin & Mabel	Longsworth, Polly. *Austin and Mabel.* New York: Farrar, Straus and Giroux, 1984.
Baym	Baym, Nina. "God, Father, and Lover in Emily Dickinson's Poetry." In Emory Elliott, ed. *Puritan Influences in American Literature.* Urbana: University of Illinois Press, 1979. Pp. 193–209.
Bench	Davis, William T. *Bench and Bar of the Commonwealth of Massachusetts.* 2 vols. Boston: Boston History Co., 1895.

Benfey	Benfey, Christopher E. G. *Emily Dickinson and the Problem of Others.* Amherst: University of Massachusetts Press, 1984.
Bernhard	Bernhard, Mary Elizabeth Kromer. "Portrait of a Family: Emily Dickinson's Norcross Connection." *New England Quarterly* 60 (Sept. 1987) 363–81.
Bio Rec	*Amherst College Biographical Record 1973.* Amherst: Trustees, 1973.
Bliss	Bliss, Daniel. *The Reminiscences of Daniel Bliss.* New York: Revell, 1920)
Brocades	Bingham, Millicent Todd. *Ancestors' Brocades: The Literary Debut of Emily Dickinson.* New York: Harper, 1945.
Buckingham	Buckingham, Willis J., ed. *Emily Dickinson's Reception in the 1890s: A Documentary History.* Pittsburgh: University of Pittsburgh Press, 1989.
Bullard	Bullard, Asa. *Incidents in a Busy Life. An Autobiography.* Boston: Congregational Sunday-School & Publishing Society, 1888.
Burgess	Burgess, John W. *Reminiscences of an American Scholar.* New York: AMS Press, 1966.
Calvary	Wilson, Carol Green. *Calvary through the Years.* San Francisco: Calvary Presbyterian Church, 1929 (copy at P).
Capsule	Ward, Theodora Van Wagenen. *The Capsule of the Mind: Chapters in the Life of Emily Dickinson.* Cambridge: Harvard University Press, 1961.
Carlyle's	Higginson, Thomas Wentworth. *Carlyle's Laugh and Other Surprises.* Freeport, N.Y.: Books for Libraries Press, 1968.
Carp	Carpenter, Edward W., and Charles F. Morehouse. *The History of the Town of Amherst, Massachusetts.* Amherst: Carpenter and Morehouse, 1896.
Cody	Cody, John. *After Great Pain: The Inner Life of Emily Dickinson.* Cambridge: Harvard University Press, 1971.
Comic Power	Juhasz, Suzanne, Cristanne Miller, and Martha Nell Smith. *Comic Power in Emily Dickinson.* Austin: University of Texas Press, 1993.
Conant	Conant, Frank P. *God's Stewards: Samuel and Emily Williston.* Easthampton, Mass.: Williston Northampton School, 1991.
Conforti	Conforti, Joseph A. *Jonathan Edwards, Religious Tradition, and American Culture.* Chapel Hill: University of North Carolina Press, 1995.
Cooke	Cooke, George. "Reminiscences of the North Parish, Amherst, Mass., from Oct. 1838 to March 1858" (1883). AAS.
"Country Girl"	Bianchi, Martha Dickinson. "Recollections of a Country Girl 18__ to 1900 (1935)." Bianchi Coll.
Craik, *Head*	[Craik, Dinah Mulock]. *The Head of the Family. A Novel.* New York: Harper, 1852.
Craik, *Olive*	[Craik, Dinah Mulock]. *Olive. A Novel.* 3 vols. London: Chapman & Hall, 1850.
Cullum	Cullum, George W. *Biographical Register of the Officers and Graduates of the U.S. Military Academy at West Point, N.Y.* New York: Van Nostrand, 1868.
DAB	*Dictionary of American Biography*
Dall	Lavinia Norcross Dickinson to Caroline H. Dall, Jan. 29, 1895,

Emily Dickinson Collection (no. 7658), Clifton Waller Barrett Library, The Albert H. Small Special Collections Library, University of Virginia Library.

Dandurand   Dandurand, Karen. "Dickinson and the Public." In Martin Orzeck and Robert Weisbuch, ed. *Dickinson and Audience.* Ann Arbor: University of Michigan Press, 1996. Pp. 255–77.

Desc   Smith, Elinor V., comp. *Descendants of Nathaniel Dickinson.* N.p.: Dickinson Family Assoc., 1978.

Diary   Lavinia Norcross Dickinson's 1851 diary. H.

Discourses   *Discourses, and Speeches, Delivered at the Celebration of the Semi-Centennial Anniversary of Monson Academy, Monson, Mass., July 18th and 19th, 1854.* New York: Gray, 1855.

Dobson   Dobson, Joanne. *Dickinson and the Strategies of Reticence.* Bloomington: Indiana University Press, 1989.

Eberwein   Eberwein, Jane Donahue. *Dickinson: Strategies of Limitation.* Amherst: University of Massachusetts Press, 1985.

EDE   Eberwein, Jane Donahue, ed. *An Emily Dickinson Encyclopedia.* Westport, Conn.: Greenwood Press, 1998.

EDIS Bull   *Emily Dickinson International Society Bulletin*

EDJ   *Emily Dickinson Journal*

Endow   King, Stanley. *A History of the Endowment of Amherst College.* Amherst: Amherst College, 1950.

END's Bible   Edward Dickinson's family record in Emily Norcross Dickinson's Bible. New York: Daniel D. Smith, 1825. EDR 1.6.6.

England   England, Martha Winburn. "Emily Dickinson and Isaac Watts: Puritan Hymnodists." *Bulletin of the New York Public Library* 69 (Feb. 1965) 83–116.

"Evangel"   Habegger, Alfred. "Evangelicalism and Its Discontents: Hannah Porter versus Emily Dickinson." *New England Quarterly* 70 (Sept. 1997) 386–414.

FF   Bianchi, Martha Dickinson. *Emily Dickinson Face to Face.* Boston: Houghton Mifflin, 1932.

The following ledgers from the Dickinsons' church are at J,
under MS:Amherst–First Church:

First #1   Records, 1820–1855.

First #2   Records, 1854–1890.

First #3   Directories ("Catalogue of the Pastors and Deacons and Members . . .").

First #4   Records, 1840–1881 (Parish Record Book).

First #5   Membership, ca. 1830–1880 ("A Register of Families and Individuals in the Parish . . .")

FN   Jenkins, MacGregor. *Emily Dickinson: Friend and Neighbor.* Boston: Little, Brown, 1939.

FN/ED   Frances Norcross's transcribed excerpts from Emily Dickinson's letters to her and Louisa Norcross, MLT Papers 69:19. (This item forms part of MLT/ED, listed below.)

Funeral   *Funeral Services of the Rev. Charles Wadsworth . . . of Philadelphia, April 4, 1882. Address by the Rev. John DeWitt.* Philadelphia: Presbyterian Printing Co., [1882].

Gelpi   Gelpi, Albert J. *Emily Dickinson: The Mind of the Poet.* Cambridge: Harvard University Press, 1965.

Gillett   "Early Recollections of Mrs. Edward Bates Gillett" (transcript). Westfield Athenaeum, Westfield, Mass.

God's Culture   Wadsworth, Charles. *God's Culture. Extracts from a Sermon.* Philadelphia: Bradley, 1876.

Graves   Graves, Gertrude M. "A Cousin's Memories of Emily Dickinson." *Boston Sunday Globe,* Jan. 12, 1930, p. 41.

Green   Green, Clara Bellinger. "A Reminiscence of Emily Dickinson." *The Bookman* (New York) 60 (Nov. 1924) 291–93.

Hammond   Hammond, William Gardiner. *Remembrance of Amherst: An Undergraduate's Diary 1846–1848.* George F. Whicher, ed. New York: Columbia University Press, 1946.

Hart   Hart, Ellen Louise. "The Encoding of Homoerotic Desire: Emily Dickinson's Letters and Poems to Susan Dickinson, 1850–1886." *Tulsa Studies in Women's Literature* 9.2 (fall 1990) 251–72.

HFE   *Hampshire and Franklin Express* (Amherst newspaper, 1844–1868, including *Hampshire Express*)

Higgins   Higgins, David. *Portrait of Emily Dickinson: The Poet and Her Prose.* New Brunswick, N.J.: Rutgers University Press, 1967.

Him   Himelhoch, Myra, and Rebecca Patterson. "The Dating of Emily Dickinson's Letters to the Bowles Family, 1858–1862." *Emily Dickinson Bulletin* 5, no. 20 (March 1972) 1–28.

Hist   *An Historical Review. One Hundred and Fiftieth Anniversary of the First Church of Christ in Amherst, Massachusetts. November 7, 1889.* Amherst: Amherst Record, 1890.

Hist Amh Coll   Tyler, William S. *History of Amherst College during Its First Half Century.* Springfield, Mass.: Bryan, 1873.

Homans   Homans, Margaret. *Women Writers and Poetic Identity: Dorothy Wordsworth, Emily Brontë, and Emily Dickinson.* Princeton: Princeton University Press, 1980.

Home   Bingham, Millicent Todd. *Emily Dickinson's Home: Letters of Edward Dickinson and His Family with Documentation and Comment.* New York: Harper, 1955.

House-Keeping   Lyman, Joseph B., and Laura E. Lyman. *The Philosophy of House-Keeping: A Scientific and Practical Manual.* Hartford: Goodwin and Betts, 1867.

HSR   Stachiw, Myron, Claire Dempsey, and Tom Paske. "Historic Structure Report." Unpublished document in the collection of the Dickinson Homestead.

Imagery   Patterson, Rebecca. *Emily Dickinson's Imagery.* Amherst: University of Massachusetts Press, 1979.

JL/ED   Joseph B. Lyman's transcribed excerpts or "snatches" from Emily Dickinson's letters, Lyman Papers 4:64 (first published in *Lyman Let* [see below], 69–79).

Jones   Jones, Rowena Revis. "The Preparation of a Poet: Puritan Directions in Emily Dickinson's Education." *Studies in the American Renaissance* (1982) 285–324.

Kellogg　　　Kellogg, Alfred H. *A Sermon Commemorative of the Life and Character of the Rev. Lyman Coleman.* Easton, Pa.: Trustees of Lafayette College, 1882.

Lease　　　Lease, Benjamin. *Emily Dickinson's Readings of Men and Books: Sacred Soundings.* London: Macmillan, 1990.

Let　　　*The Letters of Emily Dickinson.* Thomas H. Johnson and Theodora Ward, eds. 3 vols. Cambridge: Belknap Press of Harvard University Press, 1958.

Let (Holl)　　　*Emily Dickinson's Letters to Dr. and Mrs. Josiah Gilbert Holland.* Theodora Van Wagenen Ward, ed. Cambridge: Harvard University Press, 1951.

Let (1894)　　　*Letters of Emily Dickinson.* Mabel Loomis Todd, ed. 2 vols. Boston: Roberts Brothers, 1894.

Let (1931)　　　*The Letters of Emily Dickinson.* Mabel Loomis Todd, ed. New York: Harper, 1931.

Leyda　　　Leyda, Jay. *The Years and Hours of Emily Dickinson.* 2 vols. New Haven: Yale University Press, 1960.

Lindberg-Seyersted　　　Lindberg-Seyersted, Brita. *The Voice of the Poet: Aspects of Style in the Poetry of Emily Dickinson.* Uppsala, Sweden: 1968.

LL　　　Bianchi, Martha Dickinson. *The Life and Letters of Emily Dickinson.* Boston: Houghton Mifflin, 1924.

Loeffelholz　　　Loeffelholz, Mary. *Dickinson and the Boundaries of Feminist Theory.* Urbana: University of Illinois Press, 1991.

"Lost Homes"　　　Habegger, Alfred. "How the Dickinsons Lost Their Homes." *ESQ* 44.3 (1998) 160–97.

Lowenberg　　　Lowenberg, Carlton. *Emily Dickinson's Textbooks.* Lafayette, Calif.: Carlton Lowenberg, 1986.

Lyman Let　　　Sewall, Richard B. *The Lyman Letters: New Light on Emily Dickinson and Her Family.* Amherst: University of Massachusetts Press, 1965.

Manual　　　*A Manual of the Congregational Church of Monson . . . for 1874.* Springfield, Mass.: Bryan, 1875.

Mass Reports　　　*Massachusetts Reports* (available at Massachusetts State Library)

Master Let　　　Dickinson, Emily. *The Master Letters of Emily Dickinson.* R. W. Franklin, ed. Amherst: Amherst College Press, 1986.

MB　　　*The Manuscript Books of Emily Dickinson.* R. W. Franklin, ed. 2 vols. Cambridge: Belknap Press of Harvard University Press, 1981.

McIntosh　　　McIntosh, James. *Nimble Believing: Dickinson and the Unknown.* Ann Arbor: University of Michigan Press, 2000.

"Medicine"　　　Hirschhorn, Norbert, and Polly Longsworth. " 'Medicine Posthumous': A New Look at Emily Dickinson's Medical Conditions." *New England Quarterly* 69 (June 1996) 299–316.

Mer　　　Merriam, George S. *The Life and Times of Samuel Bowles.* 2 vols. New York: Century, 1885.

Mercy Phil　　　[Jackson, Helen Hunt.] *Mercy Philbrick's Choice.* Boston: Roberts, 1876.

MHJL　　　Mount Holyoke Journal Letter for 1847–1848, transcript by Helen M. Gidley, MH.

Miller   Miller, Cristanne. *Emily Dickinson: A Poet's Grammar.* Cambridge: Harvard University Press, 1987.

Mitchell   Mitchell, Domhnall. *Emily Dickinson: Monarch of Perception.* Amherst: University of Massachusetts Press, 2000.

MLT/ED   Printer's copy, mostly in MLT's hand, for *Let* (1894), MLT Papers, boxes 68–69.

Moseley   Moseley, Laura Hadley, ed. *Diary 1843–1852 of James Hadley, Tutor and Professor of Greek in Yale College.* New Haven: Yale University Press, 1951.

Murray   Murray, Aífe. "Miss Margaret's Emily Dickinson." *Signs* 24 (spring 1999) 697–732.

Nason   Nason, Emma Huntington. *Old Hallowell on the Kennebec.* Augusta, Me.: Burleigh & Flynt, 1909.

NEI   *New-England Inquirer* (first Amherst newspaper, 1826–1828).

Nettleton   Tyler, Bennet. *Memoir of the Life and Character of Rev. Asahel Nettleton.* Boston: Congregational Publishing Society, 1879.

Obit Record   *Obituary Record of Graduates of Yale College Deceased from June, 1870, to June, 1880.* New Haven: Tuttle, Morehouse & Taylor, 1880.

Open Me   *Open Me Carefully: Emily Dickinson's Intimate Letters to Susan Huntington Dickinson.* Ellen Louise Hart and Martha Nell Smith, eds. Ashfield, Mass.: Paris Press, 1998.

Other Bullards   *Other Bullards: A Genealogy.* Port Austin, Mich.: E. J. Bullard, 1928.

Passion   Farr, Judith. *The Passion of Emily Dickinson.* Cambridge: Harvard University Press, 1992.

Poems   *The Poems of Emily Dickinson.* Thomas H. Johnson, ed. 3 vols. Cambridge: Belknap Press of Harvard University Press, 1955.

Pollak   Pollak, Vivian R. *Dickinson: The Anxiety of Gender.* Ithaca: Cornell University Press, 1984.

PP   Pollak, Vivian R., ed. *A Poet's Parents: The Courtship Letters of Emily Norcross and Edward Dickinson.* Chapel Hill: University of North Carolina Press, 1988.

"Putnam"   Hart, Ellen Louise. "The Elizabeth Whitney Putnam Manuscripts and New Strategies for Editing Emily Dickinson's Letters." *EDJ* 4.1 (1995) 44–64.

Reid   Reid, Mary J. "Julia C. R. Dorr and Some of Her Poet Contemporaries." *Midland Monthly* 3 (June 1895) 499–507.

Remin   Hitchcock, Edward. *Reminiscences of Amherst College.* Northampton: Bridgman & Childs, 1863.

Reunion   *Reunion of the Dickinson Family, at Amherst, Mass., August 8th and 9th, 1883.* N.p.: Binghamton Publishing, 1884.

Rev   Bingham, Millicent Todd. *Emily Dickinson: A Revelation.* New York: Harper, 1954.

Rich   Rich, Adrienne. " 'Vesuvius at Home': The Power of Emily Dickinson." *Parnassus* 5 (winter 1976) 49–74.

Riddle   Patterson, Rebecca. *The Riddle of Emily Dickinson.* Boston: Houghton Mifflin, 1951.

"Root"   Franklin, R. W. "Emily Dickinson to Abiah Root: Ten Reconstructed Letters." *Emily Dickinson Journal* 4.1 (1995) 1–43.

Rowing   Smith, Martha Nell. *Rowing in Eden: Rereading Emily Dickinson.* Austin: University of Texas Press, 1992.

Sargent   Sargent, David W., Jr. "The Railroad Mania in Amherst." *Bulletin of the Railway and Locomotive Historical Society* no. 47. (1938) 11–45.

Sewall   Sewall, Richard B. *The Life of Emily Dickinson.* Cambridge: Harvard University Press, 1994. First published 1974, 1980.

Shurr   Shurr, William H. *The Marriage of Emily Dickinson: A Study of the Fascicles.* Lexington: University Press of Kentucky, 1983.

Smith   Smith, James Avery, comp. "Families of Amherst, Massachusetts: A Genealogical Outline of Individuals and Families residing at Amherst . . . through 1850." 4 vols. Amherst: James Avery Smith, 1984. Copy at J.

SR   *Springfield Republican* (newspaper)

St. Armand   St. Armand, Barton Levi. *Emily Dickinson and Her Culture.* Cambridge, Eng.: Cambridge University Press, 1984.

Sullivan   Sullivan, David. "Suing Sue: Emily Dickinson Addressing Susan Gilbert." *Emily Dickinson Journal* 5.1 (1996) 45–70.

Sweetser   Sweetser, Philip S. *Seth Sweetser and His Descendants.* Philadelphia: Integrity, n.d.

Talbot   Talbot, Norman. "The Child, the Actress and Miss Emily Dickinson." *Southern Review* (Adelaide, Australia) 5.2 (June 1972) 102–124.

This Was a Poet Whicher, George Frisbie. *This Was a Poet: A Critical Biography of Emily Dickinson.* Philadelphia: Dufour, 1952. First published 1938.

Tracts   *Tracts of the American Tract Society. General Series.* New York: American Tract Society, n.d.

Trustees Min   "Minutes of the Board of Trustees of Amherst College 1825–1923" (annotated typescript). A.

Turner   Turner, Clara Newman. ["My Personal Acquaintance with Emily Dickinson"]. bMS Am 1118.7, H.[2]

Uno   Uno, Hiroko. *Emily Dickinson Visits Boston.* Kyoto: Yamaguchi, 1990.

Var   Dickinson, Emily. *The Poems of Emily Dickinson: Variorum Edition.* R. W. Franklin, ed. 3 vols. Cambridge: Belknap Press of Harvard University Press, 1998.

Walker   Walker, Cheryl. *The Nightingale's Burden.* Bloomington: Indiana University Press, 1982.

Watts & Select Worcester, Samuel. *The Psalms, Hymns, and Spiritual Songs, of the Rev. Isaac Watts, D.D. to Which Are Added Select Hymns, from Other Authors.* Boston: Crocker & Brewster, 1852.

---

2. This essay, introduced by Clara Newman Pearl, is printed in part in Sewall 265–75, where it is mistakenly credited to J. A typescript containing the introduction and an insert on ED's domestic habits (the latter omitted by Sewall) is in the MTB Papers 101:565. Another version of Pearl's introduction is in the possession of Mary C. Pearl.

Weisbuch   Weisbuch, Robert. *Emily Dickinson's Poetry.* Chicago: University of Chicago Press, 1975.

Wells   Wells, Anna Mary. *Dear Preceptor: The Life and Times of Thomas Wentworth Higginson.* Boston: Houghton Mifflin, 1963.

Werner   Werner, Marta L. *Emily Dickinson's Open Folios: Scenes of Reading, Surfaces of Writing.* Ann Arbor: University of Michigan Press, 1995.

Wolff   Wolff, Cynthia Griffin. *Emily Dickinson.* Reading, Mass.: Addison-Wesley, 1988.

World   Longsworth, Polly. *The World of Emily Dickinson.* New York: Norton, 1990.

Notes

Introduction

xii groundbreaking 1975 article: Carroll Smith-Rosenberg, "The Female World of Love and Ritual: Relations between Women in Nineteenth-Century America," *Signs* 1.1 (1975) 1–29.

xii "At certain levels": George Steiner, *On Difficulty and Other Essays* (New York: Oxford University Press, 1978) 45.

xiii invites and deflects such intimacy: See Suzanne Juhasz, "The Big Tease," in *Comic Power*.

xiii "a chronology of composition," "her art did not change": David Porter, *Dickinson: The Modern Idiom* (Cambridge: Harvard University Press, 1981) 9, 5. Porter's second statement presupposes the chronology whose possibility the first statement denies. Another who believes ED's verse "continues to resist narratives of chronological development" is Shira Wolosky, "Emily Dickinson's Manuscript Body: History/Textuality/Gender," *EDJ* 8.2 (1999) 89. Among the relatively few critics who make a case for development is James McIntosh in his admirable *Nimble Believing: Dickinson and the Unknown* (Ann Arbor: University of Michigan Press, 2000) 36–37.

xiv set it up in type: On the debate over typographic representation, see in particular *Rowing*, chapter 2, and Mitchell, chapter 7.

xv footnote 1: MLT Papers, boxes 68–69.

Chapter 1

3 parish of Billingborough: Clifford L. Stott, "The Correct English Origins of Nathaniel Dickinson and William Gull, Settlers of Wethersfield and Hadley," *New England Historical and Genealogical Register* 152 (April 1998) 159–78. Before this article appeared, it was assumed Nathaniel migrated in 1630.

4 smallpox-infected blankets: Francis Parkman, *The Conspiracy of Pontiac* (Boston: Little, Brown, 1906) 2:45.

4 Dickinson grit: Cooke 20.

4 Dickinson reunion: *Reunion* 54, 55, 5.

5 father's toast: *Celebration of the Two Hundredth Anniversary of . . . Hadley* (Northampton: Bridgman & Childs, 1859) 77–79.

6 227 poems in 1862: *Var* 1533.

6 "the land of the fathers": Charles Hammond to SCB, 11-11-1850, SCB Papers 4:98.

7 After graduating from Dartmouth: SFD to Tilton Eastman, 5-1-1797, Ms. 797301, D; *Reunion* 172; *Hist Amh Coll* 119. The last source may have begun the story that SFD's religious teacher was the Reverend Timothy Dickinson, an older brother. SFD still had "a debility of body" on 7-4-1897 (SFD, *An Oration in Cele-bration of American Independence* [Northampton: Butler, 1797] 5).

7 footnote 1: *The Works of Nathanael Emmons*, Jacob Ide, ed. (Boston: Crocker & Brewster, 1842) 1:lxxvii–lxxviii.

7 "for entering the world": SFD to Tilton Eastman, 5-1-1797, D.

8 But Squire Dickinson: *Reunion* 174; Card index of legislators, MA State Lib; Jour-nal of the MA Senate 48 (May 1827–March 1828) 123, 284, 288, 304, 359, MA State Lib; *NEI* 10-30-1828; *Hampshire Gazette* 10-29-1828; *Greenfield Gazette and Franklin Herald* 10-21-, 11-4-, 11-11-1828; SFD, *An Address Delivered at Northampton, before the Hampshire, Hampden and Franklin, Agricultural Society* (Amherst: Adams, 1831); CDS to EdD, 5-12-1835, H. Wolff 25 makes the impos-sible claim that SFD ran for the U.S. Senate.

8 woman Samuel married: For the date of the marriage, see END's Bible. *Desc* 206 and some other sources have 3-31-1802.

8 Lucretia Gunn: CDS to EdD, 5-12-1835, LGD to EdD, 12-5-, 7-8-1820, H; First #1, 5; *FF* 87–88 (but MDB's vivid claims are not always veracious). SFD was twenty-two when he joined Amherst's First Church in June 1798, according to a copy of an early list of members (MS:Boltwood, LM–Amherst Vital Records–Notebook, loose sheets, etc., J). That means he could not have been a deacon at twenty-one, as claimed since 1873 (*Hist Amh Coll* 119).

9 Toward his children: SFD to EdD, 12-17-1819, 1-2-1820, 4-10-, 4-11-1823, H.

9 By 1813 Samuel had: HSR; LDB to EdD, June 1821, 1-15-1823, H.

10 In 1817, well before: Hampshire Co. RD 40:463. Since the mortgage, dated 4-16-1817, preceded the 11-18-1817 meeting at which academy trustees approved the initial fund-raising campaign, the tradition that SFD went broke because of his philanthropy seems questionable.

11 Second Great Awakening: See William G. McLoughlin, *Revivals, Awakenings, and Reform: An Essay on Religion and Social Change in America, 1607–1977* (Chicago: University of Chicago Press, 1978); Nancy A. Hewitt, *Women's Activism and Social Change: Rochester, New York, 1822–1872* (Ithaca: Cornell University Press, 1984).

11 "We have seen error": Noah Webster, *A Plea for a Miserable World* (Boston: Lincoln, 1820) 32.

11 organized Amherst Academy: *Amh Acad* 11–12.

12 a fellow enthusiast: For Samuel and Graves as founders, see *Remin* 5; *Hist Amh Coll* 115, 120.

12 "wide-spread defection": quoted in *Hist Amh Coll* 117.

12 subscription drive and guaranty bond: The 1818 bond is often confused with the raising of a similar sum in 1824, when a legislative committee inspected the books. Hitchcock (*Remin* 121) seems responsible for this confusion, which reappears in Theodore Baird, "A Dry and Thirsty Land," *Essays on Amherst's History* (Amherst: Vista Trust, 1978) 117. The account of the 1824 episode in Wolff 20 is not trust-worthy: trustee Sampson Wilder alone backed dubious pledges with hard cash (*Endow* 30–32), and SFD did *not* join in the substitute subscription, his financial situation having become far too desperate. The best documentary sources on early

capital campaigns are in Early History Collection—Amherst College Inception, A: "Copy of Noah Webster's notes for the history of Amherst Academy / Amherst College," pp. 3–29, 58, 1:1, and "Charity Fund of Amherst College," pp. 20–22, 3:3. See also Heman Humphrey, *Sketches of the Early History of Amherst College* (Northampton [1905]) 3–7, 25–27, 32; *Hist Amh Coll* 649–56.

12 When South College: *Hist Amh Coll* 62, 121; LGD and LDB to EdD, 12-5-1820, H. The bank in question was probably the Sunderland Bank, whose founder and president was Nathaniel Smith (*Endow* 29).

13 footnote 3: SFD, *Address Delivered*, 36–37.

13 Zeal also tends: *Remin* 119–20; LDB to EdD, June 1821, H; *Hist Amh Coll* 74; Hezekiah Wright Strong, 1822 Account Book, 5-30, 5-31, 6-6, Boltwood Collection, J.

13 The idea behind: Joseph Hardy Neesima, *My Younger Days* (Kyoto: Doshisha Alumni Association, 1934); *Hist Amh Coll* 120.

14 Yale vs. Amherst: Three key sources in this section, all at Y-MSSA, are Yale's annual catalogs from 1819 to 1823; the "Book of Averages" (grades) for the class entering in 1819; Bursar's Records, Yale Coll. Student Accounts, Term bill charges 1818–1836, GN YRG 5-B, Ser II, 64:68. The last of these, not consulted by previous biographers, clears up the confusion as to which terms EdD spent at Yale.

14 When Edward left for Yale: William L. Kingsley, ed., *Yale College: A Sketch of Its History* (New York: Holt, 1879) 1:134, 135; *The Laws of Yale College* (New Haven: Journal Office, 1817) 11, 26–27, 29; SFD to EdD, 12-17-1819, H.

14 But Friend Dick: SFD to EdD, 12-17-1819, 1-2-1820, George Hanners to EdD, 4-3-1820, H; *Catalogue of the Faculty and Students of Yale College, November, 1819* 13–14.

15 an historic revival: *Nettleton* 85; Professor Goodrich, "Narrative of Revivals of Religion in Yale College," *American Quarterly Register* 10 (Feb. 1838) 304–305; Hanners to EdD, 4-3-1820, H; "The Ringleader," *Tracts*, vol. 10, no. 355; Brooks Mather Kelley, *Yale: A History* (New Haven: Yale University Press, 1974) 145; David Greene, *A Sermon at the Funeral of the Rev. Daniel Crosby* (Boston, 1843) 7, 34; SFD to EdD, 2-9-1821, H.

15 footnote 4: SFD to EdD, 2-10-1823, H.

16 "*necessity*," "take a room": SFD to EdD, 9-4-, 7-22-1821, H.

16 his debating society: For EdD's membership in Brothers, see his lists of expenses, first terms of sophomore and senior years, H.

16 "would not be beneficial": Kingsley, *Yale College* 1:319.

16 "to leave an institution": Osmyn Baker to EdD, 11-24-1821, H.

16 Edward's next-younger: William Dickinson to EdD, 9-25-1821, H.

16 footnote 5: *Worcester Evening Gazette* 9-7-1887; Leyda 2:138.

17 Although Edward was already: *Amh Acad* 72; *Hist Amh Coll* 101; S. H. Riddel to EdD, 12-23-[1822 (EdD's probable mistake for 1821)], Baker to EdD, 11-24-1821, H. Riddel was a roommate in summer 1820 (Bursar's Records, term bills, 9-13-1820, Y-MSSA).

17 The final humiliation: *Catalogue of the Officers and Students of Yale College, November, 1822* 4; SFD to EdD, 11-17-1822, Baker to EdD, 11-16-1822, H; Bursar's Records, Term bills, 1-7-, 4-30-, 9-8-1823, folio box 1, fd 2, Y-MSSA.

18 Academically, Edward: Book of Averages, 1819, Y-MSSA; SFD to EdD, 11-17-1822, H; List of appointments for 1823 Yale Commencement, H. The myth that EdD "graduated with the highest honor," begun by *Amh Rec* 10-11-1871, reap-

peared in a 6-17-1874 obituary in the *Boston Morning Journal* and from there made its way into twentieth-century scholarship. The story was discredited in 1974 by Sewall (46), whose account of EdD's education was in other respects misleading (e.g., overlooking the junior year in Amherst). Ignoring Sewall, Wolff reinstated the valedictorian myth in 1988 (23).

18 footnote 6: Wolff 21, 22.

19 real estate transactions: Hampshire Co. RD 51:628, 90; 53:642, 54:115, 438; "Lost Homes" 166–72.

19 There is no doubt: Peter J. Coleman, *Debtors and Creditors in America: Insolvency, Imprisonment for Debt, and Bankruptcy, 1607–1900* (Madison: State Historical Society of Wisconsin, 1974) 48–50; Massachusetts, An Act for the Relief of Insolvent Debtors, and for the More Equal Distribution of Their Effects, Statutes (1838) chap. 163. In 1827–1828 Lucinda and her children left Amherst to join the household of a married daughter in Knoxville, Tennessee; by 1837 Oliver's assessed Hadley real estate had a fourth of its 1826 value ("Lost Homes" 172–73, 194).

19 "I know well": Baker to EdD, 4-24-1824, H.

19 A further complication: *Reunion* 175; SFD to EdD, 1-24-1824, H.

20 For troubles with Clark, see George Shepard, "Biographical Sketch," in Daniel A. Clark, *Complete Works* (New York: Baker & Scribner, 1848) 1:xlv; First #1, 79-80; folders "Material on case against Rev. Daniel A. Clark" and "Remarks in re Mr Clark," H; *Hist Amh Coll* 110. Ashmun to EdD, postmarked 3-4-[1824], H, calls Clark's acquittal a "misfortune." The minister presently accepted a call from Bennington, Vermont.

20 For SFD's troubles with Strong, see *Reunion* 173; Hampshire County Court of Common Pleas, Record Book no. 22, folios 123, 124, MA Arch; Hampshire Co. RD 53:521-22; Hampshire Co. RP, Estate of Hezekiah W. Strong, 144:6 1/2; Folder on Amherst Postmastership, H.

21 brothers left Amherst: Wolff's view that EdD alone stood by his father as the other sons "deserted" him (24–25) distorts the motives and actions of all concerned. Wolff quotes SFD Jr's letter to EdD from Macon, GA, 2-23-1831, H ("a cursed fool if I had stayed in Amherst") as evidence of a wish to distance himself from his father's failure. But the same letter shows that SFD Jr had been humiliated by his *own* experience with Erastus Graves and hoped to reestablish his reputation for business acumen before coming home. (According to John Montague Smith, *History of the Town of Sunderland* [Greenfield, Mass.: Hall, 1899] 365, Erastus Graves "failed in business, rem[oved]. to Macon, Ga.") As for brother William, in 1827 he reportedly wished to return to Amherst so that he and EdD could "gratify the wishes of our family & friends by settling ourselves in business, at home" (*PP* 102). EdD's own persistence in seeking an opening away from Amherst may be estimated from the many discouraging letters he received (e.g., Fr. B. Stebbins to EdD, 4-28-1826, H).

22 There was a definite military: *Let* 254, 470; EdD's commission, H; 10-4-1824, George Dickinson to EdD, 9-1-, 9-12-, Sept. 1825, Hollis Witt to EdD, 9-23-1825, H; EdD's signed issues of *Boston Courier*, 6-24-1830, 8-17-1835, and Greenfield *Gazette and Mercury,* 1-30-1838, box labeled "Dickinson Library. Misc. Pamphlets, Articles, & Lists," H; Solomon Warriner, Jr., to EdD, 2-27-, 3-27-1827, H; EdD, training-day speech at Amh 9-30-1828 [looks like 1838], H. Two articles on militia reform in *NEI,* 2-2-, 10-19-1827, may be by EdD.

22 Early in 1826 Major: Warriner to EdD, 1-17-1827, H; EdD, Complaint, H; Henry Chapin, Order to arrest, H; *Discourses* 19.

23 "the Intellectual Powers": "Order of Exercises at the First Anniversary of the Collegiate Charity Institution, Amherst, August 28, 1822" (Northampton, 1822), A; EdD, "A Colloquy on a comparative view of the intellectual powers of the sexes," H.

Chapter 2

25 local property tax list: Myra Moulton, comp., "County and Town Tax for 1834," M.

26 The figure for Joel: Hampden County Probate Court, Estate of JN, Case 8347, inventory; Bernhard 366; JN, daybook no. 11, Monson Historical Society.

26 Joel was also a pillar: *History of the Connecticut Valley in Massachusetts* (Philadelphia: Everts, 1879) 2:1021; "Records of the Union Charitable Society," 5-17-1818, Monson Ch; Record book 2 ("Congregational Church 1806–1864") 84, Monson Ch.

26 his gifts amounting: *History of the Connecticut Valley,* 2:1020; Bernhard 369; Charles Hammond to SCB, 5-9-1846, SCB Papers 4:93.

27 "Humble and retiring": [Alfred Ely], obituary of Betsey Norcross, Springfield *Journal,* 9-16-1829 (attribution in Joel W. Norcross, "Fay Family" [1887], 395, NEHGS).

27 "carrier of Dickinson traits": MTB in *Home* 4.

27 footnote 1: Wolff 40; Cody 42; Bernhard; Ackmann.

28 The Praying Circle was begun: "Journal of the first Female Praying Circle—Monson—From April 1827 to August 1829," 1–2, Monson Ch; "Evangel" 390–93.

28 The journal shows how effective: "Journal" 12, 10, 50–51.

28 At the time: *Manual* 38–40; Alfred Ely, *Two Sermons* (Boston: Mudge, 1858) 27.

29 One of the Circle's seven: "Journal" 3; Hezekiah Butterworth, *The Story of the Hymns* (New York: American Tract Society, 1875) 48–50; "Rev. S.R. Brown, D. D." *Missionary Herald* 76 (Aug. 1880) 294; Asahel Nettleton, *Village Hymns for Social Worship* (New York, 1826) 223. Nettleton indicated Brown's authorship with a "B." Later hymnals identified her as "Mrs. Brown," "P.H.B.," or "Brown": Thomas Hastings, *The Mother's Hymn Book* (New York: Haven, 1835) 75; James H. Linsley and Gustavus F. Davis, *Select Hymns* (Hartford: Canfield & Robins, 1839) 296–97; [Elias Nason], *The Congregational Hymn Book* (Boston: Jewett, 1857) 562. An 1892 reference book (John Julian, *A Dictionary of Hymnology* [New York: Dover, 1957] 185), considered her the best early female American hymnist.

30 Her lyric was published: Gillett 36–37; SB Let #2 (1-2-[1859]); *Let* 235. ED was quoting from memory a couplet from Simon Browne's "Frequent the Day of God Returns": "Where the assembly ne'er breaks up, / The Sabbath ne'er shall end" (*Village Hymns* 388).

30 footnote 2: *Discourses* 4.

31 Each of Dickinson's grandmothers: Bernhard 368; [Ely], obituary of Betsey Norcross. In a statistical retrospect, Ely noted that "the largest number who have died [in Monson], between the ages of sixteen and forty, have been removed by fevers and consumption. The number by consumption has been not a large proportion of the whole" (*A Sermon Preached the Sabbath Preceding the Ordination* [West Brookfield, Mass.: Mirick, 1843] 11).

31 "how much care": LNN to EdD and END, 12-14-1835. On boarders, see LNN to END, 8-29-1823, H.

32 The earliest trace: "Monson Academy in 1819," 1902 clipping, M; "Monson Academy History," *SR,* 6-12-1904. Erasmus, JN's youngest brother, did not join Monson's First Church until 1825 (*Manual* 37). Student "E. Norcross" was probably not

Elvira: born 1801, she was too old for the daughterly parts given END and would have been designated "Miss." The original 1819 catalog Ackmann cites (45) cannot be found at the Wilbraham-Monson Academy library.

In Monson, as elsewhere, the Second Great Awakening chilled an earlier secular openness. An old "Catalogue of Books proposed for the Monson Social Library" (found in one of JN's ledgers, Monson Historical Society) lists such popular novels as *The Turkish Spy, The Hapless Orphans, The Haunted Priory.* The Norcrosses' few books now at M include *The Female Marine* (1816), about a woman's adventures in men's wear. Signed "A. Norcross," it was perhaps acquired by Austin before he joined the church in 1819 (*Manual* 35). An 1820 sermon by the Reverend Ely set forth the orthodox position that "novels, stories, romances . . . are calculated to corrupt the heart and render the imagination and the passions ungovernable" ("On the Second Centennial Anniversary of the Landing of the Pilgrim Fathers" [ts], 1, M).

32 The next trace: *Catalogue of the Trustees, Instructors, and of the Classes of Students Who Have Fitted for College, in Monson Academy* (Springfield, Mass.: Taylor, 1851) 8; END's school report, H; "Records of the Monson Sabbath School Committee," 13, Monson Ch. A loose page in a Norcross family Bible (M) records END's 1804 birth as "Emela" Norcross. Torn from another and older Bible (published 1793), the page preserves the family's first spelling of the name.

33 But the teacher's painful: END, sermon notes, H; LNN to END, 8-29-1823, H.

33 Remarkably, after marrying: *Let* 45. Mrs. Hunt died in Amherst 9-8-1861. For proof she was Caroline P. Dutch, see "Deaths Registered in the Town of Amherst" (J); *Vital Records of Bradford* (Topsfield, Mass., 1907) 44; Smith 409. EdD informed END shortly before their wedding that Mrs. Hunt had given birth to a son and was "quite comfortable" (*PP* 194).

33 Emily Norcross's one surviving: END, "On Amusements," H. The 1827 watercolor Sewall attributes to END (facing 77) cannot be found at the library he credits, H, or for that matter at A, J, M, or the Dickinson Homestead.

34 All her life Emily Norcross: WON to END, 3-14-, 8-1-1824, LNN to EdD, 10-25-1829, 7-22-1830, H; Leyda 1:31.

35 The most revealing pieces: END, sermon notes, H. Those in pencil were found in the same folder as END, "On Amusements."

36 In 1853, when Austin: *Let* 257; END to EdD, Sunday eve [1-7-1838], H; "Root" 18; Phyllis McGinley, *A Pocketful of Wry* (New York: Duell, Sloan and Pearce, 1940). For a discussion of ED's sense of humor, see *Comic Power.*

36 Emily Norcross's longest absence: "Catalogue of the Members of Rev. Claudius Herrick's School for Young Ladies," terms beginning April 1810, April 1811, 5-8-1820, 9-18-1820, 4-21-1823, 5-15-1826, CT Misc 25:278; Charles Barney Whittelsey, *Genealogy of the Whittelsey-Whittlesey Family* (Hartford: Case, Lockwood & Brainard, 1898) 56; CT Headstone 82:182; Will of Chauncey Whittlesey, New Haven Probate Dist, #11435, CT State Lib; Olivia Flynt to END, 6-17-1826, H.

36 Although Emily made "but few": Olivia Flynt to END, 6-17-1826, LNN to END, 7-22-1830, H.

37 Like many of Herrick's pupils: WON to END, 8-1-, 11-1-1824, H. Given END's work assignments, it seems unfair to charge her with being "harried and self-absorbed" (Pollak 49).

37   Yet her own letters: *Home* 25; Olivia Flynt to END, 6-17-1826, H.

37   "Do you remember": *Let* 433.

Chapter 3

39   Nowhere do we get: EdD used the blank space on END's first letter for a running account of his visits and letters. Except for this log and one missing letter, the entire correspondence is available in *PP.*

39   On February 8: Solomon Warriner, Jr., to EdD, 2-8-1826, H; *PP* 3–4.

40   It isn't known: *PP* 5.

40   Northampton Law School: *PP* 32; *Hampshire Gazette* 7-2-1823, 7-27-1825, 5-13-1829, 9-6-1886 (p. 15), 2-22-1887.

40   "could not consistent," "without any one persons": *PP* 12–13.

40   Because Edward saw the exchange: *PP* 22, 53–54, 49, 120, 103, 126; SFD to Tilton Eastman, 5-1-1797, Ms. 797301, D.

41   Four months after Edward: *PP* 18–20.

41   footnote 1: *PP* 18; *Let* 612, 634.

41   In some respects: *Let* 610. EdD breezily asked END to "give my respects to everybody that has any thing to do with you or me. . . . I am as unceremonious as ever" (*PP* 104). A message by President John Quincy Adams that lacked "the formality of a laboured introduction" struck him as admirably "plain, simple & business-like" ("*President's Message*" [ms.], H; *NEI* 12-15-1826).

42   During the couple's two-year: *PP* 136, 145, 56, 128.

42   Still, not only was Emily: *PP* 133, 206, 13 (spelling and punctuation corrected).

43   Edward's proposal of marriage: *PP* 34, 37. Pollak's claim that "there is no indication" (*PP* 27) END read the "pamphlets" overrides END's own statement to the contrary. These were issues of a new monthly, *The Casket,* later *Graham's Magazine,* borrowed by EdD from a student (*PP* 101, 131); WON, too, referred to them as pamphlets (WON to EdD, 6-5-1827, H). An early contributor sounds like EdD: "Every female should be so educated, that she will make a good wife. . . . The duty of a female does not require that she should address the public, or speak in the halls of legislation" ("Female Education," *Casket* 1 [March 1826] 86).

44   Edward sent his formal: *PP* 39, 42–43, 44; EdD's business card, H. SFD had erected the building and owned an interest in it (Hampshire Co. RD 54:76, 58:104).

44   The result: *PP* 48–49, 56.

44   Although the couple was now: WON to EdD, 6-5-1827, H; *PP* 61, 96.

45   Edward had always: LDB to EdD, 1-15-1823, H; MDN to EdD, 1-25-1828, H; Turner 4; CDS to EdD, 5-12-1835, H; CDS to parents and EDC, begun 6-15-1835, ED953 A; CDS to JAS, 10-20-1835, ED954 A.

46   One of several ironies: Ann Hobart, "Hannah More," *Dictionary of Literary Biography* (Detroit: Gale Research, 1992) 116:202–215; [More], *Coelebs in Search of a Wife* (London: Cadell & Davies, 1809) 1:131–32. The Dickinsons' copy of the novel (Boston: West et al., 1820), missing, was apparently "inscribed by several persons, including Wm Dickinson" (Alfred Leete Hampson to Professor West, 9-26-1934, H).

46   footnote 2: William B. Sprague, *Letters on Practical Subjects, to a Daughter* (Albany: Pease, 1851) 78, EDR 3.5.1.

47   His forum was Amherst's: Carp 193; *NEI* 1-5-1827. Unless stated otherwise, cited

issues of *NEI* are at AAS. Others beside EdD took the pseudonym of Coelebs to state their preferences in female character; see "The Country Maiden," *Litchfield Enquirer* 2-2-1832.

47 Even in 1827: *NEI* 1-5-1827, 3-13-1828; *PP* 104–105; EdD, unpublished response to "Tabitha," 5-11-1827, H; *NEI* 5-11-1827.

48 In his third paper: EdD, ms. of Coelebs #3, H.

48 The ferocity implicit: EdD, unpublished Coelebs #4, H.

48 Like the reply: EdD's outline notes for Coelebs #5, H.

48 After the essay appeared: *PP* 101, 35, 121.

49 footnote 3: *NEI* 4-20-1827.

49 In fact, Edward repeatedly: *PP* 10, 55, 86, 16; *Let* 475. EdD's *Thaddeus*, acquired 1827, is at EDR 3.1.25. Pollak assumes these novels were not welcomed by END, who in fact found *Hope Leslie* "quite interesting" (*PP* 17, 123).

49 "How does it affect": EdD, ms. of Coelebs #4, H; *NEI* 2-23-1827.

50 "buys me many Books": *Let* 404.

50 Just east: "Lost Homes" 174 ff; *PP* 108.

51 "have a voice in the style": *PP* 174.

51 There was also the question: LDB to END, Tuesday, n.d., H; EdD's log on END to EdD, 3-1-[1826], H; *PP* 173; MDN to EdD, 10-13-1829, H. Spending two days in Monson immediately after the 1827 Commencement, Warriner described END as "fatigued" by her Amherst visit (letter to EdD, 8-30-1827, H).

51 Finally, in January 1828: MDN to EdD, 1-25-1828, H; *PP* 182.

52 In the courtship's final months: *PP* 162, 177, 168; END to EdD, Sat [1-5-1828], H.

52 In answering this letter: *PP* 173, 180, 186.

53 When Joel Norcross: *PP* 188; EdD to JN, 3-6-1828, J.

53 Just as Lavinia was: JN to EdD, 3-28-1828, H; *PP* 204.

54 "the house has been cleaned": *PP* 209.

54 Emily made it clear: *PP* 206; *Let* 639.

54 footnote 4: *PP* 128, 134, 139.

54 On May 6: *NEI* 5-8-1828. Monson town records give a spelling of "Emely" and a date of 5-7, probably the day the wedding was recorded ("Intentions of Marriage and Marriages," book 2).

55 "thoroughly repaired": Warriner to EdD, 5-13-1828, H.

56 Eliza Coleman's wedding: Leyda 2:29. Years later, in a memorandum added to L762 (Za Dickinson, Y-BRBL), Eudocia Flynt vividly recalled the torrential rains the day of the wedding.

Chapter 4

57 "Father had failed & mother said": *Let* 48–49.

58 When Emily Norcross left: Town of Amherst, valuations for taxes, 1828, J; Journal of the MA Senate 49 (May 1828 to March 1829) 18, 23, 29, 50, MA State Lib. For some reason, 1827 and 1828 valuations don't hold SFD, EdD, or anyone else accountable for the Dickinsons' part of Jemima Montague's house.

58 Then, on June 11: Journal of the MA Senate 49:130; *NEI* 6-26-1828. Dated 6-18-1828, the notice last appeared 9-11. The school was to open 9-1.

58 That the Squire was officially: *NEI* 7-17-, 8-28-1828; *PP* 146–47; *Greenfield Gazette and Franklin Herald* 11-11-1828. EdD signed the final request for those in debt to the paper to pay up (*NEI* 11-13-1828, New-York Historical Society).

59 The inexorable legal: Hampshire Co. RD 58:561. On 10-4-1826 SFD had "sold" the Homestead and the thirty-acre place east of Jemima Montague to Oliver Smith for $500 (Hampshire Co. RD 55:273). Though the conveyance was recorded, Smith didn't have valid title until SFD made a marginal addition on 11-1-1828—the same day Smith's sale of the Homestead was recorded in Northampton. In the interim, Amherst's property valuations continued to hold SFD, not Smith, liable for taxes on the Homestead.

59 On December 8: EdD to JN, 12-8-1828, J.

60 Edward's relations with his: EdD to JN, 3-3-1830, Monson Historical Society. The terms of the agreement aren't known.

60 Among the congratulatory notes: Albert and Loring Norcross to END and EdD, 5-17-1828, H.

60 1,343 Bible verses: "Records of the Monson Sabbath School Committee," 29-30, Monson Ch.

60 The second of Lavinia's: LNN to END, 5-21-[1828], "Thursday eve" [Sept.–Oct. 1828], H. The decline of Candace Packard (d. 12-20-1828) and the end of Prudence Smith's service with the Frinks help date the "Thursday eve" letter.

61 What chiefly worried: LNN to END, 8-30-[1828], 10-30-1828, H. LNN may have known END was some three months pregnant.

61 After the laborious wife: LNN to END, 8-30-1828, "Thursday eve" [Sept.–Oct. 1828], "Thursday noon" [winter 1828–1829], 12-20-[1828], 2-12-[1829], 3-17-1829, H. The "Thursday noon" letter was written during sleighing season and before Betsey Norcross's death on 9-5-1829.

62 On Emily's side: Gillett 5; EdD to END, 9-23-1828, LNN to END, 12-20-[1828], 3-17-1829, EdD to END, 6-7-1829, H. Summer term began 6-3-1829. Henry Morris was a son of Judge Oliver Morris and Caroline Bliss; Richard Bliss, of Caroline's brother George. Thomas B. Warren, "Springfield Families" (D.A.R. copy), 1:77, Connecticut Valley Historical Museum, Springfield; Charles Wells Chapin, *Sketches of the Old Inhabitants . . . of Old Springfield* (Springfield 1893) 57–59, 280–81.

62 The household manual: Carolyn L. Karcher, *The First Woman in the Republic: A Cultural Biography of Lydia Maria Child* (Durham, N.C.: Duke University Press, 1994) 129; [Child], *The Frugal Housewife. Dedicated to Those Who Are Not Ashamed of Economy* (Boston: Carter, Hendee & Babcock, 1831) v, 3, 8, 11–12, 18. Signs of use in END's copy (Boston: Carter & Hendee, 1830), EDR 4.2.3, are on 65, 74, 103, 117–18.

63 This frugality came to look: JL/ED; JN, record of Loring's debits, 4-1-1827, Monson Historical Society; EdD to END, 1-12-1837 [1838], H.

63 "Mother would send her love": *Let* 377.

64 On April 16, 1829: EdD to END, 6-7-1829, LNN to EdD, 5-4-1829, LNN to END, 2-22-1830, LNN to EdD, 7-22-1830, H.

64 The baby was coddled: EdD to END, 6-7-1829, H; *PP* 185; LNN to END, 7-19-1829, H.

64 In Amherst's property: Town of Amherst, valuations for taxes, 1829, J; LNN to END, 12-20-[1828], JN to EdD, 2-26-1829, H.

65 By mid-July Betsey: LNN to END, 7-19-1829, 7-30-, 8-18-[1829], H.

65 Remarkably, it was that summer: WON to EdD, "Saturday Morning" [9-5-1829], H. The revival "commenced about the middle of July" (Book 2, "Congregational Church 1806–1864," 12-6-1829, Monson Ch).

65 But as of September: WON to END, 9-1-1829, H.

65 Taking her baby: WON to EdD, 9-5-1829, LNN to EdD, 10-25-1829, H; *Nettleton* 140–41. MDN's report of hearing "good news of Lavinia" (MDN to EdD, 10-13-1829, H) is the earliest reference to her conversion. LNN joined the church in December (*Manual* 39).

66 For Lavinia, the drama: Examining Committee Records, vol. 1, 11-12-1835, Bowd St Ch.

66 Hoping to communicate her new: LNN to EdD, 10-25-1829, LNN to END, 4-22-[1829], H.

66 Lavinia composed a poem: H.

67 Unlike Edward's father: Town of Amherst, valuations for taxes, 1827, 1828, J; EdD to END, 6-7-1829, H. For Nathan Dickinson's later history, see Robert F. Eldredge, *Past and Present of Macomb County, Michigan* (Chicago: S. J. Clarke, 1905) 337–38; Elizabeth Kane Buzzelli, *A History of the Romeo Community School District 1824–1976* (Romeo, Mich.: Romeo Community Schools' Board of Education, 1976) 20–22.

68 As before, Edward turned: EdD to JN, 3-3-1830, Monson Historical Society. Complete text in "Lost Homes" 183–84.

68 Answering at once: JN to EdD, 3-8-1830, H; preliminary draft at Monson Historical Society.

69 In the end Edward made: Hampshire Co. RD 63:422–23.

69 In May Edward took: *PP* 111; EdD to END, 5-19-1830, H; *New York Evening Post* 5-19-1830; George C. D. Odell, *Annals of the New York Stage* (New York: Columbia University Press, 1928) 3:461.

70 That summer, when Emily: LNN to EdD, 7-22-1830, LNN to END, 8-2-1830, MDN to EdD, 5-3-1835, LNN to END, 8-31-1830, H.

70 Following the move: EdD to JN, 8-11-1830, J; LNN to END, 8-31-1830, H. According to HSR, the central hallway now has a different configuration. Ordinarily, "the city" designated industrial North Amherst.

70 That fall it was learned: Leyda 1:117; LNN to END, 12-6-1830, H; Isaac Parsons, *Memoir of the Life and Character of Rev. Joseph Vaill* (New York: Taylor & Dodd, 1839). See pp. 65–69 for letters to SVN.

70 To receive such a bride: Unsigned ledger, p. 40, Monson Historical Society (attributed to Charles B. Jones by Grace Makepeace); LNN to END, 11-19-[1830], 12-6-1830, H.

71 Notwithstanding: Isaac G. Cutler, "List of Women Delivered," J; END's Bible. The middle name is definitely spelled with an "s."

71 footnote 1: Leyda 1:16; Leyda's notes, MTB Papers 106:666; obituary of Flora Stebbins Gregory, *Amh Rec,* 9-12-1946; Hampshire Co. RP, Estate of Lafayette C. Stebbins; Amherst Vital Records, birth of Flora D. Stebbins on 6-14-1871 and death of Lafayette C. Stebbins on 6-19-1872, J; Amherst directory for 1869; 4-8-1867 marriage intention of Lafayette C. Stebbins and Flora E. Lovett, Town Clerk, Wendell Depot, Massachusetts.

71 From all the signs: END to EdD, postmarked 6-1-[1831], H.

Chapter 5

75 "would be a very good Boy": *Let* 454.

75 The pleasure grew with age: *Let* 704; *FN* 50–53; *Let* 703.

76   "blighted childhood": Sewall 333.

76   "I never had a mother": *Let* 475.

76   "pity her very much": "Root" 11.

77   parents bereft of their children: *Desc* 206; Smith 510; Charles B. Sumner, *A Sermon on the Life and Character of Mrs. Hannah Porter* (Northampton: Bridgman & Childs, 1870) 15; Conant 24, 40–41; END to EdD, Tuesday [2-20-1838], EdD to END, 2-22-, 2-25-1838, H; *Other Bullards* 18; Typed notes on Newman family (1946) 4, Andover Historical Society; Clara C. Pearl to MTB, 11-2-1945, MTB Papers 84:258a ("[I was] told long ago that there were three (3) babies who died in infancy"); EdD to END, 2-11-1835, H.

77   footnote 1: John Harley Warner, *The Therapeutic Perspective: Medical Practice, Knowledge, and Identity in America, 1820–1885* (Cambridge: Harvard University Press, 1986) 62.

77   Little Emily was two: LNN to END, [July–early August 1833, dated by Commencement and Maria Fanning Norcross's 8-8-1833 birth], MDN to EdD, Dec. 1822, Ashmun to EdD (" 'Oh terque, quaterque beati' are those that didn't get their heads broke when I got my leg"), 9-24-1823, H; *PP* 52; EdD's file of remedies, H; EdD to JN, 2-5-1838, J; *Let* 902. *Amh Rec*, 10-14-, 11-11-1885, reported that Dr. Joseph DeVore was suspected in the death of Harriet O. Merrill, who lived near ED on Maple Street.

78   Father's basic remedy: EDC to WAD, 5-10-1842, LNN to END, 11-11-[1833], LNN to EdD, postmarked 1-7-[1834? year inferred from reference to Colonel Barr in LNN to END, 12-3-1833], H. See also LNN to END, 2-28-[1834], H: "Your husband had much to say to me about being married about being crazy &c."

78   "watched": See SFD to EdD, 12-17-1819, 1-2-1820, H. For EdD's care of brother William, SFD, and a cousin, see *PP* 142, 178. Sue's manuscript essay on nurses, 3–4, H, reveals that men were hired as watchers. Wolff's claim that EdD showed little sympathy with suffering and that "during every severe illness some woman or other kept a 'night watch' " (49–50) illustrates the tyranny of received ideas.

79   "if any of you are sick": EdD to END, 2-7-1837, H.

79   "I would not neglect": EdD to WAD, 5-26-1874, ED926 A. Cf. WAD to Olmsted, 5-29-1874, Olmsted Papers, Container 15.

79   One reason Edward wanted: EdD to END, 5-19-1830, 9-7-1835, H; Hannah Terry to Mary Shepard, 9-12-[1835], Bolt 4:7. For other letters bearing on this trip, see SVN to END, 8-6-1835, SVN to LNN, 10-13-1835 (with note from LNN to END dated "Thursday P.M."), H.

79   In Amherst, having: EdD to END, 9-11-[1835], 7-1-1836, H.

79   "but *this* visit": EdD to END, 6-7-1829, H. In extenuation, EdD's hope that Betsey "return with you & stay with us a while, for her health" shows he didn't realize the gravity of her case.

80   footnote 2: EdD to END, 1-3-1837 [1838], 2-25-1838, END to EdD, Friday [1-5-1838], Tuesday [4-3-1838], H.

80   One of the fundamental: EdD to END, 2-25-, 2-9-1838, H.

80   On July 3, 1831: First #1.

81   Mrs. Dickinson entered: Book No. 1, 1826–1849, Records #2, 1826–1891, Amh Coll Ch; EdD to LNN, 11-21-1831, J.

81   As for Edward: *PP* 85, 52–53, 104; EdD to END, 3-18-1838, H; Examining Committee Records, vol. 2, 11-11-1841, Bowd St Ch; *Historical Manual of the South Church in Andover* (Andover: Draper, 1859) 163; First #3, no. 821; Book No. 1, 7-

18-1835, Amh Coll Ch; JAS to CDS, 11-12-1834, ED963 A. JAS and END joined Amherst's First Church the same day.

82 One ironic result: EdD to JN, 2-13-1832, J.

82 "Now if you cant": LNN to END, "Thursday eve" [12-20-1832], H. Dated by Deodatus Dutton's death, *New York Evening Post* 12-17-1832.

82 ran a notice: *Hampshire Gazette* 2-27-1833.

82 The day after this announcement: Isaac G. Cutler, "List of Women Delivered," J; END's Bible; LNN to END, 5-29-, 5-25-[1833], H.

83 Once again, the growing family: Hampshire Co. RD 71:89–90; "Col. David Mack, the Faithful Steward," *Tracts,* vol. 12, no. 487; Deed of gift signed 6-29-1833, Hampshire Co. RD 70:203; *Home* 502.

83 footnote 3: LNN to END, 2-28-[1834], H.

84 From the beginning: LNN to END, 10-3-[1831], 8-3-[1832], "Thursday eve" [12-20-1832], H.

84 Loring Norcross: Loring to END, 5-31-1828, H. Born 10-17-1808, Loring lost his father, William, in 1813. In 1816 his mother, Oril (Orril, Oral), married Daniel Burt, who died in 1823, leaving Loring again fatherless (*Vital Records of Brimfield* [Boston: NEHGS, 1931] 113, 227, 275; Joel W. Norcross, "The History and Genealogy of the Norcross Family," 2:108, NEHGS). Records of JN's guardianship, with the original 1813 appointment, are at Monson Historical Society.

84 Uncertain it was "right": LNN to END, 6-11-1833, H; JAS to CDS, 11-12-1834, ED963 A; Intentions of Marriage and Marriages, Book 2, 10-11-1834 ("Lorin Norcross and Lovina Norcross"), Monson Town Hall; *Desc* 206–207.

84 Lavinia took another chance: LNN to END, 5-20-[1833], H. All information in this section about ED's 1833 visit to Monson comes from LNN to END or EdD, 5-9,20,25,29 and 6-11, H.

85 footnote 4: SVN to EdD and END, 2-18-1836, 5-1-1835, H; Leyda 1:31.

85 "pat" read as "slap": Leyda 1:21; Sewall 324.

85 footnote 5: Wolff 59–61.

86 "fond of her child": EdD to END, 1-9-1838, H.

86 In fall Lavinia wished: LNN to END, 10-30-1833, LNN to EdD, 4-5-1834, H.

86 Although Congregationalists: First #1, 21, 188 (1834 Articles of Faith). According to " 'Infant Baptism,' " *Sabbath School Visiter* 9 (1841) 22, "the rite is falling into disuse in the Congregational churches." A First Parish register dating from 1880 has ED baptized in 1831 but gives no month or day (First #5, 1). This vague, retroactive compilation clearly has less authority than earlier documents. "Amherst Births, Deaths, Marriages [1838–1854]," J, shows Vin but not WAD or ED as baptized. The same is true for the original church ledger, the one primary source. In 1831, as this ledger shows, several couples who had recently joined the church had their previous children baptized. Mary and John Sidney Adams joined in August, and in September had two children baptized. Horace and Alma Kellogg joined that summer, and in October had four children baptized. Lucretia and Morton Salman Dickinson joined in August, and in October had four children baptized. EdD's cousin Nathan and wife, Mary Ann, joined in October, and the following July had three children baptized. Perhaps the reason the two older Dickinson children weren't given the rite is that their father was still a nonmember: 1831 shows no retroactive baptisms in "divided" families (First #1, 10–13, 21).

87 Meanwhile, Samuel Fowler: Bullard 119; "Report of Committee on Burying Yard," 1.19 Committee Reports (1788–1838), Amherst Town Clerk; EdD to JN, 12-21-

1833, J. On the Lane rebellion, see Gilbert H. Barnes & Dwight L. Dumond, *Letters of Theodore Dwight Weld, Angelina Grimké Weld, and Sarah Grimké 1822–1844* (New York: Appleton-Century, 1934) 1:132–46; Benjamin P. Thomas, *Theodore Weld: Crusader for Freedom* (New Brunswick, N.J.: Rutgers University Press, 1950) 43–44, 70–71; Lawrence Thomas Lesick, *The Lane Rebels* (Metuchen, N.J.: Scarecrow, 1980) 72, 128.

87 Soon, it was time: LNN to END, 3-22-[1834], LNN to EdD, 4-5-1834 ("I suppose I never shall visit you again in the part you now occupy"), JAS to EdD, 5-2-1834, H; *Hist* 65. Leyda's entry for 1-5-1833 (1:19) obviously belongs in 1834.

88 As a structural: HSR; EdD to END, 1-3-1837 [1838], H. See also EdD to END, 1-5-1838, END to EdD, "Friday eve" [1-12-1838], H.

88 Judging from a startlingly: EdD to JN, 12-21-1833, J; Amherst Town Records, vol. 2 (3-5-1832) 30, Town Hall vault; *Amh Acad* 193; "Copies of Records of Amherst College," Trustees [General Files], box 1, Votes (Ms. copies), A.

89 One month after this appointment: EdD to END, 9-7-1835, H; JN's note in SVN to EdD and END, 11-26-1835, H. On 10-26-1835 JN sold eight shares in the Monson Woolen Manufacturing Co. for $4,000 (Monson Historical Society). Five days later he sold the Norcross house for $5,000 (Hampden Co. RD 95:447).

89 In Amherst, the mania: David Junior and Samuel E. Mack to EdD, 6-16-1836, H. EdD's earliest known purchase dates from before 9-20-1836 (Ottawa Co., MI, RD A:582). His acquisitions are hard to trace for two reasons: grantee indexes name only the first partner in a group buy, and a fire destroyed Kent County, MI, deeds in the 1870s.

89 "So your Western": JAS to EdD, 1-9-1835 [1836], David Junior and Samuel E. Mack to EdD, 6-16-1836, H; Hubbard Winslow, *Christianity Applied to Our Civil and Social Relations* (Boston: William Peirce, 1835) 174; LNN to EdD and END, "Sun. eve" [10-16,18-1836], H. LNN urged EdD and END to read Winslow's book (letter of 12-14-1835, H).

90 In Amherst, Edward's land: Hampshire Co. RD 77:162, 166; EdD to JN, 3-3-1830, Monson Historical Society.

90 Unlike Edward, whose: LNN to END, 5-29-[1833], EdD to END, 2-25-1838, H.

90 In spite of the Dickinsons': Asa Bullard and LDB to EdD, 1-15-1836, SVN to EdD and END, 2-18-1836, LNN to EdD and END, 2-15-1836, H.

91 "I would not that servile": [Lydia Maria Child], *The Frugal Housewife* (Boston: Carter & Hendee, 1830) 103, EDR 4.2.3.

91 As Edward's letters home: EdD to END, 1-21-1838, H; John S. C. Abbott, *The Mother at Home; or the Principles of Maternal Duty* (Boston: Crocker & Brewster, 1833) 60, 95, 93, 101, EDR 1.2.7.

92 This two-phase sequence: *Let* 475.

92 In fact, the forty-year-old: *Let* 475; TWH, "A Shadow," *Atlantic Monthly* 26 (July 1870) 4–10; *Let* 612; EdD to END, 2-9-1838, H.

93 We have a very revealing: EdD to END, 9-11-[1835] (cf. EdD to END, 7-1-1836), H. A few years later Helen Fiske's mother dreamed she lost her trunk while traveling (DWVF to HHJ [transcript], 10-23,24-1842, HHJ Papers 2:1).

93 Although most of Dickinson's: *Let* 928 (PF117, first excision as in ED878 A); *Let* 576.

93 "When I was a baby": *Let* 515.

Chapter 6

96 One Sunday in 1839: EdD to END, 1-12-1839, H.
96 Before Emily Dickinson went: EdD to END, 9-7-1835, H; Reports defining district
     boundaries, 1.19 Committee Reports (1788–1838), Amherst Town Clerk; Minutes
     for 6-27-1826, 9-17-1829, 4-24-1847, Amherst–School Committee–West Middle
     District 1826–1864, J; #242, Amherst Historical Commission–Historic Resources, J.
     For a possible teacher, see Paulina Sellon–Bills and Receipts, J. On textbooks, see
     Jones 296–98; Lowenberg.
97 The reason for thinking: Amherst Town Records, vol. 2 (3-5-1832) 30, Town Hall
     vault; *Northampton Courier* 9-14-, 9-28-1841; *Life and Works of Horace Mann* (Cam-
     bridge: Published for the Editor, 1867) 2:212–16. MDB's claim that the Dickinson
     "children went to the public schools like all the other children of their time in New
     England towns" (*LL* 15) sounds typically slapdash, yet it is unlikely ED went to the
     leading alternative, a tiny school run by Emily and Julia Nelson (see CDS to EdD,
     5-12-1835, A) and patronized by the Hitchcock and Fiske families. The detailed
     retrospects of EH Jr (Notebook "B+," 15–16, 35, Doc Hitch 7:26) and HHJ ("The
     First Time," *St. Nicholas* 4 [May 1877] 473–79) do not even glance at ED. The
     Emily Dickinson listed in Amherst Female Seminary's 1834–35 catalog (J) was not
     ED, who always had a middle initial in catalogs and other public or official docu-
     ments. Still operating in 1837 (*Hampshire Gazette* 4-19-1837), this couldn't have
     been the school she and WAD *both* attended (EdD to END, 1-17-1838, H).
97 Curiously, the one point: EdD to END, 9-7-1835, LNN to EdD and END, 12-14-
     1835, EdD to END, 1-5-, 1-17-1838, H.
97 Because of the sickness: END to EdD, Friday [1-5-], Sunday [1-21-1838], EdD to
     END, 2-16-, 3-14-1838, H.
98 Other parents: EH Jr, Notebook "B+," 13–14, 26, Doc Hitch 7:26. Gillett 29 re-
     called skating as flatly disallowed for girls.
98 Some of the general assumptions: EdD to END, 2-9-, 1-9-1838, H; *Revised
     Statutes of . . . Massachusetts* (Boston State Printers: 1836) 219.
98 Emily's first letter: fMS Am 1118.4 (L53), H. A facsimile is in *World* 22.
99 *Parley's Magazine:* EdD to END, 2-16-1838, H; "Something about the Month of
     February," *Parley's Magazine* 6 (1838) 52.
99 Edward's purpose in bringing: John A. Vaughan, *Mistakes of Parents* no. 296 (New
     York: American Tract Society, n.d.), Bianchi Coll (collected in *Tracts,* vol. 8, no. 16);
     EdD to END, 2-25-, 2-9-1838, H.
100 "Against Scoffing": Isaac Watts, *Divine and Moral Songs for Children* (New York:
     American Tract Society, n.d.) 29; St. Armand 131, 333.
100 her Church's Sabbath School: In 1833–1834 the superintendent was William S.
     Tyler, later professor of Greek; in 1834–1835, Ebenezer Burgess, later missionary to
     India. There was a class for children who had "scarcely learned to read"; George
     Boltwood attended at three and a half (William S. Tyler, ms. articles on Amherst
     Sabbath School and on George Boltwood, Tyler Papers 5:5). During an 1836 cam-
     paign "to revive" the Sabbath School, all parents were visited and urged to send their
     children (First #1, 4-14-, 4-29-1836).
100 "I believe the love of": *Let* 372. Misdated by editors, this letter, L230, was probably
     written in late 1879 or early 1880. If the "Miss W" of the printer's copy (FN/ED
     402) was Maria Whitney, the letter can't have been sent in winter 1860–1861 (*Let*
     [1894] 236) or early March 1861 (*Let* 372): she didn't enter the Dickinson world till

mid-1862 (Chap. 18) and can't be linked to the Norcross cousins before 1875 (MW to James L. Whitney, Sunday [3-6-1875, misdated 3-31-1875], WDW Papers 22:593). The "Friday class" was a weekly religious discussion group in Concord's Unitarian First Parish. The experimental informal meetings began in October 1879 and were shifted to Thursday in 1883. "Well attended" from the start, they proved unusually "social and conversational"; Ellen Emerson was a regular participant. The churches previously attended by the Norcrosses, Boston's Bowdoin Street and Cambridgeport's Prospect Street societies, both orthodox, do not seem to have had any kind of "Friday class." *Concord Freeman* 10-9-1879, 11-24-1882, 10-19-1883; First Parish in Concord, Annual Reports for years ending 4-1-1880 (4), 4-1-1881 (3–4), 4-1-1883 (8), Concord Free Public Lib; Emerson 5-4-1881, 1-18-1883.

100 Another of Watts's moral: Watts, *Divine and Moral Songs* 26; *Let* 701 (spatial arrangement based on Ms Am 1118.5 [B177], H).

101 footnote 1: Bullard 72, 89, 90, 117, 9, 128–29; James Avery Smith, *The History of the Black Population of Amherst* (Boston: NEHGS, 1999) 70.

101 sending "the Sabbath School Visiter": EdD to END, 2-7-1837, H.

101 The January issue: the monthly stories are from *Sabbath School Visiter* 5 (1837) 7–11, 29–31, 63–64, 84–85, 97–98, 135–37, 145–46, 157–59, 176, 201–202.

103 footnote 2: *Sabbath School Visiter* 9 (1841) 165.

103 "the *separations* death occasions," "utterly worthless": *Sabbath School Visiter* 9 (1841) 124, 173.

103 In the Dickinsons' commerce: EdD to END, 1-16-1839, H.

103 Tellingly, Emily was: EdD to END, 2-9-1838, H (the "little children" were Louisa, two, and William, five months [*Other Bullards* 18]); END to EdD, Tuesday [4-3-1838], H. Other letters reflecting the Dickinson-Bullard relationship are LNN to END, 4-12-, 12-14-1835, Asa Bullard and/or LDB to EdD, 1-15-1836, 9-11-1837, May 1838, END to EdD, Sun [1-7-1838], H; see also *Home* 318.

104 In the mid-1830s: Loring to EdD, 5-12-1835, H; CDS to parents and EDC, letter begun 6-15-1835, ED953 A; SVN to LNN, 9-13-1835, LNN to EdD and END, 11-20-1835 (misdated 1838 by H), CDS to EdD, 4-25-1836, David Junior and Samuel E. Mack to EdD, 6-16-1836, H.

104 footnote 3: Christopher Clark, *The Roots of Rural Capitalism: Western Massachusetts 1780–1860* (Ithaca: Cornell University Press, 1990) 137.

105 In the winter of 1837–1838: EdD to END, 2-13-, 2-16-1838, H; *Hampshire Gazette* 2-14-1838.

105 footnote 4: Hampshire Co RD 83:8.

105 The news from Ohio: CDS to EdD, 5-12-1835, H; *Hist Amh Coll* 245–46; JAS to EdD, 8-28-1834, H.

105 In 1836 the former Squire: SFD Jr to JAS, 9-6-1836, A; END's Bible.

106 The shocked responses: LDB to EdD, May 1838, H; CDS and MDN to LGD and EDC, 4-29-1838, ED956 A.

106 Samuel's college accounts: *Home* 19–20; Excerpts from Trustees Records of Western Reserve College, MTB Papers 101:559; CDS and MDN to LGD and EDC, 4-29-1838, A; CDS to EdD, 5-12-1835, H; EdD to END, 1-12-1839, H; George William Montague, *Montague Family of America* (Amherst: Press of J. E. Williams, 1886); *EDE* (Dandurand) 76; LGD to EdD, 9-22-, 12-19-1839, H.

107 footnote 5: See MDN and LGD to EdD, 3-15-1821, H.

107 "It would be best": LGD to EdD, 9-22-1839, MDN to EdD, 5-3-1835, SVN to EdD and END, 2-18-1836, LNN to END, 10-26-[1838], H; END's Bible; EDC,

annual reports for 1875–1878, *Home for Aged Females* (Worcester: Press of Chas. Hamilton, 1882), AAS.

107 The Dickinson girls visited: EdD to JN, 9-6-1838, J; *Let* 567; *EDE* (Dandurand) 76; Lucien Marcus Underwood, *The Underwood Families of America* (Lancaster, Pa.: New Era, 1913) 1:180–82; Francis H. Underwood, *Quabbin: The Story of a Small Town* (Boston: Lee and Shepard, 1893) 66.

108 The boom years ended: EdD to JN, 5-16-1837, J; Hubbard Winslow, *Rejoice with Trembling* (Boston: Perkins & Marvin, 1837) 9.

108 The resulting depression: Boston directories, 1835–1839; LNN to END, Friday [11-9-1838], Loring to EdD, 10-22-1839, H; Hampden County Probate Court, Estate of JN, Case 8347, will.

109 In Brooklyn and New York: NYC directories, 1833/34–1839/40; EdD to END, 1-16-1839, H; Luke Sweetser to JAS, 11-2-1839 (ts), MTB Papers 102:570; JAS to EdD, 11-8-1839, H; Mark Haskell Newman to JAS, 11-13-1839, ED982 A; *Home* 506 (based on Carp 328–29); First #3, nos. 1060, 1061 (JAS and CDS joined 4-30-1841, were dismissed 1842); JAS, "To My Wife," ED964 A. JAS's absence from New York City and Brooklyn directories for 1840/41 (canvassing completed by summer) puts him in Massachusetts by May or June 1840. A daughter, Mary Newman Sweetser, was born there 8-11-1840 (1850 federal census, Brooklyn, ward 3, dwelling 958; *Sweetser* 122). He reappears in Brooklyn in the 1842/43 directory as "Sweetser Jn A, clerk." By 3-3-1843, as a letter from Abel Sweetser discloses, he had "gone into business again . . . I hope your trials in your children & property have been truly sanctified to you" (to JAS [ts], MTB Papers 102:570).

110 one-issue representative: EdD to END, 1-17-1838, H.

110 At this period: George S. Boutwell, *Reminiscences of Sixty Years in Public Affairs* (New York: McClure, Phillips, 1902) 1:71; EdD to END, 2-13-1838, H; Journal of the MA House (1838) 443, *Documents Printed by Order of the House* (1838), no. 45, Journal of the MA House (1839) 214–15, *Documents Printed by Order of the Senate* (1839), no. 27, MA State Lib. See also *Remin* 289; *Hist Amh Coll* 262–63.

111 "imagine[d] I could tell him": END to EdD, Saturday [1-19-1839], H.

111 Several months before: First #1, from 9-14-1837 to 1-1-1838; EdD to END, 1-17-, 1-21-, 2-9-1838, END to EdD, Sunday [1-7-1838], 2-16-[1838], H.

111 What particularly weighed: EdD to END, 1-21-1838 (cf. 3-18-1838), H; *Let* 920.

112 "passed in a wilderness": JL/ED.

112 Given the good working relations: EdD to END, 2-16-1838, END to EdD, Sunday [2-18-1838], Wednesday [2-7-1838], H.

113 But Mrs. Dickinson's times: EdD to END, 1-16-1839, END to EdD, Tuesday [2-20-1838], EdD to END, 3-18-, 1-9-1838, H.

113 Since the First Church: *Hist* 81; EdD to END, 4-1-, 2-22-1838, H.

114 racing to the post office: END to EdD, Friday [1-12-1838], H.

115 But in 1838 it looks: EdD to END, 1-5-, 4-1-1838, EDC to WAD, 4-21-1842, H.

115 The same picture: END to EdD, 2-16-, Tuesday [3-20-], Sunday [1-7-], Sunday [1-21-1838], H.

116 In her maturity: *Let* 928; Sewall 322–23; Elizabeth Barrett Browning, *Aurora Leigh* (New York: Francis, 1859) 104, A (book 3, ll. 854–55).

117 Before Emily's adolescence: *Let* 622, 920 (PF51, corrected against ED880 A).

117 "I always ran Home": *Let* 517–18.

117 "haunted me when": *Let* 663. See 2 Samuel 18. McIntosh 97–110 has a good discussion of ED's Moses poems.

118 Yet, along with the sympathy: First #1, 187; *Let* 756.

118 "There's none can know": Watts and Select 2:298; Leyda 1:51. On ED and Watts, see especially England.

119 following the regular Sunday morning meeting: *Hist* 76.

119 On January 7, 1838: END to EdD, Sun [1-7-1838], H; ED to MW, n.d., MS Am 1118.10 (8), H (passage omitted from L591); *Let* 835. Leyda 1:39–40 was the first to link END's letter to ED's memory. See also *Let* 524–25.

Chapter 7

123 West Street: James Avery Smith, "A Record of the Streets . . . of Amherst" (1991), J. In 1851 ED thought of it as West Street (*Let* 125). The name was Pleasant Street by the time the 1869 Amherst directory was published.

123 It was in January: Leyda 1:58; *Let* 411; *Capsule* 93; Barbara N. Parker, "The Dickinson Portraits by Otis A. Bullard, *Harvard Library Bulletin* 6 (winter 1952) 133–37. The flowers in ED's hand and book may be moss roses (*Capsule* 4).

124 Orthodox in doctrine: Aaron Merrick Colton, *The Old Meeting House* (New York: Worthington, 1890) 287–88, 80. For a detailed obituary endorsed by Colton's family (Mary C. Bassett to C. C. Carpenter, 5-12-1895, Andover Alumni), see *SR* 5-1-1895.

125 In early 1840: *Andover* 167, 179, 185; Colton, "Boldness in the Preacher," *American Biblical Repository*, Ser. 2, vol. 1 (April 1839) 342.

125 Then, the Reverend Josiah: *Hist* 71–72.

125 Edward probably made: First #4, 4.

126 The section from "Tuesday, June" to "ran away the first night" relies on *Hist* 72–73.

126 This was the man: *Let* 58, 120; First #1, 8-19-1852.

127 "Oh thou who sittest": *Let* 763.

127 Along with style: Colton, "Boldness," 343–44; [Colton], *In Memoriam. Dea. Walter Colton, Georgia, Vermont* (n.p.: for the family, by A. M. and G. Q. Colton [ca. 1863]) 24 (copy at CL); Jane Donahue Eberwein, "Ministerial Interviews and Fathers in Faith," *EDJ* 9.2 (2000) 10–11; *Let* 460, 631. ED first approached the idea in 1864, with Sue: "That is why I prefer the Power – for Power is Glory, when it likes, and Dominion, too" (*Let* 432). On "the Glory," see Gary Lee Stonum, *The Dickinson Sublime* (Madison: University of Wisconsin Press, 1990) 59ff.

128 In spring 1839: Hampshire Co. RD 85:167; *Home* 63; E.D.–House 31 Pleasant St., J. See also E.D.–Leyda, Jay, J; Bigelow, Orvis F.–Deeds, J.

128 In making this purchase: Hampshire Co. RD 85:168, 87:232–33, 166:584, 560; EdD to JN, 3-14-1839, J; Hampden Co. Probate Court, Estate of JN, Case 8347, will; Conveyance, EdD to WAD, 4-5-1864, B (mention of sale to Newman estate). As evidence of EdD's reputation for probity, when Nathan settled in MI in 1841 he left a sweeping power of attorney in EdD's hands, in spite of conflicts of interest (Hampshire Co. RD 95:116).

129 Judging from a remark: Loring to EdD, 3-20-1840, H; Cooke 2:14; *Let* 919.

129 As befitted a rising: EdD to ED, 6-4-1844, H; Leyda 1:lv; *Let* 16; Smith 742; EDC to WAD, 4-21-1842, H; *Let* 3, 7.

129 footnote 1: Isaac G. Cutler, "List of Women Delivered," J; *Let* 561; MDB to Ned Dickinson, n.d., Bianchi Coll.

130 "Jumping" was how: Gillett 9, 41, 49.

130 "How I wish you were": *Let* 320. It isn't likely ED was thinking of her year at Mount Holyoke, when she and Jane, a Senior, roomed in the same large building.

130 But it never quite became: Hampshire Co. RD 98:421, 304.

131 In fall 1841: Journal of the MA Senate (1842), MA State Lib.

131 The other senator: Mark Hopkins, *An Address, Delivered at the Dedication of Willis-ton Seminary . . . December 1, 1841* (Northampton: Butler, 1841); Williston catalog for 1841–42, Williston Northampton School Lib; "Amherst Academy," *Hampshire Gazette* 11-9-1841; EdD to WAD, 4-14-1842, H. Williston's spring term ran from 2-24-1842 to 5-11-1842. Ordinarily, pupils were not to enroll for less than a term. Still, Johnson notwithstanding (*Let* 8), it isn't known whether WAD returned for summer term (5-26-1842 to 8-10-1842). All we can infer from his inclusion in the first catalog is that he attended for at least part of the year. His name also appears in the fall 1844 and 1844–45 catalogs.

131 Unlike Amherst Academy: *Constitution of Williston Seminary* (Northampton: Met-calf, 1856) 6–8, 15; JL to Timothy Lyman, 2-13-1844, Lyman Papers, box 1; Carp 1:149; EH Jr. to Orra White Hitchcock, 5-8-1844, Edward and Orra White Hitch-cock Papers 25:8, A; Albert Montague to Phila Montague, 9-5-1842, Williston Northampton School Lib.

132 Austin roomed in the: Conant 56; EdD to WAD (care of Luther Clapp), 4-14-1842, H.

132 The letter concluded with: EdD to WAD, 4-14-1842, H; Smith 395-96; EdD to ED, 5-24-1844, H.

133 All of the other letters: EDC to WAD, 5-10-1842, END to WAD, Tuesday [5-3?-1842], H.

133 footnote 2: School report on WAD, H.

133 footnote 3: EDC to WAD, 4-21-, 5-10-1842, H; EdD to JN, 9-22-1841, J; DWVF to HHJ (tr), Monday [9-5-1842], HHJ Papers 2:1.

133 Making a Hurrah with Pen and Ink: All quotations in this section are from *Let* 3–7, except as noted.

134 footnote 4: EDC to WAD, 4-21-1842, H.

136 signed as a legal witness: Lapeer Co., MI, RD E:509.

136 Austin and Lavinia also: Hampshire Co. RD 98:313; Ottawa Co., MI, RD E:537.

137 vocabulary of law and business: William Howard, "Emily Dickinson's Poetic Vo-cabulary," *PMLA* 72 (March 1957) 233.

Chapter 8

139 By today's standards: *Amh Acad* 100; Leyda's notes of minutes of trustees of Amherst Academy, 9-6-1838, MTB Papers, box 104 [the minutes, at one time in the Hitchcock Memorial Room, Amherst College, have eluded me]; *Catalogue of the Trustees, Instructors, and Students of Amherst Academy. For the Year Ending July 1841* (Amherst: Adams, 1841) 11, J. This and catalogs for years ending July 1842, August 1843, and August 1847, all at J, are cited without further notice.

140 Emily was fortunate: *Amh Acad* 74–75, 96; *Catalogue of Amherst Female Seminary* (Amherst: Adams, 1835), J; Harriet Martineau, *Retrospect of Western Travel* (New York: Haskell House, 1969), 84–85. Since the report dates from 1835, the girls could not have come from Amherst Academy, as assumed by Sewall 347.

140 Latin was taught: EH Jr, Notebook "B+," 43–46, Doc Hitch 7:26; *Let* 7.

140 The catalog for 1840–41: J. S. Everett's tuition receipt for term ending 11-3-1841, H (the term began 8-18 [*Hampshire Gazette* 7-20-1841]); *Let* 7; "Root" 11. ED's long illness and many absences from September 1845 to December 1846 may have ended

Latin for her. When Vin resumed the language in 1848–1849 (catalog for that year, J), she got as far as Virgil (JL to Laura Baker, 3-30-1857, Lyman Papers 2:26).

141 A surviving school edition: J. G. Cooper, ed., *Publii Virgilii Maronis Opera, or the Works of Virgil* (New York: White, 1838) 615, flyleaf, A; Grace E. Perkinson, *Latin Scholars at the Academy: A Monograph on an Emily Dickinson Textbook* (Deer Isle, Me.: Skyefield Press, 1986); *Sweetser* 113; Bliss 61; "Root" 15, 11; *Let* 17; William Cowper, *The Task*, 2:1. The catalogs that put ED in Classical (1841–1842, 1842–1843) have Abby in English, while that for 1846–1847 reverses their curricular placements. There are no catalogs for 1845, the year ED and Abby studied closely together.

141 Lois A. Cuddy: "The Latin Imprint on Emily Dickinson's Poetry: Theory and Practice," *American Literature* 50 (March 1978) 75, 82.

142 Fr1365: Text from *The Poems of Emily Dickinson: Reading Edition*, R. W. Franklin, ed. (Cambridge: Belknap Press of Harvard University Press, 1999).

142 Emily probably studied: *Let* 7, 45; "Root" 11–12, 32. The oratory text was Ebenezer Porter's *The Rhetorical Reader, Consisting of Instructions for Regulating the Voice*, which employed certain notations to guide speakers. An acute accent placed over an emphasized word stood for a "rising inflection"; a grave accent, for a "falling" one. Edith Perry Stamm Wylder argued in *The Last Face: Emily Dickinson's Manuscripts* (Albuquerque: University of New Mexico Press, 1971) that ED's dashes and dash-like marks derived from these accents. One reason the argument is unconvincing is that accents placed above words cannot be equated with dashes placed after them. At the time, educated Americans often used dashes instead of standard punctuation. ED carried this widespread custom to an idiosyncratic extreme.

142 One of the school's: George Howland, *Practical Hints for the Teachers of Public Schools* (New York: Appleton, 1898) 84; Hiroko Uno, "Geology in Emily Dickinson's Poetry," *Memoirs of Faculty of Education, Shiga University* 48:2 (1998) 83–92.

143 Hitchcock's great point: Even though Hitchcock was not on the Amherst Academy faculty, he forms the centerpiece of Sewall's discussion of ED's schooling (342–57); see also Jones 311–13. On science texts, see Lowenberg; on the impact of science, Hiroko Uno's "Geology" and "Optical Instruments and 'Compound Vision' in Emily Dickinson's Poetry," *Studies in English Literature* (Japan) 64:2 (January 1988) 227–43.

143 Virtually all academy textbooks: Jones 304, 308; Mary H. Jones to Emma Willard, 9-18-1843, 6-16-1848, Willard Papers.

144 Edward on prudential committee: *Amh Acad* 98.

144 During Emily's first three years: EH Jr, Notebook "B+," 37, Doc Hitch 7:26; Harriet W. Fowler to Eliza W. Jones, 12-27-[1841], FF Papers, box 8. Here and below, teachers are identified primarily from annual catalogs and notices in *Hampshire Gazette* 8-26-, 11-18-1840; 2-17-, 7-20-, 11-9-1841; 4-5-, 7-26-, 11-8-1842.

145 "distinguished reputation": *Hampshire Gazette* 2-17-1841.

145 Jennette P. Dickinson: *Desc* 469.

145 Clearly, the dominant: Smith 409; *Andover* 76. Hunt's husband, pastor of Amherst's small North Church, died in 1837.

145 Hunt's career during Emily's: *Hampshire Gazette* 7-27-1841 (cf. *Amh Acad* 104); EH Jr, Notebook "B+," 37, Doc Hitch 7:26; Cooke 36-37; DWVF to HHJ, 10-23-1842, 5-[8]-1843 (tr), HHJ Papers 2:1; *Let* 17.

146 With Hunt's departure: *Amh Acad* 105.

146 Elizabeth C. Adams: Lis [Elizabeth B. Tyler] to EEF, Sunday, Nov. 1843, EFF Papers, box 1; *Hampshire Gazette* 2-13-, 8-20-1844. Adams is "Betsey" (b. 1810) in *Vital Records of Conway* (Boston: NEHGS, 1943) 9, and *Manual of the Congregational Church Conway Mass* (Springfield, Mass.: 1870) 12. She was forty in the 1850 federal census for Conway, MA, family 309. In Syracuse, she and her mother probably resided with brother Elisha Clark Adams ("Census of Onondaga County for 1840," Newton E. King, comp., Onondaga County Historical Society, Syracuse, New York). *Early Records of the First Presbyterian Church of Syracuse,* A. J. Northrup, ed. (Syracuse: Genealogical Society of Central New York, 1902) 30, lists as a member "Elizabeth Adams, July 5 [1840], by letter from Congregational Church, Conway, Mass." Adams's teaching career before moving back to Massachusetts is documented by clippings from 1840 to 1842 in the Syracuse Academy file, Onondaga County Historical Society.

146 Jeremiah Taylor: FHB to LMB, 11-13-1844, Jeremiah Taylor to LMB, 4-2-1844, Bolt 5:4.

146 Lyman Coleman: Kellogg 6; Lyman Coleman, *Farewell Sermon* (Belchertown, Mass.: 1832), Stone House Museum, Belchertown; Lyman Coleman to Samuel Miller, Feb. 1844, Samuel Miller Papers, box 5, Princeton University Special Collections. See also *DAB* 2:293-94; Lyman Coleman, *Genealogy of the Lyman Family* (Albany: Munsell, 1872) 344–45; *Amh Rec* 3-29-1882.

147 "to dispense with a female": *Amh Acad* 107.

147 "assisted by a young Lady": *HFE* 3-24-1845.

147 Still, Emily was not inclined: "Root" 11; *Let* 16.

147 But Coleman was too distracted: Amherst College catalogs for 1844–1845, 1845–1846, A; *Amh Acad* 108; JL to Timothy Lyman, 3-12-1846, Lyman Papers, box 1. Rumored to be joining David Pratt's Edgehill School in Princeton, Coleman instead became professor of German at the College of New Jersey 1847–1849. See Leyda 1:106; John Frelinghuysen Hageman, *History of Princeton* (Philadelphia: Lippincott, 1879) 2:221–23, 285.

147 Amherst's academy had never: Bill Book, Class Graduating 1846, Schaffer Library, Union College; *HFE* 4-17-1846; "Root" 21.

147 footnote 2: Z59 Papers of Jefferson College, 20:155, Mississippi Dept. of Archives and History.

148 Three striking facts: First six annual catalogs of Pittsfield Young Ladies' Institute, pub. 1842–1847, Berkshire Athenaeum, Pittsfield; Jeremiah Taylor to LMB, 11-9-1844, Bolt 5:4 (Sarah Ferry's transfer); "Root" 17; *Let* 30; Springfield directory for 1846, 89, MA State Lib. Bliss (62) has Abby Wood attending school in Pittsfield, but her name doesn't appear in the first six Institute catalogs. Johnson says Harriet and Sarah attended "a school for girls in Pittsfield" (*Let* 26), but the institute's early catalogs don't record Harriet, and the Sarah A. Tracy in the first two catalogs was someone else. See *EDE* (Tice) 291.

148 The Dickinsons' real and imaginary: "Root" 16, 17.

148 longest forced absence: "Root" 14, 17, 22; *Let* 36; *HFE* 4-17-, 11-12-1846.

149 Adams was still preceptress: Charles S. Pease, *History of Conway* (Springfield, Mass.: Springfield Printing and Binding Co., 1917) 278; *HFE* 2-11-1847 (term began March 3); *Let* 45; Smith 795.

150 When Jesse Andrews left: "Root" 22. Humphrey was appointed principal between the 4-17-1846 *HFE* notice and Olivia Coleman's letter calling him "the great man of the Academy" (to EFF, 6-[23-1846], EFF Papers, box 3, gen. corr. n.d.).

150   Although she had said this: "Root" 20; *Let* 45; EdD to Alfred Norcross, 2-19-1847, J; *Let* 60.

150   Dickinson and Humphrey shared: Heman Humphrey, certificate of withdrawal for Leonard Humphrey, 8-16-1843, ED Collection–Vertical File–Humphrey, Leonard, J; "Root" 26. Humphrey's fraternity, to which WAD belonged, wore mourning for thirty days (Memorial of Leonard Humphrey, 1-14-1851, Ibid, J). Henry Boynton Smith lamented him as "so full of life and thought and promise . . . the foremost man among the late graduates" (Elizabeth L. Smith, ed., *Henry Boynton Smith. His Life and Work* [New York: Armstrong, 1881] 162).

150   "Oh! I do love": *Let* 38, 404.

151   "it is my nature": "Root" 20.

151   Although we will always: "Root" 11, 21; *Let* 17, 46.

152   The other teacher who recognized: Daniel T. Fiske to MLT, 2-6-1894, ED Todd 346, A (published in *Brocades* 253); "Root" 32; *Let* 928 (PF115, punctuated as in ED877 A).

152   footnote 3: *Congregational Year-Book* (1904) 24.

152   One reason her frailty: "A Lecture on *Physical Education*," ca. 1841, Daniel T. Fiske Papers, Franklin Trask Lib., Andover Newton Theological School.

153   "already gasping": *Let* 16 [corrected against fMS Am 1118.4 (L55), H].

154   Herbarium: In dealing with this collection (H), I have had to rely on Edward L. Davis's species list as corrected by Ray Angelo (H), photos of the pages (H), and a brief inspection of the cover and p. 1 (which seems to have erasures). The herbarium has not been thoroughly studied.

154   Although it isn't known: EdD to END, 6-7-1829, H; *Let* 7; "Root" 10–11.

155   The textbook in use: Academy catalogs for years ending July 1841, July 1842, August 1843; Emanuel D. Rudolph, "Almira Hart Lincoln Phelps (1793–1884) and the Spread of Botany in Nineteenth Century America," *American Journal of Botany* 71(8) (1984) 1162; Ruth Galpin, "Mrs. Almira Hart Lincoln Phelps" (1914), Emma Willard School Lib; *HFE* 3-24-1845.

155   The author of several: Almira H. Lincoln Phelps, *Familiar Lectures on Botany* (New York: Huntington & Savage, 1845) 14, 13; Amos Eaton, *Manual of Botany, for North America* (Albany: Steele, 1836) 8.

155   Emily followed Eaton's advice: ED's herbarium, 20, 26, 23, 33, 40, 46, 30, H.

156   An early poem makes fun: "Mrs. Phelps continued for pedagogical reasons to use the formula of introducing plant classification using the Linnaean system, long after others had abandoned it" (Rudolph, "Almira Hart Lincoln Phelps," 1164).

156   One aspect of: *Let* 567, 928–29, 552–53; ED's herbarium, 17, 19, H; Lawrence Newcomb, *Newcomb's Wildflower Guide* (Boston: Little, Brown, 1977). A second and unnamed *fimbriata* (?) is on 27.

157   In later years: *Let* 588 (ED had earlier given TWH "a Daphne odora," 519), 829, 568 (also 510), 740; TWH, "The Procession of the Flowers," *Atlantic Monthly* 10 (Dec. 1862) 655; Allen 70. See also Paula Bennett, *Emily Dickinson: Woman Poet* (Iowa City: University of Iowa Press, 1990).

157   footnote 4: Robert L. Gonsor, "Nature, Science and Emily Dickinson" (M.A. thesis, University of Massachusetts–Amherst, 1961) 36.

158   "When Flowers annually died": *Let* 573.

158   footnote 5: *Let* 574.

158   Chances are: *Let* 36; Reid 506; *Let* (1894) 126–27. In spring 1848, ED gathered

flowers on restorative walks in Amherst and South Hadley ("Root" 25). Some specimens may date from then.

158   Since many wild plants: *Let* (1894) 126–27; Allen 71; Edward Hitchcock, *Catalogue of Plants . . . in the Vicinity of Amherst College* (Amherst: Adams, 1829); ED's herbarium, 16, 25, 10, 20, 61, H. For one of the few treatments of ED's poetic use of a given species (fringed gentian), see Mary Loeffelholz, "Corollas of Autumn: Reading Franklin's Dickinson," *EDJ* 8.2 (1999) 59–69.

159   "the love of native": Phelps, *Familiar Lectures,* 31.

159   As for the fear: *Let* 415; *FF* 27.

159   footnote 7: *Let* 281.

161   Having a taste: "Root" 9; *Let* 17; "Root" 21.

162   What Emily had to say: "Root" 11.

162   But there were times: "Root" 8; *Let* 28.

163   In poetry, Emily's early: *Let* 37, 39; "Root" 21, 15.

163   footnote 8: *Let 35;* Florence Vane, "Are We Almost There? a Touching Ballad" (Boston: Ditson, 1845), BPL.

163   The girl's trip-wire: *Let* (1894) 127–28; Amherst College catalogs for 1842–1843, 1843–1844, 1844–1845; obituaries of Spofford '40, Alumni/ae Biographical Files, A.

164   However, it was prose: "Root" 7.

164   Amherst Academy stimulated: O. J. Jonas[?] to Lucy Root, 12-1-1838 (ts), MTB Papers 106:166; *Let* (1894) 128–29, 35. The last issue of *Forest Leaves* EFF recalled seeing was at the Maplewood Institute, where "they started a similar paper." The detail rings true, Maplewood being the later name of the Pittsfield Institute to which Fanny Montague transferred, evidently carrying the idea for the student paper. An account of her appears in Margie H. Luckett, ed., *Maryland Women* (Baltimore, 1931) 450–56.

164   footnote 9: *Let* (1894) 129.

165   described at age fourteen: "Root" 16.

Chapter 9

167   In 1846 Emily confided: *Let* 27, 30.

168   Little is known about: *Let* 31. Jacob Holt professed faith 1-2-1842, after the 1841 revival. If that was the period of ED's conversion, we would have a basis for her obscure friendship with Holt, and also her copying a poem of his into her Bible after he died in 1848. Another possible date for her conversion is summer 1842, when religion was "the only topic of conversation" at college (Timothy Lyman to JL, 6-18-1842, Lyman Papers, box 1) and some of ED's older acquaintances, including EFF, were saved. First #3; *Let* 52, 53, 57, 64; *HFE* 5-18-, 6-8-1848; Leyda 1:liv; Smith 346, 389; Records #2, 1826–1891, 11-6-1842, Amh Coll Ch.

168   This brief taste: First #3; *Let* 27–28. Among many discussions of ED's Calvinist experience, see *Capsule* 20; Regina Siegfried, "Conspicuous by Her Absence: Amherst's Religious Tradition and Emily Dickinson's Own Growth in Faith" (dissertation, St. Louis University, 1982); Jane Donahue Eberwein, " 'Graphicer for Grace': Emily Dickinson's Calvinist Language," *Studies in Puritan American Spirituality* 1 (1990) 170–201.

168   footnote 1: Heman Humphrey, *Revival Conversations* (Boston: Samuel N. Dickinson, 1844) 9, 12, 13.

169   "no Verse in the Bible": *Let* 751.

169 "I have just seen": "Root" 17; *Let* 26.

169 But of course some deaths: *Let* (1931) 441.

170 At the time, careful attention: Harriet W. Fowler to Eliza M. Judkins, 10-1-1842,
FF Papers, box 3. Judkins had taught at Amherst Academy the previous year.

170 "People *always* are dying": Mary Shepard to Hannah Terry, 9-15-1843, Bolt 5:3. Cf.
Let 16, 38.

170 Deborah Fiske, the gifted: EH Jr, Notebook "B+," 13, Doc Hitch 7:26; DWVF to
Harriet W. Fowler, n.d., FF Papers, box 8; DWVF to Nathan Fiske, "Wed. aft," [8-
2-1843], Friday afternoon [8-4-1843], HHJ Papers 1:6; Martha V. Hooker to
DWVF, 11-2-1843, HHJ Papers 2:2; diary of Nathan Fiske, 5-29-1844, pp. 101,
110–12, HHJ Papers 8:3; DWVF to END, [12-25-1843], H.

170 Emily probably attended: Heman Humphrey, *The Woman That Feareth the Lord. A
Discourse Delivered at the Funeral of Mrs. D. W. V. Fiske, February 21, 1844* (Amherst:
Adams, 1844) 11, 38–39, 22, 34. END's copy is at *AC8 H8855 844w, H.

171 Next came: [Henry Jones, ed.], *Memorials of Mrs. Harriet W. Fowler . . . Deceased
March 30, 1844* (printed 1845) 14, 40, 10, 11, Gordon L. Ford's copy, FF Papers,
box 8; Harriet W. Fowler to Eliza W. Jones, 2-[8]-1839, FF Papers, box 8; [Edward
Hitchcock], obituary, *New-York Observer* 22 (4-13-1844) 59 (authorship acknowledged *Remin* 382); Jeremiah Taylor to LMB, 4-2-1844, Bolt 5:4.

171 Ann and Helen Fiske: "N.P.W." to EFF, 11-16-[1844], EFF Papers 3:3; "Root" 15.

172 In April came the: *EDE* (Tice) 146; Sylvester Judd, *History of Hadley* (Northampton: Metcalf, 1863), 488; *Let* 32; Amherst Vital Records, J. Sophia was born 6-14-
1828 (Smith 388).

172 On the night of: Lucius Boltwood to LMB, 4-28-1844 (misdated 4-24 in Leyda
1:85), Bolt 5:4; *Let* 32.

173 Letting herself be led away: *Let* 32.

173 But there was one more: *Hampshire Gazette* 7-2-1844; Amherst Vital Records, J;
Smith 712–13.

174 In a letter: *Let* 583, 737; Amherst–Second Church–Records–1809–1845, pp. 29,
105, J. The other possibility is Dr. William F. Sellon's death from "erysipelas in the
head." Because he gave no "evidence of being prepared," his death was "a melancholy one" (DWVF to Elizabeth G. Terry, 1-12-1843, HHJ Papers 2:3).

175 So Independent She Don't: Unless otherwise identified, all quotations in this section are from END and/or EdD to ED, Sunday [5-19-1844], 5-24-1844, Monday
[5-27-1844], 6-4-1844, H. Though END is known to have written ED in later
years—e.g., fall 1847 (*Let* 51)—these are her last letters to have survived.

176 "your Bond to your Brother": MLT/ED 746. Printer's copy is quoted for this, the
one missing letter (L827) to the Clark brothers.

176 Another of Father's recommendations: EdD to END, 9-7-1835, H; EdD, "The importance of providing an Asylum," student essays, H.

177 She returned home: *Let* 39; "Root" 32-33; *Let* (1894) 131.

177 footnote 3: *Let* 198.

177 The girl was Abiah: *Let* 39; James Pierce Root, *Root Genealogical Records* (New
York: Root, 1870) 423; "Root" 9, 11. Abiah's letters to ED are gone, but some Root
family letters are preserved at *93M-224, H. On MLT's finding Abiah as an old
woman, see *Let* (1931) xv–xvi. On the editing of ED's letters to Abiah, see MLT's
diary, Nov. 1892, MLT Papers 40:15; *Brocades* 206–209; "Root" 1–6.

178 "How happy we all": "Root" 11; *Let* (1894) 131; *Home* 413.

178 footnote 4: EdD to ED, 6-4-1844, H; *Hampshire Gazette* 5-14-, 8-20-1844; "Root" 22.

178 "sat together in school": Henry Wadsworth Longfellow, *Kavanagh, A Tale* (Boston: Ticknor, Reed, and Fields, 1849) 39, Dickinson family copy at Za L860 849b, copy 3, Y-BRBL. The novel interpreted the friendship in the usual way, as practice for marriage.

178 "the 'five' ": *Let* 32.

179 "making fun," "as consistent," "alias Virgil": "Root" 7.

179 footnote 5: Mary Shepard to Hannah Terry, 9-15-1843, Hannah Terry to Mary Shepard, 9-12-[1835], Bolt 5:3, 4:7.

179 The letters in which: *Let* 17 (corrected against fMS Am 1118.4 [L55], H), 46. Cody, believing the "five" lasted for years, concluded that ED's affection was "symptomatic of an abnormally prolonged period of sexual latency" (105, 109).

179 footnote 6: Smith 284; Leyda 1:195, 208; *Home* 221; Amherst Academy catalogs for fall 1848 and year ending August 1849, J.

180 Also painful was the impact: "Root" 18; *Let* 28.

180 Since Abiah was not yet: *Let* 28.

180 By the time Emily wrote: *Let* 30–31. Sarah S. Tracy, daughter of a minister, was praised at her death as "foremost in all the good works" of the Washington Street Congregational Church (*Beverly Times* 7-18-1916).

180 There are indications: *Let* 37–38, 98.

181 "Did we not find": *Let* 923.

181 "Why did you not come back": *Let* 71.

182 "rough & uncultivated manners": *Let* 55.

182 "most of the girls," "Ladys Sewing": "Root" 18.

182 The society that perhaps meant: *Let* 55, 50, 475.

182 We find a faint trace: John Pendleton Kennedy, *Swallow Barn* (Philadelphia: Carey & Lea, 1832) 2:153, EDR 2.4.19; Leyda 1:90. I am unable to attribute the book's other penciled marginalia.

183 Our best insights: Ebenezer W. Bullard to Joseph Bullard, 1-15-1829, Beecher Family Papers 17:671, Y-MSSA; *Let* 56; *HFE* 8-6-1846, 8-5-1847. On the Governor's Council, see 1820 MA Constitution, Part II, Chap. II, Sect. III; Nathaniel P. Banks, "Address to the Council . . . upon the organization of the executive council," *Acts and Resolves* (Boston: State Printer, 1859) 575; William L. Reed, "The Governor's Council," Pam 353.9M3 G72g 194-B, MA State Lib.

183 footnote 7: Matt 4:6; Luke 4:10; *Let* 774, 865, 877, 887; *Lyman Let* 52.

184 The rule at home: EdD to Alfred Norcross, 12-9-1846, J; JL to Timothy Lyman, 3-12-, 4-7-1846, Lyman Papers, box 1; Governor's Council, 1846, Minutes, MA Arch. Amherst's sixteen-week term, commencing 12-10-1845 (*HFE* 11-21-1845), would have ended 3-31-1846. In *Lyman Let* 6–7, Sewall assigns a passage from JL's key 4-7-1846 letter to 2-13-1844, producing serious distortions in chronology and his relations with the Dickinson children.

184 The young man who now: Moseley 261; JL to Timothy Lyman, 3-12-1846, Lyman Papers, box 1; JL to Laura Baker, 3-15-1858, Lyman Papers 2:37. The 1845–1846 Williston catalog has JL attending that year, which in his case means summer term, beginning 5-27-1846.

185 There was none of this: JL to Laura Baker, 7-30-[1856] (2:23), JL to mother, 10-11-1849 (box 1), JL to Timothy Lyman, 12-20-1848 (box 1), Lyman Papers.

185 Unlike Abiah: JL to Timothy Lyman, [Feb. or early March 1849], Lyman Papers 1:11. Though Sewall makes this an "early letter" from Yale (*Lyman Let* 58), it dates from JL's junior year. The reply, admitting "some exceptions" to female shallowness (Timothy Lyman to JL, 3-13-1849, 1:12) gives the approximate date.

185 Proud of his conquests: "Bon" [Daniel Bonbright?] to JL, 1-23-1851, Lyman Papers, box 1.

186 After the Civil War: JL/ED. Trying to date the passage, Sewall reasoned in *Lyman Let* 78–79 that, while the "trivial" subject points to girlhood, the "firm" and accurate language is "far from girlish." I would guess that "calix" is a trace of ED's girlhood interest in botany. Certainly, no later letter is as exact as one from 1848 listing spring flowers—"trailing arbutus, adder's tongue, yellow violets, liver leaf, blood root" ("Root" 25).

187 early daguerreotype: Mary Elizabeth Kromer Bernhard, "Lost and Found: Emily Dickinson's Unknown Daguerreotypist," *New England Quarterly* 72 (Dec. 1999) 594–601; EdD to Alfred Norcross, 2-10-, 2-19-1847, J; *Let* 411; *World.* The story of the daguerreotype's accidental preservation is told by Bernhard in a review of *World* in *New England Quarterly* 64 (June 1991) 332–34.

188 footnote 8: *Let* 415.

Chapter 10

191 "after this independent": MW to WDW, 1-29-[1875], WDW Papers 22:582.

191 This statement helps explain: *Eleventh Annual Catalogue of the Mount Holyoke Female Seminary* (Amherst: Adams, 1848); *Let* 54.

192 Mount Holyoke toughened: *Let* 59, 54, 49; MHJL 3-3-1848.

192 footnote 1: Noah Webster, *An American Dictionary of the English Language* (Amherst: Adams, 1844) 2:813.

193 letters Dickinson sent from school: ED's letters to others—Mary Warner, Abby Wood, Jacob Holt, EDC, great-uncle Zebina Montague (*Let* 51-52, 70)—have not survived.

193 "enjoyed the solitude finely": *Let* 48.

193 "found them about": *Let* 54.

193 "My good angel only waits": *Let* 63.

193 Her roommate was: *One Hundred Year Biographical Directory of Mount Holyoke College 1837–1937* (South Hadley, Mass.: Alumnae Assoc., 1937); Mary Lyon to Susanna Fitch, 9-17-1848, ML Coll. Having inherited a substantial fraction of JN's large estate, ELN also received financial help from Stearns (Hampden Co. Probate Court, Estate of JN [Case 8347], Guardianship of ELN [Case 8345]). Her Ohio teaching stint, perhaps at Granville Female Academy (Ackmann 78), was quite brief, starting after February 1849 (Sarah Jane Anderson to HP, 2-15-1849, Alumnae) and ending before 10-27-1850 (Leyda's notes of Eudocia Flynt's diaries, MTB Papers, box 104).

194 footnote 2: LNN to END, 4-12-1835, H.

194 In character, Cousin Emily: ELN to HP, 12-25-1846, Alumnae; Circular headed "Candidates for Mount Holyoke Female Seminary" on which Mary Lyon wrote a letter in 1847, ML Coll; *Let* 54, 61.

194 This cousin's presence: *Let* 53, 55.

194 Homesickness notwithstanding: *Let* 52, 54, 55.

195 In December, having passed: *Let* 57, 59, 54; "Root" 26; MHJL 5-17-, 2-22-1848.

Edward Hitchcock regularly lectured on physiology at Mount Holyoke with the aid of a "mannekin," but he is not mentioned in MHJL for 1847–1848.

195 "boarding school": "Root" 24.

195 As at Amherst: *Let* 60; Turner 7; MCW to Fidelia Fiske, 3-9-1848, MCW Papers.

195 As the mid-year exams: *Let* 60, 51 (punctuated as in ED552 A).

196 "You know Sarah": "Root" 21.

197 Her dream was conservative: Rufus Anderson, *An Address, Delivered in South Hadley* (Boston: Perkins & Marvin, 1839) 6.

197 As practical and tireless: HP to Mary Lyon, 5-11-1837, AP Papers; "Evangel" 394–395. On Mount Holyoke's Edwardsianism, see Conforti, chap. 4.

197 On the surface: "Evangel" 397–398.

198 It was never quite clear: Charles Hammond to SCB, 11-2-1846, SCB Papers 4:93; HP to Mary Lyon, 4-4-1837, AP Papers.

198 For Porter as for Lyon: Heman Humphrey, *The Shining Path. A Sermon . . . at the Funeral of Miss Mary Lyon* (Northampton: Metcalf, 1849) 14; Elizabeth Alden Green, *Mary Lyon and Mount Holyoke: Opening the Gates* (Hanover, N.H.: University Press of New England, 1979) 246–47.

198 Such rooms were Porter's: HP to Mary Lyon, "Tuesday morn" [1842], AP Papers.

199 This passage suggests: MHJL 12-23-1847, 1-4-1848.

199 Mount Holyoke's teachers kept: MHJL 10-2-1847.

199 Frequent meetings were convened: MHJL 10-11-, 10-14-, 10-18-1847.

200 The seminary had scores: MHJL 7-15-1848, 11-4-1847.

200 Judging from the comprehensive: *Let* 54–55.

200 A third of Emily's: *Let* 58–60. The sentences quoted last were written sideways on the top of p. 1 (fMS Am 1118.4 [L59], H).

201 The ordeal began: MHJL 12-20-1847. In February, informing WAD of the Reverend Belden's rumored "call to settle" in South Hadley, ED wrote, "if he accepts, I hope it will, WILL not be until my year is out" (*Let* 64). Her animosity was spurred not only by his role in the revival and by her church's longstanding disdain for Amherst's East Parish, but (probably) by the memory of his sermon at Martha Dwight Strong's funeral. In Mary Shepard's eyes, Belden was "good—but uncultivated" (Leyda 1:89).

201 In 1924 Martha Dickinson Bianchi: *LL* 26; Sydney R. McLean, "Emily Dickinson at Mount Holyoke," *New England Quarterly* 7 (March 1934) 32–35; Leyda 1:136; Turner 7; "Root" 25.

201 footnote 3: Journal of Harriette A. Wells, 12-25-1845, MH; MHJL 12-25-1847; "Root" 18; *Let* 46.

202 As the twenty-fourth approached: MHJL 12-21-, 12-23-1847.

202 On Christmas Eve: MHJL 12-24-1847.

202 During Porter's first four days: MHJL 12-27-1847; Sarah Jane Anderson to HP, 1-17-1848, Alumnae.

202 The first to: MHJL, 1-11-1848; ELN to HP, 1-11-1848, Alumnae.

203 "intended to write": ibid.

203 Six days later: Sarah Jane Anderson to HP, 1-17-1848, Alumnae; *Let* 473.

203 The previous school year: ELN to HP, 12-25-1846, Alumnae; Sarah Jane Anderson to HP, 1-17-1848, Alumnae; MCW to HP, [Feb. 1848] (dated by Jason Whitman's death in Lexington 1-25-1848 [MVR-Deaths 33:29]), MCW Papers.

204 On the same day: MCW to HP, [1-17-1848], MCW Papers; "Root" 25. McLean's 1934 article, "Emily Dickinson at Mount Holyoke," accepted MCW's rumor and

concluded ED "caught at" (39) some kind of Christian faith. McLean did not cite and may not have been aware of the two passages (*Let* 60; "Root" 25) disclosing the poet's unconverted state. The former was still unpublished; the latter had appeared as an undated fragment in *Let* (1931) 28 and was therefore useless.

204   "This term is the longest": *Let* 59. See also 62.

205   In May, after the revival: "Root" 25.

205   When the long first term: *Let* 62–63.

206   a sparkling mime: *Home* 90.

206   In February she received: *Let* 62 (punctuated as in ED555 A); "Root" 11; *Let* 64.

206   All we have: Frederick J. Bliss to Claribel Smith, 3-17-1913, MTB Papers 85:265; *Let* 63.

207   Her caution is evident: *Let* 57 (cf. 63); Amherst College Exhibition program, 4-1-1848, H; *Let* 68; MHJL 5-30-1848.

207   footnote 4: *Let* 64; MCW to HP, [2-19-1848?], MCW Papers.

207   Austin's one surviving: *Home* 82–83. WAD separated the sentences with a passage of his own but indicated they had been contiguous.

208   footnote 5: *Var* 1153-54.

208   If the teacher: MHJL 12-14-1847, 4-24-, 5-24-, 5-25-1848.

209   The letter Emily sent: *Let* 68 (punctuated as in ED556 A); MHJL 4-26-1848. ED's recuperative period at home began 3-25 and ended 5-12, when students returned for Mount Holyoke's third term ("Root" 23-24; MHJL 3-17-, 5-12-1848).

209   footnote 6: *Eleventh Annual Catalogue* 15; *Let* 69.

209   Another onerous rule: EH Jr, Notebook "A," Doc Hitch 7:22; *Let* 69–70.

211   social activism: See Miller 166–67. Erkkila's important essay interpreting ED as a product of her class, "Emily Dickinson and Class," *American Literary History* 4 (spring 1992) 1–27, pays no attention, strangely enough, to what its key word meant to *her*.

211   Emilie Led Off in Triumph: All ED quotes are from "Root" 23–26.

211   *The Princess:* Reviewed in *HFE* 3-30-1848. For Sue's response to Tennyson's poem, see Chap. 12.

212   footnote 7: *Let* 162–63; *Home* 54.

Chapter 11

213   She got a taste: *Catalogue of the Officers and Members of Ipswich Female Seminary, for the Year Ending Nov. 12, 1850* (Boston: Damrell & Moore, 1850) 4, 9, 10, Ipswich Public Lib.; *HFE* 3-8-, 3-15-1850 (facsimile in Leyda 1:170); *Let* 97–99.

214   her friend Jane Humphrey: *HFE* 8-11-1848, 2-9-, 5-18-, 8-10-1849; Amherst Academy catalogs for fall 1848 and for year ending August 1849, J; *Let* 196.

214   When Abiah came back: For ED's relations with Abiah Root, see *Let* 85; "Root" 25.

215   footnote 1: *Catalogue of the Alpha Delta Phi* (Utica: Curtiss & Childs, 1870) 38–42; Hammond 304.

215   ascent of Mount Holyoke: Summit 10-9-[1849].

215   *"Candy Pulling!!":* Fr1389; facsimile of invitation in Leyda 1:167.

215   Between Emily and the more: *Let* 75, 85, 96; *Bio Rec* 56, 59; ED886 A. The sincere-spite note has been mistakenly grouped with ED's aphoristic scraps (*Let* 929).

216   "We are anticipating": Dated 12-20 in *Lyman Let* 12, the letter can only have been written in 1848: in 1846 WAD didn't room with Thompson; in 1847 ED wasn't

home; in 1849 Vin wasn't in "Boston, spending a few weeks," but at Ipswich Seminary.

216 Elbridge Gridley Bowdoin: Leyda 1:xxxi; *Let* (1894) 137. Bowdoin joined the First Parish between 1840 and 1858 (First #4, 9) but his name is absent from the church roll (First #3).

216 Benjamin Franklin Newton: Worcester Vital Statistics 1719–1890, microfiche #11, 118, AAS; Ermina Newton Leonard, *Newton Genealogy* (De Pere, Wisc.: Bernard Ammidon Leonard, 1915) 133; *This Was a Poet* 85–86; First Unitarian Church, Worcester, Octavo #9, 3-24-1853, AAS; Church of the Unity, Worcester, Octavo #2 and Folio #2, AAS. Whicher's *This Was a Poet* and "Emily Dickinson's Earliest Friend," *American Literature* 6 (March 1934) 3–17, remain the primary discussions of Newton. Whicher's one misstep, traceable to MDB's faulty dating in *FF* 177–81, was identifying Newton as ED's "beautiful, new, friend" in 1852 (*Let* 183).

216 "a social partition line": Mer 1:345

216 Writing to a stranger: *Let* 282, 52. Others who studied law with EdD were Ithamar F. Conkey, James W. Boyden, Baalis and John E. Sanford (later speaker of the Massachusetts House), John Milton Emerson, William Howland, and WAD. Josiah G. Holland, *History of Western Massachusetts* (Springfield, Mass.: Bowles 1855) 2:173–74; *Bench* 2:373–74; *Let* 126, 134.

217 "All can write autographs": Tipped on endpaper of ED's copy of Emerson's *Poems* (Boston: Munroe, 1847), EDR 1.2.4. Facsimile in Leyda 1:158. ED's album does not survive.

217 "universally esteemed": William Lincoln, *History of Worcester* (Worcester, Mass.: Charles Hersey, 1862) 386.

217 Dickinson's tribute to her friend: *Let* 282; *Mercy Phil* 88.

218 It is thought: *Let* 404, 737.

218 "Eternity," "dreadful": *Let* 28.

219 familiar with "We Are Seven": *Let* 215.

219 The one book: *Let* 84. Newton's "Miscellaneous Books" were appraised at only $20. The value of his law library dropped from $20 to $10 when it was discovered that his Kent's *Commentaries* was borrowed (Schedule A). Worcester Co. RP, Papers of Administration for Benjamin F. Newton, #43070.

219 a liberating effect: For Emerson's influence on ED, see *This Was a Poet* 189–205; Gelpi, chap. 4; Karl Keller, *The Only Kangaroo among the Beauty: Emily Dickinson and America* (Baltimore: Johns Hopkins University Press, 1979), chap. 6; Joanne Feit Diehl, *Dickinson and the Romantic Imagination* (Princeton: Princeton University Press, 1981), chap. 5; McIntosh 14–20.

220 review of *Representative Men: Indicator* 2 (Feb. 1850) 214-20. The only evidence I find for Leyda's attribution of this to George H. Gould (1:167) is in *Indicator* 2:283.

221 "Ralph Waldo Emerson – whose name": *Let* 727.

221 "Your letter gave no Drunkenness": *Let* 408.

221 "My earliest friend wrote me": *Let* 551.

222 In summer 1849: *Let* 475; Rev. of *Kavanagh, Indicator* 2 (July 1849) 57 (I know of no basis for Leyda's attribution to Gould [1:157]); *Let* 648. On ED and *Kavanagh*, see Sewall 683–88.

223 The tiny but emphatic: Henry Wadsworth Longfellow, *Kavanagh, A Tale* (Boston: Ticknor, Reed, and Fields, 1849), Za L860 849b, copy 3, Y-BRBL. Marks referred

to are on pp. 39, between lines 9 and 10; 137, between lines 12 and 13; 129, line 22; 181, line 6.

223   footnote 2: ED's marks: *Kavanagh,* pp. 129, line 9; 138, between lines 22 and 23; 117, between lines 19 and 20, Y-BRBL.

223   Was she thinking: *Kavanagh* 80; *Let* 264.

223   *Picciola: Let* 75 (also 206–207). "X. B. Saintine" was the pseudonym of Joseph Xavier Boniface, whose *Picciola, the Prisoner of Fenestrella* was brought out in many editions from 1839 by Lea & Blanchard of Philadelphia. On prisons and ED, see Loeffelholz 106–111.

225   A book that engaged: *Littell's Living Age* 20 (3-17-1849) 505–507; [William G. Hammond], "Jane Eyre," *Indicator* 1 (June 1848) 29 (attribution in copy at A); Delia Torrey to Eudocia Carter Converse (Flynt), 6-1-1848, CT Misc. 23:457, Y-MSSA.

225   "If all these leaves were altars": *Let* 77 (punctuated as in ED793 A).

226   The tantalizing question: [Hammond], "Jane Eyre," 30; *SR* 1-24-1851.

226   Carlo: Allen 73; Leyda 2:21; *Jane Eyre,* chap. 30; *Indicator* 2 (Feb. 1850) 223. Another dog named Carlo is in [Donald Grant Mitchell], *Reveries of a Bachelor* (New York: Baker & Scribner, 1850) 29. Although this book appeared some months after ED's dog was named, the original magazine essay had a Carlo ("A Bachelor's Reverie," *Southern Literary Messenger* 15 [Sept. 1849] 604). There's a still earlier Carlo, a dancing dog, in chap. 18 of Dickens's *Old Curiosity Shop* (1840–41), which ED read.

226   In the copy: Charlotte Brontë, *Jane Eyre* (New York: Harper, 1864) 418, EDR 2.2.11; *Passion* 202–218; *Let* 562. Rochester's exact words: "I feel your benefits no burden, Jane" (chap. 15).

227   *Villette:* Charlotte Brontë, *Villette* (New York: Harper, 1859), EDR 2.2.14.

227   The pleasing stimulus: Mary Warner Crowell to Sue, 3-17-[1896], Bianchi Coll; *Let* 83–84.

228   Yet, even as Emily launched: *Let* 83; Leyda 1:157.

228   "Your *first* words": *Let* 93.

228   Joel Warren Norcross: Boston directories from 1849 to 1851; Joel W. Norcross, "The History and Genealogy of the Norcross Family," 2:101–102, NEHGS; Leyda 1:156; *Let* 77–81.

229   "uncontrolled," "I have no Tribunal": *Let* 409.

229   Twelve days after writing Joel: *Let* 85, 83.

230   On the whole, though: "Root" 13, 16–17; *Let* 83–84, 90.

231   letter she sent Abiah: *Let* 86–90. For a technical psychoanalytic handling of L31, see Cody 174–77. Homans's discussion of it and other spring 1850 letters seems more acute but doesn't persuade me that the "long, big shining fibre" is the redeemed snake/phallus (166–74).

232   "more affectionately than wont": "Root" 32.

232   Valentine season: *HFE* 1-30-1852; *Let* 63, 76.

233   footnote 3: *Let* 110 (punctuated as in ED795 A); Hammond 59.

233   "*curling hair*": MDB noted that in middle age ED's hair "retained its rather wavy, clustering tendency" and was "never flattened down or strained back" (*FF* 18). Maria Avery Howard remembered "red, short curls over a low brow" (quoted in Lydia Avery Coonley to MLT [copy], ED Tr65 A). But see *Brocades* 268.

233   "full of 'fun' ": *Brocades* 206. See also *Let* (1894) 125.

234   On the problematic female subject in Fr1, see Margaret Homans, " 'Oh, Vision of

Language!' Dickinson's Poems of Love and Death," *Feminist Critics Read Emily Dickinson,* Suzanne Juhasz, ed. (Bloomington: Indiana University Press, 1983) 115–17.

234 At some point: *Let* (1894) 130; "Root" 27.

234 Her other Valentine: *Indicator* 2 (Feb. 1850) 223–24.

235 footnote 4: Alice Eaton McBee II, *From Utopia to Florence: The Story of a Transcendentalist Community in Northampton, Mass. 1830–1852* (Northampton: [Smith College,] 1947) 32–33, 49, 62–63; *Obit Record* 337.

235 footnote 5: Hubbard Winslow, *Woman As She Should Be* (Boston: Carter, 1838) 24.

236 Two months later Emily sent: *Let* 95.

236 Looking back from the 1880s: [Edward Payson Crowell], *Memorial of Professor Aaron Warner* (Amherst, 1884) 49; *Indicator* 2:193, 211, 199, 223–24.

237 Van Twiller/Henry Shipley: *Indicator* 2:31, 283; Hammond 133, 169, 211, 218, 228–29; San Francisco *Alta California* 7-11-1857; William S. Tyler to Joab Tyler, 4-17-1850, Tyler Papers 2:15. Though he didn't name Shipley, Tyler went on to say he was "converted the day before the term ended." One of three Seniors who joined the college church by profession on 6-23-1850 (Book No. 1, 1826–1849, Amh Coll Ch), Shipley alone was seen as brilliant.

237 "roguish," "stolen": *Let* (1894) 129.

237 In the April letter: *Let* 95, punctuated as in fMS Am 1118.4 (L65), H. The letter's contents support Johnson's date, 4-3-1850, but the ms. appears to read "April 30. 1850."

238 Who was the Valentine's: "Memoranda relating to Beneficiaries of the Charity Fund," Amherst College: Early History 3:9, A; *Bio Rec* 61–62; *Brocades* 254–55; *Indicator* 2:30, 283; C. M. Southgate, "A Prince . . . in Israel" (clipping), Gould '50, Alumni/ae Biographical Files, A; Franklin P. Rice, *The Worcester of Eighteen Hundred and Ninety-Eight* (Worcester: Blanchard, 1899) 627–30; Ellery Bicknell Crane, *Genealogical and Personal Memoirs of Worcester County* (New York: Lewis, 1907) 3:37; Leyda 1:206–207; WAD to ED and Vin (rough notes beginning "Girls—write often") [Dec. 1853], H.

238 Writing Abiah in early May: *Let* 98; Vryling Wilder Buffum to Genevieve Taggard, 3-6-, 3-25-1930, Mary Lee Hall to Taggard, 12-2-1929, 3-7-1930, Taggard Papers.

239 "Our father": Dall; *Brocades* 319.

239 footnote 6: Dall; Mariette Jameson to JFJ, 5-16-[1886], Container 7, Jameson Papers.

239 There was definitely something: *Let* 95, 99, 282.

239 Some believe her visionary: Favoring poetic vocation are *Imagery* 6 and Sewall 391–98.

240 Vinnie's change of heart: *Home* 86, 90, 96.

241 Before this surrender: *Home* 88; *HFE* 1-10-1851; *Hist* 77.

241 With that, a revival began: *Hist Amh Coll* 341; Tyler to Tyler, 4-17-1850, A; Book No. 1, 1826–1849, Amh Coll Ch.

241 footnote 7: [Sacramento] *Themis* 12-6-1890; *HFE* 12-16-1859.

242 By then the fervor: *Let* 94; Allen 22; *HFE* 1-10-1851; FHB to LMB, 5-30-1850 (cf. Jeremiah Taylor to LMB, 11-18-1850, Bolt 6:4).

242 footnote 8: Leyda 1:178; Nellie M. Gould to George F. Whicher, 2-19-1930, Taggard Papers.

242 As was always the case: *Let* 94, 99.

243 In March or April: *Home* 98.

243 newly found . . . letter from Austin: WAD to EFF, [March or April 1850], Thomas

Cooper Library, University of South Carolina; Ezra Greenspan, "More New Dickinson Family Letters," *EDIS Bull* 8.2 (1996) 9, 23. Vin was home for spring recess
March 20–April 17 (*Home* 97).

243   Austin's description of his sister: *Let* 90. The handwriting (ms. at NYPL) is earlier
than that in ED's other letters to EFF. The "g" and "y" have a deep and relatively un-
slanted descender, rising in an unbroken loop to the right; by 1851 ED formed these
letters differently. Snow fell in Springfield early on March 1, on the nights of March
6 and 11, and on March 18 (*SR* 3-2,8,13,19-1850).

244   "How lonely this world": *Let* 94.

Chapter 12

245   As the product of a: *Lyman Let* 34; Cody 220; *Let* 241, also 211.

246   footnote 1: *Var* 53–55.

246   In her reading, Dickinson tended: *Let* 111, 126, 155.

247   quoted no poem more often: To Abiah, WAD, Sue, and EFF (*Let* 100).

247   But it is hard: *Light in the Valley* (Philadelphia: American Baptist Publication Soc.,
1852); [Matilda Anne MacKarness], "*Only*" (Boston: Munroe, 1850); MacKarness,
The House on the Rock (Boston: Munroe, 1852) 156; *Let* 195.

248   footnote 2: Georgiana Fullerton, *Lady-Bird: A Tale* (London: Moxon, 1852); WAD
to Sue (draft, #42, "I've just come in"), H.

248   Dickinson is not known: *Let* 212, also 205.

248   Another and more appealing: Craik, *Head* 19; Sally Mitchell, *Dinah Mulock Craik*
(Boston: Twayne, 1983) 31–34.

249   In April 1852: *Let* 195; Craik, *Olive* 1:113, 196–97; 2:52, 55. See the excellent discussion in *Dinah Mulock Craik* 29–31. The novelist's father, an unhinged evangelical fanatic, had deserted his family (Aleyn Lyell Reade, *The Mellards* [London:
Arden Press, 1915]).

249   The most immediately inspiring: Diary 2–22; Ik. Marvel [Donald Grant Mitchell],
Reveries of a Bachelor: or a Book of the Heart (New York: Baker & Scribner, 1850)
15–49.

249   "thought and passion": *Reveries* 56.

249   "Bachelor's Reveries" headed: WAD to Sue (draft), [Oct 13–15, 1851], H. Dated by
EdD's visit to WAD "last Wednesday" (cf. *Let* 142) and in conjunction with *Home*
186, 188.

250   Those made by Emily: *Reveries* 224, 240, 85, Za M692 850rb, copy 1, Y-BRBL.
Similar marks are on 18, 74, 77, 85, 174, 245.

250   "exquisite writing": *Let* 178.

250   The young woman's enjoyment: *Let* 144.

250   One reason Emily turned: "Root" 29; *Let* 130, 129; "Root" 31.

251   A year or two after: *Let* 178, 237–38, 161. WAD's 1851 *Dream Life*, signed by him,
is otherwise unmarked (EDR 4.4.8).

251   When Edward was in: Diary 3-27, 3-25, 12-16 (on 3-28 Beecher was to give "his
celebrated lecture on *Character*" in Northampton [*Northampton Gazette* 3-25-
1851]); *Home* 238–39; *Let* 136, 150–51.

252   On the whole: *Let* 128, 139, 148.

252   The worst thing Father did: *Home* 239, 235; *Let* 194, 147, 198.

253   jotted on her program: "Exhibition of the Eclectic Society," 11-26-1850, ED60 A.
Leyda found the program in the Alpha Delta Phi files in the old Memorabilia

Room at A (Leyda to MTB, 10-25-1951, MTB Papers 84:236). Perhaps the era-sure was made when the program was given to college archives. The first two quotes appear in [John E. Sanford], "Aaron Burr," *Indicator* 3 (Feb. 1851) 200, 201, which has "villain," not "rascal."

254 A contemporaneous letter: "Root" 28, 33; Leyda 1:226. By May 1852 the friendship had "freshened" again ("Root" 33).

254 Vinnie was given a diary: Jane Hitchcock to Vin, n.d. [1-1-1851], H.

254 The one organized group: Diary 6-10, 13; *Let* (1894) 129–30. Vin attended 3-11; 4-11; 5-30; 6-3,10,20,24; 7-8,11,15,25 (Diary).

255 Dickinson would not be: *Let* 114, 116; Diary 6-20; *Home* 149.

255 A kind of daily telegraph: *Let* 127; Diary 9-26 (Ware), 11-7 (quarrel). Vin saw Sue 1-9,17,22,25; 2-1,13,19,22,28; 3-11,13,27; 4-3,16,17,19,24,25; 5-1,3,6,13; 6-11,19,24; 7-8,12,31; 8-5,6,9,12,15,20,26; 9-1,2,4 (Diary).

255 Omitting a trip to Boston: Diary 2-20,27; 3-5,24,25; 5-8,15; 6-5,23; 8-2,12,13,25; 9-8; 10-10; 11-1; 12-16,25; *Home* 174; *Lyman Let* 18; *Let* 129–30; *HFE* 8-15-1851. ED's account of a gathering at the Havens' looks secondhand, relying on Vin's re-port (*Let* 116; Diary 6-17). I also exclude a family trip to Northampton and East-hampton 9-25.

255 footnote 3: 1850 federal census, Suffolk Co., ward 5, dwelling 833; 1851 Boston di-rectory; "Memoranda" ledger, Bowd St Ch; *Let* 80.

256 The pressure to stay: *Let* 111, 197; EdD to END, 1-21-1838, H.

256 Staying home from group: *Home* 239; *Let* 122, 200, 181, 140 (also "Root" 29), 187.

257 Emily's view: *Let* 141, 632 (punctuated as in Za Dickinson, folder 1, Y-BRBL), 160, 151; *Home* 186.

257 Dickinson could not always: *Let* 185–86.

257 footnote 4: *House Keeping* 399.

258 Such considerations: Mary Adèle Allen, "The First President's House—A Remi-niscence," *Amherst Graduates' Quarterly* (Feb. 1937) 97; Harriet W. Fowler to Wor-thington G. Chauncey, 2-11-1840, EFF to J. W. Hand, 2-16-1840, FF Papers, box 8; Lyman Coleman to EFF, 9-15-, 9-18-1847, EFF Papers; William C. Fowler to EFF, 9-29-, 10-12-1847, EFF Papers, box 4; EFF to George Eliot (draft), 1873, EFF Papers, box 3. No extant Dickinson family letter speaks of ED's school tri-umphs.

258 "seemed more sincere": *Let* 151. Leonard Humphrey thought EFF a hypocrite (Leyda 1:106).

258 Emily Fowler and Francis March: M.E.B. [Mary E. Blake] to EFF, 11-13-1850, "Aunt Laura" [Flynt] to EFF, 2-19-1852, EFF Papers, box 1; W. W. Fowler to Gor-don L. Ford, 1-4-1852, Ford to Francis A. March, 3-15-1853, GLF Papers, box 1; Mary H. Jones to Emma Willard, 3-31-1852, 12-[19]-1853, Willard Papers; Leyda 1:296; *Addresses Delivered at a Celebration in Honor of Prof. Francis A. March* (Easton, Pa.: Lafayette Press, 1895) 16. Doggett & Rode's 1851–1852 New York directory has March and Ford sharing an office at 7 Broad St.

258 "Havana – and writes encouragingly": ED585 A ("Havana" misread as "Harvard" in *Let* 180).

259 "very much to hear how Mr M": ED to EFF, Sunday [May 1852], ED72 A.

259 footnote 5: *Let* (1894) 144; *Let* 293–94; ED72 A; *Home* 239; John Lancaster, "An Emily Dickinson Discrepancy," *Newsletter of the Friends of the Amherst College Li-brary* 11 (1983) 13.

259　"dont weep, for you will": *Let* 218.

259　What Dickinson didn't know: William C. Fowler to Gordon L. Ford, 3-12-1852, GLF Papers, box 1; *Let* 193; *Home* 298; *Let* 254.

259　footnote 6: *Addresses Delivered* 15–22, 69–73.

259　eighteen times: Diary 1-23; 2-13,25; 3-6,31; 4-4,7,12; 6-13,27,30; 7-15; 8-20,21; 11-16; 12-4,6?,23,31.

259　"stay a long while": *Let* 273 (ms. at Za Dickinson, Y-BRBL). Written before Thanksgiving, L143 must be from 1852: ED would not have offered "comfort" just prior to EFF's 12-16-1853 wedding.

259　The most interesting: *Let* 184 (corrected against holograph at NYPL). The sheet is 65 mm wide and 100 mm high.

260　"was exquisitely neat": *Let* (1894) 131.

261　Vinnie's diary and Emily's letters: Diary 2-20; 3-13,17; 4-16, 7-22; *Let* 122, 123, 127, 118.

261　The trip finally: 1846 trip: *Let* 36–37; Thomas Bender, "The 'Rural' Cemetery Movement," in *Material Life in America, 1600–1860,* Robert Blair St. George, ed. (Boston: Northeastern University Press, 1988), 505–518. 1851 trip: *Let* 132, 135–36, 141; Diary, Sept. 4-22; ad for *Othello* at Boston Museum, *Boston Daily Advertiser* 9-9-1851; WAD to Sue (draft, "Sue I am perfectly disappointed"), Thursday [9-25-1851], H; *Let* 407. Particularly useful is Uno 17–57.

262　Wesselhoeft was consulted: Diary 9-18,21,23; 10-27; 11-1; 12-17,23; *Home* 175; *Let* 171–72; Norbert Hirschhorn, "Was It Tuberculosis? Another Glimpse at Emily Dickinson's Health," *New England Quarterly* 72 (March 1999) 102–118; DWVF to HHF (transcript), Wednesday [10-20-1841], HHJ Papers 2:1; James Jackson, *Letters to a Young Physician* (Boston: Phillips, Sampson, 1856) 175–76. In spite of his age, Jackson was still practicing in 1851; see James Jackson Putnam, *A Memoir of Dr. James Jackson* (Boston: Houghton, Mifflin, 1905) 371–73.

262　As for glycerine: "Glycerine" and "Glycerine Internally," *Boston Medical and Surgical Journal* 41 (8-29-1849) 86, and 53 (1-24-1856) 536; Hirschhorn 109. ED's fine skin: *Let* (1931) xix, 130; Leyda 2:475. Johnson flatly declared for dry skin (*Let* 279).

262　That fall, Edward informed: WAD to Sue (draft), [Oct. 13–15, 1851], H; *Home* 174; *Let* 143, 159, 174, 179, 192, 200, 259, 263, 271, 278–79, 281.

263　"try to get stout": "Root" 31.

263　Loring's bankruptcy: Insolvency papers for Norcross & Wood are in Suffolk County Insolvency Records, docket 1708, box 3924. The present shelf location at the State Records Center is T203G02. Access is through Archives and Records Preservation, Supreme Judicial Court, 1300 New Court House, Boston.

263　As the assessed valuation: 1839–1846 valuations of Norcross & Wood, 22 Kilby St., Ward 8, Boston, City Clerk, Archives and Records Management; Norcross & Wood insolvency papers; An Act for the Relief of Insolvent Debtors (1838); *Boston Daily Advertiser* 7-8,15,22-1851; Diary 7-10; *Let* 123–24.

263　Because of the trust: Norcross & Wood insolvency papers; Suffolk County Probate, Estate of LNN, Case 43154; *Boston Daily Advertiser* 1-9-1852.

264　Did anyone talk: *Let* 139; *Home* 168, 214, 261, 313.

264　"Affection her strength": Sue, notes on ED, H. Martha Nell Smith calls this document "Notes toward a Volume of Emily Dickinson's Writings" at jefferson.village. virginia.edu/dickinson/susan/.

265　Susan Gilbert was born: Smith 309; Francis M. Thompson, *History of Greenfield*

(Greenfield, 1904) 2:777, 1169; *Austin & Mabel* 70. MLT and MTB made much of Sue's "lordly bearing and obscure parentage to which she never referred" (*Brocades* 6).

265   footnote 7: *Obit Record,* Class of 1828; Allyn S. Kellogg, *Memorials of Elder John White and His Descendants* (Hartford: Case, Lockwood, 1860) 100; 1870 federal census, Mich., Grand Rapids, ward 3, family 143.

265   Because Susan was only: Sue to TDG, Sunday [Sept. 1850], H; SB Let #114 [3-14-1864]; Sue to TDG, 10-22-[1851], Sue to Ned Dickinson, Grand Rapids, Wednesday [5-29-1878], H; George C. D. Odell, *Annals of the New York Stage* (New York: Columbia University Press, 1938) 10:398; "Annals" 24. Sue's mother but not father joined Greenfield's Second Congregational Church (*Manual of the Second Congregational Church in Greenfield* [Greenfield: Eastman, 1858] 4).

266   Fully orphaned by her father's death: *Vital Records of Greenfield* (Boston, 1915); Amherst Academy catalog for 1846–1847, J (Geneva given as Sue's home); Utica Female Academy catalogs for 1848–1849 (Oneida County Historical Soc.) and 1849–1850 (Utica Imprints Collection, Utica Public Lib.) (both give Amherst as Sue's home); M. M. Bagg, ed., *Memorial History of Utica* (Syracuse: D. Mason, 1892) 464-65; S. E. Clarke, "An Old-Time School," *Town Topics and Current Events of the Mohawk Valley* (Nov. 1928) 11, 26; Henry Home, Lord Kames, *Elements of Criticism* (New York: Huntington & Savage, 1847), back board, EDR 2.4.17. Also inscribed in this textbook is a list of the seven "Intellectual Gems," Sue included, who were "Members of Miss Kelly's class in Kames—July 13th. 1848."

MDB's obit of Sue says she was "so good in mathematics that Prof [James] Hadley of Yale . . . who for a time gave her instruction, told her that she ought to go to Yale college" (*SR* 5-13-1913). Two decades later, improving the story, MDB claimed she had been taught by Yale's president (*FF* 144–45). In fact, Sue was taught botany and chemistry by another man, Professor James Hadley of Geneva College (Sue, "A Memoir of Dr Elizabeth Blackwell," H; Archives, Hobart and William Smith Colleges).

266   when an important new book came out: For Sue's interest in *Titan,* see SB Let #16 [1-5-1863], #33 [1-15-1863], #24 [1-16-1863], #18 [2-7-1863]. On Sue's intellectual presence for ED, see *Passion* 114–115.

266   In 1848, the year: Alfred Tennyson, *The Princess; a Medley* (Boston: Ticknor, 1848) 11, 75, 89, 30, 94, 159, EDR 3.5.21.

267   Susan was in her teens: EH Jr, Notebook "A," Doc Hitch 7:22; Diary 2-27 (also 7-17); *Let* 300; MGS to TDG, 3-12?,13-[1855], H. MGS's mention of "Dwighty" (Dwight G. Cutler, b. 5-14-1852) and an essay on Mary Wortley Montagu (*Littell's Living Age* 29 [6-14-1851] 481-96) rule out 1849 as the year (Leyda 1:156).

267   footnote 8: Mass. Vol. 46, p. 5, Dun.

267   In April 1849: Harriet M. Cutler, Mary Gilbert, MGS, and Sue to TDG and Frank Gilbert, April [1849], H. Dated by Kellogg robbery (*HFE* 4-20-1849) and George Cutler's 5-23-1849 marriage.

268   Sister Martha, with her poor: MGS to EH Jr, [11-28-1850], H; *Let* 895; EH Jr, Notebook "B+," [56], Doc Hitch 7:26; John E. Sanford to EH Jr, 9-4-1850, Doc Hitch 13:30.

The Smith family memorial, Glenwood Cemetery, Geneva, N.Y., has MGS born 4-13-1827. In federal and state censuses of 1860, 1865, and 1870, she gave her age as thirty-two, thirty-seven, and forty-two. The official census date falling in midsummer, these ages are consistent with a birth date in the second half of 1827 or first half of 1828.

268 The reason Sue was: Greenfield *Gazette and Courier* 8-5-1850; SCB to Joseph Bartlett, 7-24-1850, SCB Papers, box 9; Sue to TDG, Sunday [Sept. 1850], H. Mary had married SCB's brother-in-law, SJL, Sept 1849.

268 It was in this time: *Let* 102; Henry Wadsworth Longfellow, *Kavanagh, A Tale* (Boston: Ticknor, Reed, and Fields, 1849) 82; MGS to EH Jr, [11-28-1850], H; Sanford to EH Jr, 9-4-1850, Doc Hitch 13:30.

268 footnote 9: *Let* 101-2; Leyda 1:185; *Open Me* 7; MGS to EH Jr, [11-28-1850], Sue to TDG, 1-18-1851, H; Diary 2-27.

269 The sheltered Dickinson siblings: WAD to Sue (draft), 12-11-1850, WAD to Sue, (draft, "I have so much"), Sunday [Oct. 1851], H.

269 Before Martha left: Leyda 1:177; WAD to Sue (draft), 10-29-1850, H.

270 Meanwhile, Vinnie and Emily: *Home* 109; *Let* 100–101; *HFE* 7-19-, 8-2,23-1850.

270 footnote 10: EDC to WAD, postmarked 12-11-1850, ED946 A, and 6-30-1851, ED947 A.

270 In November the fall term: Leyda 1:183.

270 The romance was conducted: MGS to EH Jr, [11-28-1850], H; Leyda 1:192.

271 In good weather: *Let* 202, 194, 111, 114, 125. See *Home* 242 for an instance of WAD's concealment of his relations with Sue.

271 Suddenly restless: *Annual Circular and Catalogue of the Utica Female Academy for 1848–9* 5; Sue to TDG, [between 6-19- and 7-14-1851], 9-17-[1851], H.

271 Mr. and Mrs. Archer's: Baltimore *American & Commercial Daily Advertiser* 7-4-, 8-28-1851; Catalogs for Archer's Academy for 1848–1849 and 1855–1856, Maryland Historical Soc.; 1850 federal census, Baltimore City, ward 10, dwelling 464.

272 The public institution: Boston School Committee Minutes, vol 6, 1-21-1851 and pp. 127–28, 157, 242–43, and printed report on attendance, loose papers, 1851–1852, Ms.Bos. SC, BPL, courtesy of the Trustees; typed notes, MTB Papers 102:573.

272 For Austin, classroom: *Let* 119; WAD to Sue (draft), [Oct. 13–15, 1851], H.

272 Writing home, the young man: *Let* 113, 119 (corrected against ED562 A); also 116, 124–25, 151. ED's defective pen in L45 left her upper strokes mostly invisible, leading Johnson to read "darling" as "daring."

273 This callous nativism: *Let* 148, 137, 152, 162, 170, 141, 146. Vin, too, missed WAD "dreadfully" (*Home* 268).

273 footnote 11: Betsy Erkkila, "Emily Dickinson and Class," *American Literary History* 4 (spring 1992) 10.

273 footnote 12: Jackson, *Letters to a Young Physician* 87.

273 When she learned: *Let* 148–49 (ED573 A). Cf. Homans 195.

274 To focus on her invitation's: *Let* 112, 116, 235; *Home* 206.

274 This captive fixation: *Let* 115 (corrected against ED561 A), 117.

274 footnote 13: Vin to WAD, 6-30-1851, ED562d-e A; Leyda 1:203.

274 Stung, Emily began: *Let* 117, 296; WAD to Sue (draft), [Oct. 13-15, 1851], H.

275 The great sensation: *Hampshire Gazette* 7-8-1851; *Let* 121.

275 In Sue's absence: *Let* 205 (compared to ED591 A), 209.

275 The "childish fancies" passage: *Reveries* 54; *Let* 177, 208, 169.

276 Once, anticipating: *Let* 169; WAD to Sue (draft, Cambridge, after a Boston ju-

bilee), H. Cody (191) speaks of Sue's need to "moderate . . . the wooing that besieged her from both quarters."

276 Ten years later: *Let* 737, 193, 201, 203.

277 When her friend's return: *Let* 209–210. ED's best readers recognize her hesitation
between "the need for integration with something else and the assertion of self-
contained individuality" (Gelpi 3), or alternatively, the "need to give herself up in ecstatic union and the desire to remain separate" (Miller 118).

277 Emily's terror: *Let* 195; Craik, *Head* 23; *Metamorphoses* Book 4. These connections
were first brought to light in Marianne Noble's excellent *The Masochistic Pleasures of
Sentimental Literature* (Princeton: Princeton University Press, 2000) 147–51.

278 footnote 15: Craik, *Olive* 1:81.

278 Yet the confidante: *Let* 215. How little ED knew appears in her effort to stimulate
Sue's interest in Henry Root (*Let* 183).

Chapter 13

281 peaches, grapes: For the produce, see *Let* 137, 308; *SR* 10-20-1854, 9-12-1859;
HFE 9-2-1853; Leyda 1:255. Bread: *Let* 153, 240; Leyda 2:232; *Housekeeping* 167.

281 The table itself: *Let* 268; *Home* 313.

281 Fall is Austin's season: Quinquennial File (WAD), Joel Parker & Theophilus Parsons, Petition of 9-29-1854, Harvard Corp., "College Papers" (1854) 323, Harvard
University Archives; *Let* 244, 231, 269; *Home* 312.

282 Sometimes Emily is the first: *Let* 204, 276, 286.

282 In December 1852: *The New York Times* 12-23-1852; Newman family data, MTB
Papers 84:258a; Archive of Mary Pearl; Hampshire Co. RP, Estate of Mark H.
Newman, 230:65; *Let* 227, 245, 269. The Irish maid may have been Mary
[F?]awk, age twenty-seven in 1850 federal census, Brooklyn, ward 11, dwelling
1153. No published account of the Newman orphans can be relied on, least of all
EDE 207, which installs the two youngest girls "at the Homestead . . . from 1853
to 1858."

282 The Dickinson children did not: *Let* 227; *Home* 268, 318; *Let* 245. The Sweetser
children came to Amherst for the summer when their parents, CDS and JAS, sailed
for Liverpool on the *Arctic* on 4-30-1853 (*New York Tribune* 5-2-1853).

283 Inevitably, Mrs. Fay detected: *Home* 358–59.

283 For Edward, the real problem: Kings Co. (NY) Surrogate's Court, Will of Mark H.
Newman, 14:273; Brooklyn RD 357:215, 494:514, 497:156, 503:493; *Supreme
Court, County of Kings. Edward Dickinson, as Sole Executor and Trustee . . . Plaintiff,
against Mark Haskell Newman . . . and Others, Defendants. Summons and Complaint*
(New York: Bryant, 1858), Mary Pearl; [Clara Newman (Carleton) Pearl], brief un-
titled memoir, Mary Pearl. The case papers cannot be found in the Kings County
Supreme Court records.

In 1854, when the Newman estate was worth $68,000, EdD's net worth was
$21,500. The latter figure excludes his $4,000 life insurance policy, which he
counted as an asset, but allows his optimistic valuation of Michigan land and
railroad bonds. Kings County (NY) Surrogate's Court, Room 109, Decrees
on Final Accounting 2:257–59; EdD's 1854 inventory, Bianchi Coll.

When EdD was belatedly advised of Newman's debts to his alma mater,
his response was fair and expeditious: see EdD to Joseph McKeen, 2-11-

1853, "Letters re the will . . . of Mark H. Newman," Administrative Papers of Leonard Woods, Bowdoin College Archives.

284 A very different set: First #1, 8-19-1852; EdD to SCB, 9-27-1852, SCB Papers 4:98; *Let* 120.

284 Meanwhile, the performances: Cooke 24; Smith 144–45; E. S. Wright, *A Discourse on the Life and Character of the Late Rev. Phinehas Cooke* (Rutland, Vt.: Tuttle, 1855); Phinehas Cooke, *A Discourse Delivered in Saxton's Village* (Bellows Falls, Vt.: Blake, Cutler, 1824); Cooke, *A Farewell Sermon, Delivered at Acworth* (Windsor, N.H.: Chronicle Press, 1829) 27; Lucius Boltwood to FHB, 3-30-1853, Bolt 6:7; MVR-Deaths 76:1; *HFE* 5-6-1853; *Home* 268. Cf. Diary 2-9.

285 footnote 1: *Home* 267; MS:Amherst–First Church–Treasurer–Records 1839–1862 [parish audit], J; MS:Amherst–First Church–Ministers–Misc., folder 1, J.

285 Another supply preacher: Andover Alumni; *Let* 251–52.

286 footnote 2: *Speech of Hon. George T. Davis, of Massachusetts, in Reply to Hon. Robert Rantoul, Jr.* (Washington, D.C.: Gideon, 1852) 4.

286 Such outbursts: "Amherst College. Prize Declamation. Aug. 6th, 1850," General Files–Student Parody and Satire–Mock Programs, A.

286 Edward headed the search: First #4, 4-6-, 5-24-1853; Leyda 1:281; *Let* 258, 291.

286 Although Dickinson often turned: *Let* 291, 284, 229. EdD owned pews 60, 62, 64, 66: EdD's inventories for 1850, 1851, Bianchi Coll; Hampshire Co. RD 148:120; First #4, 12-21-1860; *Hist* 58.

287 footnote 3: *Let* 229.

287 By 1860 the Reverend Dwight: George C. Shepard, Diary, 8-20-1854, Bolt 36:4; *Hist Amh Coll* 509.

287 Emily eventually lost: Edward S. Dwight, *A Teaching Ministry the Conservators of the Social Welfare* (Augusta, Me.: Johnson, 1852) 14.

288 "the finest Lawyer," "the apex": *Let* 270.

288 On one intriguing: Supreme Judicial Court for Franklin County, Deposition of Deborah Weston (questions 33, 29, 30), docket no. 13, 1853 Sept., *Prudence W. Eastman* v. *John Eastman,* Divorce, MA Arch; *SR* 9-19-1853. The Amherst-born minister was father by a previous marriage of Julia and Sarah Eastman, founders of Dana Hall School, Wellesley. ED's interest in *SR* was stimulated by a visit to the Hollands (*Let* 264), which Eudocia Flynt's diary places in mid-September 1853 (Leyda 1:282–83)—just before the trial.

288 After earlier failures: Sargent; Trustees–Prudential Committee–transcript of minutes, 11-14-1851, A; *Endow* 54–56.

289 footnote 4: Supreme Judicial Court for Hampshire County, Record Book No. 6, 75–82, MA Arch; *Mass Reports* 63:596–603. For other suits against the A&B that EdD helped defeat, see *Mass Reports* 70:61, 74:529.

289 In February 1852: *HFE* 2-6-1852; *Home* 219.

290 "Every body is wide awake": *Let* 173–74. Colonel Horace Smith, in his seventies, lived across the street.

290 "Father was as usual": *Let* 254.

290 The original idea: Sargent 22–23; *Home* 307; *SR* 5-15-1858, p. 8; Mass. Vol. 46, p. 12, Dun; EdD, 1855 inventory, Bianchi Coll. The A&B was later acquired by the New London line for a fraction of its original cost (*SR* 12-17-1863). The president of the engulfing company was Gordon L. Ford, Emily Fowler's husband.

291 In Dickinson's well-known: Charles R. Anderson, *Emily Dickinson's Poetry: Stairway of Surprise* (New York: Holt, Rinehart & Winston, 1960) 16; Mitchell 41.

292 "to connect with": *Mercy Phil* 40–41. The river road went through Northampton, seven miles distant by stage.

293 "my dearest earthly friend": *Let* 764.

293 Not being a career politician: EdD, "Umpireship" (?), college papers, H; James Avery Smith, *The History of the Black Population of Amherst* (Boston: NEHGS, 1999) 29. All his life EdD kept the Greenfield *Gazette and Mercury* for 1-10-1838, which printed the first of six anti-abolitionist and antislavery essays by "M"; above the masthead he wrote "Maj. Dickinson" (box labeled "Dickinson Library. Misc. Pamphlets, Articles, & Lists," H).

293 Straddling the difficulty: Leyda 1:225, 335; Mer 1:93; William Chauncey Fowler, *The Sectional Controversy* (New York: Scribner, 1862); Hinton R. Helper, *Impending Crisis of the South* (New York: Burdick, 1857) 240–41, Dickinson books, box 98, Bianchi Coll. For background, see Daniel Walker Howe, *The Political Culture of the American Whigs* (Chicago: University of Chicago Press, 1979).

293 When Edward went to Baltimore: *Let* 213.

294 footnote 5: *Let* 287, 218, 277, 337.

294 won by a plurality: Leyda 1:255; *HFE* 12-17-1852; *SR* 12-9,10,14,15-1852; *Boston Daily Evening Traveller* 12-14-1852.

294 Emily apparently got word: *Let* 216–17, corrected against MS Am 1118.5 (B176), H; Leyda 1:259.

295 Edward left for Washington: *Home* 323; *Let* 275 (caption as in ED167 A); William A. Craigie and James R. Hulbert, *A Dictionary of American English on Historical Principles* (Chicago: University of Chicago Press, 1944) 4:2485. For a good facsimile and unlikely interpretation of ED's drawing, see *Comic Power* 74–76.

295 She was also caricaturing: *Home* 329, 385; Hampshire County Court of Common Pleas, February term 1854, Record Book No. 1, *Blanchard* v. *Kingsbury,* pp. 6–7, MA Arch. The referees' 1-6-1854 meeting in South Hadley figures in ED's 1–5 letter: "Father and mother are going to South Hadley tomorrow, to be gone all day" (*Let* 281). The next meeting was in EdD's office on 2-17.

295 It was perhaps during: SJL to MLB, 2-11-1854, SCB Papers 2:50; *Home* 339.

295 This journey, the longest: *Let* 288–92; *Home* 344.

296 Seventy-five years later: Graves; *Let* 328 (punctuated as in MS Am 1118.1 [4], H).

296 Sue's report of the nights: Sue to MLB, Tues, postmarked April 24 [1854], SCB Papers 2:53. ED's fear of dark: *Let* 351, 354, 404, 424, 537.

296 footnote 6: Sue, fragments of compositions, H.

296 In Washington, Edward was: *Home* 529; *Memorial Biographies of the New England Historic Genealogical Society* (Boston: NEHGS, 1885) 4:55–68; [Charles Stearns], *Report of the Case of Charles Stearns against J. W. Ripley* (Springfield, Mass.: Wilson, 1851); [Stearns], *The National Armories, A Review of the System of Superintendency* (Springfield, Mass.: Wilson, 1852); [Stearns], *Letter to Samuel Bowles. Second Edition* (Springfield, Mass.: Wilson, 1854); *SR* 11-3-1854.

297 As a young man: EdD, "Militia Law," "Are military academies beneficial to this country?" Yale compositions and disputes, H; Solomon Warriner, Jr., to EdD, 2-7-, 3-27-1827, H; *Home* 552.

297 Edward made these statements: *Home* 542-45, 548. The most adequate account of EdD's term in the House remains *Home,* chapters 20, 25, 26, appendices 3, 4.

297 But we must not forget: *Home* 387, 561–63; *Biographical Directory of the United States Congress* (Washington, D.C.: U.S. Government Printing Office, 1989) 957. EdD and Hoar had served together on the Governor's Council in 1845 and 1846.

298 The morning after: Henry Wilson, *History of the Rise and Fall of the Slave Power in America* (Boston: Houghton Mifflin, 1874) 2:411; *Mer* 1:117; *SR* 10-17,21,25,30-; 11-1-1854.

298 In his reelection bid: *SR* 11-8,9,13,14,15-1854; *HFE* 11-10-1854; Albert Bushnell Hart, ed., *Commonwealth History of Massachusetts* (New York: Russell & Russell, 1966) 4:490.

299 The 10th's defeated: EdD to Salmon P. Chase, 7-23-1855, 1-23-1860, Ser. 1, 10:683, 13:443, Salmon P. Chase Papers, LC; *Home* 568–69; SB Let #59.3, 8-2 [1865] ("forgetfulness" misread as "fruitfulness" in *FF* 150 and Leyda 2:101); EdD to Alexander H. Bullock, 2-6-1869, Bullock Papers.

299 "high, strong ground": *Home* 385.

300 In July 1852: MGS to TDG, 7-16-[1852], H; *Let* 195.

300 Technically mistaken: Sue to EH Jr, 1-13-1853, Doc Hitch 8:10; WAD to Sue (draft, "I will state"), H; Jane Hitchcock to Ann Fiske, 11-7-1852, HHJ Papers 2:35; WAD to Sue (draft, "Your own heart tells"), H. WAD to MGS (draft, lightly cross-ruled in blue, with small paste-on), H, tells how the couple reached an understanding and refers to the "long winter" as still ahead.

301 Becoming more confidential: WAD to Sue (draft, "Your own heart tells"), H; Elizabeth Barrett Browning, *Prometheus Bound, and Other Poems* (New York: Francis, 1851), EDR 3.2.2. Quotations from *Complete Poetical Works* (Boston: Houghton Mifflin, 1900) 215, 222.

302 Although the couple's: WAD to Sue (draft on ruled blue paper), WAD to MGS (draft), Sunday 3-27-[1853], H. In this last, firmly dated draft, WAD apologizes for "my so long silence" in answering two congratulatory letters from MGS—"words that told me you were glad I loved Sue, & she loves me." This document implies the couple became engaged well before their rendezvous at the Revere Hotel on 3-23-1853, the date usually given (*Imagery* 91; *Open Me* xxxii).

302 In addition to surrendering: WAD to MGS (draft), 3-27-[1853], WAD to Sue (draft), [4-2-1853, dated by Fast Day, 4-7-1853], WAD to Sue (draft, "Again, my own darling"), H.

302 In February 1853: *Let* 221–22. As in *Let* 118, the "Youth" is not ED but WAD, then in Amherst.

303 footnote 7: ED607 A; *Let* 254; *Home* 295; *Let* (1931) 62–63. The first strong presentation of the case for ED's homoerotic love of Sue was Lilian Faderman's "Emily Dickinson's Letters to Sue," *Massachusetts Review* 18 (summer 1977) 197–225. In arguing for ED's "lesbian passion," Martha Nell Smith has given wide currency to her suspicion that seven obliterated lines in L116, which speaks of "a dreadful feeling," expressed the poet's uncensored reaction to the engagement: the erased segment "might be a witness to the passion she had for Susan. It might be angry." A glance at the letter, written a few months after the poet learned of the engagement, suggests the "dreadful feeling" concerned her fear that Father might see Austin's remarks about her and wildflowers. Philip Weiss, "Beethoven's Hair Tells All!" *The New York Times Magazine* 11-29-1998, 113; ED601 A; *Let* 243; *Home* 279.

303 Subsequent letters show: *Let* 223, 266, 241, 233, 229; *Home* 268; WAD to Sue (draft, "It seems sometimes"), Monday [late April 1853], H.

304   footnote 8: WAD to MGS (draft), 3-27-[1853], H.

304   Sue's response to all this: *Let* 223, 228; *Home* 268. Even though MDB misdated L103, she realized it implied ED's knowledge of the engagement (*FF* 188–89).

304   A letter of Sue's: Sue to MLB, Saturday [3-26-1853], SCB Papers 2:53; WAD to Sue (draft), [4-2-1853], H.

305   In spite of: *Let* 229, 239, 245; WAD to Sue (draft, no. 25, "Dinner is over"), Friday [4-22-1853], H.

305   And so she overdid: *Let* 248, 256, 252, 254; *Let* (1894) 129. See also Cody 231–32.

305   After Austin scolded: *Home* 298; *Let* 255-56. The quarrel shows up in WAD to Sue (draft, no. 27), [5-6?-1853 (Leyda 1:272)], H.

Chapter 14

307   On June 9, 1853: *Let* 254, 262; *Home* 294, 308.

308   When Abiah Root invited: *Let* 299, 307–308, 310; Springfield directory for 1853–1854.

308   Unlike Dickinson: Obituary, *New York Evening Post,* cited in H. M. Plunkett, *Josiah Gilbert Holland* (New York: Scribners, 1894) 193–94; *Let* 324, 713, 537, 111; Frank Barrows Makepeace, *The North Congregational Church Springfield . . . Fiftieth Anniversary* (Springfield, Mass.: the Church, [1896]) 33.

308   "If it wasn't": *Let* 264.

309   In her letters: *Let* 264, 309; Plunkett, *Holland* 117.

309   Much shorter than: Plunkett, *Holland* 25; H. M. P[lunkett], "Elizabeth Holland," *Berkshire Sun* 4-30-1896; *Let* 715, 688.

310   The fundamental text: Horace Bushnell, *God in Christ* (Hartford, Ct.: Brown and Parsons, 1849) 44, 46, 55, 73, 84–85, 295; Donald A. Crosby, *Horace Bushnell's Theory of Language* (The Hague: Mouton, 1975).

311   The year after: "Root" 29; *Let* 346; George H. Gould, *In What Life Consists and Other Sermons* (Boston: Pilgrim Press, 1903) 3.

311   But the most important: Edwards A. Park, *Memorial Collection of Sermons* (Boston: Pilgrim Press, 1902) 95, 111; Park, "Introductory Essay," in Henry C. Fish, *Pulpit Eloquence of the Nineteenth Century* (Cleveland: Barton, 1907); Crosby 87–93. On Park's relation to Edwardsian thought, see Conforti, chap. 5.

312   Putting such ideas: Richard Salter Storrs, "Tribute," in *Memorial Collection* 12; Elizabeth L. Smith, ed., *Henry Boynton Smith. His Life and Work* (New York: Armstrong, 1881) 95.

312   On November 20, 1853: *Let* 272, 502–503; Leyda 1:287; *Home* 318.

312   Given this enthusiasm: *HFE* 11-25-, 12-2-1853 (a "condensed report").

313   "*BFN* – is *married*": *Let* 116 (corrected against ED561 A). A Unitarian clergyman married the couple on 6-4-1851. The official record says the bride, Sarah W. Rugg, was thirty-one (MVR-Marriages 56:199), a year older than Newton. In fact, she was forty-one.

313   "Love from us all": *Let* 236. "Pace" (ED597 A), which I find indecipherable, was apparently legible for Johnson and Leyda.

313   After reflecting on: *Let* 282–84. Sue left for Manchester, N.H., between January 10 and January 15: see *Let* 283–84; Sue to MLB, 1-10-1854, Sue to SCB, Tuesday (postmarked 1-24-[1854]), SJL to MLB, 1-10-1854, SCB Papers 2:53, 2:50.

314   What Dickinson didn't: Octavo no. 9, Records of the First Unitarian Church, Worcester, AAS: *Brocades* 256; MVR-Deaths 494:356. If Sarah was "more nurse

than wife" (*This Was a Poet*, 86), the life insurance may have been her promised remuneration.

314 The thank-you letter: ED to [E. E. Hale?], 2-14-[1854], A. Newly discovered, this letter, like the next one, is not in Johnson. See Diana Wagner and Marcy Tanter, "New Dickinson Letter Clarifies Hale Correspondence," *EDJ* 7.1 (1998) 110–17.

315 A few years later: EdD to E. E. Hale, [spring 1858?], courtesy Lilly Library, Indiana University, Bloomington, Ind.

315 The poet's most intriguing: *Let* 282; obituary of Williams Emmons, *Hallowell Gazette* 10-20-1855; Nason 151–53; Mary Vaughan Marvin, *Benjamin Vaughan 1751–1835* (Hallowell, Me.: Printed for the family, 1979); John H. Sheppard, *Reminiscences of the Vaughan Family* (Boston: David Clapp, 1865). The Vaughans' library was open "to any boy or girl desirous to learn" (HVE, *Address and Poem at the Dedication of the Hallowell Library* [Portland, Me.: Hoyt, Fogg & Donham, 1880] 23).

315 footnote 2: Nason 140, 153.

316 Henry seems to have: Hammond 241–42; Amherst College catalogs for 1851–1852, 1852–1853, 1853–1854, A; *Let* 174, 183, 214. A letter in HVE's alumni file (A) implies he planned to take the entrance exams in 1850, and he appears in the 1850–1851 catalog. But *Bio Rec* 72 and his class obituary have him entering in 1851.

316 The notes Emily sent: *Let* 246, 247, 280. In *Var* 9 Franklin sees these passages as evidence she was sewing into booklets the sheets on which she copied her poems. His transcription of the last hard-to-read phrase from MS Am 1118 (4), H, looks more accurate than Johnson's or Leyda's (1:292).

317 As Emily knew: HVE et al., "Report on the Establishment of a College Magazine" (in HVE's hand), 9-26-1853, General Files–Publications–Information about College Publications, A. His prize essays included "Sympathy in Action" (*Let* 246) and "Sources of Originality" (1854 Commencement program).

317 Two of Emmons's essays: N. S. S. [HVE], "Poetry the Voice of Sorrow," *Amherst Collegiate Magazine* 1 (Oct. 1853) 20–25; *The Poems of Elizabeth Barrett Browning* (New York: Francis, 1852) 2:202, EDR 2.2.24. In ED's later treatment of Jacob's wrestling with the angel, "A little east of Jordan" (Fr145), the depiction of sunrise on hills and mountain (absent from Genesis 32:24–32) recalls the conclusion of Emmons's "The Words of Rock Rimmon." But there is no wrestling with sorrow in her strikingly lighthearted poem.

317 As Dickinson moved: "Vision of Poets," lines 728, 428–29, 557–58. Vivian R. Pollak, "Dickinson, Poe, and Barrett Browning: A Clarification," *New England Quarterly* 54 (March 1981) 124, notes the parallel between Dickinson's enigmatic "I died for beauty but was scarce" (Fr448) and a tercet in "Vision": "These were poets true, / Who died for Beauty as martyrs do / For Truth—the ends being scarcely two" (lines 289–91). These, the poem's most heavily marked lines in Sue's copy, would be quoted in an essay read by ED, [Kate Field], "Elizabeth Barrett Browning," *Atlantic Monthly* 8 (Sept. 1861) 368.

318 The second essay: *HFE* 6-9-1854; *SR* 6-10-1854; *Remin* 245.

318 Though Dickinson wouldn't: [HVE], "The Words of Rock Rimmon," *Collegiate* 1 (July 1854) 247–49; Pollak 123. The tercet isn't marked in Sue's copy. "There are some mountains," wrote J. T. Headley in *The Sacred Mountains* (New York: Scribners, 1854) 13, "that seem almost conscious beings, and if they *would* but speak . . . the traveller . . . would tremble with awe."

319 He graduated in August: *SR* 7-11-1861; ED's Bible, EDR 1.1.10; *Let* 302. When

TWH asked ED in 1862 who her companions were, the answer began, "Hills – Sir" (*Let* 404). "What distinguishes her prophetic poetry," writes Beth Maclay Doriani, "is her preservation of a female identity for her prophetic persona, even as that voice draws on and adjusts the style and devices usually preferred by male prophets" (*Emily Dickinson: Daughter of Prophecy* [Amherst: University of Massachusetts Press, 1996] 19).

319 Contributing to the pensive: *Let* 301; "Van" [HVE], untitled paragraph, *Collegiate* 1 (May 1854) 171. HVE's editorial pseudonym was Vandunke (*Collegiate* 1:62). One of his known pieces, "The Poetry of Martial Enthusiasm," was signed "Van."

319 For Dickinson, a great many: *Let* 303. MS Am 1118 (7), H, has "resemblance."

320 footnote 3: *Let* 601; *Imagery* chap. 3; MHJL 10-18-1847; Aurelia G. Scott, "Emily Dickinson's 'Three Gems,' " *New England Quarterly* 16 (Dec. 1943) 627–28; Sewall 413–14.

321 "We used to think": JL/ED.

321 Writing Sue in late: *Let* 304, corrected against fMS Am 1118.4 (L21), H. Johnson's unauthorized paragraph break after "honey" obscures the link between Emmons and the imagery. This important letter is misdated 1851–1852 in *Rowing* 165 and silently excluded from *Open Me.*

322 "made [her]self sick," "for a year": Sue to TDG, Sunday 8-13-[1854], H. Sue felt oppressed by her "*sewing,* that inexhaustible labor . . . that stretches away before my tired needles" (Sue to EH Jr, 1-13-1853, Doc Hitch 8:10). A few months later, recycling the image, she changed "tired" to "crooked" (Sue to SCB [spring 1853, misdated ca. 1851], SCB Papers 2:53). "Susie is all worn out sewing," ED wrote WAD Nov. 1853; "she seems very lonely without you, and . . . more depressed than is usual" (*Let* 272).

322 from "man's requirements" to "don't get *nervous*": Cody 207; *Let* 298; Sue to TDG, 8-13-, 9-4-[1854], H; Sue to EH Jr, Geneva, Tuesday [Sept. 1854], Doc Hitch 8:10. Cody gave the first cogent analysis of Sue's situation.

322 This illness brought out: Sue to TDG, 8-13-[1854], H; Sue to MLB, 12-5-[1854], SCB Papers 2:53; Eugenia Learned James, *The Learned Family in America 1630–1967* (n.p.: Setco Printing Co., 1967) 58.

323 dating the poet's two letters mentioning the quarrel: L173 has been dated about 1854 (Johnson, Franklin), late September? 1854 (Leyda), and "mid-1850s" (*Open Me* 69). Its script resembles that of L172 (written soon after 1854 Commencement) but differs in retaining vestigial features of ED's earlier hand. The initial stroke of "Y" in "Yet" (poem) and "You" has the wedgelike look that had been common in 1852; L172 has no instances of this. The descender of "g" or "y," which by 1854 usually terminated with a graceful sweep to the left, had in 1851 always turned to the right. L173 shows the older form in the last letters of "Tuesday morning," which curve right; L172 does not, except for a faint hint in "day." A third diagnostic feature, terminal "s," is tiny and unconnected in L173, but in L172 (with one exception) is larger, clearer, and differently formed. These three features make L173 slightly earlier than L172.

The similarities in the paper of L173 and L169—the latter obviously dating from mid-August 1854—suggest the former also comes from that period. The two sheets are not the same size, but both have gilt edges and the same chain-line interval and boss ("SUPER FINE PAPER LONDON" around a diagonal "MOINIER"). Both show parts of the same large watermark, a crown above a post-horn and cursive "M" (cf. design #639, Thomas L. Gravell & George Miller, *A Catalogue of American Watermarks 1690–1835* [New York: Garland, 1979] 137). ED's only other letters with this boss and watermark are L168 and L170, from during and soon after Commencement week 1854. L168, L169, L170, L172, and L173 are all at H: MS Am 1118 (13), (14), (3), & fMS Am 1118.4 (L21), (L17).

323　from "Sue – you can go" to "Return": *Let* 305–307; "Root" 28.

324　"private message": Miller 15. In Farr's terms, ED's "art is founded on thrilling loss, thrilled sublimation" (*Passion* 182). Elizabeth Hewitt, "Dickinson's Lyrical Letters and the Poetics of Correspondence," *Arizona Quarterly* 52 (spring 1996) 30, proposes that ED's "poetry compensates for a failed correspondence."

324　If Eliza Coleman had learned: Leyda 1:319; *Let* 302.

325　In late August: *Let* 304–305. WAD's drafts (H) about someone's interrupted " 'Spiritual converse' with my sister," one of which is dated 9-23, do not concern this quarrel. Mistakenly assigned by Leyda to 1854 (1:316), they date from 1851. Proof lies in WAD's statement that "your card will find me at 19 Hancock St"—Mrs. Lucy Reed's boardinghouse and his address for most of his schoolteaching year (*Let* 153; Boston directories for 1851, 1852). WAD was writing an unidentified male friend of ED or Vin.

325　Sue did write: *Let* 310–11.

325　By late January: *Let* 315.

Chapter 15

328　Representative Dickinson and his: "Arrivals at Principal Hotels," Washington *Evening Star*, 2-10-1855, p. 1; *Let* 316. The *Star*'s mistake—"E Dickinson & daughters, N H"—shows how hard it was to decipher EdD's scribble in the hotel register. Date of Sue and Martha's return: SJL to MLB, 2-5-1855, SCB Papers.

328　This note of discomfiture: *Let* 317, 319; *LL* 46.

328　Dickinson's only known: *Independent* 7 (5-24-1855) 166; *Let* 319, 299.

329　Her one account: *Let* 317; Cullum 2:240.

329　What little we know: Washington *Evening Star* 2-5-, 1-24-1855; H. Trusta [Elizabeth Stuart Phelps], *The Last Leaf from Sunny Side* (Boston: Phillips, Sampson, 1854), J; Note by Jeanie Ashley Bates Greenough, ED Collection 31:2, A (her father and EdD sat on the Governor's Council in 1845); Henrietta R. Mack Eliot to Julian [Mack], 5-14-1932, MTB Papers 104:629. TDG came to Washington at the end of February, dined with EdD, and perhaps saw ED (Sue to TDG, 3-6-1855, H). ED may also have met Ben C. Eastman, a Wisconsin congressman originally from Maine (*Biographical Directory of the United States Congress 1774–1989* [Washington, D.C.: U.S. Government Printing Office, 1989]). At some point, Ben's wife, Charlotte Sewall Eastman, became friends with ED and Vin. She was from Hallowell, Maine, where her husband had been mentored by HVE's father, Williams Emmons. Nason 135; *Vital Records of Hallowell Maine* (Maine Historical Soc. 1924) 260; 1850 federal census, WI, Grant Co., Platteville, 98; Leyda 1:xliii.

330　After three weeks: Philadelphia directories for 1854, 1855; "Minutes of the First Presbytery of Philadelphia 1850–56," 3, 39, 58–59, 62, 70, P; notices for Presbyterian Institute, *The Presbyterian*, 9-7-1850, 9-9-1854, 9-8-1855; Kellogg 11. Sunday, 3-18-1855, Johnson's conjectured date for L179, written "just five weeks" after ED left Amherst, seems unlikely, partly because EdD avoided traveling on Sunday. If he and his daughters left home on Friday, February 9, they could have reached Washington by February 10. EdD's last recorded activity in the House, three days before adjournment, was on March 1 (*Home* 567). If he, ED, and Vin left for Philadelphia the next day, Friday, March 2, that would be consistent all around and yield a date of Friday, March 16, for L179.

330 Although the sequence: *Funeral* 23; *Let* 727, 753, 764, 737; A. Mary F. Robinson, *Emily Brontë* (London: Allen, 1883) 104. CW performed a wedding February 28 and gave a benefit sermon at the Broad Street Presbyterian Church the evening of March 18 (Philadelphia *Public Ledger* 3-1,17-1855). I haven't been given access to the records of the Arch Street Church (then located above Tenth Street) to verify the longstanding assumption that the Colemans were members. Their next church, South Congregational, Middletown, Connecticut, has no letters of transfer for them (Jonathan B. Dean-Lee to author, 2-7-2000).

330 Judging from contemporary: Leyda 2:112; *Funeral* 15, 16; [George Burrowes], *Impressions of Dr. Wadsworth as a Preacher* (San Francisco: Towne & Bacon, 1863) 5; *Let* 744–45, 762. CW's few extant letters are at A, P, Historical Society of PA, and alumni files at Hamilton College and PTS. I haven't located those quoted by Sewall 730–38.

331 Her care not to encroach: TWH, "Emily Dickinson's Letters," *Atlantic Monthly* 68 (Oct. 1891) 453; CW to William E. Schenck, Nov. 1878, CW's alumni file, PTS; *Let* 737.

331 No doubt Wadsworth had: *Barbour's Collection of Connecticut Town Vital Records* 32–34, 226; Alain C. White, *The History of the Town of Litchfield* (Litchfield, Conn.: Enquirer, 1920) 128–29, 190; Elijah Wadsworth & Co., ledger 1798–1802, Litchfield Historical Soc.; Paul Meibert Miller, "Charles Wadsworth, Spiritual Preceptor to Emily Dickinson" (thesis, San Francisco State, 1987) 27; CW to Edith and Charlie, Sewall 736; Charles Thomas Payne, *Litchfield and Morris Inscriptions* (Litchfield, Ct.: Dwight C. Kilbourn, 1905) 142; Henry Wadsworth probate, 14:491–92; 15:37, 100, 128; 16:219; 22:589–90, Probate Court, District of Litchfield; Laurens P. Hickock, "List of Deaths and Marriages," 2, 24, First Ecclesiastical Soc. of Litchfield, Litchfield Historical Soc.; *Litchfield Enquirer* 12-18-1834; *Let* 742.

332 Leaving Litchfield: *Necrological Report . . . of Princeton Theological Seminary* (Philadelphia, 1882) 39–40; William Pilcher to William E. Schenck, 11-27-1878, CW's alumni file, PTS; Milton C. Sernett, *Abolition's Axe: Beriah Green, Oneida Institute, and the Black Freedom Struggle* (Syracuse: Syracuse University Press, 1986) 31–38; Moseley 99; Miller, "Charles Wadsworth," 29.

The identity of "Sedley" is established by a small scrapbook of sermons and newspaper poems (ZIZ n.c.19, NYPL). Most of CW's poetic output appeared in the *Litchfield Enquirer*: 2-16-, 4-12,19-, 5-17-, 9-20-1832; 5-8,22-1834; 1-22-1835; 4-21-, 8-18-, 9-15-1836; 7-6-, 9-21-1837; 11-22-, 12-20-1838 (cf. 12-6-1838). Three poems appeared in the Utica *Record of Genius* 1 (12-22-1832; 2-2-, 4-27-1833) 138, 162, 110 [210]. The scrapbook poem "Death," dated Litchfield 1831 thus his earliest known work, appeared in the *Religious Intelligencer*. Another scrapbook poem, "The Spirit of Night" (Sewall 740–41), had an as yet unidentified outlet.

One year after CW died, ED told MW that one of her "lost" used to visit the Adirondacks (*Let* 793). In "Scraps," *Litchfield Enquirer*, 9-15-1836,

CW wrote, "I stood upon Lake George's shore," making him ED's only other friend with an Adirondacks connection.

"To ____ ____ ____" was published in *Litchfield Enquirer* 4-19-1832 and *Record of Genius* 1 (12-22-1832) 138. A copy of the latter in Utica Imprints Collection, Utica Public Lib., has two old and interesting inscriptions: "Mr [C?] O P" penciled in the title's blanks and "S.P." inked beside the masthead. These may designate Chester Parks and daughter Sally. She died 5-21-1832 at age nineteen (in the cholera epidemic?) and was buried in Grand View Cemetery, Whitesboro. D.A.R., "Cemetery, Church & Town Records of New York," vol. 4; Sue Lorraine to author, 3-16-2000.

332 Having gained a name: CW, *A Sermon Preached in the Arch Street Presbyterian Church . . . Thanksgiving . . . 1852* (Philadelphia: Moran & Sickels, 1852) 19; *Religious Glorying. A Sermon . . . Thanksgiving . . . 1857* (Philadelphia: Bradley, 1857) 5–6; "The Feast of Harvest," first preached 1858 and collected in CW, *Sermons* (San Francisco: A. Roman, 1869) 297; *Address Delivered in Calvary Church . . . Services of Gen. George Wright* (San Francisco: Bancroft, 1865) 9. In 1850, surprised at CW's loss of interest in poetry, the Yale professor James Hadley recalled that he once seemed, intellectually, "so immeasurably superior" (Mosely 95, 97). CW's eulogist described his faith as "the termination of an awful struggle of his spirit, upward out of unbelief" (*Funeral* 25).

333 As preacher: CW, *A Sermon Preached in the First Presbyterian Church, on the Occasion of the Installation* (San Francisco: Sterett & Cubery, 1867) 20; *Funeral* 30; Charles Wadsworth, Jr., *How to Get Muscular* (New York: Randolph, 1891) dedication.

333 to send the poet on January 4: Leyda 1:352.

334 "reached out eagerly": *Home* 375.

334 In May 1853: *Let* 250, 118, 127; Sue, "Two Generations of Amherst Society," *Essays on Amherst's History* (Amherst: Vista Trust, 1978) 184. At Springfield's Third National Exhibition of Horses, EdD entered his six-year-old Morgan gelding, Billy, in the class of "Family Horses, Roadsters" (*SR* 9-17-1858).

334 Austin also presented himself: Louise Torrey Taft to Alphonso Taft, 7-20/21-1854, MTB Papers 104:630; SJL to MLB, 2-11-1854, SCB Papers 2:50; Sue to Frank Gilbert, 1-6-1854, H.

335 footnote 1: Mrs. Edward Hitchcock, comp., *The Genealogy of the Hitchcock Family* (Amherst: Carpenter & Morehouse, 1894) 467–68; *Let* 311 (punctuated as in fMS Am 1118.4 [L6], H).

335 After all, how manly: Sue to Frank Gilbert, 1-6-1854, H; WAD to MGS (draft, "If you'll forgive"), [1-5-1854, "two weeks" before term's end at Harvard 1-19-1854], H; *Let* 311, 315.

335 John Cody has cogently argued: Cody 196, 207, 206; WAD to Sue (draft), Selected Papers of SHD (microfilm), Bianchi Coll. MDB gave a sanitized account of her parents' courtship in *FF*, chap. 3.

335 In religious matters: Cody 197; Peter Bayne, *The Christian Life Social and Individual* (Boston: Gould & Lincoln, 1856) iii, Hampson B-6, Bianchi Coll; WAD to Sue, #34, Selected Papers of SHD (microfilm), Bianchi Coll.

336 And thus it came: WAD, confession of faith (draft), H; First #3.

337 footnote 2: Leyda 2:228–29.

337 Betrayal had been: *Let* 502–503. Another of Park's famous sermons (known by ED?) was "Peter's Denials of His Lord."

337 Five years after Austin's confession: *Let* 377.

337 "The Babies we *were*": "Root" 28.

338 "come home as we used": *Let* 134–35.

338 In 1855, a year after: Henrietta Mack Eliot to Grace Eliot Scott, 1-15-1915, ED
     Collection 32:10, A; Hampshire Co. RP, Estate of David Mack, 93:1; Harriet P.
     Mack deed to Samuel E. Mack, 5-1-1855, Bianchi Coll; *HFE* 4-20-1855; Hannah
     Terry to Mary Shepard, 4-27-1855, Bolt 7:2; Hampshire Co. RD 160:446-47;
     220:349.

338 There is no mystery: *HFE* 5-18-1855; Leyda 1:339; HSR; *Let* 321.

339 A couple of weeks: *History of Floyd County, Iowa* (Chicago: Inter–State, 1882) 902;
     Allen 23; *Hist* 58; Salem Hammond to Amherst Selectmen (EdD's copy), 10-12-
     1858, Bianchi Coll; *Let* 195, 329; Revelation 3:12.

339 Informing her brother: Sue to Frank Gilbert and TDG [mid-May? 1855 (Leyda's
     date)], H; Leyda 1:305; WAD to Sue (draft, "And this week"), Monday [4-25-
     1853], H.

340 The house was paid for: EdD paid for construction partly by selling the Nathan
     Dickinson place to the Newman estate in March 1856 (Hampshire Co. RD
     166:584, 560). A 1-1-1868 bond for a deed (Bianchi Coll), apparently inoperative,
     committed EdD to sell the Evergreens to WAD for $3,000, due in two years; see
     Gregory Farmer, "Land Is the Only Thing That Lasts," *EDIS Bull* 11.1 (May/June
     1999) 7. For the Evergreens' design, construction, and landscaping, see WAD to
     TDG (Sue's copy), n.d., H; Sue to TDG, [after Oct. 1855 cattle show], H; *HFE*
     4-18-1856; Gregory Farmer, "Evergreens Update: Dreaming in Color," *Dickinson
     Homestead* (newsletter) 3.2 (fall 1999); SB Let #53, 12-14-[1864] ("your rhododen-
     dron"), #59.3, 8-2-[1865] ("new shrub for Austin"). Native rhododendrons were
     seen as threatened (TWH, "The Procession of the Flowers," *Atlantic Monthly* 10
     [Dec. 1862] 654). WAD was active in the Amherst Ornamental Tree Association,
     organized 1857 (Allen 72; Carp 408–411).

340 footnote 3: Clifford E. Clark, Jr., "Domestic Architecture as an Index to Social His-
     tory: The Romantic Revival and the Cult of Domesticity in America, 1840–1870,"
     in *Material Life in America, 1600–1860,* Robert Blair St. George, ed. (Boston:
     Northeastern University Press, 1988) 537.

340 In November 1855: Leyda 1:338. WAD's grove of evergreens: *Let* 254, 256, 258,
     296, 315.

341 The poet's one account: *Let* 323–24.

341 That said, the determined gaiety: *Let* 324.

341 Dickinson's sketchy account: *Let* 337.

342 "Our mother had": Dall.

342 "Eliza Coleman is visiting": Jane Hitchcock to Ann Fiske Banfield, 9-24-1856,
     HHJ Papers 2:35.

342 At the end of 1857: Samuel E. Mack to EdD, 12-28-1857, Bianchi Coll; Summit,
     8-20-1859; Mary Shepard to LMB, 2-15-1860, Bolt 8:3; Mary Shepard to END,
     "Friday morning" [2-10-1860], H.

343 In later years: AOT to John Tyler, 7-21-[1876], 11-6-[1877], Tyler Papers 3:15,16;
     Sue to MLB and SCB, [5-19-1856 (Leyda's date)], SCB Papers 2:53; Sue to EFF
     [received 6-10-1856], EFF Papers.

343 footnote 4: *Let* 380.

344 "I do not go out": LNN to END, 2-15-1836, H.

344 Another event that: Boston School Committee Minutes, vol 6, Ms.Bos.SC, BPL;

Israel Lombard, Diary, 12-31-1854, Israel Lombard Papers, AAS; Records for Cases 3867, *Patterson et al. v. Norcross,* and 4091, *Winslow Whittemore et al. v. Norcross,* Nov. 1855 term, Suffolk Co. Superior Court, MA Arch; 1855–1858 valuations, Ward 5, Boston, City Clerk, Archives & Records Management; 1856 Boston directory. Loring's business address from 1857 on, 104 Federal, shows he was working for Holmes Ammidown, a large wholesaler of cottons and woollens. Eudocia Flynt's 1854 diary reporting Loring's failure (Leyda 1:315) has vanished.

344   footnote 5: *Let* 260; Hampden Co. Probate Court, Estate of SVN, Case 8351.

344   Capping that, however: Hampden Co. Probate Court, Estate of JN, Case 8347, will; Loring & Albert's Petition to Supreme Judicial Court for Suffolk Co., #672 Equity & Probate, 1849 March, MA Arch; Essex Co. (NJ) RD Z-6:329-30. EdD to Alfred Norcross, 11-22-1847, J, recommending generous treatment of the impecunious WON, throws a favorable light on EdD.

345   It was Loring's one smart: Essex Co. (NJ) RD, D9 204:30–31, 306–308; *Charles Frederick Norcross et al. v. Loren Norcross et al.,* Supreme Judicial Court for Hampden Co., Record Book Sept. 1857–April 1859, case 46, p. 138, MA Arch. EdD's argument was that since Loring and Albert had been enjoined from putting trust money in New Jersey, the investment *must* have been their own. I learned of the case from cryptic entries in Henry Fanning Norcross's 1857 journal (3-17, 4-6, 5-29), kindly made available by Priscilla Chatfield.

345   Loring's sorry financial: *Let* 421 (punctuated as in FN/ED, 430 verso). Anna Mary Wells's surmise that the destruction of letters was meant to conceal ED's mental illness illustrates the common practice of converting missing documentation into positive evidence of what one suspects ("Was Emily Dickinson Psychotic?" *American Imago* 19 [winter 1962] 309–321).

346   Does Edward's defense: St. Armand 307–309. The argument is that EdD made two different inventories in 1857, owing to (and thus disclosing) his shifty finances. The mistake is that the last digit of 1851 for that year's inventory was read as a 7 (Inventories, Bianchi Coll). The story has found wide acceptance among Dickinson scholars.

346   It's pointless to charge: *SR* 5-27-1859; New England Vol. 26, p. 240a, Dun.

346   Still, the man was: Hampshire Co. RD 166:584, 560; Town of Amherst, valuations for taxes, year ending June 1855, J. In 1856 the Dickinson meadow and remodeled Homestead were together valued at $6,900. The Newman house remained at $3,200 through 1859.

346   An even more ambiguous: *SR* 1-18, 26-, 10-15-1858; 1-12-, 12-16-1859; Sargent 29-30. The cover-up is evident in *HFE* 1-22-, 2-5-, 10-15-, 11-12-1858.

347   footnote 6: *Endow* 54–56.

347   Because there seem to be: JL to Laura Baker, 5-24-1857, Lyman Papers 2:28. The envelope, a photo of which is in *Lyman Let* 26–27, invalidates Franklin's statement that "there is no document by Dickinson of any kind" from 1857 (*Var* 10). On 3-6-1857 JL wrote his mother, "the Dickinson people still remember me and write me letters" (Lyman Papers 2:26).

348   Which is not to say: *Let* 323, 327–28; JL to Laura Baker, 2-27-1858, Lyman Papers 2:36.

348   This, the one contemporary: *Remin* 186; *SR* 4-22-1858; Anon., *Memorial of the Revival in Plymouth Church, Brooklyn, during the Early Part of the Year 1858* (New York: Clark, Austin & Smith, 1859) 41, 59; CW, "The Feast of Harvest," *Sermons* (San Francisco: A. Roman, 1869) 298; H.J. [Henry James, Sr.], "American Revivals and

European Torpor," *New-York Tribune*, 5-1-1858. Edward S. Dwight surmised the 1857 panic helped bring on the revival (*Hist* 81).

348 In Amherst, the excitement: *SR* 4-22-, 5-4-, 6-5-1858; First #3; *Let* 346. L185, hard to date, could have been prompted by the 1858 revival. The second paragraph is close to L190 [summer 1858] but also to L184 [April 1856].

349 It may have been: Leyda 1:lxxvii; [CW] to "Miss Dickenson," n.d., ED1012 A. Facsimile in *Home* 370–71.

349 Although scholars have varied: Leyda 2:283; CW to [?], 12-19-?, Historical Society of Pennsylvania.

350 "Much has occurred": *Let* 335.

350 footnote 7: "Root" 26.

350 The note to Master: *Master Let* 5–19. Scholars concur in assigning the script to 1858. This and the Sweetser letter (J) are on the same paper: no boss, 123 × 187 mm, blue rules on pp. 2–3 with 8 mm spacing.

351 In the draft Dickinson says: *Master Let* 14–15.

351 The other letter, to Sweetser: *Let* 335–36, corrected against holograph (J). Sweetser's address: Trow's New York City directories for 1857–1858, 1858–1859.

352 Letters that fall: *Let* 340, 341; ED to [EFF?], tipped in EFF's copy of ED's 1890 *Poems*, Thomas Cooper Lib., University of South Carolina.

352 Why did the poet's: *Hist Am Coll* 396; *SR* 2-3-1855, 7-1-, 8-13-1858. I can't substantiate Leyda's plausible claim (1:357) that abolitionist Wendell Phillips's speech on 8-11-1858 (*HFE* 8-13-1858) caused Sweetser to withdraw his support. In August 1859 the trustees thanked him for his contributions (Trustees Min 3:651).

353 In 1858, apparently in summer: *Var* 11, passim.

353 Although Dickinson sent hundreds: *Let* 408; *Brocades* 166. See also *Imagery* 5; Karen Dandurand, "Why Dickinson Did Not Publish" (Ph.D. dissertation: University of Massachusetts–Amherst, 1984); Dobson 128–30.

354 footnote 8: *SR* 4-16-1859. Cf. Leyda 2:88.

354 seven seem designed to introduce gifts: Fr7, Fr8, Fr9, Fr10, Fr11, Fr15, Fr17. Other poems transcribed before "about late summer" were Fr3, Fr6, Fr12, Fr13, Fr14, Fr16, Fr18, Fr19, Fr20.

356 "If those I loved were lost": *Poems* 27–28; *Var* 11 (facsimile on 10).

Chapter 16

359 As if the Boston Norcrosses: *Let* 346. Vin left before Christmas 1858 (*Let* 354); L202, L204, L206 refer to her absence. L199, dated 1-4-1859 by Johnson, places her, confusingly, at home. In fact, this letter was written the following winter (see below, pp. 388, 712).

359 The older sister had become: JL/ED.

360 Austin seemed in no doubt: [Coventry Patmore], *The Angel in the House: The Betrothal* (Boston: Ticknor & Fields, 1857) 108, 33, EDR 4.4.20; ED's obituary, *SR* 5-18-1886.

361 Keenly aware of the risks SB Let #1 [5-15-1859], #2, 1-2-[1859]. Date of stillbirth from MVR-Deaths 129:240.

361 footnote 1: MLT Papers 103:259.

362 By now, Austin's feelings: Edward Hitchcock and Jane E. Hitchcock to EH Jr, 12-7-1860, Edward and Orra White Hitchcock Papers, Ser. 2, 4:43, A.

362 A further irony: FHB to Thomas K. Boltwood, 10-24-1858, Bolt 8:1; Brooklyn RD

497:156-58. Catharine Newman was gone from Amherst by February 1859, when Asa Bullard witnessed her signature in Boston (Ibid). On 12-30-1859 she transferred from Amherst's First Church to the Bullards' Prospect Street Church in Cambridgeport (First #2).

362 What evidence there is: *Let* 358, 340. After 1854, there are only three extant letters from ED to WAD.

362 A month later: FHB to Thomas H. Boltwood, 10-24-1858, Bolt 8:1; *Let* 341; SB Let #2.1, 1-16-[1859]. Harriet and an eight-year-old boy died 11-1-1858 (Amherst Vital Records, J). From July 31 to year's end, the town had twelve deaths from scarlet fever, with several more the next year (*SR* 1-8-, 2-14,25-1859).

363 footnote 2: *Let* 422, 724.

363 If Emily depended: *Let* 339; Martha Nell Smith, " 'Open Me Carefully': Emily's Book for Susan," *EDIS Bull* 10.1 (May/June 1998) 12–13, 22; *Open Me* xii–xiv, passim.

365 footnote 3: *MB* 1:28.

365 This pledge of allegiance: Sullivan proposes that "Sue's name begins to stand for an abstract idea of friendship rather than a particular friend" (45).

366 "we will lie side by side": *Let* 201.

367 by Franklin's count: *Var* 1550.

368 "poetry workshop" theory: *Rowing* chap. 5.

372 The reverse of Emily Norcross: "Annals"; Sue, untitled fragment, "I shall never forget," H. Kingsley date from Mer 2:336–37.

372 Of course, the Evergreens: Allen 73 (Mary Adelia James married Moses Adams Allen 8-31-1858 and joined Amherst's First Church January[?] 1859 [International Genealogical Index; First #5, 51]); *Let* 347, 345 (for date, see p. 388); "Annals"; Leyda 1:350–51; WAD to Sue, "What larks!" 10-31-[1865], H; *HFE* 10-19,26-1865.

373 One of the few: Henry Home, Lord Kames, *Elements of Criticism* (New York: Huntington & Savage, 1847), EDR 2.4.17; Margaret C. Haynes, comp., "Christ Episcopal Church, Cooperstown, New York, Volume I of Parish Register," 10-29-1855, 3:8, New York State Historical Assoc.; *Cherry Valley Gazette* 11-7-1855; [Cooperstown] *Republican and Democrat* 5-30-1857; [Cooperstown] *Freeman's Journal* 6-5-1857; Jane Averell, diary, 6-11,13-, 11-27-1855, New York State Historical Assoc. Dr. Campbell L. Turner died in Boston 5-26-1857.

373 In January 1859: Catharine Scott Turner Anthon to Sue, 9-6-[?], Anthon to MDB, 10-8-[postmarked 1914], H; *LL* 64; *Let* 359–360. Facsimile of woodcut and note in *LL*, facing 156. Anthon's three visits can be dated by SB Let. First visit: #2.1, 1-16-[1859], #5.1 [2-4-1859], #3 [2-16-1859]. Second: #15 [10-17-1861], #15.1 [late Oct. or early Nov. 1861]. Third: #16.1 [1-9-1863], #33 [1-15-1863], #23.2 [1-29-1863], #18 [2-7-1863].

373 Far more humiliating: S. G. Buckingham, *Discourse at the Funeral of Reuben Atwater Chapman* (Springfield, Mass.: Bryan, 1874); *Let* 348. Chapman's law partner was George Ashmun (*Bench* 1:245).

374 After Kate was back in: *Let* 349–50, corrected against Anthon's tr, H. Her other copy (Tr60 A) has "like" instead of "take." The inconsistencies in Anthon's copies of L222 (rend/send) show that ED's hand sometimes defeated her. That Anthon was ED's one great passion is the thesis of *Riddle*.

374 Dickinson's three later letters: *Let* 365. In interpreting the Daisy mounds passage, I have adapted the reading in Pollak 87–88.

375 Who could keep pace: *Let* 355, 365.

375 Emily-the-lynx's: Katharine [sic] Mary Anthon, travel diaries, 12-20-1872, 3-30-, 6-8-1873, New York State Historical Assoc.

375 Another person who entered: Mer 2:79; *Let* 662. *Capsule* 150–69 remains one of the soundest treatments of ED's relations with SB. Less reliable are the accounts in *Passion* and *EDE*.

376 Sue's draft essay: "Annals" ("lady" dropped in revision); *SR* 6-29-, 7-1-1858; *HFE* 7-2-1858. There is no other possible occasion for SB's first visit. The first year mowing machines were tried out in Amherst (*HFE* 7-18-1856), *SR* did not cover the event. In summer 1857 SB was in Boston running the *Traveller* (Mer 1:181–83).

376 Two years earlier: *HFE* 8-1-, 9-5-1856; First #4, 2-2-, 4-14-, 7-28-1856; *Let* 339. As Himelhoch and Patterson first realized, L189 and L193 were written *after* the Bowleses' summer 1859 visit (Him 2). If that visit took place in June during the first haying, we would have a motive for ED's abrupt mention of the second haying.

376 Both Samuel and his wife: *Unity Church Manual* (Springfield, Mass., 1886) 103–104; *Let* 339, 335, 358; Theodore Parker, *The Two Christmas Celebrations* (Boston: Rufus Leighton, Jr., 1859) 18, 15. On Unitarianism and ED, see Rowena Revis Jones, "A Taste for 'Poison': Dickinson's Departure from Orthodoxy," *EDJ* 2.1 (1993) 47–64. On the complexities of ED's religious views, see McIntosh 41–71.

377 "that rare type": John J. Scanlon, *The Passing of the Springfield Republican* (Amherst: Amherst College, 1950) 17.

377 But the man was canny: *SR* 8-13-1861; Ashmun to Banks, 8-14-1861, Nathaniel P. Banks Papers, Rare Book, Manuscript, and Special Collections Lib., Duke Univ.; M. A. DeWolfe Howe, *Later Years of the Saturday Club 1870–1920* (Boston: Houghton Mifflin, 1927) 202.

377 The editor could not: *Westfield News Letter* 5-26-1858 (slang); MW to WDW, 2-22-1872, WDW Papers 17:431; *Let* 367; *SR* 8-10-1860.

378 The 163 letters: SB Let #61.1, 6-27-1866, #90 [6]-7-[1863]; Sewall 469; SB Let #86 [3-28-1862] (first-naming), #44, 2-26-[1864] (temptation), #18 [2-7-1863] (aristocrats), #80.2 [5?-26?-1876?] (Queen). #90 is dated by Summit 6-9-1863. #80.2 is dated in conjunction with #80.1 [Nov. 1876] (identical paper type), #71.2 [6-3-1876], and MW's return from Paris ca. 5-10-1876.

378 spoken of only eleven times: omitting vague references to "the girls," etc., we have the following in SB Let:

#5.1	[2-4-1859]	"never forgets my spiritual longings"
#1.1	6-1-[1859]	"Emily's beautiful thought"
#13	[10-12?-1861]	"Thank Emily & Vinnie"
#19.1	[4-9-1862]	"kind & rich note, & Emily's"
#21, 21.1	[5]-12-[1862]	regards to ED among others
#22	7-13-[1862]	"one of her little gems"
#16.1	[1-9-1863]	"Queen Recluse"
#26	[5-2-1863]	"savage, turbulent . . . as Emily"
#59	[2]-12-[1864]	"love to Emily & Vinnie"
#51	[12-3-1864]	"gems for the '*Springfield Musket*' "
#59.3	8-2-[1865]	"eyes for Emily"

379 Accompanied by Mary: SB Let #2, 1-2-[1859]. SB's sign-off—"Let Mrs Bowles & myself be warmly remembered to father & mother *& sisters;* and for yourself & wife receive new assurances of *our joint* regard & affection" [italics added]—invalidates

the view that Mary's first visit was in summer 1859 (*Riddle* 123, 131; Him 2; *Var* 40, 127). This mistake undergirds Franklin's chronology of ED's 1858–1859 poems.

379   The poet's connection: *Let* 342, 358. Johnson's date for L196, December 1858, should be corrected to ca. December 1859 (Him 9; *Var* 1575).

380   "If it had no pencil": It isn't clear why Dickinson scholars assume this poem, once owned by the Bowles family, was sent to SB. The ms. does not identify him as the recipient, there are no known poems or letters from ED calling him "sweet," and once, when she sent him a stanza that originally had this endearment, she changed it to "sir" (Fr635B). For David Higgins, convinced SB was Master, Fr184 was the clinching evidence (Higgins 118).

> Since a few poems sent to Sue were turned over to the Bowleses, she is another possible recipient. Once, she sent WAD a "pencil to 'keep until I see you,'" an act he interpreted as a hint he had not kept up his end of the correspondence. WAD to Sue (draft), 12-11-1850, H.

380   In spite of this persistence: SB Let #5.1 [2-4-1859]; *FF* 149. #5.1 is dated by Edward Hitchcock's recovery from a nearly fatal illness (*HFE* 1-28-, 2-4-1859), a Harvest Club meeting concerning fruit (*SR* 2-12-1859), and a February 3 performance by Mrs. Sinclair (*SR* 2-1,4-1859).

380   Friendship entered a new: MVR-Deaths 129:240; SB Let #1.1, 6-1-[1859]; *Let* 351–52, 416. L205, misdated April 1859 by Johnson and Leyda, alludes to Mary's stillbirth in May and summer trip to Amherst (Him 2). The gems, heavy hearts, and apology for writing often place it soon after L189 and L193. The probable date: September–October 1859.

381   The stillbirth had been: Mer 1:171; *Let* 334. The visit has been dated June or July 1859 (Him 2; *Var* 40). Another possibility is late August. Mary Bowles to Mary Clemmer Ames [week of August 21, 1859], Ames Papers, speaks of a packed trunk and a reluctance to leave home. The letter can be dated by the expected publication "in Saturday's paper" of Ames's "Mamie and the Morning Glories" (*SR* 8-27-1859). If the trip this letter anticipated was the one that brought Mary to Amherst, the resulting series of letters from ED, starting with L189, began about the end of August.

381   Comparing a yellow and purple: *Let* 334, 601.

381   footnote 8: *Let* (1894) 212.

381   Fr60A: Franklin's date, "about early 1859," isn't consistent with his view that ED had not yet met Mary. The paper (187 × 122 mm, no watermark or boss, rules not quite 8 mm apart) is identical to that of L205 [Sept.–Oct. 1859]. The two sheets' irregularly spaced rules perfectly match. Given the ease with which, in the pen-lining process, the long and delicate pen points could be bent (whether separate or in a "comb"), this congruence suggests the sheets were inked at the same time and belonged to the same batch of purchased stationery.

382   The first communication: Him 8; *Let* 338 (corrected against ED646 A). The pamphlet's publication was announced in *SR* 8-13-1859. ED's mention of the second haying and first frost ("Summer stopped") suggests a date soon after 8-17, when it froze in Northampton (*SR* 8-18,22-1859). Ordinarily, Springfield had its first frost a month later (*SR* 10-23-1861). SB must have called during Commencement (*SR* 8-11,12-1859).

382   "We want to see you": *Let* 339.

382   After 1860, we have only one: *Let* 386, 737.

382 A complicating element: Mer 1:317, 2:149, 390–93. In 1863 SB recommended a Miss Nellie Loomis for a Treasury Department clerkship (SB to Charles Sumner, 4-25-1863, Sumner Papers). He was an early proponent of coeducation at Amherst College (Mer 2:80). His biographer thought his "relation to his daughters partook of the motherly quality" (Mer 2:329). MW agreed (letter to EBW, 12-12-1867, WDW Papers, box 13).

383 footnote 9: Mer 2:153; Lucia Runkle to SB, 4-5-[1874?], SB Papers 2:27. On Runkle, see SR 1-19-1902, p. 5.

383 On women's issues: Hampden Co. RD 157:391; "Women in Literature," SR 8-7-1858; "The Woman Question," 65, JGH Papers, box 1. Sewall, disregarding Holland's part ownership and the paper's division of labor (laid out in SR 1-22-1859), called it a "one-man daily" run by someone who was "poor at delegating responsibility" (466, 469). Blaming SB for "When Should We Write" (489–90, 742) and the newspaper's taste in poetry, he devised a tragic sequence in which the editor had a harmful effect on an aspiring poet who was "deeply in love with him" (473) and needed his help to fulfill "a consuming passion: the publication of her poems" (475).

> Theodora Ward, the Hollands' granddaughter, doubted there was a "break" in ED's friendship with them [Let (Holl) 68]. Four poems (Fr495A, Fr795A, Fr796A, Fr807B) went to them in 1862 and 1864. The important L269 has been variously dated 1859, 1861, and 1862 (Let (Holl) 55–56, Let (1894) 175, Let 413).

383 Unlike Holland: JGH to SB, 4-2-1860, SB Papers 1:3; Mer 1:63–64; "When Should We Write," SR 7-7-1860; Obituary, New Bedford Morning Mercury 2-20-1897. For a few of Cooke's contributions, see SR 3-7-1851, 8-25-1855, 8-21-1858, 12-3-1859. She was an "Editor" in the 1860 federal census (Springfield, dwelling 2428, page dated 7-27-1860) and the 1865 state census (Springfield, ward 3, dwelling 237). "Fidelia" in all official records, she usually signed as F.H.C. or Mrs. F. H. Cooke. Two decades after her departure from Springfield, George S. Merriam remembered her as "Frances" (Mer 1:388)—an error perpetuated in Him 22 and Var 239.

384 footnote 10: See Susan Howe, The Birth-Mark: Unsettling the Wilderness in American Literary History (Hanover, N.H.: Wesleyan University Press, 1993); Werner; EDE (Hart) 93–95. For vigorous questionings of the manuscript/print theory, see Shira Wolosky, "Emily Dickinson's Manuscript Body: History/Textuality/Gender," EDJ 8.2 (1999) 87–99; Mitchell, chap. 7.

384 "Enclosed in this was": F.H.C. to SB, verso of ED796 A.

384 The most prolific: Ames, "Mamie and the Morning Glories," SR, 8-27-1859; Let 357, 377. ED's phrase for the butterfly, "a vest like a Turk," points to the mourning cloak, Nymphalis antiopa, common in Amherst. Ames contributed thirty racy New York letters to SR from January to mid-July 1859, quitting when she broke into the top-paying New York Ledger (Westfield News Letter 6-22-1859). Her true metier was not poetry but essayistic journalism. On her debt to SB, see Edmund Hudson, An American Woman's Life and Work: A Memorial of Mary Clemmer (Boston: Ticknor, 1886) 67, 97–99.

385 footnote 11: SB Let #40 [12-13-1863], dated by the 12-16-1863 wedding of Hannah Schermerhorn, Mary Bowles's sister.

385 Dickinson's copy of: Aurora Leigh (New York: Francis, 1859) A; Imagery 79; SR 11-3-1869. My source in quoting Aurora Leigh is the 1996 Norton Critical Edition.

385 Once, in 1851: *Let* 147. CL has an anonymous twelve-page tract, "She Hath Done What She Could" (no pub., n.d.). Another, " *'She Hath Done What She Could,' or the Duty and Responsibility of Woman* (Raleigh: Galles, 1847), is at SNF.p-Box 3, Rare Books & Manuscripts, NYPL.

386 The main reason: *Aurora Leigh* (1859) 10, 15, A (marks). ED's later references to the poem focus on Marian Erle's confinement: Jack L. Capps, *Emily Dickinson's Reading 1836–1886* (Cambridge: Harvard University Press, 1966) 167–68.

387 Though the poem credits: *SR* 8-20-1859; *Aurora Leigh* (New York: Francis, 1857) 275–76, EDR 2.2.21. This, Sue's copy, has many more marks than ED's. Leyda's handy list of ED's marked passages, all in the poem's first half, is in MTB Papers 82:190.

388 For anyone growing up: *Let* 345, corrected against FN/ED 393. Flynt's diary confirms the Norcrosses were in western Massachusetts 10-11-1859: "Loring Nor+ & Daughters called—*all* returned to Boston this p.m." (Leyda's notes, MTB Papers, box 104).

388 After making this warily hedged: *Let* 345, corrected against FN/ED 393; M.C.A. [Ames], "Letters from New York," *SR* 1-15-1859; theatre billings in *Boston Daily Evening Traveller* and *Boston Daily Advertiser;* Leota S. Driver, *Fanny Kemble* (New York: Negro Universities Press, 1969), 173–74. L199 was dated January 1859 in *Let* (1894) 229. Johnson narrowed the date to ca. 1-4-1859 on the basis of ED's mention of snow. But Kemble didn't read in Boston that winter. The correct date may be 12-29-1859, a snowy day (*SR* 1-2-1860).

 L199 goes against the older view that ED "accepts and works within the conditions of a patriarchal universe" (Adalaide Morris, " 'The Love of Thee – a Prism Be,' *Feminist Critics Read Emily Dickinson,* Suzanne Juhasz, ed. [Bloomington: Indiana University Press, 1983] 109). Baym, more discerning, also gave undue emphasis to ED's childish side.

389 footnote 12: "Annals"; ED's obituary, *SR* 5-18-1886; SB to Mary Clemmer Ames, 12-14-1863, Ames Papers.

389 It is not the case: Dandurand; Dobson 128–30.

390 *Miss Gilbert's Career:* JGH, *Miss Gilbert's Career: An American Story* (New York: Scribners, 1860) 87, 388–89, 378, 466. Sue's presentation copy is unmarked (EDR 1.4.17).

390 On October 10: *SR* 9-8,29-, 10-10,13-1860; Mer 1:317. On 12-13-1860, Flynt (diary) "Completed 'Miss Gilbert's Career,' liked it exceedingly" (MTB's notes, MTB Papers 101:560). The sermonizing and weak characterization of hero and heroine were criticized in *Atlantic Monthly* 7 (Jan. 1861) 125–26.

390 bequeathed two books: They were William Patten, *Memoirs of Mrs. Ruth Patten, of Hartford* (Hartford: Canfield, 1834), and Hannah More's much reprinted *Strictures on Education.* SVN called Patten "a venerable old lady whom I dearly loved in my schooldays" and described More's book as "a valuable work [ED] would no doubt appreciate" (Copy of SVN's will, Norcross Estate folder, M). These bequests are missing from the will as probated.

391 "Dear Mr Bowles": *Let* 366, corrected against ms., Y-BRBL. *SR* 8-7-1860 puts SB in Amherst on Sunday, 8-5-1860. Flynt's diary (Leyda 2:17) puts him there Wednesday, 10-3-1860. He was back the next Wednesday for the district's Republican Convention (*SR* 10-11-1860). Soon after, there was a three-week public lecture series on Tuesday and Friday on "Great Representative Women" (*SR* and *HFE,*

both 10-19-1860). If L223 was written in October, these lectures may have been a factor in the quarrel.

Chapter 17

394 Lavinia Norcross was known: Leyda 2:8; *Let* 361–62.

394 footnote 1: FN/ED 393, 399, 414, 434, 455, 465, 483. "Louisa" appears in the following legal documents: 1862 and 1863 petitions (Suffolk Co. Probate, #43154 [LNN's will], #44460 [Loring's Papers of Administration]); 1863 deed (Norfolk Co. RD 316:114); 1888 will (copy at Concord Free Public Lib.); 1888 mortgage (Middlesex Co. RD 1879:563-65). The 1880 census has "Louisa" (Middlesex Co., Concord, dwelling 331), as do the records of the Concord Saturday Club and a list of participants in the 1879 Concord School of Philosophy (Concord Free Public Lib.). Ellen Emerson used "Louisa" in writing Edith Forbes, 1-18-1883, Emerson (checked against holograph in possession of Roger L. Gregg). She was sometimes called Louise but that was not the usual form.

394 The effort to absorb: *Let* 368; Matt. 10:29.

395 Two years later: MVR-Deaths 156:226; Leyda's notes of Flynt's diary, 5-5-1862, MTB Papers, box 104; ED to Joel W. Norcross, [early May 1862], bMS Am 1118.7, H; Polly Longsworth, " 'Upon Concluded Lives' ": New Letters of Emily Dickinson," *EDIS Bull* 7.1 (May/June 1995) 2–4. Lamira Jones Norcross died 5-4-1862.

395 The sinister word: *Let* 376, 407. "They're so happy" may refer to Eliza Coleman Dudley, married 6-6-1861 and consumptive.

396 When Loring died: *Let* 420–22; Fr528. Punctuation of L278 as in FN/ED 430.

396 footnote 2: FN/ED 434.

396 Lavinia had placed: Suffolk Co. Probate, #43154, #44460; Suffolk Co. RD, 1850 plan of Chester Square, book 615, 818:246, 829:114–15; Essex Co. RD 964:52, 985:47. A Medway property that LNN acquired in 1855 for $6,000 was sold by Louisa in June 1863 for $5,000 (Norfolk Co. RD 234:205, 316:113-15).

397 The truly fearful: *HFE* 1-9-1852, *SR* 5-17-1858; Fr60; *Let* 412, 397; *Let* (1894) 229.

397 Of all the Homestead's guests: "Country Girl" 82–83.

397 Yet the orphaned: *Let* 406–407, 424–25, 407 (corrected against FN/ED 416). L264 and L267 probably date from 1863, not 1862. Since Vin was home in early summer 1862 (*Let* 410), ED did not require her cousins for that year's commencement. In 1863, however, Vin was gone by late May (424). Other details pointing to 1863 are the sweetpeas (411, 427) and the advice of a Boston doctor (411, 425). "My double flower, that . . . comes up when Emily seeks it most" (408) refers to *both* cousins; but in 1862 only Louisa came (410). On the annual Dickinson reception, see *SR* 7-10-1873.

398 That all three: *Let* 368; Boston directory for 1860–1861; *Var* 1555; L.N. [Louisa Norcross], "Housework Defended," *Woman's Journal* 35 (3-26-1904) 98; Gary Scharnhorst, "A Glimpse of Dickinson at Work," *American Literature* 57 (Oct. 1985) 483–85. For a thirdhand and thus less credible report, see Martha Ackmann, " 'I'm Glad I Finally Surfaced': A Norcross Descendent [sic] Remembers Emily Dickinson," *EDJ* 5.2 (1996) 123.

398 What kind of oral: Mary J. Reid, "Julia C. R. Dorr and Some of Her Poet Contemporaries," *Midland Monthly* 3 (June 1895) 506; Reid to MLT, 12–5–1894, Todd 465

A; Mary Loeffelholz, "Prospects for the Study of Emily Dickinson," *Resources for American Literary Study* 25.1 (1999) 6.

398 A common past: *Let* 421 (cf. 410), 376 (corrected against FN/ED 406); [Julia Ward Howe], "George Sand," *Atlantic Monthly* 8 (Nov. 1861) 521–22; First Parish of Concord, Report for year ending April 1888, Concord Free Public Lib. Vaill's old-fashioned style is evident in his *A Sermon Delivered at Palmer* (Springfield, Mass.: Bowles, 1861).

399 As for religion: Examining Committee Records, vol. 3, Nov. 1859, Bowd St Ch; *Manual of the First Evangelical Congregational Church in Cambridgeport* (Cambridge: Riverside Press, 1870) 49–62. With mergers and dwindling membership, the latter society is now the North-Prospect United Church of Christ (Congregational), 1803 Massachusetts Ave., Cambridge. Among its few records is a typed membership list mentioning Louisa's belated transfer to Concord's "Old Parish Church" on 7-26-1912.

399 Those who believe: *Let* 397–98; ED to Joel W. Norcross [early May 1862]; *Let* 436.

400 footnote 5: *Let* 436; Leyda 2:72; *SR* 12-20-1862. Shira Wolosky, *Emily Dickinson: A Voice of War* (New Haven: Yale University Press, 1984), stands as the pioneering but thinly contextualized treatment of ED and the Civil War.

401 As the North moved: Mer 1:264; *Boston Courier Report of the Union Meeting . . . Dec. 8th, 1859* (Boston, 1859) 9, 28–29; *SR* 9-12,13,15,18,25-1860, 11-7-1860; *Let* 368.

401 The next year: *SR* 9-14,28-1861, 10-2,4,19-1861; *Northampton Free Press* 10-4,11,18-1861; *HFE* 10-25-1861. EdD's friend, Otis P. Lord, remained a strong Belleverett (*HFE* 9-13-1861).

402 Yet, even as Edward: *HFE* 7-18-1862; EdD to Charles Sumner, 5-12-1862, 7-20-1868, Sumner Papers; George C. Shepard, diary, 7-24-1864, Bolt 36:11. Inaccurate transcriptions of the letters to Sumner are in Norbert Hirschhorn, "New Finds in Dickinson Family Correspondence," *EDIS Bull* 7.1 (May/June 1995) 5.

402 Emily's position relative: *Let* 416, 377.

402 In February and March: Karen Dandurand, "New Dickinson Civil War Publications," *American Literature* 56 (March 1984) 17–27; *Riddle* 172. Storrs became a trustee 7-8-1863 but attended no meetings (Trustees Min) before ED's poems appeared in *Drum Beat*.

403 Perhaps, but letters from: *SR* 12-20-1864; SB *Let* #23.1 [12-8-1864], #53, 12-14-[1864], #54 [12-15-1864], #51 [12-3-1864]; *Springfield Musket* 12-20,21,22,23-1864. #51 ("give us some gems") is dated in part by a postponed trip to Boston (cf. #23.1); "Musket" was first deciphered by Karen Dandurand.

403 And yet, like them: *Let* 386 (punctuation as in FN/ED 410 verso), 420 (capitalization as in uncat ZA MS 77 Hooker, Y-BRBL).

404 Whether deliberately: *MB* 511–13.

405 Dickinson's productivity: *Poems* 1209; *Var* 1533. Franklin's count is based on earliest known manuscripts.

406 "tug for a life": *Let* 345.

406 "The Malay took the pearl": J. W. Watson, "Pearls and Gems," *Harper's Monthly* 21 (Nov. 1860) 764, 771; Fr5; *Let* 350; *Passion* 147–50. See also "Diamonds and Pearls," *Atlantic Monthly* 7 (March 1861) 361–71.

406 "Don't you think . . . these brief": *Let* 130.

407 "cut to the heart": Dall.

408   instances of the word "hurt": S. P. Rosenbaum, *A Concordance to the Poems of Emily Dickinson* (Ithaca: Cornell University Press, 1964) 367; dates from *Var.*

409   "Character is the creature": CW, *Religious Glorying* (Philadelphia: Bradley, 1857) 9.

409   "Wife": Shurr gives the fullest and most attentive treatment of this cycle but tends to override historical reality and take ED's imaginative transformations literally. The "wife" poems are Fr185 (J461), Fr194 (J1072), Fr225 (J199), Fr267 (J1737).

410   proposed . . . that the lover was a woman: *Rowing* 113–18. Smith makes a fixed rule out of ED's gender play: in "the Dickinson lexicon . . . a powerful *she* is *he*" (116). In fact, this is Smith's lexicon, not the poet's, who did not insist on uniform semantic equivalences.

410   Another possibility: *Let* 182 (also 208, 229); Cody 256. See also Anna Mary Wells, "Was Emily Dickinson Psychotic?" *American Imago* 19 (1962) 309–321.

411   Edward Dickinson, always so quick: EdD, "The importance of providing an Asylum for the insane," H; *HFE* 8-27-1858; *SR* 5-26-1859; EdD to Pliny Earle, 2-28-1870, Earle Papers 2:1; Earle to EdD, 10-5-1864, Bianchi Coll; [Joseph Delafield], *The Parish Will Case before the Surrogate of the City of New York. Medical Opinions upon the Mental Competency of Mr. Parish* (New York: Trow, 1857). Institutionalized members of locally prominent families included George Montague's son Charles Clinton; a son of Judge Reuben A. Chapman; a sister of William A. Stearns; and Thomas K. Boltwood (George Montague to Earle, 12-25-1876, Chapman to Earle, 1-5-, 5-4-1866, EH Jr to Earle, 3-11-1874, Boltwood to Earle, 7-30-1870, Earle Papers 5:2, 4:1).

> James W. Boyden, editor of *The Evidence of the Validity of the Will of Oliver Smith* (Amherst: Nims, 1847), is one of the more intriguing shadows in Dickinson family history. Judging from EdD's 1861 inventory, he apparently accepted notes in 1860 from this Amherst attorney with a face value of $14,400. There is no 1862 inventory—the first break in the series. By the following year, the notes had been downgraded from assets to "unproductive, doubtful" (EdD, Inventories for 1861, 1863, Bianchi Coll). The money was never recovered, and there seems to have been no lawsuit. This, EdD's biggest loss, remains a complete mystery.
>
> Boyden's wife, Eliza, daughter of Judge John Dickinson, died in 1857. Two years later the widower moved to Chicago. By September 1860 he was secretly engaged to Frances S. Kingsbury, of Beverly. He returned to Amherst in spring 1861 with the intention of staying, got married in Framingham on 6-19 (the day Sue gave birth), and was back in Chicago by August. A Boyden family history presents him as a brilliant, unexplained failure. LMB to Clara B. Williams Boltwood 9-10-1860, Bolt 9:1; *SR* 11-7-1859; *HFE* 4-12-, 8-2-1861; Hampshire Co. RP, Estate of John Dickinson, 192:33; Wallace C. Boyden, *Thomas Boyden and His Descendants* (Boston, 1901) 215–16; Albert Boyden, *Here and There in the Family Tree* (Salem, Mass.: Newcomb & Gauss, 1949) 26–30.

411   footnote 6: EdD to Pliny Earle, 1-6-, 3-27-1868, Earle Papers 2:1.

412   The most suggestive: Shurr 10-17, rightly emphasizing this poem, links it to the nearly contemporaneous Fr267, "Rearrange a 'wife's' affection!"

414   In this work Dickinson presents herself: *Let* 230; *Mass Reports* 81:582; *HFE* 8-9-1861.

415   footnote 8: Rachel Blau DuPlessis, *Writing beyond the Ending: Narrative Strategies of Twentieth-Century Women Writers* (Bloomington: Indiana University Press, 1985).

416   "Saxon" is marked: In addition to pointing to CW, this word in conjunction with "the English language" suggests an awareness of Francis A. March's 1860 Commencement speech (reported in detail in *SR* 8-9-1860) on the place of Anglo-Saxon in the development of English. See also *Addresses Delivered at a Celebration in Honor of Prof. Francis A. March* (Easton, Pa.: Lafayette Press, 1895) 72.

416   The links between: *Master Let* 23, 33. Prior to this 1986 publication, it was thought the penciled draft followed the two in ink. Since Franklin did not address the differences in kind between ED's penciled and inked scripts, the question of sequence remains unsettled. On ED's "Daisy," see Homans 201–205.

417   Even apart from the wounded: *Master Let* 42, 34, 23.

417   Readers are shocked: *Master Let* 42, 28.

417   Paradoxically, Dickinson makes: *Let* 737; *Master Let* 41.

418   footnote 9: *Rowing* 113.

418   Although the writer calls herself: *Master Let* 38.

418   To date, there is only: *Let* 744; *Master Let* 34–37.

419   The Master drafts quote: *Master Let* 38; [CW] to "Miss Dickenson," n.d., ED1012 A.

419   Following Wadsworth's death: *Let* 742. CW's mother died on either 9-29 (*Hartford Daily Courant* 10-12-1859, *Waterbury American* 10-14-1859) or 10-1 (CT Headstone 67:117). On the problem of documenting CW's first visit to ED, see George F. Whicher to MTB, 4-17-1936, MTB Papers 86:303.

419   In the other recollection: *Let* 738; Edith M. (Clark) Nyman, "Lt. William Clarke of Northampton, Mass. and his Descendants through 6 generations in New England," 2:85, 125, Forbes Lib., Northampton; Brooklyn directories from 1872–1873; "Death of Charles H. Clark," *SR* 3-18-1915; *Northampton Business Directory . . . 1860–1861* (Northampton: Trumbull & Gere, 1860) 31, Historic Northampton; Hampshire Co. RD 249:189, 425:305; Eleanor Terry Lincoln and John Abel Pinto, *This, the House We Live in: the Smith College Campus from 1871 to 1982* (Northampton: Smith College, 1983) 50. The tale MDB recounted in *LL* 47 of Vinnie's sudden appearance at the Evergreens—" 'Sue, come! That man is here!—Father and Mother are away, and I am afraid Emily will go away with him!' "—can't be taken seriously, even if shifted from mid-1850s to early October 1861 (Leyda 2:34).

420   Like Wadsworth, with his: *Catalogue of the University of the City of New York* (New York, 1858) 10; Obituary of Charles Clark, *Hampshire Gazette and Northampton Courier* 2-19-1889; Henry R. Stiles, *A History of the City of Brooklyn* (Brooklyn, 1870) 3:744; Lincoln and Pinto, *This, the House*, 50; "Clark Estate to Charity," *The New York Times* 4-10-1915, p. 18.

420   One of the poet's memorable: *Let* 764, 738; Notices for Clark and Brownell's Classical and English School, *Brooklyn Daily Eagle*, 9-3-1858, 9-6-1859, 9-10-1860, 9-4-1862, 9-7-1863. 1864 may be excluded, as Clark ran the school by himself in its last year, 1863–1864; see [James S. Knowlson, James D. Clark, and Frederic J. Parsons, Committee], *A Biographical Record of the Kappa Alpha Society in Williams College* (New York; the Society, 1881) 126.

421   footnote 10: "no near relatives": *SR* 3-18-1915; *Hampshire Gazette and Northampton Courier* 3-23-1915. For a brief account of the photograph, see Appendix 1.

421   "Wadsworth would seem": Gelpi 21. *This Was a Poet*, antedating the publication of the Master drafts, gave a remarkably astute treatment of ED's relationship to CW.

421 Whether or not: Among the views on this question, Ward's summation is one of the soundest: "whatever the complications in her personal relations, they were only the outward manifestations of a deep psychic disturbance marking the transition from a youthful phase to one more mature." *Let* (*Holl*) 67.

422 Soon after November: MVR-Deaths, 138:346; *Let* 361, 354. After Elizabeth Holland gave birth, Vin hoped she "did not pass through very 'deep waters' " (Vin to Holland [transcription], n.d., MTB Papers 86:298).

422 The lost-at-sea image: *Let* 356, 364; Henry James, *A Small Boy and Others* (New York: Scribners, 1913) 278; *SR* 10-12,13,16,17,25-1854; *HFE* 10-14-1854; Benjamin W. Dwight, *The History of the Descendants of John Dwight of Dedham* (New York: Trow, 1874) 2:868, 878; *New York Tribune* 5-2-1853.

423 As Dickinson drifted: *Master Let* 26; *Let* 364; SB Let #8 [6-11-1861], #9 [6-22-1861], #59.3, 8-2-[1865].

424 What Dickinson wanted: *Let* 363. Franklin's date, about spring 1861 (*Var* 251), makes the poem contemporaneous with the Master draft, "Oh! did I offend it" (*Master Let* 7).

424 The closest she came: *Let* 394. Of Franklin's two dates for L250, about 1861 and spring 1861 (*Var* 228, 1575), the more specific one seems better. The ms. shows no apostrophe in "*Heres*" (ED678 A).

425 If Dickinson wanted: *Let* 354, 394. Fr187B and Fr194A (ED679 & ED678, A) are on the same kind of paper, have the same script, and were written with a pen that left a small blot at the start of some strokes.

425 footnote 11: [Fidelia H. Cooke], "Over the Border," *SR* 6-1-1861; SB Let #81 [31 May 1861].

425 Responsive as Bowles was: SB Let #12 [10-1- or 10-8-1861], #15.2 [2-5- or 3-5-1862], #80 [April 1861, after SB's quarrel with F. D. Huntington (Mer 2:397–401)].

426 footnote 12: SB Let #62 [10-2-1866].

426 His crisis began: Mer 1:310; *Northampton Free Press* 6-11-1861; Mer 1:320-28; SB Let #11 [9-30-1861, dated by marriage of Catharine James and William H. Prince on 9-25-1861], #15 [10-17-1861], #15.1 [late Oct.? 1861]. The date usually given for SB's visit to Amherst and resulting sciatica is "early spring" 1861 (Mer 1:310). The true date, early February, is established by weather reports in *SR* and SB's 2-26 statement that he had "thrown my sciatica" (Mer 1:318). Nathaniel P. Banks wrote from Chicago, "The sciatica is a fearful master and I am glad to know you are well again" (Banks to SB, 3-5-1861, SB Papers 1:3).

427 Emily's many letters: *Let* 382, 383, 476.

427 One of many reasons: *Let* 371, 419.

427 All the same, Dickinson: *Let* 382, 395; Mer 1:330; Sue to [SB], 12-25-[1861], uncat ZA MS 77, Hooker, Y-BRBL. L252 has been dated early 1862 (Johnson), late December 1862 (Leyda), and ca. 1861 (Franklin). Himelhoch, spotting a parallel phrase in L246 (postmarked 1-3-1862), proposed 1-2?-1862 (Him 15). Sue's mention of the picture points to soon after Christmas 1861. On the torment of adequately thanking SB, see *Let* 393, 395, 437.

428 "I do not ask": *Let* 389.

428 "more stupendous": *Let* 436.

428 There is a recurring: *Let* 335, 390, 402, 393.

429 footnote 13: *SR* 7-20-1861; Mer 1:324.

429 By now the Evergreens': Sue to [SB], 12-25-[1861], Y-BRBL; *SR* 2-9-1861.

430 So far, neither spouse: Sue to [SB], 12-25-[1861], Y-BRBL; WAD to Sue, Palmer
     Depot [4-18-1861], WAD to Sue, postmarked 3-17-1863, H; SB Let #74 [2-14?-
     1875, dated by SB's 2-9 birthday]. The Palmer Depot letter is dated by troop move-
     ments (*SR* 4-18-1861). MTB, no doubt echoing MLT, claimed WAD was
     disappointed "early" in his marriage (*Home* 55). Farr makes the same claim for Sue
     (*Passion* 154), with as little real evidence.

430 As the end: SB Let #8 [6-11-1861, dated by defeat at Fort Monroe]; *Let* 437–38.
     L300 has the handwriting of 1861 and the same paper as L188 (moved to 1861 by
     Franklin). ED's surprise at SB's collapse, together with WAD's seeing SB on Satur-
     day, yields a date soon after 6-8-1861.

430 Incapacitated as he was: SB Let #7 [6-16-1861], #93 [ca. 6-18-1861], #9 [6-22-
     1861]. #93 is on the same Carsons Congress paper as #9, the slightly irregular pen
     rules perfectly matching. These two letters, SB's only ones using this stock, were
     written during his Berkshire trip.

431 One of the most troubling: SJL to MLB, 6-13-1852, SCB Papers 2:50; Smith fam-
     ily monument, Glenwood Cemetery, Geneva, NY; MGS to Sue and Harriet Cut-
     ler, [summer 1861], H; SB Let #15.1 [late Oct.? 1861].

431 Provisionally called Jacky: SB Let #13, 10-12-1861.

431 Four months after the birth: Abbie Shaw to Sue, 10-22-1861, H; *Let* 486; SB Let
     #19 [3-26-1862]. When Sue reread SB's letters in 1905 (Leyda 2:150), she may
     have destroyed offending passages.

431 The baby's first nurse: Obituary of Abbie Shaw, *SR* 2-16-1891; Will of Louisa
     Greene Shaw (copy), T. P. Ravenel Papers, Georgia Historical Society; Joseph Car-
     valho III, *Black Families in Hampden County, Massachusetts 1650–1855* (NEHGS
     and Institute for Massachusetts Studies, Westfield State College, 1984) 93, 115;
     Springfield directories from 1856–1857; SB Let #7.1 [6-6-1861], #7 [6-16-1861].

432 At first, Sue was charmed: Sue, untitled draft essay on nurses, H.

432 Abbie's successor: Sue, untitled draft essay on nurses, H; SB Let #11 [9-30-1861],
     #15.1 [late Oct.? 1861]. Cf. #106 [8-14-1861].

433 The third nurse: SB Let #15.1 [late Oct.? 1861], #86 [3-28-1862].

433 As this complicated: Abbie Shaw to Sue, 10-22-1861, Maggie [Conroy?] to
     Jacky/Ned, 5-11?-1862, H. Shaw's letter is in the script of her new employer, Julia
     W. Coggershall, who lived on the Hudson south of Poughkeepsie (1860 federal
     census, Town of Poughkeepsie, family 1151).

434 The split that opened: *Let* 711, 385, 396.

435 The following April: *Let* 404; San Francisco *Daily Alta California* 9-25- 10-1-1861;
     William Anderson Scott, *My Residence in and Departure from California* (Paris:
     printed by E. Brière, 1861); *Calvary* 12-13.

     However, in his 2-5-1860 anniversary sermon at Arch Street, CW predicted
     that by 1870 "probably another preacher" would be in charge (CW, *Eben-
     Ezer* [Philadelphia: Helfenstein, 1860] 27). This may have been a veiled ex-
     pression of his readiness to leave.

436 "the meaning goes out": *Let* 919. Cf. William C. Fowler to his son, William W., 12-
     12-1856, FF Papers, box 8: "Almost every one has a breaking down."

436 The one extant note: Sue to ED, "I have intended," H. In height, the three scissored
     fragments (which perfectly fit) come to 177 mm, the usual vertical dimension of
     queen's head stationery. Contrary to the inference in Walker 90, nothing is lost aside
     from "for."

438　The range of interpretation: Heman Humphrey, *The Woman that Feareth the Lord* (Amherst: Adams, 1844) 8; TWH, *The Results of Spiritualism* (New York: Munson, 1859) 11; *Let* 386 (punctuation as in FN/ED 410 verso).

439　"I am not suited": *Let* 379–80 (MS Am 1118.5 [B74b], H). That the pen rules perfectly match those of Sue's "I have intended" note indicates the two sheets were probably manufactured as part of the same batch.

439　Johnson's placement: *Let* 379; *Var* 161; Sue to [SB], 12-25-[1861], Y-BRBL. The letter has the same paper as Sue's "I have intended" and "I am not suited" and also the early December note to EdD concerning Jacky/Ned's name (H). Each sheet has the same irregularity on pages 2–3, the rules being out of parallel with top and bottom, rising slightly to the right. These features support the notes' contemporaneity. Sue's "Never mind Emily" (MS Am 1118.5 [B94], H), on the upside-down bottom half of a leaf of queen's head stationery (thus lacking the boss), shows the identical irregularity.

439　footnote 16: *Let* 434.

440　"Your praise is good": *Var* 162.

440　"Why Susie – think of it": *Let* 315.

440　"makes my whole body": *Let* 473–74.

441　"Could I make you": *Var* 162. For two very different treatments of "Safe in their alabaster chambers," see *Rowing* 190–96 and Mitchell, chap. 9.

441　The two women stubbornly: When the poem appeared in *SR* 3-1-1862, it was dated, mysteriously, "*Pelham Hill, June, 1861.*" Franklin connects this with SB's visit to Amherst that month but clouds the picture (*Var* 160) by bringing in the Orient Hotel, dedicated July 4 and opened soon after. This resort was not situated on Pelham Hill, a name reserved even then for higher Pelham center (Carlene Riccelli, "Place-Names of Pelham," 11, J). All local newspapers placed the hotel at Pelham Springs or Hygeian Springs, near the base of Mount Orient (*Northampton Free Press* 6-4-, 7-2-, 7-5-1861; *Hampshire Gazette* 7-16-1861, 3-1-1881; *HFE* 7-19-1861). Only the more distant *SR*—Franklin's one source—situated the hotel on Pelham Hill (3-14-, 7-6-1861).

　　Pelham's central burying ground was on the flat summit of Pelham Hill. The date assigned the poem may commemorate a side trip there by SB on 6-17-1861, the day he stopped at the Evergreens on his way north with Edward B. Gillett (SB Let #8 [6-16-1861], #93 [ca. 6-18-1861]). The public reference to this visit, two days before Ned's birth, would have had a special meaning for Sue.

Chapter 18

442　In faraway San Francisco: San Francisco *Daily Alta California* 12-10-1861, 4-3-, 5-27-, 6-1-1862; George Burrowes, "My early labors in San Francisco," 85, P; Questionnaire, CW's alumni file, PTS; *New York Tribune* 4-29-, 5-2-1862; *This Was a Poet* 324. *Calvary* 12–13 prints a letter from CW dated 4-8-1862.

443　Prior to Wadsworth's: *Let* 390, 396; SB Let #15.3 [3-21-1862].

443　Presently, Dickinson thought: *Let* 398. The Hollands' granddaughter, Theodora Ward, first surmised the meaning of these obscure requests to SB (*Capsule* 157–58); see also Shurr 141.

443　What Wadsworth's departure: *Let* 404, 460. The postmark of L261, misread by

Johnson (*Let* 405) and Franklin (*Var* 136), is Palmer APR 28 1862 (MS. Am. 1093 [4], BPL).

444   That Bowles also sailed: SB *Let* #15.3 [3-21-1862], #15.2 [2-5- or 3-5-1862]; *Let* 604; Frederick Law Olmsted to SB, 9-26-1865, Container 10, Olmsted Papers.

444   By the time Bowles: SB *Let* #86 [3-28-1862], #109, postmarked 4-3-1862; *Let* 402–403 (corrected against ED681 A). MDB's color-word for ED's eyes was "wine-brown" (*FF* 86). #86 is dated by Frazar Stearns's death ("the great Amherst bereavement") and a fast day on 4-3-1862. Johnson's claim that SB visited Amherst on 4-5-1862 is mistaken.

445   On April 5: SB *Let* #109, postmarked 4-3-1862, #19.1 [4-9-1862].

445   Soon after Samuel sailed: *Let* 405–406.

445   For once, Mary replied: *Let* 410; SB *Let* #21.1 and #21 (both belong to the same letter), "April [lapse for May] 12," [1862]; #20, Vevey, 9-15-[1862]. ED probably read SB's enthusiastic response to Paris before asking "how Amherst looked, in your memory."

446   The letter from Samuel: SB *Let* #20, 9-15-[1862]; #22, Black Forest, 7-13-[1862]. Leyda 2:68 mistakenly incorporated the message for ED (part of #22) into the later #20.

446   How appreciative was he: SB *Let* #21 [5]-12-[1862]; *Let* 382.

446   After the editor came: SB *Let* #23 [11-22-1862]; Mer 2:79; *Let* 419–20.

447   "the vagaries of fine womanhood": SB *Let* #16 [1-5-1863]. Dated by slightly later letters, trips to Boston, the framing of pictures, Catharine Scott Turner's expected visit, Charles H. Sweetser's work at *SR*, and Sue's interest in Jean Paul's *Titan* (reviewed in *Atlantic Monthly* 11 [Jan. 1863] 136–39).

447   "To the [Newman] girls": SB *Let* #16.1, Fri. [1-9-1863]. Misdated March? 1863 in Leyda 2:76, this letter was written two or three days after MW left Northampton for New Haven to assist her brother and sister-in-law in a double emergency—the birth of a child a month early on 1-6-1863 and the stroke suffered that day by father-in-law Roger Sherman Baldwin. The date is confirmed by Sue's return from Long Island, Catharine Scott Turner's anticipated visit, and the framing of a picture SB calls *Rebecca* (unframed in #16 [1-5-1863]). The sequence of letters is: #41 [12-28-1862], #16, #16.1, #33 [1-15-1863], #24 [1-16], #23.2 [1-29], #25 [2-2], #18 [2-7], #111 [2-19].

Like Old Hundred, China was a standard hymn tune. Leyda's misreading, "Aleluia" [sic], is not only too long for the script, but the initial letter, comparable to the C of "Col. Lincoln" (in #16), doesn't resemble SB's usual capital A. More seriously, Leyda's failure to italicize *Maiden's* loses the crucial nuance.

SB's praise of Mrs. Gillett's "sly humanity" suggests his uneasiness with ED's absolutism: "Too perfect goodness is for admiration, not for love" (SB *Let* #86 [3-28-1862]).

448   When Bowles visited: Annie Adams Fields, diary, 1-30-1867, Annie Fields Papers, MHS. According to Johnson (*Let* 961), ED sent four letters to SB in 1863 and 1864. Of these, L299 and L300 have been moved to 1861 by Leyda (2:28) and Franklin (*Var* 1575), and L283 to 1862 by Franklin (Var 302). The fourth, an impersonal note accompanying END's gift of apples (L284), is shown in facsimile in *Let* (1894) 218.

450   On his side: SB *Let* #26 [5-2-1863]; *Let* 420. #26 is dated by Elizabeth Chapman's marriage on 4-16 and Fast Day on 4-30 (*SR* 4-17, 23-1863).

450　But Bowles no longer: SB Let #90 [6]-7-[1863], #36.1 [12-18-1863], #59 [2]-12-[1864]. #90 is dated by SB's signature on the Mountain House register (Summit 6-9-1863).

451　footnote 1: Mer 2:66.

451　The April that removed: TWH, *Atlantic Essays* (Boston: Osgood, 1871), 75, 79, 92, 76; *Let* 573, 405. In quoting, ED replaced "seek" with "presume" and shortened "time and deliberation."

452　Like Ralph Waldo Emerson: TWH, *Atlantic Essays* 186. On TWH's radicalism, see Tilden G. Edelstein, *Strange Enthusiasm: A Life of Thomas Wentworth Higginson* (New Haven: Yale University Press, 1968); Howard N. Meyer, ed., *The Magnificent Activist: The Writings of Thomas Wentworth Higginson* (n.p.: Da Capo, 2000).

452　During the four years: *SR* 2-27-1858; SB Let #15.2 [2-5- or 3-5-1862].

452　An admirer of Thoreau: [TWH], "My Out-Door Study," *Atlantic Monthly* 8 (Sept. 1861) 302; Sewall 549. See Wells, chap. 7.

453　Further qualifying: TWH, *Atlantic Essays* 106, 102; EdD, "A Colloquy on A comparative view of the intellectual powers of the sexes," H.

453　On April 15: *Let* 403. Ms. Am 1093 (1), BPL, has a comma after "occupied."

453　As one might have guessed: [TWH], "Gymnastics," *Atlantic Monthly* 7 (March 1861), 283–302; *Let* 403. Talbot 106–107 has a discerning analysis of ED's first four submissions.

454　posted in nearby Palmer: Johnson substituted Amherst for Palmer on the postmarks of L261, L265, and L274 (*Let* 405, 409, 417). L268, loosely dated July 1862 in *Let* 411 and *Var* 259, was postmarked Palmer July 2[2?] (interpreted as 22 by BPL's accession catalogue). Ms. Am. 1093 (4), (8), (9), (16).

454　Hadley and Middletown postmarks: L314, L316, L319, L323; Ms. Am. 1093 (21), (23), (25), (30), BPL. Ackmann (229) suggests the 1867 Middletown letter was posted by the Norcross cousins.

454　Although Higginson's letters: *Let* 404, 408.

454　Convinced by Higginson's: *Let* 404–405, 408–409.

455　"When I state myself": *Let* 412. For helpful discussions of this passage, see Lindberg-Seyersted 24–31 and Benfey 127.

455　Inevitably, the letters: *Let* 404, 415.

456　"as to the 'innocent' ": *Brocades* 166–67.

456　Of course, Dickinson threw: *Let* 404; *SR* 6-16-1860.

457　Regarding another daring: *Let* 404; "Circumstance," *Atlantic Monthly* 5 (May 1860) 558–65; S.H.D. [Sue], "Harriet Prescott's Early Work," *SR* 2-1-1903. Prescott aroused great interest in the early 1860s: "The style of this writer is remarkable. We are told that she seems to herself to be the medium of some occult power, suggesting thoughts and images over which she has but an imperfect control" (*SR* 9-8-1860).

457　The critical surgery: *Carlyle's* 256; *Let* 415.

458　"that curious tilt": Talbot 109.

458　But it goes deeper: Fr284; *Let* 737, 404, 414. The poems submitted with L271 were Fr336A, Fr381A, and probably Fr359A and Fr401, all dating from summer 1862.

459　In late 1862: Cullum 2:240; Edelstein, *Strange Enthusiasm* 255–57; *Let* 423–24, 436; [TWH], "The Procession of the Flowers," *Atlantic Monthly* 10 (Dec. 1862) 649–57.

459　*The Friendships of Women:* William R. Alger, *The Friendships of Women* (Boston:

Roberts, 1868). Modern discussions of ED's female friendships include *Riddle; Imagery;* Lillian Faderman's groundbreaking "Emily Dickinson's Letters to Sue Gilbert," *Massachusetts Review* 18 (1977) 197–225; *Rowing; Passion* (proposing a "two loves" theory, SB and Sue); *Open Me.*

459 On July 10: Leyda 2:62, 64; *Let* 414. Flynt was nine years older than ED; Mary Bowles, three. Sylvia Henneberg, "Neither Lesbian nor Straight: Multiple *Eroticisms* in Emily Dickinson's Love Poetry," *EDJ* 4.2 (1995) 6–11, considers Fr380.

460 footnote 3: *Var* 406; Za Dickinson, Y-BRBL.

460 Dickinson showed a more: Anna Newman to Sue, Saturday [3-14-1863], enclosed with WAD to Sue, same date, H; Clara Newman Pearl, introduction to Clara Newman Turner, "My Personal Acquaintance with Emily Dickinson," MTB Papers 101:565.

461 Clara's interest in: Maggie [Conroy?] to Jacky/Ned, 5-11-1862, H; SB Let #16.1 [1-9-1863], #17, 3-9-[1863]; Turner 12, 15–16.

461 The poet's friendship: *SR* 4-12-1862; *Let* 451–52. Assigned to 1866 by Johnson, L317 was correctly dated in *Imagery* 25, 27.

461 About the time: MW to WDW, [5-7-1862], 3-13-[1863], MW to EBW, 1-12-[1864], MW to WDW, [9-28-1862], WDW Papers, boxes 8, 9.

462 When Whitney reported: SB Let #20, 9-15-[1862]; "Annals" 4. L230, possibly naming MW and misassigned to 1861 (*Let* 372), was written after the Norcross cousins moved to Concord in the 1870s; see pp. 673–74.

462 Fr430A: The hypothesis that the poem was meant for SB or Sue ("Putnam" 48) is highly unlikely: there is no solid evidence; the paper, thick and very white (MS Am 1118.10 [2], H), is unlike that used in ED's messages to either correspondent; and none of ED's mss. in MW's possession is known to have been sent first to others.

463 Fr566A: Two plausible dates are late June and early September 1863. On 6-24-1863 MW and the Bowleses visited the Evergreens at the start of a ten-day jaunt (Josiah Whitney, Sr., to WDW, 6-27-1863, WDW Papers 9:174; SB Let #27 [7-4-1863]); visit misdated 7-2?-1863 in Leyda 2:80. On 9-3-1863, writing Harriet Cutler, MGS had reason to think "Maria is with Sue" ("Thursday P.M.," H); letter dated by Susan Gilbert Smith's birth on 9-8-1863 and A. H. Barber's death on 9-5-1863 (*Geneva Gazette* 9-11-1863).

463 The third poem: *Poems* 634; *Var* 768; Josiah Whitney, Sr., to WDW, 7-14-1863, MW to EBW, 7-17-[1863], WDW Papers 9:175; WAD to Sue, "It is 20 minutes," Thursday [2-11-1864], H. WAD's letter, wrongly assigned to 3-15?-1863 by Leyda 2:76, is dated by the Academy of Music's *Faust* (*The New York Times* 2-12-1864) and MW's going to New Haven with SB (MW to WDW, Wednesday [2-10-1864], WDW Papers, box 9).

463 Fr813A: MS Am 1118.10 (4), H. The poem, dated "about 1864" in *Var,* is on the same paper (gilt-edged but cheap-looking, 97–99 × 152–155 mm, embossed "PARIS" in stippled oval) as Fr724A ("about 1863," MS Am 1118.3 [368], H) and four poems from early 1864—Fr794A (Lehigh University), Fr803A, Fr804A, and Fr805 (ED698, ED699, ED469, A). All but Fr794A are in pencil. 2-11-1864, the day WAD said good-bye to MW, would be a plausible date for Fr813A.

464 "To lose what we," "the parting of those": *Let* 532, 716.

464 The three Whitney: "The Flatbush Shooting Affair," *Brooklyn Eagle* 3-22-1864; SB Let #112 [3-22-1864], #82 [last half of June 1864]; *Let* 434. "Sorry to miss Flat-

bush friends," SB wrote in #82, dated by his approaching move on 7-9 and the 7-1 rain ending a drouth.

> Gertrude Phebe (Lefferts) Vanderbilt was active in charities and the author of books on Flatbush history and a first-person novel about a tough Irish newsboy saved by his Sunday School teacher, *Jack's Story As Told by Himself* (New York: Board of Publication R. C. A., 1872). On her connections, see her *Social History of Flatbush* (New York: Appleton, 1881) 204–206, 232; A. V. Phillips, *The Lott Family in America* (Trenton: Travers Book Store, 1942), 73; the articles on her husband in *Brooklyn Daily Eagle* 5-17-1877; *Riddle* 171–74.

464　On March 18: *HFE* 3-24-1865; MVR-Deaths 184:1; SB Let #56 [May 1 or 8, 1865], #104 [5-14-1865]. #56, anticipating the Colfax expedition, was written five days after #75 [4-26- or 5-3-1865].

465　That spring Emily: *Let* 441, 442.

465　Another tragic Gilbert: *Let* 444. The child's dates (9-8-1863, 11-3-1865) are on the Smith family monument, Glenwood Cemetery, Geneva, NY.

466　"Stroke the cool forehead": In 1859, decrying the fear of "immediate contact" with a corpse, Higginson urged: "Face it as it is, touch that quiet hand, it will not hurt you. Smooth that soft hair: God did not mean us to shrink from it."

471　In 1924: *LL* 46–47; *FF* 51–53. Two "corroborating" letters quoted by MDB are Virginia Fendley Dickinson to Virginia Dickinson Reynolds, postmarked 11-?-1930, and Reynolds to MDB, 10-7-1930, bMS Am 1118.97, 3:100, 3:99, H. For the noxious effects of MDB's account of the Wadsworth romance on ED's early textbook presentation, see Tom Cross, Reed Smith, and Elmer C. Stauffer, *American Writers: Good Reading for High Schools* (Boston: Ginn, 1931) 578.

472　footnote 5: Craik, *Olive* 3:54, 62–63, 69.

472　Fr905: See the helpful reading in *Comic Power* 44–47.

474　Fr554: My understanding of the poem is indebted to the clarifying exegesis in Walker 112–15.

474　Fr802: I use ED's alternative for the original "And is the Soul at Home."

478　"spasmodic," "I am in danger": *Let* 409.

478　Fr754: It is unlikely the poem addresses Sue (*Passion* 143–45): there is no evidence it was sent to her, and the lover appears from *outside* school.

483　From late April . . . October in 1865: *Let* 429, 431, 435–36, 440, 444. In early 1864 Mary Bowles was afflicted with painfully "inflamed eyes" (SB Let #44, 2-26-[1864], #46 [3-10-1864], #103 [3-11-1864]).

484　There is no record: *Let* 430, 433, 439 (punctuated as in FN/ED 442); *Let* (1931) xiv; JL/ED.

484　Dr. Williams's office: *Let* 432; [Henry W. Williams], "Female Physicians," *Boston Medical and Surgical Journal* 54 (4-3-1856) 3 [his italics].

485　exotropia: Martin Wand and Richard B. Sewall, " 'Eyes Be Blind, Heart Be Still': A New Perspective on Emily Dickinson's Eye Problem," *New England Quarterly* 52 (Sept. 1979) 400–406. See also James R. Guthrie, *Emily Dickinson's Vision: Illness and Identity in Her Poetry* (Gainesville: University Press of Florida, 1998). Mary Elizabeth Kromer Bernhard has presented sound objections to the exotropia theory in "A Response to 'Eyes Be Blind, Heart Be Still,' " *New England Quarterly* 55 (March 1982) 112–14.

485   anterior uveitis: "Medicine" 300–309; Henry Willard Williams, *A Practical Guide to the Study of the Diseases of the Eye* (Boston: Ticknor & Fields, 1862) 122–25; *Let* 433 (punctuated as in ED629 A).

485   It so happens: Anon., "Notes on Dr Williams lecture on Rheumatic iritis, Apr 27. 1865," B MS misc. W, Boston Medical Library in the Francis A. Countway Library of Medicine; Robert Christison, *A Dispensatory, or Commentary on the Pharmacopoeias of Great Britain and the United States* (Philadelphia: Lea & Blanchard, 1848) 281; Williams, *Practical* 125–27; *Let* 439.

486   Dickinson's living arrangements: *Let* 431; Uno 58–79; 1865 MA census, Middlesex Co., Cambridge, Ward 2, dwellings 532–537, 3; G. M. Hopkins, *Atlas of the City of Cambridge* (Philadelphia: Griffin Morgan Hopkins, 1873); Cambridge directories for 1863–1864 (MA State Lib) and 1865–1866 to 1872 (Cambridge City Lib). The change in street number was discovered by Uno 58–61.

486   A presentation inscription: Charlotte Brontë, *Jane Eyre* (New York: Harper, 1864), EDR 2.2.11; Charlotte Sewall Eastman to ED and Vin, 10-21-1872, H; *Let* 443, 435, 442.

486   As for Bowles: SB *Let* #50 [7-7-1864], #75 [4-26- or 5-3-1865], #59.3, 8-2-[1865].

487   Dickinson's statement: *Let* 433; 1865 MA census, Middlesex Co., Cambridge, Ward 2, dwelling 534; Cambridge Tax Rolls, 1865, Ward 2, p. 5; Rosalba Peale Smith Proell, "3. Sparks Street," *Publications,* Cambridge Historical Soc., 22 (1932) 51; Cambridge directories for 1882 and 1883; Louise Bangs's death notice, *Cambridge Chronicle* 4-26-1884.

487   Most of what: *Let* 430, 443 (punctuated as in ED 632 A), 435 (punctuated as in ED 631 A).

487   The letters to Sue: *Let* 430 (Hawthorne connection made in *Open Me* 131), 432, 121. ED wrote "Whem my Hands," then made a small penciled line canceling the last stroke of "m" (MS Am 1118.5 [B56], H). Except for *Open Me* 131, which gets it right, the word has been misread as "Where."

488   footnote 7: *Let* 419.

488   If Vinnie and Sue: *Let* 434, 430.

488   No matter whom: *Let* 433, 434 (question mark as in MS Am 1118.5 [B179], H, and *Open Me* 133).

489   In her one letter: *Let* 431, 404.

489   As for those guests: *Var* 1541. Fr576B, Fr871, Fr940, Fr942, Fr1027, Fr1028, and Fr1029 seem to touch on her eye trouble.

490   Another answer: *Let* 345; Emerson 4-6-, 1-18-1883. ED also listened to Louisa's piano playing: "How I miss ten robins that never flew from the rosewood nest!" (*Let* 439).

490   Certain at age twenty: *Let* (1894) 129; JL/ED; *Let* 440, 474, 471. There is no basis for John Evangelist Walsh's claim that Lord read Shakespeare to ED in Cambridge (*The Hidden Life of Emily Dickinson* [New York: Simon & Schuster, 1971], 190–93).

490   footnote 8: SB *Let* #6 [5-15-1861].

491   Among the plays: *Boston Daily Advertiser* 12-16-1859; JL/ED; Judith Farr, "Emily Dickinson's 'Engulfing' Play: *Antony and Cleopatra,*" *Tulsa Studies in Women's Literature* 9 (fall 1990) 231–50; Shakespeare, *Dramatic Works* (Boston: Phillips, Sampson, 1856) 6:123, 160, EDR 4.6.2; *Let* 791.

492   footnote 9: *Var* 832–33; *Let* 302. On WAD's feelings for crickets, see Peter Gay, *The Bourgeois Experience* (New York: Oxford University Press, 1986) 2:283–84.

492 Fr895D: A discerning treatment of the poem is in John Robinson, *Emily Dickinson: Looking to Canaan* (London: Faber, 1986) 173–77.

Chapter 19

497 When the large: *Let* 449–51; *Poems* 753; Fr895D and E.

497 Carlo's death marked: *Let* 454, 450–51.

498 dormancy or even exhaustion: *Capsule* 80; Johnson in *Let* 448; Murray.

499 seven poems written in the first-person singular: Fr1122, Fr1129, Fr1132, Fr1145, Fr1147, Fr1151, Fr1154.

500 a signal pride: *Let* 475; *Home* 414.

500 the more famous "My life had stood": For three notable wrestlings with this poem, see Rich, Weisbuch 25–39, and especially Miller 122–26.

501 A few months: Leyda 2:99, 102; "Margaret (Colossus) had in 9 yrs," MLT's notes of Vin's remarks, MLT Papers 82:402; WAD to Sue, 10-31-[1865], H (dated by Abby Fiske Adams's 11-1-1865 marriage [MVR-Marriages 181:2]). WAD's and others' diarrhea—"a river right through my stomach"—may explain two-year-old Susan's death on 11-3-1865.

501 Chances are: *Let* 427, 444; "This self-same Margaret," MLT's notes of Vin's remarks, MLT Papers 82:402. Immediately succeeding Margaret was a certain Hannah (*Let* 454; *FF* 24).

502 footnote 1: FN/ED 423.

502 It was not until: For a dressmaker's account, see Leyda 2:109.

502 "The art of making perfect bread": *House-Keeping* 157; Turner 1; *Let* 474.

502 The longest chapter: *House-Keeping* 233–300; *Let* 493, 783, 474; Allen 74.

503 In February 1869: Margaret Maher to Clarinda Boltwood, 3-2-, 4-6-1869, Bolt 12:5. The story has been beautifully told in Jay Leyda, "Miss Emily's Maggie," *New World Writing: Third Mentor Selection* (New York: New American Library, 1953) 255–67, and in Murray.

503 Another time never: Margaret Maher to Clarinda Boltwood, 4-6-, 6-22-1869, Bolt 12:5; "Statement of Finance" (1896) accompanying "Inventory of Lavinia N. Dickinson's property after Settlement with the Estate of Wm A. Dickinson," Bianchi Coll; *Home* 477.

504 "Tim is washing": *Let* 466.

504 "Complacency! My Father!": *Let* 350.

505 As a man of property: EdD to Alfred Norcross, 12-27-1867, 3-27-1868, J; EdD to Austin Graves, 5-18-1866, MTB Papers 99:517; *Amh Rec* 12-3-1868; EdD, Inventories, Bianchi Coll; EdD to Pliny Earle, various dates, Earle Papers 2:1.

505 Edward's biggest achievement: SB Let #91 [1-25-1864]; Leyda 2:85; Henry F. French to Frederick Law Olmsted, 7-30-1866, EdD to Olmsted, 10-22-1866, Container 10, Olmsted Papers.

505 Father's distinctive voice: EdD to SB, 12-25-1868, uncat ZA MS 77, Hooker, Y-BRBL. Potosí also appears in Fr118 and *Let* 352.

506 The second letter: *Worcester Daily Spy* 1-8-1869; EdD to Alexander H. Bullock, 2-6-1869, Bullock Papers. On Bullock's refusal to commute Edward W. Green's death sentence for shooting a bank officer in Malden, see the Governor's speech to Executive Council, 2-27-1866, Bullock Papers 2:4; *SR* 4-21-1866.

506 Although Edward and Austin: Mer 2:79–80; *SR* 2-21-1865; First #4, 1-2-1866, 4-9,15,18-1867; *SR* 9-24-1868; Allen 30; Leyda 2:133.

507   Unlike his father: WAD to Sue, [2-10-1864, dated by MW's trip to California], 10-31-[1865], H.

507   In her long: *SR* 5-18-1886, 2-14-1866; *Let* 450; Green 292. On lineation, see *Rowing* 67–69; Mitchell, chapter 7. Franklin calls ED's stated fear that TWH might see the poem a "pretext" (*Var* 953) for writing him. But L316 shows she had recently heard from him and had ample reason to write.

508   In September: SB Let #89 [9-29-1866]; *HFE* 12-6-1866; *Let* 464. #89 is dated by the postmark, an accident with a runaway horse, and SB Let #62, #60.

508   Dickinson's messages to Sue: *Let* 457, 458, 455, 464.

510   The friendship went back: *Let* 300–301, 349–50, 364–65, 445–46; Leyda 1:345, 349, 2:10–12; Charles Phelps [Susan's older brother], "Journal of Farm Works," 12-1-, 12-5-1865 (transcribed by Jane S. Scott); *SR* 12-5-1865; *Hampshire Gazette* 12-5-1865; *HFE* 12-7-1865, 8-2-1866. Leyda's "Dr [*Fish*]" (2:103) is incorrect. The other poem headed "December 5th" was Fr1216C. All three poems I link to Phelps were entrusted to friends.

511   After 1865: Mer 2:60–61; SB Let #31, 9-1-[1867?], #66 [9]-24-[1868], #85 [3-21-1867], #98 [10-16-1869, the day after the Bowleses returned home from the West (Mer 2:147)]. In dating #31, 1863 is ruled out by the reference to MGS, who gave birth in Geneva 9-8-1863 and didn't visit Amherst that August or September (MGS to Harriet Cutler, "Thursday P.M.," [9-3-1863 (for date, see p. 722)], H.) The years 1862, 1865, 1868, 1869, and 1870 are ruled out by SB's travels, and 1864 and 1866 are unlikely. The opening suggests Sue took offense at a risqué passage in SB Let #61.3 (no. 2) [7-24-1867, dated by envelope postmarked 7-25-1867 and by Mer 2:55].

511   Judging from the remnants: Ackmann 212, 229; *Hartford Courant* 7-4-1867; Leyda 2:124; *Let* 456 (punctuated as in FN's transcription, Tr50 A), 368.

512   A Norcross family letter: Joel W. Norcross to Alfred Norcross, "Friday aft" [3-13-1868], J; *Let* 459.

512   In spring 1869: *Let* 465–66.

512   The spirited letters: *Let* 444, 449, 452.

513   Once, after Elizabeth: *Let* 455.

513   Nothing made: Alumni file for Perez Dickinson Cowan, PTS; Burgess 45; [Cowan], *James H. Cowan* (Boston: Frank Wood, 1883) 43; *Let* 463. Nannie died 6-21-1869 (Cowan, comp., "The Cowan Family," 10, Knox County Public Lib.).

514   From the dying: Diane Price Herndl, *Figuring Feminine Illness in American Fiction and Culture, 1840–1940* (Chapel Hill: University of North Carolina Press, 1993); JL to Laura Baker, 5-9-1858 (2:39), JL/ED (4:64), Laura B. Lyman to Alfred B. Crandell, 6-5-1886 (5:80), Lyman Papers.

516   But the white attire: *Let* 370; *Lyman Let* 68; Sewall 448.

516   Dickinson's one surviving: "New Dress Replica on Display," *Dickinson Homestead* (newsletter) 4.1 (spring 2000); Mary E. Safranski Derrick, "In Just the Dress [Her] Century Wore: Emily Dickinson's White Dress," unpublished paper (Dickinson Homestead); *Let* 427. The Amherst Historical Society owns the dress. The Homestead has an exact replica on display.

516   footnote 2: Nason 135; Charlotte Sewall Eastman to ED and Vin, Venice, 10-21-1872, H.

516   A fastidious: "Was She a Recluse?" Portland *Sunday Oregonian* 3-19-1899, p. 22; Leyda 2:120; E. F. Strickland to MDB, 9-2-[1920s?], 3:119, bMS Am 1118.97, H. JL's letters from 1865 (Lyman Papers, box 4) make it unlikely that he visited ED in Cambridgeport that summer.

517   Although Dr. Williams: *Var* 1541; *Let* 450.

517   Was Dickinson's health: EdD to Alfred Norcross, 3-16-, 3-27-1868, J; *Let* 457, 459, 466, 471 (corrected against and supplemented by FN/ED 453).

518   Fr1129: After writing line 4, "With the austerer sweet," ED at once composed a substitute, "With this sufficient Sweet," before going on to the second stanza. MS Am 1118.3 (271), H.

518   "I gave my part": *Let* 419.

518   Yet most of the poems: *Let* 464, 455; Ellen E. Dickinson, "Emily Dickinson," *Boston Evening Transcript* 9-28-1894, p. 4; Leyda 2:141.

518   footnote 3: *Let* 692.

519   Dickinson's impetus: *Let* 463; Leyda 2:143.

519   In late 1865: *Var* 994; *Philadelphia Inquirer* 4-10-1869; Clifford Merrill Drury, *William Anderson Scott: "No Ordinary Man"* (Glendale, Calif.: Arthur H. Clark, 1967) 292; San Francisco *Daily Morning Call* 6-30-1869; San Francisco *Daily Alta California* 6-30-, 7-1-1869; *The New York Times* 7-24-1869, p. 8. Johnson linked Fr1143 and Fr1186 to CW in *Poems* 794, 790, xxiv.

520   Fr1143: I give what looks like ED's preferred alternatives in the ms. (ED435 A).

520   footnote 4: San Francisco *Daily Morning Call* 6-27-1869.

520   Another poem on renewal: *Var* 1015; Leyda 2:149.

521   Instead, her most enlivening: Leyda 2:132; *Let* 462.

521   It is a mark: *Let* 460, 453, 450.

521   Her strong refusal: *Let* 460–62. See *Let* 379–80, 517–20, 725–26, 840–42, 866–69 for the other letters and ED's replies. On "the 'Power,'" see Chapter 7 and *Let* 432, 631.

522   To be sure: *Let* 460.

522   In August 1870: *Let* 472–73; TWH, "Charlotte Prince Hawes," *The Radical* (Jan. 1867) 284.

523   The visitor's wife: "Recent Deaths," Boston *Daily Evening Traveller* 9-4-1877; *SR* 9-14-1877, p. 4; *Let* 473, 476.

523   The Dickinsons' home: On Stoddard, see Alfred Habegger, *Henry James and the "Woman Business"* (Cambridge: Cambridge University Press, 1989), chap. 4.

523   In the entry hall: *Let* 473–75.

524   The next day: *Let* 475.

524   Only after: *Let* 476; *Carlyle's* 276. Originally, instead of the insinuating "something abnormal," TWH wrote "an abnormal life" ("Emily Dickinson's Letters," *Atlantic Monthly* 68 [Oct. 1891] 453).

Chapter 20

531   Long after her death: *FF* 48; "Country Girl" 115

532   In 1870: TWH, "The Door Unlatched," "The Gate Unlatched," *Woman's Journal* (1-15-1870, 7-9-1870); *Let* 480, 481.

533   the only pre-1865 poem she is thought: *Var* 1536.

534   footnote 4: *FN* 94.

535   The 1852 note: *Let* 184 (discussed Chapter 12).

535   Meanwhile, a poem: *SR* 7-18-1882; EFF, "Eheu! Emily Dickinson!" *SR* 1-11-1891; Bliss 62.

536   A third visitor: In *Riddle* (9, 224, 283–84, 329) Patterson conjectured that Anthon returned 1876–1877 and made the link with Fr1429 (which Franklin dates about 1877). In Patterson's view, ED felt Anthon committed "Treason" by spurning the

poet's lesbian desire. As I see it, the poem concerns a plurality of loved ones and her own pattern of avoidance, and accuses no one of treason.

536 These lines: *Let* 510 (quoting I John 4:10).

537 "It was a return": *Capsule* 94.

537 In 1930: Austin Baxter Keep to George F. Whicher (copy), 11-30-1930, MTB Papers 86:303. I think it is unlikely the "exquisite note" was the one accompanying Fr1455B (*Var* 1275–76).

538 At church: Vin to Nora Green, 1-14-1899, J; Green 291–92; 1870 federal census, Amherst, family 359; *Let* 599; Leyda 2:266, 273; "Country Girl" 11. Clara was the one person who both met ED and reviewed early books about her: see Clara Bellinger Green, "Guesses and Memories," Boston *Herald* 5-10-1930, p. 17; Green to Genevieve Taggard, 4[5]-4-1930, Taggard Papers.

538 footnote 5: *FF* 35.

538 In 1882 or 1883: William T. Mather to MDB, postmarked 12-16-1936, 2:79, bMS Am 1118.97, H; Sewall 296.

539 Once, when: Annie Holland Howe to MDB, 8-4-1931, 2:57, bMS Am 1118.97, H; *FF* 25. Leyda 2:115 dates the encounter July 1866, when Annie, b. 9-15-1851, was fourteen (Gilbert Warren Chapin, *The Chapin Book* [Hartford: Chapin Family Association, 1924] 1:998).

539 This dark hallway: *FF* 25–30.

539 To judge from: *Let* 508, 485 (cf. 567), 514 (cf. 524).

540 "inveterate readers": Allen 41, 43.

540 cultivated Sarah Tuckerman: James S. Cushing, *The Genealogy of the Cushing Family* (Montreal: Perrault, 1905) 171–72; MVR-Marriages 80:57; HFE 2-22-, 4-18-1856, 12-31-1858; Sue, "Architecture," fragments, H; 1870 federal census, Amherst, dwelling 202; Burgess 57.

540 This phrase aptly describes: *Let* 520, 487; Adelaide Hills to ED, n.d., ED163 A. Henry F. Hills first shows up in New York directories in 1871.

541 But there was an: *FF* 9–10 (cf. ED, *The Single Hound* [Boston: Little, Brown, 1914] xv); *Let* 862 (punctuated as in MS Am 1118.10 [13], H).

541 Although Dickinson showed: Frances Hodgson Burnett to Myra, 4-7-1918, Bianchi Misc. 4, bMS Am 1118.98, H; Leyda 2:322 ("box" misread as "bow").

541 Heading the list: First Church of Christ in Pittsfield, *Proceedings in Commemoration of Its One Hundred and Fiftieth Anniversary* (Pittsfield, Mass.: Sun Printing Co., 1914) 85; Allen 37; Clarinda Boltwood to LMB, 5-4-1867, Bolt 11:1; *FN* 75–78; *Let* 464. In Pittsfield, the Jenkinses had a cook, a chambermaid, and a nurse (1880 federal census, district 59, dwelling 104)—a large domestic staff for a minister.

542 It was perhaps: Jonathan Jenkins, memorial sermon for EdD, H; *Let* 473, 505–506, 548; EdD, pledge, H (facsimile in Leyda 2:200); *FN* 80–82. Sweetser's name, dropped in *Let* (1894) 279 and FN/ED 495, was plausibly restored by Johnson. She struck an Amherst girl as "from another world in the elegance of her beautiful laces and rustling silks" (Allen 43). Like ED (*Let* 470), Bianchi made fun of her size and gait: "She walked . . . with a dipping motion, up and down—something like a dumpling in boiled water" ("Country Girl" 22–23).

542 Sue's daughter had: *FF* 8–9; *Let* 543. For SB's birthday messages to Sue, see #36.1 [12-18-1863]; #52, 12-19-1864; #64 [12]-18-[1867]; #66.1, 12-23-1867; #67.1 [12]-14-[1869]; #116 [12-17-1872]; #77 [12-22-1872].

543 footnote 6: *Passion* 145–46; Charles Wadsworth, Jr., *How to Get Muscular* (New York: Randolph, 1891), dedication.

544 "pretty thoroughly": AOT to John Tyler, 9-13-[1876], Tyler Papers 3:15. The source of the report was a neighbor, Richard H. Mather. After moving to Pittsfield in 1877, the Jenkinses remained friends, naming their third child after WAD.

544 Emily's letters to Louisa: *Let* 470–71, 515–16, 543, 504; *FN* 37. For the cousins' Berkeley Hotel residence, see "Country Girl" 83–84 and Boston directories for 1873 and 1874. L442, previously dated summer 1875, was probably written in May. "The very weather that I lived with you" points to this month, which ED thought of as "the peculiar anniversary of your loving kindness to me" (*Let* 471). MW had visited the Norcrosses on 4-18-1875: see MW to James L. Whitney, Sun [3-6-1875] (misdated 3-31 by Y-MSSA and 3-1 by Leyda 2:232), WDW Papers 22:593. In L410 "J____ W____" must be James L. Whitney, a librarian. FN/ED 467 suggests that ED wrote "Tidings of a book" to explain her message to him. The phrase should not accompany her signature, as in *Let* 523.

544 footnote 7: Marion V. Dudley, *Poems* (Milwaukee: Cramer, Aikens & Cramer, 1885) 41; Frederick I. Olson, "My Search for Mrs. Dudley," *Historical Messenger of the Milwaukee County Historical Society* 13 (Dec. 1959) 11–15.

545 When others broke: *Let* 500, 84; Elizabeth Stuart Phelps, *Hedged In* (Boston: Fields, Osgood, 1870). The name was reduced to its initial for *Let* (1894).

545 This tartness: *Let* 678, 668–69.

546 Few aspects: Baym 194; *Let* 473.

546 What we know: Buckingham 215–17; MVR-Births 215:57; 1870 federal census, Amherst, dwelling 316; *FN* 72–73.

547 Oddly enough: Buckingham 216; *FN* 39–42; *Let* 559.

547 footnote 8: MDB to Ned, 8-2-1876, Bianchi Coll.

547 "Aunt Emily stood": *FF* 6; *FN* 31–36, 67–68.

548 Never moody: *FN* 58, 32–33.

548 Once, when little Gilbert: "Country Girl" 64–65.

548 Curiosity was growing: *FF* 50; WAD to EFF, [March or April, 1850], Thomas Cooper Lib, University of South Carolina.

549 How did Edward feel: *FF* 24–25; [Alexander H. Bullock], "Mrs. Davis," Worcester *Daily Spy* 1-25-1872; EdD to Bullock, 2-3-1872, Bullock Papers. EdD's "almost perfect woman" echoes Alonzo Hill's *The Perfect Man* (New York: Norton, 1854), a funeral sermon on Davis's husband.

549 As a trustee: William H. Ladd to Alexander H. Bullock, 10-4-1871, Julia Ward Howe and Lucy Stone to Bullock, 6-17-1874, Bullock Papers 1:6, 1:5; "The Committees," *Boston Daily Advertiser* 2-19-1874; EdD to WAD, 2-18-1874, ED915 A.

550 There is a family story: MLT's notes of Vin's remarks, MLT Papers 82:402.

551 "The Vein cannot thank": *Let* 479.

551 A few years earlier: *Let* 453, 481.

551 Dickinson's ambition: *Let* 491.

553 When Higginson: *Let* 525 (cf. 500); TWH's diary, 12-3,4-1873, bMS Am 1162 (11) 1873, H; *Brocades* 63, 128–29. TWH may have been entertained at the Evergreens, to judge by SB Let #68 [12-2-1873]: "Another day, when there is no stranger."

553 footnote 9: Leyda 2:112.

553 On his side: *Let* 570, 518–20.

554 Dickinson's reply: *Let* 517–18. On letter and poem, see Loeffelholz 134–35.

555 Hunt had grown up: EH Jr, Notebook "B+," 14, Doc Hitch 7:26; Ruth Odell, *Helen Hunt Jackson* (New York: Appleton-Century, 1939) 57–61; Leyda 2:14, 213; *Let* 475–76; Wells 185, 198.

555 footnote 11: *Catalogue One: Women Authors Published by Roberts Brothers* (Brockton, Mass.: John William Pye Rare Books, [1991?]) 16.

556 As a professional: HHJ to James T. Fields, 11-16-1870, Huntington Lib; EFF to Horace Scudder (draft), box 3, gen. corr. n.d., EFF Papers; HHJ to Thomas Niles, 11-18-1876, Preston-Dodge Family Papers, MHS; [Harriet W. Preston], rev. of *Mercy Phil, Atlantic Monthly* 39 (Feb. 1877) 243 (attribution in *Atlantic Index* 1857–1888, 141); AOT to John Tyler, 2-4-[1877], Tyler Papers 3:16 (cf. Leyda 2:295–97). Henry James's (suitably) contemptuous review appeared in *The Nation*.

556 Higginson started things: *Let* 545, 461; unused envelope addressed to HHJ in "Bethleem" on which ED drafted Fr1183B and Fr1184; HHJ to James T. Fields, Bethlehem, NH, 7-29- to 11-16-1870, Huntington Lib; Odell, *Helen Hunt Jackson* 129–30; Leyda 2:204–205, 210.

557 Whatever the answer: *Let* 544–45.

557 Others had said this: *Let* 404–405; Leyda 2:239, 193; *Let* (1931) 131. In *SR* 11-25-1879 it was said (by SB's son?) that "a great poet from among our women has not yet entered in the lists of expectation."

558 And Helen would not: *Let* 563, 565.

558 Unable to field: *Let* 563, 565, 573.

558 As the 1878 publication date: *Let* 624, 625.

559 When *A Masque*: "Success," *A Masque of Poets* (Boston: Roberts, 1878) 174; Thomas Niles to ED, 1-15-1879, H; *Catalogue One*.

559 Perhaps not: *FF* 30.

559 In March 1871: Leyda 2:172; *Let* 486; "Pen Pictures of the Prominent Men of Amherst. No. II. Honorable Edward Dickinson," *Amh Rec* 10-11-1871.

559 When Edward tried: *SR* 7-11-1872; Trustees Min 4:797, 806–807; SB Let #97.1, 11-26-1872, #68 [12-2-1873]; *Endow* 65–67, 104; *Mass Reports* 229:392. On the stringpulling: SB Let #77 [12-22-1872], #101 [7-15-1873]; Richard H. Mather to Julius H. Seelye, 12-27-1872, Seelye Papers 2:2; SB to Alexander H. Bullock, 11-18-1873, Bullock Papers 1:2.

560 Ironically, as Edward: *Home* 441–44; *Amh Rec* 10-29-1873; *Boston Evening Journal* 11-7-1873. On Hoosac Tunnel: *The New York Times* 4-24-1873 (5), 5-2-1873 (4), 5-30-1873 (1), 11-28-1873 (5), 2-21-1874 (1), 9-12-1874 (6).

560 Although the Panic: *Let* 511, 515; EdD to WAD, postmarked 1-21-1874, ED911 A.

560 It was in the middle: "Disappearance of Mr. Sweetzer," clipping in EDC's scrapbook, MTB Papers 101:567; "INFORMATION WANTED," *New York Herald* 1-23,24,25-1874; "A Missing Merchant," *Herald* 1-24-1874; "$250 Reward," *Herald* 1-26,27,28-1874.

561 Although a Mulberry Street: Nivens George, detective, *Trow's New York City Directory* for 1873–1874, 973.

561 From time to time: *Let* 521, 662–63 (cf. 543), 528; *Amh Rec* 4-29-1874; *SR* 6-19-1874.

562 The next morning: Leyda 2:223–24; *Boston Morning Journal* 6-17-1874; MLT to TWH, 7-9-1891, TWH Papers, BPL.

562 Emily was at supper: *Let* 526.

562 Three days later: *FF* 13; *SR* 6-20-1874; Leyda 2:225.

562 She also could not: Leyda 2:226–27; Jenkins, memorial sermon, H; *Home* 219.

562 The *Springfield Republican's*: *SR* 6-17-1874.

563 It is a tribute: Jenkins, memorial sermon, H.

563 bought large life insurance policies: EdD, inventory for 1851, Bianchi Coll. EdD's 1858 inventory shows the insurer as State Mutual Life Assurance Co. All American Financial, today's successor company, has not been able to find the policy.

563 "it is doubtful": JGH, "The Woman Question," JGH Papers, box 1.

564 In Edward's case: Hampshire Co. RP, Estate of EdD, 192:6, WAD's 1874 petition (copy) and Vin's 1895 statement (copy); Vryling Wilder Buffum to Genevieve Taggard, 3-6-1930, Taggard Papers. MDB misleadingly claimed that ED and Vin "were never dependent upon their brother financially in any way" (FF 142).

564 footnote 13: Let 596 (misdated by Johnson); FF 250; SR 12-12-1876; Amh Rec 12-18-1876; EdD, inventory for 1873, Bianchi Coll; WAD's record of EdD's estate, H.

564 A defect in this: FHB to LMB, 11-24-1876, Bolt 15:1; AOT to John Tyler, 11-26-1876, 6-11-[1878], Tyler Papers 3:15, 3:17; Ned to MDB, postmarked 1-7-1889, Bianchi Coll; Ned to MDB, Wed evening [1890s], Bianchi Coll. The gravity of WAD's illness is indicated by SB Let #80.1 [Nov.? 1876].

565 footnote 14: FF 173; MDB, "Indian Summer," New England Magazine 17.2 (Oct. 1897) 212.

565 The striking anomaly: Forgery noted by Leyda 2:229. EFF to Mary, 1-25-[1881], 3:1, to Mr. Loper (draft), n.d., box 3, EFF Papers.

566 The first time Mattie: FF 32; Let 537, 528.

566 A bulwark was gone: Let 551, 529, 559; LL 100; Let 600.

566 footnote 15: Helen Jameson to JFJ, 11-14-1882, Container 5, Jameson Papers.

566 The last books: Let 547.

567 The most powerful: Brocades 128–30; Poems 960–62; Var 1247–49; Let 525, 528.

568 footnote 16: On James W. Boyden, see above, p. 715.

568 The letter to Higginson: Let 583.

569 Knowing how: SB Let #69, 11-24-1874 (cf. Let 557); FF 13; Let 852, 683.

569 The deadliest calendar day: Let 526, 542, 635, 588, 627; Var 1533.

569 At Edward's funeral: Let 526–27.

570 Now that she: Let 540.

570 Eighteen seventy-five was a: Mer 2:319–20; SB Let #71 [8-8?-1875], #71.1, 8-4-[1875]. For other pertinent letters, see SB Let #124 [summer 1875?], #80.2 [5-26-1876?], #71.2 [6-3-1876], #76 [12-14-1876]).

570 By 1877 he was: SR 6-27,28-1877; Leyda 2:275–77; Graves; FF 62–63; Let 589–90; SB Let #119, Wednesday, 7-4-[1877]. July 4 fell on Wednesday in 1866 and 1877. 1866 is ruled out by the postage stamps (first issued 1870–1871) and by what is said about Edward B. Gillett.

571 For Emily, the interview: Mer 2:426; William S. Robinson, "Warrington" Pen-Portraits (Boston: Mrs. W. S. Robinson, 1877) 163–66; Let 588–89.

571 The editor's own gallant: Mer 2:419, 426 (cf. Higgins 230–31); SR 10-19-1861. There is no question the letter went to ED, who alluded to it twice before its publication: about 1884 she spoke of "the Warrington Words" (SB's excerpt from "Warrington" Pen-Portraits), and in January 1885 she quoted "greatly impressive to me" (Let 828, 856). Sue (Leyda 2:277–78) could not have been the recipient: SB's letters to her in the 1870s were far more direct and ungloved.

572 Higginson was sent: Var 1252; Let 573, 627, 569, 570.

572 Since Dickinson's letters: For ED's use of the Hollands as intermediaries, see Let 737, 562, 596, 608, 648, 689, 575; Let (Holl) 106, 162. For an attempt to discredit Ward's report of the family tradition that Elizabeth Holland facilitated ED's correspondence with CW, see Sewall 593 and Richard B. Sewall, "In Search of Emily

Dickinson," in *Extraordinary Lives: The Art and Craft of American Biography,* William Zinsser, ed. (New York: American Heritage, 1986) 84. For ED's use of other intermediaries, see *Let* 523, 549, 656, 668, 702, 703, 740, 772, 778, 793. Mary Lee Hall's tale of Luke Sweetser's part in ED's romantic correspondence (Leyda 2:359–60) probably reflects Hall's own conspiratorial bent.

573 footnote 17: ED222 A (Fr1570A).

573 footnote 18: ED277 A; *Var* 1224–25.

574 "The Sermon you failed": *Let* 572–73; *God's Culture.* The end of ED's sentence—"and 'Corn in the Ear,' Audacity, these inclement Days"—quotes this sermon: "as if the Omniscient Husbandman did not know when his immortal grapes are purple, and his corn in the ear!" (7).

574 footnote 19: George F. Whicher, "Pursuit of the Overtakeless," *Nation* 169 (7-2-1949) 14–15.

575 On December 10: MVR-Deaths 292:275.

Chapter 21

576 Lizzie Mather: Henry F. Hills to Adelaide Hills, 10-31-1877, Hills Papers 3:1; AOT to John Tyler, Tuesday A.M. [10-30-1877], Tyler Papers 3:16; MVR-Deaths 293:2; *Let* 595.

576 Two months later: AOT to John Tyler, 1-1-1888 [1878], Tyler Papers 3:17; *Let* 595–96.

577 When Maria Whitney: MW to WDW, 10-28-1877, WDW Papers 26:733 (see also 26:736, 739; 27:743, 749); Sue to SB, 12-11-[1877], Hooker, uncat ZA MS 77, Y-BRBL; Dr. David P. Smith to Sue, 12-29-1877, bMS Am 1118.8, fd 17, H; Mary Clemmer [Ames], "Forever Lives the King," *Poems of Life and Nature* (Boston: Osgood, 1883) 61; *Let* 595; MVR-Deaths 301:347; *Amh Rec* 1-23-1878.

577 footnote 1: MLT/ED 695.

577 It is clear: *Let* 600; Fr1314C; *Let* 601, 620–21.

578 "my dearest friend": MW to [SB], [late April 1875, after Concord centennial of 4-19], Hooker, uncat ZA MS 77, Y-BRBL.

578 footnote 2: WDW Papers, boxes 8–25; *Passion* 207.

578 lived with the family: See MW's letters to WDW or EBW from 2-10-[1867], box 12, to 3–10–1868, box 13, WDW Papers. MW to EBW, 8-11-[1867], misdated 1862 by Y-MSSA, is in box 9. On the rumors, see MW to EBW, 3-10-1868, 13:293, and "Sat P.M." [3-14?-1868] (misdated 1863? by Y-MSSA).

579 "with peculiar," "sweet," "long fidelity": *Let* 623. For a thinly contextualized and often conjectural survey of ED's mss. to MW, see "Putnam."

579 Yet it is true: Mer *passim;* SB Let #16 [1-5-1863], #16.1 [1-9-1863], #126 [mid-April 1867]; MW to EBW, 1-27-[1878], WDW Papers 46:1409. For two major statements on the friendship, see SB Let #44, 2-26-[1864]; MW to WDW, 9-13-[1865], WDW Papers 11:215.

579 "I have thought": ED to MW, [early 1878], MS Am 1118.10 (6), H (*Let* 602).

580 To "hope you": ED to MW, [early 1878?], MS Am 1118.10 (8), H; MW to Sue, 11-25-[1895], Bianchi Coll. L591 is dated early 1879? in *Let* 634 and ca. December 1878 in *Var* 1294–95. Two considerations point to an earlier date: it appears the correspondence was just getting under way, and "we cannot believe for each other" shows up in a June 1878 letter (*Let* 612).

580 "I lend you": ED to MW [early 1878], MS Am 1118.10 (7), H. Only the last five

words appear in *Let* 603. Hart's surmise ("Putnam" 58) that ED "lent" a rose doesn't do justice to the occasion and is otherwise unconvincing.

581 "dreamed Saturday": ED to MW [fall 1884], MS Am 1118.10 (12), H (passage omitted in *Let* 848). Contrary to *Passion* 244, nothing in the WDW Papers suggests MW "was still mourning" SB in 1885.

581 footnote 3: "Putnam"; *Let* (1894) 349–50; "Newspaper Employees Buy Church Window," *SR* 5-28-1961; *Selections from the American Collection of the Museum of Fine Arts and the George Walter Vincent Smith Art Museum* (Springfield, Mass.: Springfield Library and Museums Association, 1999) 250–52.

581 Dickinson had many: ED to MW, MS Am 1118.10 (13), (8), H (*Let* 862, 634).

581 Whitney came to Amherst: WAD's 1880 diary, 3-27,28,29,30, 7-31, 8-1, MLT Papers 101:243; MW to James D. Whitney, 3-31-[1880] (29:834), 5-21-[1880] (29:840), MW to EBW, 4-4-[1880] (46:1407), 4-10-[1880] (46:1409), WDW to EBW, 7-31-1880 (29:848) [speaks of chintz: hence ED's "sewing"?], MW to EBW, Wed P.M. [8-4-1880] (46:1407), WDW Papers; *Let* 661–62. L643 is assigned to June in *Let* 661 and *Var* 1333.

582 footnote 4: *Let* 758.

582 A letter reacting: MW to EBW, 1-28-[1883], 5-21-[1883], WDW Papers 46:1408, 1407. The story is told in family correspondence from 5-19-1882 to 6-13-1883, boxes 32–33, 46. See especially MW to WDW or EBW, 6-28-[1882] (32:919), 7-29-[1882] (32:922), 10-23-[1882] (46:1408), 11-4-[1882] (32:932), and EBW to WDW, 3-12-[1883] (33:943). MW to WDW, 10-16-[1882] (32:930), implies MW was too busy to visit Amherst after returning from Europe.

582 This ordeal: *Let* 776–77. Johnson explained this letter by MW's interest in the Children's Aid Society. His context for L815 seems equally speculative: WAD saw MW in Cambridge 2-5-1883 (WAD's diary, MTB Papers 101:245), but I find no evidence she visited Amherst that spring or that ED wouldn't see her (*Let* 771).

582 footnote 5: MLT/ED 706.

583 "went into camp": *Let* 848.

583 "I feel Barefoot": *Var* 1250.

583 "I am glad": *Let* 793–94.

584 Born in 1812: *Proceedings of the Bar of the Commonwealth, and of the Supreme Judicial Court, at Boston. On the Death of Otis Phillips Lord, LL.D. March, 1884* 4, 6; *Proceedings of the Essex Bar Association, and of the Supreme Judicial Court, at Salem . . . April, 1884* 43. Bound together at CL.

584 An old-line Whig: *Bench* 1:420; *Proceedings of the Whig State Convention Held at Worcester, Oct. 2d, 1855* (Boston: Office of the Boston Courier, 1855) 14–15; *SR* 7-10-1862; Edgar J. Sherman et al. to Essex Co. Commissioners, 1-1-1875 (copy), MTB Papers 99:522; *SR* 9-24-1874.

585 In private life: *Proceedings of the Essex Bar* 35, 38; "Annals"; Watts & Select 375.

585 footnote 6: "Annals"; Watts and Select 465.

586 The judge had a memory: MVR-Deaths 365:90; *Let* 883.

586 Like Dickinson: Lord, "Memoir of Asahel Huntington," *Historical Collections of the Essex Institute* 11 (July, Oct. 1871) 92–93; James Guthrie, "Law, Property, and Provincialism in Dickinson's Poems and Letters to Judge Otis Phillips Lord," *EDJ* 5.1 (1996) 27–44. Conceivably, Fr728 could concern Judge Reuben A. Chapman.

586 The first solid: Lord's envelope to ED, postmarked Salem November 10 and variously assigned to 1872 (*Var* 1090), 1873 (Leyda 2:210), and 1873 or later (*Rev* 71); *Let* 509 (cf. *FF* 235; "Country Girl" 40–41), 730 (ED424 A, on reverse of Fr1337),

548; Leyda 2:236–37; ED's will, fms Am 1118.4 [L32]; Lord to Vin, [early Feb.? 1877] (dated by Jenkins's imminent departure), H; MVR-Deaths 292:275 (cancer). Although MLT's working list of correspondents for the last three chapters of *Let* (1894) includes "Mrs Lord, 1874," the published work has no letters identified as written to her; see MLT Papers 69:25.

587　fair copies that can be dated: *Let* 727–28, 730–31, 753. Werner 288 astutely questioned whether the second half of L750 (from "Door either," *Let* 728) belongs with the first half. It was in fact written on 11-11-1882 (see footnote 13).

587　assigned the earliest manuscripts: *Let* 614–15, 618; Leyda 2:305–306; Werner A757. The paper of the first part of L560 (ED736–736a A) has exactly the same dimensions, 127.5 × 204.5, as Fr1488C (ED322 A) and Fr1489B (ED816 A), both about 1879. The paper of the last part of L560 (ED736b A) is identical (127 × 204) to that of Fr1525 A (ED427 A), about 1880. That of the first and last parts of L561 (ED737–737a A) is identical (125.5 × 203.5) to Fr1494 (ED340 A) (about 1879) and Fr1462C (ED41 A) (securely dated Dec. 1880). The reason Lord cannot be Master is that Master resided out of New England (*Master Let* 42). I see no real basis for the supposition (Wolff 401) that ED's passion for Lord antedated Elizabeth's death.

587　"It sometimes seems": *Let* 744.

587　"the Lords": WAD's 1880 diary, MLT Papers 101:243; *Amh Rec* 8-25-1880. *Amh Rec* and *SR* do not mention any Lord visits to Amherst in August 1878 and 1879.

587　"I designed": *Let* 567. Variously misdated 1884 (*Let* [1894] 411) and 1876 (Leyda 2:258), L478 was written Sept. 4, 5, or 6, 1880. The relatives mentioned in the first sentence were Thankful and Oliver Eastman Smith of Hadley (MLT/ED 862).

587　The next day the pastor: *SR* 9-1-1880; *Presbyterian Reunion: A Memorial Volume. 1837–1871* (New York: De Witt C. Lent, 1870) 513–14; *Andover* 110. The Sweetsers' church membership is established in "Disappearance of Mr. Sweetzer," clipping in EDC's scrapbook, MTB Papers 101:567.

588　On September 23: WAD's 1880 diary, MLT Papers 101:243 (cf *FF* 36). WAD's diaries for other years (101:244, 245) show Lord visited April 14–17, 1882, and September 8–12, 1883. No diaries survive for the 1870s, 1881, or 1885.

588　Shakespeare concordance: Mrs. Cowden Clarke, *The Complete Concordance to Shakspere* (Boston: Little, Brown, 1877), EDR 2.6.5. Inscription in Sue's hand: "Emily Dickinson from Judge Otis P. Lord. 1880." Leyda 2:336 guessed it was a Christmas gift. The 860-page book shows no signs of use.

588　The letter to Lord: Werner A734, A734a, A735a; *Rev* [75]; Werner 14, 35, 301. Werner's signal contribution is to call attention to the visual qualities of ED's manuscripts and probe the constructions of earlier editions. Unlike them, however, *Open Folios* does no new archival work of the kind that ascertains dates, explains allusions, clarifies meaning. At times, the book bends the historical record, as when claiming that, "according to Bingham [Todd], the drafts and fragments of the Lord letters had been entrusted, *possibly by Dickinson herself,* to her brother" (Werner 43). If Bingham made the major but unfounded surmise I italicize, I don't know where. And a few transcriptions seem faulty: "severely" for "serenely," A440; "now" for "won," A479; "makes" for "make," A758a.

589　"the prank of the Heart": *Master Let* 37.

589　"almost feared Language": Werner A754.

589　In spite of: Werner A739, A740 (*Let* 617). Werner 287 makes a strong argument that "Dont you know" doesn't belong with the rest of L562.

589 footnote 9: Werner A739; *FF* 48.

590 footnote 10: Werner A744e (*Let* 727); *Rev* 59; Leyda 2:375–76; Dinah Craik, *The Head of the Family. A Novel* (New York: Harper, n.d.) 106.

590 As for what: Werner A740a–b; [Coventry Patmore], *The Angel in the House: The Betrothal* (Boston: Ticknor & Fields, 1857) 108, EDR 4.4.20.

590 Alternatively: Werner A749d–e.

591 The basic understanding: Werner A757, A737; Abby Farley to Ned Dickinson, 4-8-1883, H. "Little hussy" is supposed to have been spoken to Miriam Manning Kimball Stockton, who repeated it to MTB in 1936, all according to *Rev* 23.

591 Among her ruses: *Let* 703; Werner A745b, A748a–b, A753.

592 This dream reaction: Werner A753a; TWH's diary, 5-19-1886, bMS Am 1162, H; Ruth Kimball Smith to MTB, 12-19-1954, MTB Papers 85:265. The mother, Mary Merrill Kimball, came from Danvers; one of her great-grandfathers, John Kimball (1780–1871) was Lord's maternal uncle (Ruth Kimball Smith's alumna folder, Radcliffe College Archives; MVR-Births 532:521, 232:186; Leonard Allison Morrison and Stephen Paschall Sharples, *History of the Kimball Family in America* [Boston: Damrell & Upham, 1897]).

592 Whether or not: *Let* 486; Werner A742b; *Let* 861, 824.

592 footnote 12: ED to [E. E. Hale?], 2-14-[1854], quoted above p. 315; *Indicator* 2 (Feb. 1850) 223 ("*such* an one"); Craik, *Olive* 2:158, 288; 3:29, 232.

593 Emily proved: *Bench* 1:420; *Proceedings of the Essex Bar Association* 35. Lord's retirement was spurred by declining health and Democrat Benjamin F. Butler's election as Governor (*Amh Rec* 12-6-1882).

593 Dickinson's decision: Wolff 404; *Let* 559. *Capsule* 100–103 has a sensitive assessment of the relationship with Lord.

593 One of the things: Obituary of CW, *Philadelphia Inquirer* 4-3-1882; San Francisco *Daily Morning Call* 6-27-1869; *Funeral* 23–24. See also Vivian R. Pollak, "After Calvary: The Last Years of ED's 'Dearest Earthly Friend,' " *Dickinson Studies* no. 34 (1978) 13–18.

594 The next summer: *Let* 738, 901.

594 But he gave: *Let* 738; *Funeral* 24–25; *Philadelphia Inquirer* 4-3-1882.

594 The last words: "Charles Wadsworth," *The Presbyterian* 4-8-1882, 10; *Let* 901.

594 It is a curious: *Let* 737; Werner A734, A744d–e.

595 The one acquaintance: *Obituary Record of Donors and Alumni of Williams College 1882–3* 320–21; Brooklyn directories from 1872–1873; CW, *Sermons* (Philadelphia: Presbyterian Publishing Co., 1882) 170, 218.

595 "The Friend": MLT/ED 747. The words follow "voice is able?" and precede "Are you certain" in L827.

595 The Clark correspondence: *Let* 745, 778.

597 "The sea had been passed": J. T. Headley, *The Sacred Mountains* (New York: Scribner, 1854) 68; Amherst College Library Accession Book, vol. 4, #11595, A.

597 Two years after: *Let* 815, 817, 820, 818.

598 What had happened: Werner A742e–f, A740.

598 footnote 13: *Let* 728; Werner A742d; *Boston Daily Globe, SR,* and *Amh Rec* for 11-8-1882; Howard P. Nash, Jr., *Stormy Petrel: The Life and Times of General Benjamin F. Butler* (Madison, N.J.: Fairleigh Dickinson University Press, 1969) 279; "Mr. William Dickinson," *Worcester Evening Gazette* 9-7-1887; Psalm 118:22; Luke 20:17; Acts 4:11; I Peter 2:7.

599 Fr1265: Harold Bloom's promising exegesis falters when it propounds an exact ref-

erent for each "this" (*The Western Canon* [New York: Harcourt Brace, 1994] 299–300). Like some other poems never sent out by ED, Fr1265 probably wasn't meant to be understood by readers.

600   "Till the first friend dies": *Let* 817.

600   only one or two more treatments of love: Fr1631, Fr1642.

Chapter 22

603   take the royalties: See Elizabeth Horan's indispensable "To Market: The Dickinson Copyright Wars," *EDJ* 5.1 (1996) 88–120.

603   And yet Bianchi: *FF* 46, 66, 54; *Let* 875.

604   would burn her papers: *FF* 59–60; *Let* (1931) 246; *Brocades* 16–17; Murray 726–27.

604   One way to try: *Let* 700; Thomas Niles to ED, 4-24-1882, H.

604   From Blind's: Mathilde Blind, *George Eliot* (Boston: Little, Brown, 1910), 19, 56; *Let* 769. "Niger Fig" does not seem to be a varietal name. In *Henderson's Handbook of Plants and General Horticulture* (New York: Peter Henderson, 1890) 276, "niger" is a descriptive term meaning "black, or black a little tinged with gray."

605   Robinson's biography: *Let* 721, 775; A[gnes] Mary F. Robinson, *Emily Brontë* (Boston: Roberts, 1883) 141, 142, 218. On "strange power," see Loeffelholz 130.

606   At the Mansion: Mariette Jameson to JFJ, 11-19-[1882], Container 5, Jameson Papers; *Let* 676, 643 (corrected against FN/ED 506), 774.

606   From all sides: *Let* 693, 676; WAD to Clara Newman Turner, 5-29-1885, MLT Papers 97:159; Turner to WAD, [March 1884?], MTB Papers 104:632.

607   helped look after her bedridden mother: *Amh Rec* 9-8-1880; *Let* 675, 475.

607   The old blockage: *Let* 750, 689.

607   "We were never intimate": *Let* 754–55.

608   The troubles next door: EdD to WAD, 5-26-1874, ED926 A; Elizabeth Seelye to Julius H. Seelye, 2-11,14-1877, Seelye Papers 5:13; WAD's 1880 diary, 1-19, 6-6, 7-9, 1883 diary, 3-12,13, MLT Papers 101:243, 245; Richard Quain, ed., *A Dictionary of Medicine* (New York: Appleton, 1883), 1354–63; *FF* 66–67. WAD's diary places Ned's one rheumatic episode for the year in March 1883, when the window would not have been open or a rosebush blooming—two of MDB's details. Could her anecdote be based on an epileptic attack, disguised as rheumatism?

608   little direct contact: WAD's 1880 diary, 12–19; *Let* 756; *LL* 52; Beaconsfield, Benjamin Disraeli, First Earl of, *Endymion* (New York: Appleton, 1880), EDR 1.2.25. The book shows no signs of use. For ED's "whom seeing not," see *Let* 679, 724.

609   footnote 1: *EDE* (Lombardo) 15–16; wedding announcement and clipping, Hills Papers 7:11; Horan 93.

609   Perhaps one reason: *Let* 612, 828 (cf. *Austin & Mabel* 182), 893, 829.

610   By this time: WAD's 1880 diary, 2-28, 6-17; 1882 diary, 6-19, 10-17, MLT Papers 101:244; WAD to Henry F. Hills, 3-23-1880, Hills Papers 6:12; WAD [to Sue], 10-19-[1882], H; envelope to Sue in Grand Rapids, postmarked 10-19, H.

610   By a happy chance: Werner A742c–d (*Let* 728). The draft was composed 11-11-1882. ED's "The Air is soft as Italy" accords with WAD's description of the "warm, soft" weather (1882 diary, 11-10). Frances Hersey cannily guessed the draft's context and date (letter to MTB, 3-24-1957, MTB Papers 83:216).

610   footnote 2: MLT's 1882 diary, 11-10, MLT Papers 39:4.

611   But sides were what: MLT's 1882 diary, 3-25, 9-10; 1881 diary, 10-3, MLT Papers

39:3; Leyda 2:354, 357, 361. For a shrewd firsthand appraisal of MLT, see Frances Hersey to MTB, 11-18-[1952], MTB Papers 83:213.

611 The family had such distinction: Leyda 2:354; MLT's and WAD's 1882 diaries, 9-11-1882. For detailed accounts of the affair, see *Austin & Mabel;* Peter Gay, *The Bourgeois Experience* (New York: Oxford University Press, 1984) 1:71–108.

611 The affair had all: WAD to MLT, March? 1883 (copy), 7-12-1883, MLT Papers 94:77, 78; WAD's 1883 diary, 6-21, 12-13; *Austin & Mabel* 149–54.

612 footnote 3: Quoted from *Austin & Mabel* 233.

612 Years passed: Sewall 298–99; *Austin & Mabel* 175; Sue to MDB, "Sunday eve" [folds show the letter goes with an envelope postmarked 12-8-1884, a Monday], H.

612 Outside the family: Amherst Savings Bank Records–Customer–Loan, nos. 679, 722, J; Deed of 6-8-1886, Hampshire Co. RD 404:89; EH Jr to WAD, 3-16-1889, Doc Hitch 14:19. After WAD died, EH Jr spoke of the constant "coming together of him & myself" in running the college (to Charles M. Pratt, 9-1-1895, Doc Hitch 14:42). In the one comment Longsworth cites to prove the affair was known, Mariette Jameson is bent on *dismissing* the "mean things said by the lower classes" about the couple (*Austin & Mabel* 121).

613 In her later years: *Let* 622, 790, 641; *LL* 55.

613 The question stands: *Let* 765, 781, 882; *Austin & Mabel* 216, 226, 208. Longsworth's claim that ED was "fully aware" (64) has yet to be substantiated.

614 How we answer: *Let* 733; *FF* facing 176; *Open Me* 293. In *FF* 176, MDB put on record Sue's selective destruction of ED's mss.

615 many enemies: Those highly critical of Sue included AOT, James I. Cooper, Mary Lee Hall, Mary A. Jordan, Clara Newman Turner, and Anna Newman Carleton (Leyda 2:257, 299, 408; Sewall 252–64; Turner). "Much to my disgust, I am invited . . . to tea at our detestable neighbor's," says the diary of JFJ, who considered Sue "the biggest liar in town" (6-23-1883, Container 2, Jameson Papers). John W. Burgess admired her as a brilliant "social leader," but was dubious about her "exceedingly vivid" imagination (Burgess 60).

615 More devastating: MGS to Sue, "Wed. P.M." [10-17-1883], H; F. W. Mather to Sue, 10-15-1883, Bianchi Coll.

615 In fall 1883: Ned Gilbert to Gilbert Dickinson, 10-5-1883, Bianchi Coll; "Country Girl" 116–17; MLT's 1883 diary, 10-6; MGS to Sue, "Sat. morning" [10-6-1883], "Friday A.M." [10-12-1883], H.

615 For the one: WAD's 1883 diary, 12-13; MGS to Sue, "Sunday P.M." [11-25-1883], H; "Country Girl" 120.

616 But the suffering: Mariette Jameson to JFJ, 10-14-[1883], Container 6, Jameson Papers; Vin to [Rev. and Mrs. Forrest F. Emerson], 11-16-[1883], 1-24-[1884], Emily Dickinson Collection (#7658), Clifton Waller Barrett Library, The Albert H. Small Special Collections Library, University of Virginia Library; *Let* 721.

616 The poet's response: *Let* 572–73; *God's Culture* 5, 8; CW, *Sermons* (Philadelphia: Presbyterian Publishing Co., 1882), 233; *Let* 799, 620, 866. For commentary on L868, see Talbot 120–23.

617 Later messages: *Let* 800–801; *FF* 172.

618 footnote 6: "Country Girl" 118.

618 Dickinson wrote Elizabeth: *Let* 803. Later, more realistically, she interpreted Gib's raving as involving his agemates (*Let* 891).

619 The severe illnesses: Sue to MDB, "Your Tuesday's letter," "Wed Eve" [8-6-1884?

(Leyda 2:427)], H; *FF* 249; Sue to MDB, "Your Sat. letter," Tuesday [Aug.? 1884], H; Sue to MDB, "Of course my dear," Thursday P.M. [12-4-1884], H; "Country Girl" 141; Ned to MDB, 5-14-[1885], Bianchi Coll; Sue to MDB, "Why you got" and "I am up dear" [March 1885], H; WAD's 1884 diary, 12-19, MLT Papers 102:246; *Let* 848, 879.

619 One of the most difficult: "Dwight," *SR* 5-15-1913; *Let* 830, 463, 780; Fr1658; *Open Me* 256-57. Hart (251–52, 262–68) maintains that the entire communication is a poem, that we must retain ED's lineation, and that the message is erotic, one of many "coded declarations of desire." To my ear, the third sentence ("To believe") fails to scan (on ED's meters, see Lindberg-Seyersted 118–55). Nor do I see anything in the message about a heavenly union with Sue (on this point Pollak 137 was right). The problem is that Hart grounds her reading on a hidden "code" known to her but not to others such as Johnson, whose different take can be explained by his being "unfamiliar" with the "language" and maybe "uncomfortable with it" (Hart 267). For another (but frightfully intricate) reading of L912, see Sullivan 48–57.

620 "off charnel steps": *Let* 436.

621 "Not to outgrow": *Let* 899.

621 When Sarah Tuckerman's: *Let* 898, 903; *The Interpreter's Bible*, George Arthur Buttrick, et al., eds. (New York: Abingdon-Cokesbury, 1951) 722–23; Wolff 144–47. Barrett Browning had compared the poet-hero to Jacob in "A Vision of Poets" (ll. 793–95).

622 The physician who chiefly: MVR-Deaths 374:1; Leyda 2:474; Quain, *Dictionary of Medicine*, 174–82, J.

622 There are other reasons: MVR-Deaths, vol. 374.

623 More material reasons: "Medicine" 309–316.

623 After Bowles died: *Let* 611 (cf. 920 [PF52]), 823, 843.

623 This was her way: WAD's 1884 diary, 6-14; *Let* 826–28.

623 The one poem she is known: *Let* 826–27, 802, 840.

624 On October 12: WAD's 1884 diary, 10-12; Sue to MDB, 10-13-1884, H; Sue to MDB, "Wed. 2 PM," postmarked 10-22-[1884], H; Vin to Clara Newman Turner and Anna Newman Carleton, 1-23-[1885], H; Mariette Jameson to JFJ, 5-16-[1886], Container 7, Jameson Papers.

624 footnote 8: Leyda 1:xxix; E.D.–Leyda, Jay, J; Kate Boyle in conversation. Bigelow resided in the Dickinsons' former home on Pleasant Street.

624 This sense of lurking danger: *Let* 889, 888.

625 On November 30: MLT's 1885 diary, 11-30, MLT Papers 39:7; WAD's 1886 diary, 1-19, 2-10,24, 3-18, 4–4,6,9, MLT Papers 102:247.

625 In spring, feeling better: *Let* 897, 900, 901.

625 In the end: *Let* 906, 856; John Frederick Fargus ["Hugh Conway"], *Called Back* (New York: Holt, 1884).

626 On the morning of May 13: WAD's 1886 diary, 5-13; *SR* 5-17-1886.

626 The next day: WAD's 1886 diary, 5-14,15; MLT's 1886 diary, 5-14, MLT Papers 39:8; Leyda 2:472.

627 obituary, laying out, funeral, and interment: [Sue], "Miss Emily Dickinson of Amherst," *SR* 5-18-1886; *FF* 61; E. F. Strickland to MDB, postmarked 9-2-[1920s?], 3:119, bMS Am 1118.97, H; *World* 112; Mariette Jameson to JFJ, 5-23-1886, Container 7, Jameson Papers; TWH's 1886 diary, 5-19, bMS Am 1162, H; MLT's 1886 diary, 5-19. I know of no basis for the claim that Sue "prepared the body for burial" (Hart 257), let alone that she "swaddled" it (*Open Me* 265).

628 Going through: *Brocades* 86–87; *Open Me* xvi–xvii; William Dean Howells to MLT, 10-28-1890, ED Todd454 A; Howells, "Editor's Study," *Harper's New Monthly Magazine* 82 (Jan. 1891) 318–20; Buckingham.

628 When Austin: *Brocades;* Horan; *Open Me* xiv–xv; Josephine Pollitt Pohl, unpublished chapter or essay beginning "The lovers of Emily Dickinson," Josephine Pollitt Pohl Papers Relating to Emily Dickinson, Brown University Library.

Notes for Photo Section

2, top left	Below the silhouette: "Emily E. Dickinson." Above: "Executed by Charles Temple, a native of Smyrna. 1845."
2, top right	Daguerreotype by William C. North. See Mary Elizabeth Kromer Bernhard, "Lost and Found: Emily Dickinson's Unknown Daguerreotypist," *New England Quarterly* 72 (Dec. 1999) 594-601.
3, top left	Ibid.
3, top right	Assigned by some to 1853, EdD's photo was taken in 1874, when he "sat for his picture . . . for the first time in many, many years" (Turner). The name of the studio is printed on the back of the BPL's *carte de visite*: Marshall, Tremont Street, Boston—Augustus Marshall's business address 1867-1882.
3, bottom left	*Let* 237–38.
3, bottom right	*Let* 127.
4, middle left	Obituary, *Worcester Evening Gazette* 9-7-1887.
4, bottom right	*Let* 561.
5, bottom	Clara Carleton Pearl to MTB, 7-31-1946, MTB Papers 84:258a; *Let* 463.
7, bottom	Emerson 4-6-1883. The studio address stamped on the back of the photo—Allen & Horton, 13 Winter Street, Boston—dates it 1861-1863.
8, top	EH Jr, Notebook "B+" 43-44, Doc Hitch 7:26.
9, top right	HVE, "Poetry the Voice of Sorrow," *Amherst Collegiate Magazine* 1 (Oct. 1853) 22.
9, bottom right	*Let* 205.
10, top right	Elizabeth L. Smith, ed., *Henry Boynton Smith. His Life and Work* (New York: Armstrong, 1881) 95.
10, bottom	[George Burrowes], *Impressions of Dr. Wadsworth as a Preacher* (San Francisco: Towne & Bacon, 1863) 14.
11, top	*Let* 688.
11, bottom left	*SR* 10-13-1860
11, bottom right	SB Let #6 [5-15-1861].
14, top right	*Let* 751.
14, bottom left	Part of a large group photo from July 1882: "The Shutesbury School of Philosophy."
16, top	*Proceedings of the Bar of the Commonwealth, and of the Supreme Judicial Court, at Boston. On the Death of Otis Phillips Lord, LL.D. March, 1884* 16, CL.

Index of First Lines to Poems .

Index

Permissions and Photo Credits

Permissions

The author is indebted to the following for permission to quote unpublished material:

American Antiquarian Society
Amherst College Library, Archives and Special Collections
Franklin Trask Library, Andover Newton Theological School, Newton, Mass.
Baker Library, Harvard Business School
Boston Public Library/Rare Books Department. Courtesy of the Trustees.
Brown University Library
Special Collections, Tutt Library, Colorado College, Colorado Springs, Colo.
Congregational Library, Boston
The Boston Medical Library in the Francis A. Countway Library of Medicine, Boston
Dartmouth College Library
Burton Historical Collection, Detroit Public Library
Rare Book, Manuscript, and Special Collections Library, Duke University
Dun & Bradstreet Company
The Ralph Waldo Emerson Memorial Association
First Church of Monson, Mass.
Georgia Historical Society
Rutherford B. Hayes Presidential Center
Houghton Library, Harvard University
Lilly Library, Indiana University, Bloomington, In.
Special Collections, Jones Library, Amherst
Massachusetts Archives, Boston
Massachusetts Historical Society
Monson Free Library, Monson, Mass.
Monson Historical Society, Monson, Mass.
Mount Holyoke College Archives and Special Collections
Manuscripts and Archives Division, New York Public Library, Astor, Lenox, and Tilden Foundations
New York State Historical Association, Cooperstown, N.Y.
Mary C. Pearl

Photo Credits

Photo Section

Page 7

Upper left: Monson Free Library.
Upper right and bottom: Alice V. Yarick.

Page 8

Top: Amherst College Archives and Special Collections. By permission of the Trustees of Amherst College.
Bottom left: Public Domain, attained from *Amh Acad.*
Bottom right: Public Domain, attained from *Let* (1931).

Page 9

Top left: Manuscripts and Archives, Yale University Library, Historical Picture Collection.
Top right: Amherst College Archives and Special Collections. By permission of the Trustees of Amherst College.
Bottom left and bottom right: By permission of the Houghton Library, Harvard University, bMS Am 1118.99b.

Page 10

Top left: Manuscripts and Archives, Yale University Library, Todd-Bingham Picture Collection.
Top right: Franklin Trask Library, Andover Newton Theological School.
Bottom: Presbyterian Historical Society, Presbyterian Church (U.S.A.) Philadelphia.

Page 11

All photos: By permission of the Houghton Library, Harvard University, bMS Am 1118.99b.

Page 12

Top: Colorado College, Tutt Library, Special Collections, Helen Hunt Jackson Papers 12:3.
Bottom left: Smith College, Mortimer Rare Book Room.
Bottom right: By permission of the Houghton Library, Harvard University, bMS Am 1118.7, box 2.

Page 13

Top: Manuscripts and Archives, Yale University Library, Todd-Bingham Picture Collection.
Bottom: By permission of the Jones Library, Inc., Amherst, Mass.

Page 14

Top left, top right, and bottom left: By permission of the Houghton Library, Harvard University, bMS Am 1118.99b.
Bottom right: Manuscripts and Archives, Yale University Library, Todd-Bingham Picture Collection.

Page 15

Top left: Brown University Library, Martha Dickinson Bianchi Collection.
Top right: Manuscripts and Archives, Yale University Library, Todd-Bingham Picture Collection.
Bottom: By permission of the Houghton Library, Harvard University, bMS Am 1118.99b.

Page 16

Top and bottom: Manuscripts and Archives, Yale University Library, Todd-Bingham Picture Collection.

Part Title Pages

Part 1: Public Domain, attained from *Reunion*.

Part 2: By permission of the Jones Library, Inc., Amherst, Mass.

Part 3: Manuscripts and Archives, Yale University Library, Todd-Bingham Picture Collection.

Part 4: Mount Holyoke College Archives and Special Collections, Seminary Building Records 9:6 (Series 5).

Part 5: By permission of the Houghton Library, Harvard University, L 4.

Part 6: By permission of the Houghton Library, Harvard University, H154.

Part 7: Boston Public Library/Rare Books Department, Ms. Am 1093 (50). Courtesy of the Trustees.

ALFRED HABEGGER has been a backpacker, butterfly collector, and scholar of nineteenth-century American literature. Formerly a professor of English at the University of Kansas, he has won numerous research fellowships; in 1972–1973 he was Fulbright Lecturer in Bucharest. He lives with his wife, Nellie, in a log house they built together in northeastern Oregon. His previous books include an award-winning biography, *The Father: A Life of Henry James, Sr.* He has two grown children.

ABOUT THE TYPE

This book was set in Caslon, a typeface first designed in 1722 by William Caslon. Its widespread use by most English printers in the early eighteenth century soon supplanted the Dutch typefaces that had formerly prevailed. The roman is considered a "workhorse" type-face due to its pleasant, open appearance, while the italic is exceedingly decorative.